Information Management: A Strategic Approach

Information Management: A Strategic Approach

Edited by
Douglas Schwartz

www.willfordpress.com

Published by Willford Press,
118-35 Queens Blvd., Suite 400,
Forest Hills, NY 11375, USA

ISBN: 978-1-68285-577-5

Cataloging-in-Publication Data

Information management : a strategic approach / edited by Douglas Schwartz.
p. cm.
Includes bibliographical references and index.
ISBN 978-1-68285-577-5
1. Information resources management. 2. Management information systems.
3. Information technology. 4. Strategic planning. I. Schwartz, Douglas.
HF5548.2 .I54 2019
658.054--dc21

For information on all Willford Press publications
visit our website at www.willfordpress.com

Contents

Preface

This book elucidates new techniques of information management and their applications in a multidisciplinary manner. Managing the acquisition, dispersion and archiving of information related to an organization is referred to as information management. Due to technological advancements, ways to manage and share information have also changed. The field of information management uses concepts and systems of knowledge management for the effective administration of data. It also incorporates the practices of behavioral science for the handling of information and decision making. This book is compiled to provide the reader new insights into the field while also elaborating some crucial concepts. As this field is emerging at a rapid pace, the contents of this book will help the readers understand the modern principles and applications of the subject.

All of the data presented henceforth, was collaborated in the wake of recent advancements in the field. The aim of this book is to present the diversified developments from across the globe in a comprehensible manner. The opinions expressed in each chapter belong solely to the contributing authors. Their interpretations of the topics are the integral part of this book, which I have carefully compiled for a better understanding of the readers.

At the end, I would like to thank all those who dedicated their time and efforts for the successful completion of this book. I also wish to convey my gratitude towards my friends and family who supported me at every step.

Editor

Factors influencing Internet banking adoption in South African rural areas

Authors:
Thinamano C. Ramavhona[1]
Sello Mokwena[1]

Affiliations:
[1]Department of Informatics, Tshwane University of Technology, South Africa

Corresponding author:
Thinamano Ramavhona,
cyril.ramavhona@gmail.com

Background: The banking industry globally provides Internet banking to offer their customers easy access to banking services. The banks in South Africa, like their counterparts in other parts of the world, offer Internet banking to customers. However, the majority of South Africans in rural areas do not adopt and use Internet banking despite its convenience, the availability of Internet banking infrastructure, the effort of banks in promoting Internet banking awareness and Internet security.

Objectives: This research investigated factors which influence the adoption and use of Internet banking in the context of South African rural areas.

Method: In this study, a quantitative research approach was used. Data were collected through questionnaires and analysed using Statistical Package for Social Sciences (SPSS) tool.

Results: The perceived compatibility, trialability and external variables such as awareness and security were found to have significant influence in the adoption of Internet banking in South African rural areas, whereas relative advantage was found not to be a significant factor. Security and the complexity of Internet banking were also revealed as some of the factors hampering the intention to adopt Internet banking in South African rural areas.

Conclusion: The lack of awareness on Internet banking services and its benefits such as its convenience and the possibility to conduct banking transactions from any location with Internet is found to be the reason for South African rural area retail bank consumers' reluctance to adopt Internet banking. The majority of retail bank customers in South African rural areas do not use Internet banking because of the lack of resources, such as computers with Internet access. The security of transactions conducted over the Internet is the main concern and significant element that customers consider before adopting Internet banking in South African rural areas as they perceive it as being easily exposed to fraud. As a result, this perception erodes retail bank customers' confidence to adopt Internet banking. The majority of retail bank customers in South African rural areas will be willing to adopt Internet banking if their lifestyle, values and specific need are met. Retail bank customers in South African rural areas will adopt Internet banking if the Internet banking processes are simplified and user-friendly.

Introduction

The banking industry worldwide provides Internet banking to offer customers easy access to banking services (Adapa 2011). Internet banking was first introduced around the early 1980s and started gaining momentum in developing countries in the mid-1990s (Peterson 2006). Internet banking has transformed the way banks conduct their business, and has expanded their consumer base, which includes rural areas (Gonzalez, Dentiste & Rhonda 2008; Peterson 2006). Internet banking allows bank customers to transact on their accounts without physically visiting the banks by using the bank's software over the Internet (Zheng 2010). Internet banking customers access bank accounts from a remote location as long as there is Internet access (ABSA Bank 2011:1). The main benefit of Internet banking is that it is cheap and offers its users services that are convenient and not limited to time and place (Brogdon 1999:4; Wu 2005). Internet banking can be used to conduct banking transactions such as checking balances, transferring money and paying utility bills without physically visiting a branch (FNB 2011:2). Internet banking improves client safety by reducing the need to carry large amounts of cash (Wu 2005:13). The accessibility of Internet banking in rural areas is hindered by a number of factors which impede constructive use of Internet services (Cloete & Ramburn 2006:4).

South Africa has four major banks: Amalgamated Banks of South Africa (ABSA), Standard Bank, Nedbank and First National Bank (FNB). ABSA Bank was the first to offer limited transactions online in late 1996 and was followed by Nedbank which offered full Internet services in early 1997. Standard Bank introduced Internet banking services in July 1997 and later FNB added its working sites to the web in August 1997 (Singh 2004:190).

In South Africa, about 22 million people, 38.3% of the population reside in rural areas and 61.7% live in urban areas (Stats SA 2011). The rural population is not equally distributed over the provinces. Limpopo and KwaZulu-Natal provinces have the highest proportion of rural dwellers (Stats SA 2011). South African banks provide their rural customers with Internet banking in order to enable them to perform bank transactions through the bank's website without visiting a physical branch (Wang *et al.* 2003:22; Zheng, 2010). The Internet banking infrastructural distribution in South African rural areas is different from that in urban areas or other countries because of its demographic factors and Internet infrastructure (Green & Van Belle 2002). Little research has been conducted on Internet banking in South Africa (Wu 2005). The adoption of Internet banking by consumers in rural areas is lower than that of urban areas (Masocha *et al.* 2010), despite the benefits of Internet banking. There are still customers who prefer the traditional banking methods (Munusamy 2012).

Background

South Africans in rural areas are not adopting Internet banking despite the availability of Internet banking infrastructure and the efforts of banks in promoting Internet banking awareness, security and the convenience of the system. The aim of this study was to investigate factors that may influence the adoption and use of Internet banking in the context of South African rural areas. To conceptualise the theoretical and practical framework for the above stated problem, the following question guided the research: Why are South Africans in rural areas not adopting and using Internet banking despite the availability of Internet banking infrastructure and the effort of banks in promoting Internet banking awareness, security and the convenience of the system?

Literature review

Internet banking

Internet banking is described as the delivery of information or services by the banks to their customers using computers or mobile phones via the Internet (Daniel 1999:73). Internet banking is a banking service, which gives consumers a platform to perform banking functions online (Onay & Ozsoz 2013; Ongkasuwan 2002:3). According to Kyobutungi (2014) and Wang *et al.* (2003), Internet banking allows users to undertake financial transactions without the need to physically visit the bank. Consumers' migration to Internet banking is boosted by the ability to conduct banking transactions 24 h a day, anywhere, faster and with lower cost compared to using traditional bank branches (ABSA Online 2015; Sayar & Wolfe 2007). Redlinghuis and Rensleigh (2010) shared the same sentiment that convenience is one of the key factors for customers. This is reflected and supported in the study conducted by Yuan, Lee and Kim (2010), where it was found that the 'implementation of Internet banking eliminated the constraints associated with time and place'. Although customers in both rural and urban areas are expected to enjoy numerous benefits as a result of the implementation of Internet banking, there are various challenges that hamper the use of Internet banking services for rural customers.

Challenges with Internet banking

The limited access to computers and the Internet by South African public dwelling in rural areas is one of the serious inhibitors of information technology innovations in South Africa (April & Cradock 2000). This has implications for the Internet banking industry. Lack of infrastructure in rural areas results in the public not being able to gain access to Internet banking services. Infrastructural inadequacy is a widespread challenge, particularly in the former homeland rural areas of South Africa such as Limpopo province (Kgantsi & Mokoene 1997).

Opportunities for Internet banking in rural settings

There is telecommunication infrastructure to support Internet banking in rural areas. This infrastructure includes the use of mobile phones and personal computers (AFDB 2010).

Internet banking refers to the ways in which bank customers both in urban and rural areas can access their bank accounts via the bank's website through personal computers and mobile phones without being physically present at the bank's branch (Leow 1999).

Telecommunication and banking services have created opportunities for the emergence of mobile banking. Mobile banking services provide customers convenience together with cost savings. According to the International Telecommunication Union (ITU) report, 'there is a significant growth in the use of mobile phones, with mobile-cellular penetration rates stand at 96% globally; 128% in developed countries; and 89% in developing countries with South Africa included' (ITU 2013). Mobile phones can be used as Internet banking terminals. This will enable user access to financial services and provide fundamental services such as instant access to any bank account and the ability to make payments and transfers remotely (AFDB 2010).

The Wallis Report (1997) has indicated that the level of Internet banking security is the key factor in determining customers' decision in using Internet banking. The study conducted in Australia by O'Connell (1996) pointed out that security concern was the leading cause of the slow adoption of Internet banking in the country. Internet banking security is considered the main challenge by potential users when considering Internet banking in South African rural areas. South African banks offer clients security such as a personal identification number (PIN) in order to prevent unauthorised access to their accounts (Martins, Martins & Olivier 2001:32), as well as one time pin (OTP) (which is a single, unique and time-sensitive PIN) used as added security on online banking. According to Pather (2007), the OTP has proved to be successful in preventing online fraud in the South African banking sector.

Cost is one of the key factors that stimulate the consumer adoption of innovation. It has been stated in Wallis Report (1997) that if consumers are to use new technologies, the technologies must be reasonably priced compared to their alternatives. A study conducted by Bareczal and Ellen (1997:137) indicates that consumers may be reluctant to adopt a new innovation, such as Internet banking, unless it reduces their costs and does not require them to change their behaviour when using it.

The consumers' adoption or rejection of a new innovation such as Internet banking starts when the consumer becomes aware of the innovation (Rogers & Shoemaker 1971). Several studies have been conducted that empirically supported the idea that consumer knowledge and awareness had an effect on Internet banking adoption (Polatoglu & Ekin 2001; Sathye 1999).

Demographic features of Internet banking adopters

Demography can be defined as a study of human population statistics which include size, age, sex, race, location, occupation, income and education (Loudon & DellaBitta 1993:35). Each of these features influences the nature of consumers' needs and wants, and the ability to purchase products or services. South Africa has high inequality standard of living between urban and rural areas. The consumer demographic factors related to this study are age, education level, income and occupation. Most of the consumers who use Internet banking services are usually highly educated, with higher income and having better occupations than non-users (Karjaluoto 2002:359).

Theoretical foundations

Diffusion of innovation theory attempts to identify patterns and rates of adoption of innovation (Rogers 1995). There are five characteristics of innovations which influence individuals in the adoption of new innovation:

- Relative advantage, defined as an extent to which an innovation is perceived as being better than its previous innovation or existing counterparts, usually expressed in terms of economic and social benefits such as cost savings and convenience (Rogers 1995).
- Compatibility, which is defined as an extent to which an innovation is perceived as consistent with the existing values, past experiences and needs of potential adopters (Rogers 1983, 1995). It is measured in terms of how innovation fits into individual life situations.
- Complexity is defined as an extent to which the consumer considers the innovation to be difficult to use. It is measured in terms of innovations' levels of complexity experienced by potential adopters (Rogers 1995).
- According to Rogers (1983), 'triability contributes to achieving some sort of comfort among the customers and the users who may later become more willing to adopt this innovation'.
- Observability, which is the degree to which the results of an innovation are visible to others. In the context of this study, individuals normally do banking transactions privately; this transaction is not observable and visible to others because of security reasons (Tan & Teo 2000), and therefore the observation element is removed from this study about Internet banking adoption in rural areas.
- Two external factors *Awareness* and *Security* have been added in this study, as they are also critical factors in the diffusion of innovations such as Internet banking.
- Security of Internet banking refers to the threat and risks of identity theft and fraud that the individuals are exposed to and the measures to safeguard Internet banking (Kalakota & Whinston 1997).

Several researchers have applied diffusion of innovation theory. Moore and Benbasat (1991) applied it in their study of instrument development. Tan and Teo (2000), Taylor and Todd (1995) used it as a part of their research models. The individual characteristics, relative advantage, compatibility and complexity, together with the external factors awareness and security were critical in this study in a quest to identify factors influencing the adoption of Internet banking in South African rural areas.

Research method and design

Hypothesis of this research

In this study, six hypotheses have been derived from the research questions and objective of this study.

The previous research study conducted by Sohail and Shanmugham (2003) on Internet banking has revealed that awareness of the benefits and advantages of Internet banking has an influence on the customer's adoption of Internet banking. This has been supported by other previous studies which indicated that the lack of awareness of Internet banking and its benefits was revealed as a reason for individuals' reluctance to adopt Internet banking (Sathye 1999). Hence, this study hypothesises that:

> **Hypothesis 1:** Awareness of Internet banking positively affects the adoption and use of Internet banking in South African rural areas.

Gerrard and Cunningham (2003:8) recognise perceived relative advantage as an important factor influencing the adoption of Internet banking. Relative advantage is measured in terms of innovations' economic profitability, time saving, and decrease in discomfort and effort (Rogers 1983:217). This has been asserted by Agarwal and Prasad (1998:222) who have indicated that 'relative usefulness of an innovation is positively related to its rate of adoption'. Hence, this study hypothesises that:

> **Hypothesis 2:** Relative advantage affects the intention to adopt and use Internet banking in South African rural areas.

A number of previous researchers revealed that compatibility is one of the main factors that promote the diffusion of innovation to consumers. Compatibility leads to the rapid adoption of any new ideas or technologies. The study conducted by Kolodinsky, Hogarth and Hilgert (2004) identified compatibility as having a positively significant relationship with Internet banking adoption, while the study conducted by Gounaris and Koritos (2008) has found compatibility as insignificant to the adoption of Internet banking. Therefore, this study hypothesises that:

> **Hypothesis 3:** Compatibility affects the adoption and use of Internet banking in South African rural areas.

Rogers (1983:230) has argued that the adoption of innovation will be less likely if it is perceived as being complex or difficult to use. In addition, Wu (2005) also indicated that the adoption of Internet banking is far more likely to occur if the Internet banking processes are simple and user-friendly. Hence, this study hypothesises that:

> **Hypothesis 4:** Complexity affects the adoption and use of Internet banking in South African rural areas.

According to Tan and Teo (2000), 'if the user got the chance to try a new technology, this would lessen his feelings of fear concerning the usage of this technology'. In the previous study conducted by Hernandez and Mazoon (2007), trialability has been revealed as a significant factor in the adoption of Internet banking. This study also hypothesises trialability effect on Internet banking adoption as follows:

> **Hypothesis 5:** Trialability of Internet banking positively influences the adoption of Internet banking in South African rural areas.

Sathye (1999) has indicated that the majority of users avoided Internet banking adoption because of the concern about security of transactions over the Internet. Several previous researchers showed that the issue of security is more critical in Internet banking adoption because transactions on Internet banking comprise sensitive information and individuals involved in the financial transaction are concerned about access by fraudsters to sensitive files and information transferred via the Internet (Alsajjan & Dennis 2009; Suh & Han 2002). Hence, this study hypothesises that:

> **Hypothesis 6:** Internet banking security affects the intention to adopt and use Internet banking in South African rural areas.

Research methodology

This research aimed to identify the factors influencing the adoption of Internet banking in South African rural areas. The researcher adopted a cross-sectional approach during data collection. A sample size of 400 respondents was targeted. Data collection for this study was restricted to Limpopo province because it is one of the provinces with the highest proportion of rural dwellers (Stats SA 2011). A non-probability sampling method was used. This sampling method relies on the personal judgement of the researcher rather than chance to select sample elements (Malhotra 1999:334; Mokwena 2011:142). A closed item self-administered questionnaire was used as a main method to collect responses from school teachers.

The five-point Likert scale was used in the questionnaire for statements that required scaling to determine Internet banking customers' perceptions and non-Internet banking customers' perceptions and attitudes. The researcher used strongly agree (SA), agree (A), uncertain (U), disagree (D) and strongly disagree (SD) codes throughout where statements required respondents to choose one of these options. A pilot survey was conducted. In the pre-pilot study, the questionnaire was administered to a small group of respondents who were retail bank customers (teachers) from four schools in rural areas of Limpopo province in order to determine whether the questions were understandable as well as to test whether survey procedures worked.

The survey questionnaire was pilot tested and reviewed before it was finalised. Permission from the Provincial Department of Education was secured to collect research data from teachers.

A total of 400 questionnaires were distributed by the researcher to 45 schools in the rural areas of Limpopo province of South Africa. Out of 201 (50.25%) responses received, 41 (10.25%) were not useable, and 159 (39.5%) questionnaires were not returned. The study therefore used the remaining 160 responses that were useable. Data preparation, which includes coding, capturing and editing of the data, was conducted, and the data were captured using Microsoft Excel and then imported to SPSS 22 for analysis.

Data analysis and results

Description of respondents

IBM SPSS 22 was used for analysis of the demographics of the collected data. The majority of respondents were males (55.6%) and 44.4% were females. The majority of respondents were between the ages of 26 and 35 years (37.5%), followed by 36–45 years (26.3%); the age group of 18–25 years accounted for 18.8%, while that of 46–55 years accounted for 13.1% and over 56 years accounted for 4.4%.

Of the respondents, 40.6% had diplomas, 29.4% had bachelor degrees, 11.9% had certificates and 9.4% had postgraduate degrees.

All the respondents were employed, with full-time employees accounting for 92.5% and part-timers or interns accounting for 7.5% of the respondents. The majority of respondents (66.9%) earned an income of R4000 and above, followed by 15.6% of respondents earning between R3000 and R3999, 7.5% respondents earning between R2000 and R2999, while 2.5% of the respondents earned between R0 and R1999.

Internet banking usage and experience of the respondents

The majority of respondents (70.6%) indicated that they have never used Internet banking, while 62.5% of respondents cited that they do not have computers with Internet access in order to access Internet banking and as a result preferred visiting bank branches physically. Only 27.5% respondents indicated that they were using or used Internet banking before.

The relative advantages of Internet banking

A total of 57.5% of respondents indicated that Internet banking makes it easier for them to conduct their banking transactions in rural areas, only 16.3% of respondents were uncertain, whereas 26.3% disagreed with the statements. Once again, more than 50% of respondents indicated that Internet banking gives them greater control in managing their finances more efficiently.

The complexity of Internet banking

The majority of respondents (40%) indicated that they disagree that Internet banking programme makes it easy to manage their finances in rural areas, only 22.5% of respondents were uncertain, while 37.6% of respondents agreed that an Internet banking programme makes it easy to manage their finances in rural areas. While the majority of respondents (44.3%) indicated that Internet banking process is simple, only 41.9 of respondents indicated that they were uncertain, while 13.8% disagreed with the statements. The majority of respondents (37.7%) indicated that learning to use Internet banking is easy and only 25% of respondents indicated that they were uncertain about the statement, while 37.5% disagreed with the statements.

The compatibility of Internet banking

The majority of respondents (58.2%) indicated that using Internet banking to do their banking business fits into their work style, only 14.4% of respondents were uncertain, while 27.6% disagreed with the statements. Once again, the majority of respondents (63.8%) indicated that Internet banking is more convenient than queuing in the bank, and only 12.5% of respondents were uncertain, while 23.8% disagreed that Internet banking is more convenient than queuing in the bank branches. Of the respondents, 81.4% indicated that Internet banking could save them time and travelling costs in rural areas, only 16.2% of respondents were uncertain, while 2.4% disagreed that Internet banking could save them time and travelling cost.

The trialability of Internet banking

At least 63.8% of respondents indicated that they want to be able to try Internet banking for at least 1 month, while 33.6% of respondents were uncertain. Other respondents did not want to try Internet banking. Once again, the majority of respondents (62.5%) indicated that they want to be able to use Internet banking on a trial basis to see what it can do; only 13.8% of respondents indicated that they were uncertain, while 23.8% disagreed with the statements.

The awareness of Internet banking

The majority of respondents (58.8%) indicated that they were aware of Internet banking and the facilities it offers; only 10.0% of respondents were uncertain, while 31.3% of respondents disagreed with the statements. Once again, 56.9% of respondents indicated that they were aware of what needs to be done in order to become an Internet banking user; only 16.3% of respondents were uncertain, while 26.9% of respondents disagreed with the statements. The majority of respondents (53.2%) indicated that they were aware of the services that could be used through Internet banking, only 18.8% of respondents were uncertain, while 28.1% disagreed with the statements.

Security on Internet banking

The majority of respondents (56.9%) disagreed that using Internet banking is as safe as visiting the bank branches physically, only 15.0% of respondents were uncertain, while 28.2% agreed that using Internet banking is as safe as visiting the bank branches physically. Once again, 50.7% of respondents indicated that the banks offering Internet banking have not set security measures to protect their bank customers, only 19.4% of respondents were uncertain, while 30.0% of respondents disagreed with the statements.

Intention to adopt Internet banking service

The majority of respondents (61.9%) indicated that they have intentions to use Internet banking service in the near future, only 11.9% of respondents were uncertain, while 26.2% indicated that they were not planning to use Internet banking service in the near future.

Reliability test

The reliability test was conducted using Cronbach's alphas to test all the constructs used in this study for internal consistency. The alpha value for the measures in this study has ranged from 0.724 to 0.956, as reflected in Table 1. All the constructs have Cronbach's alpha value of more than 0.7; therefore, no internal consistency problems were found in further statistical analysis in the study.

Correlation analysis

Pearson's correlation analysis was used to determine the relationship between different variables in the study, which included relative advantage, compatibility, complexity, trialability, awareness, security and adoption of Internet banking. The correlation in the study checked the directions and strength of relationships that exist among the study variables. See Table 2 for the correlation analysis results.

TABLE 1: Reliability analysis using Cronbach's alpha.

Item statistics	Indicator	Mean	SD	α
Relative advantage	RELAD1	2.53	1.273	
	RELAD2	2.67	1.242	0.956
	RELAD3	2.66	1.253	
Compatibility	COMPA1	2.56	1.262	
	COMPA2	2.36	1.210	0.948
	COMPA3	2.28	1.202	
	COMPA4	2.57	1.232	
Complexity	COMPL1	2.95	1.179	
	COMPL2	2.91	1.187	0.918
	COMPL3	2.91	1.198	
Trialability	TRI1	2.39	1.279	
	TRI2	2.44	1.282	0.724
	TRI3	3.36	1.481	
Security	SEC1	3.31	1.245	0.838
	SEC2	3.27	1.237	
Awareness	AW1	2.58	1.262	
	AW2	2.52	1.239	0.927
	AW3	2.56	1.222	
Intention to adopt IB	IB1	2.39	1.279	
	IB2	2.44	1.282	0.724
	IB3	3.36	1.481	

Source: Ramavhona, T.C. & Mokwena, S.N., 2014, *Factors influencing internet banking adoption in South African rural areas*, Master's dissertation, Tshwane University of Technology, Tshwane, viewed 09 November 2016, from http://encore.tut.ac.za/iii/cpro/DigitalItemViewPage.external?lang=eng&sp=1001585&sp=T&suite=def

AW, awareness; COMPA, compatibility; COMPL, complexity; IB, Internet banking; RELAD, relative advantage; SD, standard deviation; SEC, security; TRI, trialability.

TABLE 2: Correlation analysis results in the study.

Variables		1	2	3	4	5	6	7
Relative advantage	Pearson's correlation	1	-	-	-	-	-	-
Compatibility	Pearson's correlation	0.856*	1	-	-	-	-	-
Complexity	Pearson's correlation	0.599*	0.619*	1	-	-	-	-
Trialability	Pearson's correlation	0.636*	0.640*	0.612*	1	-	-	-
Awareness	Pearson's correlation	0.551*	0.546*	0.534*	0.560*	1	-	-
Security	Pearson's correlation	0.403*	0.416*	0.619*	0.476*	0.374*	1	-
Intention to banking adoption	Pearson's correlation	0.658*	0.669*	0.534*	0.704*	0.607*	0.489*	1

Source: Ramavhona, T.C. & Mokwena, S.N., 2014, *Factors influencing internet banking adoption in South African rural areas*, Master's dissertation, Tshwane University of Technology, Tshwane, viewed 09 November 2016, from http://encore.tut.ac.za/iii/cpro/DigitalItemViewPage.external?lang=eng&sp=1001585&sp=T&suite=def

*, Correlation is significant at the 0.01 level (2-tailed).

Regression analysis

Regression analysis was used to determine the degree to which relative advantage, complexity, compatibility, trialability, awareness and security influenced the adoption of Internet banking in South African rural areas. The results as shown in Table 3 indicated that the predictor variables (relative advantage, compatibility, complexity, trialability, awareness and security) in this study accounted for at least 61.6% of the variance of Internet banking adoption (adjusted R-squared = 0.616). The result further showed trialability and awareness as the main predictor of Internet banking, followed by security and compatibility, respectively. Relative advantage and complexity were found not to be significant predictors of Internet banking adoption in South African rural areas. The regression model was also observed to be significant (sig < 0.000) and could be used reliably to make conclusions and recommendations for the banks in line with Internet banking adoption.

Conclusions and recommendations

Hypothesis testing

Six hypotheses were formulated for this research and linear regression analysis was used to test these hypotheses by regressing each of the independent variables against the adoption of dependent variables. The finding of this study as indicated in Table 4 shows that the intention to adopt Internet banking services can be predicted by awareness, compatibility, trialability and security, but not by relative advantage and complexity.

Conclusions in relation to the research problem

The research problem which this study sought to find answers to was the following: Why are South Africans in rural areas are not adopting and using Internet banking despite the availability of Internet banking infrastructure and the effort of banks in promoting Internet banking awareness, security and the convenience of the system? The overall conclusions of this study based on the findings presented in the previous sections are summarised below.

The demographic factors such as age, education, occupation and the level of income have an effect on the adoption of Internet banking in rural areas. The factors such as perceived compatibility, perceived trialability and external variables (awareness and security) were found to

TABLE 3: Results of regression analysis model in the study.

Model	Unstandardised coefficients		Unstandardised coefficients	*T*	Sig	Dependent variable: intention of adoption of Internet banking
	B	Std. error	Beta			
(Constant)	-1.683	0.652	-	-2.582	0.011	-
Relative advantage	0.145	0.106	0.134	1.364	0.175	-
Compatibility	0.177	0.085	0.208	2.081	0.039	-
Complexity	-0.130	0.090	-0.110	-1.446	0.150	-
Trialability	0.419	0.086	0.350	4.854	0.000	-
Awareness	0.247	0.071	0.220	3.449	0.001	-
Security	0.284	0.107	0.168	2.650	0.009	-
R-squared	-	-	-	-	-	0.631
Adjusted R-squared	-	-	-	-	-	0.616
F. Change	-	-	-	-	-	43.540
Sig	-	-	-	-	-	0.000

Source: Ramavhona, T.C. & Mokwena, S.N., 2014, *Factors influencing internet banking adoption in South African rural areas*, Master's dissertation, Tshwane University of Technology, Tshwane, viewed 09 November 2016, from http://encore.tut.ac.za/iii/cpro/DigitalItemViewPage.external?lang=eng&sp=1001585&sp=T&suite=def

T, this t-test compares the value of the Y-intercept with 0. If it is significant, then it means that the value of the Y-intercept is significantly different from 0; Sig, Significance; B, this is the unstandardized regression coefficient (B); Std. Error, standard error of the mean, also called the standard deviation of the mean, is a method used to estimate the standard deviation of a sampling distribution; R-Squared, R-squared is the fraction by which the variance of the errors is less than the variance of the dependent variable; F. Change, A significant 'F Change' value means that there has been a significant improvement in model fit.

TABLE 4: Hypothesis acceptance and rejection test remarks.

Hypothesis	Variable	Beta	*p*	Remarks
1	Awareness	0.220	0.001	Supported
2	Relative advantage	0.134	0.175	Not supported
3	Compatibility	0.208	0.039	Supported
4	Complexity	-0.110	0.150	Not supported
5	Trialability	0.350	0.000	Supported
6	Security	0.168	0.009	Supported

Source: Ramavhona, T.C. & Mokwena, S.N., 2014, *Factors influencing internet banking adoption in South African rural areas*, Master's dissertation, Tshwane University of Technology, Tshwane, viewed 09 November 2016, from http://encore.tut.ac.za/iii/cpro/DigitalItemViewPage.external?lang=eng&sp=1001585&sp=T&suite=def

have significant influence on the adoption of Internet banking in South African rural areas. However, relative advantage and complexity were found not to be significant factors influencing the adoption of Internet banking in South African rural areas. It has been found that the majority of respondents from South African rural areas have never used Internet banking, due to customers' lack of resources such as computers with Internet access and costs. Security and the complexity of Internet banking was revealed as one of the factors hampering the intention to adopt Internet banking in South African rural areas because the bank customers perceived Internet banking as unsafe, that the banks offering Internet banking have not yet set enough security measures to protect customers and that Internet banking is difficult to use and not user-friendly.

Acknowledgements

Competing interests

The authors declare that they have no financial or personal relationships which may have inappropriately influenced them in writing this article.

Authors' contributions

T.R. was the main author of this article and conducted most of the research in regard to the article, while S.M. was the co-author of this article, performing most of the supervisory role on the article.

References

ABSA Bank, 2011, *Absa electronic banking brochure*. ABSA Bank.

ABSA Online, 2015, *ABSA online Internet banking/the way internet banking meant to be*, viewed 30 January 2015, from http://www.absa.co.za/Absacoza/Individual/Ways-to-Bank/Anytime,-Anywhere/Absa-Online

Adapa, S., 2011, 'Continued and frequent use of Internet banking by Australian consumers: Identification of the factor components', *Journal of Internet Banking and Commerce* 16(2), 1–22.

AFDB, 2010, 'Africa Economic Brief', *African Development Bank* 1(8), 1–16, viewed 29 Nov. 2016, from http://www.afdb.org/fileadmin/uploads/afdb/Documents/Publications/John%20brief%201_John%20brief%201.pdf

Agarwal, R. & Prasad, J., 1998, 'A conceptual and operational definition of personal innovativeness in the domain of information technology', *Information Systems Research* 9, 204–224. http://dx.doi.org/10.1287/isre.9.2.204

Alsajjan, B. & Dennis, C., 2009, 'Internet banking acceptance model: Cross-market examination', *Journal of Business Research* 5(5), 257–272.

April, A.K. & Cradock, J., 2000, *E-business – Redefining the corporate landscape*, Butterworths, Durban.

Bareczal, G. & Ellen, P., 1997, 'Developing typologies of consumer motives for use of technologically base banking services', *Journal of Business Research* 38, 131–139. http://dx.doi.org/10.1016/S0148-2963(96)00032-X

Brogdon, C., 1999, *Banking and the Internet: Past, present, and possibility*, viewed 23 April 2011, from http://www-db.stanford.edu.html

Cloete, E. & Ramburn, H., 2006, 'Determinants of Internet banking: Consumers' versus banks perspective', in *Proceedings of the 8th Annual Conference on World Wide Web Applications*, Bloemfontein, South Africa, 06–08 September.

Daniel, E., 1999, 'Provision of electronic banking in the UK and the Republic of Ireland', *The International Journal of Bank Marketing* 17(2), 72–83. http://dx.doi.org/10.1108/02652329910258934

First National Bank (FNB), 2011a, *Online banking*, viewed 15 July 2011, from https://www.fnb.co.za/channel/online-banking.html

First National Bank (FNB), 2011b, *One time pin (OTP)*, viewed 18 October 2011, from https://www.online.fnb.co.za/rhelp0/zob/security/one_time_pin.htm

Gerrard, P. & Cunningham, J.B., 2003, 'The diffusion of internet banking among Singapore consumers', *The International Journal of Banking Marketing*, viewed 25 April 2013, from http://www.proquest.umi.com/pqdweb?index

Green, S. & Van Belle, J.P., 2002, *Customer expectations of internet banking in South Africa*, viewed 2 February 2012, from http://www.commerce.uct.ac.za/informationsystems/staff/personalpages/jvbelle/pubs/f-VanBelleJeanPaul2.pdf

Gonzalez, M.E., Dentiste, M.R. & Rhonda, M.W., 2008, 'An alternative approach in service quality: An e-banking case study', *The Quality Management Journal* 15(1), 41.

Gounaris, S. & Koritos, C., 2008, 'Investigating the drivers of internet banking adoption decision', *International Journal of Bank Marketing* 26(5), 282–304. http://dx.doi.org/10.1108/02652320810894370

Hernandez, J. & Mazzon, J., 2007, 'Adoption of internet banking: Proposition and implementation of an integrated methodology approach', *Marketing* 25(2), 72–88.

ITU, 2013, *World in 2013 ICT facts and figures*, viewed, from http://www.itu.int/en/ITU-D/Statistics/Documents/facts/ICTFactsFigures2013-e.pdf

Kalakota, R. & Whinston, A., 1997, *Electronic commerce: A manager's guide*, Addison Wesley, Reading, MA.

Karjaluoto, H., 2002, 'Selection criteria for a mode of bill payment: Empirical investigation among Finnish Bank customers', *International Journal of Retail and Distribution Management* 30(6), 331–339. http://dx.doi.org/10.1108/09590550210429540

Kgantsi, M. & Mokoene, S., 1997, 'South African farmer support services: An end-user perspective', unpublished research report, Development Bank of Southern Africa.

Kolodinsky, J., Hogarth, J. & Hilgert, M., 2004, 'The adoption of electronic banking technologies by US consumers', *Marketing* 22(4), 238–259. http://dx.doi.org/10.1108/02652320410542536

Kyobutungi, A., 2014, *Internet banking and customer satisfaction of commercial banks in Uganda: A case study of Centenary Rural Development Bank in Mbarara municipality*, viewed from http://www.academia.edu/7388611/internet_banking_and_customer_satisfaction_of_commerical_banks_in_uganda_a_case_study_of_centenary_rural_development_bankin_mbarara_municipality

Leow, H.B., 1999, 'New distribution channels in banking services', *Bankers Journal Malaysia* 110, 48–56.

Loudon, D. & DellaBitta, A., 1993, *Consumer behavior*, McGraw Hill, Singapore.

Malhotra, N., 1999, *Marketing research: An applied orientation*, Prentice Hall, Upper Saddle River, NJ.

Martins, A., Martins, N. & Olivier, M.S., 2001, 'Consumer perception of electronic-commerce', *South African Computer Journal* 27, 27–33.

Masocha, R., Chiliya, N. & Zindiye, S., 2010, *E-banking adoption by customers in the rural milieus of South Africa: A case of Alice*, Eastern Cape, South Africa.

Mokwena, S.N., 2011, 'Factors influencing the acceptance and use of a school administration and management system in South African high schools', Unpublished PhD thesis, Tshwane University of Technology, Pretoria.

Moore, G.C. & Benbasat, I., 1991, 'Development of an instrument to measure the perceptions of adopting an information technology innovation', *Information Systems Research* 2(3), 192–222.

Munusamy, J., 2012, 'Perceived barriers of innovative banking among Malaysian retail banking customers', *Journal of Internet Banking and Commerce* 17(1), 1–15.

Onay, C. & Ozsoz, E., 2013, 'The impact of Internet-banking on brick and mortar branches: The case of turkey', *Journal of Financial Services Research* 44(2), 187–204. http://dx.doi.org/10.1007/s10693-011-0124-9

O'Connell, B., 1996, 'Australian banking on the Internet – Fact or fiction?', *The Australian Banker* 110(6), 212–214.

Ongkasuwan, M. & Tantichattanon, W., 2002, 'A comparative study of Internet banking in Thailand', paper presented at The First National Conference on Electronic Business, Bangkok, 24–25th October.

Pather, P., 2007, *The way business is moving*, viewed 24 December 2011, from www.Netdotwork.co.za/news/aspx?pklnewsid=26579

Peterson, M., 2006, *A brief history of internet banking*, Ezine Articles, viewed 14 February 2011, from http://ezinearticles.com

Polatoglu, V.N. & Ekin, S., 2001, 'An Empirical Investigation of the Turkish Consumers' Acceptance of Internet Banking Services', *International Journal of Bank Marketing* 19(4), 156–161.

Ramavhona, T.C. & Mokwena, S.N., 2014, *Factors influencing internet banking adoption in South African rural areas*, Master's dissertation, Tshwane University of Technology, Tshwane, viewed 09 November 2016, from http://encore.tut.ac.za/iii/cpro/DigitalItemViewPage.external?lang=eng&sp=1001585&sp=T&suite=def

Redlinghuis, A. & Rensleigh, C., 2010, 'Customer perceptions on Internet banking information protection', *South African Journal of Information Management* 12(1), 1–6.

Rogers, E.M., 1983, *Diffusion of innovations*, 3rd edn., Free Press, New York.

Rogers, E.M., 1995, *Diffusion of innovations*, 4th edn., Free Press, New York.

Rogers, E.M. & Shoemaker, F.F., 1971, *Communications of innovations: A cross-cultural approach*, Free Press, New York.

Sathye, M., 1999, 'Adoption of internet banking by Australian consumers: An empirical investigation', *International Journal of Bank Marketing* 17(7), 324–334. http://dx.doi.org/10.1108/02652329910305689

Sayar, C. & Wolfe, S., 2007, 'Internet banking market performance: Turkey versus the UK', *International Journal of Bank Marketing* 25(3), 122–141. http://dx.doi.org/10.1108/02652320710739841

Statistics South Africa, 2011, *Census 2011: Community profiles*, Stats SA, Pretoria.

Sohail, M.S. & Shanmugham, B., 2003, 'E-banking and customer preferences in Malaysia: An empirical investigation', *Information Sciences* 150, 207–217. http://dx.doi.org/10.1016/S0020-0255(02)00378-X

Singh, A., 2004, 'Trend in South African Internet banking', *Aslib Proceedings*, 56(3), 187–196.

Suh, B. & Han, I., 2002, 'Effect of trust on customer acceptance of Internet banking', Electronic Commerce Research and Applications 1(2002), 247–263.

Taylor, S. & Todd, P., 1995, 'Understanding information technology usage: A test of competing models', *Information Systems Research* 6(2), 144–176.

Tan, M. & Teo, T.S.H., 2000, 'Factors influencing the adoption of Internet banking', *Journal of the Association for Information Systems* 1(5), 22–38.

Wang, Y., Wang, Y., Lin, H. & Tang, T., 2003, 'Determinants of user acceptance of Internet banking: An empirical study', *International Journal of Bank Marketing* 14(5), 501–519, viewed 14 February 2011, from http://ijmbr.srbiau.ac.ir/pdf_64_f2e1cffc35d055294267fe8a6e1fa0f9.html

Wallis Report, 1997, *The financial system inquiry final report*, AGPS, Canberra.

Wu, J., 2005, *Factors that influence the adoption of Internet banking by South Africans in the EThekwini metropolitan region*, viewed 24 December 2011, from http://ir.dut.ac.za/bitstream/handle/10321/114/Wu_2005.pdf?sequence=13

Yuan, X., Lee, H.S. & Kim, S.Y., 2010, 'Present and future of internet banking in China', *Journal of Internet Banking and Commerce* 15(1), 1–10.

Zheng, L.N., 2010, *An empirical analysis of factors that influence the adoption of internet banking in China: A case study of Zhengzhou*, viewed from https://researcharchive.lincoln.ac.nz/bitstream/10182/2633/3/Zheng_MCM.pdf

2

An investigation into the usage of mobile phones among technical and vocational educational and training students in South Africa

Authors:
Herring Shava[1]
Willie Chinyamurindi[1]
Anathi Somdyala[2]

Affiliations:
[1]Department of Business Management, University of Fort Hare, South Africa

[2]Business Management Unit, East London Management Institute, South Africa

Corresponding author:
Willie Chinyamurindi,
chinyaz@gmail.com

Background: Information and Communication Technologies (ICTs) are gaining popularity in South Africa; this includes the use of mobile phones and the Internet. Mobile phones also seem to be popular with the student cohort of the South African population, especially for communication purposes. Empirical evidence affirms the importance of mobile phones to this cohort, including the need to research further how these groups use and experience such devices.

Objectives: This study seeks to provide an understanding of how mobile phone features, the motivation to use and time spent on a mobile phone influence behavioural intention to use mobile phones among a sample of technical and vocational educational and training (TVET) students in the Eastern Cape Province of South Africa.

Method: A survey was carried out with 161 TVET students through a self-administered questionnaire completed by each respondent. Pre-testing and pilot testing of measures were conducted using a sample of final-year students using mobile phones who fit the same characteristics as the intended sample. To arrive at findings, data analysis was undertaken through the Chi-square test.

Results: Descriptive results of the study reveal that the majority of mobile phones owned by TVET students were in the category of smartphones, bearing modern features that facilitate instant messaging, exchange of data and information as well as speedy access to information via the Internet.

Conclusion: Inferential results of the study indicate that the more features a mobile phone has, the higher the desire to make use of the phone for communication purposes. Furthermore, motivation and time were found to play insignificant roles in influencing student utilisation of mobile phones for communication purposes.

Introduction

The use of Information and Communication Technologies (ICTs) has become popular in modern society, and the mobile phone has become one of the most 'ubiquitous' devices found in most parts of the world (Li *et al.* 2012:469). This is a stark contrast to earlier held views of mobile phones as gadgets that would not attract much ownership (Karim, Darus & Hussin 2006). One cohort popular for using such ICTs includes young adults and students. Skiba's study (2014) focusing on connectivity through applications designed for mobile devices found that 79% of tertiary-level students own the newly innovated smartphones. Head and Ziolkowski (2012:2331) not only affirm the importance of mobile phones to this cohort but also the need to research how these groups 'value the feature richness of their devices'. This appears to be a consistent view among scholars attributing the need to investigate the impact technology may have in different communities (Chen & Katz 2009; Katz 2006). Skiba (2014) further suggests that youths attending tertiary institutions value interaction to the extent that 70% were found to be utilising mobile phones during class sessions.

This study seeks to extend the knowledge base of mobile phone usage and student behaviour in two important ways. Firstly, this study seeks to establish what students are using their mobile phones for. Secondly, this study seeks to understand individual usage of the mobile phone and its relation to phone features and individual-specific factors such as motivation and time. The findings of the study have important implications for educators, marketers and communication researchers involved in studying the student market and their communication patterns.

The rest of the study is organised in the following manner: discussion of the background on technical and vocational educational and training (TVET) and review of literature on mobile phone usage and student population leading to the study's hypotheses. Thereafter, the research methodology, results, discussion and implication of the study as well as limitations are discussed. The last sections focus on areas for future research and the study's conclusion.

Technical and vocational educational and training sector

The TVET sector is mapped in such a way that each curriculum on offer is based on a job title, thereby playing a critical role in the development of a country through the production of skilled and semi-skilled manpower (Chua & Jamil 2012). TVET colleges in South Africa emerged from the famous public Further Education and Training (FET) college system. These FETs were established to help develop practical vocational skills in sectors such as agriculture, arts and culture, business, commerce and management, education, training and development, engineering, manufacturing and technology, services, building construction and security (Fisher, Jaff, Powell & Hall 2003).

Within higher education, calls have been made for research aimed at furthering understanding of the adoption and utilisation of technology (Chinyamurindi & Shava 2015; Hsiao & Yang 2011), especially within institutions and among students given the varied popularity of technology not just for learning purposes (Park 2009).

Mobile phones and the student population

Students have been found to have strong consumption behaviour with regard to their usage of mobile phones (Jamal *et al.* 2012). Such a practice is believed to be universal and cuts across various barriers, thus making students an important target market (Jurisic & Azevedo 2011). Prior research has revealed that mobile phone usage enhances a student's learning experience and increases a student's attention to school work and participation in learning activities (Eteokleous & Ktoridou 2009).

The popularity of mobile phones among the student market could be due to a number of reasons. Chen and Katz (2009) found the popularity of the mobile phone to be due to students' need to communicate with family while they are away studying. Baysal, Sahenk and Hazneci (2010) attribute mobile phone features to the popularity of mobile phones. This includes features such as making voice calls, sending messages, live chat, playing music, playing video games, the Internet and telephone banking services. The presence of such features makes mobile phones influential in everyday communication (Pourrazavi *et al.* 2014) among younger generations (Hakoama & Hakoyama 2011). All this has led to the emergence of the smartphone – a phone that has the ability to not only enhance interpersonal communication but also incorporate a range of multimedia tools (Ting *et al.* 2011).

Furthermore, mobile phones appear popular among students given their ability to link users to social networks for the purpose of human interaction (Walsh, White & Young 2010). Others attribute factors such as convenience, mobility, safety and networking as contributing significantly to the popularity of mobile phones (Ling 2004).

Determinants of mobile phone usage

This section presents the key theoretical underpinnings of intention to use information technology products and services, focusing on intention to use within the mobile phone context. A focus on factors that influence the adoption of technology is argued as important, not just for the full utilisation, but also acceptance of the technology (Hsiao & Yang 2011). Furthermore, it may help grasp a picture not just into usage of mobile phones but also the decision processes users of such technology go through. This section pays attention first to the dependent variable, which is behavioural intention to use (BIU).

Behavioural intention to use

An important theoretical consideration specific to the utilisation of technology is the Technology Acceptance Model (TAM) (Venkatesh & Davis 2000). This model consists of two beliefs, namely: perceived usefulness and perceived ease of use of the application. These two determine attitudes towards the adoption of a new technology. The attitude towards adoption depicts the prospective adopter's positive or negative orientation and/or behaviour towards adopting a new technology (Venkatesh & Davis 2000). Usage could also be influenced by an individual's perception of the ability to use the technology (Compeau & Higgins 1995). Subsequently, all these elements of TAM can serve as predictors of human behaviour (Fishbein & Ajzen 1975; Lee & Lehto 2013) or BIU, thus resulting in TAM being seen as a useful predictor in explaining human behaviour concerning technology acceptance (Agundo-Peregrina, Hernández-García & Pascual-Miguel 2014; Chen, Li & Li 2011; Chinyamurindi & Louw 2010; Chinyamurindi & Shava 2015; Saadé, Nebebe & Tan 2007).

The TAM is built around the theory of reasoned action (TRA) (Fishbein & Ajzen 1975), which suggests that individual behaviour is initiated by the intention to perform a particular task. The result of this is that individual behavioural intention determines one's attitude and subjective norms regarding the behaviour in question (Fishbein & Ajzen 1975). The TRA also posits that intention to act determines behaviour, and a causal link is believed to exist between the two (Venkatesh & Davis 2000). The attitude-behavioural intention relationship, as espoused in the TAM constructs, assumes that all intentions to use technology are equal and can be formed on the basis of positive usage of the technology. This study, therefore, seeks to test if mobile phone features, motivation and time (all independent variables) can be associated with the BIU (dependent variable) mobile phones.

Mobile phone features

Research indicates that the amount of features on a mobile phone is related to the lifetime of the mobile phone (Li *et al.* 2012). Added to this, empirical evidence shows successful usage or adoption of a technology to be dependent on its full utilisation (Ilechukwu 2013; Nwogu, Udoye & Oguejiofor 2014). In essence, the more features a mobile phone has, the more time the phone may remain in the hands of the user. This appears to be supported by the economic theory suggesting that product features and attributes are linked to consumer demand given the additive utility function (Lancaster 1971). Building on the previous statement, Head and Ziolkowski (2012) suggest that there is a positive relationship between mobile phone features and consumer usage of the product. From a marketing point of view, this may create a competitive advantage that helps phone manufacturers stand out from their competitors (Mukherjee & Hoyer 2001).

Furthermore, research shows the mobile phone to be more popular for leisure than for school- or work-related causes (Lepp *et al.* 2013). Economicides and Grouspoulou (2009) found that students tend to consider the following features important: battery life, mp3 player, video camera, Bluetooth and chatting sites. The features favoured appear to be those that encourage interactivity, simplicity and the availability of up-to-date information (Wanajak 2011). In support of the previous notion, a South African study undertaken to determine mobile application and/or features preferred by university students found that features that provide students with access to information and entertainment were downloaded more than other features (Potgieter 2015).

Given that the majority of mobile phone features appear to support a leisure cause also found to be popular among students (Mannell 2007), it can be expected that mobile phone features will be related to BIU. The thinking here could be that a high number of mobile phone features reflect the phone's expanded functionality (Lepp *et al.* 2015). Therefore, it is expected that:

Hypothesis 1: An association can be found between mobile phone features and BIU.

Motivation

Motivation refers to 'the reasons underlying behaviour' (Guay *et al.* 2010:712) and directs humans (Gredler, Broussard & Garrison 2004). Motivation can be viewed as influencing individual behaviour to use mobile phones. Individuals should be willing and able to use these technologies by accepting them as this will lead to improved efficiency (Keeton 2008). In the context of this study, motivational factors are those that move individuals to use their phones (Van Biljon 2006). The thinking here could be that individual motivation needs to exist as a fundamental technology adoption requirement (Qualasvirta 2005).

Bandura (1986) highlighted that motivation, either as external (observing others) or internal (individual self-efficacy), affects intention and adoption of behaviour. This view has been supported in a number of empirical studies (Peters *et al.* 2006; Wang, Lin & Luarn 2006). In some studies (Li *et al.* 2012), the motivation to change a mobile phone was motivated by the phone being damaged. In essence, lack of functionality resulted in no usage of the phone and, in turn, created no further motivation for using such a device.

However, using the choice task complexity theory (Johnson & Payne 1985), motivation and time can be influenced by complexity of the mobile phone as a physical product and its features. The thinking here could be that the greater the product feature and its complexity, the more consumer effort needed. In essence, Wright (1975) theorised that consumers usually wish to minimise decision efforts. Resultantly, mobile phones that come with features that require much effort and time may be avoided because of their complexity (Dellaert & Stremersch 2005) and trigger anxiety or stress (Mick & Fournier 1998). This can often lead to feature fatigue when too many features make a product overwhelming, thereby causing dissatisfaction (Thompson, Hamilton & Rust 2005).

An attitude towards mobile phone usage may be formed as a result. Using the TRA (Ajzen & Fishbein 1980) based on the attitude (positive or negative), this may affect intention to perform a behaviour. The presence or absence of motivation has been found to influence satisfaction or dissatisfaction (Zhang & Von Dran 2000). In some cases, lack of motivation to use technology can often result in resistance to use the technology based on user perceptions (Desmet & Parente 2012). Thus, the usage of mobile phones can serve as a motivational utility value in meeting individual needs (Jokela 2004; Kang 2014). Given this, it can be expected that:

Hypothesis 2: An association can be found between motivation and BIU.

Time

The mobile phone is an anytime and anywhere tool, thus boosting the tendency to do things discreetly as well as openly. The Internet has removed a geographical boundary, which means students have an abundance of information at their disposal accessed at their convenience (Caronia & Caron 2004). Among students, time limitations have been found to affect how students use mobile phones (Lightner, Benander & Kramer 2008). However, the Salesforce Marketing Cloud (2014) reports that people between the ages of 18 and 25, on average, utilise phones for 5.2 hours per day. The majority of TVET students in South Africa fall within this age category. Therefore, it is expected that:

Hypothesis 3: An association can be found between time and BIU.

The hypothesised relationships are described graphically in Figure 1. The research seeks to answer the following questions: (1) What are the salient factors that influence the BIU mobile phones among a sample of TVET students in South Africa? (2) What are the sampled TVET students using mobile phones for?

Research methodology

This section highlights the research paradigm, research design, research respondents, measuring instrument, the research procedure and statistical analysis adopted in this study.

Research paradigm

Researchers adopted the post-positivist approach. To successfully undertake this research, researchers recognised that 'all cause and effect is a probability that may or may not occur' (Creswell 2013:23–24). The post-positivist approach is a shift from traditional positivism (Philips & Burbules 2000). Post-positivists argue that it is rather unlikely for an individual to be absolutely positive about claims that other people make in respect of knowledge, specifically when human behaviour is the subject under scrutiny as is the case in this study (Creswell 2014; Philips & Burbules 2000).

Research design

The study adopted the survey research design. Survey research enables the researcher to gather quantitative data with regard to 'trends, attitudes or opinions' by examining a subset of a population, which is the case in this study (Creswell 2014:13). To achieve this, a self-administered questionnaire was used, given that it allowed for investigating the associations between the determinants and BIU mobile phones within the sample. Furthermore, questionnaires were a cost-effective method, thereby allowing a wider reach (Jack & Clarke 1998). Finally, responses were gathered in a standardised manner as the study adopted existing TAM measures.

Research respondents

The sample consisted of 161 TVET students studying in institutions located in East London and consisted of 76 male participants (n = 76) and 85 female participants (n = 85). The respondents responded to a 34-item self-administered questionnaire. The questionnaire was made available to the students through a trained data collector employed for this project and a former student of the TVET College. Students were first asked to respond to some descriptive questions and thereafter to a series of questions on a five-point Likert scale.

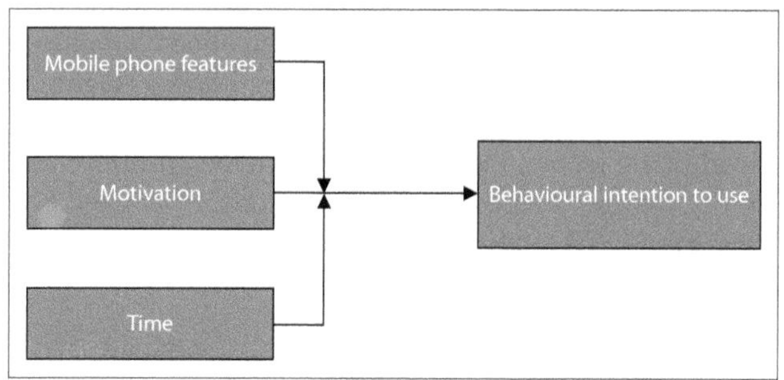

FIGURE 1: Theoretical model.

Measuring instrument

In an attempt to ensure content validity of the scales, items represented the concept of which generalisations were to be made. The researchers selected items that were either mainly adapted from previous studies or from the previous application of the TAM (Compeau & Higgins 1995; Davis 1989; Kyobe & Shongwe 2011; Ong & Lai 2006; Venkatesh & Davis 1996). Validated items adapted from prior studies were used to measure mobile phone features, time, motivation and BIU.

In terms of the reliability of the measure, sufficient reliability was found (mobile phone features – 0.71; time – 0.70; motivation – 0.73 and BIU – 0.77). The reliability of the measures in this study showed sufficient reliability as per the recommended threshold of 0.70 (Streiner 1993). Pre-testing and pilot testing of measures were conducted using a sample of final-year students using mobile phones who fit the same characteristics as the intended sample at a private TVET College in East London. Academics from the education and computer science fields from the University of Fort Hare (Alice and East London Campuses) were also consulted to give their input on the study instrument. The questionnaire items were modified to make them relevant to the context of the intended study based upon the feedback.

Research procedure

Permission was granted from the participating TVET College, and relevant ethical clearance was obtained. The research assistant was assisted by a former TVET student in collecting data. The former TVET student was also trained and briefed on the study and expectations. The research assistant and the former TVET student approached potential respondents and introduced themselves and stated the objectives of the study. Potential respondents were informed of the expectations from them and the recourse (including their rights) they could exercise if they wanted to withdraw from the study. Participation in the research was voluntary, and this was communicated to the respondents through the research assistant; respondents could withdraw at any time. To ensure anonymity and confidentiality, participants were informed not to endorse their names, signatures or nicknames on questionnaires.

Statistical analyses

Data analysis was carried out using IBM Statistical Package for Social Sciences Version 22.0. Cronbach's alpha coefficients (α) were used to assess the internal consistency of the measuring instruments (Clark & Watson 1995). Statistical analysis also involved generating a descriptive picture concerning the phenomena under study. Inferential statistics were used to determine the association between the dependent and the independent variables. Inferential statistics assist in generalising findings from the sample to the larger population (Wiid & Diggines 2013). Relying on inferential statistics further helped the researchers to come to conclusions from observations about the population of the study (Babbie 1992). The study data did not violate the assumption of normality. Using the Kolmogorov–Smirnov statistic, a non-significant value of 0.2 larger than 0.05 was found (Field 2013). Furthermore, the Chi-square test of independence, a parametric statistic was used to statistically analyse the study's hypotheses (Pallant 2010).

Results

Furthermore, the research sought to establish, through descriptive statistics, what features did the mobile phones for TVET students have. Table 1 summarises the results. Table 2 reveals what TVET students used their mobile phones for based on the features on their phones.

Table 1 indicates that the majority of mobile phones were in the category of smartphones and bearing modern features that facilitate instant messaging (chat features). The majority of these phones also had a camera, Bluetooth and GPS applications installed. Most importantly, Table 1 indicates that the majority of mobile phones were equipped with Internet browsers enabling TVET students' easy and speedy access of information via the Internet.

Besides traditional mobile uses such as voice calling and messaging, Table 2 summarises other major uses of mobile phones by TVET students. The study's findings reveal that besides voice calling and messaging, the majority of students utilise mobile phones for chatting purposes. Chatting is effectively carried out through various phone features and/or applications compatible to different phone models. The applications range from Facebook, BBM to WhatsApp among others. TVET students also use mobile phones for entertainment purposes. The majority of phones have music player applications installed. For the user to use the music player feature, he or she has to upload music and have it stored within. However, other Internet sites or applications such as YouTube and iTunes enable the user to access music online for entertainment purposes without uploading it, thereby making entertainment the second major use of mobile phones among TVET students. From Table 2, emailing became the third major use of mobile phones among TVET students. Emailing is predominantly carried out through Gmail and Yahoo mail. Moreover, mobile phones are being used to gather information on the Internet for various purposes, depending on the lifestyle of the mobile phone owner. Some use the mobile phone to access weather updates and for comparing product and/or service prices, and others use the mobile phone to gather information on health-related issues, thus making use of the WebMD site.

In testing hypotheses 1, 2 and 3, the Chi-square test was used. Table 3 reflects the results of the analyses.

To test hypothesis 1, the association between mobile phone features and BIU, a Chi-square test for independence indicated a statistically significant association between mobile phone features and BIU mobile phones, as shown in

TABLE 1: Mobile phone features.

Descriptive statistics	Frequency	%
Phone type		
Smartphone	150	93
Non-smartphone	11	7
Chat feature on phone		
Yes	133	83
No	28	17
MMS		0
Yes	134	83
No	27	17
Internet on phone		
Yes	159	99
No	2	1
Camera on phone		
Yes	159	99
No	2	1
Bluetooth on phone		
Yes	158	98
No	3	2
GPS on phone		
Yes	126	78
No	35	22
Live TV on phone		
Yes	38	24
No	123	76

TABLE 2: Major uses of mobile phones among TVET students.

Category of use	Application and/or feature and/or site	Frequency
Social media	Facebook	104
	Twitter	38
	Instagram	14
	BBM	69
	WhatsApp	125
	2go	8
	WeChat	9
	Mxit	11
	Skype	3
Entertainment	Shazam	4
	YouTube	36
	iTunes	3
	Zonkewap	12
	Kasi mp3	3
	Toxicwap	17
Online shopping	Bid or Buy	6
	Gumtree	8
Emailing	Gmail	15
	Yahoo mail	8
	Webmail	6
General Internet search	Online news	3
	WebMD	2
	Wiki answers	2
	Price check	3
	Bodybuilder	4
	Weather	3

TABLE 3: Chi-square tests.

Variables	Hypothesis 1: MPF -> BIU	Hypothesis 2: M -> BIU	Hypothesis 3: T -> BIU
Pearson Chi-square	174.989[a]	39.748[b]	67.527[c]
Likelihood ratio	133.21	44.134	68.996
Linear-by-linear association	1.286	0.416	0.292
Number of valid cases	161	161	161
Asymptotic Significance (2 sided)	0.012	0.939	0.391

MPF, Mobile phone features; BIU, Behavioural intention to use; M, Motivation; T, Time.
a, 166 cells (98.8%) have expected count less than 5 (the minimum expected count is 0.1); b, 61 cells (84.7%) have expected count less than 5 (the minimum expected count is 0.1); c, 75 (89.3%) have expected count less than 5 (the minimum expected count is 0.1).

Table 3, $X^2(n = 161) = 174.989, p = 0.012$. Therefore, hypothesis 1 stating that a significant association can be found between mobile phone features and BIU, is supported. The conclusion here is that the more mobile phone features present on the phone, the higher the BIU the phone for communication purposes. With regard to hypothesis 2, the aim was to test the association between motivation and BIU. The Chi-square test results revealed no statistically significant association between motivation and BIU, $X^2 (n = 161) = 39.748, p = 0.939$. These results indicate that motivation plays a minor role in influencing students to utilise their phones for communicating purposes. Finally, hypothesis 3 tested the association between time and BIU mobile phones by students. Results further revealed no statistically significant association between time and BIU, $X^2 (n = 161) = 67.527, p = 0.391$. The statistical findings reveal that there is no evidence to support hypothesis 3. The results indicate that time plays a minor role in influencing students to utilise their phones for communication purposes. Based on the findings, a conclusion was reached that student communication via mobile phones is seldom a time-related factor. However, due to the desire to know more, students find themselves downloading more features (Potgieter 2015) and exploring various other features installed on their phones at great length and with enthusiasm independent of time.

Discussion

The presence of various mobile phone features appears to heighten the intention to use mobile phones. Therefore, this study concurs with other empirical studies, for example, those by Li *et al.* (2012), Ilechukwu (2013) and Nwogu *et al.* (2014), which concluded that the greater the amount of features on a mobile phone, the higher the behavioural intention to utilise that device for various communicating purposes. Uniquely in this study, this happens within a South African TVET setting, a notion which no other studies have explored before. The findings of this study are also in line with the assumptions of the economic theory suggesting that product features and attributes are linked to consumer demand given the additive utility function. Results further revealed no statistically significant association between motivation and BIU. Earlier on, in accordance with empirical evidence, it was argued that motivational factors are those that move individuals to use their phone (Qualasvirta 2005; Van Biljon 2006). This implied that individual motivational needs had to exist as a fundamental technology adoption requirement. Given the findings of this study, and contrary to literature, it can be argued that modern mobile phones are, themselves, a motivational tool. In this era of smartphones, mobile phones do more than work as a communication device but also as a tool to support the learner in realising his or her potential. For example, the use of modern mobile phones has proven to offer new educational opportunities. Thus, the use of smartphones or mobile phones in TVET has a positive effect on learning and cultivating the desire to learn. It is widely acknowledged that not all students respond to the new institution's settings (a new environment of learning and/or teaching techniques) in the same manner. Some students find it hard to adjust to the new environment and/or teaching techniques, but with the use of smartphones, students play a significant role in their own learning in various and rewarding methods. With mobile phones in their hands, students have realised, nurtured and demonstrated skills essential to their success in both academic and professional fields.

Contribution

A contribution of this study lies in its shift from previous empirical studies with regard to the task complexity theory (Johnson & Payne 1985). The assumptions of the task complexity theory adopted in this study were that motivation and time can be influenced (negatively) by complexity of the mobile phone as a physical product and its features. As elaborated earlier, the thinking was that the greater the product feature and its complexity, the more consumer effort is needed. Wright (1975) further theorised that consumers usually wish to minimise decision efforts. Therefore, other scholars such as Mick and Fournier (1998) and Dellaert and Stremersch (2005) came to the conclusion that mobile phone features that require much effort and time may be avoided due to their complexity as they trigger anxiety or stress. Thompson *et al.* (2005) further suggested that complexity or too many features could lead to feature fatigue, thus making a product overwhelming and thereby causing dissatisfaction. The findings of this study, in contrast to the task complexity theory, are that students are very passionate about smartphones as they regard them as tools of their era. More often, students find themselves exploring at great length various features installed in modern mobile phones, thus supporting the view that the more mobile phone features, the higher the BIU.

Implications for theory

Based on the findings, the research contributes to literature on education and technology, communication as well as marketing. The assumptions of the task complexity theory stating that consumers will avoid complex products were not supported in this study. Phones with more features qualify to be regarded as complex products and resultantly, making use of such phones is also a complex task. On the contrary, students were found to be comfortable in utilising complex products, as evident in higher ratings of BIU.

Implications for practice

The findings of this study provide evidence and data that can be used by practitioners with interest in technology usage by students. The findings reveal that owing to various features on smartphones, students now have access to the Internet. Estimates by the Groupe Speciale Association (GSMA 2014) suggest that between the year 2014 and 2020, sub-Saharan Africa will realise an exponential growth unlike any region, globally, with regard to connectivity through smartphones. Around 525 000 000 connections will be through smartphones, making it the most convenient gadget to conclude business and personal transactions via the Internet. Hence, marketers of educational material can exploit this function and target student groups making use of platforms such as social networking features found on mobile devices for the purpose of advertising.

Given that mobile phone features were found also to be associated with BIU, communication experts can utilise interactive features to gather insights on ever-changing consumer tastes and preferences among youth. In addition, Mukherjee and Hoyer (2001) point out that products which are a result of high innovation such as smartphones, as evident by the volume of application software which they can accommodate, can create a competitive advantage that help marketers to penetrate the student and/or youth market easily. The findings of this study serve as an eye opener to various practitioners with varying interests. For example, the South African student market, largely representing the youth, adopts products that promote interaction between peers in the same manner as other regional and international markets. Hence, to marketers of mobile phones who would like to pursue global and regional markets, the local market's behaviour can prove to be a useful secondary research platform.

Limitations

A limitation exists with the present research. The results of this research are not generalisable to the entire population of TVET students in South Africa. Caution should be exercised when interpreting and making implications based on this.

Future research

Despite the limitation that exists with the current research, future research can be suggested to improve on such. Furthermore, a qualitative study would aid in understanding underlying motivations for mobile phone usage among students.

Conclusion

The use of mobile phones outside communication purposes can bring added value to the TVET system in South Africa. Thus, if the responsible authorities in the TVET sector adopt the relevant framework and incorporate the use of communication application software (Facebook, Twitter, LinkedIn, WhatsApp, Skype, Viber and BBM among others) that come along with modern mobile phones into the TVET system, such software can prove to be of great use in the form of student support and guiding tools.

Acknowledgements

Competing interests

The authors declare that they have no financial or personal relationships which may have inappropriately influenced them in writing this article.

Authors' contributions

H.S. was the project leader assisted by A.S. W.C. was responsible for the data collection and assisted H.S. with the data analysis. H.S. and W.C. were involved in the final write up of the project.

References

Agundo-Peregrina, Á.F., Hernández-García, A. & Pascual-Miguel, F.J., 2014, 'Behavioral intention, use behavior and the acceptance of electronic learning systems: Differences between higher education and lifelong learning', *Computers in Human Behavior* 34, 301–314. http://dx.doi.org/10.1016/j.chb.2013.10.035

Ajzen, I. & Fishbein, M., 1980, *Understanding attitudes and predicting social behaviour*, Prentice-Hallm, Englewood Cliffs, NJ.

Babbie, E., 1992, *The practice of social research*, Belmont, Wadsworth, OH.

Bandura, A., 1986, *Social foundations of thought and action: A social cognitive theory*, Prentice-Hall, Englewood Cliffs, NJ.

Baysal, Z.N., Sahenk, S.S. & Hazneci, Y.O., 2010, 'Evaluation of the primary school level students' attitudes towards mobile phones', *Procedia Social and Behavioral Sciences* 2, 4279–4284. http://dx.doi.org/10.1016/j.sbspro.2010.03.679

Caronia, L. & Caron, A.H., 2004, 'Constructing a specific culture: Young people's use of the mobile phone as a social performance', *Convergence: The International Journal of Research into New Media Technologies* 10(2), 28–61. http://dx.doi.org/10.1177/135485650401000204

Chen, S.H., Li, S.H. & Li C.Y., 2011, 'Recent related research in technology acceptance model: A literature review', *Australian Journal of Business and Management Research* 1(9), 124–127.

Chen, Y.F. & Katz, J.E., 2009, 'Extending family to school life: College students' use of the mobile phone', *International Journal of Human-Computer Studies* 67(2), 179–191. http://dx.doi.org/10.1016/j.ijhcs.2008.09.002

Chinyamurindi, W. & Shava, H., 2015, 'An investigation into e-learning acceptance and gender amongst final year students', *South African Journal of Information Management* 17(1), 1–9. http://dx.doi.org/10.4102/sajim.v17i1.635

Chinyamurindi, W.T. & Louw, G.J., 2010, 'Gender differences in technology acceptance in selected South African companies: Implications for electronic learning: Original research', *SA Journal of Human Resource Management* 8(1), 1–7. http://dx.doi.org/10.4102/sajhrm.v8i1.204

Chua, J.H. & Jamil, H., 2012, 'Factors influencing the Technological Pedagogical Content Knowledge (TPACK) among TVET instructors in Malaysian TVET institution', *Procedia Social and Behavioral Sciences* 69, 1539–1547. http://dx.doi.org/10.1016/j.sbspro.2012.12.096

Clark, L.A. & Watson, D., 1995, 'Constructing validity: Basic issues in scale development', *Psychological Assessment* 7, 309–319. http://dx.doi.org/10.1037/1040-3590.7.3.309

Compeau, D.R. & Higgins, C.A., 1995, 'Computer self-efficacy: Development of a measure and initial test', *MIS Quarterly* 19(2), 189–211. http://dx.doi.org/10.2307/249688

Creswell, J.W., 2013, *Qualitative inquiry & research design: Choosing among five approaches*. 3rd edn., Sage, Thousand Oaks, CA.

Creswell, J.W., 2014, *Research design: Qualitative, quantitative and mixed methods approaches*, 4th edn., Sage, Thousand Oaks, CA.

Davis, F., 1989, 'Perceived usefulness, perceived ease of use, and user acceptance of information technology', *MIS Quarterly* 13(3), 318–339. http://dx.doi.org/10.2307/249008

Dellaert, B.G.C. & Stremersch, S., 2005, 'Marketing mass-customized products: Striking a balance between utility and complexity', *Journal of Marketing Research* XLII May, 219–227. http://dx.doi.org/10.1509/jmkr.42.2.219.62293

Desmet, K. & Parente S., 2012, 'The evolution of markets and the revolution of industry: A unified theory of growth', *Journal of Economic Growth* 17(3), 205–234. http://dx.doi.org/10.1007/s10887-012-9080-y

Economicides, A.A. & Grouspoulou, A., 2009, 'Students thoughts about the importance and costs of their mobile devices features and services', *Telematics Inform* 26, 57–84. http://dx.doi.org/10.1016/j.tele.2008.01.001

Eteokleous, N. & Ktoridou, D., 2009, 'Investigating mobile devices integration in higher education in Cyprus: Faculty perspectives', *International Journal of Interactive Mobile Technologies* 3(1), 38–48. http://dx.doi.org/10.3991/ijim.v3i1.762

Field, A., 2013, *Discovering statistics using IBM SPSS statistics*, 4th edn., Sage, London.

Fishbein, M. & Ajzen, I., 1975, *Belief, attitude, intention, and behaviour: An introduction to theory and research*, Addison-Wesley, Reading, MA.

Fisher, G., Jaff, R., Powell, L., & Hall, G., 2003, 'Public further education and training colleges', in Human Research Council (Ed.) *Human Resources Development Review 2003: Education, employment and skills in South Africa*, HSRC Press, Cape Town HSRC and East Lansing; Michigan State University Press.

Gredler, M.E., Broussard, S.C. & Garrison, M.E.B., 2004, 'The relationship between classroom motivation and academic achievement in elementary school aged children', *Family and Consumer Sciences Research Journal* 33(2), 106–120. http://dx.doi.org/10.1177/1077727X04269573

GSMA, 2014, *The mobile economy: Sub-Saharan Africa 2014*, viewed 21 October 2015, from http://ssa.gsmamobileeconomy.com/

Guay, F., Chanal., J., Ratelle, C.F., Marsh, H.W., Larose, S. & Boivin, M., 2010, 'Intrinsic, identified, and controlled types of motivation for school subjects in young elementary school children', *British Journal of Educational Psychology* 80(4), 711–735. http://dx.doi.org/10.1348/000709910X499084

Hakoama, M. & Hakoyama, S., 2011, 'The impact of cell phone use on social networking and development among college students', *American Association of Behavioral and Social Sciences Journal* 15, 1–20.

Head, M. & Ziolkowski, N., 2012, 'Understanding student attitudes of mobile phone features: Rethinking adoption through conjoint, cluster and SEM analyses', *Computers in Human Behavior* 28(6), 2331–2339. http://dx.doi.org/10.1016/j.chb.2012.07.003

Hsiao, C.H. & Yang, C., 2011, 'The intellectual development of the technology acceptance model: A co-citation analysis', *International Journal of Information Management* 31(2), 128–136. http://dx.doi.org/10.1016/j.ijinfomgt.2010.07.003

Ilechukwu, L.C., 2013, 'The assessment of utilisation of e-learning opportunities for effective teaching and learning of religion in Nigerian tertiary institutions', *European Journal of Educational Studies* 5(3), 343–359.

Jack, B. & Clarke, A., 1998, 'The purpose and the use of questionnaires in research', *Professional Nurse* 14(3), 176–179.

Jamal, A., Sedie, R., Haleem, K.A. & Hafiz, N., 2012, 'Patterns of use of "smart phones" among female medical students and self-reported effects', *Journal of Taibah University Medical Sciences* 7(1), 45–49. http://dx.doi.org/10.1016/j.jtumed.2012.07.001

Johnson, E.J. & Payne, J.W., 1985, 'Effort and accuracy in choice', *Management Science* 31(3), 395–414. http://dx.doi.org/10.1287/mnsc.31.4.395

Jokela, T., 2004, 'When good things happen to bad products: Where are the benefits of usability in the consumer appliance market?', *Interactions* 11(6), 28–35. http://dx.doi.org/10.1145/1029036.1029050

Jurisic, B. & Azevedo, A., 2011, 'Building customer–brand relationships in the mobile communications market: The role of brand tribalism and brand reputation', *Brand Management* 18(4/5), 349–366. http://dx.doi.org/10.1057/bm.2010.37

Kang, S., 2014, 'Factors influencing intention of mobile application use', *International Journal of Mobile Communications* 12(4), 360–379. http://dx.doi.org/10.1504/IJMC.2014.063653

Karim, A., Darus, S.H. & Hussin, R., 2006, 'Mobile phone applications in academic library services: A students' feedback survey', *Campus-Wide Information Systems* 23(1), 35–51. http://dx.doi.org/10.1108/10650740610639723

Katz, J.E., 2006, 'Mobile communication and the transformation of daily life: The next phase of research on mobiles', *Knowledge, Technology & Policy* 19(1), 63–71. http://dx.doi.org/10.1007/s12130-006-1016-4

Keeton, K.E., 2008, 'An extension of the UTAUT model: How organizational factors and individual differences influence technology acceptance', PhD Dissertation, University of Houston.

Kyobe, M.E. & Shongwe, M.M., 2011, 'Investigating the extent to which mobile phones reduce knowledge transfer barriers in student project teams', *South African Journal of Information Management* 13(1), 1–10. http://dx.doi.org/10.4102/sajim.v13i1.424

Lancaster, K., 1971, *Consumer demand: A new approach*, Columbia University Press, New York.

Lee, D.Y. & Lehto, M.R., 2013, 'User acceptance of YouTube for procedural learning: An extension of the Technology Acceptance Model', *Computers and Education* 61, 193–208. http://dx.doi.org/10.1016/j.compedu.2012.10.001

Lepp, A., Barkley, J.E., Sanders, G.J., Rebold, M. & Gates, P., 2013, 'The relationship between cell phone use, physical and sedentary activity, and cardiorespiratory fitness in a sample of U.S. college students', *International Journal of Behavioural Nutrition and Physical Activity* 10, 79. http://dx.doi.org/10.1186/1479-5868-10-79

Lepp, A., Li, J., Barkley, J.E. & Salehi-Esfahani, S., 2015, 'Exploring the relationships between college students' cell phone use, personality and leisure', *Computers in Human Behaviour* 43, 210–219. http://dx.doi.org/10.1016/j.chb.2014.11.006

Li, B., Yang, J., Song, X. & Lu, B., 2012, 'Survey on disposal behaviour and awareness of mobile phones in Chinese university students', *Procedia Environmental Sciences* 16, 469–476. http://dx.doi.org/10.1016/j.proenv.2012.10.064

Lightner, R., Benander, R. & Kramer, E.F., 2008, *Faculty and student attitudes about transfer of learning*, viewed 11 February 2015, from http://www.insightjournal.net/Volume3/FacultyStudentAttitudesTransferLearning.pdf

Ling, R., 2004, *The mobile connection: The cell phone's impact on society*, Morgan Kaufmann Publishers, San Francisco, CA.

Mannell, R.C., 2007, 'Leisure, health and well-being', *World Leisure Journal* 49(3), 114–128. http://dx.doi.org/10.1080/04419057.2007.9674499

Mick, D.G. & Fournier, S., 1998, 'Paradoxes of technology: Consumer cognizance, emotions, and coping strategies', *Journal of Consumer Research* 25, 123–143. http://dx.doi.org/10.1086/209531

Mukherjee, A. & Hoyer, W.D., 2001, 'The effect of novel attributes on product evaluation', *Journal of Consumer Research* 28, 462–472. http://dx.doi.org/10.1086/323733

Nwogu, U.F., Udoye, N.R. & Oguejiofor, C.S., 2014, 'Towards utilisation of e-learning in preparing business education students for the world of work', *African Education Review* 8(3), 155–164. http://dx.doi.org/10.4314/afrrev.v8i3.13

Ong, C.S. & Lai, J.Y., 2006, 'Gender differences in perceptions and relationships among dominants of e-learning acceptance', *Computers in Human Behaviour* 22(5), 816–829. http://dx.doi.org/10.1016/j.chb.2004.03.006

Pallant, J., 2010, *SPSS survival manual: A step by step guide to data analysis using SPSS*, 4th edn., McGraw-Hill, Maidenhead.

Park, S.Y., 2009, 'An analysis of the technology acceptance model in understanding university students' behavioural intention to use e-learning', *Educational Technology and Society* 12(3), 150–162.

Peters, O., Rickes, M., Jockel, S., Von Criegerna, C. & Van Deursen, A., 2006, 'Explaining and analyzing audiences: A social cognitive approach to selectivity and media use', *Communications* 31, 279–308. http://dx.doi.org/10.1515/COMMUN.2006.019

Philips, D.C. & Burbules, N.C., 2000, *Postpositicism and educational research*, Rowman & Littlefield, Lanham, MD.

Potgieter, A., 2015, 'The mobile application preferences of undergraduate university students: A longitudinal study', *South African Journal of Information Management* 17(1), 650.

Pourrazavi, S., Allahverdipour, H., Jafarabadi, M.S. & Matlabi, H., 2014, 'A socio-cognitive inquiry of excessive mobile phone use', *Asian Journal of Psychiatry* 10, 84–89. http://dx.doi.org/10.1016/j.ajp.2014.02.009

Qualasvirta, A., 2005, 'Grounding the innovation of future technologies', *Human Technology* 1(1), 58–75. http://dx.doi.org/10.17011/ht/urn.2005126

Saadé, R.G., Nebebe, F. & Tan, W., 2007, 'Viability of the technology acceptance model in multimedia learning environments: A comparative study', *Interdisciplinary Journal of Knowledge and Learning Objects* 3(1), 175–184.

Salesforce Marketing Cloud, 2014, *2014 mobile behaviour report*, viewed 15 October 2015, from http://www.exacttarget.com/2014-mobile-behavior-report

Skiba, D.J., 2014, 'The connected age: Mobile apps and consumer engagement', *Nursing Education Perspectives* 35(3), 199–201. http://dx.doi.org/10.5480/1536-5026-35.3.199

Streiner, D.L., 1993, 'A checklist for evaluating the usefulness of rating scales', *Canadian Journal of Psychiatry* 38(2),140–148. PMid:8467441

Thompson, D.V., Hamilton, R.W. & Rust, R.T., 2005, 'Feature fatigue: When product capabilities become too much of a good thing', *Journal of Marketing Research* XLII, November, 431–442. http://dx.doi.org/10.1509/jmkr.2005.42.4.431

Ting, D.H., Lim, S.F., Patanmacia, T.S., Low, C.G. & Ker, G.C., 2011, 'Dependency on smartphone and the impact on purchase behaviour', *Young Consumers: Insight and Ideas for Responsible Marketers* 12(3), 193–203. http://dx.doi.org/10.1108/17473611111163250

Van Biljon, J.A., 2006, 'A model for representing the motivational and cultural factors that influence mobile phone usage variety', Doctoral Dissertation, viewed 3 January 2015, from http://uir.unisa.ac.za/xmlui/bitstream/handle/10500/2149/thesis.pdf?sequence=1

Venkatesh, V. & Davis, F.D., 1996, 'A model of the antecedents of perceived ease of use: Development and test', *Decision sciences* 27(3), 451–481. http://dx.doi.org/10.1111/j.1540-5915.1996.tb00860.x

Venkatesh, V. & Davis, F.D., 2000, 'A theoretical extension of the technology acceptance model: Four longitudinal field studies', *Management Science* 46(2), 186–204. http://dx.doi.org/10.1287/mnsc.46.2.186.11926

Walsh, S.P., White, K.M. & Young, R., 2010, 'Needing to connect: The effect of self and others on young people's involvement with their mobile phones', *Australian Journal of Psychology* 62(4), 194–203. http://dx.doi.org/10.1080/00049530903567229

Wanajak, K., 2011, 'Internet use and its impact on secondary school students in chainmail, Thailand', PhD Thesis, Edith Cowan University, Australia.

Wang, Y.S., Lin, H.H. & Luarn, P., 2006, 'Predicting consumer intention to use mobile service', *Information Systems Journal* 16, 157–179. http://dx.doi.org/10.1111/j.1365-2575.2006.00213.x

Wiid, J. & Diggines, C., 2013, *Marketing research*, 2nd edn., Juta, Cape Town.

Wright, P., 1975, 'Consumer choice strategies: Simplifying vs. optimizing', *Journal of Marketing Research* 12, 60–67. http://dx.doi.org/10.2307/3150659

Zhang, P. & von Dran, G.M., 2000, 'Satisfactor and dissatisfactorers: A two-factor model for website design and evaluation', *Journal of the American Society for Information Science* 51(4), 1253–1268. http://dx.doi.org/10.1002/1097-4571(2000)9999:9999<::AID-ASI1039>3.0.CO;2-O

3

Students' perceptions of the infopreneurship education in the Department of Records and Archives Management at the National University of Science and Technology

Authors:
Peterson Dewah[1]
Stephen Mutula[1]

Affiliations:
[1]School of Social Sciences, Information Studies Programme, University of KwaZulu-Natal, South Africa

Corresponding author:
Peterson Dewah,
dewah@ukzn.ac.za

Background: The infopreneurship education course forms part of the final year Bachelor of Science Honours Degree in Records and Archives Management (BScRAM) at the National University of Science (NUST). The course looks unique and out of place in relation to other records and archives courses which specifically focus on the management of records and archives.

Objectives: The study examined the students' perceptions regarding the relevance of the infopreneurship course in the BScRAM that is offered in the Department of Records and Archives Management at NUST, Zimbabwe. The aim of the study was to determine student evaluation of relevance of the course to the BScRAM.

Method: Both quantitative and qualitative methods of collecting data were used. Using a census method, data was collected through a focus group interview and a self-administered questionnaire from a study population that comprised 17 students who were in their final year of the BScRAM at NUST.

Results: The results revealed students found the infopreneurial education module quite relevant to their degree. Although the lecturer was helpful in providing resources, students felt that they needed to visit some infopreneurial businesses for familiarisation and looked forward to having guest lecturers from the infopreneurial world.

Conclusion: Although the BScRAM was not well known at high school level, students found the infopreneurial education in this degree quite stimulating. Having gone through an infopreneurship course, students were prepared to undertake infopreneurial businesses after graduating from the university.

Introduction

The term infopreneur is derived from information and entrepreneur. Entrepreneurship is the process of starting a business, based around an innovative product, process, or service. Weber (2012) defines entrepreneurship as the discovery, evaluation, and exploitation of opportunities to create future goods and services by a natural individual through the creation of a new organisation. Infopreneur refers to an entrepreneur who makes a living by producing, collecting, gathering, repacking, disseminating, developing, and selling information and information products and services for a profit, in most cases via the internet (Du Toit 2000; Chandler 2007; Lahm & Stowe 2011). Infopreneurship is part of what Ocholla (1999) described as information consultancy and brokerage. An entrepreneurial personality identifies with a set of traits such as need for achievement, locus of control, risk-taking propensity, desire for autonomy, over-optimistic about chances of being successful, and tolerance for ambiguity (Storey & Greene 2010) among other useful traits that make an individual a successful entrepreneur in information.

Universities worldwide use various methods to teach entrepreneurship. Many scholars and educators agree that entrepreneurship education is intended to encourage and stimulate the creation of new ventures through increasing students' awareness of entrepreneurship as a process and a distinct career possibility (Kassean *et al.* 2015; Blenker *et al.* 2006). Entrepreneurship education culminates in establishment of business for the purposes of profit making and growth, and self-employment in contrast to organisational employment. In Weber's (2012) view entrepreneurship education has two purposes: (1) to increase students' entrepreneurial skills and (2) to provide impetus to those who are suited to entrepreneurship while discouraging those who are not. Individuals engage in infopreneurship for various reasons, chief among them being unemployment and the desire to be self-employed.

A study conducted in Botswana, Ocholla (1999; 1998) identified a host of some reasons for engaging in infopreneurship including the following:

- decline of resources to sustain wage employment in the public and private sector
- increase in unemployment calling for self-employment
- dead end jobs retarding professional and career growth
- the inability of existing information provision centres to provide information services needed, and increased demand for specialised information services
- the willingness of information consumers to pay for consultancy services and recognition that information is a commodity that can create wealth
- acceptance that information is power necessary for individuals and firms to stay in the market and to keep the competition off-balance
- interest in self-employment; inadequate incomes force income earners to sell skills and knowledge for additional earnings
- social change witnessed in the creation of small businesses
- encouragement by entrepreneurs who buy expertise, hire consultants, and avoid obligations for hiring staff on a long-term basis
- increased need for proper information management
- size and complexity of the information industry (Ocholla 1999; 1998).

Other areas of infopreneurship could include internet providers; e-services and m-services; computer troubleshooting services; helping junior students write research proposals, essays, and reports; proofreading; editing (Ramugondo 2010); and such areas as e-books and e-publishing; business analyst consultancy; web newsletters, access achieved through subscription; and online solutions through recorded videos, for example on how to reference, how to publish online, and how to write a winning research proposal (Chandler 2007).

In a Botswana study Ocholla (1999; 1998) identified research in information related fields such as:

- user studies and market analysis
- compilation of bibliographic lists
- provision of current business information
- compilation of directories
- publishing, for instance desktop publishing
- translation services; information repackaging
- writing, editing, proofreading; collection management
- records management; management of service established through consultancy services
- cataloguing
- document delivery services
- development of specialised libraries from scratch
- software creation and development; development vocabularies
- search and retrieval of information
- conduct staff training
- newspaper clipping services
- online searching; organisation of files and planning of paper flow
- organisation of seminars, workshops and conferences and preparation of proceedings, provision of current awareness and alerting information services among others.

Information consultancy can provide a wide range of services in Records and Archives Management (RAM), for instance filing, reorganising the registry, automating records offices, digitisation projects of records or archives, and training services, among others.

Contextual setting: Teaching infopreneurship in the Records and Archives Management Department at the National University of Science and Technology

The National University of Science and Technology (NUST) was founded in 1988. Its vision is 'to be a world-class centre of excellence in teaching, research, innovation and entrepreneurship for sustainable development' (NUST 2015) and its mission statement is to 'contribute positively towards the advancement of humanity through the provision of knowledge based solutions to scientific, technological, economic and social challenges'. NUST hopes to achieve its mission and goals through a coterie of core values, namely honesty and integrity, innovativeness, excellence and diligence, intellectual freedom, equity, and social, and environmental responsibility.

The NUST is comprised of seven faculties (Applied Sciences, Commerce, Communication & Information Science, Built Environment, Medicine, Industrial Technology, and Faculty of Technical Teacher Education) consisting of 32 different departments. A run through the university's yearbook reveals that the majority of the departments teach entrepreneurial courses to either undergraduates or postgraduate students. Cited in Keat, Selvarajah and Meyer (2011), observes that courses in entrepreneurship are also becoming popular at college and university levels. Regarding entrepreneurship education Blenker's *et al.* (2006) assume that entrepreneurship or enterprising behaviour characteristics, competencies, and skills can be learned and taught. Kirby (2007) argues that in this era of rapid change universities should develop in students the abilities to see opportunities, cope with uncertainty, and bring about change through innovation.

The department of Records and Archives Management (RAM) is housed under the Faculty of Communication and Information Science together with the departments of Library and Information Science, Journalism and Media Studies, and Publishing. In the first semester of their final year RAM students cover Management of Records Centres, Information Economics, Marketing of Information Products and Services, Management of Health Information, and infopreneurship courses. At the time of the study the department had seven lecturers, two staff development fellows, three teaching assistants, and one research fellow (NUST 2015). Johannisson (1991) and as cited in Fayolle, Gailly and Lassas-Clerc (2007) are of the opinion that the impact of students' perceptions of entrepreneurship, along with resources and other support mechanisms available in the university environment, can positively influence student attitudes towards entrepreneurial careers. Fayolle *et al.* (2007) opine that the significant differences between students who have taken entrepreneurship courses and those who have not can be explained by the educational variables (course content, teaching methods, teacher profile, resources, and support) and the direct intentional and behavioural antecedents (attitudes, values, knowledge, and so on).

Weber (2012) has observed that although students express interest about entrepreneurship, they lack information and as such entrepreneurship courses may provide a welcome source of information and skills. An infopreneurship course was introduced to the RAM Department in 2011 and to date it has had four cohorts of graduates. This was in line with the vision, mission, and core values of NUST which entail equipping NUST graduates with entrepreneurial skills in order to start their own businesses and fend for themselves rather than seek to be employed by others. Keat *et al.* (2011) are of the view that many universities and colleges around the world have introduced entrepreneurial courses to students in an effort to promote entrepreneurship as well as a professional entrepreneurship career. Blenker *et al.* (2006) reveal that traditionally universities have focused on teaching students what the university finds necessary.

Weber (2012) identified six elements of entrepreneurship education:

- objectives that are pursued
- faculty or teaching team who will be imparting it
- participant students
- content of the course
- teaching methods
- specific support activities for the participants to start their ventures.

The course description clearly outlines that after studying this course, among other outcomes and expectations, students should be able to conceptualise the current world in which people work with information as a living function; discuss the characteristics of an information society and give reasoned views of whether Zimbabwe or part of the country, measures up to these characteristics; set up an information business; and develop a business plan. Various methods are designed to assist students learn entrepreneurial skills. Kassean *et al.* (2015) suggest that many entrepreneurship programs aim to expose students to role models in the form of guest speakers, consulting projects, and mentoring programs. Education, training, and mentoring for aspiring and established entrepreneurs are intended to develop entrepreneurs (Henry & Letch 2007).

The 2014 course outline had six units:

- the information world
- business of information
- entrepreneurship and information
- starting and managing a new business
- business ethics
- developing a business plan.

Chandler and Jansen (1992) cited in Carrier (2007) are of the view that entrepreneurs must acquire three types of competencies, namely entrepreneurial, managerial, and technical competencies.

It was noticeable that topics such as risk taking and market research were absent from the course outline. Kyro and Tapani (2007) observe that risk-taking from learning and teaching perspectives has been a neglected area in entrepreneurship education research such that they believe risk-taking is a competence that can be both taught and learned. With regards to marketing, Hills, Hultman and Miles (2007) have noted that marketing educators, using traditional marketing principles, typically encourage students to develop a marketing plan. An important part of marketing education focuses on how companies obtain information about the environment (Hills *et al.* 2007). The course outline gives some activities and cases as a way to enhance learning. Assignment topics are listed so that students choose and answer them as part of their coursework. Assessment of the course is well explained in the course outline. A reference list is appended to assist students in their further research. The infopreneurship course is offered in the first semester of the fourth/final year and to date the RAM department has graduated four streams in this course. It remains to be seen how many graduates have started their businesses. Maybe this deserves a follow-up study by another researcher. Kirby (2007) suggests that to develop an individual who can identify opportunities requires a change in the courses, the process of learning, and in some cases the place where learning takes place.

Statement of the problem

The infopreneurship course forms part of the final year Bachelor of Science Honours Degree in Records and Archives Management (BScRAM). The course looks unique and out of place in relation to other courses which specifically focus on the management of records and archives. Because of substantial changes, transformations, and demands on an entrepreneur's skills and abilities, entrepreneurship educators need to formulate flexible strategies to allow for continual redesign of organisations, and find alternative and non-traditional methods of teaching entrepreneurship. Absence of some key topics such as risk and market research requires an inquiry on students' perceptions on the infopreneurship course. As such the study aimed at assessing the RAM students' perceptions on the infopreneurship course that forms part of their courses in the final year of BScRAM.

Research questions

The main research question this paper sought to address was: what are the RAM students' perceptions on the infopreneurship education course offered in the study of records and archives management degree? The following specific research questions are addressed.

- What motivated students to enrol for the BSc degree in Records and Archives Management at NUST?
- How relevant is the infopreneurship course in the study of Records and Archives Management?
- Do resources suffice to assist students undertaking the course?
- What challenges do final/fourth year students face in undertaking this course?
- Would the students want to become infopreneurs after graduation?
- What recommendations can be made to the RAM department to facilitate smooth running of the course?

In spite of the fact that entrepreneurship is offered to students across the university faculties, this study was delimited to the Faculty of Communication and Information Science's Records and Archives Management Department. Anecdotal evidence by one of the researchers who is a member of staff in that faculty pointed to the fact that the RAM department was the only department that offered an infopreneurship module in that faculty at the time of the study and only at fourth/final year level. The other departments (Library and Information Science, Publishing Studies, and Media and Journalism) shop for the entrepreneurship course from the Faculty of Commerce.

Methodology

The study used both quantitative and qualitative methods of collecting data. A self-administered questionnaire was distributed to all the 17 fourth/final year students who were taking the infopreneurship module during the final year of their degree. The study used the census method. The census was appropriate to this small and heterogeneous group of 17 students. The students completed and returned the questionnaires through their class representative. Sixteen completed questionnaire copies were returned and one student did not return the questionnaire. This gave a response rate of 94%. Quantitative data was analysed statistically using SPSS version 18, whereas qualitative data was analysed thematically. The researcher conducted a focus group interview with six students (two males and four females) to seek clarifications on certain questions. The interview lasted for 90 min.

Data gathered revealed that all students were Zimbabweans and enrolled for the BSc Honours degree in Records and Archives Management at this university in 2011. Eleven female and 5 male fourth and/or final year students took part in the study. Fourteen (87.5%) respondents were between the ages of 22–24 years, 1 (6.2%), was in the 19–21 year age group, and 1 (6.2%), was above 25 years of age.

Data presentation and analysis

Students' motivation for enrolling for the Bachelor of Science Honours Degree in Records and Archives Management

Students were asked to give their reasons for choosing and enrolling for the BScRAM at NUST. This was a qualitative question. Student responses were put under themes and the following are responses from the questionnaire and focus group interview: 'it is an emerging professional discipline in Zimbabwe'; 'the university chose the programme for me'; 'the management of records is applicable to many organisations'; 'I was fascinated about the programme'; 'the programme is not yet flooded on the market'; 'I saw the newspaper advert'; 'somebody encouraged me'; 'mentor advised me to take the degree programme'. It also emerged that the majority of the students who took part in the focus group interview wanted degree programmes that are offered in the Faculty of Commerce at the same university. The degrees they mentioned included, BSc Honours Marketing, BSc Honours Accounting and BSc Honours Business Management.

Relevancy of the infopreneurship education in records and archives

Given that it is a course slightly different from other courses that are found in the BScRAM, students were asked if they think it was a relevant course in RAM. The responses from both questionnaire and interviews revealed that students found it very relevant in the degree programme and in preparing them for future life. Their answers were grouped thus 'equips with knowledge in infopreneurial activity'; 'role of information professional is changing with technology' and 'learned creative analytical skills' (Figure 1).

From the interviews students pointed out that the BScRAM provides them with basic foundation knowledge in the management of records. Infopreneurship then gives skills to

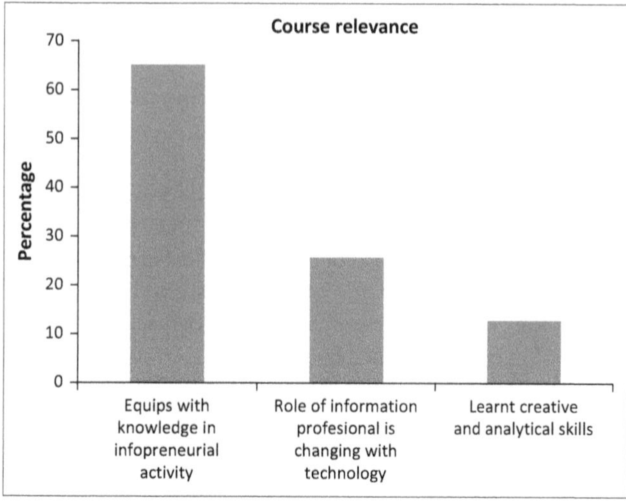

FIGURE 1: Relevancy of the infopreneurship course in records and archives (N = 16).

sell information and skills to start their own businesses through good proposal writing. Students went on to suggest that in a university they may start businesses to proofread research projects. In view of all these they concluded that infopreneurship was a relevant course to them.

The questionnaire provided the students with a list of all the six units that they covered as stated in the course outline. Students were then asked to identify those units which they found relevant and or irrelevant to the BScRAM. Results indicate that students found all the five units (the information world; business of information; entrepreneurship and information; starting and managing a new business; business ethics, and developing a business plan) to be relevant and appropriate to be taught in the course.

Students' evaluation of the infopreneurship course

The course Infoprenuership (Code IRA 4104) was offered to fourth and/or final year students in the first semester in 2014. Students were then asked for their opinions on how they found this course. The question required them to fill in their opinions in the spaces provided. A qualitative analysis grouped the responses under seven themes and this was presented diagrammatically in Figure 2. Students' views were as follows: 'very interesting course' (9: 56%); 'promotes innovation' (2: 13%); 'highlights gaps that can be exploited' (1: 6%); 'equips with entrepreneurial skills' (1: 6%); 'easy to understand' (1: 6%), 'good foundation' (1: 6%) and 'fair' (1: 6%). The students' views are presented in Figure 2.

During the focus group interview students made the following additional comments: 'the course was an eye-opener'; 'I was fascinated'; 'I saw other job opportunities to earn money' and 'the course opened avenues for RAM graduates to do something' suggesting that the Theory of Planned Behaviour is appropriate in predicting entrepreneurial activity (Weber 2012) as future behaviour of students.

Infopreneurship course content

In view of what was covered in their course outline students were asked to tick those topics that they felt needed to be

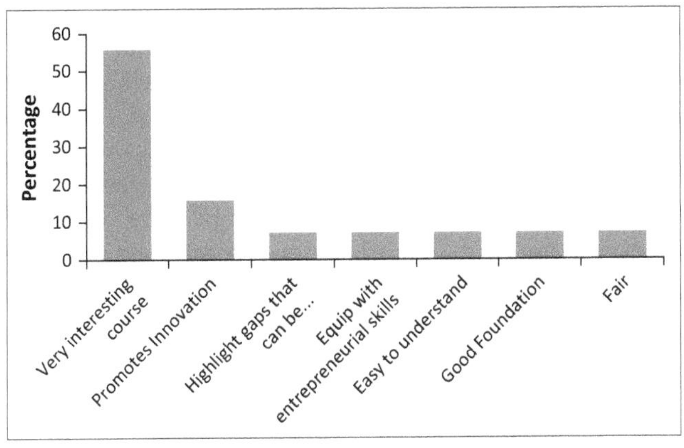

FIGURE 2: Students' evaluation of infopreneurship course (N = 16).

added to the course content. In the responses 'strongly agree' and 'agree' were treated as 'agree'. Similarly 'disagree' and 'strongly disagree' were treated as 'disagree'. Results indicated that the majority of students agreed that risk and the entrepreneur (15: 93%), infopreneurship in Zimbabwe (14: 87%) were frequently mentioned, followed by market research (13: 81.3%). The others were entrepreneurship (11: 68%), marketing management (10: 62.6%), personnel management (8: 50%), and financial management (9: 56.3%). Students were not sure if financial management (6: 37.5%), personnel management (5: 31.3%), marketing management (4: 25%), entrepreneurship (4: 25%), market research (2: 12.5%) and infopreneurship in Zimbabwe (2: 12.5%) could be added to the infopreneurship course. Nobody objected/disagreed to the inclusion of financial management, risk and the entrepreneur, and infopreneurship in Zimbabwe. Three (18.8%) students disagreed that personnel management could be added. There were single objections to the inclusion of market research (1: 6.3%), marketing management (1: 6.3%), and entrepreneurship (1: 6.3%) topics. Teaching these topics to students is consistent with Chandler and Jansen's (1992) view as cited in Carrier (2007) that entrepreneurs must acquire entrepreneurial, managerial, and technical competencies.

The focus group interview revealed that respondents disagreed (3: 18.8%) that personnel management should be added to course outline because the students cover this title in a shopped module (Principles of Management and Business Ethics) from the faculty of commerce. The five (31.3%) respondents who remained neutral probably thought there could be something special/unique with personnel management in infopreneurship or that it was not necessary to do personnel management again. During the interview students pointed out that considering the Zimbabwean economic situation, another topic called 'Information in Zimbabwe' needed to be added.

During the focus group interview students revealed that risk and the entrepreneur must be included because 'information has its risks' and therefore needed 'risk takers'. The absence of risk as a topic in the course confirms Kyro and Tapani's (2007) view that students' feelings and perceptions about risk-taking, uncertainty, and insecurity are rarely studied in entrepreneurship research yet they are valid in entrepreneurship education. Respondents also suggested that market research was important because the infopreneur needs to 'know what consumers want' confirming Hills *et al.* (2007) observation that marketing research is the leading source of information about the environment.

Challenges faced by the fourth or final year students in undertaking this course

In view of challenges of taking a relatively new course in the university curricula, respondents were asked to rate the lecturer's support in helping the student's education on infopreneurship. Data obtained revealed that the lecturer

TABLE 1: Courses to be added to the existing course outline (N = 16).

Suggested courses to be added	Strongly agree		Agree		Neutral		Disagree		Strongly disagree	
	n	%	*n*	%	*n*	%	*n*	%	*n*	%
Financial Management	3	18.8	6	37.5	6	37.5	-	-	-	-
Risk and the entrepreneur	12	75	3	18.8	-		-	-	-	-
Infopreneurship in Zimbabwe	12	75	2	12.5	2	12.5	-	-	-	-
Market research	9	56.3	4	25	2	12.5	1	6.3	-	-
Marketing Management	5	31.3	5	31.3	4	25	-	-	1	6.3
Personnel Management	4	25	4	25	5	31.3	2	12.5	1	6.3
Entrepreneurship	4	25	7	43.8	4	25	-	-	1	6.3

TABLE 2: Lecturer's support (N = 16).

Lecturer's activities and initiatives	Not helpful at all		Not sure		Helpful		Very helpful		Extremely helpful	
	n	%	*n*	%	*n*	%	*n*	%	*n*	%
Conducted lectures	-	-	-	-	2	12.5	9	56.3	5	31.3
Provided books	-	-	-	-	6	37.5	3	18.8	6	37.5
Provided journal articles	-	-	-	-	4	25	3	18.8	9	56.3
Provided course outline	-	-	-	-	3	18.8	3	18.8	10	62.5
Provided practical speeches by Infopreneurs	6	37.5	4	25	2	12.5	-	-	2	12.5
Group visits to Information businesses	7	43.8	3	18.8	1	6.3	1	6.3	2	12.5
Lecturer related his own infopreneurship experience	2	12.5	3	18.8	5	31.3	1	6.3	3	18.8

was helpful by conducting lectures 16 (100%), providing books 16 (100%), providing journal articles 16 (100%), and providing the course outline (100%). Dilts and Fowler (1999), cited in Fayolle *et al.* (2007), have shown that certain teaching methods such as traineeships and field learning are more successful than others at preparing students for an entrepreneurial career. Respondents felt that the lecturer was not helpful in providing practical talks from infopreneurs 10 (62.6%) and yet Carrier (2007) is of the view that very rich, well known, and successful entrepreneurs can be excellent motivational speakers and role models for students, making students aware of the intrinsic rewards of self-employment. Respondents also felt that the lecturer was not assisting in group visits to information businesses 10 (62.6%), and in relating his own infopreneurship experience 5 (31.3%). Apart from imparting knowledge in the class, educators are given the responsibility to mould the personality and characters of students (Keat *et al.* 2011).

Fayolle, *et al.* (2007) opine that the educational variables such as course content, teaching methods, teacher profile, resources, and support have significant differences between students who have taken entrepreneurship courses and those who have not. During the focus group interview students clarified that they really needed to visit some infopreneurial businesses to familiarise with what actually happens in such businesses so that they could establish their own in future. It was also clarified during this interview that the respondents meant 'not helpful' when they said 'not sure'.

The focus group interview also revealed that students expected to be tasked to engage in more hands-on approaches and practicals such as selling information, books, and websites. Students also indicated that they expected to gain more exposure to infopreneurship businesses. This is consistent with Blenker *et al.* (2006), who suggest that experience has to be brought in from elsewhere in the form of guest lecturers from the 'real world'. The other aspect that emerged was that the module lacked resources such as books. Students pointed out that some of the recommended articles could not be accessed because their university (NUST) did not subscribe to the databases where the articles could be downloaded. Keat *et al.* (2011) argue that the ultimate aim of entrepreneurial programmes is to stimulate entrepreneurship awareness among students that, in turn, would increase their interest in entrepreneurship.

At the end of the questionnaire students were asked to make any other comment on the course Infopreneurship. The following is a summary of the respondents' comments with regards to the course: 'Can the course have some element of practicality in it in order to put theory into practice?'; 'The course is very helpful to us as students because we can actually start our businesses, be self-employed, after finishing degrees instead of sitting at home due to lack of employment in the country'; 'It is a relevant course regarding the unemployment levels in Zimbabwe'; 'It is a very good course which teaches relevant skills and is administered with simplicity that allows understanding by lecturer which is very helpful'; 'The course should involve aspects relating to financial management as well as risk management to ensure that the student is equipped with skills involved within the business'; 'It is a good course which can assist students to better manage their own businesses. However, students need visits to infopreneurship organizations'; 'lectures should have some practicals and students must be tasked to start businesses like what happens with the students for the BSc Honours Applied Chemistry entrepreneurship course'; 'The course should be complimented with systematic tours to infopreneurial firms and have seminars with practical infopreneurship'. This was consistent with Kassean *et al.* (2015) who note that for an entrepreneurship education programme to be effective, scholars have argued that it must emphasise actions in entrepreneurial ways and separate from traditional hallmarks such as business plan writing.

Would you start your own business after taking and completing the Infopreneurship course?

Respondents were asked if they would want to become infopreneurs after graduation. All 16 (100%) students responded in the affirmative. Focus group interview data confirmed the questionnaire data. Table 3 presents the results from the focus group.

The results are consistent with Weber (2012) who opines that having gone through a course, students may now be more able to decide for the 'right' career path. The results confirm Ajzen's (1991) theory of planned behaviour that the formation of entrepreneurial intentions depends on perceived desirability, perceived social norm, and perceived behavioural control towards the behaviour in question.

Conclusions and recommendations

The paper is based on the study that aimed at investigating the NUST RAM students' perceptions on the infopreneurship course that is offered in their final year of BScRAM. It sought to address the following research questions.

- What motivates students to enrol for the BSc Honours Degree in RAM?
- Is the Infopreneurship Module a relevant course in the study of records and archives?
- What available resources are there for the teaching of the Infopreneurship course considering that it is a fairly new course?
- What challenges do part 4 students face when undertaking this course?

Results indicate that the majority of students did not apply to enrol for this degree, but found the infopreneurial module quite interesting, an eye-opener and relevant to their degree. The other finding was that the lecturer was helpful in providing to students such resources as books and electronic resources but students felt that they needed to visit some infopreneurial businesses for the purposes of familiarisation. They also looked forward to having guest lecturers from the real infopreneurial world. In line with the theory of planned behaviour and having gone through the infopreneurship course, students were prepared to undertake infopreneurial business after graduating from the university. The study proposed some recommendations for the programme.

TABLE 3: Respondents' view on starting an Infopreneurial business (N = 6).

Respondent	Respondents' view
R1	The course is very helpful to us as students because we can actually start our businesses, be self-employed, after finishing degrees instead of sitting at home due to lack of employment in the country
R2	It is a very good course for students as it prepares us with the necessary tools to engage into the real world and be better prepared for what life has to offer
R3	The course is relevant especially to prepare students who are about to finish their first degrees
R4	It is a good course which can assist students to better manage their own businesses

Considering that students did not choose BScRAM as a first choice degree on application, the study recommends that the department of RAM can engage in advocacy to market the programme in order to bring awareness to high school students on the programme. This will motivate students to enrol for a programme of their choice. In view of the fact that students have found the course relevant to their degree programme (BScRAM) and in life, the study recommends that NUST may provide students with an opportunity and resources to start businesses such as to proofread final year students' research projects. Given the finding that infopreneurship is a relatively new discipline and as such resources are still scarce, the study recommends that NUST purchase some books relevant for the course. The study also recommends the subscription to some databases to assist in accessing some important online articles and e-books on infopreneurship. Another recommendation is the inclusion of varying teaching methods and activities in infopreneurship education that may include motivational speeches by successful infopreneurs, visits to infopreneurial businesses, and practicals such as drawing up a business plan or business proposal writing identified in local or international newspapers. The BSc RAM graduates would want to become infopreneurs in the future. In view of this conclusion the study recommends that the lecturers should regularly update the course outline to include some important topics on contemporary issues so that the entrepreneurial graduates will not face serious challenges in the field.

Acknowledgements

Competing interests

The authors declare that they have no financial or personal relationships which may have inappropriately influenced them in writing this article.

Authors' contributions

D.P., a postdoctoral scholar, conducted the study as part of his postdoctoral studies at University of KwaZulu-Natal. M.S.M., the dean and head of School of Social Sciences and Humanities at University of KwaZulu-Natal, supervised the postdoctoral work.

References

Ajzen, I., 1991, 'The theory of planned behavior', *Organizational Behavior and Human Decision Process* 50, 179–211.

Ann, J. & Carland, J. (eds.), 2010, *Proceedings of the Allied Academies Internet Conference*, Vol. 12, pp. 1–171, 14–17 April 2010, New Orleans: Louisiana.

Blenker, P., Dreisler, P., Faergeman, H.M. & Kjeldsen, J., 2006, 'Learning and teaching entrepreneurship: Dilemmas, reflections and strategies', in A. Fayolle & H. Klandt (eds.), *International entrepreneurship education: Issues and newness*, pp. 21–34, Chetelham (UK): Edward Elgar Publishing Limited. http://dx.doi.org/10.4337/9781847201652.00008

Carrier, C., 2007, 'Strategies for teaching entrepreneurship', in A. Fayolle (ed.), *Handbook of research in entrepreneurship education, volume 1: A general perspective*, pp. 143–159. Chetelham (UK): Edward Elgar Publishing Limited.

Chandler, G.N. & Jansen, E., 1992, 'The founder's self-assessed competence and venture performance', *Journal of Business Venturing* 7(3), 223–236. http://dx.doi.org/10.1016/0883-9026(92)90028-P

Chandler, S., 2007, *From entrepreneur to infopreneur: Make money with books, eBooks and information products*, Wiley, London.

Dilts, J.C. & Fowler, S.M., 1999, 'Internships: Preparing students for an entrepreneurial career', *Journal of Business and Entrepreneurship* 11(1), 51–63.

Du Toit, A., 2000, 'Teaching infopreneurship: Students' perspectives', *Aslib Proceedings* 52(2), 83–90. http://dx.doi.org/10.1108/EUM0000000007003

Fayolle, A., Gailly, B. & Lassas-Clerc, N., 2007, 'Towards a new methodology to assess the entrepreneurship teaching programmes', in A. Fayolle (ed.), *Handbook of research in entrepreneurship education, volume 1: A general perspective*, pp. 187–197, Chetelham (UK): Edward Elgar Publishing Limited. http://dx.doi.org/10.4337/9781847205377.00019

Henry, C.H. & Letch, C. M., 2007, 'Evaluating entrepreneurship education and training: Implications for programme design', in A. Fayolle (ed.), *Handbook of research in entrepreneurship education, volume 1: A general perspective*, pp. 248–260. Chetelham (UK): http://dx.doi.org/10.4337/9781847205377.00024.

Hills, G., Hultman, C. & Miles, M., 2007, 'Entrepreneurial marketing and university education', in Alain Fayolle (ed.), *Handbook of research in entrepreneurship education, volume 1, a general perspective*, pp. 219–229, Edward Elgar Publ. Ltd, Cheltenham, UK (in US: Edward 7 Elgar Publishing Inc., Northampton, MA).

Johannisson, B., 1991, 'University training for entrepreneurship: Swedish approaches', *Journal of Entrepreneurship and Regional Development* 3(1), 67–82. http://dx.doi.org/10.1080/08985629100000005

Kassean, H., Vanevenhoven, J., Liguori, E. & Winkel, D.E., 2015, 'Entrepreneurship education: A need for reflection, real-world experience and action', *International Journal of Entrepreneurial Behavior & Research* 21(5), 690–708. http://dx.doi.org/10.1108/IJEBR-07-2014-0123

Keat, O.Y., Selvarajah, C. & Meyer, D., 2011, 'Inclination towards entrepreneurship among university students: An empirical study of Malaysian university students', *International Journal of Business and Social Science* 2(4), 207–220.

Kirby, D., 2007, 'Changing the entrepreneurship education paradigm', in A. Fayolle (ed.), *Handbook of research in entrepreneurship education, volume 1: A general perspective*, pp. 21–45. Chetelham (UK): http://dx.doi.org/10.4337/9781847205377.00010

Kyro, P. & Tapani, A., 2007, 'Learning risk-taking competences', in A. Fayolle (ed.), *Handbook of research in entrepreneurship education, volume 1: A general perspective*, pp. 283–306. Chetelham (UK):http://dx.doi.org/10.4337/9781847205377.00026

Lahm, R.J. Jr. & Stowe, C.R.B., 2011, 'Infopreneurship: Roots, evolution, and revolution', *Entrepreneurial Executive* 16, 107–119.

National University of Science and Technology (NUST), 2015, *Records and archives management*, viewed 20 March 2015, from http://www.nust.ac.zw/index.php/medicine/communication-information-science/records-archives-management

Ocholla, D.N., 1998, 'Information consultancy and brokerage in Botswana', *Journal of Information Science* 24(2), 83–95. http://dx.doi.org/10.1177/016555159802400203

Ocholla, D.N., 1999, 'Information intermediaries in the next millennium: An agenda for action for the development of information consultancy and brokerage in Africa', *Library Management* 20(2), 105–114. http://dx.doi.org/10.1177/016555159802400203

Ramugondo, L.S., 2010, 'An exploratory study of infopreneurship as a job option for Library and Information Science students: A literature review', paper presented at the 11th DIS Annual Conference 2010, Richardsbay, University of Zululand, South Africa, 02–03 September.

Storey, D.J. & Greene, F.J., 2010, *Small business and entrepreneurship*, Pearson Education Limited. Harlow, Essex UK.

Weber, R., 2012, *Evaluating entrepreneurship education*, Springer Gabler, Wiesbaden. http://dx.doi.org/10.1007/978-3-8349-3654-7

4

Developing a competitive intelligence strategy framework supporting the competitive intelligence needs of a financial institution's decision makers

Authors:
Tanya du Plessis[1]
Mzoxolo Gulwa[1]

Affiliations:
[1]Department of Information and Knowledge Management, University of Johannesburg, South Africa

Corresponding author:
Tanya du Plessis,
tduplessis@uj.ac.za

Background: For competitive intelligence (CI) to have the greatest contribution to strategic management, CI professionals require an in-depth understanding of the CI needs of decision makers. CI professionals have to carefully plan how to best inform corporate decision-making. A strategy framework is a planning tool which can be used to explore ways to enhance an organisation's strategic planning capabilities.

Objective: To investigate the CI needs of a financial institution's decision makers in order to develop a CI strategy framework. To present the strategy framework as a planning tool to CI professionals in the financial services industry as well as mapping the process of developing a planning tool, thereby enabling a financial institution's CI capability to better meet the CI needs of decision makers.

Method: The guiding paradigm of interpretivist research directed the research design of a single qualitative case study, using an inductive approach. Qualitative data analysis techniques were used, which included the use of numerical data, to develop a planning tool for CI professionals based on a thorough understanding of the CI needs of decision makers.

Results: Decision makers place considerable value on CI in terms of its contribution to strategy development, decision-making, gaining advantage over competitors and enhancing the financial performance of the organisation. Relationships between concepts and patterns or trends that were identified and utilised to establish themes in the data resulted in a 12-point strategy framework.

Conclusion: A financial institution's CI capability can be enhanced to better meet the CI needs of the organisation's decision makers when CI professionals carefully plan their approach of informing corporate decision-making. This paper presents a 12-point CI strategy framework as a planning tool for CI professionals.

Introduction

In recent years the global competitive scenario has grown in fierceness and intricacy (Zenaide & Castro 2015:11). Phenomena such as globalisation, deregulation, dematerialisation, emerging economies, rapidly changing consumer behaviour, disruptive innovation and shortened life cycles of several products point to a hard-to-foresee panorama. Ghannay and Mamlouk (2015:35) add that 'organisations are struggling to survive in today's competitive business world', and that 'becoming and remaining competitive requires a conscious and continuous design for competitive advantage'.

Companies with the ability to emerge stronger from difficult economic conditions are those that, on the basis of correctly organised intelligence, base their new business plans on value, innovation and correct competitive strategy, followed by implementation and successful realisation in the market place (Bartes 2014b:1243). The emphasis is on having a basis of correctly organised intelligence. It is thus of critical importance that competitive intelligence (CI) professionals have a plan that will successfully elevate the synergies between CI and strategic management.

For CI to have the greatest contribution to strategic management, CI professionals need an in-depth understanding of the CI needs of decision makers as well as the decision-making value they associate with CI. CI professionals have to carefully plan how to best inform corporate decision-making and a planning tool would be useful. A strategy framework is a planning tool which can be used to explore ways to enhance an organisation's strategic planning capabilities.

This paper presents a strategy framework that could be used as a planning tool by CI professionals in the financial services industry.

The paper begins by stating the research question and objective, followed by a brief review of the value of CI in decision-making according to existing literature. The research methodology section motivates the research design, a single qualitative case study. The analysis of results and presentation of key findings section is followed by a 12-point CI strategy framework which was developed as a result of this study's inductive research approach. Lastly, the delimitation of the study is stated, the paper is concluded and recommendations are made as well as suggestions for further research.

Research question and objective

It is not always clear how CI professionals should best approach informing corporate decision-making. The main research question of the study was: *How can the competitive intelligence needs of decision makers at a financial institution be better met?* and data was collected in order to address these three sub-problems: (1) What are the CI needs of a financial institution's (FI's) decision makers? (2) What actions or elements constitute a strategy framework to be used as a planning tool by CI professionals in the financial services industry? (3) What does the process entail of developing a planning tool aimed at enabling a FI's CI capability to better meet the CI needs of decision makers?

The research objective was threefold: (1) investigating the CI needs of a FI's decision makers in order to develop a CI strategy framework, (2) presenting the strategy framework as a planning tool to CI professionals in the financial services industry and (3) mapping the process of developing a planning tool by which a FI's CI capability would be enabled to better meet the CI needs of decision makers. The research objective originated from existing knowledge of the value of CI in decision-making.

Value of competitive intelligence in decision-making

The value of CI in decision-making has been investigated and reported extensively in the studies of Du Toit and Muller (2004), Muller (2006), Botha and Boon (2008), Fleisher and Wright (2009), Heppes and Du Toit (2009), Wright, Eid and Fleisher (2009), Strauss and Du Toit (2010) and Du Toit and Sewdass (2014), to mention a few. Every business confronts some set of crucial business issues and strategic decisions i.e. a unique combination of specific competitive changes that need to be explored and specific choices that need to be made. Each business issue or strategic decision must be supported by vital, forward-looking intelligence (Fahey & Herring 2007:13).

Fahey (2009:12) and Laney (2016) mention analysis tools and techniques that use data sources, technology and gathering methods unimaginable a generation ago; these tools now offer executives tantalising clues to new opportunities to achieve competitive advantage. However, companies consistently struggle to ensure that decision makers have timely and relevant intelligence for making strategic decisions (Naidoo 2003:61; Begg & Du Toit 2007:2; Laney 2016). Strategic decisions by definition concern tomorrow and they have far-reaching consequences for the future, which means that unpredictable changes in the areas of technology, demography, economy, globalisation and the environment need to be taken into account (Botterhuis *et al.* 2009:1).

Calof and Wright (2008:724) cited a study which found that CI supports strategic decisions in the areas of corporate or business strategy, sales or business development, market entry decisions, product development, research and development, technology decisions, mergers and acquisitions decisions, due diligence, joint venture decisions and regulators/legal responses. This reveals that CI influences a wide range of decision-making areas and is a vital ingredient in the formulation of business strategy (Calof & Wright 2008:724).

The more information about the internal and external organisational environment that is considered within decision-making processes, the better the conclusions are about possible consequences of alternative actions leading to more successful decisions (Schiefer 2013:9). Lowenthal (2008:313) states that a key role of CI is to reduce uncertainty. In tough times, CI activity therefore has to increase in both intensity and frequency of supporting decision-making. Decision makers want to know what is happening as well as what is likely to happen in the near and far future.

Duvenage (2010:34) suggests that the decision-making 'window' is only open for a very short time due to the increasing speed with which transactions and events occur throughout the world as a result of the Internet, multimedia and other networks. Individuals and organisations are overwhelmed because events and patterns are enfolding so rapidly and non-linearly, leading to confusion, anxiety and ultimately decision paralysis. According to Duvenage (2010:34), the immediacy trend has an impact on intelligence as CI professionals have to compete with media and other information brokers who communicate and disseminate information on world events instantaneously through the multimedia, Internet and cell phone technology. This information is sometimes labelled, positioned and sold as intelligence (Duvenage 2010:34). This type of 'intelligence' is available to all in abundance. Instead, the value of CI in decision-making begins with establishing the relationship between strategic management and CI based on a thorough understanding of the specific CI needs of decision makers. This study set out to investigate decision makers' CI needs in order to develop a CI strategy framework. Qualitative inquiry was chosen as the appropriate research approach.

Research methodology

The interpretivist research paradigm directed the research design. A single qualitative case study research strategy was used with an inductive approach. A primary purpose of the inductive approach is to allow research findings to emerge from the frequent, dominant or significant themes inherent in raw data, without the restraints imposed by structured methodologies (Thomas 2003:2; Yin 2003; Saunders, Lewis & Thornhill 2012:126). An inductive approach was suitable because the research intended to develop a CI strategy framework of relevance to a specific FI where no existing research on the CI needs of decision makers at the case organisation had been done previously.

The methods applied were aimed at collecting data that would contribute to action plans aimed at enhancing the CI services currently provided to decision makers at the case organisation. Qualitative data analysis techniques were used, which included the use of numerical data because quantification gives precision to statements, it enables themes in data to emerge with more clarity and highlights the meaning of findings by providing focus (Bauer, Gaskell & Allum 2000:3–18; Sandelowski, Voils & Knafl 2009:208). Maxwell (2010:480) states that the use of numerical data in qualitative research is a legitimate and valuable research strategy as this ensures that the process and procedures are orientated properly.

In order for this study to develop a planning tool for CI professionals, numerical data had to be collected that would provide a thorough understanding of the CI needs of decision makers. A self-administered questionnaire, including structured questions, was used as a data collection method. The population was the case organisation's managerial component and out of the targeted sample of 500 managers and executives, 124 respondents returned the questionnaire. Although the response rate was only 25%, data analysis remained important to the case organisation because no other similar investigation had been conducted to date.

Questions were aimed at testing participants' understanding of strategic management ideals and establishing their CI needs in terms of topics and frequencies. Data was first statistically analysed as part of the scientific process of qualitative data analysis aimed at identifying relationships between concepts and patterns or trends and using these to establish themes in the data. A 12-point CI strategy framework was then developed based on qualitative data analysis of empirical data and literature review with an inductive approach.

Analysis and discussion of results

In this study, the analysis and discussion of results formed an interrelated and interactive set of processes and findings typical of qualitative inquiry with an inductive approach (Saunders, Lewis & Thornhill 2009:488). It was first established that a strategy framework is a planning tool which can be used to explore ways to enhance an organisation's strategic planning capabilities (Gould & Desjardins 2015:319). From a planning perspective, a strategy framework aids decision makers in choosing a course of action for their organisation. The difference between a 'strategy framework' and 'framework' should be noted; the first is described as a 'planning tool' and is a precursor of the latter. The latter is a complete structure or system-wide comprehensive plan aimed at continuous improvement, comprised of all relevant entities and activities, including guiding principles for understanding, defining, capturing, documenting and categorising how various parts and processes of a complex system work together to achieve desired objectives (Fullan 2007:36; Ternes 2012:25). This study sets out to develop a planning tool and not a system-wide comprehensive plan.

The results of the literature review provide evidence of the value of CI in decision-making. CI has long been recognised as a strategic management tool and is one of the fastest growing fields in the business world (Schiefer 2013:9; Ghannay & Mamlouk 2015:35). Globalisation and the development of the future competitive environment is one of the key factors affecting the growth of the CI practice (Bartes 2014a:1234). Although the literature provides evidence for a relationship between CI and strategic management, it is not clear whether the synergy between strategic management and CI is recognised by decision makers to their benefit. Also, it is not clear how much value is placed on CI by business leaders in terms of CI's contribution to strategy development and decision-making processes, the organisation's quest for competitive advantage and on its overall success. For CI professionals to have the greatest contribution to their clients, i.e. decision makers, they need an understanding of the nature of those needs and insight into how their CI outputs are used by decision makers. Armed with this knowledge, CI professionals will be able to design CI services that truly meet decision makers' CI needs.

Key findings of the empirical research are that managers and executives at the case organisation, in this paper referred to as the FI, place considerable value on CI in terms of its contribution to strategy development, decision-making, gaining advantage over competitors and enhancing the financial performance of the organisation. The following 12 themes emerged from the data.

Understanding of the role of competitive intelligence in strategic management [#1]

Managers and executives at the FI were in unquestionable agreement on the statements implying synergy between strategic management and CI, but CI professionals should not assume that decision makers with evident understanding of strategic management, will also understand the role of CI in strategic management. More specifically, CI professionals should begin by ensuring that decision makers know what is meant by CI, that is, CI as a service, process, product and capability.

Value placed on competitive intelligence by decision makers [#2]

Managers and executives at the FI placed considerable value on CI in terms of its contribution to strategy development, decision-making, gaining advantage over competitors, and enhancing the financial performance of the FI and therefore to the overall success of the FI. However, relatively lower percentages were recorded for both managers and executives in terms of indicating that CI is *very* important to enhancing the FI's financial performance (cf. Gulwa 2015:39–92).

Use of competitive intelligence in decision-making [#3]

Managers and executives at the FI most often used CI for strategic and operational decision-making – this was established through data collected and analysed using quantitative data analysis techniques in qualitative inquiry (cf. Gulwa 2015:39–92), which is essential for the inductive integrity of the findings. This study finds that the growing competition on world markets increases the demands on the information needs of managers and executives which exact the subsequent increase in the level of use of CI.

Identifying the actual competitive intelligence needs of decision makers [#4]

Identifying the actual CI needs of decision makers entails knowing their preferred frequency intervals of obtaining intelligence on diverse topics, as illustrated in Figure 1. For example, the most important topics relating to the FI's competitive environment were political developments, macroeconomic trends, changing customer needs, legal/regulatory changes, local competitors and operational risk, but not at the same frequency intervals, also varying at executive and manager decision-making levels.

Figure 1 informs the development of a planning tool for CI professionals. In their planning, CI professionals have to make provision for determining decision makers' frequency preferences with reference to receiving intelligence on specific topics at different decision-making levels at varying intervals.

Extent to which competitive intelligence needs of decision makers are being met [#5]

A planning tool for CI should include a measure of determining the gap between what intelligence decision makers require, and what they are actually receiving. For example, gap analysis could be done to determine if there is discrepancy between what managers and executives require in terms of the elements of the financial services industry competitive environment and the topics specific to competitors. The gap analysis, presented in Figure 2, focused on what CI is required and received monthly as this is the interval that was preferred overall by both respondent groups.

For example, in terms of the priority elements of the financial services competitive environment, it was found that on changing customer needs, the gap is significant for both managers (27.8) and executives (27) in terms of what they require and currently received monthly (Figure 2). The case organisation has a number of teams that are mandated to develop this type of intelligence. However, based on the gap analysis it would seem that their outputs are not successfully reaching the FI's managers and executives.

In relation to intelligence on legal and/or regulatory changes, the needs of executives are being met as there is only a gap of 3.2. However, those of managers are not being met as a gap of 26.2 was recorded (Figure 2). Insights on legal and/or regulatory changes are largely developed by legal teams that are attached to specific business units within the company. Based on the results of the gap analysis, it would seem that their outputs are not reaching managers and executives in areas of the organisation outside the teams the legal staff are attached to.

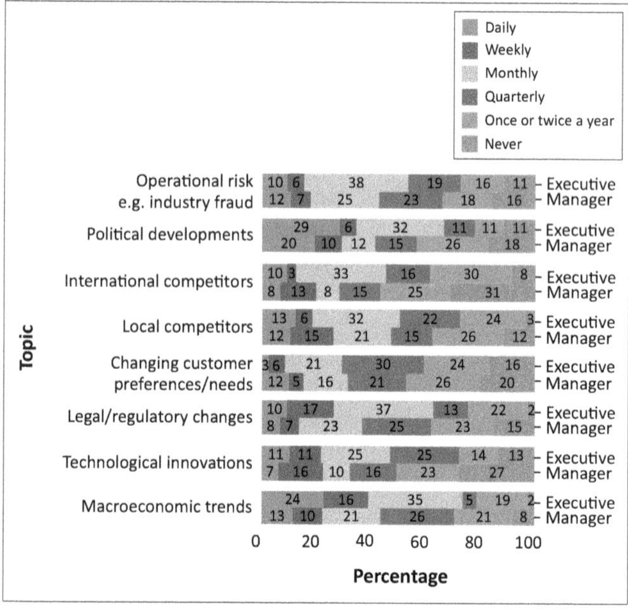

FIGURE 1: Comparison of frequency preference to receiving intelligence on specific topics.

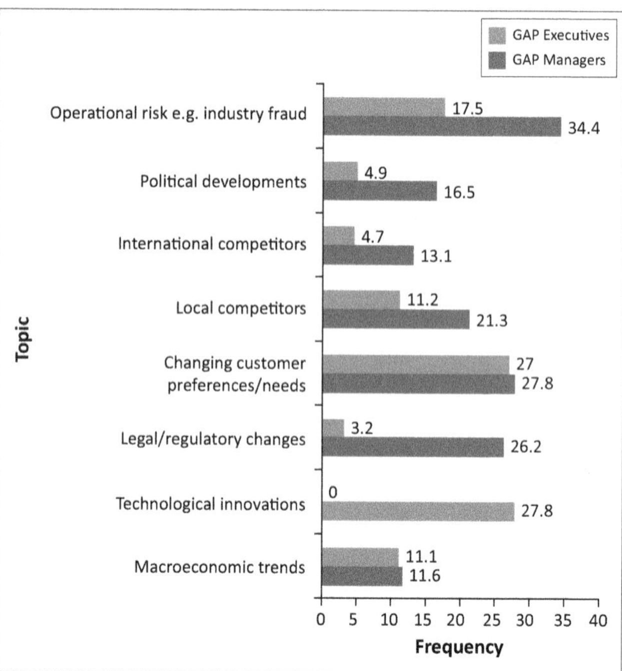

FIGURE 2: Gap between what intelligence decision makers required and what they were actually receiving.

In addressing CI needs on local competitors, there is a gap of 21.3 in terms of intelligence received by managers and what they require. The margin is smaller in terms of executives at 11.2 on the topic of local competitors (Figure 2). Insights on this topic are developed throughout the FI, however in an uncoordinated manner. In terms of intelligence on macroeconomic trends, the CI needs of both groups of respondents are being met. The reason could be that information and intelligence on macroeconomic trends is largely available from both internal and external sources to the FI.

In terms of the priority topics that relate to competitors, the main concern was on the gap in the intelligence required and currently received on the topics on product and price comparison against competitors. Although this type of intelligence is developed in some areas of the FI, it is not done to the required extent; and, when it is done the outputs are not effectively reaching managers and executives.

The above gap analysis was discussed in order to explain the process of measuring the gap between what intelligence decision makers require, and what intelligence they are actually receiving. The process of developing a planning tool for CI professionals includes the process of gap analysis. Gap analysis is an important practice to be included in a CI strategy framework.

So far, five themes emerging from the empirical data have been analysed and discussed as themes for inclusion in the CI strategy framework. Now, the qualitative data analysis continues, further linking the empirical data and the literature review findings which incorporate the Key Intelligence Topics (KITs) process (Herring 1999:4), as well as an adaptation of the hallmarks of excellence in competitive intelligence (Best Practices 2008). The seminal work of Herring (1999) promoted the KITs process which is aimed at identification and prioritisation of CI needs of decision makers. According to Herring (1999:4–6), a company's CI needs can be generally assigned into one of three functional categories, (1) strategic decisions and actions, including the development of strategic plans and strategies, (2) early-warning topics, including competitor initiatives, technological surprise and government actions and (3) descriptions of the key players in the specific marketplace, including competitors, customers, suppliers, regulators and potential partners, packaged in the preferred format in order to save the decision maker's time.

For example, executives usually would not have time to read and review large amounts of competitive data and information produced by CI teams. Rather, what they need is insight, that is, a new understanding, complete with its implications relevant to a specific business issue or topic (Fahey 2009:13). Proficiency in providing decision makers with insight begins with building strong relationships with a few customers and building a reputation based on the hallmarks of excellence as illustrated in Figure 3.

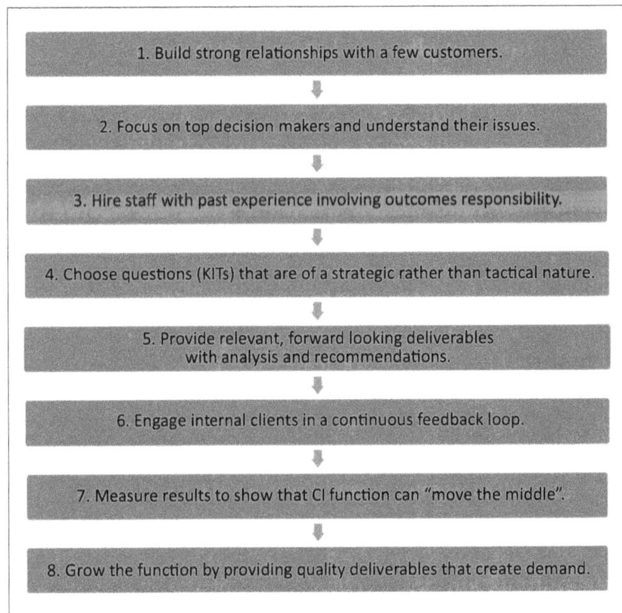

Source: Adapted from Best Practices, 2008, 'How successful companies create and develop a high-value CI function to drive better business decisions', viewed 19 November 2015, from http://www.slideshare.net/bestpracticesllc/psm-302-a-competitive-intelligence

FIGURE 3: Hallmarks of excellence in competitive intelligence.

The comprehensive literature review conducted by Pellisier and Nenzhelele (2013:1–6), critically reviews the CI process and reiterates the hallmarks of CI excellence, illustrated in Figure 3. In order to achieve these hallmarks of excellence requires CI education. Also, the promotion of CI services should be included in the CI strategy framework.

Competitive intelligence education and promotion of available competitive intelligence services [#6]

A number of respondents indicated that they are self-reliant in terms of where they get CI from. The problem with this is the issue of duplication, where managers and executives will work on developing CI outputs that are already available somewhere else in the organisation. One reason for self-reliance could be that some managers and executives are not aware of existing CI services inside the FI. Indeed promotion of existing CI services will go a long way in resolving this problem.

The central CI team runs an internal course on CI which is aimed at upskilling employees with basic CI skills so that they can conduct their own CI when the need arises. The importance of ensuring that the CI they need is not already available somewhere else in the organisation is emphasised. However, the internal CI training programme should be run more vigorously going forward and as part of its content it should drive awareness on the role of CI in strategic management and successful execution of business.

Auditing of available competitive intelligence services within the financial institution [#7]

The findings indicated that CI outputs are being created throughout the case organisation. A need exists to identify who is developing these outputs, what topics are addressed by these CI outputs, where are these outputs stored and who is currently receiving and or using these outputs. In addition, an audit can determine what CI reports have been acquired from external suppliers and where these reports are being stored. This will help ensure that such reports, usually purchased at high cost, are leveraged across the entire organisation. Furthermore, it is necessary to eliminate, or at least reduce, duplication of instances where intelligence is bought from third parties when the same intelligence has already been developed internally.

Collaboration between competitive intelligence teams [#8]

Within the FI, a number of teams are producing CI that is focusing on specific elements of the competitive environment. For example, legal teams produce intelligence on changing regulations, market research teams produce insights on changing customer needs and the central CI team has a focus on producing intelligence pertaining to competitors. These teams need to collaborate more effectively as it is evident that their outputs are not reaching some of the managers and executives who need their outputs to support their strategic management duties.

Review of scope of the central competitive intelligence team [#9]

Based on the topics identified by managers and executives as *very* important to receive intelligence on, the central CI team needs to review the topics they have been covering in their CI reports. Through quantitative data analysis it became evident that the FI's managers and executives perceive product and price comparison as the most important topics to get intelligence on, however, through gap analysis, significant gaps were found in terms of what is required and what is currently received as far as these two topics are concerned. Thus, both the process of developing a planning tool and the eventual CI strategy framework should include continuous review of the scope of the CI team.

Improvement on distribution of competitive intelligence outputs [#10]

From the empirical data a clear observation was made of the actual CI needs of decision makers (Figure 1). As mentioned above, the use of CI was established through data collected and analysed using quantitative data analysis techniques in qualitative inquiry (Gulwa 2015:39–92), which is essential for the inductive integrity of research findings. Based on these findings, an improvement on the distribution of CI outputs is required, as recommended in the conclusion section of this paper.

Capacity of the competitive intelligence team [#11]

A significant number of managers and executives indicated that the CI they were receiving internally was not timeous (cf. Gulwa 2015:87–88). For example, in terms of frequency requirements, decision makers mostly preferred monthly outputs (Figure 1). However, the central CI team recently had to change the frequency of its *Strategic Competitive Intelligence Report* to publication once every second month due to capacity challenges. Indeed, with more staff members the CI team would be in a position to again release the FI's *Strategic Competitive Intelligence Report* on a monthly basis and ensure that it covers the priority topics of decision makers as per the results of this research.

Presentation of research results [#12]

The need was identified to present these research results to the FI's managers and executives. Typically the CI cycle includes a continuous feedback loop, mentioned in this paper as the sixth hallmark of excellence (Figure 3). Again, the comprehensive literature review conducted by Pellisier and Nenzhelele (2013:1–6), emphasised both aspects of obtaining feedback as well as giving feedback, as critical CI processes. Thus, '*Presentation of research results*' was identified as the last of the 12 themes emerging from the empirical study.

The above discussion has covered the research objective of investigating the CI needs of a FI's decision makers in order to develop a CI strategy framework.

Competitive intelligence strategy framework

A CI strategy framework was developed based on the data that was collected, analysed and logically arranged according to themes. Each theme forms a component of the 12-point CI strategy framework developed as a result of this study (Figure 4).

Put together, the 12 points of the CI strategy framework form a balanced approach to CI service delivery. CI professionals could benefit from using Figure 4 as a planning tool. Also, CI professionals could use this study as map of the process of developing a CI strategy framework. The researchers found that the centre point of the process was [#1] understanding of

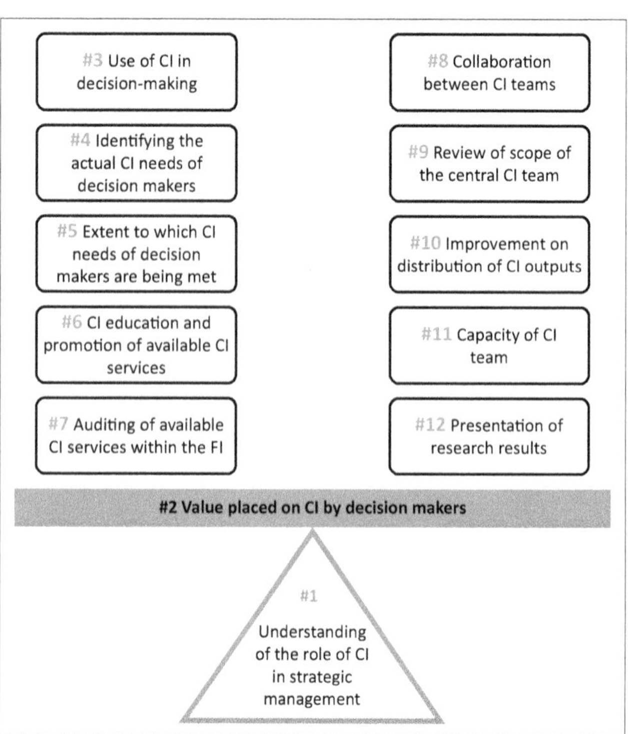

FIGURE 4: CI strategy framework.

the role of CI in strategic management on which balances, [#2] the value decision makers place on CI; and, the value [#2] rests squarely on the fine balancing of the other 10 points of the CI strategy framework, [#3] to [#12]. The emphasis is on balance; when an imbalance is noticed the relevant corrective action could be taken, for example, the case organisation may have to adjust according to the recommendations made in the concluding section of this paper.

Conclusion and recommendations

In conclusion, a FI's CI capability can be enhanced to better meet the CI needs of the organisation's decision makers when CI professionals carefully plan their approach of informing corporate decision-making. This paper presented a 12-point CI strategy framework as a planning tool for CI professionals, summarised in Figure 4. The layout of Figure 4 simultaneously serves the purpose of mapping the process of developing a CI strategy framework – *emphasising that an imbalance is an indication of specific action to be taken.*

This study recommends specific action in terms of [#6] CI education and promotion of available CI services. The CI team of the case organisation should play a proactive role in educating and promoting to managers and executives the value of CI to decision-making and its contribution to the performance of the organisation. Elevated awareness through education can increase the appreciation of CI efforts from the CI function as well as the use of its outputs aimed at elevating synergies between CI and strategic management.

In terms of [#7] auditing of available CI services, it is recommended the FI determines what CI reports have been acquired from external suppliers and where these reports are being stored. This will help ensure that such reports are leveraged across the organisation and help reduce duplication in cases where intelligence is bought from third parties.

Also, the scope of the central CI team [#9] may need revision. Although the central CI team should continue covering the topics identified in [#4] and [#5], it should also ensure that it develops to a greater extent intelligence on product and price comparison against competitors. Product and price comparison were the most important topics to get intelligence on for both managers and executives and there were significant gaps in terms of what is required and what is currently received as far as these two topics are concerned. Another suggestion to ensure coverage of both priority topics on competitors as well as the elements of the financial services industry competitive environment will be for the central CI team to selectively summarise and integrate relevant insights on changing customer needs, regulatory changes and macroeconomic trends into its competitor intelligence focused reports. Doing so will ensure that the needs of decision makers are addressed in a more effective way. The new-look intelligence products as suggested in this section should then be distributed widely to cover CI needs of decision makers across business units and geographies the FI operates in.

In terms of [#10] the improvement on distribution of CI outputs, the first step would be to compare the existing subscription lists which are used by the central CI team and other CI teams at the FI to distribute their respective outputs against the targeted sample of this research. This action will ensure that the current CI needs of these decision makers are proactively met. As an end result, decision makers will spend less time in producing their own input and rather focus their time on their core strategic management duties, thereby leveraging the synergy of CI and strategic management. In addition, a central electronic repository should be used by the central CI team and other producers of CI within the organisation. This will ensure that managers and executives across the FI are made familiar with only one source of available CI thus eliminating duplication of CI efforts and acquisition of CI from outside, which might already exist internally.

In terms of [#11] increasing the capacity of the central CI team, an imbalance was noted in the ability to cover the priority topics relating to competitors in a proactive manner. A need exists for a bigger central CI team that will have more capacity to develop required intelligence products on time and distribute these across the organisation in a format that is preferred by decision makers. One preferred format was oral presentations. It is difficult to deliver on this requirement when the team has limited capacity. With more capacity the team would be able to increase its efforts in promoting collaboration of CI activities across the organisation. Lastly, it is recommended the research results are presented to decision makers [#12] in order to achieve the fine balance of the value placed on CI by decision makers [#2].

A number of potential areas for further research were identified. Firstly, to explore the decision-making process of managers and executives to better understand at what stage they actually use CI when making strategic and operational decisions. This will help CI teams to ensure they provide timely CI that supports decision-making. Secondly, to find out whether the managers and executives who claimed to have acquired CI reports from external suppliers had commissioned specific CI research and what CI topics did they commission on. Answers to this question will provide insights into those topics decision makers can do without. Thirdly, finding out which external newsletters managers and executives are subscribing to will help the CI team to ensure that the most useful external newsletters are shared with relevant audiences internally. In addition, this will provide insights into topics that are important for decision makers to receive information and CI on. Lastly, now that a CI strategy framework has been developed, this planning tool needs to be implemented and evaluated by the case organisation's CI professionals. Thereafter the planning tool has to be expanded into a comprehensive framework aimed at enhancing the organisation's strategic planning capabilities.

Limitations of the study

The data analysis and discussion of results present an interpretation of a single case organisation, therefore the findings cannot be generalised for other companies and industries. However, other organisations may benefit from the idea of a balanced process mapped out by this study.

Acknowledgements

Competing interests

The authors declare that they have no financial or personal relationships which may have inappropriately influenced them in writing this article.

Authors' contributions

Briefly summarise the nature of the contribution made by each of the authors listed, along the lines of the following: T.d.P. Master's study supervisor; M.G. Master of Commerce study, with specialisation in strategic management.

References

Bartes, F., 2014a, 'Defining a basis for the new concept of competitive intelligence', *Universitatis Agriculturae et Silviculturae Mendelianae Brunensis* 62(6), 1233–1242. http://dx.doi.org/10.11118/actaun201462061233

Bartes, F., 2014b, 'The objectives of competitive intelligence as part of a corporate development strategy', *Universitatis Agriculturae et Silviculturae Mendelianae Brunensis* 62(6), 1243–1250. http://dx.doi.org/10.11118/actaun201462061243

Bauer, M.W., Gaskell, G. & Allum, N.C., 2000, 'Quality, quantity and knowledge interests: Avoiding confusions', in W.M. Bauer & G. Gaskell (eds.), *Qualitative researching with text, image and sound: A practical handbook,* pp. 3–18, Sage, London.

Begg, M. & Du Toit, A.S.A., 2007, 'Level of importance attached to competitive intelligence at a mass import retail organisation', *South African Journal of Information Management*, 9(4), viewed 14 April 2014, from http://www.sajim.co.za/index.php/SAJIM/article/viewFile/196/196

Best Practices, 2008, 'How successful companies create and develop a high-value CI function to drive better business decisions', viewed 19 November 2015, from http://www.slideshare.net/bestpracticesllc/psm-302-a-competitive-intelligence

Botha, D.F. & Boon, J.A., 2008, 'Competitive intelligence in support of strategic training and learning', *South African Journal of Information Management* 10(3), 1–6. http://dx.doi.org/10.4102/sajim.v10i3.325

Botterhuis, L., Van der Duin, P., De Ruijter, P. & Van Wijck, P., 2009, 'Monitoring the future: Building an early warning system for the Dutch Ministry of Justice', *Futures* 1–12.

Calof, J.L. & Wright, S., 2008, 'Competitive intelligence: A practitioner, academic and interdisciplinary perspective', *European Journal of Marketing* 42(7/8), 717–730. http://dx.doi.org/10.1108/03090560810877114

Du Toit, A. & Muller, M.L., 2004, 'Organizational structure of competitive intelligence activities: A South African case study', *South African Journal of Information Management* 6(3), 1–13. http://dx.doi.org/10.4102/sajim.v6i3.308

Du Toit, A.S.A. & Sewdass, N., 2014, 'Competitive intelligence practices in Brazil: An exploratory study', *Mousaion* 32(1), 85–98.

Duvenage, M.A., 2010, 'Intelligence analysis in the knowledge age: An analysis of the challenges facing the practice of intelligence analysis', Master's Thesis, University of Stellenbosch.

Fahey, L., 2009, 'Exploring "analytics" to make better decisions – The questions executives need to ask', *Strategy & Leadership* 37(5), 12–18. http://dx.doi.org/10.1108/10878570910986434

Fahey, L. & Herring, J., 2007, 'Intelligence teams', *Strategy & Leadership* 35(1), 13–20. http://dx.doi.org/10.1108/10878570710717245

Fleisher, C.S. & Wright, S., 2009, 'Examining differences in competitive intelligence practice: China, Japan, and the West', *Thunderbird International Business Review* 51(3), 249–261. http://dx.doi.org/10.1002/tie.20263

Fullan, M., 2007, 'Change theory as a force for school improvement (Chapter 3)', in J.M. Burger, C.F. Webber & P. Klinck, (eds.), *Intelligent leadership: Constructs for thinking education leaders,* Springer, Dordrecht.

Ghannay, J.C. & Mamlouk, Z.B.A., 2015, 'Influence of organisational culture on competitive intelligence practice: A conceptual framework', *International Journal of Innovation, Management and Technology* 6, 35–45.

Gould, A.M. & Desjardins, G., 2015, 'A spring-clean of Michael Porter's Attic', *Competitiveness Review* 25(3), 310–323. http://dx.doi.org/10.1108/CR-04-2014-0008

Gulwa, M., 2015, 'Developing a competitive intelligence strategy framework', M Com minor dissertation, University of Johannesburg, Department of Business Management.

Heppes, D. & Du Toit, A., 2009, 'Level of maturity of the competitive intelligence function: Case study of a retail bank in South Africa', *Aslib Proceedings: New Information Perspectives* 61(1), 48–66. http://dx.doi.org/10.1108/00012530910932285

Herring, J.P., 1999, 'Key intelligence process: A process to identify and define intelligence needs', *Competitive Intelligence Review* 10(2), 4–14. http://dx.doi.org/10.1002/(SICI)1520-6386(199932)10:2%3C4::AID-CIR3%3E3.0.CO;2-C

Laney, D., 2016, 'Use predictive analytics to help you capitalize on business moments', viewed 19 April 2016, from www.gartner.com

Lowenthal, M.M., 2008, 'Towards a reasonable standard for analysis: How right, how often on which issues?', *Intelligence and national security* 23(3), 303–315. http://dx.doi.org/10.1080/02684520802121190

Maxwell, J.A., 2010, 'Using numbers in qualitative research', *Qualitative Inquiry* 16(6), 475–482. http://dx.doi.org/10.1177/1077800410364740

Muller, M.L., 2006, 'Parts of competitive intelligence: Competitor intelligence', *South African Journal of Information Management* 8(1), 1–5. http://dx.doi.org/10.4102/sajim.v8i1.209

Naidoo, A., 2003, 'The impact of competitive intelligence practices on strategic decision-making', Master's Dissertation, University of KwaZulu-Natal, KwaZulu-Natal.

Pellisier, R. & Nenzhelele, T.E., 2013, 'Towards a universal competitive intelligence process model', *South African Journal of Information Management* 15(2), 1–7. http://dx.doi.org/10.4102/sajim.v15i2.567

Sandelowski, M., Voils, C.I. & Knafl, G., 2009, 'On quantitizing', *Journal of Mixed Methods Research* 3, 208–222. http://dx.doi.org/10.1177/1558689809334210

Saunders, M., Lewis, P. & Thornhill, A., 2009, *Research methods for business students,* 5th ed., Prentice Hall, London.

Saunders, M., Lewis, P. & Thornhill, A., 2012, *Research methods for business students,* 6th ed., Pearson, Harlow, England.

Schiefer, C., 2013, 'Role of CI in strategic purchasing decisions and its influence on suppliers resource allocation', Master's thesis, University of Twente, Berlin.

Strauss, A.C. & Du Toit, A.S.A., 2010, 'Competitive intelligence skills needed to enhance South Africa's competitiveness', *Aslib Proceedings: New Information Perspective* 62(3), 302–320. http://dx.doi.org/10.1108/00012531011046925

Ternes, C.D. Jr., 2012, 'Confirming the Stankosky knowledge management framework', Doctor of Science dissertation, Faculty of Engineering and Applied Science, George Washington University.

Thomas, D.R., 2003, 'A general inductive approach for qualitative data analysis', viewed 25 April 2015, from http://www.frankumstein.com/PDF/.../Inductive%20Content%20Analysis.pdf

Wright, S., Eid, E.R. & Fleisher, C.S., 2009, 'Competitive intelligence in practice: Empirical evidence from the UK retail banking sector', *Journal of Marketing Management* 25(9/10), 941–964.

Yin, R.K., 2003, *Case study research: Design and methods,* 3rd ed., Sage, Thousand Oaks, CA.

Zenaide, V. & Castro, L.T., 2015, 'Scenario of business practices in competitive intelligence within the telecommunication industry', *African Journal of Business Management* 9(6), 311–322. http://dx.doi.org/10.5897/AJBM2014.7653

5

Middle manager role and contribution towards the competitive intelligence process: A case of Irish subsidiaries

Author:
Willie Chinyamurindi[1]

Affiliation:
[1]Department of Business Management, University of Fort Hare, South Africa

Corresponding author:
Willie Chinyamurindi,
chinyaz@gmail.com

Background: Calls have been made especially during a period of global competition and economic austerity for research that focuses on how competitive intelligence (CI) is actually generated within organisations.

Objectives: The aim of this study was to understand the views and experiences of middle managers with regard to their role and contribution towards the CI process within Irish subsidiaries of the Multinational Corporation (MNC).

Method: The study adopts a qualitative approach using the semi-structured interview technique to generate narratives and themes around how CI is generated using a sample of 15 middle managers drawn from five participating Irish subsidiaries.

Results: Based on the analysis of the narratives of the middle managers, three main themes emerged as findings. Firstly, the process of gathering CI was facilitated by the reliance on internal and external tools. Secondly, information gathered from the use of such tools was then communicated by middle managers to top managers to inform the making of strategic decisions. Thus, (and thirdly), middle managers were found to occupy an important role not only through the execution of their management duties but by extending this influence towards the generation of information deemed to affect the competitive position of not just the subsidiary but also the parent company.

Conclusion: The study concludes by focusing on the implications and recommendations based on the three themes drawn from the empirical data.

Introduction

The role and contribution of middle managers towards the strategic planning process is receiving empirical attention in multiple contexts (e.g. Rouleau & Balogun 2011; Salih & Doll 2013; Teulier & Rouleau 2013). This study extends this focus by paying attention to the role and contribution of middle managers towards the competitive intelligence (CI) process as a component of how strategy is realised within organisations. There is need to clarify some key concepts that appear constantly in this article.

Firstly, CI is widely discussed in the extant literature. Herring (2007) argues for CI as a strategic tool used to facilitate the identification of potential opportunities and threats. Thus, a useful platform of generating data that determines not only the performance of the organisation's CI (Xu *et al.* 2011) but also its competitiveness in relation to other players in the same industry (Du Toit & Sewdass 2014:1). In essence, strategic planning (including efforts towards CI) is a skill for survival and success in an uncertain world (Salih & Doll 2013), hence the need to pay attention to them. The second key concept in this article is the resource-based view (RBV) of the firm proposed by Barney (1991). The underlying premise with the RBV is the need to strategically position a firm's resources and its interaction with the environment (internal and external) as a basis for attaining competitiveness (Xu *et al.* 2011).

In essence, CI relies on resources. Some scholars praise the role and existence of human capital within the organisation as important in gathering, organising and utilising information (Xu *et al.* 2011). This places such human capital as important players within organisations through a resource allocation role (Mariadoss *et al.* 2014). Resources within an organisation such as employees and managers are key in determining the competitiveness of the firm through the use of tools such as competitor analysis and an analysis of wider industry trends (Opait *et al.* 2016). Herring (2007:26) argues for the importance of CI: 'information costs money, while intelligence makes money. Moreover, intelligence that makes money for a company is valued intelligence'. Resources (the presence and utilisation of them) have a bearing in determining competitiveness.

A general research question was proposed: What are the views and experiences of middle managers with regard to their role and contribution towards the competitive intelligence process within Irish subsidiaries?

In following from previous studies (e.g. Salih & Doll 2013:32), a broad research question was set to 'elicit a wide range of views and perceptions' around the phenomena understudy. The structure followed in this article is firstly, to put this research into context. Secondly, the theoretical framework underlying this study is presented, leading to the justification of the research question. Thirdly, the research design and methodology section follows. Finally, the results, discussion and a conclusion are presented.

Putting this research into context

The author of this article was based in Ireland for a period of 2 years when this study was conducted. The context in which this study was conducted was based on Multinational Corporation (MNC), where the subsidiary level was used as the unit of analysis. The MNC can be conceptualised as a collection of globally dispersed units possessing distinctive resources (Noble 1999). Though emphasis is on the distinctive resources, it is worth to mention that subsidiaries by function are not meant to exist in isolation but operating with various corporate units and business actors (Noble, Sinha & Kumar 2002). Thus, this study is contextualised within the MNC (and subsidiary level) context in understanding aspects of competitiveness and the role of middle managers. The main reason for this has to do with the acknowledgement of the need for subsidiaries as an extension for the MNC to grow. White and Poynter (1984) suggested that this can happen within the subsidiary through: (1) the start-up of sales activities in new geographical markets which is represented by a change in scope, (2) a change in product scope where the subsidiary has to extend a product line (product modifications) or introduce new product areas, and (3) through an extension of basic value chain activities, such as primary activities (inbound logistics, operations, outbound logistics, marketing and sales or service) or support activities like procurement, technological development, human resources management or infrastructure. Thus, through such efforts, a subsidiary is being competitive and yielding benefit not just for its own operation but that of the parent company (Dörrenbächer & Geppert 2009).

Furthermore, the competitive orientation of a subsidiary can be thought of as encompassing the extent to which the subsidiary not only understands its strengths and weaknesses but also the tactical and strategic capabilities of both current and potential competitors (Noble *et al.* 2002). Competitive intensity is high when competitor's actions contribute to market uncertainty and customer needs are constantly in flux (Calof & Wright 2008). The noted challenge for firms is to reduce costs and come to the market quickly and introduce innovative products (Nam *et al.* 2014). In highly competitive situations, competitive advantage is gained through increased knowledge assets and decreased fixed assets (Barney 1991). Given this, a research question proposed for this study reads: What are the views and experiences of middle managers with regards to their role and contribution towards the competitive intelligence process within Irish subsidiaries?

Theoretical background

This study considers two main views around aspects on how organisations can be competitive, especially within the MNC. Thus, an eclectic view stemming from previous studies and theorising is preferred. For instance, Amit and Schoemaker (1993) investigated the influences of attaining strategic assets and organisational rent and attributed this to the resources available to the firm, the nature of the industry and managerial decisions. Within the same vein, Birkinshaw (1997) found factors within the subsidiary's local market, internal market (relationships within the MNC) and the global market to be influential towards quests around competitiveness. From this, subsidiaries engage in a process of learning from their environment, thereby allowing them to not only be innovative but also competitive (Saka-Helmhout 2010).

The first consideration gives credence to the presence or absence of resources (physical or human) within the subsidiary as a basis for competitiveness or the lack of it.

In essence, as argued by Barney (1991), it all depends on how resources available to the firm are rare, their ability to be imitated and also how easily such resources can be substituted as a basis for a firm's success and failure. Even though the RBV is a theory of the firm, it is applicable to explain how not only subsidiary strategy but also issues of competitiveness in subsidiaries develop (Birkinshaw 1997). Linked to the RBV is the consideration of management as a driving force of the resources. This becomes the second theoretical consideration; the focus here is on the link between resources and management as influencing not only the development of strategy but also how firms create a competitive advantage in doing so. Thus, another important resource is the role played by management in not only realising strategy but also competitiveness (O'Brien & Meadows 2013).

Competitive intelligence and management influence

The management literature identifies a range of sources by which firms can attain a competitive advantage. The emphasis is on the firm's resources as a potential source of attaining a competitive advantage (Barney 1991). However, for these resources to be effectively utilised, other management theorists argue for the need for compatibility or congruence of the organisational components to attain a competitive advantage (Argote 1982). The thinking here is that the experience, skills, levels of management and components within the organisation exert a significant effect towards a firm's quest for competitiveness. Given this, efforts towards strategic planning (including CI) are viewed as practice, as something managers use to enact change and also help firms perform (Lechner & Floyd, 2012).

The concept of competitiveness is one that is receiving attention either at an individual, organisational or country level. The barometer of measuring competitiveness at these three levels is through productivity and effectiveness (Hart & Spero 1997). One such enabler of an organisation's competitiveness, as argued by Gilad (2011), is the strategic decision-making capability, which is a tool that seeks to generate intelligence and secure a position in spite of changing market conditions. The ultimate aim is to stay ahead of competitors with a thrust towards short- and long-term strategic planning (Dishman & Pearson 2003). It is envisaged that within organisations, the drivers of efforts towards CI are managers (Nikolaos 2012). CI, thus, emerges as a tool in the hand of managers to be able to not only anticipate environmental change but respond to it (Viviers, Muller & Du Toit 2005). CI is also a useful tool in the hand of managers to improve decision-making and the attainment of company targets (Du Toit & Sewdass 2014). Furthermore, Calof and Wright (2008:717) argue for the process of CI not to be an avenue of an elite or the privileged few but to be integrated with the 'knowledge of everyone in the company'.

Middle manager role and contribution

A middle manager consists of the tier of management between 'the first level supervisor' and upper management who exercise 'company-wide responsibilities' (Herzing & Jimmieson 2006:628). The main activity base of middle managers, as argued by Floyd and Wooldridge (1994), is to implement those decisions proposed from a higher tier of management above them. In achieving this, middle managers appear to be driven not from the authority above them but the knowledge they have and their ability to be both strategic and operational (Salih & Doll 2013). Thus, through their activity base, middle managers are involved in CI efforts through their influence towards top managers (Noble 1999). Middle managers are also seekers and implementers of innovations (Bourne & Walker 2005). Furthermore, Floyd and Lane (2000) argue for middle managers as an important mediator between top managers and those below them. This allows middle managers to expend upwards and downwards influence, especially in strategy formulation and implementation (Wooldridge, Schmid & Floyd 2008).

A number of scholars make an argument for the importance of middle managers to processes where CI is generated for organisational decision-making (e.g. Wooldridge *et al.* 2008; Elbanna 2016; Kealy 2015). Furthermore, calls have been raised in understanding further not only the contribution of middle managers but also their interaction with other actors (such as top managers) within organisations in not only generating CI but enacting change across the organisation (Balogun 2003; Floyd & Wooldridge 1994; Raes *et al.* 2011; Salih & Doll 2013).

Research methodology

This study adopted the philosophy of interpretivism which seeks to pave a way in which meaning is interpreted from the lens of the individual (Creswell 2014). Interpretivism is praised as a useful philosophy in understanding complex phenomena and coming to a holistic, rich and in-depth understanding of such phenomena (Creswell 2014). The rationale for this is motivated by the objectives of this study which are exploratory in nature and seeking to gain an understanding of a behaviour (i.e. the views and experiences of middle managers with regard to their role and contribution towards the CI process within Irish subsidiaries) not to predict behaviour (a predominantly positivist stance). Furthermore, the qualitative approach is also adopted and motivated by the need to study 'real people, real problems and real organisations' (Edmondson & McManus 2007:1155). Such efforts are applauded as they can be forerunners in theory development (Eisenhardt 1989). Within the management sciences, especially the strategy literature, such approaches are receiving attention (Salih & Doll 2013).

Data collection and analysis

In achieving the aims of this research, semi-structured interviews were used as a tool for data collection. Interviews help in arriving to an understanding around the depth and complexity of the phenomena under investigation (Creswell 2014). Furthermore, semi-structured interviews boast in allowing for some flexibility in the quality of data that can be collected (Creswell 2014). This can be helpful for the interviewee as they have 'freedom' to express and ascribe meaning to the topic understudy (Noaks & Wincup 2004:80). A trigger question was asked to initiate the process: 'Can you please tell me a bit about yourself and your role within the MNC?' The duration of each interview was between 1 h and 1.5 h.

A total of 15 middle managers from five Irish subsidiaries took part in the research (see Table 1). The convenience sampling approach was adopted. The thinking here was to access a sample that is 'available and accessible' to the study (Cohen, Manion & Morrison 2007). The participants were provided with an outline of the key interview questions in advance of the interview so that they had adequate time for preparation and reflection prior to the interview.

All interviews were conducted at sites where the interviewees deemed as comfortable as it is recommended that interviews of this type take place in a setting natural to the interviewee (Creswell 2014). Given this, participant work sites were used for all interviews. The study paid focus to an inclusion and exclusion standard. Participants had to be middle managers within MNCs in Ireland. Participants were excluded if they did not meet this criterion.

The interviews were exported into QSR International's NVivo 9, a data analysis and management software package for the purpose of data analysis useful when dealing with a lot of text, graphic, audio and video data (Reuben & Bobat 2014). A data analysis procedure based on three levels of meaning-making, as adopted in previous research, was used (Chinyamurindi 2012; McCormack 2000).

Level 1 was helpful in developing a good understanding of the contribution and experience of the middle manager to the CI process as per each participant story. This was done by re-reading each interview and listening to audio recordings. This process allowed for the identification of 'markers' in the stories (McCormack 2000:221) and answered questions about each interview, such as 'what kind of story is this?' (Thornhill, Clare & May 2004:188). Level 2 was achieved through classifying responses from participants into meaningful categories (Nachmias & Nachmias 1996). Finally, in level 3, the researcher analysed the content of the gathered narrative accounts and themes (McCormack 2000). This was done by identifying themes and using quotes based on consistencies across participant stories (Rhodes 2000). Table 2 presents a summary of the data analysis process.

In ensuring concerns around reliability and validity, some steps were taken. Firstly, ethics approval for the research was granted by the Dublin Institute of Technology in Ireland (where the researcher was based). Furthermore, each company, through their representative, had to give consent before data were collected. Secondly, the interview questions were pre-tested using a sample of five managers (non-participants) who fitted the same profile as those interviewed in the main part of the research. Thirdly, to ensure credible data, all interview data were recorded and transcribed verbatim within 24 h. Fourthly, the study relied on multiple participants per participating MNCs. Finally, following transcription of data, participants were emailed a copy of the transcription to verify accuracy as per the interview. All these practices are recommended procedures when conducting research, especially qualitative research (Eisenhardt 1989).

TABLE 1: Participant characteristics.

Company†	Details of company	Middle manager position of participants
Alpha¶	World leader in manufacturing of plastic pipe systems with parent company in the Netherlands.	Strategy‡ Marketing‡ Supply Chain§
Beta¶	Global manufacturer and supplier of medical equipment with parent company in the United States.	Production‡ Supply Chain‡
Gamma¶	Airline service company and specialised aircraft parts manufacturer with parent company in Germany.	Marketing‡ Production‡ Supply Chain‡ Strategy‡ Quality Assurance‡
Delta¶	Management consulting and technology services company with parent company in the United States.	Quality Assurance‡ Sales & Marketing‡ Information Management§
Lamda¶	Biopharmaceutical company with parent company in the United Kingdom.	Finance§ Strategy & Information‡

†, n = 15; ‡, Male participant; §, Female participant; ¶, Pseudonym.

TABLE 2: Data analysis: Levels of meaning-making.

Meaning-making	Description
Level 1	Each interview is written as a brief vignette. Thereafter, each vignette is then developed into a longer narrative about each participant.
Level 2	Narrative themes are then conveyed by participants and their experience of career development. Thereafter, preliminary themes are then compared across participants.
Level 3	An analysis of the themes from cross-case comparison begins, and illustrating quotes and stories are used.

Source: McCormack, C., 2000, 'From interview transcript to interpretative story: Part 1. Viewing the transcript through multiple lenses', *Field Methods* 12(4), 282–297. http://dx.doi.org/10.1177/1525822X0001200402

Findings

Based on the narratives of the 15 middle managers, three themes emerged. Firstly, the process of gathering CI was facilitated by the reliance on internal and external tools. Secondly, information gathered from the use of such tools was then communicated by middle managers to top managers to inform the making of strategic decisions. Thus, (and thirdly), middle managers were found to occupy an important role not only through the execution of their management duties but by extending this influence to the generation of information deemed to affect the competitive position of not just the subsidiary but also the parent company.

Generating competitive intelligence

Middle managers were requested to indicate how CI was generated within the subsidiary. Figure 1 gives a breakdown of the strategy tools and techniques used when generating CI based on the question posed to middle managers specific to the tools and techniques being used within the subsidiary as per the working year.

From Figure 1, three strategic tools and/or techniques stand out in terms of their use by the middle managers in generating CI, namely:

- Strengths, Weaknesses, Opportunities, Threats (SWOT) analysis
- Reliance on an internal knowledge base
- Scenario planning.

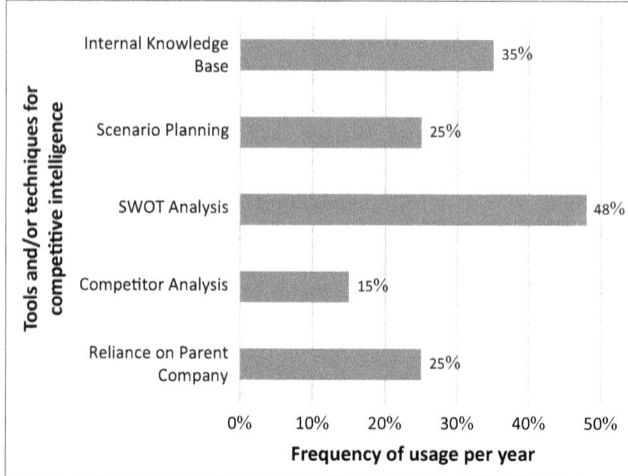

FIGURE 1: Strategic tools and/or techniques used in generating competitive intelligence.

A sizeable fraction of the middle managers relied on the established techniques used by their parent company to gather data deemed strategic in CI building; next to this, competitor analysis is used by almost a third of the organisations when coming up with strategy. Thus, the data in Figure 1 show that middle managers use and have a wide knowledge of tools and techniques and use these to suit existing business objectives and processes. Further to this, participants were asked to show (if any) the extent to which they use such strategic tools, not just for CI but also for the development of strategy.

Common themes that emerged as to the extent of use of strategic tools for CI were twofold (see Table 3 for illustrating quotes):

- Strategy tools serving as a supportive role to the business objectives and targets of the subsidiary
- Strategy tools serving as a facilitative role towards decision-making.

Middle manager role in competitive intelligence

A third theme based on the data analysis was around the role of middle managers to the CI processes. Middle managers were found to occupy an important role not only through the execution of their management duties but by extending this influence to the generation of information deemed to affect the competitive position of not just the subsidiary but also the parent company. Within this, middle managers exercise upwards and downwards influence in supporting CI processes.

TABLE 3: Role of strategy tools and techniques in competitive intelligence.

Role of strategy tools and techniques	Illustrating quotes
Strategy tools serving as a supportive role to the business objectives and targets of the subsidiary.	'We use SWOT to measure market share and to respond to our customer needs' (Beta respondent 1).
	'The SWOT is used to decide on which manufacturers we can build a relationship with based upon the elements of the SWOT' (Delta respondent 1).
Strategy tools serving as a facilitative role towards decision-making.	'We develop our own methodologies, tools and techniques to guide us through the process of strategy development' (Alpha respondent 1).
	'We make time to study different scenarios and select one which best meets our position and intended action' (Beta respondent 2).

Within upwards influence, the middle manager acted and served as a consultant to the top management team by supplying information required in generating information for CI. One middle manager put it simply: 'all I do is supply the parent company with detailed financial packs with information they may use to come up with decisions and this is done on a monthly basis'. (*Lamda Respondent*). Table 4 shows some quotes on how middle managers exercised upwards influence.

In the second role, the middle manager exerted downwards influence towards strategy development and CI processes. The empirical data shown in Table 4 illustrate that the middle manager in this role acts as the facilitator of the strategy dealing with any perceived obstacles that emerge when pursuing this deliberate strategy. The behaviours reflected in this theme included motivating lower level managers to meet strategic goals and even come up with means through which the subsidiary can compete better. Other behaviours included negotiating with outsiders and channelling employee efforts towards the turn out of the deliberate strategy.

Discussion

The aim of this study was to understand the views and experiences of middle managers with regard to their role and contribution towards the CI process within Irish subsidiaries of the MNC.

TABLE 4: Middle manager role in competitive intelligence.

Name of company	Representative comments
Alpha	'We play along any possible scenarios so that all avenues are explored. From this a possible strategy is mapped out and smaller projects emerge to support this overall strategy' (upwards and downwards influence [Strategy Manager]).
	'My role is as middle manager is just to take what comes from our senior management, so there is no need to change or review an intended path...' (upwards influence [Marketing Manager]).
Beta	'I prepare some notes to give and lease with the MD through market rundowns... the aim is for me to help them (strategy formulation team consisting of top management team) understand the language of the business, the strategy, the interactions and relationships, the causality and what's going on out there' (upwards and downwards influence [Production Manager]).
	'I gather information about the market place because I am the person on the ground, so I give feedback on this about the possibility of markets opening up or about the possibility of new developments or even aspects of expansion. This information is then used for strategy planning...' (upwards influence [Supply Chain Manager]).
Gamma	'We supply information to our parent company about an overview of what we do here and this is used when making decisions' (upwards influence [Marketing Manager]).
	'I am always reacting to what senior management would have given us, the budget of the year is my "bible" and guide. I look at issues like how many engines are we going to produce, how does that compare to what we did last year or the year before and are there any resource issues that are coming up on this new budget' (upwards and downwards influence [Production Manager]).
Delta	'I work within a quality assurance department.... my role is to negotiate with contract manufacturers ... and the availability of support functions to ... the overall organisation' (upwards and downwards influence [Quality Assurance Manager]).
	'I occupy the role of directing the sales and marketing aspects of our group and I work with people who interact directly with the business strategy.... We are implementing processes that reflect traits of being innovative using centralised organisational structures' (upwards and downwards influence [Sales & Marketing Manager]).
Lamda	'All I do is supply the parent company with detailed financial packs with information they may use to come up with decisions and this is done on a monthly basis' (upwards influence [Finance Manager]).
	'We then look at how we can be part of this strategic plan [from the parent] based upon the services and products we provide... it is very much to the region as to how you realise that plan. There is a large degree of autonomy given to the region to manage its operations and profitability'. (upwards and downwards influence [Strategy & Information Manager]).

Contributions

The study valued the role and contribution of middle managers, especially relying on internal and external tools not only as a basis of efforts towards strategy development but also as a capability for attaining a competitive position (O'Brien & Meadows 2013). In this study, middle managers are illustrated as using these tools as a basis for attaining a competitive position for the subsidiary. In this regard, tools used by subsidiary managers existed also as a way of helping the subsidiary identify its strengths and weaknesses in relation to the competition (Noble *et al.* 2002) and a basis for innovation (Nam *et al.* 2014).

The study uniquely illustrates the value that middle managers place on internal sources and tools for gathering information rather than on external sources and tools in generating CI. This could be that internal sources and tools of gathering CI are more personal and most immediate to middle managers. Thus, internal sources and tools have been illustrated in this study to not only enhancing strategic decision-making (Gilad 2011) but also offering a way for middle managers (and the entire MNC) to understand the local, internal and global markets (Birkinshaw 1997).

For instance, in this study subsidiaries had within them a reference point internally that served as a source of information in generating CI. Such reference points due to their experience were better informed within the subsidiary in introducing not only new products but also product modifications (White & Poynter 1984). Put differently, information generated internally and externally provides a basis through which the subsidiary learns (Saka-Helmhout 2010) and, by doing so, responds to uncertainty (Viviers *et al.* 2005). Through such efforts of learning, subsidiaries are not only improving their decision-making capability (Du Toit & Sewdass 2014) but also positioning themselves as competitive players in an uncertain environment.

Finally, this study extends understanding on the role of middle managers in organisations that has continued (e.g. Balogun 2003; Floyd & Wooldridge 1994; Raes *et al.* 2011; Salih & Doll 2013). The study has not only contributed towards the literature with regard to the strategy development process but also reveals how a middle manager's role and contribution relate with CI generation. In essence, middle managers exist as an important resource (Barney 1991) that can be used to achieve competitiveness for the organisation (Lechner & Floyd 2012). Thus, this study, through the themes presented, posits middle managers as drivers of the CI agenda within the MNC subsidiary through their role and contribution to such a process (Nikolaos 2012).

Implications

The study has a number of implications. Firstly, the study focuses on the strategic importance of middle managers not only in how strategy turns out but also in generating CI. The implication here is that organisations need to be aware of the position of influence that middle managers occupy and their relation with regard to top managers, lower managers and employees. The findings of this study show that middle managers are a bridge between the upper and lower echelons of the organisation, and exert upwards and downwards influence with regard to efforts of being competitive. The results of this study also reinforced the idea of middle managers not only providing information to upper management for strategy formulation but also being actively involved in implementing these strategic outcomes.

The second managerial implication is the influence of the environment on subsidiary management and the process of CI. Subsidiary management needs to constantly monitor and scan their environment to help get the best and accurate information to be used with regard to strategy decision-making. To this end, the results of the study highlight the need for organisations to constantly keep an ear on the ground as a basis for remaining competitive.

The third managerial implication, linked to the second one, concerns the tools and techniques for gathering data from the environment to not only make strategic decisions but generate information that makes the subsidiary competitive. Due to the uncertainty in the environment, multiple methods of gathering information are preferred as they help offering a more accurate means of understanding data from the environment. Thus, usage of multiple tools and sources can help unearth new strategic insights and opportunities for subsidiary management and competitiveness.

Limitations

Some limitations exist with this work. Firstly, the study was interpretive and based on a specific context and has used a specific local example; the problem with this is that it cannot be assumed that the same observable patterns will emerge in the future. This plays well with the fact that only five subsidiaries (15 middle managers) took part in the study and hence the results may not be applicable not only to other subsidiaries but countries as well. Secondly, a small sample size was used for this study. Regardless of these limitations, the study has enhanced understanding in the experience in terms of the role and contribution of middle managers to the process of CI.

Future research could use a larger sample size in an attempt to obtain normative data. Future research may also benefit by improving from the methodology used in this study and incorporate a triangulation approach which could involve a combination of qualitative and quantitative research methods. Future research could also investigate the effects of national culture on CI generation as a basis to account for the role of macro factors not only on the strategy development processes but also for CI. Future research could also provide insight into the applicability of the study's results for samples from similar industries as well as various contexts. It is envisioned that this can help with comparability and enhance an understanding of CI processes within the same industries or different contexts.

Conclusion

The compelling theme that emerges from this study is that middle managers are an important conduit in the decisions that determine not only subsidiary performance but the competitiveness of the subsidiary within the MNC. One such way that this has been illustrated to happen through CI. It would appear that through their strategic position within the organisation, middle managers exert an influence towards efforts of CI. Strategic tools and techniques exist as key tools in the generation of data that helps determining the competitiveness of the subsidiary. Notably, the reliance on the tried and trusted sources of data generation such as internal expertise is given priority. This study heightens awareness to the issue that the middle manager is not dead but active. CI generation exists as one such useful activity that gives life to the middle-management tier.

Acknowledgements

Competing interests

The author declares that he has no financial or personal relationships which may have inappropriately influenced him in writing this article.

References

Amit, R. & Schoemaker, P.J.H., 1993, 'Strategic assets and organisational rent', *Strategic Management Journal* 14(1), 33–46. http://dx.doi.org/10.1002/smj.4250140105

Argote, L., 1982, 'Input uncertainty and organisational coordination in hospital emergency service units', *Administrative Science Quarterly* 27, 420–434. http://dx.doi.org/10.2307/2392320

Balogun, J., 2003, 'From blaming the middle to harnessing its potential: Creating change intermediaries', *British Journal of Management* 14(1), 69–83. http://dx.doi.org/10.1111/1467-8551.00266

Barney, J.B. 1991, 'Firm resources and sustained competitive advantage', *Journal of Management* 17(1), 99–120. http://dx.doi.org/10.1177/014920639101700108

Birkinshaw, J., 1997, 'Entrepreneurship in multinational corporations: The characteristics of subsidiary initiatives', *Strategic Management Journal* 18(3), 207–229. http://dx.doi.org/10.1002/(SICI)1097-0266(199703)18:3<207::AID-SMJ864>3.0.CO;2-Q

Bourne, L. & Walker, D.H.T., 2005, 'The paradox of project control', *Team Performance Management* 11, 157–178. http://dx.doi.org/10.1108/13527590510617747

Calof, J.L. & Wright, S., 2008, 'Competitive intelligence: A practitioner, academic and inter-disciplinary perspective', *European Journal of Marketing* 42(7/8), 717–730. http://dx.doi.org/10.1108/03090560810877114

Chinyamurindi, W.T. 2012, 'An investigation of career change using a narrative and story-telling inquiry', *South African Journal of Human Resource Management* 10(2), 1–11. http://dx.doi.org/10.4102/sajhrm.v10i2.447

Cohen, L., Manion, L. & Morrison, K., 2007, *Research methods in education,* 6th edn., Routledge-Falmer, London.

Creswell, J.W., 2014, *Research design: Qualitative, quantitative, and mixed methods approaches*, 4th edn., Sage, Thousand Oaks, CA.

Dishman, P. & Pearson, T., 2003, 'Assessing intelligence as learning within an industrial marketing group: A pilot study', *Industrial Marketing Management* 32(7), 615–620. http://dx.doi.org/10.1016/S0019-8501(03)00030-0

Dörrenbächer, C. & Geppert, M., 2009, 'A micro-political perspective on subsidiary initiative taking: Evidence from German-owned subsidiaries in France', *European Management Journal* 27(2), 100–112. http://dx.doi.org/10.1016/j.emj.2008.06.004

Du Toit, A.S.A. & Sewdass, N., 2014, 'A comparison of competitive intelligence activities in Brazil, Malaysia, Morocco and South Africa', *Acta Commercii* 14(1), 1–7. http://dx.doi.org/10.4102/ac.v14i1.234

Edmondson, A.C. & McManus, S.E., 2007, 'Methodological fit in management field research', *Academy of Management Review 32*(4), 1155–1179. http://dx.doi.org/10.5465/AMR.2007.26586086

Eisenhardt, K.M. 1989, 'Building theories from case study research', *Academy of Management Review* 14(4), 532–550.

Elbanna, S. 2016, 'Manager's autonomy, strategic control, organizational politics and strategic planning effectiveness: An empirical investigation into the missing links in the hotel sector', *Tourism Management* 52, 210–220. http://dx.doi.org/10.1016/j.tourman.2015.06.025

Floyd, S.W. & Lane, P.J., 2000, 'Strategising throughout the organisation: Managing role conflict in strategic renewal', *Academy of Management Review* 25, 154–177.

Floyd, S.W. & Wooldridge, B., 1994, 'Dinosaurs or dynamos? Recognising middle management's strategic role', *Academy of Management Executive* 8(1), 47–57.

Gilad, B., 2011, 'Strategy without intelligence, intelligence without strategy', *Business Strategy Series* 12(1), 4–11. http://dx.doi.org/10.1108/17515631111106821

Hart, J. & Spero, J., 1997, *The politics of international economic relations*, 5th edn., Bedford/St. Martin's Press, New York.

Herring, J.P., 2007, 'How much is your competitive intelligence worth?', *Competitive Intelligence Magazine* 10(2), 23–26.

Herzing, S.E. & Jimmieson N.L., 2006, 'Middle managers' uncertainty management during organisational change', *Leadership & Organisation Development Journal* 27(8), 628–645. http://dx.doi.org/10.1108/01437730610709264

Kealy, T., 2015, 'Do middle managers contribute to their organisation's strategy?', *International Journal of Humanities and Social Science* 5(1), 108–116.

Lechner, C. & Floyd, S.W., 2012, 'Group influence activities and the performance of strategic initiatives', *Strategic Management Journal* 33, 478–495. http://dx.doi.org/10.1002/smj.959

Mariadoss, B.J., Milewicz, C., Lee, S. & Sahaym, A., 2014, 'Sales person competitive intelligence & performance: The role of product knowledge and sales force automation usage', *Industrial Marketing Management* 43, 136–145. http://dx.doi.org/10.1016/j.indmarman.2013.08.005

McCormack, C., 2000, 'From interview transcript to interpretative story: Part 1. Viewing the transcript through multiple lenses', *Field Methods* 12(4), 282–297. http://dx.doi.org/10.1177/1525822X0001200402

Nam, D., Parboteeah, K.P., Cullen, J.B. & Johnson, J.L., 2014, 'Cross-national differences in firms undertaking innovation initiatives: An application of institutional anomie theory', *Journal of International Management* 20, 91–106. http://dx.doi.org/10.1016/j.intman.2013.05.001

Nachmias, F.C. & Nachmias, D., 1996, *Research methods in the social sciences,* 5th edn., Worth Publishers, New York.

Nikolaos, T., 2012, 'Competitive intelligence: Concept, context and a case of its application', *Science Journal of Business Management* 2, 1–15.

Noaks, L. & Wincup, E., 2004, *Criminological research: Understanding qualitative methods,* Sage, London.

Noble, C.H., 1999, 'The eclectic roots of strategy implementation research', *Journal of Business Research* 45, 119–134. http://dx.doi.org/10.1016/S0148-2963(97)00231-2

Noble, C.H., Sinha, R.K. & Kumar, A., 2002, 'Market orientation and alternative strategic orientations: A longitudinal assessment of performance implications', *Journal of Marketing* 66(4), 25–40. http://dx.doi.org/10.1509/jmkg.66.4.25.18513

O'Brien, F. & Meadows, M., 2013, 'Scenario orientation and use to support strategy development', *Technological Forecasting and Social Change* 80(4), 643–656. http://dx.doi.org/10.1016/j.techfore.2012.06.006

Opait, G., Bleoju, G., Nistor, R. & Capatina, A., 2016, 'The influences of competitive intelligence budgets on information energy dynamics', *Journal of Business Review* 69, 1682–1689.

Raes, A.M., Heijltjes, M.G., Glunk, U. & Roe, R.A., 2011, 'The interface of the top management team and middle managers: A process model', *Academy of Management Review* 36(1), 102–126. http://dx.doi.org/10.5465/amr.2009.0088

Reuben, S. & Bobat, S., 2014, 'Constructing racial hierarchies of skill-experiencing affirmative action in a South African organisation: A qualitative review', *South African Journal of Industrial Psychology* 40(1), 1–12. http://dx.doi.org/10.4102/sajip.v40i1.1158

Rhodes, H., 2000, 'Mid-life career change to home-based self-employment in a group of women', Master's thesis, Department of Sociology, Simon Fraser University.

Rouleau, L. & Balogun, J., 2011, 'Middle managers, strategic sense-making, and discursive competence', *Journal of Management Studies* 48(5), 953–983. http://dx.doi.org/10.1111/j.1467-6486.2010.00941.x

Saka-Helmhout, A., 2010, 'Organisational learning as a situated routine-based activity in international settings', *Journal of World Business* 45, 41–48. http://dx.doi.org/10.1016/j.jwb.2009.04.009

Salih, A. & Doll, Y., 2013, 'A middle management perspective on strategy implementation', *International Journal of Business and Management* 8(22), 32–39. http://dx.doi.org/10.5539/ijbm.v8n22p32

Teulier, R. & Rouleau, L., 2013, 'Middle managers' sense-making and interorganisational change initiation: Translation spaces and editing practices', *Journal of Change Management* 13(3), 308–337. http://dx.doi.org/10.1080/14697017.2013.822674

Thornhill, H., Clare, L. & May, R., 2004, 'Escape, enlightenment and endurance: Narratives of recovery from psychosis', *Anthropology and Medicine* 11, 181–199. http://dx.doi.org/10.1080/13648470410001678677

Viviers, W., Muller, M.L. & Du Toit, A.S.A., 2005, 'Competitive intelligence: An instrument to enhance competitiveness in South Africa', *South African Journal of Economic and Management Sciences* 8(2), 246–254.

White, R.E. & Poynter, T.A., 1984, 'Strategies for foreign-owned subsidiaries in Canada', *Business Quarterly* Summer, 59–69.

Wooldridge, B., Schmidt, T. & Floyd, S., 2008, 'The middle management perspective on strategy process: Contributions, synthesis, and future research', *Journal of Management* 34(6), 1190–1221. http://dx.doi.org/10.1177/0149206308324326

Xu, K., Liao, S.S., Li, J. & Song, Y., 2011, 'Mining comparative opinions from customer reviews for competitive intelligence', *Decision Support System* 50, 743–754. http://dx.doi.org/10.1016/j.dss.2010.08.021

6

Utilisation of poultry management information in three rural districts of Tanzania

Authors:
Grace Msoffe[1]
Patrick Ngulube[2]

Affiliations:
[1]University of Dodoma Library, University of Dodoma, United Republic of Tanzania

[2]Department of Interdisciplinary Research and Postgraduate Studies, University of South Africa, South Africa

Corresponding author:
Patrick Ngulube,
ngulup@unisa.ac.za

Background: In Tanzania, poultry farming plays an important role in improving rural livelihoods and contributes to the national economy. Promoting utilisation of poultry management information can support farmers in making good decisions and translate into efficiency in poultry production.

Objective: Being part of a PhD project, this study assessed the utilisation of poultry management information among farmers in three rural districts of Tanzania. The objective was to establish the extent of information use, types of information used, the constraints faced by farmers in using information and the strategies used by information providers to ensure farmers use the information.

Method: Quantitative and qualitative data were collected using questionnaires, focus group discussions and interviews. Quantitative data were analysed using the SPSS© software, and the meaning of qualitative data was established using content analysis.

Results: The findings revealed that most of the farmers used poultry management information. Information on disease control, poultry protection and markets was the most used. Information on poultry production and hatching were the least used. Poultry farmers faced various challenges in the course of using poultry management information. Most of the challenges were linked to poverty, ignorance and limited literacy.

Conclusion: The study concludes that farmers in the surveyed communities had limited skills on utilising information. The findings necessitate a need for information providers to ensure that farmers are well informed of the benefits of utilising information. It is recommended that imparting skills for information use be considered as part of information provision in rural communities, as it would facilitate use of information.

Introduction

Information use is often linked to information need, as information is needed so that it can be used (Meho & Hass 2001). It is mainly concerned with what happens with the information after it has been acquired, and how it is applied to accomplishing a specific goal and/or solving a particular problem (Bartlett & Toms 2005). An informed person is able to make better decisions in accomplishing a certain task or solving a problem and accruing the benefits associated with information use (Potnis 2014).

Improvement in agricultural production requires utilisation of agricultural information (Olaniyi & Adewale 2011). The use of agricultural information enhances farming productivity by assisting farmers to make proper decisions regarding their farming activities (Bachhav 2012). Similarly, a community that recognises and uses information has a greater chance for development (Kamba 2009). Thus, it is important for the poultry farmers to utilise information with the purpose of improving poultry production for the benefit of farmers, communities and the nation at large. Poultry farmers need a wide variety of information to increase their knowledge on poultry management (Temba et al. 2016). The use of poultry management information helps to increase poultry production, which translates into the improvement of farmers' standard of living and the national economy.

Poultry production is an important sector of Tanzania's economy (Temba et al. 2016). At the turn of the century, the poultry industry in Tanzania was estimated to be 40.5 billion Tanzania shillings, worth USD 50.6 million (Minga et al. 2000). It contributes about 3% of the agricultural GDP and 1% of national domestic product (FAO 2011). It comprises commercial poultry production and traditional poultry production. Commercial poultry production is more prominent in urban and peri-urban areas. Traditional poultry production is mostly practised in rural areas, contributing about 70% of the flock, and 100% of poultry meat and eggs consumed in rural areas and 20% in urban areas (Boki 2000; United Republic of Tanzania 2006). Traditional poultry production is an important farming activity in the rural areas because it can be afforded by the poor rural farmers (Guèye 2000). Poultry production is an important source of income for most of the rural poor households and plays an essential role in improving household income and alleviating poverty (Knueppel et al. 2009, 2010). This is because of an increasing urban demand for traditionally kept poultry, which is stimulating trade from rural areas to urban areas and creating opportunities for rural farmers to sell more poultry at a better price (Msoffe 2015). It is an important source of protein-rich food acting as an effective way to reduce food insecurity and malnutrition in the rural areas (Knueppel et al. 2009).

Despite the importance of the traditional poultry production for economic development, there has been low poultry production in rural Tanzania. The use of poultry management information among farmers will always lead to increased poultry productivity (Ofuoku, Emah & Itedjere 2008). The low poultry production implies that poultry management information is not adequately utilised by farmers. Thus, it is important to investigate the information utilisation in the rural areas of Tanzania. The study assessed the extent of information use, types of information used, the constraints faced by farmers in using information and the strategies used by information providers to ensure farmers use the information. The findings could be useful in taking measures to ensure information that reaches the rural farmers is effectively utilised.

Methodology

This study used a quantitative approach to large extent. A survey research strategy was used, and it was supplemented by methodological triangulation with the intention that the methods will converge to support the objectives of the study (Leedy & Ormrod 2005:99). Using a purposive sampling technique, three rural districts in Tanzania were selected to include those that were involved in the poultry management programmes; and from each of the selected districts, one ward with higher poultry production was selected. From each of the selected wards, three villages with well-established poultry production were selected. The districts selected for the study were Iringa rural, Morogoro rural and Mvomero. The villages involved in the study included Fulwe, Mikese and Mkambarani in Morogoro rural; Mafuluto, Malinzanga and Nyamahana in Iringa rural; and Changarawe, Tangeni and Vikenge in Mvomero. Simple random sampling technique was used to select farmers. A total of 360 farmers participated in questionnaire survey.

The purposive sampling technique was used to select individuals for focus group discussions (FGDs) and interviews. A sample of 160 farmers was purposively drawn from the participants of questionnaire survey to take part in FGDs. Sixteen FGDs were held. The typical case sampling technique was used to select information providers (extension officers, researchers, local leaders). Twenty-two information providers participated in the interviews.

The triangulation of data collection instruments facilitated the collection of reliable data. Multiple research instruments were used to cross-check and verify the reliability of research tools and the validity of the collected data (McNeil & Chapman 2005). The use of FGDs and interviews facilitated face-to-face communication between the first author and participants, which enabled the first author to explain questions, depending on the level of understanding of the participants. Likewise, questionnaires were administered during face-to-face interaction between the first author and respondents. Furthermore, FGDs were used to validate information collected by means of the questionnaire. Similarly, data from interviews with information providers were used to clarify the different findings from the questionnaire administered to farmers.

Quantitative and qualitative data were collected through questionnaires, FGDs and interviews. The FGDs and interviews were used to supplement data gained through questionnaires. The quantitative data were collected through close-ended questions in questionnaires. Qualitative data were collected through FGDs, interviews and open-ended questions in questionnaires. Quantitative data were analysed using SPSS®, and qualitative data were analysed using content analysis as suggested by Ngulube (2015). Quantitative data analysis involved descriptive and inferential numeric analysis, while qualitative data analysis involved description and thematic text analysis. Frequencies, percentages and forms of graphic presentation and narrative descriptions were used for data presentation. The study was guided by the following research questions:

- Do farmers use the poultry management information that they access?
- What types of poultry management information are used by farmers?
- What are the factors hindering farmers from using poultry management information?
- What are the strategies used by information providers in ensuring that farmers use information?

Findings and discussions

Starting with a discussion of the characteristics of the poultry farmers and information providers who participated in the study, this section discusses the findings based on the four research questions that informed the study.

Characteristics of poultry farmers

A total of 360 poultry farmers participated in the survey questionnaire. The mean age of the respondents was 39 years,

TABLE 1: Characteristics of poultry farmers (N = 360).

Variable	Categories	Frequency (N)	%
Gender	Men	189	52.5
	Women	171	47.5
Age (years)	Below 18	2	0.6
	18–37	173	48.1
	38–57	130	36.1
	58 and above	55	15.2
Educational levels†	Post-secondary education	4	1.1
	Secondary education	22	6.1
	Primary education	287	79.7
	Informal education	4	1.1
Occupation	Crop farming and livestock keeping	341	94.7
	Livestock keeping and small business	13	3.6
	Livestock keeping and skilled work	6	1.7

†, Forty-three respondents were illiterate.

where the majority (303, 84.1%) were aged between 18 and 57 years (Table 1). Most of the respondents had primary education, few had secondary education, whereas 43 (11.9%) were illiterate. Men dominated the formal education category. Respondents with primary education comprised 131 (36.4%) women and 156 (43.3%) men, while those with secondary education comprised 9 (2.5%) women and 13 (3.6%) men. The majority of the respondents were involved in mixed farming (crop farming and livestock keeping). Some farmers were involved in livestock keeping and small businesses, while few farmers did livestock keeping and skilled work (See Table 1).

Characteristics of information providers

Twenty-two information providers participated in the semi-structured interviews. The mean age of the respondents was 42 years. The majority of the respondents were between 35 and 55 years, and few respondents were above 55 years. They comprised village executive officers, researchers, district agricultural officers, extension officers and a ward executive officer (See Table 2).

Use of poultry management information

The findings revealed that majority of the respondents (332, 92.2%) accessed poultry management information. Out of those who accessed information, more than half (187, 56.3%, n = 332) used the poultry management information they acquired. Most of the respondents (146, 78.1%, n = 187) indicated that the information assisted them to solve the problems and provide better management of their poultry. Some respondents (41, 21.9%, n = 187) indicated that the information was not helpful in solving their problems. The findings demonstrate that accessing information does not guarantee that the information will be utilised for solving the problems and improving poultry production. Coudel and Tonneau (2010:63) emphasised that 'information may seem appropriate, usable, relevant, but it can only be useful if the actors have the capacity to use it and if their environment offers them the opportunity to use it'. This calls for information providers to devise follow-up strategies to ensure that farmers are able to use the information they access.

TABLE 2: Characteristics of information providers (N = 22).

Variables	Frequency (N)	%
Gender		
Men	15	68.2
Women	7	31.8
Age		
35–55 years	18	81.8
Above 55 years	4	18.2
Educational levels		
Degree	6	27.3
Secondary education	6	27.3
Tertiary certificate	4	18.2
Diploma	3	13.6
Primary education	3	13.6
Job		
Village executive officers	9	40.9
Researchers	6	27.3
District agricultural officers	3	13.6
Extension officers	3	13.6
Ward executive officer	1	4.5

TABLE 3: Information use by education categories (N = 187).

Educational levels	Frequency (N)	%
Post-secondary education	4	2.1
Secondary education	22	11.8
Primary education	159	85
Informal education	1	0.5
Illiterate	1	0.5

The optimal use of information can be realised if information is disseminated in the formats that are desirable by the target audience. This may be achieved with full participation of all stakeholders such as rural farmers, researchers and various information providers (Kalusopa 2005). In order for users to access and use information, they must have economic resources, skills, technology and social resources (Heeks 2005). It is therefore important to take into consideration all the factors influencing the use of poultry management information in rural areas. Regular follow-ups may shed light on what changes need to be applied in order for the information to be useful; this may entail changing the format or the delivery method.

Table 3 illustrates the information use by education categories. The findings suggest that farmers' educational levels have an influence on the utilisation of poultry management information. There was a variation in the use of information across different education categories. Farmers with primary education and secondary education were the majority among those who utilised information, in comparison to illiterate farmers and those who had informal education. All the farmers with secondary and post-secondary education used the information (See Table 3). On the other hand, more men (101, 54%) utilised information compared to women (86, 46%). As the demographic characteristics show that men dominated the formal education categories, it is imperative to attribute their use of information with their level of education.

These findings are inconsistent with those of Olaniyi and Adewale (2012), who reported that there was no relationship between educational level and level of utilisation of agricultural information. The difference may be attributed to the fact that the respondents in the study of Olaniyi and Adewale (2012) were rural youth, while this study dealt with all age categories. Thus, educational levels in this study may seem to be important, particularly because of the disparity in terms of level of understanding. It is probable that youth educational levels did not have significant differences as far as understanding and using agricultural information are concerned.

Farmers' ability to access and use information is highly dependent on educational level (Eze et al. 2006; Fawole 2006; Waller et al. 1998). This implies that inadequate knowledge to use the information is directly related to the educational levels of farmers. This is consistent with Ofuoku et al. (2008), who assert that the higher level of formal education has a positive influence on farmers' use of information.

Most of the farmers in rural areas of Tanzania had little education as shown in their demographic characteristics (Table 1). With low level of education, it is not guaranteed that the farmers would have the ability to access and use information disseminated in various formats. This partly explains the low poultry productivity in the rural areas. The situation is directly related to the inadequate use of information caused by limited educational levels of the majority of rural farmers in Tanzania. It is therefore crucial for information dissemination services to take into consideration the farmers' literacy level to enable effective utilisation of information.

Types of information used by poultry farmers

The findings (Figure 1) established that information on poultry disease control was the most used – 187 (100%, n = 187). Other types of information that were highly used were information on poultry protection and markets. The least used information was information on poultry production and hatching. Figure 1 presents the detailed findings on the types of poultry management information used by farmers in the surveyed communities.

The findings from FGDs indicated that there was low use of information on poultry feeding and nutrition and information on poultry housing and shelter. Most farmers used information on poultry disease control and were not willing to provide proper feeds and housing for the poultry. Also, some farmers especially in Mafuluto village were not interested in using conventional methods for prevention of poultry diseases because they had experienced massive loss of their poultry when vaccines were used previously. Thus, they were reluctant to use

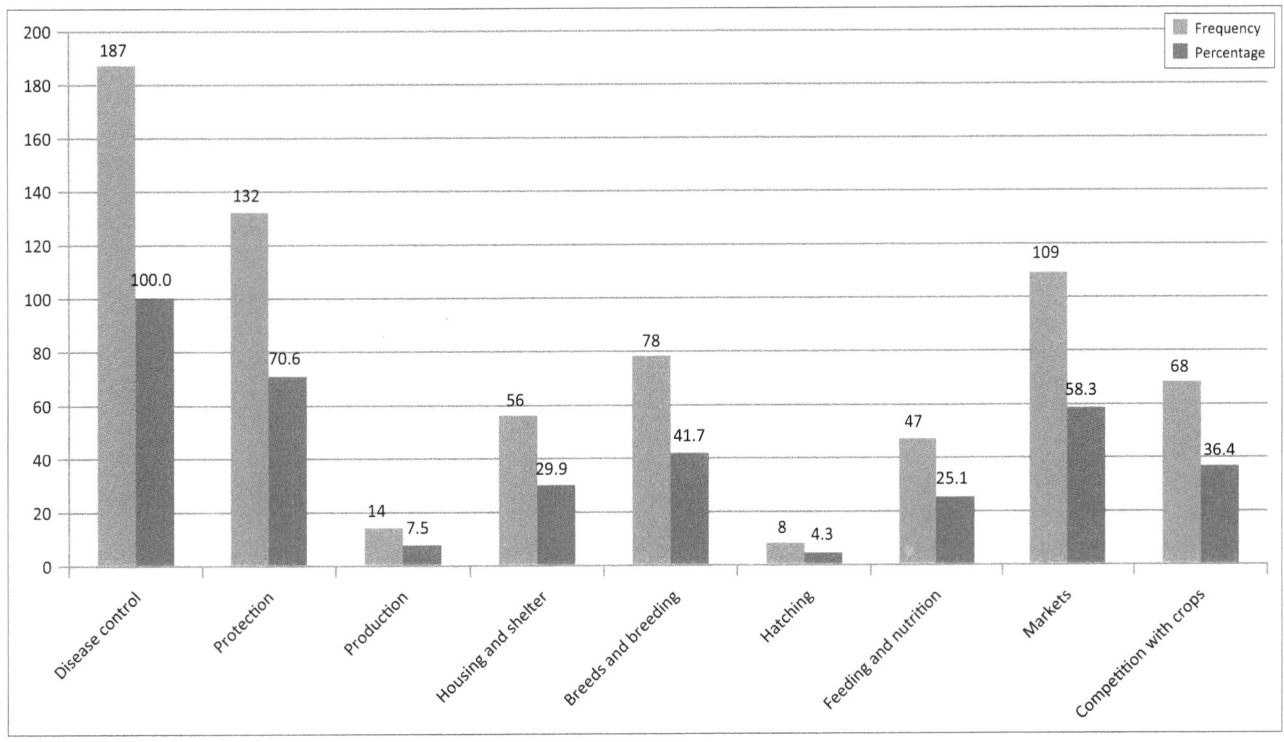

Note: Multiple responses were possible.

FIGURE 1: Types of information used by poultry farmers (N = 187).

any information they received from the extension officer. Some of the typical responses were:

> 'We have used vaccines previously, and as a result all the poultry died because of Newcastle disease. Now, we only want to use the traditional methods to prevent loss of poultry.' [Female, 50 years old, primary education level]

> 'Implementing some of the advices from extension officers is expensive, and some of us cannot afford. For instance building a house for the poultry is expensive.' [Male, 55 years old, illiterate]

> 'It is expensive to get food for the poultry, why should I feed them while they can easily find their own food?' [Female, 43 years old, primary education level]

It was evident from the findings that farmers mainly applied information that had direct impacts on their farming activities. The most used information was the one that directly affected the poultry health and production. For instance, information on diseases that caused death of poultry, information on poultry protection which was crucial for poultry safety and information on poultry markets which was necessary for selling poultry products. These findings agree with that of Byamugisha, Ikoja-Odongo and Nasinyama (2010) who found that farmers mainly used information on controlling animal diseases (51.5%) and controlling crop diseases (48.2%). This implies that information use indicates information needs of poultry farmers and the value poultry farmers attached to particular information.

On the other hand, other types of information were rarely used by farmers. These findings suggest that farmers chose certain information to be more important than the others and utilised those which they considered to be important. For instance, traditionally farmers have been rearing poultry leaving them to find food for themselves. Thus, information on feeding and nutrition would not be taken as an important practice especially if it requires money to buy the feed. In such a situation, it takes a knowledgeable farmer who understands the importance of utilising such information to pay for the recommended inputs. The implication is that poultry farmers need more education and training to make them understand the importance of various farming practices. This calls for the information providers to devise strategies to ensure that farmers understand the benefits of utilising the information.

The findings also demonstrate that the cost associated with utilising information was considered to be an important reason for the failure to use information. Some of the farmers were constrained by the cost of inputs needed to utilise the information. According to Opara (2010), the income level of farmers is very important in facilitating agricultural information use. Opara (2010) emphasises that farmers with a better income are more likely to spend money on looking for information, utilising it and buying the required inputs. An increase in level of utilisation of agricultural information leads to improved productivity (Olaniyi & Adewale 2012), which in turn leads to improved income (Lwoga et al. 2011). With improved income, the farmer will be able to spend more money on the utilisation of agricultural information, which will further increase agricultural productivity and income. However, most farmers in rural areas of Tanzania had very little income. Thus, the majority of rural farmers could not afford to pay the cost of accessing information and buying the inputs needed to utilise the information. Even when the information was provided free of charge, they could rarely afford to buy the required inputs.

Strategies used by information providers to ensure utilisation of information

The majority of the information providers (17, 77.3%, $n = 22$) indicated that they had no strategies for ensuring that farmers used the information. Few information providers (5, 22.7%) pointed out that they had strategies. The strategies they used (Table 4) were: following up the farmers, practising together with farmers, demonstrating during the seminars and requesting for feedback from farmers. A researcher in Mvomero district organised school children and built a poultry house at their school. He supplied the building materials and bought the poultry and feeds for starting the project. This was a strategy to encourage students and farmers to learn from the school poultry project. Students learnt how to manage poultry and transferred the knowledge to their homes. Through this strategy, many farmers started to use the information after seeing the benefits of using the information at the school poultry project.

These findings (Table 4) indicate that most information providers disseminated information to the rural communities without strategies for ensuring that farmers utilise the information. The findings demonstrate further that face-to-face communication was the main method used by information providers to make follow-ups on the utilisation of information in the surveyed rural communities. Taking the school poultry project as an example of a successful strategy, it is evident that poultry farmers were ignorant about the benefits of utilising such information. They utilised the knowledge after becoming aware of the benefits of utilising information on best farming practices. Therefore, there is a need for information providers to educate farmers on the benefits of utilising information on farming practices.

TABLE 4: Strategies used by information providers to ensure information is utilised ($N = 22$).

Strategies	Frequency (N)	%
Following up the farmers	5	22.7
Practising together with farmers	4	18.2
Demonstrating during the seminars	4	18.2
Requesting for feedback from farmers	3	13.6
School poultry project	1	4.5

Note: Multiple responses were possible.

Factors that hinder the use of poultry management information

More than half of the surveyed farmers (228, 63.3%) responded to the question on factors that hindered the use of poultry management information. The majority of the respondents indicated that limited assistance from experts and lack of skills on how to use the information were the main barriers. Other factors were limited literacy levels, unreliable information, low economic status, and lack of cooperation among farmers. Figure 2 shows the findings on factors that hinder the use of poultry management information.

Data from FGDs confirmed that the unavailability of assistance from experts such as extension officers was a major factor which limited farmers from using poultry management information. Other factors that hindered farmers from using poultry management information in descending order of importance were: lack of cooperation among poultry farmers, unreliability of the information, poor economic status, high cost of implementing the information and unavailability of poultry treatment drugs in the community. Some of the typical responses were:

> 'They only give us information, but we don't know how to use it. For instance, I read a poster on vaccination of poultry against Newcastle disease. I buy the drug, vaccinate the poultry, and they die. They should demonstrate to us how to do it, when to do it, and how often we should do it.'

> 'There is a long distance from our community to the drug store. It is a day trip which requires funds for transport. Even if I get information, it is difficult to use it, because there is no drug store in our community, and I cannot afford the transport cost to town.'

The barriers identified in this study are similar to the obstacles reported by Odini (2014). Odini (2014) found that illiteracy, ignorance, poverty, inaccessibility of information and unreliable information were among the main barriers to female farmers' use of information in Kenya. The findings demonstrate that the factors hindering the use of poultry management information mainly originate from illiteracy and poverty among the rural farmers. Similar observations were made by Opara (2010), who asserted that low literacy and high poverty levels of farmers could affect their access to and use of agricultural information. Likewise, Dorsch (2000) reported that cost of information, lack of skills and geographical isolation were among the major hindrances to information use. Mtega (2012) also stressed that literacy levels of information seekers limit the utilisation of information.

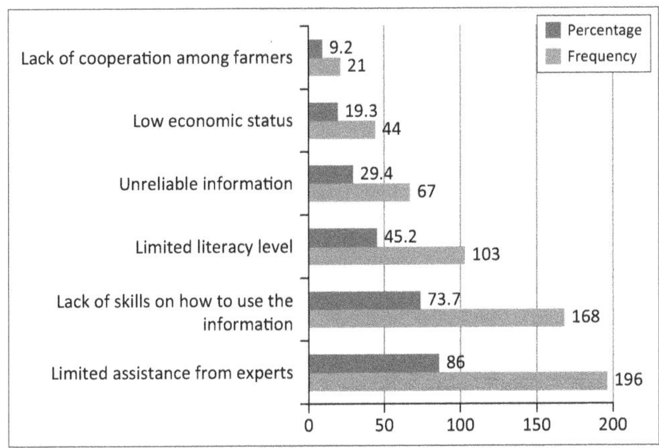

Note: Multiple responses were possible.

FIGURE 2: Factors that hinder the use of poultry management information (N = 228).

The findings also indicate that farmers needed assistance from experts to use information, and they lacked skills on how to use the information. Accessed information can be effectively used by farmers if they know how to use it. Meyer (2005) emphasised that receivers of information must know how to use the information, otherwise the information will be useless. Mtega (2012) highlighted the fact that information can only be useful when effectively interpreted by the receivers. The implication is that farmers lack knowledge on how to use the accessed information. This situation is exacerbated by the fact that most of the farmers have low literacy levels, as reported in previous sections. Limited literacy level was one of the most cited barriers to information use.

The findings from interviews with information providers indicated that the low literacy level of farmers was the main barrier to information use. This indicates that farmers need knowledge to enable their effective utilisation of information. Imparting the needed knowledge to farmers can be achieved through seminars, training and demonstration. Thus, information providers need to consider having more seminars, training courses and demonstrations to increase farmers' skills on how to use the information that they receive. This is supported by Opara (2010), who emphasised that education gives an individual the ability to seek and use information.

The need for training and demonstration was also highlighted by some of the farmers in the surveyed communities, as clarified in the typical responses from the FGDs. One of the farmers stated that:

> 'They only give us information, but we don't know how to use it.'

Thus, training of farmers is an important issue to be considered for the effective utilisation of poultry management information in the surveyed communities. Farmers indicated limited assistance from experts and lack of skills as their major hindrance for information utilisation. In this case, the extension officers are the main experts in rural areas; hence they have a responsibility of shaping the future of information utilisation for increased poultry production. This implies that the extension officers have to put more effort into training farmers to utilise the information they acquire.

Furthermore, the study findings indicate that poverty among the rural population had a great influence on the way in which farmers utilised poultry management information.

The findings revealed that poor economic status and the high cost of employing the suggested farming practices were among the most cited barriers to information use. This is an indication that poverty has an effect on information use. Similarly, Opara (2010) cited poverty as one of the main variables hindering information use. Daudu, Chado and Igbashal (2009) reported that financial difficulty was the major constraint to farmers' use of information in Benue State, Nigeria.

Thus, there is a need to find ways to make information services and agricultural inputs more affordable to rural farmers. This can be achieved through government subsidisation of agricultural inputs and all information products distributed to the rural areas. Availability of farming inputs such as poultry vaccines at a subsidised price could enhance the use of poultry management information in the surveyed rural communities. However, eradicating poverty in rural areas is the only permanent solution.

Conclusion

The findings suggest that farmers tended to use information that had direct impact on their farming activities. The high use of information on poultry disease control and poultry protection explains the need to ensure poultry are healthy and protected, while markets bring monetary gains. The low use of information on poultry production and hatching spells out lack of knowledge on the benefits of utilising such information. This implies that farmers use information they perceive as important to their farming activities. The study concludes that farmers were ignorant on the importance of utilising information, and information providers inadequately supported them. The situation calls attention to the government and other institutions responsible for information provision to facilitate information utilisation by ensuring that farmers are well informed. Based on the findings, information utilisation seemed to be determined by various factors, including inadequate knowledge and economic resources. It is therefore important to educate farmers by providing seminars and demonstrations using participatory approaches. It would also be important to adjust the planning for information dissemination by taking into consideration the factors that influence information utilisation.

Recommendations

- Information providers should conduct regular training on how to use the information, and have follow-up strategies to ensure that farmers are able to utilise the information.
- Information providers should devise better strategies for informing farmers on the benefits of information utilisation, such as farmers' field schools.
- Although oral communication seems to be popular in rural areas, the study recommends use of a variety of sources to complement each other. For instance, the use of print media to supplement oral messages communicated during the meeting or demonstration. It is also recommended that information be delivered in a variety of formats to accommodate various education categories of farmers.
- The government should subsidise the resources which are needed for effective functioning of the information system in rural areas.
- Capacity building should be the priority of the government, local authorities and other responsible institutions. This should involve providing training for farmers as well as the information providers. The training programmes for farmers should be geared towards imparting knowledge and skills for accessing and using information. The training programmes for information providers should focus on improving and updating their information provision skills. These programmes should be continuous to strengthen and update the knowledge base of both farmers and information providers in rural areas.

Acknowledgements

Competing interests

The authors declare that they have no financial or personal relationships which may have inappropriately influenced them in writing this article.

Authors' contributions

P.N. was the project leader and assisted in the conceptualisation and execution of the project including dealing with correspondence from the editorial board. G.M. was responsible for data collection, analysis and drawing conclusion from the data. This was part of the project that formed the PhD study of G.M.

References

Bachhav, N.B., 2012, 'Information needs of the rural farmers: A study from Maharashtra, India: A survey', *Library Philosophy and Practice*, Paper 866, viewed 20 July 2013, from http://digitalcommons.unl.edu/libphilprac/866

Bartlett, J.C. & Toms, E.G., 2005, 'How is information used? Applying task analysis to understanding information use', in CAIS Conference Proceedings: Data, information and knowledge in a networked world, viewed 12 June 2011, from http://www.cais-csi.ca/proceedings/2005/bartlett_2005.pdf

Boki, J.K., 2000, 'Poultry industry in Tanzania with emphasis on small-scale rural poultry. smallholder poultry project eastern and southern Africa', *Journal of International Development* 14(2), 23–35.

Byamugisha, H.M., Ikoja-Odongo, R. & Nasinyama, G.W., 2010, 'Information needs and use among urban farmers in Kampala City in Uganda', *Library and Information Research* 34(108), 18–32.

Coudel, E. & Tonneau, P., 2010, 'How can information contribute to innovative learning processes? Insight from a farmer university in Brazil', *Agricultural Information Worldwide* 3(2), 56–63.

Daudu, S., Chado, S.S. & Igbashal, A.A., 2009, 'Agricultural information sources utilized by farmers in Benue State, Nigeria', *Publication Agriculture and Technology* 5(1), 39–48.

Dorsch, J.L., 2000, 'Information needs of rural health professionals: A review of the literature', *Bulletin of the Medical Library Association* 88(4), 346–354, viewed 15 September 2013, from http://www.ncbi.nlm.nih.gov/pmc/articles/PMC35256/pdf/i0025-7338-088-04-0346.pdf

Eze, C.C., Ibekwe, U.C., Onoh, P.O. & Nwajiuba, C.U., 2006, 'Determinants of adoption of improved cassava production technologies among farmers in Enugu State of Nigeria', *Global Approaches to Extension Practice* 2(1), 37–44.

Fawole, O.P., 2006, 'Poultry farmers' utilization of information in Lagelu local government area, Oyo State of Nigeria', *International Journal of Poultry Science* 5(5), 499–501. https://doi.org/10.3923/ijps.2006.499.501

Food and Agriculture Organisation (FAO), 2011, *Animal Husbandry and Animal Health Division- Poultry Sector Country Review for Tanzania*, FAO, Rome.

Guèye, E.F., 2000, 'The role of family poultry in poverty alleviation, food security and the promotion of gender equality in rural Africa', *Outlook on Agriculture* 29(2), 129–136. https://doi.org/10.5367/000000000101293130

Heeks, R., 2005, 'Foundations of ICTs in development: The information chain', *eDevelopment Briefing* 3, 1–2.

Kalusopa, T., 2005, 'The challenges of utilizing information communication technologies (ICTs) for the small-scale farmers in Zambia', *Library Hi Tech* 23(3), 414–424. https://doi.org/10.1108/07378830510621810

Kamba, M.A., 2009, *Access to information: The dilemma for rural community development in Africa*, viewed 2 June 2014, from https://smartech.gatech.edu/jspui/bitstream/1853/36694/1/1238296264_MA.pdf

Knueppel, D., Cardona, C., Msofffe, G.E.P., Demment, M. & Kaiser, L., 2010, 'Impact of vaccination against chicken Newcastle disease on food intake and food security in rural households in Tanzania', *Food and Nutrition Bulletin* 31(3), 436–445. https://doi.org/10.1177/156482651003100306

Knueppel, D., Coppolillo, P., Msago, O.A., Msoffe, P.L., Mutekanga, D. & Cardona, C., 2009, *Improving Poultry Production for Sustainability in the Ruaha Landscape, Tanzania*, viewed 5 June 2014, from http://files.figshare.com/483963/CaseStudy_ImprovingPoultryProduction_Tanzania.pdf

Leedy, P.D. & Ormrod, J.E., 2005, *Practical research: Planning and design*, 8th edn., Pearson Education, Upper Saddle Rive, NJ.

Lwoga, E.T., Stilwell, C. & Ngulube, P., 2011, 'Access and use of agricultural information and knowledge in Tanzania', *Library review* 60(5), 383–395. https://doi.org/10.1108/00242531111135263

McNeil, P. & Chapman, S., 2005, *Research methods*, 3rd edn., Routledge, New York.

Meho, L.I. & Hass, S.W., 2001, 'Information seeking behaviour and use of social science faculty studying stateless nations: A case study', *Library and Information Science Research* 23(1), 5–25. https://doi.org/10.1016/S0740-8188(00)00065-7

Meyer, H.W.J., 2005, 'The nature of information and effective use of information in rural development', *Information Research*, 10(2), paper 214, viewed 29 November 2016, from http://InformationR.net/ir/10-2/paper214.html

Minga, U.M., Yongolo, M.G.S., Mtambo, M.M.A., Mutayoba, S.K., Lawrence, P., Mwalusanya, N.A. et al., 2000, 'The potential for rural poultry production and health in Africa', in G. Pedersen, A. Permin, & U. Minga (eds.), *Proceeding of the workshop on the possibilities for smallholder poultry projects in Eastern and Southern Africa*, pp. 83–94, The Royal Veterinary and Agricultural University, Copenhagen, Denmark.

Msoffe G.E.P., 2015, *Access and use of poultry management information in selected rural areas of Tanzania*, University of South Africa, viewed 29 November 2016, from http://uir.unisa.ac.za/handle/10500/19021

Mtega, W.P., 2012, 'Access to and usage of information among rural communities: A case study of Kilosa District Morogoro Region in Tanzania', *Partnership: The Canadian Journal of Library and Information Practice and Research* 7(1), viewed 29 November 2016, from https://journal.lib.uoguelph.ca/index.php/perj/article/view/1646/2462#.WD2cRfl95QI

Ngulube, P., 2015, 'Qualitative data analysis and interpretation: Systematic search for meaning', in E.R, Mathipa & M.T. Gumbo (eds.), *Addressing research challenges: making headway for developing researchers*, pp. 131-156. Mosala-MASEDI Publishers & Booksellers cc, Noordywk, South Africa.

Odini, S., 2014, 'Access to and use of agricultural information by small scale women farmers in support of efforts to attain food security in Vihiga County, Kenya', *Journal of Emerging Trends in Economics and Management Sciences* 5(2), 100–107.

Ofuoku, A.U., Emah, G.N. & Itedjere, B.E., 2008, 'Information utilization among rural fish farmers in Central Agricultural Zone of Delta State, Nigeria', *World Journal of Agricultural Sciences* 4(5), 558–564.

Olaniyi, O.A. & Adewale, J.G., 2011, 'Nigerian Rural Youths' utilisation of agricultural information on selected arable crops : An empirical evidence', *Agricultural Information Worldwide* 4, 81–87.

Olaniyi, O.A. & Adewale, J.G., 2012, 'Assessment of utilization of agricultural information on maize production among rural youth: Panacea for sustainable food security in Nigeria', *OIDA International Journal of Sustainable Development* 5(2), 75–86.

Opara, U.N., 2010, 'Personal and socio-economic determinants of agricultural information use by farmers in the Agricultural Development Programme (ADP) zones of Imo State, Nigeria', *Library Philosophy and Practice*, Paper 434, viewed 15 August 2013, from http://digitalcommons.unl.edu/libphilprac/434

Potnis, D.D., 2014, 'Beyond access to information: Understanding the use of information by poor female mobile users in rural India', *The Information Society* 31(1), 83–93. https://doi.org/10.1080/01972243.2014.976687

Temba, B.A., Kajuna, F.K., Pango, G.S. & Benard, R., 2016, 'Accessibility and use of information and communication tools among farmers for improving chicken production in Morogoro municipality, Tanzania', *Livestock Research for Rural Development* 28, viewed 28 November 2016, from http://lrrd.cipav.org.co/lrrd28/1/temb28011.html

United Republic of Tanzania (URT), 2006, *National livestock policy*, viewed 10 September 2011, from http://www.mifugo.go.tz/documents_storage/lLivetockPolicy.pdf

Waller, B.E., Hoya, C.W., Hendersonb, J.L., Stinnera, B. & Welty, C., 1998, 'Matching innovations with potential users, a case study of potato IPM practices', *Agriculture, Ecosystems & Environment* 70(2), 203–215. https://doi.org/10.1016/S0167-8809(98)00149-2

7

An investigation into possibilities for implementation of a virtual community of practice delivered via a mobile social network for rural community media in the Eastern Cape, South Africa

Authors:
Oliva Muwanga-Zake[1]
Marlien Herselman[1]

Affiliations:
[1]Department of Information Systems, University of Fort Hare, South Africa

Corresponding author:
Oliva Muwanga-Zake,
muwango@eskom.co.za

Background: The purpose of this article is to provide an overview of how a virtual community of practice can be delivered via a mobile social networking framework to support rural community media in the Eastern Cape Province of South Africa.

Objectives: The article presents the results of a study conducted to ascertain the possibilities of utilising mobile social networking as a means to provide access to required information and knowledge to rural community media through creation of a virtual community of practice. Improving the operational effectiveness of rural community media as a component of the rural community communication process would serve to improve the entire rural community communication process as well, making them more effective tools for availing relevant news and information to rural communities and reflecting the realities of rural communities to their broader environment.

Method: The study was conducted on rural community media small micro and medium enterprises (SMMEs) in the Eastern Cape Province of South Africa. The study applied an interpretive research philosophy, qualitative research design and multiple–case study approach. Primary data were collected through semi-structured interviews supported by a questionnaire, with secondary data collected via literature review, observation and documentation analysis.

Results: Findings were that rural community media do make use of social media and mobile devices in operating their business, require access to generic and domain specific support services and actively engage their peers and stakeholders in this respect, although no formalised structure existed. The authors' recommendation is to create a formalised virtual community of practice through the establishment of a mobile social network.

Conclusion: Because of the fact that rural community SMMEs already utilise mobile devices and social media to operate their businesses, development of a solution based on a mobile social networking platform could be a useful tool in providing support to these SMMEs.

Introduction

The International Fund for Agricultural Development (IFAD 2011:7) states that in developing countries entrepreneurs and their micro and small-scale enterprises (MSEs) are recognised as 'necessary engines for achieving national development goals such as economic growth, poverty alleviation, employment and wealth creation, leading to a more equitable distribution of income and increased productivity…'. MSEs have become a major concern in an attempt to accelerate growth rates in low-income countries such as Africa (IFAD 2011). These enterprises are faced with unique problems that affect their growth, reducing their ability to contribute effectively to economic development (IFAD 2011).

Baumgartner, Schulz and Seidl (2013) conducted a study that concluded that entrepreneurship in rural areas may not be a distinctive 'rural' phenomenon, rather 'rural' is conceptualised as specific attributes measured by specific indicators. As a result, rural entrepreneurs are seen not as following a process unique to them but rather operating within a distinctive context or environment. Rural areas are generally afflicted by the twin economic ills of poverty and unemployment, with human resources typically employed below their productive potential (The Eastern Cape Development Corporation [ECDC] 2015).

The very nature of the rural environment itself inhibits the existence and/or cultivation of precursors that could subvert poverty and encourage socio-economic development

(Duncombe 1999). Based on this, it is not surprising that entrepreneurs in rural areas face a host of difficulties (Horn & Harvey 1998). Because these businesses are small and isolated, the people and information base needed to provide expert support for critical decisions and functions do not exist internally or externally within the rural location; furthermore, the needs of the enterprise are continuing, not one-time, and if the enterprise is successful, the needs grow (Horn & Harvey 1998).

Rural areas typically share a number of common characteristics that constrain rural entrepreneurial operation, these comprise the following (Heeks 2009):

- lack of access to relevant information and knowledge
- lack of empowerment
- lack of participation and inclusion
- poor communication and information flow.

Rural community media

The authors have specifically scoped the research that informs this paper to focus on rural community media as a specialised sub-segment of entrepreneurs operating in rural areas. The reasons for this decision were in part because of the effect and impact of community media on socio-economic development because of the role they play in enabling access to information and knowledge and giving a voice to poor and isolated communities.

Opubor (2000) states that amongst other things, human communities are built on the exchange of initiatives, information and meaning in the process of defining, creating and maintaining a collective identity in the interests of survival within a specific geographical and/or cultural space. A community thus creates, and is also created by, a shared communication system, which comprises communication roles, needs and resources available to individuals and subgroups within this shared space (Opubor 2000). 'Community media should be viewed then as an element of a community communication system' ... serving as instruments for role performance and resource utilisation in response to the communication needs of individuals and institutions within the community (Opubor 2000:3). In this light, improving the operational efficiency of rural community media, as an element of the rural community communication system, will also serve to ultimately improve the efficiency of the rural community communication system as a whole.

Banda (2010) states that communication via community media could serve to build a sense of community amongst citizens. Banda (2010) further notes important implications for community media as follows:

- greater access for citizens
- more use of community voices in news stories
- the possibility of citizen ownership and operation of media platforms
- greater opportunity to experiment with more participatory approaches to communication.

South African rural community media face specific challenges based on the broader South African media context as well as the rural context within which they operate. In assessing domain specific rural community media constraints and challenges, the Print and Digital Media Transformation Task Team (PDMTT 2013) identifies major rural community media challenges as being related to the news production value chain, which comprises the following broad steps:

- create and manage content
- build awareness
- distribute
- monetise.

Uncovering means with which to support rural community media in effectively navigating their rural environment as well as accessing domain specific information and knowledge would facilitate improved operational efficiency and sustainability of these rural-based small micro and medium enterprises (SMMEs). Assessment of means to provide support to rural community media via access to relevant information and knowledge accessible through an appropriate technology based platform could aid in the development of a framework that would support rural community media through facilitating access to information and knowledge that could positively impact their operational efficiency.

Knowledge sharing and communities of practice

Communities of practice are identified as a possible means to assist rural community media with accessing relevant information and knowledge. Karvalics (2012:2) states that the notion of communities of practice is based on the field of organisational learning and refers to 'interest groups that get together at work and in social settings into which newcomers can enter and learn the sociocultural practices of the community'. Karvalics (2012:2) defines a community of practice as:

> a unique combination of three elements: a domain of knowledge, which defines a set of issues; a community of people who care about this domain; and the shared practice that they are developing to be effective in their domain.

Uriarte (2008) adds that communities of practice have been proven to be excellent means to share knowledge amongst people who share a common interest. However, adequate technology infrastructure is needed for the creation, organisation, sharing and application of knowledge (Uriarte 2008). Technology and the ability to use it and adapt it have become an important factor in generating and accessing the wealth, power and knowledge necessary for development (Pott 2003). Based on the above arguments, the policy implications and emphasis clearly relate to two things – knowledge transfer and investment in technology (Mansell 2012).

Mobile social networking

Mobile social networking is identified as a possible delivery component for development of a virtual community of practice that could assist rural community media. Social networking is a technology that is currently, pervasive, accessible and easy to use (Deloitte 2012). Social networking sites are defined as web-based services that allow users to post a profile and connect to other users (Durham, Cragg & Morrish 2009). In recent years, social media has also developed to allow for networking with professionals or same interest groups and community engagement (Durham et al. 2009). Durham et al. (2009) add that low barriers to entry allow SMMEs to utilise social media in the same ways that large enterprises do without the need for extensive resources. They (Durham et al. 2009) further advise it likely that SMMEs could benefit from social media through jointly creating value with other parties.

Social media consists of content, communities and Web 2.0 technologies (Nicholson 2011). In general, social media refers to applications that are either completely based on user-generated content or in which user-generated content and the actions of users plays a substantial role in increasing the value of the application and/or service (Nicholson 2011). Although social media was originally a tool for friends to connect, communicate and share online, it has now also been adopted as a business tool (Durham et al. 2009). Online business presence via social media is now more a norm than an exception.

Relevant literature reports that the key purpose of social media is to engage people in one of four ways (Nicholson 2011), namely communication, collaboration, education and entertainment. The main advantages of transactions via mobile technology also apply to social media, as the former appears to be a key enabler of the latter. According to Murthy (2010), these advantages include ubiquity (available everywhere), localisation (location-based engagement), personalisation (tailored to the individual) and convenience (anytime, anywhere). Trends in social media indicate increased use by a business. It is observed by Nicholson (2011) that social media has now graduated from being a fashionable trend to a strategic tool. This has resulted in increased attention from researchers and practitioners, with the former developing skills to better utilise the technology and the latter developing models to explore business value and examine aspects of use.

This paper presents outcomes of a study conducted to ascertain whether there is opportunity to utilise mobile social media to assist rural community media SMMEs in the Eastern Cape Province of South Africa, through creation of a virtual community of practice that could facilitate improved operational efficiency.

Research methodology

This research seeks to answer the following research question: How can a framework for mobile social networking support and/or enhance rural SMME's through the creation of virtual communities of practice?

The case study conducted was scoped to focus specifically on rural community media with fieldwork conducted in the Eastern Cape Province of South Africa. The research methodology applied, is based on the Saunders, Lewis and Thornhill (2015) research onion. Saunders et al. (2015) research onion comprises multiple layers demonstrating various perspectives to be considered when designing and implementing a suitable research methodology. Their (Saunders et al. 2015) research onion compares the research processes to peeling different layers of an onion until the centre has been reached. The centre of the research process depicted by the onion is the analysis of collected data, with associated subcomponents comprising research philosophy, design, approach, data collection and analysis methods make up the research onion (Saunders et al. 2015).

The study applied an interpretive research philosophy, qualitative research design and a multiple–case study approach. Primary data collected through semi-structured interview supported by a questionnaire, with secondary data collected via literature review, observation and documentation analysis. Hermeneutics was utilised as the data analysis technique where cross-case data analysis and triangulation were applied. Additional broad factors for inclusion in the study included that selected cases operate an SMME in a rural area in the Eastern Cape Province. The study was conducted in October 2015 in the Eastern Cape Province of South Africa.

Data collection methods included interview, observation and documentation review. The researcher made use of semi-structured interviews guided by a standardised questionnaire as the primary data gathering tool. Observation and document analysis were used to provide additional information. The owners of the rural community media SMMEs were interviewed, this is because of the fact that being the creator and driver of the business they would be most familiar with business operations and various constraints impacting their operational efficiency.

The author reviewed meeting minutes, business plans and the actual newspaper product. Review of the selected documentation provided a view of the manner in which the SMMEs were run, the strength of governance and management processes and the quality of the product produced as a result of these. In addition to this, the author observed the operational environment of the SMMEs to develop further understanding of the context they operate in and how it impacts them. Observation was conducted at the same time as the interviews, with pre-identified guidelines as follows:

- Which Information and Communication Technology (ICT) is used by the SMME?
- Which ICT equipment is visible?
- Which visual evidence can be viewed of management approach and/or structured operations?

The observation process conducted (Figure 1) was as follows.

The sampling technique utilised in this research was maximum variation sampling. The rural community media SMMEs selected for inclusion in this study demonstrated variation related to years of operation, number of employees and location within the Eastern Cape, South Africa. In selecting the utilised seven cases, the researcher approached key rural community media support organisations operating within the Eastern Cape, South Africa, described the nature of the study being conducted and asked that they forward a directory of rural community media that could be included. The organisations contacted were the Media Diversity and Development Agency (MDDA), Association of Independent Publishers (AIP) and Eastern Cape Communications Forum (ECCF). All rural community media SMMEs included in this study operated within the Eastern Cape, South Africa.

This study utilised cross-case analysis (and triangulation), as different cases were analysed to identify cross-cutting issues or themes. The unit of analysis for this research was identified as the rural entrepreneurs operating as rural community media SMMEs in Eastern Cape Province, South Africa. The diagram below depicts the steps taken by the author in conducting the thematic analysis based on guidelines from Creswell (2009).

In conducting the thematic analysis (Figure 2) the author developed codes or labels to identify data that were key to answering the research question. These codes or labels were then used to collate and group data extracts for further analysis. The third step of the thematic analysis involved searching the collated or grouped data for themes. Once potential themes were identified they were checked against the data set to confirm their validity and that the themes were reflective of the data that were collected. Following the process of checking and confirming the validity of each theme the author then selected a descriptive name per theme as well as developed a definition per theme. The process concluded with a write-up of the results of the thematic analysis.

Each of the resultant themes has been discussed in detail in Table 1.

Section A1: Years in operation versus size of the small micro and medium enterprise

Analysis of data obtained from Section A of the questionnaire resulted in the observation of the above mentioned theme in the data. The author observed that while Case 2 had been in operation for the longest period amongst the cases studied, 8 years, and had a total of seven employees; Case 3 had also been in operation for a period of 8 years but had only four employees. Case 5 had been in operation for 7 years and had a total of six employees, which is equal to the number of employees held by Case 4, which had only been in operation for a period of 2 years. Case 6 had been in operation for 5 years and had four employees, followed by Case 7 in operation for a total of 4 years with six employees and Case 1 in operation for 3 years with a total of four employees. As can be seen from the data shared above, there is no apparent correlation in the data between the number of years in operation and the number of employees, which may point to a growth challenge in the Eastern Cape rural community media space. It could be that the number of employees is likely determined by other factors such as cost of labour, funding availability or profitability of the business.

Section B1: Information and Communication Technology as an enabling resource

Section B data analysis revealed that all seven cases surveyed indicated a view that the use of ICT could positively impact their business operation by assisting with access to information and knowledge and by supporting communication. Case 1 held the view that ICT can be utilised

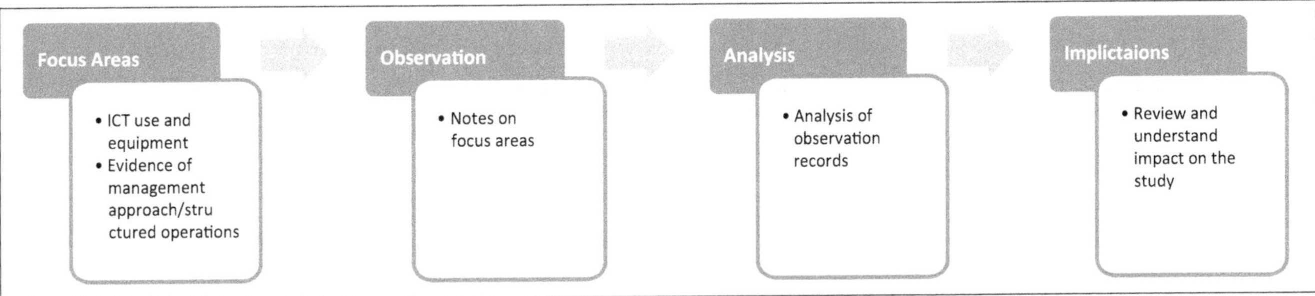

Source: Adopted from Rumo, J., 2013, *Absorptive capacity and information technology adoption strategies in Kenyan SMEs*, Unpublished work, University of Fort Hare

FIGURE 1: Observation process.

Source: Adopted from Creswell, J., 2009, *Research design*, Sage, Newbury Park, CA, United States

FIGURE 2: The thematic analysis process.

TABLE 1: Research questions and questionnaire linked to possible themes.

Section	Content	Related research sub-question	Objective	Possible themes
A	1. How long have you been in operation? 2. How many employees do you have? 3. What town/city is your business based in?	None, background questions	Understand general background	General info
B	1. Do you think ICT can facilitate engagement and access to support services, information and knowledge sharing in a manner that can assist your business? YES/NO (circle relevant) • If yes, what do you think you need in order to leverage ICT to support your business?	Sub-problem 1: What are the building blocks for a mobile social networking framework for SMMEs, which utilises virtual communities of practice as a vehicle?	Understand views on ICT capability to assist in accessing required resources	ICT as an enabling resource
C	1. Do you need business advice/support? YES/NO (circle relevant) 2. If yes, what areas do you require support in (Please tick all that apply)? • Financial Management/Funding Support • Business Planning and Management • Human Resource Management • Internal Business Process • Training (Writing/Marketing/Management etc.) • Stakeholder Engagement and Support 3. What are the most challenging issues impacting your business right now?	Sub-problem 2: What are the knowledge sharing needs of rural SMMEs?	Understand rural community media support requirements	Support requirements trends or key areas
D	1. Do you engage other community media or community media stakeholders for advice/support? YES/NO (circle relevant) • If yes, how often and what areas do you engage in for advice/support? 2. Do you feel that the advice/support/resources you need to thrive as a business are readily available/accessible? YES/NO (circle relevant) • If no, why, what are the issues/challenges impacting you in this respect?	Sub-problem 3: How can a virtual community of practice facilitate knowledge sharing, improved business support and socio-economic impact for rural SMMEs?	Understand stakeholder engagement practices and motives for initiating engagement	Stakeholder engagement practices and motives
E	1. Do you make use of your cell phone for your business? YES/NO (circle relevant) • If yes how do you use your cell phone to facilitate your business (phone calls, SMS etc.)? 2. Do you access the Internet for business purposes? YES/NO (circle relevant) • If yes, how often do you access the Internet for business purposes? • What challenges do you experience around Internet access, if any?	Sub-problem 4: How do SMME's make use of mobile social networking to enhance their businesses?	Understand the use of mobile devices and Internet access as well as challenges in accessing the Internet	Mobile and Internet use for business. challenges in Internet access
F	1. Do you make use of social media for business purposes? YES/NO (circle relevant) • If yes, which applications/sites do you make use of (Please tick all that apply)? ▪ WhatsApp ▪ MixIT ▪ Facebook ▪ LinkedIn ▪ Twitter ▪ Instagram ▪ Pinterest ▪ Other (please specify) • If yes, how do you utilise social media for business purposes (advertising, networking)? • If no, why not?	Sub-problem 5: What different social networking possibilities exist that can support SMME's?	Understanding use of social media for business	Use of social media for business

to provide access to support services, information and facilitate knowledge sharing but indicated suitable connectivity and hardware as requirements for this to happen after having experienced issues with connectivity regardless of utilising a high-speed ADSL line. Cases 2, 4 and 6 concurred that ICT can act as an enabling resource for rural community media but indicated no additional requirements for this to happen. While Case 3's views were aligned with those of Case 1 and 2 regarding the usefulness of ICTs for business, they indicated a need for training/engagement on how this can be done. Case 5 highlighted the concern of old PCs and technology being a possible impediment to fully realising the benefit of ICT application in the business context, and Case 7 shared the specific concern of the lack of a business website as a challenge to fully realising the benefits of ICT for business. It is encouraging that rural business already has an appreciation for how ICTs could be useful enabling resources for business. Some are more aware than others regarding impediments of use in rural or peri-urban settings, such as connectivity issues, aging equipment and training requirements. These issues could likely be assisted through knowledge sharing and support with stakeholders who could contribute to resolving the situation.

Section C1: Internal business process support requirements

Analysis of Section C data revealed that six of the seven cases studied indicated that they could benefit and were in need of business advice and support. Assistance with internal business processes was a cross-cutting theme in the data. Internal business process support had to do with support for certain segments of the news production value chain. A number of internal business processes were identified as areas where support is required. Case 1 specifically mentioned a requirement for support with funding, advertising and marketing. Case 2 concurred with Case 1 on advertising as an area that required additional support but added training as an additional requirement. Although Case 3 stated that they did not require additional business advice and support, they did specify a need for graphic design services to assist with the layout of their paper. Case 4 specified requirements for sales, production and distribution support, while Case 5 specified funding, business planning and management, sustainability and advertising as areas where additional support was required. Case 6 concurred with Case 1, specifying marketing and advertising as areas where additional support was required. Case 7 highlighted the need for financial management and funding, admin, sales and marketing support. Case 4 specifically stated that the structure of the market was an impediment to community media, specifically the ability to secure advertising. A specific query/concern shared by Case 4 was regarding what informs advertising buying decisions, noting a bias for established and mainstream media. Case 4 further stated that distribution channels were inaccessible and operated like a cartel with mainstream media either in tight relationships with or outright owning print and distribution channels. Cross-cutting areas mentioned more than once were advertising, marketing, funding and financial management and sales. Means with which to ensure access to support for these specific areas would be a useful and required component for a proposed solution.

Section C2: Structured operations and quality of product

An item related to internal business process, governance was identified as an element that appeared to impact ultimate quality of the end product. This theme was uncovered through assessment of the observation data and document analysis. There appeared to be correlation between cases with more structured internal business operations and a superior end product. Observation of Case 1 offices revealed a very neat and organised office area in an open-plan office, all documents were neatly filed and labelled with documentation analysis revealing regular meetings with employees and detailed tracking of minutes and action items. A detailed and comprehensive business plan that had been recently updated and a good quality product (well structured, good language and/or grammar, a number of adverts) were also observed at Case 1, serving as evidence of a good management and operating structure in place. Case 3 observations revealed a relatively neat office environment and a product of relatively good quality in terms of structure, average language and grammar but few adverts. Improvement opportunity in operations could be viewed at Case 3 as there was no evidence of regular office meetings or a comprehensive business plan; however, documentation analysis revealed periodic meetings taking place irregularly together with a high-level planning document, not detailed enough to serve as a business plan but indicative of some level of planning taking place with which to guide operational activities. Case 4 observations revealed a neat and orderly environment, access to meeting minute's revealed regular meetings with staff, with copies of their product revealing good structure, language and grammar and fair spread of adverts. Case 5 observation revealed a small, relatively untidy office space (may have been because of size), review of their product revealed relatively small newspaper in terms of number of pages and content as compared to others, not many adverts and poor grammar/structure. Case 7 observation revealed a slightly disorganised office environment, the newspaper product was relatively small and of poor quality (poor grammar and structure, with no adverts). As can be seen from the above, the data analysed suggest that rural community media could benefit from a more structured environment with appropriate governance to direct operations, given the perceived positive correlation between this and a higher quality end product.

Section D1: Stakeholder engagement

Analysis of Section D data indicated that all cases confirmed regular engagement with their stakeholders. Case 1 indicated that they engage their peers and stakeholders at least monthly for advice and support, identifying politics within the space and cartel like behaviour both by mainstream media and more established community media as challenges impacting them. Case 2 and Case 3 specified membership of the Eastern Cape Community Print Media (ECCPM), with Case 2 advising that though established this body is yet to gain traction. The AIP and MDDA were also mentioned by Case 2 as bodies approached for support. Case 4 specifically indicated membership of the AIP and involvement in state-led engagement initiatives, advising that the department of communications was active in engaging community media and creating opportunities for them to interact with the government and their peers and stakeholders to address the various issues impacting this space. Case 5 specifically indicated membership of a community media hub in the Eastern Cape, indicating that it was however not yet strong enough to effectively protect the interests of community media. Cases 6 and 7 made specific mention of AIP membership. The data revealed that all cases see stakeholder engagement as crucial for their business operation, and also that a number of cases are members of the same associations. This shows that the concept of community and working together as well as attempting to learn through engagement already exists within this environment; means to further enhance this would prove beneficial.

Section D2: Accessible versus inaccessible support services

There were mixed views on how accessible support services were, with four of the seven cases indicating that support services were not easily accessible. Cases 1, 2, 4 and 6 indicated that support is not easily accessible within the rural community media space, while Cases 3, 5 and 7 indicated the opposite. Case 2 added that obtaining access to certain support services and generally slow progress in the space were additional impediments. Case 2 further advised that they are also trying to leverage government for support/assistance and shared the concern that community media is dying because of lack of support, with a number of SMMEs having folded as a result of this. Case 6 further added that communication in the rural community media space was a major issue. The almost equal split between cases indicating ease of access to support services and cases indicating the opposite suggests that some of the cases surveyed may have knowledge or access to info that the others do not. The creation of an environment that facilitates knowledge and information sharing amongst rural community media may serve to remedy the situation.

Section E1: Cell phones and Internet use for business

All cases indicated that they made use of cell phones and accessed the Internet for business purposes. All cases specified use of cell phones (both phone and SMS services) as a business tool on a daily basis. It was also specified by all cases that the Internet is accessed daily for business purposes. Case 1 indicated cost and network issues as constraints they faced on a daily basis in this regard. Case 3 indicated a weekly cost of R100 for data bundles as a high cost given their limited funds, with their main issue regarding the Internet use being that it is expensive. Cases 4 and 5 echoed the concerns raised by Case 3 by sharing high-data costs as a concern. Case 7 specifically raised their concern regarding lack of a business website. Both Cases 2 and 6 did not indicate any specific challenges regarding the use of the Internet and cell phones for business purposes. The confirmed use of mobile devices and the Internet by all cases indicates that these may be good delivery mediums for facilitating access to required support services. Support may be required regarding the cost of access to the Internet.

Section F1: Use of social media to support business operations

All cases indicated the use of social media to support their business operations. The most utilised social media application was Facebook, followed by WhatsApp, Twitter and LinkedIn. Of specific interest is that while Facebook was used to engage externally, WhatsApp was used for internal engagement. Case 1 makes use of WhatsApp, Facebook, Twitter and LinkedIn for business purposes. WhatsApp to co-ordinate work internally and engage team members and Facebook, Twitter and LinkedIn to engage their customers and other stakeholders on their product. Case 2 makes use of WhatsApp for business purposes and also advised that they are in the process of setting up a Facebook page but are illiterate when it comes to such things and require training and support in this respect. Case 3 makes use of Facebook for business purposes and has employed a resource specifically to assist them with leveraging Facebook as a business tool. Case 4 makes use of Facebook and WhatsApp for business purposes, with Facebook utilised mainly to engage their customers and WhatsApp for co-ordinating internal operations. Case 5 makes use of Facebook and Twitter for business purposes and specifically mentioned attendance of a social media course via AIP to assist them in leveraging social media for their business. Cases 6 and 7 make use of Facebook for business purposes. Once again confirmed the use of social media for business purposes bodes well for the development of a social media–based framework in support of improved rural community media operational efficiency.

Research findings

On an average, the SMMEs surveyed were in operation for 5 years, with an average of five employees. All seven cases ($n = 37$ participants) interviewed and surveyed held the view that ICTs can facilitate access to support services, information and knowledge sharing to the benefit of their businesses. These results are depicted graphically in Figures 3 and 4.

Eighty-six percent of the cases surveying indicated a need for business support and advice. Specific support areas are depicted graphically in Figures 5 and 6.

The most challenging business areas were identified as follows: Advertising/marketing (Internal Business Process),

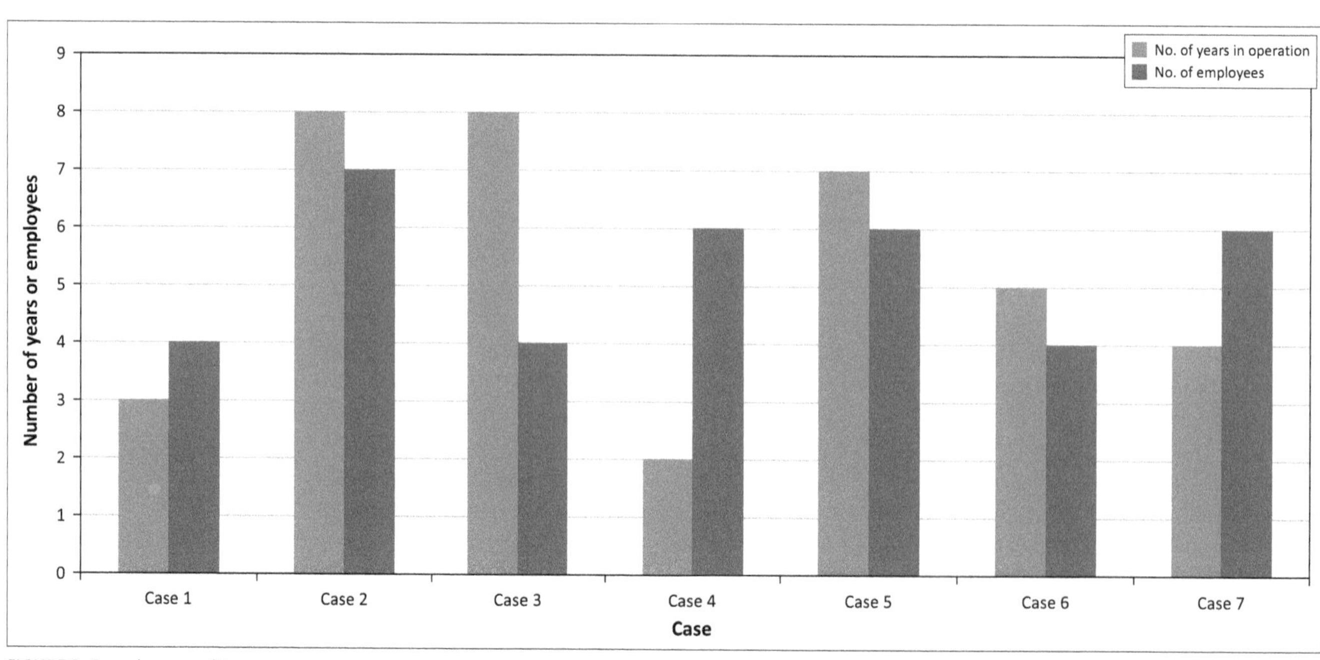

FIGURE 3: Case demographics.

Finance (Funding/Financial Management), Production and Distribution (Internal Business Process), Sustainability (Funding), Marketing (Internal Business Process) and Administration (Internal Business Process).

Hundred percent of the cases surveyed confirmed that they engage their peers and other community media stakeholders for advice and support regularly, with 57% indicating the support is not readily accessible. This depicted graphically in Figure 7 and 8.

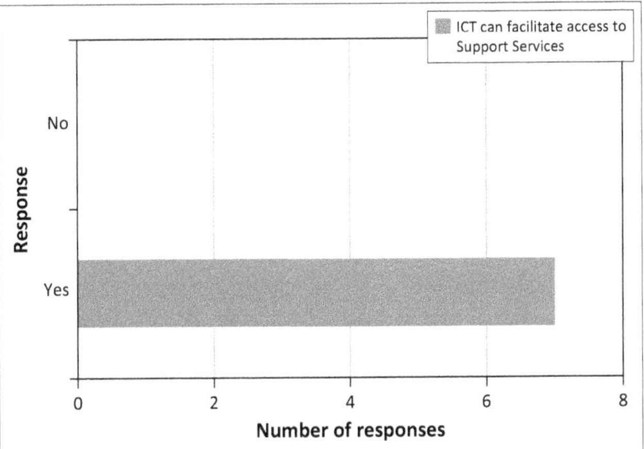

FIGURE 4: Information and Communication Technology use to access support services.

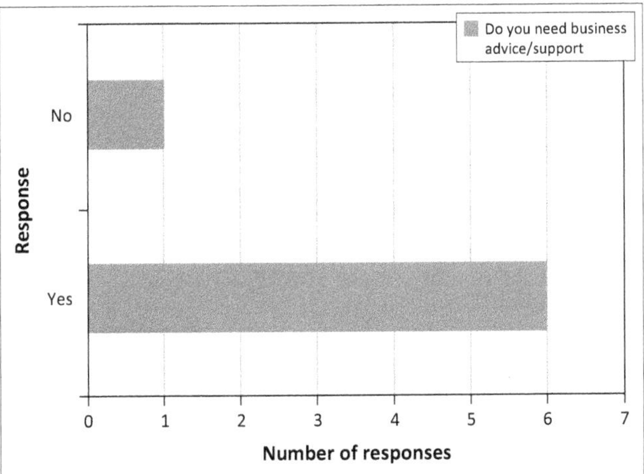

FIGURE 5: Access to business advice and support.

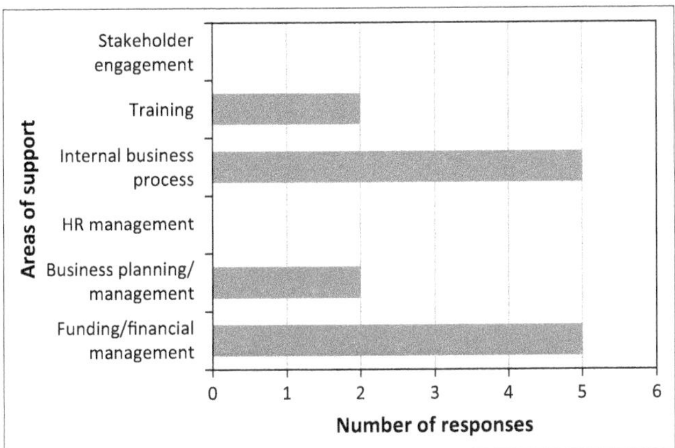

FIGURE 6: Areas for required support.

Hundred percent of the cases surveyed indicated that they made use of their cell phones and the Internet on a daily basis to operate their business. All cases surveyed made use of social media for business purposes. This is depicted graphically in Figure 9 and 10.

It can also be seen from the above that WhatsApp, Twitter and Facebook were the popular choices of social media amongst the cases surveyed. WhatsApp was mainly used to assist with internal operations and team engagement,

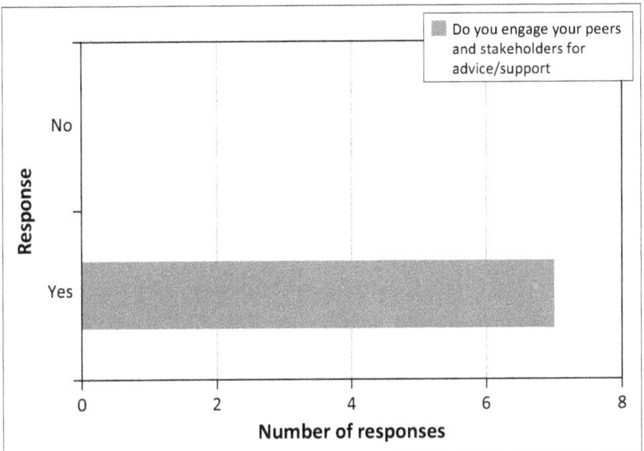

FIGURE 7: Case engagement of peers and stakeholders.

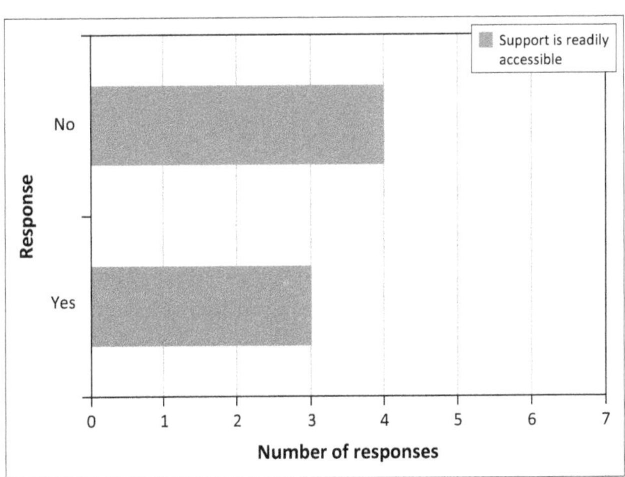

FIGURE 8: Availability of support.

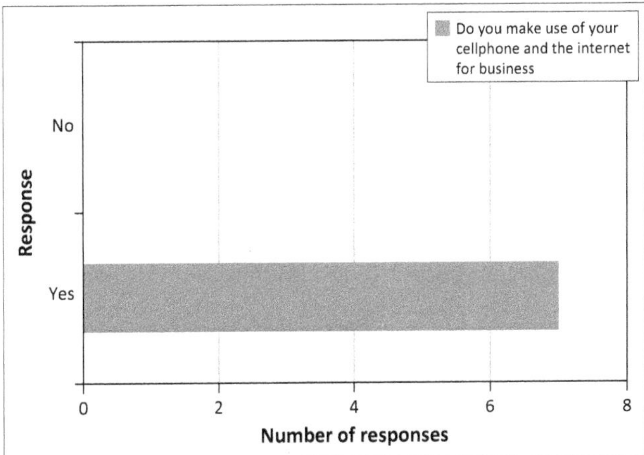

FIGURE 9: Use of cell phone and Internet for business.

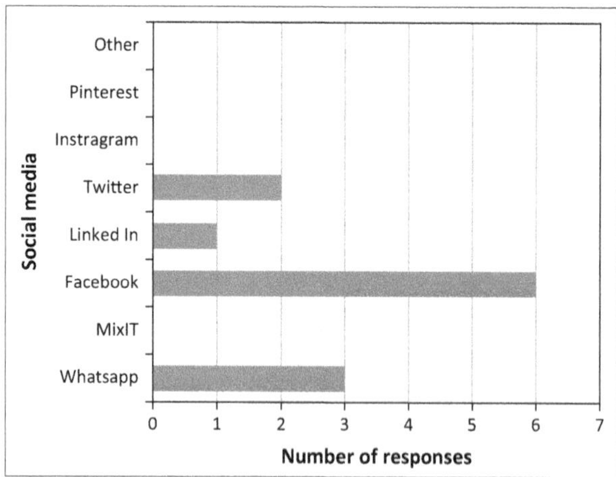

FIGURE 10: Use of social media for business.

while Facebook and Twitter were used to engage their consumers and market their product.

It was found that a virtual community of practice is a suitable vehicle for the provision of business support and advice. This is because of the fact that although the rural community media surveyed already made use of social networking and social media to enhance their business, they also access the Internet regularly and utilise their mobile devices regularly while conducting business. It was also found that there is a need for specific business support services and advice in the rural community media space in order to improve the efficiency and sustainability of these organisations.

It was concluded that the nature of the rural location generally impacted rural community media negatively because of the relative isolation and lack of support perceived by businesses operating in the area. This highlighted the need for developing means to address this issue and contribute to facilitating sustainability and growth of these businesses.

This research culminated in the development of the Rural Community Media Mobile Social Networking Framework. High-level components of the framework supported by the field work and literature include:

- Rural community media community of practice elements and/or considerations
- Rural community media business model elements and/or considerations
- Mobile social networking technology elements and/or considerations

The Rural Community Media Mobile Social Networking Framework which incorporates all the elements found in the research as necessary for the creation of a virtual community of practice, based on a mobile social networking platform, would serve to assist community media and answer the main research question as presented in the Research Methodology component of this article.

Conclusion and recommendations

The following conclusions can be drawn from the case and expert review findings:

- There is no obvious correlation between number of years in operation and number of employees indicating that there may be a challenge with business growth if an increased number of employees are seen as an indicator
- There is a view that ICT can facilitate access to support services, information and knowledge sharing
- Additional business advice and/or support is required. Internal business process (sales, marketing, advertising, distribution and production) and funding are raised by the majority of cases surveyed as specific areas where support is required, followed by training and business planning and/or management
- All cases engage their peers and stakeholders regularly for advice and support
- There are mixed views on how accessible support in the environment is with 57% indicating the view that support is not readily accessible
- All cases make use of cell phones and the Internet for business purposes; cost of data was raised as an impediment
- All cases make use of social media for business with Facebook leading, followed by WhatsApp, Twitter and LinkedIn. Of note is the use of Facebook and the like for external engagement versus the use of WhatsApp for internal engagement.

Community media seem to already attempt to collaborate and share information; therefore, an ICT platform could further enable this practice. It was found that a virtual community of practice is a suitable vehicle for the provision of business support and advice. This is because of the fact that rural community media surveyed already make use of social networking and social media to enhance their business, and they also access the Internet regularly and utilise their mobile devices regularly while conducting business. It was also found that there is a need for specific business support services and advice in the rural community media space to improve the efficiency and sustainability of these organisations. The development of a framework that could guide creation of a virtual community of practice enabled by a mobile social network would add value to the rural community media space.

Acknowledgements

Competing interests

The authors declare that they have no financial or personal relationships which may have inappropriately influenced them in writing this article.

Authors' contributions

O.M.Z., a student at the time, conducted the research. M.H. supervised the research project.

References

Banda, F., 2010, *Citizen journalism and democracy in Africa*, viewed 30 October 2015, from http://www.highwayafrica.com

Baumgartner, D., Schulz, T. & Seidl, I., 2013, 'Quantifying entrepreneurship and its impact on local economic performance: A spatial assessment in rural Switzerland', *Entrepreneurship and Rural Development* 25, 222–250. https://doi.org/10.1080/08985626.2012.710266

Creswell, J., 2009, *Research design*, Sage, Newbury Park, CA, United States.

Deloitte, 2012, *Social media in Africa,* viewed 10 July 2014, from https://ofti.org/wp-content/uploads/2012/10/Deloitte_Social-Media-Report_FINAL_20120709.pdf

Duncombe, R., 1999, *The role of information and communication technology for small, medium and micro enterprise development in Botswana*, viewed 11 January 2012, from http://www.man.ac.uk/idpm

Durham, R., Cragg, P. & Morrish, S., 2009, *Creating value: An SME and social media,* viewed 28 June 2012, from http://www.pacis-net.org/file/2011/PACIS2011-043.pdf

Heeks, R., 2009, *The ICT4D 2.0 manifesto: Where next for ICTs and international development?* viewed 12 August 2012, from http://www.sed.manchester.ac.uk/idpm/research/publications/wp/di/index.htm

Horn, R. & Harvey, G., 1998, 'The rural entrepreneurial venture: Creating the virtual mega firm', *Journal of Business Venturing* 13, 257–274. https://dx.doi.org/10.1016/S0883-9026(97)00012-8

Karvalics, L., 2012, *Transcending knowledge management, shaping knowledge governance,* viewed 13 July 2015, from http://basepub.dauphine.fr/bitstream/handle/123456789/9769/InTech-Transcending_knowledge_management_shaping_knowledge_governance.Pdf?sequence=1

Mansell, R., 2012, *ICTs, discourse and knowledge societies: Implications for policy and practice*, Intellect Ltd., Bristol, viewed 07 July 2015, from http://eprints.lse.ac.uk/39245/

Murthy, G., 2010, *AudienceScapes development research brief*, viewed 07 March 2013, from http://www.audiencescapes.org/sites/default/files/audiencescapes briefs_mobilefutures_murthygayatri.pdf

Nicholson, H., 2011, *Social media 101,* viewed 07 March 2013, http://irosteveperry.pbworks.com/w/file/fetch/58059588/social%20media%20basics.pdf

Opubor, A., 2000, *If community media is the answer, what is the question?* viewed 16 April 2014, from http://unesdoc.unesco.org/images/0018/001877/187739e.pdf

Pott, A., 2003, *Rural development and the flow of information. Do ICTs have a role?* viewed 29 September 2004, from http://www.idd.bham.ac.uk/research/dissertations/2002-2003/Alex%20pott.pdf

Rumo, J., 2013, *Absorptive capacity and information technology adoption strategies in Kenyan SMEs*, Unpublished work, University of Fort Hare.

Saunders, M., Lewis, P. & Thornhill, A., 2015, *Research methods for business students*, Pearson Education Ltd., England.

The Eastern Cape Development Corporation (ECDC), 2015, *About the Eastern Cape*, viewed from 10 June 2015, http://www.ecdc.co.za

The International Fund for Agricultural Development (IFAD), 2011, *Promoting rural enterprise growth and development: Lessons from four projects in sub-Saharan Africa*, viewed 25 March 2014, from http://www.ifad.org/pub/pa/field/2.pdf

The Print and Digital Media Transformation Task Team (PDMTT), 2013, *Report on the transformation of print and digital media*, viewed 29 April 2014, from http://www.printmedia.org.za

Uriarte, F., 2008, *Introduction to knowledge management*, ASEAN Foundation, Jakarta, Indonesia.

8

Empowering insight: The role of collaboration in the evolution of intelligence practice

Authors:
Craig Fleisher[1]
Rostyk Hursky[2]

Affiliations:
[1]Aurora WDC, United States

[2]Saskatchewan Research Council, Canada

Corresponding author:
Craig Fleisher,
craig.fleisher@aurorawdc.com

Background: Though subtle through the years, there has been a perceptible shift in competitive and market intelligence (CMI) practice from that of relying more heavily on sole operators to ones relying on collaboration. It happens within the nature of work performed inside intelligence functions, the larger organisation, and between organisations (i.e., intra-organisational). In this paper, the authors describe the change, develop a three-layered taxonomy for documenting it, and provide examples of how it impacts intelligence practice both now and possibly in the future.

Objective: To describe the increasingly evident role of collaboration and collaborative behaviour within insight producing functions in commercial, market-facing organisations. Identify evidence of collaborative intelligence practices in use across a range of different companies, industries, and geographies.

Method: The authors used a participant observation approach to developing this research. The discussion and frameworks in this study are based upon the authors' current roles, experiences and observations in leading a CMI group for a successful provincially based yet globally focused research and technology organisation, and having led interactive workshops and courses for over 100 organisations and approximately 1800 CMI analysts in over a dozen countries.

Results: The authors identified an impressive array of collaborative practices for each of the three layers of organisational environments studied. These included ones in (1) intra-process (aka, intelligence cycle) collaboration, (2) intra-organisational collaboration (i.e. within the intelligence and broader organisation) and (3) inter-organisational collaboration (i.e. between discrete organisations). These are illustrated from actual, observed, and ongoing CMI practices and are shared as examples reinforcing our view of the movement away from independent practices and approaches toward purposeful, socialised ones.

Conclusion: The evidence we have amassed provides substantial evidence of a notable and beneficial shift from doing intelligence work independently, frequently within silos, towards doing it collaboratively and across multiple types of boundaries. Intelligence practitioners are growing in their capabilities by taking advantage of emerging technologies, adapting practices imported from adjacent fields and benefitting from academic and/or scholarly research that helps push ahead the working boundaries of the field and allows it to make progress. In our view, CMI practice has recently entered a third era of evolution, one in which collaboration will continue to feature prominently, if not centrally.

Introduction

Problems requiring intelligence coordination and collaboration

The days of the solitary or lone-wolf approach to intelligence have passed. Among the key reasons for this is that the context within which the practitioner works has shifted in ways that promote the need for collaborative effort. There are many challenges that occur as a result of the lack of collaboration among intelligence practitioners. Some of these challenges that have been prominent in our experiences are described in greater detail in the following paragraphs.

Challenges caused by rivals that are increasingly complex, dynamic, fast-moving, boundary-spanning and sophisticated

Contemporary rivals are typically not static or willing to utilise incremental tactics to compete over time. Many rivals are not going to be from geographic regions that used to constrain competition geographically, and this is multiplied by the ability of digital networks and exchanges to cut across physical boundaries. Today's rivals, especially ones that aim to compete on a global or multinational basis, are not as easily defined either, as many companies are an array of networks, alliances, partnerships, subsidiaries, public or private, contracts and/or other arrangements that defy easy classification or typology. Some rivals are actually former, spun-off parts of one's own organisation! In this increasingly complex and fast-moving competitive context, it is critical that intelligence practitioners are able to collaborate across and span boundaries, and tap into factors and trends that were formerly beyond and outside the reach of any individual and their resources.

Because rivals and rivalry have gotten more complex and difficult to classify, many organisations have realised that their intelligence units do not have the resources to meet the competitive challenge being posed. Companies often have blind spots (Gilad 1994), face new competition, trends or rivals, and/or are not able to gather, analyse or communicate intelligence on a timely basis (Hackman 2011). This inflexibility in deploying practitioners or modifying competitive and market intelligence (CMI) applications and solutions, assuming these are available in the first place, has caused them to recognise collaboration as a desirable mode of operating practice.

Many intelligence problems and opportunities require a wide breath of perspectives (Heuer 2007). Collaboration is increasingly required when organisations face a context in which they lack a diversity of research or analytical approaches, lack employees who have a strong grasp of the craft of intelligence and have deep, practical experience, where only a few methods are consistently applied – thus limiting the range of insight or phenomena that can be adequately examined (Fleisher & Bensoussan 2003), or where too limited thinking is routinely applied to problems (Hackman 2011).

In light of the steady flow of demands on their time and the ever-increasing flow of data they are required to process, individual practitioners can quickly get 'stale' in their approaches to their work (Fleisher & Bensoussan 2003; Heuer 2007). Like any healthy field of practice, new developments are shared regularly by researchers, scholars and practitioners – but absent a deliberate and formal approach to collaboration, the likelihood of a practitioner gaining awareness of this new knowledge is lowered. Additionally, lacking others to challenge and test their approaches, they lose the 'sharpness' of focus that is essential to effective intelligence processing (Hackman 2011). As such, intelligence practitioners have regular needs to continuously learn about new discoveries that can improve their practice and also to obtain focused training and development in order to just 'keep up' with developments in practice and context (Fleisher 2004).

Because of the exponential growth of digital data and information that has been generated in the last decades, many practitioners are no longer able to effectively filter, organise and analyse the inflows (Davenport, Harris & Morrison 2010). This so-called fire hose of information, and the sheer volume of increased noise further hides the sought-after signal. Big data have overwhelmed many intelligence practitioners and units' ability to address it (Davenport *et al.* 2010). This phenomenon is an even bigger problem in companies that are customer facing, business to consumer focused and driven by the need to sell products and/or services. This has led to many of them seeking collaborations with, among others, professional service firms and specialised consultancies, taxonomical specialists, solution providers, aggregators and/or subscription vendors and other organisations to better respond.

Last but not least, many clients (i.e. the organisational executives or decision makers who seek out or request intelligence) have intelligence needs and problems that go beyond the ability of any sole intelligence practitioner to attain. Executives have the ability and frequently use their own networks or choose self-discovery processes they have conveniently available. For example, many executives are very comfortable using their own extensive human networks, going to a search engine, or accessing increasingly sophisticated dashboards and reporting portals. Many of these efforts are deemed to be insufficient; thus, they refer these matters to their intelligence staff. The staff member must then fully understand what actions were used by the executive and then extend their reach beyond those in order to generate higher insight quality. This can rarely, if ever, be done in the absence of collaboration.

Key benefits gained from intelligence collaboration

Our observations and experience have demonstrated that there are numerous benefits that come out of collaborative behaviour, whether among individuals inside the organisation or between different organisations in the larger commercial marketplace. Among those that witnessed most often include the following 10, listed in no specific order:

- **Collaboration ties people together for the greater good:** Collaboration enables entities to tackle problems that are too big for any single entity operating independently.
- **Financial benefits:** Collaboration can let a CMI unit stretch its resources. A good example of this is when intelligence engages individuals from outside its full-time roster, thus enabling intelligence gathering to include a wider base, more networks and extend far beyond the aegis of the full-time team members.
- **Subject matter benefits:** Collaboration has enabled CI employees and their units to gain access to otherwise unavailable topical domains and stretches the knowledge basis of existing and/or permanent employees.
- **Team-building benefits:** Collaboration can strengthen individuals' skills, as well as 'stretch' practitioners to develop competences that would go beyond what they might otherwise achieve.
- **Time benefits:** Collaboration can give an intelligence unit the ability to produce intelligence more quickly, particularly when those collaborations cross time zones. We know of some organisations that keep their CMI

projects active and working 24 hours a day because they have their Asian unit work it for 8 hours, their European unit takes over the next 8 hours, and their American unit follows through the next 8 hours, until it gets returned back to the Asian unit to begin the process anew the next day.

- **Bias reduction:** Collaboration with a greater number of arms-length or neutral participants can provide a CMI team with the ability to remain neutral and deliver a perspective on the intelligence in an environment that can become driven by personal interests, growth drivers and 'pet projects'.
- **Linkages with other organisational processes:** Reliable and effective insights that can be directly linked to the Enterprise Risk Management or Collaboration Systems, Customer Relationship Management Systems and other Management Information Systems.
- **Analysis breakthroughs:** Collaboration enables the development of new analytical models, techniques and approaches, some of which cannot be effectively done by individuals, if at all.
- **New perspectives:** Collaboration has provided intelligence teams with the ability to see a perspective from other stakeholders' eyes, utilise lessons learned and come up with best-case scenarios to adapt or apply to one's own organisation.
- **Validity and generalisability checks**: Collaborations with individuals from various sectors, industries and professions provide intelligence and insights on industry convergences or divergences.

Types of collaboration within intelligence practice: Intraprocess

There are a variety of different forms of collaboration used by intelligence practitioners and units (Hackman 2011). These range along a continuum of the degree of collaborative intensity. In other words, some forms are less intense, suggesting more informal means of regular communication and interaction, as well as a lesser degree of formalised organisational or bureaucratic mechanisms established in support of it. Others are far more intense, characterised by a high degree of formalisation, the use of scheduling and project management methods, supported by change management practices and designed to last for longer, if not indefinite, time periods. These different forms are illustrated in Box 1 (see Box 1).

We have witnessed CMI units making use of all these collaborative forms. Arguably among the most utilised of these would be Communities of Practice, as organisations create subject matter expert (SME) networks of individuals, both inside and outside the organisation, that help intelligence staff members track, monitor and assess emerging developments in specific practice areas. These networks perform both regular/routine as well as focused reconnaissance and can be made quickly available for special projects or requests. Another increasingly used form in intelligence practice is the semi-permanent insight team as described in case detail by Fleisher, Wright and Allard (2008). These are semi-permanent work teams that cut across organisational boundaries and are designed to bring cross-functional, cross-geographic perspectives to planning and strategy development.

BOX 1: Continuum of intra-organisational collaboration of intelligence functions.

Less Intensive Collaboration: → Community of Shared Interests (e.g. both internal and external subject matter expert networks), Communities of Practice (CoPs – such as R&D practitioners, regulatory advisors, sales personnel, etc.), Emergent Collaborations, Coaching Groups, Distributed Teams, (Special/Designated) Project Teams/Task Forces, Semi-Permanent Work Teams. → *More Intensive Collaboration*.

Source: Adapted from Hackman, J.R., 2011, *Collaborative intelligence: Using teams to solve hard problems*, Berrett-Koehler Publishers, San Francisco

Certain forms of collaboration have demonstrated to be especially promising in intelligence applications, those being multidisciplinary and interdisciplinary forms. Multidisciplinary collaboration means working with several disciplines but with individual goals and where the different disciplines work independently. It does not challenge disciplinary boundaries and the participants learn about each other (Choi & Pak 2006). Interdisciplinary collaboration occurs when others' boundaries are being blurred and the participants learn about and from each other (Choi & Pak 2006).

There is also a changing nature of collaboration applied with the intelligence cycle (Hackman 2011). The analysis process is a pertinent example of how this changed the nature of insights delivered by practitioners. Past competitive intelligence analysis practice emphasised independent, individual analysts producing insights. Today's analysis is more frequently generated by groups, in shared work sessions, whether in-person and face-to-face as led by facilitators or done in on-line platforms that allow for synchronous analysis to take place.

Even the nature of analytical methods used has been changed by collaboration. More social analytical methods such as war gaming, scenarios, blue and/or red teams and shadowing get greater emphasis in today's collaborative intelligence process. Even older, more static methods like SWOT, four corners or competitor profiles benefit from active collaboration by SMEs in networks using a variety of digital communication channels and specialised software applications to enliven the outputs and keep them evolving as developments warrant (Fleisher & Bensoussan 2015).

Intra-organisational collaboration

When business, competitive, economic and/or market intelligence first came to prominence as an outgrowth of public intelligence practices applied in military and defence endeavours, it was often practiced by the sole or 'lone ranger' analyst, data collectors and often managers who worked on their own and had to exhibit a wide range of different skills to execute the entire intelligence cycle. Early comprehensive research surveys of CMI practice conducted under the auspices of Strategic and Competitive Intelligence Professionals (SCIP) and related international intelligence organisations demonstrated that many earlier era business, commercial or corporate units consisted of one individual who 'did it all' (Prescott & Fleisher 1991) – and even these surveys greatly underestimated the number or percentage of sole operators because of sampling issues (i.e. surveyed SCIP members, who were more likely than the population member to work in a larger business or corporation).

Intelligence units of one were frequently tasked with developing the mission, meeting all their client's needs, developing the essential intelligence resources such as the databases, networks, subscriptions, systems and the like required to execute the basic CMI process (West 2001). Analysts were sometimes viewed as the 'geniuses' in cubicles or behind their desks, crunching the data and numbers until the wee hours of the night, working with mysterious formula, and doing 'black magic' with their 'black boxes' to produce their insights. Although we still see intelligence units-of-one show up in empirical studies of practice, hardly any CMI practitioners can be effective without working with others inside, and outside, their organisations. Today's intelligence reality shows practitioners frequently working collaboratively in teams, whether doing networking, source identification and validation, data fusion, training, special projects, management, sophisticated analysis methods like red and blue team exercises or war gaming, scientific and technology scouting or just developing enhanced insight deliverables (Fleisher *et al.* 2008; Hackman 2002, 2011).

The movement towards intelligence collaboration within and among intelligence teams began to happen in the late 1980s and has accelerated in its evolution since that time. Modifying an approach first described by Fleisher and Bensoussan (2015:62), we suggest that there have been three distinctive eras that the organisational aggregation of expertise has taken.

The first era of business and commercial competitive intelligence was nearly always done by individuals working in silos. These practitioners were expected to work intelligence problems through the entire intelligence cycle of planning, data gathering, analysis and dissemination. Collaboration, to the extent that it occurred, was nearly always practiced in a serial or sequential manner. Intelligence was generated based more on a scale basis than a scope-based one. Simpler intelligence problems, or ones that existed within mostly mature and stable contexts, and where there was a lesser degree of VUCA (aka, volatility, uncertainty, complexity, ambiguity) could be reasonably addressed through these processes. This generation was highly paper intensive and lasted until the early 1990s.

The second era of collaboration occurred following the rapid individual and organisational adoption of information technology (IT) resources and particularly those used for data transmission and information communication. E-mail, the Internet and World Wide Web, faster processing power, less expensive memory, connected desktop and organisational networks and portals, allowed for more synchronous communication around the organisational management and processing of intelligence matters. These enabled more collaboration to occur in a timelier and more frequent fashion and permitted some intelligence units to begin gaining scope advantages in their gathering (especially through automated agents or 'push' means) and processing of intelligence. Collaboration still had not achieved full and continuous levels of interactivity (e.g. 365 × 24 × 7 interaction), and the IT being utilised continued to improve at uneven rates, but intelligence executives had not yet captured the full potential benefits of collaboration throughout the intelligence cycle. This generation was dominant from the early 1990s until around the middle of the first Y2k decade.

A third distinctive era of intelligence has occurred since the latter part of the first Y2k decade. It arose concurrently with the rapid commercial growth and widespread adoption of mobile communication technology, big data technologies and enterprise collaboration systems (ECS). Smartphones, faster networks, social media (SM), transaction using mobile devices and the bigger, more detailed, timelier data it generates have been enormously helpful to intelligence practitioners. Adding to these cloud storage and access, geo-locational data developments, more powerful processing and a resurgence of artificial intelligence, machine learning, data science methods and the conditions are fertile for a highly collaborative form of intelligence operation. This generation is in evidence at some of the more advanced intelligence operations, though it is still not yet predominant among most business and commercial CMI groups.

ECS used for intelligence collaboration purposes would include combinations of groupware, software tools, the Internet, extranets and other networks needed to support enterprise-wide communications. ECS allow for the sharing of documents and knowledge to specific teams and individuals within the enterprise and are a key factor in third-era CMI practice. Enterprise collaboration software applications enable intelligence team members to collaborate on an ongoing basis by allowing them to share and/or coordinate updates to documents any time regardless of where the members are located. Examples of collaboration software include e-mail, enterprise blogs and wikis, instant messaging (IM), online whiteboards, videoconferencing, collaborative document sharing and project management tools.

Third-era intelligence collaboration functionality tends to include choices from among the following five categories:

- Messaging: E-mail, calendaring and IM.
- Team Collaboration: Intelligence portals, document repository, project management, library services, workflow and discussion threads.
- Web Conferencing: Virtual meetings, video and audio teleconferencing, shared desktop and presentation.
- Shared Data and Analytics: Cloud storage, collaborative analysis, automated filtering.
- SM: Blogs, social networking, wikis.

Multinational companies, such as Microsoft, Cisco, Web-Ex, Citrix, IBM, SAP, Oracle and others, are actively improving existing applications and developing new programmes designed to enhance collaborative productivity in this space. Additionally, these companies' solutions have also been augmented by Voice-Over-IP offerings, such as Skype, and SM offerings, such as Facebook, Instagram, Twitter, blogs and wikis. These have nearly unlimited potential to drive forward third-era intelligence collaboration.

New IT and software solutions also allow for individuals to build upon others' work while they are asleep, to autonomously update reference sources, to fuse knowledge across different data types (e.g. visual, signals, text, voice), to tap into previously inaccessible networks, to filter and move the data and information around seamlessly and instantaneously and to engage in and apply synchronous analysis methods.

For intelligence units, embracing collaboration technology is at the heart of managing data, information, intelligence and knowledge. The organisation benefits by unlocking, synthesising and sharing knowledge hidden among its employees and also discovering new sources of expertise. It also plays a fundamental role in bringing together the workforce, whether local or global, by enabling the creation of both social and professional communities of interest, and across traditional functional, geographic and market boundaries.

Linking collaboration to business processes and high-level business objectives gives intelligence staff valuable insight into the larger enterprise business scenario. This supports more effective, efficient and timely decision making. Though we are still in the earlier stages of this generation, the promise for IT, solutions, SM, VoIP and increasing mobility in intelligence remains very large and agile, early adopters stand to gain at least temporary, short-term advantages in applying the third-era resources to boost the collaborative learning potential of their intelligence processes.

Collaboration as part of the generation of organisational learning or wisdom

Collaborative learning cultures serve as a foundation of effective executive leadership through encouraging reflection and learning at all levels of the organisation (see Figure 1). Work cultures are generally viewed to be the atmosphere or climate of a work environment, perception of how it feels to work in the organisation, within a particular team or for a specific supervisor and/or the ideal operating environment required to provide a sustainable, highly effective work climate that optimises the team's potential to do its best work (Wilderom *et al.* 2011). Unfavourable work cultures tend to generate frustration, which is projected onto others, resulting in tense and problematic relations and contributing to poorer outcomes for decision makers and executives.

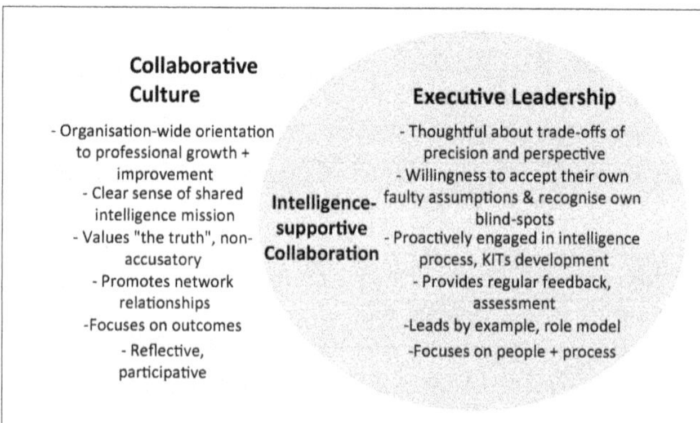

FIGURE 1: Collaboration as part of an intelligence-conducive work culture.

Many individuals' fundamental organisational needs revolve around clarity, development, meaning, purpose, development and connection. After extensive research and analysis, Gallup identified critical factors that contribute to practitioners' productive motivations, engagement and outcomes (Cotton 2012; Cotton & Hart 2011; Hart & Cotton 2003; Wagner & Harter 2006). These factors refer to practitioners:

- having clear expectations about their roles and responsibilities
- having the basic material resources to undertake work
- having regular opportunities to utilise their talents, strengths and aptitudes
- receiving feedback and recognition for good work and progress
- having a supervisor who shows interest in their professional and personal development
- having a say and having their opinions taken into account
- feeling that their role is important to the organisation
- having a commitment to the work group in order to undertake quality work, and
- having a sense of connection and someone in the organisation to confide in.

Teams can provide benefits for both organisations and collaborating employees through higher productivity, quality improvements, greater flexibility and speed, a flatter management structure, increased employee involvement and satisfaction, and lower turnover. However, teams often present greater leadership challenges than does a traditional hierarchical organisation.

Summary of intra-organisational collaboration

Reflecting on our observations and experience, we have identified several necessary conditions that organisations should have in place to be effective in this team-supportive, collaborative role.

Having the right teams in the right places

In his book *Leading Teams*, Hackman (2002) makes a distinction between 'real teams' and 'co-acting groups'. Applying his definition of co-acting groups to business organisations, practitioners may have offices located next to one another and regularly meet to share ideas, but each practitioner's analyses and deliverables are independent of the others.

However, in productive teams, members share the responsibility for the success of their decision makers. Team members rely on each other for increasing the abilities of all organisational clients. They do not view their roles as being 'my clients' and 'your clients' but rather see it as being 'our clients'. In intelligence functions, interdependence for business outcomes is the most critical hallmark of collaboration.

'Real' team members tend to talk constantly about what they have in common. Today's better intelligence solutions include collaborative communication technologies such as real-time chats, IM and real-time video teleconferences that allow for this constant communication to securely occur between organisational members. Because similarly experienced or tasked analysts, managers or researchers share regularly about their work processes, needs, networks, standards and assessments, interactive, collaborative communication mechanisms are usually the most productive configuration for effective intelligence analysis.

Building a culture where trust is central

A significant level of trust must exist among team members and between the C-suite and other executives. Executives need to empower their intelligence staff to act decisively to raise new and powerful insights, as long as their recommendations and insights can be supported by data. As Richard DuFour pointed out in Learning by Doing, even though this level of trust takes time to generate, leaders cannot wait until the perfect positive culture is in place to have intelligence operatives start the data dialogue. Struggling together to initiate the conversation – using both face-to-face and digitally supported means, implementing the decisions made during the conversations and dialogue and, most importantly, seeing executive success and support increase, are effective builders of trust.

The use of protocols

Having an agreed-upon process in place can be useful to structure difficult group conversations. In his publication *The Power of Protocols* (McDonald *et al.* 2013), Joseph McDonald and others define protocols as 'guidelines [that] everyone understands and has agreed to, leading to conversations that school people are usually not in the habit of having'.

Using this protocol, intelligence teams answer a series of questions that guide their analysis of business problems, opportunities and outcomes to identify (1) patterns of organisational intelligence strengths and weaknesses in colleagues' understanding of the deliverables being generated; (2) individual intelligence practitioners ready for enrichments and interventions, and the professional development focus that the differentiations should take; and (3) practice improvements and upgrades they will make. A focused exploration of powerful questions in a logical sequence enables intelligence teams to begin to develop the skills they need to be collaborative.

Articulate compelling reasons to perform collaborative analysis

As leaders in academe and practitioner organisations, we have pressed staff and our colleagues to conduct data-driven conversations. But in some cases, we may not have provided what Hackman (2002) and others labelled a 'compelling direction' to energise team members and engage their talents.

It is becoming increasingly clear that justifying data analysis to intelligence practitioners based on increasing satisfaction and meeting adequate unit progress or arbitrary goals is far less persuasive than basing improvement initiatives on the reason most intelligence practitioners remained in the profession – to help executives make better decisions and to underlie successful organisational actions that generate new benefits, prosperity and wealth.

Clarity about team autonomy

To enable collaborative teams to be successful, leaders must be clear about the extent of autonomy team members will have to act on the results of their dialogues, such as challenging essential assumption, concepts, practices or altering the nature of future deliverables. Either CI practitioners have the autonomy to make insights based on their data as it is processed or they must follow pacing guides that identify what must be regularly delivered. They cannot do both at the same time.

It must be clear to intelligence employees that insight teams are expected, not just permitted, to spend additional time on significant opportunities or problems that arise and/or they have identified, that some executives may not have observed or properly digested, and to modify the content, timing, intelligence methods and/or future deliverables or project assignments, based on documented client needs.

Provide ongoing coaching, mentoring and support

Because working in networks and teams can be chaotic and challenging, regular coaching from leadership team members and mentoring from more seasoned teammates is essential to sustain top performance. Process feedback about the internal operation of teams is particularly important as teams begin work in the early stages of their collaboration and struggles to establish a more collaborative environment.

Integrate self-accountability into their ongoing operations

Most teams require assistance in putting internal mechanisms in place to follow-up on outcomes decided upon during interactions and dialogues. Effective protocols often include templates that teams complete as their conversation progresses – a recommended part of the Key Intelligence Topic and/or Key Intelligence Question development process for planning intelligence projects (Herring 1999) as well as reference interviewing such as those done by special librarians (Ross 2003). As meetings end, the chair e-mails to the members the template containing the actions team members are committed to take. A copy can be forwarded to executive clients so they can better monitor and support the team's work and also allow for collaboration and discussions as the intelligence employees work through their CI process.

Follow-up is improved when team leaders document at the next team meeting the outcomes of the process improvements that they implemented. Assessment activities such as shared work sessions, 360-degree feedback, deliverable debriefs, walk-throughs and periodic reviews by the team with their executive clients can also serve to increase internal team accountability for follow-through (Rao 2014).

Communicating successes, regularly

Most business professionals recognise the importance of celebrating achievements, even the so-called smaller ones, during the early stages of any change process. However, an essential part of celebrations often overlooked is the intentional connection by executives of the specific actions of intelligence staff, such as increased collaboration across geographic and functional boundaries and leveraging structured data analyses, to the business outcomes and results that followed.

Where might an organisation identify its most potent leverage point be in increasing intelligence team performance? When a CI director reflects on the effectiveness of CI teams, it is worthwhile to determine whether their organisation's executives can answer the following queries:

- Do the intelligence teams act on a clearly articulated, compelling direction to reduce performance gaps by analysing data collaboratively?
- Are conversations, KIT development, reference interviewing and other data dialogues structured by protocols that lead decision makers to take definitive customer-focused, market-impactful actions that increase revenues and profitability?
- Also, are intelligence team members clear about leaders' expectations that they act decisively, as the data warrant, to modify their instruction to address identified weaknesses?
- Do team members have in place their own internal accountability mechanisms that result in follow-up and thoughtful reflection on what works and why?
- If these questions have definitive answers, it is a helpful indication that they will achieve higher levels of executive satisfaction and impact than those organisations that struggle with answering them.

Inter-organisational collaboration

The data and information underlying intelligence are generated every time individuals and/or organisations make a business or commercial exchange. More of it is created on a daily basis than in digital formats and around the world, then at any time in human history. In today's increasingly globally competitive marketplaces, no organisation can operate for long in isolation. Inter-organisational networks are increasingly used to accomplish business and commercial tasks, whether these are used for financial exchange and transfer, information transmission, logistics and in allowing the movement of human resources and skills. Intelligence practitioners and insight teams must increasingly work across differing cultures and languages, national and regional markets, regulatory frameworks, trade policies and the like. Very few organisations have the global expanse of resources to gather, process and analyse intelligence across all of these boundaries; therefore, collaboration has become an essential and fundamental element of conducting effective intelligence processes.

Managing networks of organisations has become a fundamental task for managers who seek to maximise their own organisation's intelligence potential. In the earlier years of the CI field, organisations used to try to manage and own as many of their own resources as possible in conducting intelligence operations. Whether this was hiring their own CMI practitioners, having an internal library or knowledge centre, maintaining large assets of subscriptions to informational resources and databases, the ability to have an independent CMI operation within larger commercial enterprises was a point of organisational pride and sometimes even thought to confer business or commercial advantage. If resources were needed to address intelligence challenges that went beyond the reach of the organisation's own resources, strict agreements could be drafted to allow for the temporary hiring of professional services firms, consultancies or other advisory bureaus. These often satisfied the needs, but frequently created a new set of transaction costs or agency problems that required new and often innovative managerial responses (Wood & Gray 1991).

In today's data-driven, insight-seeking, increasingly competitive business world, the prevailing approach to intelligence efforts, especially from organisations that do not have the 'we've got unlimited money and resources to do it all in-house' mindset, has been to seek out experts, networks and linkages to individuals who have and are willing to share insights, opinions and perspectives relative to a specific challenge or a question (Rowley & Gibbs 2008).

It can be argued that the establishment of collaborative intelligence networks and expanding CMI efforts outside of one's own organisation has been reliant solely on the CMI head within the organisation. These individuals have the awareness and whereabouts to be able to strategically develop a compelling business case for each collaborative effort and how they would benefit both or multiple stakeholders. The authors believe that the current external environment is generally not yet built and predisposed for naturally occurring collaboration with intelligence initiatives. Someone has to initiate and persistently move the effort forward, being well aware that some collaborations will come naturally, while others will take time to develop. Even when collaborating makes complete sense and the organisation does not know how it ever made it without such an effort, the natural tendency is still to try and do it alone or wait for someone to instigate the discussion.

In most instances, the CMI practitioner is really well positioned to instigate thoughts and discussions about collaboration, both within and outside of the organisation. They should be well aware of some if not most of the major stakeholders locally and potentially globally who can collaborate with them on some intelligence efforts. For smaller organisations, global CMI networks provide access to thought leadership, guidance and advice on how to approach collaboration. They also provide access to direct contacts one would never be able to connect with otherwise. Local networks require more knowledge building and educating about CMI efforts and why organisations might want to collaborate. However, it is the combination of local, national and global collaborations in CMI that provide organisations with long-lasting, future-thinking, well-rounded insights and deliverables.

Over the past few years, Saskatchewan, a Canada-based research and technology organisation's intelligence team has been making efforts to expand their intelligence network through collaborations. Based on these experiences, the authors provide an overview of the types of organisations that have been approached and the reasons behind each opportunity.

Small and medium-sized businesses as well as large enterprises

These organisations both within and outside of the key operating sectors provide access to 'on the ground' intelligence and are able to share insights on markets based on their intrinsic and vast experiences. Collaborations with key analysts, decision makers and other individuals offer the ability to understand various aspects of emerging local and national mega-trends relative to their sector, industry and area of focus.

Economic development authorities and associations

In discussion with representatives from these types of organisations, the shared intelligence is relative to local and national business drivers, attracting factors for new businesses and the retention of key businesses. These collaborations provide insights into economic indicators and trends mixed with industry-specific, sectoral and technological insights about what makes local businesses function and grow.

Research agencies and institutes responsible for economic forecasting, public policy, skill development and organisational growth

These collaborative efforts provide access to educational opportunities and thought leadership growth and expansion of the CI function locally and nationally. Through common workshops, training sessions, conference presentations and other such opportunities, organisations gain invaluable opportunities to grow one another's capabilities. Additionally, linkages with their expertise in economic forecasting, business growth and policy analysis add to the repertoire of sources and references.

Educational institutions

Connections with post-secondary institutions such as universities provide for proactive discussions revolving around growth and development of CMI capabilities within MBA, MSc, MLIS and other professional programmes. Collaborations in this sphere build an understanding of CI as it relates to business, research, STEM fields (Science, Technology, Engineering and Mathematics), R&D and strategic decision making. By utilising CMI expertise and the university's ability to deliver programmes and training courses, today's new and emerging leaders gain access to information that was not previously available to them, or would not have been presented in such format and context. Several universities also work with CMI professional services companies and commercial organisations to provide surge research, project back-up and on-the-job training for their students.

Professional service firms

There are quite a few consulting organisations responsible for providing intelligence services to those who need them. Depending on each consultant, creative collaborative relationships can be established where one is not only paying for a service but also growing a long-term capacity and gaining access to resources, databases, expertise, thought leadership and networks that are non-existent in house. These collaborations help with challenging the norms of CMI practices, they push the way things are done and expand approaches to address complex problems. These organisations also grow networks as well as help the organisation to learn about, build and grow the intelligence function.

Professional associations

Linkages with professional associations that are responsible for driving intelligence forward as a profession or incorporate CMI into their training and growth, provide individuals with a readily available source of networks and thought leaders who have been in the field for a number of years. Through these collaborative networks, CMI practitioners learn and grow their function and capabilities, are challenged on their approaches and learn some of the real-world applications of intelligence. These networks provide many globally connected, long-lasting relationships.

Other 'like' organisations

Collaborative intelligence efforts have been established to advance the knowledge and reach of CI outside of the organisation as well as expand capabilities that other organisations might not have in-house. Once again, thought leaders and practitioners from these organisations provide their own perspectives of market intelligence and on decision making and together the efforts assist with the development and rise of new business models, as well as foresight and risk warning efforts that are objective, neutral and offer a 360-degree view of the operating environment.

Summary of inter-organisational collaboration

The development of long-lasting collaborative intelligence efforts typically takes much time. It also takes a lot of effort, prior research and creative thinking to understand how the collaborations might work and what value they would add to the organisations at hand. Although time-consuming and work intensive, these collaborations can provide new perspectives, new ways of thinking and build capacity where sometimes none or little existed. Based on the authors' experiences, some of the top reasons why inter-organisational intelligence collaborations make sense and what they offer are illustrated in Table 1.

Closing thoughts on inter-organisational collaboration

Where could collaborations lead and what type of networks might be established next? Based on the need for intelligence from many stakeholders, the authors envision the possible creation of newly established industry-specific intelligence networks. These initiatives, likely taking the form of accelerators, catalysts, incubators or skunkworks, would consist of CI professionals, economists, service providers, technology developers, academia, scientists and engineers, strategists, business developers, legal, industry associations, government and others. Objectives of these networks would be to develop and grow key strategic sectors that are of importance to specific regions. These networks would focus not only on business and market intelligence in ensuring that businesses prosper and flourish but also would work towards creating environments where we would all be doing business in a setting that have social, environmental and economic impacts on communities locally, nationally and globally.

A vision of the future of a collaborative CMI

The authors' view of the future of CMI collaboration is promising. We see the following trends as being drivers over the next 5 years:

A shift will be towards collaborative CMI driving discussion and planning at community, state/province or nation-state/country levels. The utilisation of findings and analytics will help drive policy development, support the growth of new funding and programming initiatives that will sustain and support and grow RD&D, Innovation, Impacts and Social Responsibility.

The creation of new and effective Global Panels, Advisory Boards, Committees focusing on change, growth, innovation and overall positive impacts, will utilise insights generated by collaborative intelligence efforts through advising with 'topic leads' or by directly bringing collaborative CMI networks into their discussions and planning exercises.

Effective collaborative intelligence infrastructure and mobile-enabled platforms will expand for soliciting ideas, generating discussions, sharing insights and developing new methodologies and foresight. Through this platform, boundaries that existed

TABLE 1: The advantages of inter-organisational collaborations.

Reason for collaborating	What collaboration offer?
Technology, process, service innovation	Each organisation provides their expertise and viewpoint, challenging some of the norms and asking different types of questions. This can lead to new technological developments, changes to the way things are done within the organisation and develop new services. It is what each organisation takes away from the collaboration effort that is applicable and becomes invaluable.
Access to networks	Through the process of sharing of intelligence, organisations find that they are now also sharing their networks as those become relevant and applicable. Collaborations offer access to previously unavailable niche networks and information.
Thought leadership	Organisations establish themselves as thought leaders relative to their areas of expertise and grow outside of a siloed environment.
Breaking boundaries and historical work patterns	Gaining first- or second-hand access to thought leadership, new and developing knowledge and demonstrated practices allow for roadmaps permitting managed changes to occur that would otherwise be unknown.
Collaborative analytics	Thought leaders in policy, economics and finance, technology development, legal and patents, providing their perspective on similar KIQs, helps an organisation's CMI professionals develop 'complete' insights.
Bring together action-driven 'doers' and foresight-driven 'strategists'	There are individuals in organisations who do not call themselves CMI professionals and might not have CMI in their job description, but they are doing CMI. There are also those who are constantly think up new ideas, new scenarios, see the bigger picture and are able to make assumptions on things that might happen in the future. These collaborations bring various individuals together who learn and elaborate on bringing the tactical and strategic together in realising some 'blue sky' ideas and implementing them into practice.
Pre-emptiveness	The next stage to being proactive is being pre-emptive – that is, building the future's organisations through which to do business in. These futures are rarely created by one organisation alone and through inter-organisational CMI collaboration, practitioners develop an understanding together of what the reality of the future might look like and what it will take from each of the many stakeholders to contribute to building that future into a reality.
Develop a more 'all-inclusive' growth environment	When building out a vision of the future and various scenarios that might play out, consideration is given to all the future stakeholders that might be a part of an event, even before it takes place. When assumed futures become realities and various stakeholders meet, they now start with a similar and/or common mindset. Through the initial collaborations, 'right people get on the bus into their appropriate seats' much quicker (Collins 2001).
Develop a community of practice	Through initial discussions, meetings and ideation stages, individuals involved in the collaborative networks develop a Community of Practice, where ideas and thoughts are shared, and processes are written and refined. These COPs provide a reference for other stakeholders to utilise and reference.
Full access to CI, while no or little CI in-house	Organisations that become involved in these collaborative discussions might not have the need for or have the ability to have an in-house CMI individual or a team. Through collaboration these organisations are now able to gain access to a much broader community, much broader base of experts and thought leaders that provide insights and perspectives one would not have had access to otherwise.
Foresight and scenario-building capabilities	One of the main goals of CI practitioners is to provide its clients with balanced and accurate insights to better enable their decision making. CMI aims to minimise risks and maximise the opportunities. Collaborators in CMI become better in thinking and planning forward. Executives or decision makers will not refuse insights that somewhat reliably help position their organisation as a leader in the near future.
Collaborations lead to working partnerships	Through collaborative CMI, organisations create collaborative working relationships that lead to partnerships, as they explore and learn about one another's capabilities. CMI teams provide perspectives on how organisations can benefit from working together, establishing partnerships or collaborative relationships to deliver on a challenge based on their specific capabilities.

CMI, competitive and market intelligence.

in collaborating for intelligence will be pierced and individuals will be able to connect and tap into a vast array of professionals whose goals are to think and act strategically.

Acknowledgements

Competing interests

The authors declare that they have no financial or personal relationships which may have inappropriately influenced them in writing this article.

Authors' contribution

C.F. and R.H. co-developed the conceptualisation, model building, inclusion of examples and samples, and execution of the article.

References

Choi, B.C. & Pak, A.W., 2006, 'Multidisciplinarity, interdisciplinarity and transdisciplinarity in health research, services, education and policy: 1. Definitions, objectives, and evidence of effectiveness', *Clinical and Investigative Medicine* 29(6), 351–364.

Collins, J.C., 2001, *Good to great: Why some companies make the leap... and others don't*, Random House, New York.

Cotton, P., 2012, *What is good work?* viewed 12 October 2015, from http://www.thinkers.sa.gov.au/lib/pdf/MartinSeligman/sowppts/BallC_1210_Cotton.pdf

Cotton, P. & Hart, P., 2011, *Positive psychology in the workplace*, viewed 28 October 2015, from http://www.psychology.org.au/publications/inpsych/2011/april/cotton/

Davenport, T.H., Harris, J.G. & Morison, R., 2010, *Analytics at work: Smarter decisions, better results*, Harvard Business Press, Boston.

Fleisher, C.S., 2004, 'Competitive intelligence education: Competencies, sources, and trends', *Information Management* 38(2), 56–63.

Fleisher, C.S. & Bensoussan, B.E., 2003, *Strategic and competitive analysis: Methods and techniques for analyzing business competition*, p. 457, Prentice Hall, Upper Saddle River, NJ.

Fleisher, C.S. & Bensoussan, B.E., 2015, *Business and competitive analysis: Effective application of new and classic methods*, p. 590, FT Press, Upper Saddle River, NJ.

Fleisher, C.S., Wright, S. & Allard, H.T., 2008, 'The role of insight teams in integrating diverse marketing information management techniques', *European Journal of Marketing* 42(7/8), 836–851. http://dx.doi.org/10.1108/03090560810877187

Gilad, B., 1994, *Business blindspots: Replacing your company's entrenched and outdated myths, beliefs and assumptions with the realities of today's markets*, Probus Professional Publishers, Chicago.

Hackman, J.R., 2002, *Leading teams: Setting the stage for great performances*, Harvard Business Press, Boston.

Hackman, J.R., 2011, *Collaborative intelligence: Using teams to solve hard problems*, Berrett-Koehler Publishers, San Francisco.

Hart, P.M. & Cotton, P., 2003, 'Conventional wisdom is often misleading: Police stress within an organisational health framework', in M.F. Dollard, A.H. Winefield & H.R. Winefeld (Eds.), *Occupational Stress in the Service Professions*, pp. 103–141, Taylor & Francis, London.

Herring, J.P., 1999, 'Key intelligence topics: A process to identify and define intelligence needs', *Competitive Intelligence Review* 10(2), 4–14. http://dx.doi.org/10.1002/(SICI)1520-6386(199932)10:2<4::AID-CIR3>3.0.CO;2-C

Heuer R.J., Jr., 2007, Small group processes for intelligence analysis. Unpublished manuscript, Sherman Kent School of Intelligence Analysis, Central Intelligence Agency. viewed from http://www.pherson.org/LibraryH,11

McDonald, J.P., Mohr, N., Dichter, A. & McDonald, E.C., 2013, *The power of protocols: An educator's guide to better practice*, Teachers College Press, New York.

Prescott, J. & Fleisher, C., 1991, 'SCIP: Who we are, what we do', *Competitive Intelligence Review* 2(1), 22–26. http://dx.doi.org/10.1002/cir.3880020112

Rao, T.V., 2014, *HRD audit: Evaluating the human resource function for business improvement*, Sage Publications, New Delhi, India.

Ross, C.S., 2003, 'The reference interview: Why it needs to be used in every (well, almost every) reference transaction', *Reference & User Services Quarterly* 43(1), 38–43.

Rowley, J. & Gibbs, P., 2008, 'From learning organization to practically wise organization', *The learning organization* 15(5), 356–372. http://dx.doi.org/10.1108/09696470810898357

Wagner, R. & Harter, J.K., 2006, *12: The elements of great managing*, Simon and Schuster, New York, Vol. 978, No. 1-59992.

West, C., 2001, *Competitive intelligence*, Palgrave Macmillan, London, UK.

Wilderom, C.P., Härtel, C.E., Ashkanasy, N.M., Vacharkulksemsuk, T., Sekerka, L.E., & Fredrickson, B.L., 2011, 'Towards positive work cultures and climates', *The Handbook of Organizational Culture and Climate 2*, 79–84. http://dx.doi.org/10.4135/9781483307961.n5

Wood, D.J. & Gray, B., 1991, 'Toward a comprehensive theory of collaboration', *The Journal of Applied Behavioral Science* 27(2), 139–162. http://dx.doi.org/10.1177/0021886391272001

9

Incentive theory for a participatory crowdsourcing project in a developing country

Authors:
Elizabeth Bosha[1]
Liezel Cilliers[1]
Stephen Flowerday[1]

Affiliations:
[1]Department of Information Systems, University of Fort Hare, South Africa

Corresponding author:
Liezel Cilliers,
liezelcilliers@yahoo.com

Background: Urbanisation has put enormous strain on the limited resources and services provided by city management. This means that the city must find new ways to manage their resources more effectively. One option is to collect data in a smart city from the citizens in order to make better decisions about resource management.

Objectives: The aim of this study was to provide a participatory crowdsourcing incentive model that can be used by the city of East London, South Africa, to collect information continuously from citizens in order to improve public safety in the city.

Method: This study made use of a quantitative approach to gather and analyse data. Data were collected using a questionnaire sent to all 91 East London citizens who had registered on the project website. The response rate was 81.3%.

Results: A model was proposed that can be used by the city to increase the participation rate of citizens in smart city projects. Three factors: intrinsic, internalised-extrinsic and extrinsic, were identified as central to the incentive model.

Conclusion: The recommendation of the study is that city management can use the crowdsourcing participatory incentive model to ensure citizen participation in smart city projects.

Introduction

South Africa's urban population is growing, and it is anticipated that 80% of the South African population will be staying in cities by 2050 (Rand Daily Mail 2015). As more and more people are living in cities, the demand for the available resources is increasing. These resources include electricity, water, sanitation, road infrastructure and the ability to keep the city safe, such as adequate policing. These resources are finite and owing to budget constraints cannot be increased or even maintained properly (Washburn & Sindhu 2010). This means that cities must search for more innovative ways of providing services to the increasing population making use of existing resources.

Some cities have decided to become 'smarter' in order to provide better management of the city. A smart city can be defined as 'a city that uses Information and Communications Technologies (ICT) to be more interactive, efficient and making citizens more aware of what is happening in the city' (Azkuna 2012:2). A smart city allows the city to improve resource management, which ensures that better decisions can be made about existing resources (Harrison & Donnelly 2011). This results in a better quality of life for the citizens. Benefits of a smart city include citizens having better access to healthcare facilities and clean water and air as a result of reduced pollution and increased public safety (smart living) (Berst 2013).

The most important responsibility of city management is to ensure the quality of life and safety of their citizens. This can be accomplished by making use of technology that can monitor the activities that are happening in the city in real time. Citizens can report public safety issues to the city (known as participatory crowdsourcing), making use of mobile phones (Bartoli et al. 2013; Caragliu, Del Bo & Nijkamp 2011). Cities need to collect large amounts of public safety data to use for predictive analysis in order to become more proactive. Currently, most cities rely on a reactive approach to public safety. Therefore, in order to collect public safety information, incentives can be used to encourage citizens to participate in such projects. The problem, however, is that there is currently no participatory crowdsourcing incentive model that allow city management to plan for continuous public safety data collection in a developing city.

This study discusses methods that can be used by the city to encourage citizens to participate in a smart city project by continuously reporting public safety issues they witness. Thus, the objective is to develop a participatory crowdsourcing incentive model that motivates citizens to continuously report public safety issues to the city.

The next section discusses the components of a smart city, followed by the different types of crowdsourcing. Then, citizen participation in smart city projects and the theoretical foundation of the paper, Incentive Theory, is discussed. The subsequent section describes the research methodology that was followed in this study. The paper concludes with an analysis and discussion section.

Public safety in a smart city

Public safety ensures that all citizens feel protected and safe in the city by focusing on collecting information to predict and respond faster to emergencies and threats (Bartoli et al. 2013). Information can be collected about natural disasters, accidents and deliberate harmful acts by citizens. In order to ensure safer living conditions for citizens, the city has to find better ways to manage its existing resources. This can be achieved by the following: (1) identifying and addressing public safety issues in the city; (2) being able to recover faster from natural disasters; and (3) collecting public safety information provided by citizens, thereby improving the quality of life for all (Nam & Pardo 2011). A smart city approach makes use of participatory crowdsourcing which will allow city management to monitor the activities that are happening in the city (Caragliu et al. 2011; Figure 1).

According to Nam and Pardo (2011), in order for a city to become smarter, three components should be present: technology, people and institution (Figure 1). The first component is technology, which consists of hardware and software infrastructures, which allows for public safety information to be collected, processed and analysed in a city (Colldahl et al. 2013). Smart cities encourage the use of ICT to gain insights into what is happening in a city and enable decision-making based on the available information

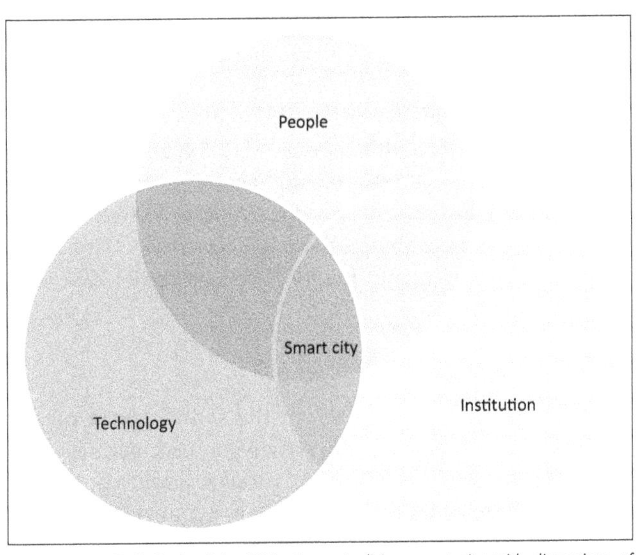

Source: Nam, T. & Pardo, T.A., 2011, *Conceptualizing smart city with dimensions of technology, people, and institutions*, New York, ACM, pp. 282–291

FIGURE 1: Three key components of a smart city concept.

(Nam & Pardo 2011). The type of technology used in a smart city includes sensors, which collect data from citizens making use of electronic devices such as mobile phones or tablets (Christin et al. 2011). Unfortunately, the cost of technology and infrastructure used in crowdsensing is prohibitive, which means that developing cities, such as East London, cannot afford to implement this solution. Sensors are also associated with privacy issues because individuals do not have control over when and what type of information is being collected (Shin et al. 2011). Apart from using sensors to collect information, citizens may also report any public safety information they witness by willingly volunteering it to city managers (participatory crowdsourcing) (Harrison & Donnelly 2011). Making use of participatory crowdsourcing eliminates the problem of privacy because citizens voluntarily report any public safety information they witness. The second component of a smart city consists of people. According to Nam and Pardo (2011), people are the major component of a smart city because they enable communication with the city. People will assist in making a city smarter by being involved in the management of the city and by providing public safety information that will assist the city managers to better utilise the city's resources. Currently, there is no functional system in place that allows the citizens of East London to report public safety issues. The institution is the third component of a smart city. The institution consists of two components: the smart community, where citizens are empowered to make use of information technology to transform and support their individual and communal quests for well-being within a community, and smart growth, which makes use of technology to assist urban planners to make use of resources more efficiently in order to improve public safety (Nam & Pardo 2011).

Crowdsourcing

Two different types of crowdsourcing have emerged from literature. These types of crowdsourcing allow for large amounts of data to be collected from the crowd (citizens). Data gathering allows citizens to be able to communicate with the city managers, and also allows the city to obtain information about the community and how people are living (Halder 2014). According to Doan et al. (2011), data can be gathered using either implicit methods (involuntary crowdsourcing) or explicit methods (participatory crowdsourcing). Implicit data collection methods make use of sensors to gather data, whereas explicit data collection methods request information from the crowd in order for the crowd to provide solutions (Doan et al. 2011). These two types of crowdsourcing are explained in the following section.

Involuntary crowdsourcing

Involuntary crowdsourcing is known in literature as opportunistic sensing or crowdsensing (Christin et al. 2011). Involuntary crowdsourcing requires less user involvement because it makes use of sensors to collect information automatically. This type of crowdsourcing allows for sharing of information about a citizen's immediate environment and experiences such as traffic information (Tomasic et al. 2014). The citizens of East London must agree to attach the devices that will record the data to their cellular phones. However, the citizens do not know when the data will be collected, which could be seen as an invasion of their privacy. The information collected from these sensors will then be processed in order to search for the required information.

Kaiserswerth (2010) reported that the city of Madrid has spent 30 million Euros to build a dashboard that is able to coordinate the police, fire, highway, hotline and ambulance units. This dashboard makes use of sensors across the city, such as traffic videos, surveillance cameras, maps with GPS data and the status and location of personnel that can be tracked through sensors in their mobile phones. This was made possible by the fact that smart technologies are able to improve both the availability and coordination of information during public safety events, thus enabling emergency services to minimise the risk and damage associated with these events.

Participatory crowdsourcing

Participatory crowdsourcing allows the crowd to provide public safety information willingly, without using any sensors. According to Cilliers and Flowerday (2014), participation is regarded as voluntary because participants can decide on what to report in terms of public safety issues they observe. Therefore, participatory crowdsourcing requires increased user involvement. With this type of crowdsourcing, the citizens can choose what they want to report and when they would like to report the data. This means that the privacy concerns mentioned in the previous section will not be relevant. Participatory crowdsourcing also has the advantage that existing cellular infrastructure can be used, which negates the cost of implementation of costly infrastructure.

In some countries, applications have been developed for individuals to inform the community if a citizen is in danger or if they witness any activity that might be a threat to their lives (Grass 2013). Examples of these countries include Haiti, Afghanistan and Chile, all of whom made use of crowdsourcing for disaster recovery by making use of the Ushahidi platform. The main objective of the Ushahidi platform was to communicate with affected citizens and to understand their community needs better. This platform allowed citizens to contribute any information related to natural or man-made disasters, thereby raising disaster awareness for other citizens (Meier 2012).

The use of participatory crowdsourcing in a city will help the city prepare for a particular situation affecting the safety of its citizens, as well as providing some insights on how to respond to an emergency situation and recover after the situation (Halder 2014). These applications ought to make it easy for public safety information to be collected continuously from the citizens.

Incentive theory, the theoretical foundation

The Incentive Theory is a motivational theory that focuses on rewards and motivation. The theory posits that people are motivated to perform tasks because of both external and intrinsic incentives (Cherry 2013). Incentives are a form of motivation that encourages people to do their best at a particular task (Brewer, Hollingsworth & Campbell 1995). These incentives may vary depending on the task to be performed.

Sincero (2012) is of the view that the Incentive Theory differs from other theories of motivation in that it views the incentive as an item that attracts a person towards it. This means that in order for East London citizens to participate, incentives have to be offered to encourage citizens to provide public safety information to the city (Cherry 2013). In this project, the incentive was in the form of a better quality of life (intrinsic) and airtime (extrinsic), which was offered to citizens who provided public safety issues they witnessed.

Types of incentives

There are various types of incentives that can be used to motivate a person to perform a task or an activity. There are three types of incentives that are identified in literature; these include intrinsic, internalised-extrinsic and extrinsic incentives.

Extrinsic incentives

According to Gassenheimer, Siguaw and Hunter (2013), citizens can be motivated by extrinsic motivators, which require an economic advantage such as money or free products from a company. In a community, citizens may be extrinsically motivated by physical rewards such as money or airtime in order for them to provide public safety information.

Brewer et al. (1995) suggest that using extrinsic incentives is more effective than intrinsic incentives because the rewards are always positive and are likely to encourage citizens to continuously participate (Brewer et al. 1995). Examples of these extrinsic incentives include monetary and tangible non-monetary incentives. The effectiveness of these types of incentives may assist by motivating East London citizens to provide public safety information. The next section discusses intrinsic incentives.

Intrinsic incentives

Intrinsic incentives are based on the satisfaction a person feels after accomplishing an activity or task because it is enjoyable (Massung et al. 2013). Intrinsic incentives are not physical because they are based on a person's feelings. Examples of intrinsic incentives include enjoyment, interest, verbal recognition, feedback, curiosity and satisfaction. Intrinsic incentives allow citizens to view their involvement as a way of assisting the city to use resources more effectively, develop relationships with other citizens and also as a way of enjoyment. Intrinsically motivated citizens are most likely to share information with the public safety crowdsourcing project.

Some citizens obtain satisfaction from the action of providing public safety information to the city. Thus, external rewards are not required in order to motivate these citizens (Massung et al. 2013). This is because citizens are motivated by the feeling of accomplishment they acquire after reporting public safety issues and also because they will experience a better quality of life.

Nov, Naaman and Ye (2009) developed a model that attempts to explain an individual's willingness to participate in a community by providing or sharing information. This model states that motivation to participate in a community is dependent on an individual's willingness to participate in community matters (Nov et al. 2009). This means that the more a person is willing to participate, the more motivated they are.

Figure 2 illustrates that there could be various intrinsic reasons why citizens participate by reporting public safety information in a community. These reasons result in increased citizen participation. The next section discusses internalised-extrinsic incentives.

Internalised-extrinsic incentives

Internalised-extrinsic incentives refer to citizens who use their contributions to gain or to improve their reputation in a community with the intention of teaching or influencing other community members (Gassenheimer et al. 2013). In a city, this incentive enables residents to provide their views on public safety matters to the city. Citizens feel that they have participated or have control over how their safety is managed in the city. These incentives enable citizens to take ownership regarding public safety services that are available to all. The next section discusses methodology.

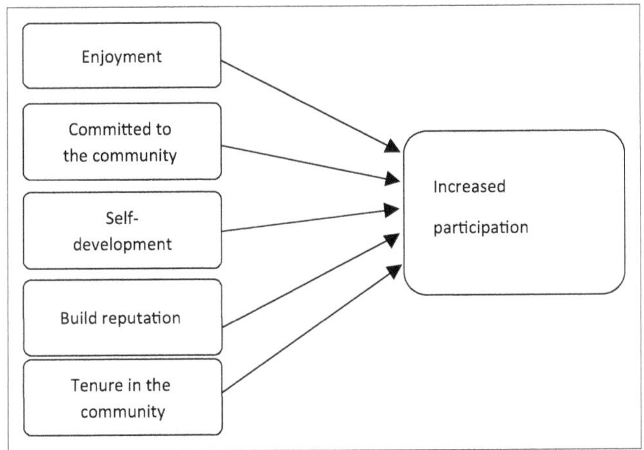

Source: Nov, O., Naaman, M. & Ye, C., 2009, 'Analysis of participation in an online photo-sharing community: A multidimensional perspective', *Journal of the American Society for Information Science and Technology*, Paris, Wiley, 1–12

FIGURE 2: Citizen community participation model.

Research methodology

This study made use of a positivist paradigm and quantitative data collection method (Collis & Hussey 2009). In this study, a literature review was used to identify the categories of the questionnaire and general insight into the research problem.

A pilot study was conducted in order to validate the questionnaire for user friendliness and ease of use. The feedback was taken into consideration and was included in the final questionnaire. Ethical approval was granted from the University Research Ethics Committee (UREC).

Participants were required to register on the project's website. A total of 91 citizens registered on the website after which they could report public safety issues via the Public Safety Smart City project (PCSS) toll-free number and a mobile site. The airtime incentive was awarded only to public safety reports that were complete, and an online questionnaire was sent to all 91 participants to investigate their reasons for participating. Seventy-four participants responded to the questionnaire. The response rate for this project was considered to be acceptable at 81.3%. The reasons for such a high response could be that people wanted to improve city, or in order to receive the airtime incentive. Only 61 of the 74 questionnaires were found to be complete. In other words, 17.5% of the questionnaires collected could not be used. The questionnaire was hosted online and technical problems such as poor network connectivity or slow processing of devices could have influenced the completion rate of the questionnaires.

Quantitative data were collected from a questionnaire. The questionnaire comprised four sections. The first section asked for the demographics of the participants (age, gender). The rest of the sections represented the intrinsic, internalised-extrinsic and extrinsic factors. The intrinsic, internalised-extrinsic and the extrinsic sections included two, three and four questions, respectively. Cronbach's alpha coefficient was used in this project to determine the reliability of the factors identified in the model. The factors that were used in this project include intrinsic, internalised-extrinsic and extrinsic factors. The intrinsic, internalised-extrinsic and extrinsic factors had Cronbach's alpha coefficients of 0.69, 0.62 and 0.58, respectively. The values of 0.70 and above represent a good level of reliability, whereas values between 0.50 and 0.69 are considered to have an acceptable level of reliability (Pallant 2010). These three factors can thus be considered to have an acceptable level of reliability. Quantitative data were analysed making use of SPSS V22, descriptive statistics (mean, median) and inferential statistics.

Results

This study sample consisted of 54.1% female and 45.9% male participants. This shows that participation between males and females was almost equal. Both males and females were aware of the Public Safety Smart City Project and therefore reported issues they witnessed.

Spearman correlation was conducted to test for the direction and strength of relationship between perceived usefulness and other variables (Figure 3). Intrinsic factors were found to be most important to increase the participation level of citizens in a smart city project. Participants found the project to be useful in terms of reporting public safety issues they witnessed. Therefore, participants indicated that they are willing to continuously provide information on public safety issues they witness.

Ethical consideration

Ethical clearance was granted by the University of Fort Hare's Research Ethical Committee. The ethical clearance number is FLO041SPID01.

Participatory crowdsourcing incentive model

The model for this project was derived from the findings of the literature review, observations and questionnaire incorporating the Incentive Theory. Spearman correlation was used to test for the direction and strength of the relationship between increased participation and other variables. The figures in the model represent the relationship between variables, whereby weak/small (r = 0.10 to 0.29), medium (r = 0.30 to 0.49) and strong/large (r = 0.50 to 1.0) (Pallant 2007) relationships are presented. The model is presented in Figure 3.

The model identifies factors that encourage citizens to provide information on public safety issues they witness to the city continuously. These factors are discussed in the next sections.

Intrinsic factors

Intrinsic incentives provide the internal feeling that a citizen feels after reporting public safety issues they observe (Brewer et al. 1995). In order for the Public Safety Participatory Crowdsourcing Incentive Model to be effective, the city has to ensure that they offer intrinsic incentives for citizens that are intrinsically motivated. These factors include: a useful way to report public safety issues, usefulness of the project,

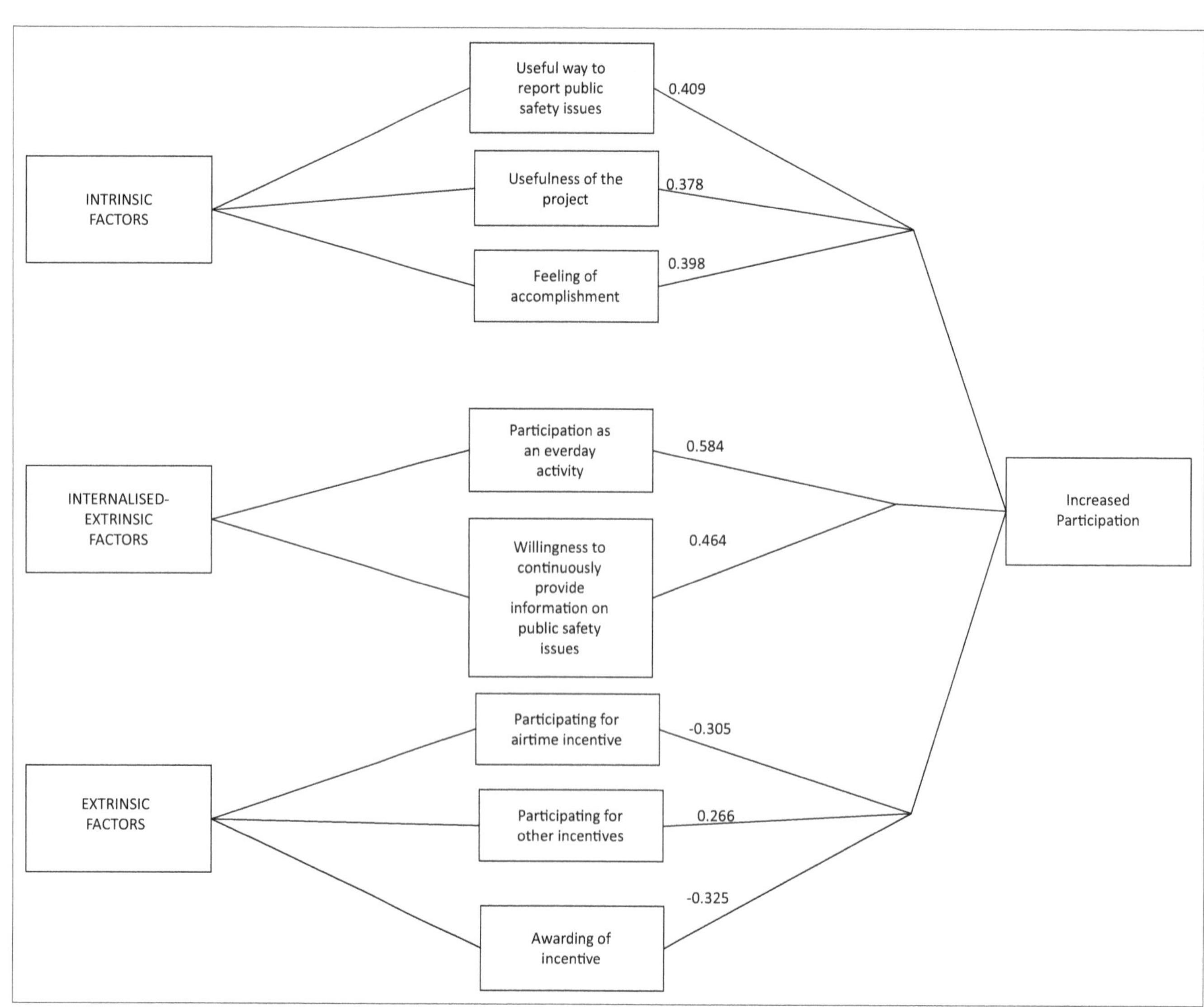

FIGURE 3: Participatory Crowdsourcing Incentive Model.

feeling of accomplishment and a city that responds to their reports.

Useful way to report public safety issues

This factor focuses on the value of the crowdsourcing system to participants. According to Gassenheimer et al. (2013), citizen involvement in city matters will allow them to use the crowdsourcing system to report issues they observe. This results in increased participation as continuous public safety information will be provided by citizens. Figure 3 illustrates a medium relationship, whereby participants indicated that participation increased because it was a useful way to report public safety issues. Therefore, it is necessary for the city to involve citizens by reporting public safety issues.

Usefulness of the project

This factor focuses on how the project was useful to citizens in terms of reporting public safety issues. Participants found this project to be useful in terms of reporting issues in order to make the city safer because previously there was no effective crowdsourcing system in place that allowed them to communicate these issues to the city. The Public Safety Smart City project made it easy to report public safety issues, thereby increasing citizen participation. This is because participants used the project's toll-free number and the mobile site which worked effectively by continuously collecting information. In 2015, East London city had an increase in recorded crime rates (7963 from 7858 crimes in 2014); therefore, the project was useful as it allowed citizens to report these crimes (Massung et al. 2013).

Feeling of accomplishment

According to the Incentive Theory, a person performs a task in order to be awarded an incentive in the end (Cherry 2013). In this case, citizens reported public safety issues in order to enjoy the feeling of accomplishment. Participants believed that the public safety project made it possible for them to provide information on the public safety issues they witnessed, thus leading to increased feelings of accomplishment. Feeling of accomplishment is important for intrinsically motivated participants who would like to provide information on public safety issues they witness. This factor is associated with the satisfaction a participant acquires after providing public safety information with the help of a well-functioning Participatory Crowdsourcing Model. The next section discusses internalised-extrinsic factors.

Internalised-extrinsic factors

Internal-extrinsic factors allow participants to take part in an activity in order to improve their reputation and to influence other citizens to make a difference in the community (Gassenheimer et al. 2013). This includes two factors that will encourage continuous public safety collection. These factors are participation as an everyday activity and willingness to provide public safety information. The next section discusses everyday activity.

Participation as an everyday activity

Everyday activity is one of the factors that ensure that the Public Safety Participatory Crowdsourcing Incentive Model is effective. This allows for the city to gather public safety information continuously from citizens. Collecting information on public safety issues regularly will assist the city to update or create new policies and operational procedures that will help reduce these issues, thereby making the city safer (Harrison & Donnelly 2011).

Willingness to report public safety issues continuously

This factor is important for the Participatory Crowdsourcing Model because it allows for public safety data to be collected from citizens continuously. The model suggests that the willingness to provide public safety issues continuously is more likely to affect citizen participation. Citizens will provide public safety information they observe regardless of whether they are being offered incentives or not, resulting in continuous public safety information being collected from citizens. The next section discusses extrinsic factors.

Extrinsic factors

Extrinsically motivated people perform an activity in order to be awarded an extrinsic incentive. Extrinsic factors consist of incentive motivation, participating for incentives. The next section discusses extrinsic motivation factors.

Participating for airtime incentive

The model illustrates that incentive motivation is less likely to be associated with increased participation. This means that majority of the participants did not report in order to be awarded the airtime incentive. Brabham (2012) states that various interviews and surveys have been conducted in order to find out what motivates people to participate in a crowdsourcing project, and it was found that there is no single motivator that encourages all participants. Therefore, the city of East London should incorporate incentives to encourage those participants who are encouraged by incentives.

Participating for other incentives: Literature suggests that participants prefer different incentives, depending on the person. Some prefer monetary incentives and some prefer non-monetary incentives (e.g. gift cards). The model found some relationship between extrinsic incentives and citizen participation. This indicates that participation levels were increased because some citizens reported in order to be awarded the airtime incentive.

Awarding of incentive

As mentioned in literature, some participants take part in an activity in order to be awarded for their performance. As illustrated in Figure 3, this factor had a negative medium relationship. This indicates that for some participants, the level of participation is not affected by the airtime they receive as their incentive. Thus, these citizens will provide public safety issues they witnessed even if they are not awarded incentives.

Conclusion

There are various public safety issues that are experienced by citizens as a result of urbanisation. In order to reduce these issues, the city can use participatory crowdsourcing to gather public safety information in a real-time and continuous basis. The city can make use of incentives as a way of encouraging citizen participation. This study explained how different types of incentives motivate citizens. The main aim for this study was to develop a crowdsourcing model that will assist the city in the continuous collection of data. The Public Safety Participatory Crowdsourcing Incentive Model was developed, and it identified different factors that that may be used to encourage citizens to continuously report public safety issues. Therefore, to improve the continuous data collection in a smart city project, the following motivators are important: intrinsic, internalised-extrinsic and extrinsic factors. The city can make use of these factors in order to keep collecting public safety reports continuously, thereby improving the quality of life of citizens.

Limitations and recommendations for future research

One of the limitations of this study was the small population size that completed the questionnaire which limits the generalisability of the results and the subsequent model. However, as the study made use of a case study approach, the results can be considered a reflection of the factors that will motivate the citizens of East London to participate in the smart city project. This study only focused on participatory crowdsourcing; crowdsensing and the use of sensors were not included in this project as participants were required to report. Using sensors could allow for more public safety data to be collected from citizens. The model developed in this study can be applied to other smart living aspects (such as health care and transport) besides public safety. Future research could focus on the appropriate incentive systems. This will guide future projects on the right or correct incentives that should be offered to participants for completing a task.

Acknowledgements

This project was funded by the National Research Foundation (NRF) and IBM and based on the research supported in part by IBM, the NRF of South Africa and the citizens of East London. The authors acknowledge that the opinions, findings, and conclusions or recommendations expressed in this article are those of the authors and that IBM and the NRF accept no liability whatsoever in this regard.

Competing interests

The authors declare that they have no financial or personal relationship(s) that may have inappropriately influenced them in writing this article.

Author's contributions

E.B. completed the research study in fulfilment of her degree requirements, and L.C. and S.F. made conceptual contributions to the project.

References

Azkuna, I., 2012, *Smart cities study: International study on the situation of ICT, innovation and knowledge in cities*, The Committee of Digital and Knowledge-based Cities of UCLG, Bilbao.

Bartoli, G., Fantacci, R., Gei, F., Marabissi, D. & Micciullo, L., 2013, 'A novel emergency management platform for smart public safety', *International Journal of Communications Systems* 28, 928–943. http://dx.doi.org/10.1002/dac.2716

Berst, J., 2013. *Smart cities readiness guide*, Seattle, WA: Smart Cities Council.

Brabham, D.C., 2012, 'Motivations for participation in a crowdsourcing application to improve public engagement in transit planning', *Journal of Applied Communication Research* 40(3), 307–328. http://dx.doi.org/10.1080/00909882.2012.693940

Brewer, E.W., Hollingsworth, C. & Campbell, A., 1995, 'Incentive motivation psychology: An exploration of corrective learning behaviour', *Journal of the Southeastern Association of Educational Opportunity Program Personnel*, XIV(1), 33–56.

Caragliu, A., Del Bo, C. & Nijkamp, P., 2011, 'Smart cities in Europe', *Journal of Urban Technology*, 18(2), pp.65–82.

Cherry, K., 2013, *The incentive theory of motivation: Are actions motivated by a desire for rewards?*, viewed 2 July 2014, from http://psychology.about.com/od/motivation/a/incentive-theory-of-motivation.htm

Christin, D., Reinhard, A., Kanhere, S.S. & Hollicka, M., 2011, 'A survey on privacy in mobile participatory sensing applications', *The Journal of Systems and Software* 84, 1928–1946. http://dx.doi.org/10.1016/j.jss.2011.06.073

Cilliers, L. & Flowerday, S., 2014, *Information security in a public safety, participatory crowdsourcing smart city project*, London, World CIS, pp. 1–5.

Colldahl, C., Frey, S. & Kelemen, J.E., 2013, *Smart cities: Strategic sustainable development for an urban world*, Blekinge Institute of Technology, Karlskrona.

Collis, J. & Hussey, R., 2009, *Business research*, 3rd edn., Palgrave Macmillan, London, UK.

Doan, A., Franklin, M.J., Kossma, D. & Kraska, T., 2011, 'Crowdsourcing applications and platforms: A data management perspective', *VLDB Endowment* 4(12), 1508–1509.

Gassenheimer, J.B., Siguaw, J.A. & Hunter, G.L., 2013, 'Exploring motivations and the capacity for business crowdsourcing', *Academy of Marketing Science* 2013(3), 205–216. http://dx.doi.org/10.1007/s13162-013-0055-8

Grass, J., 2013, *Crowdsourcing our safety*, viewed 20 October 2014, from http://whartonmagazine.com/blogs/crowdsourcing-our-safety/

Halder, B., 2014, 'Evolution of crowdsourcing: Potential data protection, privacy and security concerns under the New Media Age', *Digital Democracy and E-Government* 1(10), 377–393.

Harrison, C. & Donnelly, I.A., 2011, *A theory of smart cities*, International Society for the Systems Sciences (ISSS), Hull, UK, pp. 1–15.

Kaiserswerth, M., 2010, *Creating a smarter planet, one collaboration at a time*, IBM, Zurich.

Massung, E., Coyle, D., Cater, K.F., Jay, M. & Preist, C., 2013, *Using crowdsourcing to support pro-environmental community activism*, Paris, ACM, pp. 371–380.

Meier, P., 2012, *How crisis mapping saved lives in Haiti*, viewed 17 November 2014, from http://voices.nationalgeographic.com/2012/07/02/crisis-mapping-haiti/

Nam, T. & Pardo, T.A., 2011, *Conceptualizing smart city with dimensions of technology, people, and institutions*, New York, ACM, pp. 282–291.

Nov, O., Naaman, M. & Ye, C., 2009, 'Analysis of participation in an online photo-sharing community: A multidimensional perspective', *Journal of the American Society for Information Science and Technology*, Paris, Wiley, 1–12.

Pallant, J., 2010, *SPSS survival manual: A step by step guide to data analysis using SPSS*, 4th edn., McGraw-Hill, New York.

Rand Daily Mail, 2015, *New figures show staggering rate of urbanisation in SA*, viewed 21 January 2016, from http://www.rdm.co.za/politics/2015/05/26/new-figures-show-staggering-rate-of-urbanisation-in-sa

Shin, M., Cornelius, C., Peebles, D., Kapadia, A., Kotz, D. & Triandopoulos, N., 2011, 'AnonySense: A system for anonymous opportunistic sensing', *Journal of Pervasive and Mobile Computing* 7(1), 16–30. http://dx.doi.org/10.1016/j.pmcj.2010.04.001

Sincero, S.M., 2012, *Incentive theory of motivation*, viewed 10 July 2014, from https://explorable.com/incentive-theory-of-motivation

Tomasic, A., Zimmerman, J., Steinfeld, A. & Huang, Y., 2014, *Motivating contribution in a participatory sensing system via Quid-Pro-Quo*, ACM, Baltimore, MD.

Washburn, D. & Sindhu, U., 2010, 'Helping CIOs understand "Smart City" initiatives', *Forrester* 1(1), 1–17.

10

Evaluation of information ethical issues among undergraduate students: An exploratory study

Author:
Liezel Cilliers[1]

Affiliation:
[1]Department of Information Systems, University of Fort Hare, South Africa

Corresponding author:
Liezel Cilliers,
liezelcilliers@yahoo.com

Background: Higher education is increasingly making use of information and communication technology (ICT) to deliver educational services. Young adults at higher educational institutions are also making use of ICTs in their daily lives but are not taught how to do so ethically. Software piracy, plagiarism and cheating, while making use of ICTs, are the most common ethical dilemmas that will face digital natives.

Objective: The purpose of this article was to investigate information ethics of young adults at a higher education institution in the Eastern Cape Province of South Africa.

Method: This study made use of a positive, quantitative survey approach. A closed-ended questionnaire was distributed to a group of 312 first-year students, who had registered for a computer literacy class. A response rate of 69.2% was recorded, resulting in 216 students participating in the study. The results were analysed using descriptive and inferential (*t*-tests) statistics in SPSS V22.

Results: The results indicated that plagiarism is a problem among first-year students, and elements of authorship should be included in the curriculum. Students understood what software piracy was but did not think it was wrong to copy software from the Internet. Finally, the students understood that cheating, while making use of technology, is wrong and should be avoided.

Conclusion: The recommendation of the study then is that information ethics must be included in the undergraduate curriculum in order to prepare students to deal with these ethical problems.

Introduction

Higher education is responsible for the development of student autonomy and thereby the development of a knowledge society (Duarte 2014). In order to achieve these goals, higher education institutions (HEIs) are increasingly making use of information and communication technology (ICT) to deliver services (Alshwaier, Youssef & Emam 2012; Koch, Assuncao & Netto 2012). HEIs have become dependent on ICT to manage large amounts of data, improve the delivery of educational material, offer digital content and make classes more interactive (Koch et al. 2012).

In HEI interactive classes, young adults (typically aged between 18 and 24 years) can access information and resources making use of the ICT infrastructure. This generation is considered to comprise 'digital natives' who grew up with ICT, unlike their parents who had to learn to use new ICT services (Prensky 2001). Skiba (2014) reported that 79% of young adults own smart phones, with 70% of them using devices to stay connected in class.

This knowledge era does, however, bring about some unique challenges, such as the privacy and confidentiality of technology users as well as the accuracy of, and access to, digital technologies and ownership of such information (Halawi & McCarthy 2013; Mutula & Mmakola 2013; Sturges 2009). In order to address authorship, the flip side of plagiarism, the field of information ethics was introduced. Information ethics focuses on the relationship between the creation, organisation, dissemination and use of information, and extends to the ethical standards and moral acts controlling human behaviour around the use of such information by others without appropriate acknowledgement (Capurro 2007). Kim, Kim and Lee (2013) argued that while ethical problems in the ICT field do not differ from broader societal ethical issues, a thorough knowledge of ICT practices is necessary in order to comprehend the root cause of such ethical problems.

The two most common ethical problems faced by students in higher education are plagiarism and software piracy. Plagiarism is defined as 'The deliberate or reckless representation of another's words, thoughts, or ideas as one's own without attribution in connection with submission of academic work' (University of North Carolina 2014:1). Software piracy involves the unauthorised copying of software to avoid purchasing cost and can include copying of movies, music, games or software programs (Hsieh & Lee 2012). Leonard and Cronan (2005) suggested that the Internet makes information and software resources readily available and students, therefore, believe that it is acceptable practice to download movies or music from websites. This attitude then extends to the academic work of the student who plagiarises Internet resources. Alternatively, students can also use technology to cheat when taking tests or examinations. Underwood (2007:218) stated that ICT and Internet skills may provide students with an educational advantage, but there is also: 'recognition by students that the technologies can give them an edge, i.e. they can cheat'.

The purpose of this article is to investigate the information ethics of young adults at an HEI in the Eastern Cape Province of South Africa. While ICT has become acceptable in the higher education landscape, there is poor understanding of ethical issues for the purpose of teaching, learning and research. This is especially true in developing countries where there is also a lack of ethical education, awareness and policy regulation around the issue. Computer Science and Information Systems' lecturers in higher education have previously indicated that information ethics is an area that must be investigated and included in the curriculum in order to improve the social responsibility of young adults (Leonard & Cronan 2005; Straub & Collins 1990).

Literature review

ICT has become essential in teaching and learning at HEIs, where it is used by both staff and students as a learning, research and communication tool (Jamil, Shah & Tariq 2013b). The purpose of information technology (IT) is to generate knowledge that can be used to solve problems, unlock creativity and increase productivity (Halawi & McCarthy 2013). IT, therefore, can be defined as a set of tools that help students acquire information and perform tasks related to information processing (Haag & Keen 1996). Typical tasks that will be performed include accessing resources, completing assessments, preparing for presentations and communicating with peers or lecturers. While performing these tasks, ethical issues around acknowledging sources of information, for instance, will need to be addressed. Information ethics will guide the moral decision-making of young adults while making use of technology whether in the workplace, at school or in society in general (Jamil, Hussain & Tariq 2013a).

Ethics is considered to be the guidelines influencing human social behaviour intended to protect and fulfil the rights of individuals in a society (Marshall 1999). The definition of information ethics as proposed by Johnson (1985) was adopted for this study. Information ethics refers to a set of rules or principles used for moral decision-making regarding computer technology and computer use. Mason (1986) identified three critical areas that should be protected by information ethics, which include an individual's right to keep information about himself or herself private, the right to ascertain that the data are accurate and maintain ownership of it and an individual's right to have access to information.

Walter Maner first introduced information ethics in the mid-1970s. Maner (1995:3) stated that he: 'found it hard to convince anyone that computer ethics was anything other than an oxymoron'. Initially, the discipline only focused on the computing profession, which was responsible for the development of computer systems, but with the advent of the Internet, the emphasis soon moved to the end-users of computer and related technologies as issues such as intellectual property rights, plagiarism, software piracy and privacy had to be considered (Halawi & McCarthy 2013; Hsieh & Lee 2012). Two threats mentioned among the issues can be categorised as unethical Internet behaviour and are responsible for serious legal offenses. Freestone and Mitchell (2004) coined the term 'aberrant behaviour', which is used to describe the inappropriate use of the Internet without fear of punishment.

Meanwhile, Halawi and McCarthy (2013) stated that research in the information ethics' field is still inadequate and is mostly driven by two considerations. The first is public awareness about the vulnerability and misuse of information systems. This type of awareness depends on media coverage of specific incidents which helps to raise public awareness through discussions of how to manage these ethical issues in a more socially acceptable manner (Straub & Collins 1990). The second consideration has been the concerns of information system professionals that found the unacceptable, illegal and unethical use of computers to be problematic (Halawi & McCarthy 2013).

In order to address these concerns, Mason (1986) created a theoretical social framework to deal with ethical issues of the knowledge age. Mason identified four issues known as 'PAPA', which stand for privacy, accuracy, property and accessibility:

- Privacy deals with the decision about what information to reveal to others, under what conditions and with what safeguards.
- Accuracy refers to the authenticity, fidelity and accuracy of information.
- Property refers to who owns information, how access should be granted to this resource and what are the just and fair prices for its exchange.
- Accessibility guides the individual as to what information a person or an organisation has the right or the privilege to obtain, under what conditions and with what safeguards.

While the PAPA framework has remained popular for the last two decades to address information ethics, Halawi and McCarthy (2013) and Mason (1986) stated that with the advancements made in IT, unethical behaviour will increase. This type of unethical behaviour could include opportunistic behaviour such as hacking, spamming, denial of service attacks, identity theft and unauthorised duplications of software or content (Masrom et al. 2010). Young adults should be educated about information ethics so that they develop respect for authorship and ownership and do not indulge in opportunistic behaviour.

Pierce and Henry (1996) proposed that there are three influences that must be considered when an individual is confronted with an ethical decision related to IT or computer use. The first is the personal code of ethics which the individual develops through observation and experience. The second influence is the informal code of ethics, which is seen as acceptable behaviour in the workplace or endorsed by peers, and the third is the formal code of computer ethics which can include the institutional code or policy and legislation.

Among institutions, in particular, HEIs are increasingly concerned that the Internet will motivate students to be dishonest or unethical in their use of information. Unethical behaviour can include plagiarism, software piracy, fraud, falsification and misuse of information (Akbulut et al. 2008). Teston (2008) reported that 48% of students in the United States believe software piracy is legal. The computer curriculum, therefore, should include information ethics which will raise the awareness of these issues and increase the understanding of the implications of unethical behaviour. This will provide students with the tools to analyse and evaluate ethical dilemmas they may encounter in the field of ICT. However, at present, very few curricula include any information ethics in their list of objectives or values to be inculcated as learning outcomes (Jamil et al. 2013a).

Literature suggests that such values and attitudes have been found to be the most significant factor that will influence an individual's intention to behave ethically or unethically (Ajzen 1991; Leonard & Cronan 2005). Attitude can be influenced by five environmental factors, including societal belief system, and personal, professional, legal and business factors. The societal environment includes the social, religious and cultural values that impact the individual. Personal values are an individual's personal goals and experiences and are most often influenced by family, peers and significant others. The professional environment consists of the codes of conduct and professional expectations of an individual's profession, while the legal environment captures the law and the legislation of the country. Finally, the business environment consists of a company's stated policies which may increase the probability of ethical behaviour and persuade individuals to refrain from prohibited behaviour (Leonard & Cronan 2005).

In the business environment, cell phones are used prolifically. Young adults working and studying use them and other technologies; hence, they must be taught about information ethics in order to mitigate some of the effects experienced with plagiarism and software piracy. When young adults are taught the moral codes of handling and disseminating information, it will propagate knowledge about issues of privacy, censorship, copyright, fair use and access to information (Limo 2010). As the young adults' attitude regarding these issues change, it will also contribute to their social conduct and the growth of the knowledge era. This will ultimately lead to a morally informed society (Halawi & McCarthy 2013).

Methodology

The study made use of a positivistic, quantitative research approach. The study population consisted of 312 first-year students registered for a computer literacy course. The semester course consisted of students registered for commerce, law and social sciences degrees. The response rate of the students was 69.2% (216 students). This is considered an adequate response (Oates 2006). The study used the Cronbach's alpha coefficient to determine the reliability of the questionnaire. Cronbach's alpha values of 0.70 and above are typically employed as a rule of thumb to denote a good level of internal reliability, values between 0.50 and 0.69 denote an acceptable level of reliability and values below 0.50 denote poor and unacceptable levels of reliability. The reliability factor for the questionnaire was 0.604 which denotes an acceptable level of reliability (Bryman 2012).

As part of the course material, all the students were asked to complete an online questionnaire that evaluated their knowledge about information ethics. The questionnaire was developed and tested previously by Jamil et al. (2013a). The positivistic, quantitative approach was chosen owing to time constraints and the convenience of students, as it was accessible online. The questionnaire was designed to understand students' perceptions of information ethical behaviour in various activities that they may encounter while studying. The questionnaire consisted of two parts: Part 1 was designed to collect students' demographic information, while Part 2 comprised 14 statements on which respondents were required to respond making use of a Likert scale (1=strongly disagree to 5=strongly agree). The statements were divided into three categories: plagiarism, piracy and cheating. A pilot study was conducted prior to the distribution of the questionnaire in order to test for ambiguity, completeness and user-friendliness.

The questionnaire items were analysed making use of the Statistical Package for Social Sciences (SPSS) Version 22 in order to develop descriptive statistics (frequencies and percentages) and deferential statistics (mean, standard deviations and independent sample t-test at $\alpha = 0.05$).

Results

The aim of this article was to investigate the ethical issues that relate to the use of ICT by young adults at an HEI in the Eastern Cape Province of South Africa. The study sample consisted of 102 (47.2%) males and 114 (52.8%) females. Seventy-seven per cent of the participants were aged between 17 and 21 years. This percentage is to be expected as most students enter university after school. The 22- to 30-year age group consisted of 19.4% of the study sample, while the students that were older than 30 years were the smallest group comprising 0.03%.

Slightly more students (115, 53.2%) had attended a school in the rural areas specifically, while 101 students (46.8%) had attended a school located in an urban area. Rural schools often did not have adequate computer laboratory facilities, and this was reflected in the responses of 128 students (59.3%) who had not received computer literacy training prior to entering the university. Almost half of the students (49.5%) stated that they had no prior knowledge of computer ethics, but the vast majority (91.2%) indicated that it is important to be ethical when using a computer.

The ethical behaviour of the students was grouped into three categories: piracy of software, plagiarism and cheating. The results for each of the categories are displayed in Table 1, which shows that 59.3% of the students thought it was wrong or slightly wrong to copy software for educational purposes. Interestingly, while only 65.3% of the students thought that it was wrong to download music or movies from the Internet for personal use, 91.2% thought it was wrong to share it with friends.

The plagiarism category consisted of four questions (Table 2). The majority of the students (95.9%) thought that it was wrong to copy and paste entire pieces of work from the Internet. The percentage of students that recognised plagiarism decreased steadily as the amount of work copied decreased. This could indicate a problem as to the definition of plagiarism among the students. When asked if two lines copied from a source without acknowledging the source was acceptable, 94.4% of the students did know that this was wrong. Seventy-four per cent of the students thought that it would be unethical to copy a paragraph and change a few words without citing the source, while only 47.2% of the students indicated that it would be wrong to copy a series of paragraphs verbatim from different sources, even if the student acknowledged the sources in the reference list.

TABLE 1: Software piracy category.

Category	Wrong		Somewhat wrong		Somewhat right		Right	
	n	%	*n*	%	*n*	%	*n*	%
Copying original software for education purposes is	111	51.4	17	7.9	33	15.2	55	25.5
Downloading music or movies from Internet is	111	51.4	30	13.9	37	17.1	38	17.6
Unauthorised sharing of original software with friends is	173	80.1	24	11.1	7	3.2	12	5.6

TABLE 2: Plagiarism category.

Questions	Wrong		Somewhat wrong		Somewhat right		Right	
	n	%	*n*	%	*n*	%	*n*	%
Copying and pasting an essay from the Internet and submitting it as your own is	195	90.3	12	5.6	2	0.9	7	3.2
Copying two lines from a printed source without acknowledging the source is	177	81.9	27	12.5	10	4.7	2	0.9
Changing a few words of a paragraph copied and pasted from the Internet, so that the material does not have to be cited is	124	57.4	37	17.1	30	13.9	25	11.6
Using a series of paragraphs that have been copied and pasted from a variety of Internet sites to create a paper with acknowledgement to the sites in your bibliography is	81	37.5	21	9.7	22	10.2	92	42.6

Table 3 provides the results for the last category: cheating. The majority of the students indicated that it may be wrong to cheat. Ninety-five per cent of the students thought that it would be wrong to lie to the lecturer about handing in an assignment when they did not, while 88.9% did not approve of buying a paper or assignment online and submitting it as their own work. Ninety-nine per cent of students thought it was wrong to chat to other students during a test, making use of their mobile phones, but only 81.2% thought it would be wrong to receive the test questions from a fellow student after they had written the test.

Only 55.0% of the students indicated that it would be ethical to use a chat room to gather information for assignment purposes, while 13.4% indicated that it may be ethical. Thirty-one percent of the students felt that it was unethical to make use of chat rooms to search for information to be used for assignment purposes.

Correlation analysis tests were conducted to determine whether relationships existed between the different factors in the literature section. The correlation coefficients provide an indication of whether the relationship is positive (changes increase or decrease in the same direction) or negative (respond in opposite directions). The results for the categories piracy, plagiarism and cheating are also discussed.

Software piracy

Although the majority of students indicated in the previous section that they knew that software piracy was wrong, the results from the t-tests showed that students' attitude towards downloading music or movies from the Internet is that it is not unethical. The results indicated a positive statistically significant difference in the ethical score between students from a rural background ($t = 2.4; p < 0.05$), those that did not receive computer literacy training before entering university ($t = -2.97; p < 0.05$) and those that did not have prior knowledge of computer ethics ($t = -.97; p < 0.05$).

TABLE 3: Cheating category.

Questions	Wrong		Somewhat wrong		Somewhat right		Right	
	n	%	*n*	%	*n*	%	*n*	%
Buying a paper online and submitting it as your own is	180	83.3	12	5.6	5	2.3	19	8.8
Claiming to have attached an assignment to an email when you did not in order to have extra time to complete the work is	195	90.3	11	5.1	3	1.4	7	3.2
Carrying on an instant message conversation while taking a computerised exam is	200	92.6	14	6.5	2	0.9	0	0.0
Receiving and using an email from a friend about the questions on an exam he and/or she just completed is	183	74.7	14	6.5	3	1.4	16	7.4

Plagiarism

Plagiarism was shown to be a problem among first-year students as most of the variables tested statistically significant for this category. Students from rural areas indicated that the following actions are not considered unethical:

- Buying a paper online and submitting it as your own ($t = 1.98; p < 0.05$).
- Copying two lines from a printed source without acknowledging the source ($t = 2.29; p < 0.05$).
- Changing a few words of a paragraph copied and pasted from the Internet ($t = 2.81; p < 0.05$).
- Using a series of paragraphs that have been copied and pasted from a variety of Internet sites to create a paper with acknowledgement to the sites in your bibliography ($t = 2.61; p < 0.05$).
- Writing a summary based on an online abstract of a journal article rather than reading the article itself ($t = 4.2; p < 0.05$).

Students that did not receive any prior computer literacy training tested statistically significant for the questions 'changing a few words of a paragraph copied and pasted from the Internet' with $t = -3.44$ and $p < 0.05$, and 'using a series of paragraphs that have been copied and pasted from a variety of Internet sites to create a paper with acknowledgement to the sites in your bibliography' with $t = -2.55$ and $p < 0.05$. These results show that there is a negative relationship between lack of prior computer literacy training and the perceptions of the students regarding plagiarism.

Similarly, students that had no prior knowledge of computer ethics were found to be statistically significant for the question 'changing a few words of a paragraph copied and pasted from the Internet' ($t = -2.79$ and $p < 0.05$). In addition, students also reported that 'copying two lines from a printed source without acknowledging the source' as statistically significant ($t = -2.36; p < 0.05$). These results show that there is a negative relationship between lack of prior knowledge about computer ethics and the perceptions of the students regarding plagiarism.

Cheating

Prior knowledge of computer ethics tested statistically significant in this category. Claiming to have attached an assignment to an email when you did not in order to have extra time to complete the work tested significant for students with no prior knowledge of computer ethics ($t = -1.96; p < 0.05$) as did receiving and reading an email from a friend about the questions on an exam he/she had just completed ($t = -3.34; p < 0.05$).

Discussion

Many Computer Science and Information Systems' lecturers in higher education have previously indicated that information ethics is an area that must be investigated and included in the curriculum in order to improve the social responsibility of young adults (Halawi & McCarthy 2013; Jamil et al. 2013a; Straub & Collins 1990). This statement is supported by Masrom et al. (2010), who suggested that integrating computer ethics topics into the curricula is effective in making students aware of ethical concerns in IT. This exposure to information ethics will also impact the attitude of students towards ethical behaviour when working with a computer or digital information. The results of this study showed that while students thought it was important to be ethical when using a computer, many were not aware of plagiarism issues that may arise. If these matters are addressed early on in the curriculum, the students will be able to conduct themselves in an ethically acceptable manner as the awareness around these issues will have increased.

Previous literature proposes that the background of the students will influence their perspective of information ethics (Hsieh & Lee 2012). This was found to be true as students from rural backgrounds did not understand the ethical use of information piracy or plagiarism. This could be partly attributed to the lack of exposure to computers in rural areas. While both the national departments of Basic Education and Higher Education and Training in South Africa have adopted ICT as a means of enhancing education in the country, it is estimated that only 10% of the schools in South Africa have access to one or more computers. The reason why so few schools have computers is that the government of South Africa does not have the budget to purchase computers or provide the infrastructure necessary for ICT (Mdlongwa 2012). It is estimated that only 8.8% of schools in the Eastern Cape, the catchment area for the university in this study, has access to computers (Mdlongwa 2012). This unfortunately means that students enter higher education without the necessary computer literacy skills or exposure to topics such as information ethics.

In the previous paragraph, it was discussed how students' backgrounds influenced their perspectives on information ethics and their understanding of piracy and plagiarism. In terms of software piracy, it should be noted that young adults are the most prolific users of smart phones, which are enabled to download music and videos from the Internet (Limo 2010). Fewer students indicated that it was wrong to download these materials from the Internet for entertainment than software for other purposes, such as educational software. This can be attributed to the convenience of the Internet which makes it easy to access content and the cost of genuine software. Software piracy, therefore, has become acceptable to many of the students. Interestingly, students did not think it was acceptable to share content with their peers. Hsieh and Lee (2012) found that peer pressure can be used to reduce the rate of software piracy and to cultivate social norms. It may be possible that students do not share software as they are not sure that their peers will approve of this practice.

The issue of piracy above went hand in hand with plagiarism. Plagiarism was shown to be of concern among the cohort of students. As mentioned previously, the students from a rural background, in particular with no prior experience of computers or information ethics, did not understand why avoiding plagiarism was important. The amount of students that thought plagiarism was wrong decreased with the amount of text that was plagiarised. This means that first-year students did not understand what plagiarism is or did not appreciate the consequences of plagiarism when they enter higher education. Plagiarism, and its flip side, authorship, must therefore be included in the curriculum for these students to ensure that they abide by the rules for ethical conduct, instead of assuming that the students understand the concepts.

While ICT does provide convenience to students, in that they can access information and prepare professional documents, it also provides the opportunity to be dishonest. The students with no prior knowledge of information ethics had difficulty identifying why cheating making use of ICT was wrong. Once again, if the topic of information ethics is included in the curriculum, it will raise the awareness of these issues and provide the students with a frame of reference to determine what information ethics issues are and to prevent future unethical conduct.

Conclusion

Information ethics has become an important field in recent years as computers have become an integral part of daily life. Students in higher education are most often faced with three categories of breach of information ethics: software piracy, plagiarism and cheating. While most agree that it is important for students to understand these concepts, very few HEIs have included information ethics in their curriculum. This study has shown that while students do know what software piracy is, they do not think it is wrong to copy software from the Internet, possibly because of the convenience in doing so. Universities and colleges must teach students what authorship is in order for students not to fall prey to plagiarism and unethical behaviour. Finally, the students understood that cheating making use of technology is wrong and should be avoided.

The limitation of the article is the relatively small sample size when compared with the student population at the university and self-reported data that could lead to bias. Future opportunities for research include a longitudinal study with the same cohort of students, or an action-type research where information ethics is included in the curriculum and the knowledge of students is tested before and after the intervention.

Acknowledgements

Competing interests

The author declares that she has no financial or personal relationship(s) that may have inappropriately influenced her in writing this article.

References

Ajzen, I., 1991, 'The theory of planned behaviour', *Organizational Behavior and Human Decision Processes* 50, 179–211. http://dx.doi.org/10.1016/0749-5978(91)90020-T

Akbulut, Y., Sendag, S., Birinci, G., Kilicer, K., Sahin, M. & Odabasi, H., 2008, 'Exploring the types and reasons of Internet-triggered academic dishonesty among Turkish undergraduate students', *Computers & Education* 51(1), 463–473. http://dx.doi.org/10.1016/j.compedu.2007.06.003

Alshwaier, A., Youssef, A. & Emam, A., 2012, 'A new trend for e-learning in KSA using educational clouds', *Advanced Computing: An International Journal* 3(1), 81–97. http://dx.doi.org/10.5121/acij.2012.3107

Bryman, A., 2012, *Social research methods*, Oxford University Press, Oxford.

Capurro, R., 2007, 'Information ethics for and from Africa', *International Review of Information Ethics* 7, 1–13.

Duarte, M., 2014, 'Formative assessment in b-learing: Effectively monitoring students learning', *Second International Conference on Technological Ecosystems for Enhancing Multiculturality*, TEEM'14, Salamanca, October 1–3, pp. 1–6.

Freestone, O. & Mitchell, V., 2004, 'Generation Y attitudes towards e-ethics and internet-related misbehaviors', *Journal of Business Ethics* 54(2), 121–128. http://dx.doi.org/10.1007/s10551-004-1571-0

Haag, S. & Keen, P., 1996, *Information technology: Tomorrow's advantage today*, McGraw Hill Companies, Inc., New York.

Halawi, L. & McCarthy, R., 2013, 'Evaluation of ethical issues in the knowledge age: An exploratory study', *Issues in Information Systems* 14(1), 106–112.

Hsieh, P. & Lee, T., 2012, 'Does age matter? Students' persepctives of unauthorized software copying under legal and ethical considerations', *Asia Pacific Management Review* 17(4), 361–377.

Jamil, M., Hussain, J. & Tariq, R., 2013a, 'IT ethics: Undergraduates' perception based on their awareness', *Journal of Education and Practice* 4(12), 110–122.

Jamil, M., Shah, J.H. & Tariq, R., 2013b, 'IT ethics: Undergraduates' perception based on their awareness', *Journal of Education and Practice* 4(12), 1–14.

Johnson, D., 1985, *Computer ethics*, Prentice-Hall, Englewood Cliffs, NJ.

Kim, H., Kim, J. & Lee, W., 2013, 'IE behavior intent: A study on ICT ethics of college students in Korea', *Asia-Pacific Education Researcher* 23(2), 1–10.

Koch, F., Assuncao, M. & Netto, M., 2012, *A cost analysis of cloud computing for education*, Springer, Berlin.

Leonard, L. & Cronan, T., 2005, 'Attitude toward ethical behavior in computer use: A shifting model', *Industrial Management & Data Systems* 105(9), 1150–1171. http://dx.doi.org/10.1108/02635570510633239

Limo, A., 2010, Information ethics and the new media: Challenges and opportunities for Kenya's education sector, viewed 05 January 2016, from http://www.africainfoethics.org/pdf/2010/presentations/Limo%20paper.pdf

Maner, W., 1995, 'Unique ethical problems in information technology', *Science and Engineering Ethics* 2(2), 137–154. http://dx.doi.org/10.1007/BF02583549

Marshall, K., 1999, 'Has technology introduced new ethical problems?', *Journal of Business Ethics* 19(1), 81–90. http://dx.doi.org/10.1023/A:1006154023743

Mason, R., 1986, 'Four ethical issues of the information age', *MIS Quarterly* 10(1), 4–12. http://dx.doi.org/10.2307/248873

Masrom, M., Ismail, Z., Hussein, R. & Mohamed, N., 2010, 'An ethical assessment of computer ethics using scenario approach', *International Journal of Electronic Commerce Studies* 1(1), 25–36.

Mdlongwa, T., 2012, *Information and Communication Technology (ICT) as a means of enhancing education in schools in South Africa: Challenges, benefits and recommendations*, Africa Institute of South Africa, Johannesburg.

Mutula, S. & Mmakola, L., 2013, 'Information ethics integration in the curriculum at the University of KwaZulu Natal', *Innovations* 46, 1–18.

Oates, B., 2006, *Researching information systems and computing*, Sage, London.

Pierce, M. & Henry, J., 1996, 'Computer ethics: The role of personal, informal and formal codes', *Journal of Business Ethics* 15(4), 425–437. http://dx.doi.org/10.1007/BF00380363

Prensky, M., 2001, 'Digital natives, digital immigrants', *On the Horizon* 9(5), 1–10. http://dx.doi.org/10.1108/10748120110424816

Skiba, D., 2014, 'The connected age: Mobile apps and consumer engagement', *Nursing Educational Perspectives* 35(3), 199–201. http://dx.doi.org/10.5480/1536-5026-35.3.199

Straub, D. & Collins, R., 1990, 'Key inforamtion liability issues facing managers: Software piracy, proprietary databases, and individual rights to privacy', *MIS Quarterly* 14(2), 143–156. http://dx.doi.org/10.2307/248772

Sturges, P., 2009, 'Information ethics in the twenty first century', *Australian and Research Libraries* 40(4), 241–251. http://dx.doi.org/10.1080/00048623.2009.10721415

Teston, G., 2008, 'Software piracy among technology education students: Investigating property rights in a culture of innovation', *Journal of Technology Education* 20(1), 66–78. http://dx.doi.org/10.21061/jte.v20i1.a.5

Underwood, J., 2007, 'Rethinking the digital divide: Impacts on student-tutor relationships', *European Journal of Education* 42(2), 213–222. http://dx.doi.org/10.1111/j.1465-3435.2007.00298.x

University of North Carolina, 2014, *UNC*, The Writing Center, viewed 5 January 2016, from http://writingcenter.unc.edu/handouts/plagiarism/

11

Contribution of records management to audit opinions and accountability in government

Author:
Rodreck David[1]

Affiliations:
[1]Department of Records and Archives Management, National University of Science and Technology, Zimbabwe

Corresponding author:
Rodreck David,
rodreck.david@nust.ac.zw

Background: Auditing can support national democratic processes, national development and government good will. Supreme Audit Institutions (SAI), such as offices of Auditor General, publish consolidated reports on audit outcomes for local authorities, government departments, parastatals and related public entities. These reports identify broad areas analysed during audit exercises that often include financial management, governance, asset management, risk management, revenue collection and debt recovery. They highlight trends that were detected during audit exercises at the end of a financial year. The reports further show how records and records management affect audit exercises as well as financial management within the audited institutions.

Objectives: The intention of the research was to ascertain the contribution of records management to audit opinions and accountability in financial management in Zimbabwean government entities.

Method: A document analysis of Comptroller and Auditor General of Zimbabwe (CAGZ)'s reports was used to identify the types of decisions and recommendations (audit opinions) issued, in juxtaposition to the records management issues raised.

Results and Conclusion: This study shows that there is a strong correlation between records management concerns and audit opinions raised by the CAGZ's narrative audit reports. Inadequate records management within government entities was associated with adverse and qualified opinions and, in some cases, unqualified opinions that had emphases of matter. There was a causal loop in which lack of documentary evidence of financial activities was the source cause of poor accounting and poor audit reports. Errors resulting from incomplete or inaccurate records meant that government entities were not showing a true picture of their financial status and their financial statements could be materially misstated. As an important monitoring and control system, records management should be integrated into the accounting and auditing processes of government entities.

Introduction

Audit reports resulting from accounting information from public institutions are an indispensable information resource that can improve or advance government efforts to public democracy and development. Creditors and investors use audit reports from Supreme Audit Institutions (SAI) to make decisions on financial investments. As explained by Chen, Srinidhi and Su (2014:223), auditing derives its value by increasing the credibility of financial statements, which subsequently increases investors' reliance on them. Legislative and anti-corruption entities use financial auditing information to keep track of the actions of public administrators on behalf of concerned citizens. In the government, auditing is a check mechanism on behalf of the citizen, to ensure that public finances, resources and trust are managed in entities created to foster good governance, such as local authorities, parastatals, government departments, ministries and related government bodies.

Also, the provision of governmental accounting information to citizens supports the 'right to know' and 'to openly receive declared facts' that may lead to open deliberations by the constituents on their chosen councils and legislatures, all of which supports socio-political democracy (Stalebrink & Sacco 2007:494). Therefore, auditing of public institutions has a social role, considering that the opinions issued by the auditors help citizens to comprehend the implications of the information contained in the financial statements. It is on this basis that citizens make decisions that can alter the democratic processes, social structures and the quality of persons elected or entrusted to run public offices (Lungeanu 2015:358–359). Consequently, governmental auditing activities through an SAI and the resultant reports or information allow citizens to participate in the democratic processes such as public debates, enlightened political opinions, lobbying and voting.

Robust auditing structures can also improve a country's economic development (Abdolmohammadi & Tucker 2002). They foster accountability, transparency and good governance in financial management within public and government institutions. The value of auditing is in its ability to provide an independent guarantee of the trustworthiness of accounting information, and this fosters good management of public resources (DeFond & Zhang 2014:275). Accountability implies that organisations and individuals can 'explain their actions to others in a transparent and justifiable manner' (Ngulube 2004:24; Ngoepe & Ngulube 2013:45).

Through the mandate enshrined in *the Constitution of Zimbabwe Act* [No. 20], *the Public Finance Management Act (PFMA)* [Chapter 22: 19] and *the Audit and Exchequer Act (AEA)* [Chapter 22: 03], the Comptroller and Auditor General of Zimbabwe (CAGZ) has a vital role of facilitating good financial management and public accountability. This is pivotal in democratic governance. These Acts require accounting officers, auditors and related financial management officers to manage the resources allocated to their institutions and to be accountable for these resources. CAGZ facilitates accountability and promotes financial management in the use of public resources through carrying out and producing reports on audit outcomes in public institutions. These reports provide a narrative account of the findings, recommendation and related audit opinions of the outcomes of audit activities by the SAI in government bodies across the country. The narrative audit reports identify areas of concern and present them in major themes, stressing on specific tendencies that were noticed during audit exercise(s), as well as the overall opinion of the CAGZ. They narrate the audit findings, the recommendations made by the CAGZ as well as feedback or responses given by the management to key issues raised.

For SAIs such as CAGZ to produce effective reports, they depend on source evidence from the institutions being audited. Evidence-based reporting and the management of such evidence to be used to prove the responsibility of actions and accountability of decisions form the thrust of transparent financial management. Such evidence is found in official records that document the business actions of public service workers, particularly those involved in financial management. As such, effective management of records forms the base of financial management systems and subsequently supports audit exercises with evidence from records. Therefore, where accountability is concerned, 'lack of records management is unthinkable' (Ngoepe & Ngulube 2013:46). Records management, being the base of auditing, it is an obvious public interest too.

Mismanagement of financial records has long been known to support fraud and corruption activities (Palmer 2000; Rezaee 2005; Thurston 1997; Vanasco 1998). This often emanates from poor record-keeping systems and is worse and prevalent in the public sector in developing countries where paper records are used widely (Nengomasha 2013:2–3; Ngulube & Tafor 2006:60–70). It includes failure to create expenditure files, misfiled or non-existent account receivable and payable records, all of which often result in material misstatement of financial statements and enable fraudulent financial reporting. Maintenance of proper and adequate accounting records of financial transactions in government entities is a legal obligation through Section 35 (6) (a) of the PFMA and Section 19 of the AEA in Zimbabwe. It is not surprising that record-keeping receives a considerable amount of deserved attention by SAIs (Everett, Neu & Rahaman 2007; Ngoepe & Ngulube 2013) and that emphasis on proper record-keeping is placed in auditing standards such that some SAIs emphasise that 'a clear trail of supporting documentation that is easily available and provided timely is listed as the first of six good-practice indicators of positive audit results' (Bhana 2008:6).

This study replicates a similar one done in South Africa by Ngoepe and Ngulube (2013). In this study, a total of six narrative audit outcomes reports from the CAGZ, of national and local authorities, government departments, parastatals and related public entities for the period between 2011 and 2014 were examined using document analysis to identify the trends in audit opinions with regard to records management vis-à-vis audit opinions. The expectation was that this study would motivate further research in the area of embedding records management within financial management and auditing processes in government bodies. Audited public institutions are expected to benefit by appreciating the extent of contribution and value of records management work which is often treated with low priority (Kemoni 2007:156, 231; Smith 2007:215). The management stratum in government entities is therefore expected to use recommendations from this work to put strategies that endeavour towards unqualified audit opinions.

Research problem, hypothesis and intents

The CAGZ's opinions in several narrative reports showed her concerns on audit outcomes in several areas of financial management in the government entities. In these areas, the CAGZ had specifically identified record-keeping amongst the key areas that hindered government entities from attaining and upholding unqualified audits. There appeared to be a correlation between record-keeping and audit opinions. The extent of contribution of records management concerns to audit opinions by the CAGZ had not yet been reported in any financial, auditing or records management studies in Zimbabwe. Therefore, this study sought to analyse the narrative audit outcomes reports of the CAGZ from 2011 to 2014 to determine the extent of contribution of records management concerns to CAGZ's audit opinions and government accountability in Zimbabwe.

Considering this, the study intended to:

- establish the reporting trends in the CAGZ's narrative audit outcomes reports in relation to records management concerns from 2011 to 2014
- analyse and interpret word use metrics surrounding records management in the narrative reports
- analyse and interpret the concordance and contextual usage of record-keeping terms in audit findings
- establish a causal loop relationship between records management concerns and audit outcomes.

Research methods

This study was confined to the analysis of CAGZ's narrative audit outcomes reports for government entities that include local authorities, parastatals, state enterprises and related public entities. A total of six reports were analysed which were for the period between 2011 and 2014. A document analysis was conducted to gather relevant data about the contribution of records management concerns to audit opinions reflected in the CAGZ's reports. Document analysis is a technique that uses both quantitative and qualitative methods to understand the trend of desired issues within written or printed documents (document analysis further includes image and graphics analysis). Quantitative methods are based on statistical analysis, whereas qualitative methods hinge on semantic inferences using text retrieval and presentation techniques.

Document analysis was used because of its unobtrusive nature as it is dependent on objects (i.e. reports, books, articles, web pages, etc.) rather than humans (similar to Ngoepe & Ngulube 2013:46). This eliminated the Hawthorne or observer effect, which is a human-based reaction that would lead to bias, as humans can modify their behaviour because they are being studied (Breznau 2016:302). Also, because document analysis data sources exist before the study, they have a degree of objectivity based on the fact that the data sources were produced without the influence of their creators (Singleton & Straits 2010:403). Also, reports are often publicly available. In this case study, the CAGZ's narrative audit reports on audit outcomes available in the website (http://www.auditgen.gov.zw/index.php/reports) were used. As such, document analysis is one of the more forthright ways to trigger broader or detailed research.

The electronic reports that were in portable document format were analysed using software tools from Provalis Research (QDA Miner and WordStat) to establish the CGAZ's reporting trends on records management concerns, to analyse and interpret word use metrics surrounding records management in the narrative reports, to analyse and interpret the concordance and contextual usage of record-keeping terms in audit findings and to establish a causal loop relationship between records management concerns and audit outcomes.

Presentation of research results

The research objectives were used as a guide in presenting the results that came out of document analysis. These are presented here, with a follow up discussion of the results and their implications after which relevant conclusions and recommendations are made.

Analysis of audit opinions vis-à-vis records management concerns

Table 1 presents the CAGZ Audit Opinions and Records Management Concerns in State Enterprises and Parastatals from the 2014 Narrative Report (see Table 2 report no. 6). As shown, the correlation between records management concerns and audit outcomes was close, such that in all cases where the concerns were emphasised, there was either unqualified opinion with an emphasis of matter, a qualified opinion or an adverse opinion. Generally, the results show that there are poor regimes of records management in most government entities.

Analysis of records management concerns through text mining

Text mining was used to detect and bring out concerns raised about records management in the audit reports (Box 1). The keyword-in-context (KWIC) analysis method was used to extract specific concerns raised using keywords such as *record-keeping, record-keeping, record*, poor, keep*, maintain*, deleted, inadequate, weak*, proper, failure, financial statement, receipt, accurate*, complete*, register, book** and *document**. Frequency of word use was also used to show the level of concern around records management. Table 3 shows an extract of the top frequently used words in the six reports, highlighting the use of *record*-related terms and emphasising frequency of reference.

The strength of the relationship between words, keywords and content categories (in this case, the reports) was analysed using statistical predictors. This analysis established the occurrence of selected keywords within six cases (the reports) (Table 4). As shown in Table 4, there was a high probability of the occurrence of the words *records* and *keeping* [probability (P) = 1 in both cases] in all the reports. Simple word use frequency analysis showed that terms relating to records management where high up the graph with the word 'record' itself being the fourth frequently used word in the reports (Figure 1). A heatmap plot was used to graphically present a crosstab analysis where cell frequencies were represented by different colour-brightness or tones. The tool enabled an exploratory analysis of the functional relationships and cluster similarities between specific keywords. For instance, in the heat map in Figure 2, there was a strong emphasis on record-keeping in all the reports especially in report no. 5 (Table 2). Also, a keyword *Dendrogram* (Figure 3) was used to show the similarity relationship between words emphasised in the reports. Using a similarity index of

TABLE 1: The Comptroller and Auditor General of Zimbabwe audit opinions and records management concerns in state enterprises and parastatals from the 2014 narrative report (see Table 2, report no. 6).

Government Entities	CAGZ's audit opinions	Records management concerns
Authorities and agencies		
Agricultural Marketing Authority (AMA)	Unqualified Opinion	None Noted
Broadcasting Authority of Zimbabwe (BAZ)	Unqualified Opinion	None Noted
Civil Aviation Authority of Zimbabwe (CAAZ), 2013	Unqualified Opinion	None Noted
Environmental Management Agency, 2013	Unqualified Opinion	None Noted
Health Professions Authority (HPA)	Unqualified Opinion	None Noted
Medicines Control Authority of Zimbabwe	Unqualified Opinion	None Noted
National Biotechnology Authority, 2010–2012	Qualified	Emphasised
National Social Security Authority (NSSA), 2013	Qualified	Emphasised
Postal and Telecommunications Regulatory Authority of Zimbabwe (POTRAZ)	Qualified	Emphasised
Radiation Protection Authority of Zimbabwe, 2013	Unqualified Opinion	Noted
Zimbabwe Energy Regulatory Authority (ZERA)	Unqualified Opinion	Noted
Zimbabwe Investment Authority (ZIA)	Unqualified Opinion	Noted
Zimbabwe National Road Administration (ZINARA), 2012–2013	Qualified	Emphasised
Zimbabwe Parks and Wildlife Management Authority	Unqualified Opinion	Noted
Zimbabwe Revenue Authority (ZIMRA) & Its Subsidiary, 2013	Unqualified Opinion	Noted
Boards		
Grain Marketing Board (GMB), 2013	Qualified	Emphasised
Health Service Board (HSB), 2013	Unqualified Opinion	Noted
National Indigenisation and Economic Empowerment Board	Unqualified Opinion	Noted
Tobacco Industry and Marketing Bard (TIMB)	Unqualified Opinion	Noted
Tobacco Research Board	Unqualified Opinion	Noted
Commissions		
Anti-Corruption Commission of Zimbabwe, 2010	Adverse Opinion†	Emphasised
Competition and Tariff Commission	Unqualified Opinion	Noted
Forestry Commission	Unqualified with an Emphasis of matter	Emphasised
National Income and Pricing Commission (NIPC)	Unqualified Opinion	Noted
Securities and Exchange Commission of Zimbabwe (SECZ)	Unqualified Opinion	Noted
Investor Protection Fund (for SECZ)	Unqualified with an Emphasis of matter	Emphasised
Sports and Recreation Commission (SRC)	Unqualified Opinion	Noted
Zimbabwe Media Commission (ZMC)	Unqualified Opinion	Noted
Companies corporations		
Allied Timbers (Pvt) Ltd	Unqualified with an Emphasis of Matter	Emphasised
CMED (Pvt) Ltd	Unqualified Opinion	Noted
Cold Storage Company and its Subsidiary Wetblue Industries (Pvt) Ltd	Unqualified with an Emphasis of Matter	Emphasised
Courier Connect	Unqualified with an Emphasis of Matter	Emphasised
Deposit Protection Corporation	Unqualified Opinion	Noted
Life Long Engineering	Unqualified Opinion	Noted
Marange Resources (Pvt) Ltd, 2013	Unqualified with an Emphasis of Matter	Emphasised
Minerals Marketing Corporation of Zimbabwe (MMCZ)	Unqualified Opinion	Emphasised
Mellofield (under MMCZ)	Qualified Opinion on Legal and Regulatory Matters	Emphasised
National Oil Infrastructure Company of Zimbabwe (NOIC)	Unqualified Opinion	Noted
National Pharmaceuticals (NATPHARM)	Unqualified Opinion	Noted
National Railways of Zimbabwe (NRZ), 2013	Unqualified with an Emphasis of Matter	Emphasised
Net *One Pvt Ltd	Unqualified Opinion	Noted
New Ziana	Unqualified Opinion	Noted
Petrotrade (Pvt) Ltd, 2014	Unqualified Opinion	Noted
Powertel Communications (Pvt) Ltd, 2013	Unqualified with an Emphasis of Matter	Emphasised
Printflow (Pvt) Ltd	Unqualified Opinion	Noted
Saint Lucia Park Training and Conference Centre (Pvt) Ltd	Unqualified Opinion	Noted
TelOne (Pvt) Ltd	Unqualified with an Emphasis of Matter	Emphasised
ZESA Enterprises (ZENT) Pvt Ltd, 2013	Unqualified Opinion	Noted
ZESA Holdings	Unqualified Opinion	Noted
Zimbabwe Academic and Research Network (ZARNet) Ltd, 2011–2013	Unqualified Opinion	Emphasised
Zimbabwe Mining Development Corporation (ZMDC) and its Subsidiaries, 2013	Adverse opinion with an emphasis of matter	Emphasised
Zimbabwe Posts (Pvt) Ltd (ZIMPOST)	Qualified Opinion with an emphasis of matter	Emphasised
Zimbabwe Power Company (ZPC)	Unqualified Opinion	Noted
ZimTrade	Qualified Opinion	Emphasised
Zimbabwe Transmission and Distribution Company (ZETDC)	Unqualified Opinion	Noted
Zimbabwe United Passenger Company (ZUPCO)	Qualified Opinion	Emphasised

Table 1 continues on the next page →

TABLE 1 (*Continued*): The Comptroller and Auditor General of Zimbabwe audit opinions and records management concerns in state enterprises and parastatals from the 2014 narrative report (see Table 2, report no. 6).

Government Entities	CAGZ's audit opinions	Records management concerns
Councils		
Allied and Health Practitioners Council	Unqualified Opinion	Noted
Environmental Health and Practitioners of Zimbabwe (EHPC)	Unqualified Opinion	Noted
Medical and Dental Practitioners Council	Unqualified Opinion	Noted
Medical Rehabilitation Practitioners Council	Unqualified Opinion	Noted
National Aids Council (NAC)	Unqualified Opinion	Noted
National Arts Council of Zimbabwe (NACZ), 2013	Unqualified Opinion	Noted
Nurses Council of Zimbabwe	Unqualified Opinion	Noted
Pharmacist Council of Zimbabwe	Unqualified Opinion	Noted
Research Council of Zimbabwe (RCZ)	Unqualified Opinion	Noted
Traffic Safety Council of Zimbabwe	Unqualified Opinion	Noted
Zimbabwe Council for Higher Education (ZIMCHE)	Unqualified Opinion	Noted
Zimbabwe National Family Planning Council (ZNFPC), 2013	Unqualified Opinion	Noted
Zimbabwe School Examinations Council (ZIMSEC)	Unqualified Opinion	Noted
Financial institutions		
Agribank	Unqualified with an Emphasis of Matter	Emphasised
Infrastructure Development Bank of Zimbabwe (IDBZ)	Unqualified with an Emphasis of Matter	Emphasised
People's Own Savings Bank (POSB)	Unqualified Opinion	Noted
Small Enterprises Development Corporation (SEDCO)	Qualified Opinion	Emphasised
Ingutsheni Central Hospital	Unqualified Opinion	Noted
Parirenyatwa Group of Hospitals	Unqualified Opinion	Noted
United Bulawayo Hospitals	Adverse Opinion	Emphasised
Universities and tertiary institutions		
Bindura University of Science and Education	Unqualified Opinion	Noted
Bulawayo School of Hospitality and Tourism	Unqualified Opinion	Noted
Chinhoyi University of Technology & the Hotel	Unqualified Opinion	Noted
Great Zimbabwe University	Unqualified Opinion	Noted
Harare Institute of Technology	Unqualified Opinion	Noted
Judicial College of Zimbabwe	Unqualified Opinion	Noted
Lupane State University	Unqualified Opinion	Noted
Midlands State University	Unqualified Opinion	Noted
National University of Science and Technology	Unqualified Opinion	Noted
University of Zimbabwe	Unqualified Opinion	Noted
Zimbabwe Open University (ZOU), 2013	Unqualified Opinion	Noted
Zimbabwe School of Mines (ZSM)	Unqualified Opinion	Noted
Other		
National Galleries of Zimbabwe	Unqualified Opinion	None Noted
National Museums and Monuments of Zimbabwe (NMMZ)	Unqualified with an Emphasis of Matter	Emphasised
Scientific and Industrial Research Development Centre (SIRDC)	Unqualified Opinion	Noted

†, It was interesting to note that the Anti-Corruption Commission had an adverse opinion as well as *emphasised* records management concerns considering its role as an institution set to foster accountability and government transparency.

TABLE 2: The Comptroller and Auditor General of Zimbabwe (CAGZ) reports analysed in this study.

Report number	CAGZ reports analysed in this study
1	Narrative Report on Finance Accounts Statements in the Ministry of Finance and Economic Development 2011: • Statement of Public Financial Assets 2011 • Statement of Receipts and Disbursements 2011 • Statement of Contingent Liabilities 2011
2	Narrative Report on Finance Accounts Statements in the Ministry of Finance and Economic Development 2012: • Summary of Transactions on the Exchequer Account 2012 • Summary of Transactions on the Consolidated Revenue Fund 2012 • Statement of Public Financial Assets 2012 • Statement of Public Debt 2012 • Statement of Contingent Liabilities 2012
3	Report of the Comptroller and Auditor General for the Financial Year Ended December 31, 2011 – Narrative Report on Appropriation Accounts and Miscellaneous Funds and Donor Funded Projects Volume I of III
4	Report of the Auditor General for the Financial Year Ended December 31, 2012 – Local Authorities Volume III of III
5	Report of the Auditor General for the Financial Year Ended December 31, 2014 – Narrative Report on Appropriation Accounts and Miscellaneous Funds
6	Report of the Auditor General for the Financial Year Ended December 31, 2014 – Narrative Report on State Enterprises and Parastatals

3 and with 10 clusters, the results in Figure 3 show that *accounts, accounting, proper, system, maintenance* and *records* were correlated and commonly used together in the reports. Clearly, the above textual analysis highlights a high level of concern of records management issues raised in the reports.

Analysis of concordance and contextual usage of record-keeping terms in audit findings

All of the six reports (Table 2) analysed in this study were subjected to a concordance and contextual usage test of the word *record**. The results presented in Figures 4–9 were interesting. They pointed out all the instances in which the term appeared and the contexts in which it was used. Interestingly, the visual presentations show many cases in which the term *record** was linked to concerns such as *poor record-keeping, lack of sound record-keeping systems, inadequate*

BOX 1: Key records management concerns mined using the KWIC method.

Key records management concerns mined using the KWIC method (record-keeping, record-keeping, record*, poor, keep*, maintain*, deleted, inadequate, weak*, proper, failure, financial statement, receipt, accurate*, complete*, register, book*, document*):

- The Fund should maintain a *record* of its payments to schools in order to monitor and use the *information* for planning and budgeting purposes.
- An annual inspection of assets should be conducted and the Master Asset Register updated in order to come up with a correct *record* of assets.
- *Inadequate record-keeping.* Treasury did not *keep proper records* of account for Public Financial Assets as the *records* were fragmented in contravention of Section 35 (6) (a) of the Public Finance Management Act (Chapter 22:19).
- An annual inspection of assets should be conducted and the Master Asset *Register* should be updated in order to come up with a correct *record* of the Ministry`s assets.
- *Poor record-keeping* of property *files*. Property *files for* stand number 309, 434, 481 and 666 are yet to be updated with lease agreements.
- *Adequate books* of accounts should be *maintained* to *record* and disclose all the financial information.
- A record of all fuel coupons received and issued should be kept and regular checks by responsible officers should be carried out as a control measure.
- A *record* of security items should always be *maintained* in compliance with the provisions of Treasury Instruction 2101.
- A site visit of the Public Sector Investment Programmes (PSIP) on construction of school buildings, revealed *weaknesses* in *record-keeping* of building materials.
- As a result, there was no record for the following receipt *books 056201*–056300, 056401–056500, 725101–725200 and *invoice book* number 139501–139550 that were in use at the centre for the year under review.
- Council should *maintain* a *proper receipt book record* which shows all *receipt books* issued and returned.
- Council *maintains* the following *record books* to cater for under and over banking.
- Council should generate duplicate *record* of building inspection fees, one should be given to client and the other one should be *filed*.
- Due to *poor record-keeping* and *weak* supervisory controls, the Balance Sheet had a credit suspense account of $3536 135 (2011: $2 713 457).
- *Failure* to record and prepare financial *statements may* result in loss of transactions *information* for the years the fund has been in operation.
- *Failure* to *record* assets in the Master Assets Register may result in late detection of thefts and misuse of assets.
- Furthermore, *receipt book* number 725101–725200 was not *recorded* on the stores *register* neither is there *record* of who is currently using it.
- Good accounting practice requires that an entity should use a secure and robust accounting package to *record* and *maintain* its financial information.
- I observed that although *financial statements* were prepared from schedules *maintained* on Microsoft Excel spreadsheets no reliance could be placed on the accounts due to lack of a permanent *record*.
- In the absence of a *register* for Contingent Liabilities and sound *record-keeping* system I could not place reliance on the opening balance disclosed.
- In the absence of a sound record-*keeping system* audit could not therefore, establish the *completeness* and *accuracy* of the figures disclosed on the return submitted for audit.
- *Inadequate record-keeping* and non-disclosure of investments.
- It becomes difficult to establish the *completeness* and *accuracy* of the figures disclosed on the return submitted for audit if a sound *record-keeping* system is not in place.
- Management response – A follow up with Zimbabwe Parks and Wildlife Management Authority will be done to have a *record* of their movement and disposal.
- No *register* was maintained to *record* all private colleges *registered* with the Ministry of Higher and Tertiary Education.
- Recommendation – Council should generate duplicate *record* of building inspection fees, one should be given to client and the other one should be filed.
- Recommendation – The Fund should fully utilise the accounting system to *record* and process all financial transactions.
- Recommendation. The Local Board should enter into loan agreements when advancing loans to its staff and *maintain* a *record* of such agreements. Recommendation – The Local Board should enter into loan agreements when advancing loans to its staff and *maintain* a *record* of such agreements.
- Recommendation – The Ministry should *record* all its advance payments in a register to facilitate follow ups.
- Risk/Implication – In the absence of *proper record-keeping*, some accounting transactions might not be *recorded* and processed thereby affecting the *accuracy* and completeness of financial *information*.
- Risk/Implication – *Lack* of *proper record-keeping* system may create opportunity for fraud.
- Risk/Implication – Misappropriation of assets may occur and remain undetected as no complete *record of* assets exists.
- Risk/Implication – Misappropriation of assets may occur and remain undetected as no *complete record of* assets exists.
- Section 10 (1) of War Veterans Act [Chapter 11:15] states that *proper books* of accounts and *records should* be used to record all financial transactions of the Fund.
- Supporting *documents* must be attached to the bills of entry retained for *record-keeping*.
- Supporting *documents* must be attached to the motor vehicle change of ownership form and retained for *record-keeping*.
- The Council does not have a central record of all computers used for billing and *receipting*.
- The Ministry should put in place an effective monitoring mechanism such as maintaining a database of all the *registered businesses*, periodic inspection of the premises and a *record* of land allocated to council for residential purposes should be put in place.
- The Council should ensure that *adequate* controls and suitable accounting package are in place to allow for good *record-keeping*.
- The Fund did not *maintain* a manual cashbook and ledgers on which to *record* financial transactions.
- The Ministry did not *maintain* an up-to-date consolidated Master Asset *Register* to *record* all assets in terms of Treasury Instruction 2002.
- The anomaly could have been as a result of *poor record-keeping* or theft of the un-acquitted cash.
- The extent of guarantees and commitments disclosed may be misstated, in the absence of a sound *record-keeping* system.
- The proceeds of the sale of these stands have no *record* on council funds.
- The *register* could not give *accurate* information and dates as to movement of *records* as some sections like when the *record* was sent to High Court was left blank despite the *records* having been returned back from High Court.
- There was no improvement in *record-keeping*.
- There was no proper *accounting*, regular stock taking, complete *record-keeping*, reconciliations or even spot audits being done for the City's security items.
- There is a risk that without any *record*, the assets may be lost or misappropriated.
- There is no *record* of how these *receipt books* were transferred to Harare Institute of Technology.
- There should be a standard procedure for *recording* stocks which is uniform so that the year-end returns reflect a true *record* of the stocks on hand.
- Therefore, in the absence of a sound *record-keeping* system I could not establish the completeness and accuracy of the figures disclosed on the return submitted for audit.
- Therefore, there was no *record* of the computers that had the *receipting* module installed on them or were authorized to have this software.
- This was caused by *inadequate* supervision and *improper record-keeping*.
- This module however was not being utilised to capture and *record* such *information* of land sold and yet to be sold.
- This was caused by poor *record-keeping* and lack of supervision.
- This was caused by inadequate *record-keeping*.
- Risk/Implication Without *registers*, the Fund will not have a full *record* of Housing units and stands and details of beneficiaries of the housing scheme. This was caused by *inadequate record-keeping*.
- This was caused by *poor record-keeping*. Treasury had an *incomplete record of receipt books* issued and this was compounded by the fact that the following four receipt *books* were missing: 347701- 348000 349201- 349500 007601- 007700 007701- 007800.
- Treasury had an *incomplete record of receipt books* issued and this was compounded by the fact that the following four *receipt books* were missing: 347701- 348000 349201- 349500 007601- 007700 007701- 007800. Some receipts from the sub-offices had no master *receipts to* show that they were *receipted* at the main offices.
- When an employee's name is deleted in the system, all the *record* of payments made to such an employee are lost.
- *Register* in place to record fuel received from suppliers and issued out to users for the period January to May 2011.
- The situation did not improve owing to *inadequate records* and as a result the Ministry has been qualified on the same issue during the current year.
- Failure to carry out an annual asset assessment may result in *maintaining* or keeping redundant and unserviceable assets on *record*.
- No *record* or proof of disposal of the exhibits was availed for audit.
- Parliament of Zimbabwe did not open *books* of accounts to *record* the indebtedness of the Members of Parliament to government.
- Recommendations – An up-to-date *record* of debtors should be *maintained* so that schools do not loose potential revenue.

record-keeping or *failure to keep accurate or correct records*, all of which was common in all the six reports (Figures 4–9).

Discussion of the results

Document analysis of the narrative reports of the CAGZ strongly confirms the hypothesis of a strong correlation between record-keeping and audit opinions (Table 1). This replicates results from a similar study done in South Africa by Ngoepe and Ngulube (2013), which showed a strong link between record-keeping and audit outcomes and accountability of public institutions.

The proximity heat map analysis of word use in the six reports shows that record-keeping, evidence and recommendations were highlighted and strongly linked as shown with the lighter heat signature and cluster similarities presented in Figure 2.

In the narrative reports on state enterprises and parastatals for 2013–2014 (see Table 2, report no. 6), adverse, qualified

TABLE 3: An extract of the top frequently used words in the six reports highlighting the use of *record*-related terms emphasising frequency of reference.

Word	Frequency	Shown %	Processed %	Total %	Number cases	Cases %	TF • IDF
Financial	586	2.47	1.42	0.70	239	38.06	245.9
Records	571	2.41	1.38	0.68	432	68.79	92.8
Ministry	558	2.35	1.35	0.66	229	36.46	244.5
Management	517	2.18	1.25	0.62	281	44.75	180.6
Fund	465	1.96	1.13	0.55	152	24.20	286.5
Assets	425	1.79	1.03	0.51	141	22.45	275.7
Audit	419	1.77	1.01	0.50	219	34.87	191.7
Accounting	336	1.42	0.81	0.40	195	31.05	170.7
Statements	331	1.39	0.80	0.39	166	26.43	191.3
Council	313	1.32	0.76	0.37	89	14.17	265.6
System	297	1.25	0.72	0.35	127	20.22	206.2
Register	286	1.20	0.69	0.34	136	21.66	190
Recommendation	267	1.12	0.65	0.32	212	33.76	125.9
Account	247	1.04	0.60	0.29	127	20.22	171.5
Risk	244	1.03	0.59	0.29	185	29.46	129.5
Implication	238	1.00	0.58	0.28	199	31.69	118.8
Response	220	0.93	0.53	0.26	187	29.78	115.7
Finding	204	0.86	0.49	0.24	180	28.66	110.7
Bank	204	0.86	0.49	0.24	84	13.38	178.2
Treasury	200	0.84	0.48	0.24	128	20.38	138.1
Revenue	200	0.84	0.48	0.24	107	17.04	153.7
Public	193	0.81	0.47	0.23	101	16.08	153.2
Noted	187	0.79	0.45	0.22	146	23.25	118.5
Expenditure	185	0.78	0.45	0.22	79	12.58	166.6
Accounts	178	0.75	0.43	0.21	100	15.92	142
Ensure	176	0.74	0.43	0.21	144	22.93	112.6
Cash	174	0.73	0.42	0.21	80	12.74	155.7
Fuel	174	0.73	0.42	0.21	44	7.01	200.9
December	159	0.67	0.39	0.19	113	17.99	118.4
Record	151	0.64	0.37	0.18	126	20.06	105.3
Recorded	149	0.63	0.36	0.18	120	19.11	107.1
Result	137	0.58	0.33	0.16	121	19.27	98
Maintain	137	0.58	0.33	0.16	109	17.36	104.2
Proper	130	0.55	0.31	0.15	91	14.49	109.1
Maintained	129	0.54	0.31	0.15	107	17.04	99.1
Finance	127	0.54	0.31	0.15	90	14.33	107.2
Office	127	0.54	0.31	0.15	86	13.69	109.7
Time	126	0.53	0.31	0.15	91	14.49	105.7
Receipts	126	0.53	0.31	0.15	52	8.28	136.3
Section	124	0.52	0.30	0.15	93	14.81	102.9
Books	122	0.51	0.30	0.15	70	11.15	116.2

TF • IDF, term frequency–inverse document frequency.

and unqualified opinions which had emphases of matter were heavily linked to records management concerns, featuring absence, inadequate or lack of proper record-keeping (see Table 1). Supporting this was the text retrieval analysis of key records management concerns mined using terms: *record-keeping, record-keeping, record*, poor, keep*, maintain*, deleted, inadequate, weak*, proper, failure, financial statement, receipt, accurate*, complete*, register, book*, document** (see Box 1). The analysis shows a host of records management concerns raised characterised by comments given as follows:

- there were no up-to-date consolidated records of financial transactions
- inaccurate or insufficient information in the records
- poor record-keeping system
- absence of a sound record-keeping system
- records are manual and difficult to obtain
- warehouse records had no regular backup
- the situation did not improve owing to inadequate records, and as a result, the Ministry has been qualified on the same issue during the current year
- did not maintain adequate account records such as cash books, ledgers and related registers
- accountability of donor funds is questionable in the absence of accounting records
- failure to maintain loan guarantee records and a register will make it difficult to monitor and determine the claims and penalties when they fall due and also in the event of a dispute
- these operations are wide, complex and involve large volumes of data. Some manual records could not be retrieved upon audit request such as inventory schedules because they had been misplaced and there was no backup
- there were no records of contracts to support some of the projects that amount to US$ 2 884 372.

The above analysis is also evident when looking at the contextual usage and concordance analyses presented in

TABLE 4: Metrics analysis using statistical predictors for the occurrence of the word 'record' within six cases (the reports).

Name	Global Chi²	*p*	Max Chi²	*p*	Biserial	Predict
Account	2.97	0.7040	0.96	0.3265	1.6280	3
Accounting	5.49	0.3588	1.96	0.1615	3.0743	2 & 6
Accounts	6.52	0.2590	1.55	0.2128	2.7361	2 & 6
Act	4.91	0.4266	1.61	0.2049	2.1036	3 & 4
Agents	14.32	0.0137	14.32	0.0002	10.5376	4
Assets	4.27	0.5119	3.46	0.0628	3.2906	3
Audit	4.98	0.4181	0.67	0.4123	1.5815	2 & 6
Bank	9.60	0.0874	3.97	0.0464	4.3729	2 & 6
Cash	13.85	0.0166	5.11	0.0238	4.9631	2 & 6
Certificates	11.25	0.0466	11.25	0.0008	5.5656	3
City	9.68	0.0848	4.37	0.0366	5.8201	2 & 6
Clearing	6.43	0.2667	3.67	0.0553	5.3375	4
Construction	8.22	0.1445	7.79	0.0053	4.6308	3
Contravention	10.60	0.0599	7.60	0.0058	4.3536	3
Council	45.00	0.0000	20.30	0.0000	7.9697	2 & 6
Delays	4.19	0.5230	4.19	0.0408	4.4930	3
Department	3.30	0.6536	1.96	0.1615	3.0743	2
Disclosed	4.40	0.4927	1.82	0.1775	2.3849	5
District	6.63	0.2493	3.46	0.0628	3.2906	3
Documents	10.23	0.0688	6.39	0.0115	5.5522	4
Ensure	7.64	0.1772	1.96	0.1615	3.0743	2 & 6
Evidence	2.76	0.7364	0.53	0.4657	2.0314	4
Files	6.63	0.2493	3.46	0.0628	3.2906	3
Finance	10.54	0.0613	6.02	0.0142	3.7216	3
Financial	2.22	0.8180	1.61	0.2049	1.8112	3
Finding	23.20	0.0003	7.23	0.0072	4.7560	2 & 6
Fund	11.04	0.0506	8.76	0.0031	4.2290	3
Houses	6.43	0.2667	6.43	0.0112	4.8906	3
Housing	16.58	0.0054	16.58	0.0000	6.1780	3
Implication	11.93	0.0358	2.98	0.0842	3.3303	2
Keeping	0.00	1.0000	0.00	1.0000	0.0000	1 & 2 & 3 & 4 & 5 & 6
Maintained	4.87	0.4321	1.55	0.2128	2.7361	2 & 6
Management	14.34	0.0136	7.51	0.0061	3.6891	3
Ministry	12.41	0.0296	10.60	0.0011	4.6518	3
Noted	8.22	0.1446	3.67	0.0553	4.2089	4
Observation	3.84	0.5729	0.53	0.4657	2.0314	4
Observed	4.86	0.4327	3.46	0.0628	2.8230	3
Office	2.92	0.7130	1.61	0.2049	2.1036	3 & 4
Opinion	6.43	0.2667	3.67	0.0553	5.3375	4
Payments	5.66	0.3404	3.72	0.0536	3.2024	3
Progress	6.63	0.2493	3.46	0.0628	3.2906	3
Project	4.19	0.5230	4.19	0.0408	4.4930	3
Projects	8.78	0.1181	8.78	0.0030	5.2409	3
Proper	8.39	0.1361	1.55	0.2128	2.7361	2 & 6
Properties	8.78	0.1181	8.78	0.0030	5.2409	3
Property	16.58	0.0054	16.58	0.0000	6.1780	3
Public	14.67	0.0119	10.60	0.0011	4.6518	3
Receipts	4.58	0.4697	1.41	0.2355	3.3034	2 & 6
Recommendation	15.51	0.0084	2.98	0.0842	3.3303	2 & 6
Recommendations	1.52	0.9110	0.62	0.4292	1.3982	3
Record	0.00	1.0000	0.00	1.0000	0.0000	1 & 2 & 3 & 4 & 5 & 6
Records	3.92	0.5604	0.40	0.5272	1.3885	2 & 6
Register	2.04	0.8438	0.36	0.5501	1.6642	4
Response	18.45	0.0024	3.43	0.0640	3.5722	2 & 6
Risk	11.93	0.0358	2.98	0.0842	3.3303	2
Section	3.47	0.6284	1.61	0.2049	2.1036	3
Stand	5.89	0.3168	2.37	0.1236	4.2885	2 & 6
Stands	6.63	0.2493	3.46	0.0628	3.2906	3
Statements	6.29	0.2790	2.24	0.1344	2.8874	2 & 6
Submitted	1.28	0.9370	0.38	0.5373	1.3548	1
Suspense	1.90	0.8633	0.51	0.4745	1.5704	5
System	6.44	0.2658	2.59	0.1077	3.1028	2 & 6

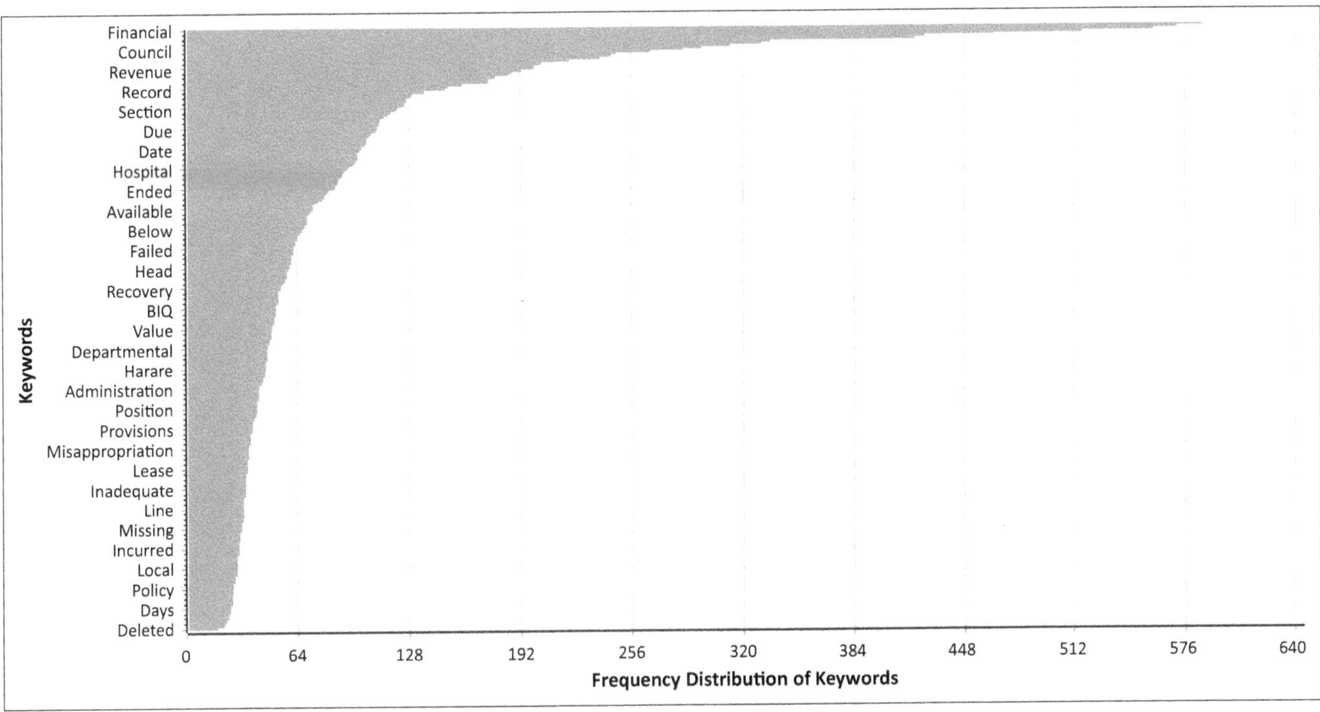

FIGURE 1: Analysis word use metrics in relation to records management issues in the narrative report.

Figures 4–9. They show that the word 'record' was heavily used in paragraph and sentence cases, which reflected concerns with regard to record-keeping. These also highlighted such issues as inadequate records, incomplete records, poor record-keeping, failure to maintain records, no improvement in record-keeping, failure to maintain up-to-date records and absence of records amongst many other challenges (see Figures 4–9). Both analyses showed a causal loop relationship between records management and auditing exercises, as well as the subsequent opinions made by the CAGZ.

Text metrics analysis using statistical methods also showed that 'record' was a heavily used word in the six reports topping amongst the top five frequently used words (Figure 1; Table 3). A further inference into this analysis through word similarity coupling and presented using a keyword *Dendrogram*, using a similarity index of 3 and with 10 clusters, showed that based on each of the six reports, 'record' was tightly coupled with words like *recommendations*, *keeping*, *fund* and *evidence* (Figure 3). Using a statistical prediction analysis enabled by WordStat, the results also show that most of the words tightly coupled with the word 'record' featured in all the reports six reports (Table 4). Again, inference into these statistical findings shows that records management was a *strong* concern in the six CAGZ narrative audit reports analysed.

Implications of the results

Government entities without records as evidence of property ownership or transactions of business with third-party institutions had no recourse in the absence of records in the event that disputes arise.

Government entities reported to have absent, incomplete or inconsistent records due to failure to maintain books of accounts, such as the cash book, relevant ledgers, expenditure vouchers, receipts and registers as well as required reconciliations, were not accountable. This was a glaring loophole for misappropriation of government or public resources as there was no evidence to charge responsible persons to be accountable for their actions. Public resources may continue to be misused with far reaching effect, particularly citizens' discontent with the effectiveness of persons running such public offices.

Lack of an integrated records management system between complementing government entities has had far reaching implications. For instance, it meant that there was no link between records of registered clients in Zimbabwe Revenue Authority's database and the companies registered with the Registrar of Companies, creating a risk that there may be more potential clients not submitting tax returns.

Government entities using paper-based, spreadsheet-based and weak payroll records processing and maintenance systems were allowing a loophole for creating 'ghost workers' as personnel profiles may easily be processed through the payroll by adding files creating or deleting electronic ones even where control systems may be in place.

Legal disputes emanating from expired lease agreements, contracts and other legally binding business transactions may be difficult to solve, resulting in a financial loss by government entities to third parties for those entities whose records were not being updated or kept sufficiently complete to serve as proof of evidence that such transactions occurred.

Absence of backups of vital records (those records without which government entities could be crippled or fail to continue) was a huge security threat and a red flag creating

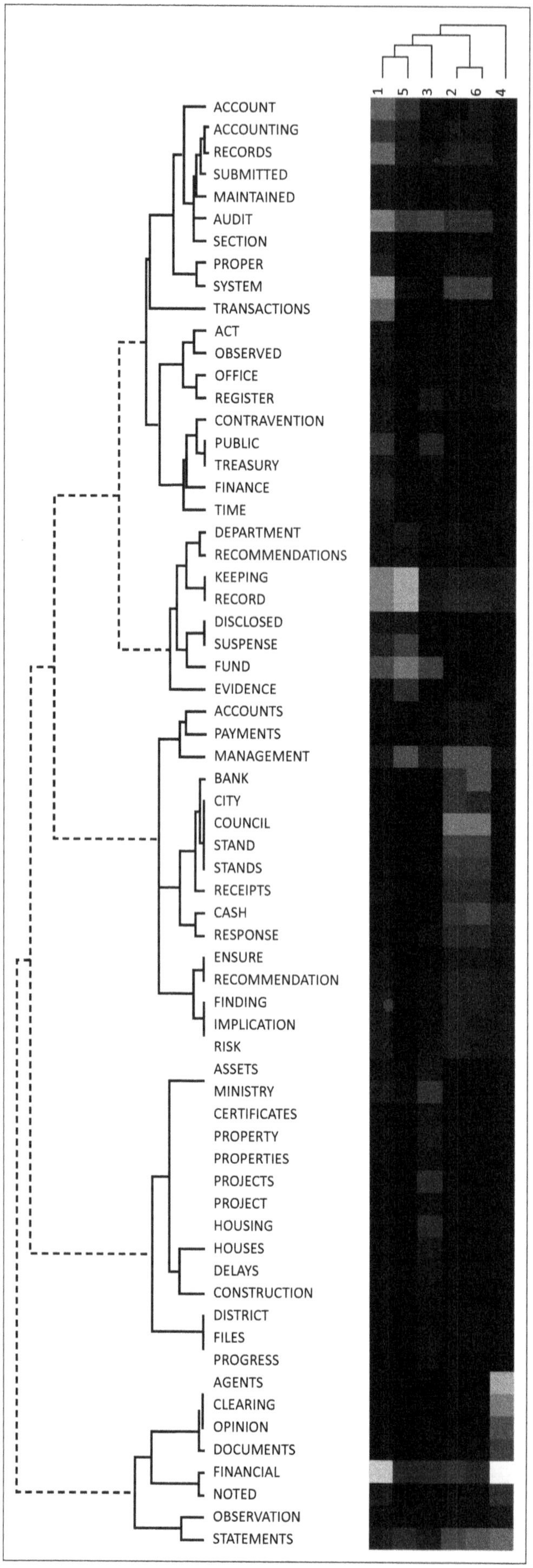

FIGURE 2: A proximity heat map showing word cluster similarities.

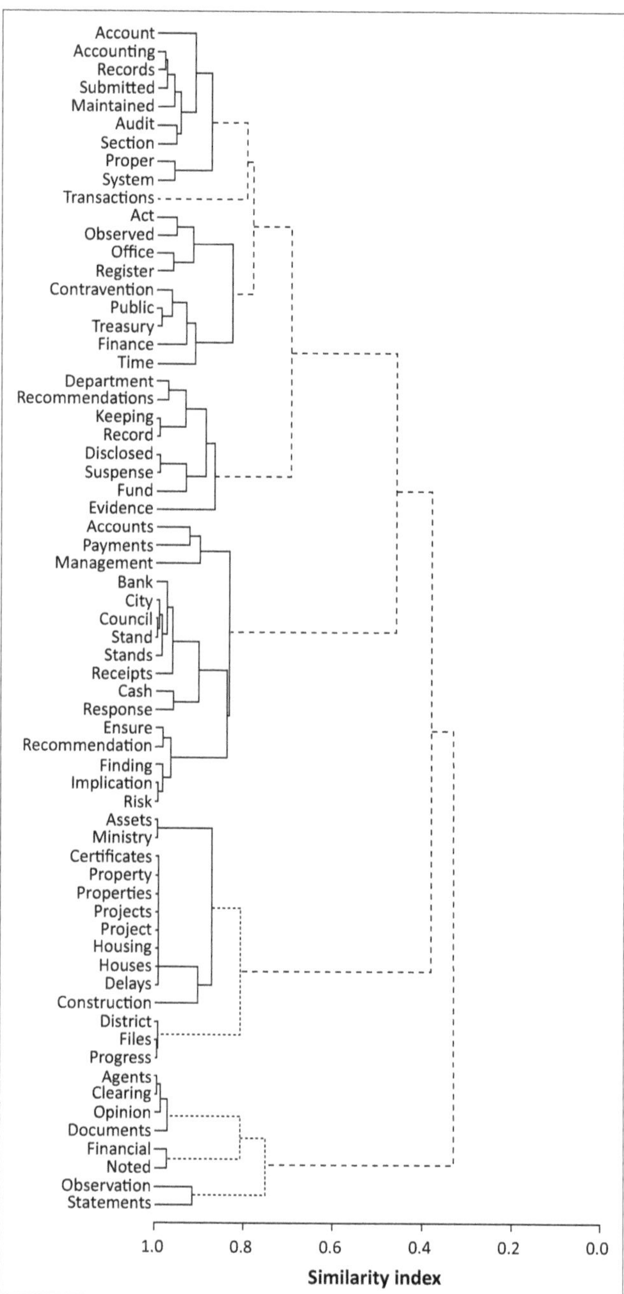

FIGURE 3: Keyword *Dendrogram* using a similarity index of 3 and with 10 clusters.

an ineffective risk management environment in which the institutions are vulnerable to sabotage and unforeseen disasters.

Government entities that were reported to have poor record-keeping systems cultivated a fraudulent environment which allowed for the concealment of fraudulent activities. Errors resulting from incomplete or inaccurate records could go undetected. This further implied that financial statements presented by such government entities were not showing a true and fair view of their financial status and their financial statements could be materially misstated.

Government entities that were not keeping proper records of account for public financial management may have been in contravention of Section 298 (1) (a), (d) and (e) of *the*

N	Concordance
1	the Public Finance Management Act [Chapter 22:19]. 1. GOVERNANCE ISSUES 1.1 RECORD KEEPING Finding A sample of revenue collections from entities listed in the
2	of loans and advances and other adjustments. 1. GOVERNANCE ISSUES 1.1 RECORD KEEPING Finding I observed that Treasury did not keep proper records of
3	The Ministry should avail documents to explain the variance of $887 614 423. 1.2 RECORD KEEPING Finding I observed with concern that a guarantees register was not
4	a database of all the registered businesses, periodic inspection of the premises and a record of land allocated to council for residential purposes should be put in place.
5	, the vendor's financial capability, experience, reference checks, previous criminal record, tax and State Procurement Board clearance. There was no selection
6	RECORDS Finding In my 2010 audit report, I highlighted the issue of poor record keeping that was characterised by numerous cases of mispostings, omissions
7	records for expenditure transactions. Risk/ Implication In the absence of proper record keeping, some accounting transactions might not be recorded and processed
8	Finance Management Act [Chapter 22:19]. Therefore, in the absence of a sound record- keeping system I could not establish the completeness and accuracy of the
9	pleas have been made to Treasury but all these have fallen on deaf ears. The record of releases from Treasury tells the story. The Department needs urgent
10	chairs) 5100000104 935 1 (Video camera) 5100000113 999 Risk/ Implication Failure to record assets in the Master Assets Register may result in late detection of thefts and
11	year were not disclosing SEDCO's outstanding repayments. Risk/ Implication Failure to record and prepare financial statements may result in loss of transactions information
12	IMPLEMENTATION OF PRIOR YEAR RECOMMENDATIONS 3.1 Inventory registers to record registration plates not being maintained and closing stock not being determined
13	was incurred for the intended purpose. There was also no register in place to record fuel received from suppliers and issued out to users for the period January to
14	on each prospective supplier before awarding supply contracts, including its track record and capacity to deliver among other critical factors. While the Ministry
15	any District or Provincial office results in the Head Office not having an up-to-date record. As part of the monitoring, sub national levels are regularly reminded to timely

FIGURE 4: The Comptroller and Auditor General of Zimbabwe Statements of Audited Financial Accounts for the year ended 31 December 2011 for government ministries.

N	Concordance
1	response A follow up with Zimbabwe Parks and Wildlife Management Authority will be done to have a record of their movement and disposal. Campfire Manager is responsible. 2 PROCUREMENT OF GOODS
2	The Local Board should enter into loan agreements when advancing loans to its staff and maintain a record of such agreements. Management response The observation was noted. All loans are being repaid,
3	aggregated onto a single land bank register. This module however was not being utilised to capture and record such information of land sold and yet to be sold. Risk/ Implication Fraud or error may go
4	record books to cater for under and over banking. Under banking invoice book Over and under banking record book or register Daily income return Cash book These records were available for your inspection.
5	and circumstances surrounding the missing receipt books. Council should maintain a proper receipt book record which shows all receipt books issued and returned. All receipt books in Council's custody should be
6	genuine cash payments by customers on settlement of monthly bills. The Council does not have a central record of all computers used for billing and receipting. In these circumstances, I was unable to satisfy
7	assets. Risk/ Implication Misappropriation of assets may occur and remain undetected as no complete record of assets exists. Recommendation A comprehensive fixed assets register covering significant asset
8	of cash deposited into the bank accounts. There was no proper accounting, regular stocktaking, complete record keeping, reconciliations or even spot audits being done for the City's security items. The City's
9	of revenue due to Council, which may go undetected. Recommendation Council should generate duplicate record of building inspection fees, one should be given to client and the other one should be filed. These
10	reconciled on a daily basis by the Revenue Clerk and the Accounts clerks. Council maintains the following record books to cater for under and over banking. Under banking invoice book Over and under banking
11	be easily misappropriated. Recommendation Council is advised to register the earth moving equipment for record purposes. Management response We agree with the observation, the transport superintendent is
12	should ensure that adequate controls and suitable accounting package are in place to allow for good record keeping. Management response The organization is in the advanced stage of implementing Pastel
13	Finding Internal control system with regards to receipting was weak. Treasury had an incomplete record of receipt books issued and this was compounded by the fact that the following four receipt books
14	without the Town Clerk's and Council's consent. The proceeds of the sale of these stands have no record on council funds. Valuation was not done by Council and Council procedure was violated. 1.8
15	of ivory. However, as at December 31, 2011 the Council did not have the ivory stock at hand and no record was kept by the Council relating to either their disposal or safe keeping. Risk/ Implication
16	was differing from the number of the actual machines that were on the ground. Therefore, there was no record of the computers that had the receipting module installed on them or were authorized to have this
17	The tender register is also a tool that ensures that previously qualified and disqualified companies are on record and known for reference in any future tender processes. Management response The observation
18	inspect one (1) available file out of sixty-five (65) stands administered. Risk/ Implication Lack of proper record keeping system may create opportunity for fraud. There may be double allocation of stands.
19	Finding I was unable to carry out any detailed tests on stand sales for the year under review as the record availed for audit examination was a tattered counter book with no details relating to date of
20	such agreements. Management response The observation was noted. All loans are being repaid, and this record is on our payroll. HWANGE LOCAL BOARD 2011 1 REVENUE COLLECTION AND DEBT RECOVERY 1.1

FIGURE 5: The Comptroller and Auditor General of Zimbabwe Narrative Report for the financial year ended 31 December 2012 for local authorities.

Constitution of Zimbabwe Act [No. 20] and were in contravention of Section 35 (6) (a) of the PFMA. By being unlawful they are vulnerable to the risk of constant litigation and financial loss. Such actions further cause bad reputation and citizen disapproval or public distrust in the persons running such public offices and hence the current government.

Recurrent records management concerns trending in the reports (2011–2014) appeared to show that despite its evident importance, the records management function is accorded low priority within government entities. There appeared to be a general lack of trained records management personnel in charge of records management within government entities as all the reports never gave such a report. Although reference to auditors, accountants and related financial officers was given, the reports were silent about records management officers. As such record-keeping duties seemed not to have human resource capacitation required to ensure that best practice record-keeping systems are put in place, with policies and structures required.

Conclusions and recommendations

This study proves the hypothesis that there is a strong correlation between records management concerns and audit opinions raised by the CAGZ narrative audit reports, which are a result of audit exercises in government entities. Absence, lack of or inadequate and inconsistent records management within government entities was associated with adverse and qualified opinions and, in some cases, unqualified opinions, which had emphases of matter. There was a causal loop in which lack of documentary evidence of financial activities was the source cause of poor accounting and poor audit reports with negative implications on governance. Even though important, records management still seems to be accorded low priority

N	Concordance
1	may result in increased project costs and contractors may withdraw their services. 2.2 Record keeping The issue of record keeping was still a challenge at the Public Works
2	Unit Vehicles is housed and maintained at Minerals Unit. The Ministry however, has a record for vehicles under the minerals unit. Most of the pool vehicles have dual number
3	to avoid being issued with duplicated receipt books in future for accountability purposes. A record of security items should always be maintained in compliance with the provisions of
4	of internal controls on procurement of fuel. -The Stores Department did not have a record of fuel drawn by the Departments outside the normal fuel procurement system.
5	direct payments made by Treasury are communicated to line ministries to enable adequate record keeping at both ends. Management should consider maintaining registers for Public
6	be understated in the financial statements. Recommendation The Fund should value and record all the assets at Khumalo Hockey Stadium in the asset register in accordance with
7	Instructions. This was evidenced by Khumalo Hockey stadium's inability to value and record all assets under its custody leading to non-disclosure of the same in the financial
8	and invoice books to Indo- Zimbabwe Centres in order to ensure that there is a correct record of the official receipt and invoice books in use. Management Response The record of
9	, schools risk failing to recover the amounts completely. Recommendations An up to date record of debtors should be maintained so that schools do not loose potential revenue. The
10	that "at the end of each term a schedule of all outstanding fees should be prepared for record purposes". This was not done because figures in the financial statements did not
11	inadequate record keeping Risk/Implication Without registers, the Fund will not have a full record of Housing units and stands and details of beneficiaries of the housing scheme.
12	are other material issues noted during the audit. 2 GOVERNANCE ISSUES 2.1 Improper Record Keeping Finding I observed with concern that Ministry officials did not maintain
13	of Treasury Instruction 2302. This was caused by inadequate supervision and improper record keeping. The Table below refers: Stand Number Location Area Remarks 1133
14	4.1 Incomplete and inaccurate financial statements The Ministry made efforts to improve record keeping and preparations of financial statements during the year following workshops
15	of Section 5.2 of the loan and performance agreements. This was caused by inadequate record keeping. Risks/Implications Outstanding loans may become irrecoverable through
16	. 3 PROGRESS IN IMPLEMENTATION OF PRIOR YEAR RECOMMENDATIONS Inadequate Record Keeping Treasury did not keep proper records of account for Public Financial Assets
17	beneficiaries were occupying Garikai/HlalaniKuhle houses. This was caused by inadequate record keeping Risk/Implication Without registers, the Fund will not have a full record of
18	cash must be discussed at a meeting of the Fund management and the minutes must record the resolution that was passed. The resolution must also state the specific amount
19	to the Harare Institute of Technology Indo-Zimbabwe Centre. As a result there was no record for the following receipt books 056201-056300, 056401-056500, 725101-725200 and
20	they were not seen when physical check of the exhibits was done in the exhibit room. No record or proof of disposal of the exhibits was availed for audit. The table 1 below refers:
21	for receipting at Harare Institute of Technology Indo-Zimbabwe Centre. There is no record of how these receipt books were transferred to Harare Institute of Technology.
22	costs and contractors may withdraw their services. 2.2 Record keeping The issue of record keeping was still a challenge at the Public Works Department as evidenced by the
23	assessment may result in maintaining or keeping redundant and unserviceable assets on record. It may also result in procuring unsuitable or excess assets. Recommendation The
24	internal controls. Risks/Implications It may be difficult to evict illegal occupants if an original record of the Fund's properties is not readily available. Rental income may be misstated if
25	and submitted to the parent Ministry. Management Response The stock balance as per record need to be adjusted by 853 658 litres which was released on February 1, 2011.
26	on which the Fund was supposed to be generating revenue. This was caused by poor record keeping. Risk/Implication There is risk that some houses could have been converted
27	provided to account for the difference. The anomaly could have been as a result of poor record keeping or theft of the unacquitted cash. Risk/Implication The Fund's financial
28	return and ascertain the status of the said provincial houses. This was caused by poor record keeping and lack of supervision. Risk/Implication Houses might have been
29	of housing properties The Ministry is still in the process of attending to the issue. 4.3 Poor record keeping of property files Property files for stand number 309, 434, 481 and 666 are
30	a shortage of architects and there were delays in payment of certificates as well as poor record keeping. 2.1 Delays in completion of construction projects The initial audit covered
31	whose cases were on warrant of arrest. The Victoria Falls Magistrates Court should record all exhibits in the register and tag them with identifiable numbers in chronological
32	, was involved in a " conflict of interest" whereby he was involved in a private survey, record number 152/2012 which he subsequently examined and approved for payment in his
33	correct record of the official receipt and invoice books in use. Management Response The record of officers who collected the receipt and invoice books in question is in the stores
34	appeals they were being caused by the accused who took time to come and inspect the record before it is sent to the High Court. I noted that Rusape Magistrates Court was not
35	accurate information and dates as to movement of records as some sections like when the record was sent to High Court was left blank despite the records having been returned
36	the documents. The delays in review were being caused by time being taken to type the record. On appeals they were being caused by the accused who took time to come and
37	book number 725101-725200 was not recorded on the stores register neither is there record of who is currently using it. 1.4 Submission of Revenue Supporting Documents
38	. The PVA screens were received well after the world cup games. The Ministry failed to record the PVA equipment in its Master Asset register. It would appear as if the Ministry
39	statements. Recommendation The Fund should fully utilise the accounting system to record and process all financial transactions. This will facilitate production of accurate and
40	environment. 1.2 Audit Information System Finding The Audit Information System is used to record user activities on the SAP application system in audit logs (trails). At the time of
41	that accounting records be maintained. The fund acquired a Promun Accounting package to record its financial information but did not fully utilise the accounting package as it was
42	information but did not fully utilise the accounting package as it was using the system to record loan debtors only. The financial statements were prepared from the cash book and
43	Revolving Fund Constitution. Parliament of Zimbabwe did not open books of accounts to record the indebtedness of the Members of Parliament to government. A nil return for the
44	records with such issue vouchers. Risk/Implication Unofficial receipt books may be used to record revenue if records of issued out receipt books are not maintained resulting in
45	the above, I noted that the Fund did not use a secure and robust accounting package to record accounting information. Ledgers were maintained on Microsoft Excel spreadsheet
46	practice requires that an entity should use a secure and robust accounting package to record and maintain its financial information. Contrary to the above, I noted that the Fund

FIGURE 6: The Comptroller and Auditor General of Zimbabwe Narrative Report for the financial year ended 31 December 2014 for appropriation accounts and miscellaneous funds.

and importance as evidenced by recurrent concerns in the 2011–2014 reports studied.

The study recommends the strengthening of the records management legislation provided for by *the National Archives of Zimbabwe Act* [Chapter 25: 06] to ensure enforceability. The National Archives of Zimbabwe (NAZ) is the regulator of records management in government and the public sector and should be engaged to ensure proper management of records. Such a recommendation was never mentioned in any of the narrative reports analysed in this study and that appears to show a disjointed relationship between the CAGZ and NAZ.

Accounting, or auditing officers are given the responsibility of records management duties as stated or otherwise implied by Section 35 (6) (a) and Section 80 (2) (a) (ii) of the PFMA. These officers' training is vested in financial management and not records management. Records management should be strengthened through human resource capacitation by employing dedicated records management officers or

N	Concordance
1	was not reconciled. The Ministry did not reconcile the variance. 2.2 Record keeping A guarantees register was not being maintained by the
2	of completing the audit. The reconciliation had still not been done. 2.3 Record Keeping Payments to other accounts figure of $367 432 750 was
3	have been used for purposes not related to the Fund. Recommendation A record of all fuel coupons received and issued should be kept and regular
4	of the Statement of Public Financial Assets. Failure to keep accurate record of investments might result in the Ministry of Finance missing
5	on August 1, 2011, however the Stadia Revolving Fund did not value and record the assets listed in the table below in the asset register in
6	the period under review. Risk/Implication There is a risk that without any record, the assets may be lost or misappropriated. Recommendation The
7	the Fund failing to take corrective actions. There was no improvement in record keeping. Management did not implement audit recommendations. 2.3
8	were being checked by the Head of Office. There was no improvement in record keeping. Management did not implement audit recommendations. 3.2
9	IN IMPLEMENTATION OF PRIOR YEAR RECOMMENDATIONS 2.1 Inadequate Record keeping The Ministry of Transport, Communication and
10	. Basis for Disclaimer of Opinion 1. GOVERNANCE ISSUES 1.1. Inadequate Record Keeping and Non-disclosure of Investments Findings 1.1.1 For the
11	no reliance could be placed on the accounts due to lack of a permanent record. Risk/Implication Unauthorized changes may be made to financial
12	Records In my previous reports, I highlighted the issues of poor record keeping characterised by numerous mispostings, omissions and
13	Vehicle Registry Department. 1.5 Suspense Account Finding Due to poor record keeping and weak supervisory controls, the Balance Sheet had a
14	in the delivery of the equipment. Recommendation The Ministry should record all its advance payments in a register to facilitate follow ups. The
15	balance. In the absence of a register for Contingent Liabilities and sound record keeping system I could not place reliance on the opening balance
16	and commitments disclosed may be misstated, in the absence of a sound record keeping system. Recommendation The Ministry should avail
17	, had a "conflict of interest" whereby he was involved in a private survey, record number 152/2012 which he subsequently examined and approved
18	have been made to Treasury but all these have fallen on deaf ears. The record of releases from Treasury tells the story. The Department needs
19	spot checks and stock takes and supervise the officers responsible for the record keeping. Investigations on discrepancies are going to be conducted
20	that an entity should use a secure and robust accounting package to record and maintain its financial information. Contrary to the above, I
21	were received well after the world cup games. The Ministry failed to record the PVA equipment in its Master Asset register. It would appear as
22	received and duly expended for the intended purposes. The failure to record fuel coupons bought was due to lax controls and failure by
23	The Fund did not maintain a manual cashbook and ledgers on which to record financial transactions. This was contrary to Treasury Instruction
24	the Fund did not use a more secure and robust accounting package to record its ledgers. Its ledgers were being maintained on Microsoft Excel
25	did not maintain an up-to-date consolidated Master Asset Register to record all assets in terms of Treasury Instruction 2002. As a result, I could
26	:15] states that proper books of accounts and records should be used to record all financial transactions of the Fund. However, contrary to this
27	stocks which is uniform so that the year-end returns reflect a true record of the stocks on hand. The Fund should on a regular basis check

FIGURE 7: The Comptroller and Auditor General of Zimbabwe Summary and Statements of Audited Financial Accounts for the year ended 31 December 2012 for government ministries.

N	Concordance
1	2012 and 2013. Attendance registers play an important role of keeping a record of attendance to board and committee meetings by members. The
2	is a holder of a current certificate and also an employer shall keep a record of the particulars of the certificate relating to such workers and shall
3	evaluate each competitive tender submitted to them during a meeting and record minutes of the evaluation process. Any tenders for the provision of
4	of the October pay sheet the Finance Manager had to remove this dummy record from the NBA payroll. 1.2 Board meetings Finding Good corporate
5	attached to the motor vehicle change of ownership form and retained for record keeping. Management response Observation noted. Officers have
6	. Supporting documents must be attached to the bills of entry retained for record keeping. Management response The delay in generating T1 of the
7	was added again but with a different code of NBA019FA and the old record was then deleted permanently on March 26, 2013. On 28 August
8	records should not be deleted even if they leave the organisation. The record should be frozen and its reactivation should only be made possible
9	banking details. When an employee's name is deleted in the system, all the record of payments made to such an employee are lost. I was therefore
10	encourage greater internal communication between departments in order to record transactions accurately. Progress made Bank reconciliation statements
11	. Declaration of interest register Finding The Company had no register to record Board members as well as members of senior management's interests

FIGURE 8: The Comptroller and Auditor General of Zimbabwe Narrative Report for the financial year ended 31 December 2014 for state enterprises and parastatals.

otherwise retraining of accounting and auditing officers to improve records management capacitation. Employment of dedicated record-keeping officers within government entities would ensure that there are responsible personnel who could be held accountable for the records management within public entities especially for managing financial records (not the accounting or finance function). These would ensure the creation of complete records, identify activities that need to be documented as well as consistent and constant updating of the records as may be required. They would ensure that

N	Concordance
1	The Ministry should compile and avail for my examination a record of salary arrears and come up with plans on how the
2	fees. 1.3 Recommendation 1.3.1 The Fund should maintain a record of its payments to schools in order to monitor and use
3	. 1.3 Recommendation 1.3.1 The Ministry should receipt and record in the sub-collectors schedule all revenue received from
4	Register should be updated in order to come up with a correct record of the Ministry`s assets. All new assets should be
5	Asset Register updated in order to come up with a correct record of assets. This will help the Office to establish whether
6	model or type. For the second year running the Office did not record assets that it purchased to guard against pilferage and/
7	which operate in Zimbabwe. No register was maintained to record all private colleges registered with the Ministry of Higher
8	4.4.1 Adequate books of accounts should be maintained to record and disclose all the financial information. EDUCATION,

FIGURE 9: The Comptroller and Auditor General of Zimbabwe Narrative Report for the financial year ended 31 December 2011 for Appropriation Accounts and Miscellaneous Funds and Donor-Funded Project.

necessary vital records identification and protection as well as disaster recovery measures are put in place to reduce security risks associated with loss of such vital documentary evidence. Such duties require qualified and trained records management officers.

The study recommends the prioritisation of the records management function within government bodies. This should be done by embedding records management operations within the financial, accounting and auditing processes of governmental bodies. Also, record-keeping systems should be mandatorily put in place with the best interest to have effective electronic systems instead of cumbersome paper-based systems, which are a huge loophole for fraud. If the above recommendations are not met, the recurrent recommendations by the CAGZ in identifying records management as one of the key sources of accountability continue to be in vain.

Acknowledgements

Competing interests

The author declares that he has no financial or personal relationships that may have inappropriately influenced him in writing this article.

References

Abdolmohammadi, M.J. & Tucker, R.R., 2002, 'The influence of accounting and auditing on a country's economic development', *Review of Accounting and Finance* 1(3), 42–53. https://doi.org/10.1108/eb026990

Audit and Exchequer Act (AEA) [Chapter 22: 03], 2001, Government of Zimbabwe, Government Printers, Harare.

Bhana, P., 2008, 'The contribution of proper record-keeping towards auditing and risk mitigation: Auditor General of South Africa's perspective', Paper presented at the Third Annual General Meeting of the South African Records Management Forum, Midrand, South Africa, 10–11th November, viewed from http://sarmaf.org.za/oid%5Cdownloads%5CSARMAF_10_Keynote%20address_06_November_2008.doc

Breznau, N. 2016. 'Secondary observer effects: idiosyncratic errors in small-N secondary data analysis', *International Journal of Social Research Methodology,* 19(3), 301–318. https://doi.org/10.1080/13645579.2014.1001221

Chen, C.J.P., Srinidhi, B. & Su, X., 2014, 'Effect of auditing: Evidence from variability of stock returns and trading volume', *China Journal of Accounting Research* 7(4), 223–245. https://doi.org/10.1016/j.cjar.2014.11.002

Constitution of Zimbabwe Act [No. 20] Act, 2013, Government of Zimbabwe, Government Printers, Harare.

DeFond, M. & Zhang, J., 2014, 'A review of archival auditing research', *Journal of Accounting and Economics* 58(2), 275–326. https://doi.org/10.1016/j.jacceco.2014.09.002

Everett, J., Neu, D. & Rahaman, A.S., 2007, 'Accounting and the global fight against corruption', *Accounting, Organizations and Society* 32(6), 513–542. https://doi.org/10.1016/j.aos.2006.07.002

Kemoni, H.N., 2007, 'Records management practices and public service delivery in Kenya', PhD thesis, University of KwaZulu-Natal, Pietermaritzburg.

Lungeanu, E., 2015, 'Considerations regarding the external public audit of reimbursable funds', *Procedia Economics and Finance* 20, 358–364. https://doi.org/10.1016/S2212-5671(15)00084-2

Nengomasha, C.T., 2013, 'The past, present and future of records and archives management in sub-Saharan Africa', *Journal of the South African Society of Archivists* 46, 2–11. https://www.ajol.info/index.php/jsasa/article/view/100084/

Ngoepe, M. & Ngulube, P., 2013, 'Contribution of record-keeping to audit opinions: An informetrics analysis of the general reports on audit outcomes of the Auditor-General of South Africa', *Journal of the Eastern and Southern Africa Regional Branch of the International Council on Archives* 32, 45–54. https://www.ajol.info/index.php/esarjo/article/view/88541

Ngulube, P., 2004, 'Fostering accountability and justice: Opportunities for records managers in changing societies', *ESARBICA Journal: Journal of the Eastern and Southern Africa Regional Branch of the International Council on Archives* 23, 23–32. https://doi.org/10.1080/00039810600691288

Ngulube, P. & Tafor, V.F., 2006, 'The management of public records and archives in the member countries of ESARBICA', *Journal of the Society of Archivists* 27(1), 57–83. https://doi.org/10.1080/00039810600691288

Palmer, M., 2000, 'Records management and accountability versus corruption, fraud and maladministration', *Records Management Journal* 10(2), 61–72. https://doi.org/10.1108/EUM0000000007256

Public Finance Management Act (PFMA) [Chapter 22: 19], 2009, Government of Zimbabwe, Government Printers, Harare.

Rezaee, Z., 2005, 'Causes, consequences, and deterrence of financial statement fraud', *Critical Perspectives on Accounting* 16(2005), 277–298. https://doi.org/10.1016/S1045-2354(03)00072-8

Singleton, R.A. & Straits, B.C., 2010, *Approaches to social research*, 5th edn., Oxford University Press, New York.

Smith, K., 2007, *Public sector records management: A practical guide*, Ashgate Publishing, Ltd., Burlington, VT.

Stalebrink, O.J. & Sacco, J.F., 2007, 'Rationalization of financial statement fraud in government: An Austrian perspective', *Critical Perspectives on Accounting* 18(4), 489–507. https://doi.org/10.1016/j.cpa.2006.01.009

Thurston, A., 1997, 'Records management as a public sector accountability function', *International Journal of Government Auditing* 24(4), 7–9. https://search.proquest.com/docview/236819139?accountid=14782

Vanasco, R.R., 1998, 'Fraud auditing', *Managerial Auditing Journal* 13(11), 4–71. https://doi.org/10.1108/02686909810198724

12

The use of mobile applications by public transport commuters in Gauteng, South Africa

Authors:
Cornelius J.P. Niemand[1]
Hlelo Chauke[1]

Affiliations:
[1]Department of Information and Knowledge Management, University of Johannesburg, South Africa

Corresponding author:
Cornelius Niemand,
corn@uj.ac.za

Background: Information and Communication Technology (ICT) has brought about a 'singularity' – that is 'an event which changes things so fundamentally that there is absolutely no going back'. The aforesaid change may be attributed to the way that the modern consumer thinks, communicates and interacts with the environment. Because businesses need to adapt and offer new, innovative ways of products and service delivery, early technology adopters are more likely to experience favourable business outcomes, including increased revenue potential and a better market position in comparison to competitors.

Objectives: The transport industry may be regarded as early adopters of new technology. Thus, the objective of this study is to determine the perceived use and usefulness of mobile applications used within the public transport industry of South Africa.

Method: This study adopted a positivist stance with a deductive research approach utilising the technology acceptance model theory as a departure point for the study. A mixed method research design was selected for this exploratory study, utilising a survey strategy comprising both closed and open-ended questions as a snapshot of the perceived usefulness of a mobile application within the South African public transport domain. A convenience sample of a hundred Gautrain commuters was selected.

Main findings: Based on descriptive statistics, the main findings of this study indicate a positive relationship between the perceived ease of use and usefulness of the Gautrain Buddy application in the dissemination of Gautrain-specific information. Some of the results of the study have also been presented at an international conference [for the conference details, please refer to the reference list Niemand and Chauke (2016)].

Conclusion: The sample of commuters forming part of the study indicates that mobile applications can be useful in the dissemination of public transport information in Gauteng, South Africa.

Introduction

The onset and rapid diffusion of Information and Communication Technology (ICT) in the last decade of the 20th century has brought about a 'singularity' – that is 'an event which changes things so fundamentally that there is absolutely no going back' within the way that the modern consumer thinks, communicates and interacts with the environment (Prensky 2001). Nicholas et al. (2003:23) concurs and adds that it is '...not just the number of people using the system that changed so dramatically, the types of people using the system changed dramatically too...'. According to Spink (2004:336), 'the growing complexity of everyday life and work environments often requires people to engage in multitasking behaviours'.

Taking the aforesaid statements into consideration, business has had to adapt to the new way consumers interact and engage with information and the brand itself. One of the most significant developments within the business environment during the last century is the ability of organisations to deliver products and or services via technological means to the consumers thereof. According to Wentzel, Diatha and Yadavalli (2013) 'computers, mobile telephones, the Internet and self-service devices are examples of technology platforms that have enabled services to be offered in new and innovative ways'. Considering that businesses need to adapt and offer new innovative ways of products and service delivery, Cusanelli (2014) postulates that early technology adopters are more likely to experience favourable business outcomes, including increased revenue potential and a better market position in comparison to competitors. The aforementioned statement is supported by a study (The Digital Dividend-First Mover Advantage) completed by the Harvard Business Review Analytic Services (n.d.).

Challenger (2015) is of the opinion that the transport industry may be regarded as early adopters of new technology. Robinson (2015) concurs and adds that mobile technology is not new to the transportation world. The author furthermore points to various examples including Qualcomm's OmniTracs™ in 1988 and UPS' roll-out of the Delivery Information Acquisition Device (DIAD) 4 years later of pioneering companies investing in mobile technology as a means to drive efficiencies and create competitive advantage. Based on the fact that the transport industry may be regarded as early adopters of technology, the main research question may be defined as:

Does the use of mobile applications assist in information dissemination within the public transport industry in Gauteng, South Africa?

The main research objectives of the study are to determine:

- What is the perceived usefulness of mobile applications in the dissemination of information in the public transport industry?
- What is the perceived ease of use of mobile application in the dissemination of information in the public transport industry?

Theoretical framing

Theoretical frameworks provide a base position from which researchers engage with and view knowledge within a particular field of study. Depending on the methodological orientation of the researcher, the same phenomenon may be viewed from varying theoretical frameworks. The aforesaid frameworks may be defined in terms of the scholarly reality within which the researcher endeavours to answer a research problem and or partly relating to the framework that the researcher consciously pursues to describe and understand the phenomenon. Considering the importance of the theoretical framework, Agherdien (2007:17) argues that frameworks may be regarded as 'epistemological devices that account for the knowledge that is produced in a study'. The objective of a theory is to guide the study and research process in three unique ways. Agherdien (2007:20) is of the opinion that a theory may pertain to and guide the philosophy of the science and the way the research is designed, the way a phenomenon is viewed within a specific academic or disciplinary stance or the way it facilitates critical review of previous research and how it relates to a specific study. In order to justify the importance of the three guiding functions of a theory, it is necessary to define the concept of a theory. Pettigrew and McKechnie (2001:62) are of the opinion that within the modern day research environment, having a theory is an indication of research importance and research respectability. The dynamic nature of research impact on how a theory will be defined, for what is acceptable as the correct theory today, may be replaced by an updated, more descriptive theory tomorrow. The aforementioned statement is justified if the definition as postulated by Flick (1998:43) in Agherdien (2007) who states that a theory may be seen as a 'versions of the world' that are said to be revised, evaluated, constructed and reconstructed on a continuous basis, is taken into account. Gorard (2004) concurs with Flick (1998:43) and postulates that a theory is 'a tentative explanation, used for as long as it usefully explains or predicts real-world events'. Pettigrew and McKechnie (2001:62) are of the opinion that a theory may be represented in a written and or graphical format.

The theoretical framing or theory used in this study is the 'technology acceptance model' (TAM). The TAM attempts to explain the phenomenon of the users' acceptance of a specific system and the subsequent use thereof. It should be noted that the TAM has been widely applied, validated and cited within the Information Management (IM) and ICT fields. The importance of aforesaid is evident from the statement by Lee, Kozar and Larsen (2003:764) indicating that 'TAM studies occupy 10% of total (leading information systems [IS] journals) publications'.

Technology acceptance model

A number of different theories have been postulated in an attempt to explain the adoption of technology by its users. According to Wentzel et al. (2013), the first attempt at explaining how users go about adopting technology was the 'Theory of Reasoned Action'. It should be noted that the Theory of Reasoned Action describes the behaviour of a user of technology from a social psychological point of view, that is, the theory attempts to identify the causes of conscious intended behaviours and maintains that these behaviours are a function of the user's attitude towards the intended behaviour. The Theory of Reasoned Action does have a limitation in its inability to explain behaviour in which people have limited control. The Theory of Reasoned Action was therefore extended to the Theory of Planned Behaviour that accounts for situations or conditions where users do not have full control over the situation.

Wentzel et al. (2013) is of the opinion that the first theory that focuses specifically on the adoption of technology by its users was introduced by Fred Davis in the late 1980s. According to Lala (2014), Davis postulated that the TAM aims 'to provide an explanation of the determinants of computer acceptance that are generally able to explain the behaviour of users of a wide range of computing technology'. Lala (2014) furthermore states that Davis postulated that the use of a system can be explained or predicted by users' motivation, which in turn, is directly influenced by an external stimulus in the form of the actual system features and capabilities. The aforementioned interaction may be graphically summarised by means of Figure 1.

Taking the aforesaid into consideration, the TAM as postulated by Davis may be regarded as a theoretical basis for specifying the casual relationship between the two main sets of constructs

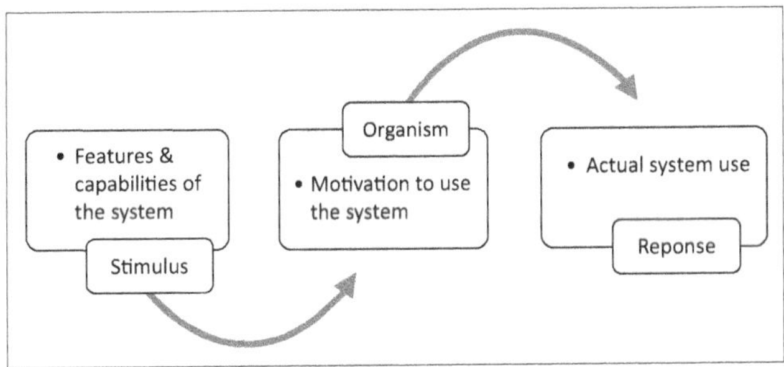

Source: Adapted from Lala, G., 2014, *The emergence and development of the technology acceptance model (TAM)*, viewed 28 January 2015, from http://0-web.b.ebscohost.com.ujlink.uj.ac.za/

FIGURE 1: Davis' conceptual model for technology acceptance.

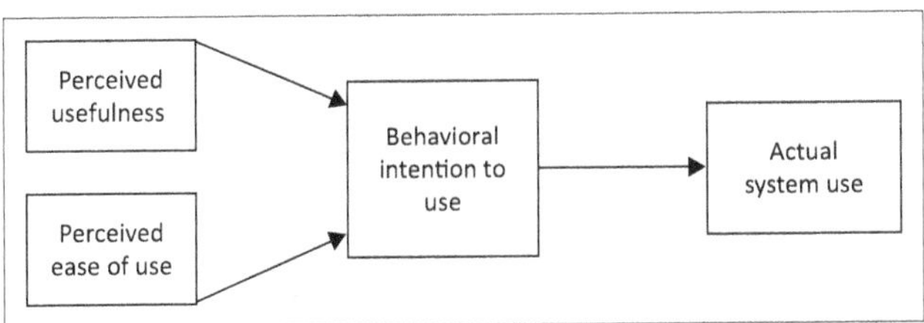

Source: Adapted from: Davis, F.D., Bagozzi, R.P. & Warshaw, P.R., 1989, 'User acceptance of computer technology: A comparison of two theoretical models', *Management Science* 35(8), 982–1003. https://doi.org/10.1287/mnsc.35.8.982

FIGURE 2: Technology acceptance model.

identified, that is, perceived usefulness and perceived use of the system. Fădor (2014:61) states that Davis defined perceived usefulness as 'the degree to which a person believes that using a particular system would enhance his performance at work' and perceived ease of use being defined as 'the degree to which a person believes that using a particular system would be free of effort'. Thus, the model states that the perceived usefulness and the perceived ease of use will predict the attitude towards the system. Fădor (2014:61) defines the attitude towards the system as 'the user's willingness to use its own system'. Furthermore the model dictates that the users' attitude and perceived usefulness will influence the behavioural intention of the users to use the system, where the actual use of the system is dictated by the behavioural intention of the users to use the system (Figure 2).

According to Radomir and Nistor (2013) over the last couple of years, several adjustments have been made to the original TAM. These adjustments include but are not limited to:

- researchers removing or adding new relationships between the variables in the model
- some researchers remove behavioural intention and actual usage behaviour from the model
- differences have also been noticed relating to external variable identification and incorporation that may influence individuals' beliefs and thus their specific behaviours
- other researchers rename behavioural intention to continuance intention when the study is conducted among users of a particular information system.

For the purpose of this study, the fundamental or initial TAM will be used to determine the perceived use and usefulness of mobile application in the public transport industry in Gauteng, South Africa.

South African transport industry

According to a PwC (n.d.) report 'the transport sector is a key contributor to South Africa's competitiveness in global markets'. The report suggests that the air and rail networks within South Africa may be regarded as the largest on the African continent. Ports and ports efficiencies has improved because of high levels of investment within this sector of the transport industry. But, because of a lack of intermodal transport infrastructure the South African economy over-relies on road transport to mitigate the legacy infrastructure issues created by its past. The crisis facing specifically public transportation in South Africa is well known and well documented (Mashiri, Moeketsi & Baloyi 2013). According to Oxford (2013) 'South Africa is a country in desperate need of a viable and sustainable public transport network'. The legacy of Apartheid is evident in the lack of basic public transport infrastructure if it is considered that approximately 15 million commuters per day (or 60% – 70% of the public and workforce) are transported via minibus taxis. Zharare, in Media Update (2011), postulates that the average commuter spends at least 3 hours per day commuting to and from work.

The South African Government has identified various initiatives to elevate the current issues in public transport and intermodal transportation linkage. The various initiatives are captured in the National Transport Master Plan 2050, also known as Natmap 2050. The Natmap 2050 guiding document focuses on the long-term governmental vision of an integrated transport network with various modes of transport complementing each other to create growth within the South African economy.

South African transport industry's regulatory composition

The South African Constitution governs the role allocation and responsibilities of the various levels of government regarding air, road, traffic management and public sector transportation. Most of the responsibility and implementation of mandates with regards to public transport resides within public entities that are overseen by the Department of Transport (DoT) on a national Governmental level.

The South African DoT's strategic goals are to (South African Government n.d.):

- ensure an efficient and integrated infrastructure network that serves as a catalyst for social and economic development
- ensure a transport sector that is safe and secure
- improve rural access, infrastructure and mobility
- improve public transport systems
- increase the contribution of the transport sector to job creation
- increase the contribution of the transport sector to environmental protection.

On a national level, the 12 entities that report to the Minister of Transport includes Airports Company of South Africa (ACSA),

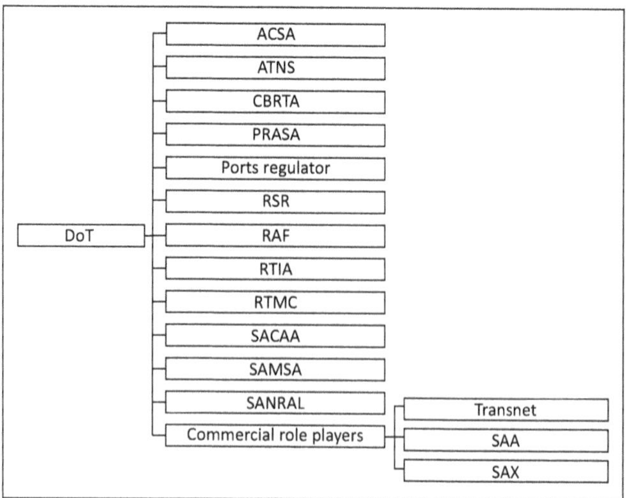

ACSA, Airports Company of South Africa; ATNS, Air Traffic and Navigation Services; CBRTA, Cross Border Road Transport Agency; PRASA, Passenger Rail Agency of South Africa; RSR, Ports Regulator, Rail Safety Regulator; RAF, Road Accident Fund; RTIA, Road Traffic Infringement Agency; RTMC, Road Traffic Management Corporation; SACAA, South African Civil Aviation Authority; SAMSA, South African Maritime Safety Authority; SANRAL, South African National Road Agency Limited.

FIGURE 3: National public entities reporting to the Department of Transport.

Air Traffic and Navigation Services (ATNS), Cross Border Road Transport Agency (CBRTA), Passenger Rail Agency of South Africa (Prasa), Ports Regulator, Rail Safety Regulator (RSR), Road Accident Fund (RAF), Road Traffic Infringement Agency (RTIA), Road Traffic Management Corporation (RTMC), South African Civil Aviation Authority (SACAA), South African Maritime Safety Authority (SAMSA) and South African National Road Agency Limited (SANRAL). The following commercial entities also report to the DoT: Transnet, South African Airways (SAA) and South African Express (SAX).

Figure 3 graphically represents the 12 national public entities that reports to the Minister of the Department of Transport.

For the purpose of this study, it should be noted that the Gautrain project is managed at the provincial level by the Gauteng Provincial Government and the Provincial Government reports at the national level to the DoT.

Gautrain project

The Gauteng Provincial Government in association with local and international stakeholders announced the Gautrain project in 2000. The aim of the project was to build one of the largest and most modern transport networks in Africa. According to Thomas (2011), the Gautrain is the continent's first high-speed rail. Construction on the project started in 2006, with the main stakeholders responsible for the construction being Bombela Consortium, a partnership between Bombardier Transportation, Bouygues Travaux Publics, Murray & Roberts, the Strategic Partners Group and RATP Development, the J&J Group and Absa Bank.

The project consisted of two phases, being constructed simultaneously. The first phase of the project, scheduled to take 45 months, was between the O.R. Tambo International Airport, Sandton and Midrand in Gauteng. Phase two of the project, scheduled to be completed within 54 months, focused on the remainder of the network.

Although the project was scheduled to be completed by 2011, the first public passenger trip was made in February 2009 on a 3-km part of the route. The first section of phase one of the project was opened for public use on the 8th of June 2010 with the remainder of the route completed by mid-2012. To date, the entire 80-km route consists of 10 operational stations in Gauteng. These stations include the following:

- Hatfield
- Pretoria
- Centurion
- Midrand
- Marlboro
- Sandton
- Rosebank
- Park Station
- Rhodesfield
- O.R. Tambo International Airport.

According to Venter (2013), the Gautrain Management Agency (GMA) projected that the Gautrain should move 100 000 people on the network per day by 2016. Recent statistics indicate that the Gautrain has to date transported 50 million passengers at an average of 1.4 million commuters per month, equating to 45 161 commuters per day (Maqutu 2016). If the aforementioned statistic is taken into consideration, the Gautrain is yet to meet its objective of transporting 100 000 commuters per day.

Although various factors may be attributed to the aforesaid, Mashiri et al. (2013) is of the opinion that technology adoption coupled with information dissemination to customers is critical for the successful operation of public transport services and in maintaining and stimulating demand for these public transport services.

Mobile applications

The rapid development of mobile phones and devices over the last decade has resulted in devices and the operating systems of these devices becoming more sophisticated, resulting in an increase in the variety of mobile applications designed for the mobile smart devices. Harris, Brookshire and Chin (2016:441) note that 'as of May 2015, Google's Google Play Market contained 1.5 million apps and Apple's App Market contained 1.4 million'.

Hoehle and Venkatesh (2015:435) state that in most developed countries, smart phone penetration rates have reached more than 100% per capita, with individuals in general owning more than one device. As smartphone penetration reaches almost 40% in South Africa (Litha Communications 2016), more and more South African consumers are downloading mobile applications to interact and engage with information on a daily basis. The aforementioned is based on the fact that according to IT News Africa (2015) the South African consumers download most of the applications available in the app stores. Kim, Wang and Malthouse (2015) argue, 'with the explosive growth of mobile technologies and app culture, customers' expectations of a useful and enjoyable mobile experience will become the norm'.

Per definition, an application may refer to software applications that have been designed to run on smaller electronic and wireless devices such as smartphones and tablets, the mobile applications may be preloaded on the mobile device or be installed from the respective application stores using the Internet. It should be noted that mobile applications serve to provide users of mobile technology with similar services to those accessed on a personal computer (PC), but with limited functionality (Technopedia n.d.). According to Morrison (2015), there are three types of mobile applications and these types of applications include:

- Native application is an application specifically created for the operating system of the mobile device.
- Web-based is an application that allows the users access to a mobile version of a functioning website.
- Hybrid application may be defined in terms of a combination of the native and hybrid forms of applications.

Recent developments within the mobile application environment allow for the incorporation of the mobile devices features into the application, examples of these application include the incorporation of the camera feature of the phone to capture and share images via application such as WhatsApp.

According to the World Economic Forum (2016), 'many smartphone users have apps for every potential task (e.g. communication, banking, fitness tracking, catching-up on news)'. Because of the diverse nature of the types of applications and their related tasks, Nickerson et al. (2007) proposes taxonomy of mobile applications to assist in the classification thereof. The taxonomy identifies the following categories of mobile applications:

- purchasing location-based contents
- mobile inventory management for a company
- product location and tracking for individuals
- mobile auctions
- mobile games
- mobile financial services
- mobile advertisement
- mobile entertainment services
- mobile personal services
- mobile distance education
- mobile product recommendation systems
- wireless patient monitoring
- mobile telemedicine.

The focus of this study relates to the use of a mobile personal service application, and more specifically the use of the Gautrain Buddy application. Nickerson et al. (2007) define a mobile personal service application

> as asynchronous, interactional, transactional (depends on what people are looking for), public, individual, non-location-based (but if the user wants to be alerted every time a potential products or service that comes within a certain distance of the current location, it will become a location-based service), non-identity-based (at least in the beginning due to privacy concerns).

Gautrain Buddy Application

The Gautrain Buddy application is an independent application created in 2013 by Theo de Bruin, aiming to improve on the Gautrain information dissemination. In 2014, the application won the MTN application of the year award. The Gautrain Buddy application displays the Gautrain timetable data on a mobile phone; it also provides notifications for scheduled trains and a fare calculator. Further features of the application include:

- seamless automatic selection of timetable(s) according to the day of week
- train and bus trips can be saved for easy access
- arrival notifications can be added
- automatic scrolling to the next trip
- the ability to view real time updates.

It important to note that this application is not affiliated to the Gauteng Provincial Government, Gauteng Management Agency, Bombela Concession Company or the Bombela Operating Company.

Methodology and research design

Mouton (2001:46) is of the opinion that 'all empirical (social) research conforms to a standard logic'. Saunders, Lewis and Thornhill (2012) concur with the aforementioned statement and postulate a high-level logical layout of the research process in the form of a 'research onion'. The research onion provides a framework of various layers of activities and choices that need to be discussed and answered before moving onto the next level or layer of research.

As represented in Figure 4, research philosophy (Saunders et al. 2012) is the first layer or activity to be considered within the research onion. The research philosophy explains the advancement of knowledge and how the research process will contribute towards the body of knowledge within a specific field of study. The importance of the research philosophy should not be underestimated for the theory identified within the research philosophy will govern the design of the research project. Saunders et al. (2012) propose that the main philosophical assumptions include:

- positivism
- realism
- interpretivism
- pragmatism.

Carnaghan (2013) concurs and adds post-positivism, social constructivism, post-modernism, feminist theories and critical theory to the list of basic philosophical assumptions.

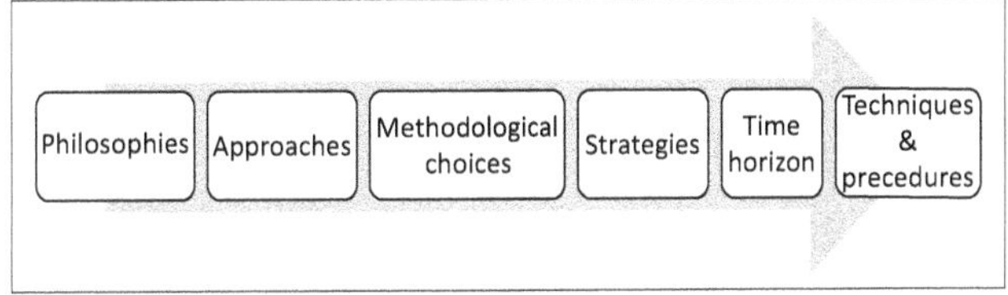

Source: Adapted from: Saunders, M., Lewis, P. & Thronhill, A., 2012, *Research methods for business students*, Pearson Education Limited, Oxford.

FIGURE 4: The research onion.

The design of the research project is portrayed in terms of the research approach that the researcher will follow. Three distinct approaches can be identified, including:

- Deductive approach is one where the researcher starts with a specific theory and designs a research strategy to test the theory.
- Inductive approach is one where the researcher starts by collecting data to explore a phenomenon and generate or build a theory (often in the form of a conceptual framework) based on the data.
- Abductive approach is one where the researcher collects data to explore a phenomenon, identify themes and explain patterns, to generate a new theory or to modify an existing theory, which is subsequently tested through additional data collection.

Following the research approach, the researcher needs to discuss the general plan on how to go about answering the research question(s). The first concept that needs to be addressed is that of quantitative (number-based research) versus qualitative (explanatory-based research) research methodology, thus defining the methodological stance of the study.

The methodological choice will inform and dictate the research strategy. The research strategy focuses on how the researcher will collect data and information to answer the research question(s). Various examples of research strategies may be identified, including but not limited to experiments, surveys, case studies and action research. An important last consideration that the research needs to take into account is the time frame of the study, that is, will it be a snapshot or multiple snapshots over a period of time. A snapshot may also be referred to as a cross-sectional study and multiple snapshots are referred to as a longitudinal study.

For the purpose of this study, the researchers adopted a positivist stance with regards to the philosophical choice of the study. The philosophical stance is based on the fact that the researchers collected data on an observable reality and searched for relationships in the data (Saunders et al. 2012:134). Based on the philosophical stance adopted by the researchers, the research approach is deductive in nature. The TAM theory is used as a departure point in understanding the perceived usefulness and ultimate use of a mobile application in the South African transport industry. The use of a deductive approach also allows for replication of the study. The research design may be defined as the general plan that the researchers will follow to answer the research question. This exploratory research applied a mixed method research design, utilising a survey strategy comprising both closed and open-ended questions in the data collection activity. The study focused on snapshot (i.e. a cross-sectional study) of how commuters perceive the usefulness of a mobile application within the South African transport industry. The total population of commuters utilising the Gautrain on a daily basis is in the range of 45 000. A convenience sample of a hundred Gautrain commuters was selected in an effort to understand the use and perceived usefulness of a mobile application in the South African public transport domain. The sample was given the questionnaire to complete at the Park Station in Johannesburg.

Limitations of the study

The study is based on the initial TAM model; it should be noted that the literature review indicated that the initial TAM model does not consider external factors that may influence individuals' beliefs with regards to ease of use and the perceived usefulness of the technology or application under investigation. Only one mobile application (the Gautrain Buddy application) was considered for the study. Due to time constraints, the study only focused on a convenience sample of a hundred commuters of the Gautrain, and it is suggested that future research incorporate a larger sample of commuters.

Results

Based on descriptive statistics, the results of the questionnaire indicated that 71% of the respondents utilise the Gautrain Buddy application. Of the 29% of respondents not using the application, more than half of them indicated that they did not know about the specific application.

The next question posed to the respondents ascertained the frequency of use of the Gautrain. The researchers divided the commuters into either frequent commuters or ad hoc commuters. The frequent commuters had to make use of the Gautrain more than once a week, with the ad hoc users only making use of the Gautrain at least once a month. Out of the population utilising the application, 78% of the commuters were frequent commuters while 22% were ad hoc commuters of the Gautrain (Figure 5).

When questioned what type of features are used most frequently, all of the respondents (i.e. regular and ad hoc users of the application) indicated that the ability to track the Gautrain bus service or schedule was the most frequently used feature. In contrast, only 67% of the application users indicated that they used the application to check the train schedule. The fare calculator was only used by 18% of the application users; this may be attributed to the fact that there is not a lot of fluctuation in terms of the set route rates. The Gautrain Buddy application notifies its users of any changes in terms of train and bus schedules as well as route fares.

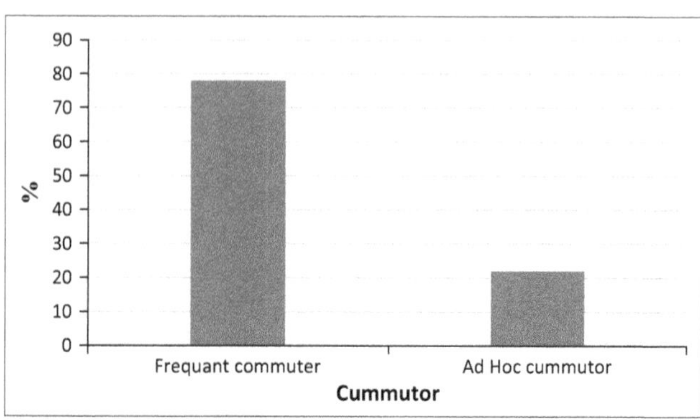

FIGURE 5: Type of commuter.

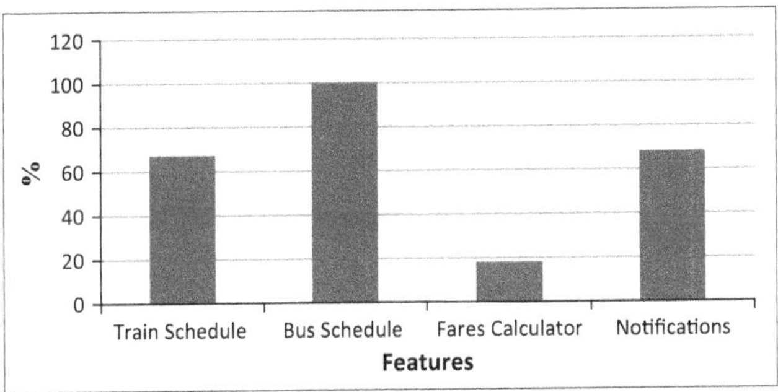

FIGURE 6: Features used.

The notification feature was used by 68% of the respondents (Figure 6).

Based on the original TAM model as postulated by Davis et al. (1989), perceived usefulness may be defined in terms of the following dimensions:

- allows for work to be completed quickly
- improves activity performance
- increases productivity
- enhances effectiveness
- makes it easier to perform activity
- is useful.

In terms of the perceived usefulness of the Gautrain Buddy application, 69% of the respondents indicated that the application is useful, with one of the respondents stating that

> 'The app tell me when the next train is leaving and where I can find the GauBus, this is information that matters to us as commuter because in order to be able to make timely decision, you need information like this as a commuter.' [Male, Student]

It should be noted that 31% of the users of the Gautrain Buddy application indicated little or no use for the application when commuting via the Gautrain. One of the respondents indicated that:

> 'it really is not effective for me, the other day the train tracker showed me that the train was still coming and still very far, only to find out that the bus has left 5 minutes ago, the app is not real time, making it not to be effective for me.' [Female, Age 23]

Focusing on the respondents that indicating that the application was useful, the researchers posed a follow-up question relating to the use of the application in planning routes and use app of travel (Figure 7).

It is evident from Figure 8 that 78% of the respondents indicated that the Gautrain Buddy application was used on a frequent basis to plan for trips and to manage the related times of departure and arrivals.

Figure 9 represents the results of the perceived ease of use of the Gautrain Buddy application. The respondents were presented with the following questions regarding the ease of use of the application:

- Was the application easy to learn?
- Was the application controllable?

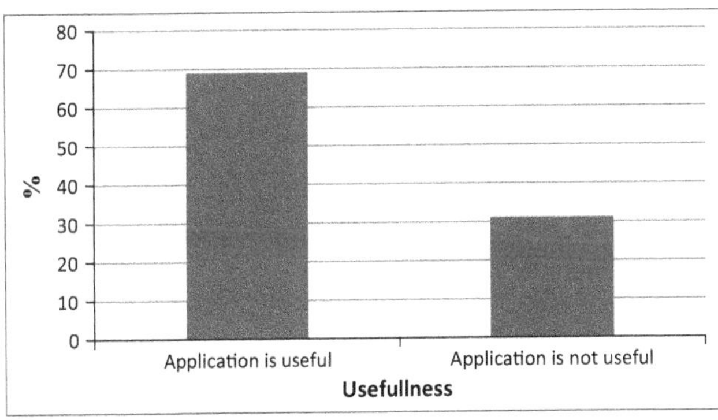

FIGURE 7: Perceived usefulness of the application.

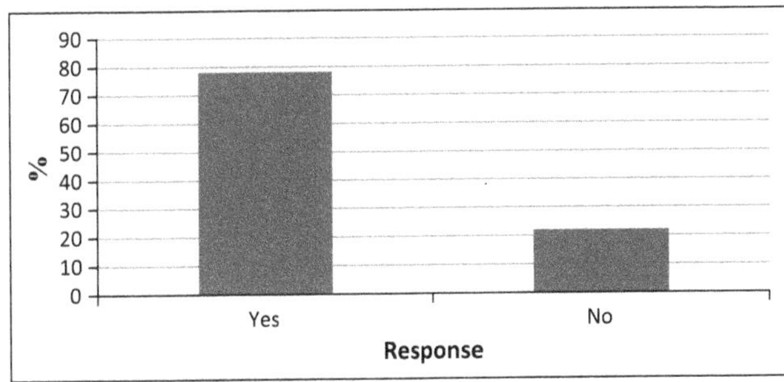

FIGURE 8: Use of the application for planning travel routes and times.

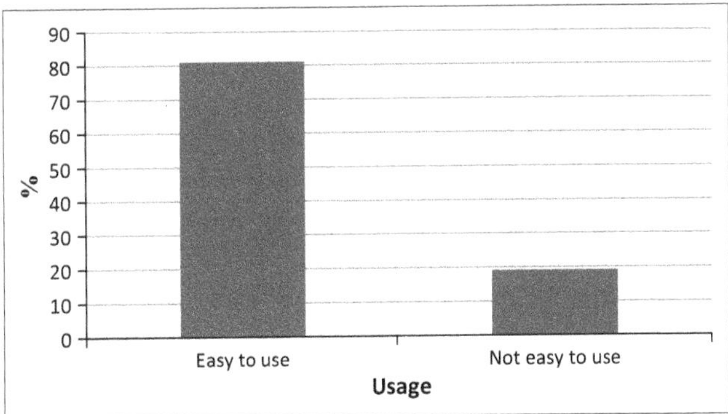

FIGURE 9: Perceived ease of use of the application.

- Was the interaction with the application clear and understandable?
- Was the application is flexible to interact with?
- Was it easy to become skilful?
- Was it easy to use?

Eighty one per cent of the respondents had a positive stance towards the perceived ease of use of the application. It should be noted that 19% of the respondents indicated that the application based on the questions posed was not easy to use.

Considering the results (the main research question, i.e., 'Does the use of mobile applications assist in information dissemination within the public transport industry in Gauteng, South Africa?'), the commuters opined that the mobile application did not facilitate the dissemination of information to a large extent. Furthermore, the respondents also indicated that the Gautrain Buddy application was easy to use based on the criteria as discussed in the TAM model. The respondents also indicated that the application was useful in assisting with the planning of trips and in the use of the Gautrain.

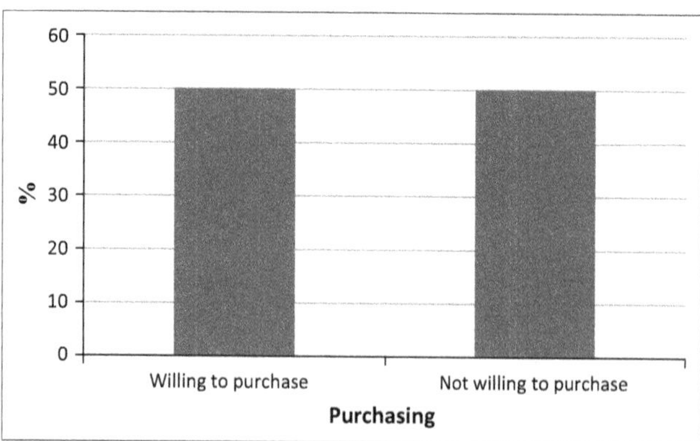

FIGURE 10: Willingness to purchase an application providing functionalities.

An interesting observation was made when the last question was posed to the respondents, that is, 'Are the respondents willing to purchase an application that offers the commuters similar functionalities?, As indicated in Figure 10, 50% of the respondents were willing to purchase the application or an application with similar features, whereas 50% of the respondents were not willing to purchase the application or an application with similar features.

Conclusion

Based on the fact that the transport industry may be regarded as early adopters of technology, this study focused on the use the Gautrain Buddy application in the dissemination of information on related Gautrain-specific information. The research findings suggest that commuters utilising the Gautrain Buddy application perceive the application as being useful in the dissemination of information. Furthermore, the research finding also suggests a positive relationship in terms of the perceived ease of use of mobile application in the dissemination of information in the public transport industry.

Acknowledgements

Competing interests

The authors declare that they have no financial or personal relationship(s) that may have inappropriately influenced them in writing this article.

Authors' contributions

C.J.P.N. was responsible for 80% and the writing of article and results. H.C. was responsible for the remaining 20%, the initial research and collecting data.

References

Agherdien, N., 2007, 'A review of theoretical frameworks in Educational Information and Communication Technology Research at leading South African Universities', Masters' dissertation, University of Johannesburg.

Carnaghan, I., 2013, *Philosophical assumptions for qualitative research*, viewed 30 January 2015, from https://www.carnaghan.com/2013/03/philosophical-assumptions-for-qualitative-research/

Challenger, 2015, *Through technology, the industry is changing*, viewed 12 January 2015, from https://www.challenger.com/changing-technology-in-trucking/

Cusanelli, M., 2014, *Survey: Early tech adopters have competitive advantage*, viewed 30 January 2015, from http://thevarguy.com/virtualization-applications-and-technologies/092214/survey-early-tech-adopters-have-competitive-advantage

Davis, F.D., Bagozzi, R.P. & Warshaw, P.R., 1989, 'User acceptance of computer technology: A comparison of two theoretical models', *Management Science* 35(8), 982–1003. https://doi.org/10.1287/mnsc.35.8.982

Fădor, A.G., 2014, 'Innovation and technology acceptance model (TAM): A theoretical approach', *Romanian Journal of Marketing* 2, 59–65.

Flick, U., 1998, *An introduction to qualitative research*, Sage, London.

Gorard, S., 2004, 'Sceptical or clerical? Theory as a barrier to the combination of research methods', *Journal of Educational Enquiry* 5(1), viewed 28 January 2016, from http://www.literacy.unisa.edu.au/jee/Papers/JEEVol5No1/Paper%201.pdf

Harris, M.A., Brookshire, R. & Chin, A.G., 2016, 'Identifying factors influencing consumers' intent to install mobile applications', *International Journal of Information Management* 36, 441–450. https://doi.org/10.1016/j.ijinfomgt.2016.02.004

Harvard Business Review Analytic Services, n.d., *The digital dividend-first mover advantage*, viewed 28 March 2015, from http://www.verizonenterprise.com/resources/insights/hbr/

Hoehle, H. & Venkatesh, V., 2015, 'Mobile application usability: Conceptualization and instrument development', *MIS Quarterly* 39(2), 435–472.

IT News Africa, 2015, *Study reveals African mobile phone usage stats*, viewed 02 January 2015, from http://www.itnewsafrica.com/2015/04/study-reveals-african-mobile-phone-usage-stats/

Kim, S.J., Wang, R.J.H. & Malthouse, E.C., 2015, 'The effects of adopting and using a brand's mobile application on customers' subsequent purchase behavior', *Journal of Interactive Marketing* 31, 28–41. https://doi.org/10.1016/j.intmar.2015.05.004

Lala, G., 2014, *The emergence and development of the technology acceptance model (TAM)*, viewed 28 January 2015, from http://0-web.b.ebscohost.com.ujlink.uj.ac.za/

Lee, Y., Kozar, K.A. & Larsen, K.R., 2003, 'The technology acceptance model: Past, present, and future', *Communications of the Association for Information Systems* 12(1), 752–780.

Litha Communications, 2016, *Technology pushes events into experience*, viewed 28 January 2016, from http://www.bizcommunity.com/Article/196/40/139697.html

Mashiri, M.A.M., Moeketsi, P.N. & Baloyi, V., 2013, *Increasing public transport market share in South Africa: The options*, viewed 28 January 2016, from http://www.thredbo-conference-series.org/downloads/thredbo6_papers/Thredbo6-theme4-Mashiri-Moeketsi-Baloyi.pdf

Maqutu, A., 2016, *Popularity of Gautrain likely to result in falling subsidies*, viewed 28 February 2016, from http://www.bdlive.co.za/business/transport/2016/01/15/popularity-of-gautrain-likely-to-result-in-falling-subsidies

Media Update, 2011, *ComutaNet's Rejoice Zharare looks at commuters and media consumption*, viewed 28 January 2015, from http://www.mediaupdate.co.za/marketing/40910/comutanets-rejoice-zharare-looks-at-commuters-and-media-consumption

Morrison, J., 2015, *What is a mobile app?*, viewed 28 January 2015, from http://blog.deepbluesky.com/blog/-/what-is-a-mobile-app_161/

Mouton, J., 2001, *How to succeed in your master's and doctoral studies: A South African guide and resource book*, Van Schaik, Johannesburg.

Nicholas, D., Dobrowolski, T., Withey, R., Russell, C., Huntington, P. & Williams, P., 2003, 'Digital information consumers, players and purchasers: Information seeking behaviour in the new digital interactive environment', *Aslib Proceedings: New Information Perspectives* 55(1/2), 23–31. https://doi.org/10.1108/00012530310462689

Nickerson, R., Varshney, U., Muntermann, J. & Isaac, H., 2007, *Towards a taxonomy of mobile applications*, viewed 20 January 2010, from https://courses.cs.washington.edu/courses/csep590b/11wi/readings/taxonomy.pdf

Niemand, C.J.P. & Chauke, H., 2016, 'An exploratory study of the use of mobile application by public transport commuters in Gauteng', 7th Biennial Conference of the Academy of World Business, Marketing and Management Development, Cracow.

Oxford, T., 2013, *The state of SA's public transport*, viewed 28 January 2016, from http://mg.co.za/article/2013-10-04-00-the-state-of-sas-public-transport

Pettigrew, K.E. & McKechnie, L., 2001, 'The use of theory in information science research', *Journal of the American Society for Information Science and Technology* 52(1), 62–73. https://doi.org/10.1002/1532-2890(2000)52:1<62::AID-ASI1061>3.0.CO;2-J

Prensky, M., 2001, *Digital native, digital immigrants*, viewed 28 January 2016, from http://pre2005.flexiblelearning.net.au/projects/resources/Digital_Natives_Digital_Immigrants.pdf

PwC, n.d., *Africa gearing up. Future prospects in Africa for the transportation & logistics industry*, viewed 28 January 2016, from https://www.pwc.co.za/en/assets/pdf/africa-gearing-up.pdf

Radomir, L. & Nistor, V.C., 2013, 'An application of technology acceptance model to Internet Banking services', International Conference 'Marketing – From information to decision' 6th Edition 2013, viewed 28 January 2016, from http://0-web.b.ebscohost.com.ujlink.uj.ac.za/

Robinson, A., 2015, *Mobile technology in transportation management & the future impact on the supply chain*, viewed 28 January 2015, from http://cerasis.com/2015/02/04/mobile-technology-in-transportation-management/

Saunders, M., Lewis, P. & Thronhill, A., 2012, *Research methods for business students*, Pearson Education Limited, Oxford.

Spink, A., 2004, 'Multitasking information behaviour and information task switching: An exploratory study', *Journal of Documentation* 60(4), 336–351. https://doi.org/10.1108/00220410410548126

South African Government, n.d., *Transport*, viewed 28 January 2016, from http://www.gov.za/about-sa/transport

Technopedia, n.d., *Mobile applications*, viewed 28 January 2016, from https://www.techopedia.com/definition/2953/mobile-application-mobile-app

Thomas, D.P., 2011, *The Gautrain project in South Africa: A cautionary tale*, viewed 28 January 2016, from http://www.tandfonline.com/doi/abs/10.1080/02589001.2013.747292?journalCode=cjca20

Venter, I., 2013, *Gautrain passenger numbers tick up, but below initial estimates*, viewed 28 January 2016, from http://www.engineeringnews.co.za/article/gautrain-2013-01

Wentzel, J.P., Diatha, K.S. & Yadavalli, V.S.S., 2013, 'An application of the extended Technology Acceptance Model in understanding technology-enabled financial service adoption in South Africa', *Development Southern Africa* 30(4–5), 659–673. https://doi.org/10.1080/0376835X.2013.830963

World Economic Forum, 2016, *The impact of digital content: Opportunities and risks of creating and sharing information online*, viewed 28 January 2015, from http://www3.weforum.org/docs/GAC16/Social_Media_Impact_Digital.pdf

13

Mobile banking in South Africa: A review and directions for future research

Authors:
Joel M. Chigada[1]
Benedikt Hirschfelder[1]

Affiliations:
[1]School of Management Studies, University of Cape Town, South Africa

Corresponding author:
Joel Chigada,
joel.chigada@uct.ac.za

Background: The purpose of this study was to review existing research on mobile banking diffusion and investigate the adoption of mobile banking in sub-Saharan Africa (SSA).

Objectives: Based on the failure of the M-Pesa in South Africa, this article also attempted to determine why mobile money service systems are difficult to apply transnationally.

Method: This was a literature survey, analysing mobile money literature during the period 2006–2016. Because of the current explosiveness of mobile money in SSA, the focus of this literature survey was limited geographically to South Africa, Zimbabwe and Kenya.

Results: The results of the literature survey and the real-world examples mainly show that a transnational application of mobile money service systems is difficult to implement.

Conclusion: This research elucidates the demand and need for mobile money service systems in SSA while underlining the explosiveness promoted mainly by rapid technological progress.

Introduction

Web 2.0 educed a widely recognised sales channel in Business-to-Consumer and business-to-business. Because of the consequently connected online payment system, the banking industry adopted and integrated online transactions into their daily business, and online banking has become a popular alternative to traditional banking (Akhter 2015; Barbesino, Camerani & Gaudino 2005; Laukkanen & Pasanen 2008). A relatively new trend, mobile banking, developed worldwide with mobile phone mobilisation. Mobile banking is defined as any mobile interaction with a money-managing institute, not necessarily a bank, which allows customers to deposit, send and withdraw money (Laukkanen & Pasanen 2008; Tobbin 2012). The Online Dictionary (2017) defines *online banking* as any banking transaction conducted over the Internet through a financial institution's website under a client's private profile. Common electronic devices used are mobile phones, smartphones and tablets. Mobile banking is a subset of Internet banking and a portable extension of it, increasing flexibility for customers and improving the services of a bank (Aker & Mbiti 2010).

With regard to research in the mobile banking field in Africa, the following key points were taken into consideration. In urban areas, the density of smartphone distribution is relatively high in comparison to rural areas where the lack of connectivity options impedes the distribution (Poushter & Oates 2015). Because of this, Africa's mobile Internet penetration is relatively low in relation to the rest of the world (Internetlivestats 2016). According to the Internet Society (2015), subdividing Africa into sub-Saharan Africa (SSA) and the Middle East and North Africa demonstrates that particularly in SSA, the penetration rate is comparatively low (Table 1).

Besides the locational circumstances, the affordability of mobile phones or telecommunication devices (smartphones or tablets) must also be considered (Brown 2014). Finally, the necessity of a bank account plays a significant role in mobile banking, particularly in the low-income class (Tobbin 2012). With regard to the points above, South African marketing practitioners have recognised this low-income banking problem and concentrated on money transfers without affiliation to a bank (Shoprite 2016) and money transfers via mobile communication companies, which assume the functions of a bank (Abbott 2015; Tobbin 2012).

Although these opportunities provide alternatives for the unbanked population, rapid technological progress predicts a promising future for mobile banking. Indeed, it has been reported that:

> The technological service access methods have already bypassed the traditional branch-based retail banking and as a consequence technology has become an increasingly essential element in the competing markets of financial services. (Laukkanen & Pasanen 2008:87)

TABLE 1: African mobile Internet penetration.

Variable	Sub-Saharan Africa (%)	Middle East and North Africa (%)
Internet users	17	39
Mobile Internet penetration	8	23
3G population coverage	35	72

Source: Internet Society, 2015, *Global internet report 2015*, viewed 25 April 2017, from http://www.internetsociety.org/globalinternetreport/#main-content

After eight years, are these insights applicable to Africa, considering the slower technological penetration? In this article, the researchers explored the following research questions concerning the literature on the implementation and adoption of mobile money in SSA, specifically in South Africa:

- Why do alternatives such as the Kenyan mobile money service provider, M-PESA, have such a large clientele?
- Which factors are crucial in the adoption of mobile money transfer systems/mobile banking?
- How do South Africans, particularly in the lower-income segment, operate with their money?

This research addressed these and related questions in its review of low-income mobile banking perspectives in SSA and elucidate the mobile banking situation in South Africa.

Research methodology and design

A systematic literature review approach was conducted where empirical data were collected through desktop research; thus, researchers were concerned about collecting data for the 2006–2016 time frame. In addition, systematic literature review allowed the researchers to formulate research questions, set inclusion/exclusion criterion and infused meta-analysis to analyse, synthesise and disseminate the findings. For this research, data were collected, analysed and interpreted using a quantitative research methodology. Data were collected from existing literature for the period 2006–2016. The researchers analysed quantitative findings from other studies in order to understand the concept of mobile banking discussed in the current study. Several studies on mobile banking in SSA were included in this study; thus, meta-analysis was infused in the study for standardised statistical procedures (see Table 2: Meta-analysis of findings). In this research, the researchers adopted a causal-comparative and descriptive research design to reveal cause and effect relationships between variables in mobile banking (van Wyk 2012). The causal-comparative and descriptive research designs helped to address the 'why' and 'how' type of research questions that informed this study. The objective was to unravel reasons why there was a slow uptake of mobile banking in SSA. However, the study also revealed that there were SSA economies that had successfully implemented these mobile money systems. The only exception was the South African project on the implementation of M-PESA which failed.

South African context of mobile banking

According to Koech (2012), in SSA, many countries exhibit a higher subscription to mobile phones than bank accounts. In

TABLE 2: Mobile phone diffusion in Africa 2014.

Country	Own a mobile phone (%)	Make or receive mobile payment (%)
Zimbabwe	93	47
Nigeria	89	15
Senegal	84	30
Ghana	83	15
Kenya	82	61
Tanzania	73	39
Uganda	65	42

Source: Based on: Gambanga, N., 2016b, *Latest POTRAZ report shows leaps in* LTE & increase in Zimbabwe's internet penetration, viewed 1 March 2017, from http://www.techzim.co.zw/2016/01/latest-potraz-report-shows-increase-in-zimbabwes-internet-penetration/; Gambanga, N., 2016c, Mobile money subscribers in Zimbabwe increase by 7.1%, viewed 1 March 2017, from http://www.techzim.co.zw/2016/01/mobile-money-subscribers-zimbabwe-increase-7-1/; Poushter, J. & Oates, R., 2015, 'Cell phones in Africa: Communication lifeline texting most common activity, but mobile money popular in several countries', viewed 22 April 2016, from http://www.pewglobal.org/2015/04/15/cell-phones-in-africa-communication-lifeline/

this context, the World Bank forecast a bright future for mobile banking as a new era of financial services, particularly in developing countries. South Africa exhibits a relatively high percentage of households with bank accounts (51% – 80%); thus, this high rate of bank account holders works against any ideas to transform the traditional banking services into mobile money. South Africa has a high mobile phone ownership (89%) and, consequently, matured mobile money services. Thus, South Africa symbolises a suitable research field (Abbott 2015; Koech 2012; Poushter & Oates 2015). Mobile banking in South Africa serves as an important interface between banks and the lower-income population by providing useful transfer, saving and investment opportunities.

The researchers suggest that mobile banking in South Africa serves the following key functions: integration into a bank system, simplification of banking, enhancement of financial opportunities and improved control of money operations. The following sections of this article review these functions and elucidate focal points. Thereafter, two real-world applications illustrate the actual state of mobile money and, finally, limitations and suggestions for future research are discussed.

Integration into mainstream banking systems

Banking has been in existence for thousands of years (Vaupel & Kaul 2016). Banks operate mainly as service providers, for example, for cash businesses and in-bank lending and have numerous functions such as monetary functions (payment transactions), investment functions (securities) and economic functions (Vaupel & Kaul 2016). The acceptance of deposits and other objects of value as well as lending are classical functions of a bank. Whereas the theory of John Maynard Keynes underlines the importance of the value stability of currencies (Mankiw 2015), the theory of Milton Friedman, mainly associated with monetarism, underlines the importance of price stability that is regulated by the government to control the amount of money in circulation (Mankiw 2015). Monetarism assumes that the combination of the government and the central bank and the accomplished money supply/control influence the gross domestic product. Therefore, banks play an important role regarding economic growth and control (Mankiw 2015).

In the period 2002–2008, South Africa as the second largest economy in Africa experienced its fastest expansion since the establishment of democracy in 1994 with an average growth rate of 4.5% (Ferreira 2016). However, this growth is declining because of the increasing gap between the rich and poor, low-skilled labour forces, the high unemployment rate, deteriorating infrastructure and the high corruption and crime rates (Ferreira 2016). The lower-income class in particular is becoming progressively appealing to banks because of: (1) growing market power, (2) growing political power, and (3) technological progress (Inglesi-Lotz, Van Eyden & Du Toit 2014; Moloi 2014; Visagie 2013). In the following sections, the researchers review each key point and elucidate how together they precipitate integration into the South African bank system.

Growing market power of the lower-income class

The growing market power of the lower-income class in South Africa is first defined. According to Visagie (2013) middle-class households (an average of four people) in South Africa have a total income of R5600 to R40 000 per month after direct income tax. Every household that has an income of less than R5600 falls into the lower-income class category. A report by BusinessTech (2016) states that 70% of the South African population earns less than R6000 per month, and thus, they fall into the lower-income class category. With regard to such a collective buying power but single buying weakness, savings accounts are rare because of the meagre lifestyle. Particularly in the lower-income class, saving schemes called stokvel[1] are more popular than traditional saving systems (UCC 2016). South African banks recognise this trend by offering tailored banking applications in order to integrate this income class.

Growing political power of the lower-income class

South Africa is a democratic country in which the political landscape is characterised by different political parties. Prior to the country's attainment of independence in 1994, the lower-income members of society were voiceless because of the oppressive apartheid regime laws (Moloi 2014). There has been a great paradigm shift in the political dispensation of the country, and previously disadvantaged members of society now wield considerable political power and have the capability to resent, resist or reject policies that infringe their rights. The dynamics in the political landscape have culminated in a number of policy reforms in the country, an indication that civil society is concerned about their well-being. Unfortunately, political change does not culminate in economic power or wealth.

Technological progress – Mobile phone or smartphone diffusion

South Africa is among the strongest economies in Africa, and Inglesi-Lotz et al. (2014) underline the importance of technological progress in the economic growth of the country. Accordingly, it is not surprising that in 2014, the mobile phone diffusion rate of 89% (of which 34% are smartphones) in South Africa was the highest in Africa (Poushter & Oates 2015). Mobile broadband subscription in particular has experienced notable growth in Africa (Screen Africa 2014). With regard to the population in South Africa, only 16.4% in metropolitan areas, 9.2% in urban areas and 2% in rural areas have Internet access at home. However, because of the progressive improvement of mobile technology, 30.8% of all households in South Africa, with 17.9% of rural households, go online using mobile devices (Statistics South Africa 2014). Furthermore, 84% of South African Internet users access the World Wide Web via mobile technology. This demonstrates the well-engineered South African mobile technological progress and the pervasiveness of mobile and smartphones (including tablets with mobile Internet access) being the most commonly used devices for Internet access.

The price of prepaid data bundles is rapidly falling because of the competitiveness in the market. In addition, smartphones are becoming progressively cheaper, which also contributes to an increase in data usage (Euromonitor 2015). Seventy-eight percent of South African Facebook users, for example, access this social media platform from their mobile and smartphones. Regarding the social network and micro-blogging service Twitter, 85% of people access this social media platform from their mobile phones (Bluemagnet 2014). South African companies are increasingly integrating social media marketing into their promotional mix and extending their social media budget, particularly for online content marketing and multimedia content (Poushter & Oates 2015). One such South African industry that is progressively making use of the online service and application is the banking sector (Maduku 2014). Because of the aim of reducing the expenses that customers incur by visiting branch offices and the decrease in cost of mobile phone technology, Internet banking has become a popular alternative to traditional banking in South Africa (Karjaluoto, Mattila & Pento 2002; Maduku 2014).

Simplification of banking

Considering the technological progress concerning mobile banking, mobile phones and smartphones as relatively young service communication channels offer potential in banking (Abbott 2015; Akturan & Tezcan 2012; Laukkanen & Lauronen 2005). According to Laukkanen and Pasanen (2008) and Akturan and Tezcan (2012), the main reasons for mobile banking adoption are convenience, access to banking services at any time of the day or night and minimisation of effort, time and consultation costs. Considering these facts, we acknowledge that South African mobile banking: (1) improves banking skills, (2) simplifies bank account maintenance, and (3) simplifies money transfers.

South African banks enable local citizens as well as foreigners to open bank accounts. To do this, South Africans must provide proof of income, address and identity; the most important criteria for a foreigner is a valid visa (AnswersAfrica 2013). However, because of the relatively open entry requirements

1. *Stokvel:* a rotating credit union.

(valid passport) and the accomplished tourist visa (90 days), South Africa is at odds with a high number of illegal immigrants who are not leaving the country after their visas have expired (Department of Home Affairs 2016). Many people regard the South African economy as an income-earning opportunity because the economy is classified as developing and highly successful in Africa (KEDO 2013). Thus, the need for money transfer to the home country for family support is high. Knowing the situation and the resulting illegal unbanked people, marketing practitioners recognising this trend offer money transfer systems for the unbanked (FinScope 2014). The method in which mobile banking addresses this system and (1) improves private banking skills, (2) simplifies bank account maintenance, and (3) simplifies money transfers is discussed in the following subsections.

Improvement of banking skills

Because private banking can include complex calculations, a bank account is, in most cases, also accompanied by a private banking consultant (Seidel & Liebetrau 2015). While the service intensity varies based on salary level and the use of services, the philosophy of banks does not differ from the traditional customer concept of 'customer is king' (Seidel & Liebetrau 2015). However, accomplished with the user-friendly interface of Web 2.0, online banking together with the 'do-it-yourself' mentality that is rewarded with no consulting costs has become a popular alternative to traditional face-to-face banking (Khrais 2015; Laforet & Li 2005). Particularly for basic transactions, more and more customers are making use of online banking or mobile banking, which is being rapidly pitched by banks offering online banking websites and mobile banking applications with user-friendly interfaces (Khrais 2015; Raitani & Vyas 2014). On the one hand, banks might reduce the consulting efforts required for basic transactions, and on the other hand, customers will gain more confidence concerning independent banking, therefore, improving their banking skills.

Simplification of bank account maintenance

As is apparent from the previous section, the user-friendly interface encourages people to adopt independent online/mobile banking (Khrais 2015; Raitani & Vyas 2014). The convenience of accessing a bank account at any time in order to track and administer finances might simplify the maintenance of private bank accounts. The most decisive point for the use of online or mobile banking is the time-saving aspect (Abbott 2015). Research concerning the effectiveness of smartphone applications illustrates the sophistication of tablet and smartphone use in life-improving matters (Couse & Chen 2010; Granado-Font et al. 2015). Particularly in South Africa, where 84% of the Internet users access the World Wide Web via mobile technology, online or mobile banking might simplify bank account maintenance.

Simplification of money transfers

In earlier times, bank transactions were connected with much paper work and associated with time-consuming, in-house, drop-off costs. Moreover, the receiving party had to wait at least 1 or 2 days for transactions to be completed. Today, online or mobile banking allows customers to transfer money, including international transactions, within a day (Seidel & Liebetrau 2015). Furthermore, clear, structured interfaces with explanatory images allow people even with little Internet experience, to make a transaction (Abbott 2015). Concerning Internet security, a transaction authentication number (TAN) serving as a one-time password, authorises the transaction. This TAN is mostly generated by a TAN-Generator or sent via a text message to the customer's mobile phone. Theoretically, this means online or mobile banking simplifies money transfers. This might be underlined, for example, by an online banking penetration of 90% in Norway, 85% in the Netherlands and a demonstrated 46% average in the European Union in 2015 (Statista 2015). In South Africa, there are currently four options for customers to access their accounts independently. Access can be via a computer, a tablet, a mobile phone or a smartphone. The five most popular banks in South Africa are ABSA, Capitec, First National Bank, Nedbank and Standard Bank. All provide mobile applications (Columinate 2015).

An upcoming option that simplifies money transfers is low-value, real-time, person-to-person payment, also known as mobile money (Abbott 2015). Real-time payments allow users to send or receive money with their feature phones, smartphones or tablet computers. Successfully adopted by more than 2500 US banks currently, the largest real-time, person-to-person payment network in the western world has been built, where mobile money has become rapidly popular. Particularly successful in introducing financial services to the lower-income class and to the unbanked, mobile money has become a popular banking instrument (Abbott 2015). Mobile money allows cashless consumers to transfer or pay varying amounts by using their mobile devices (Seidel & Liebetrau 2015).

Application of mobile money in sub-Saharan Africa

As a consequence of the relatively high mobile phone density in SSA and the consumer demand that is driven by the need for secure cash transactions and the simplification of banking, mobile money has become rapidly popular (Laukkanen & Pasanen 2008; Poushter & Oates 2015). However, the adoption level differs significantly from country to country.

M-Pesa

An African example for mobile money adoption is the Kenyan SMS-based money transfer system known as M-Pesa, where M stands for *Mobile* and *Pesa* means money in KiSwahili. This system was launched in March 2007 by the telecommunication company Safaricom (Bengelstorff 2015). By using the mobile phone number as a virtual bank account number, M-Pesa allows individuals to deposit, save, send and withdraw money via their mobile phones. Figure 1 illustrates the simplicity of using M-Pesa (Bengelstorff 2015). Particularly for the unbanked, M-Pesa facilitates the exchange of money without physically having to visit a banking

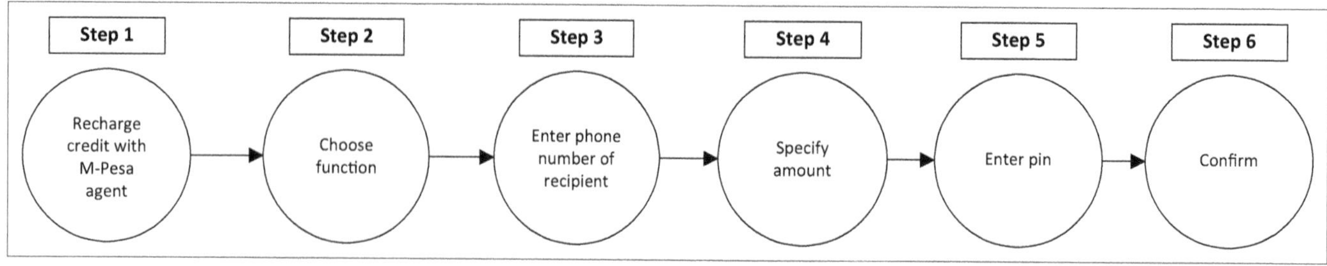

Source: Bengelstorff, A., 2015, *A global success from Kenya*, viewed 8 June 2016, from https://www.credit-suisse.com/us/en/news-and-expertise/banking/articles/news-and-expertise/2015/08/en/a-global-success-from-kenya.html

FIGURE 1: Six payment steps of M-Pesa.

institution. Considering that most of Kenya's population are farmers who live in the countryside and are subjected to long distances to the nearest banking institution, the options to move cash are uncertain and risky. In contrast to methods such as sending cash with a bus driver or sending a postal money order, M-Pesa only requires a mobile phone with a Safaricom number to 'move cash' virtually over long distances, including transnationally. Thus, M-Pesa facilitates the safe storage and transfer of money. Furthermore, a reliable and safe storage mechanism may increase the household savings. In addition, M-Pesa allows families progressive mobility by sending members to high-paying jobs at distant locations. Another economic benefit of M-Pesa is that it increases the security of subscribers, particularly in the poorer segments of the population. For example, M-Pesa allows taxi drivers to deal with less cash, which has been found to be the reason for muggings. These facts might be underpinned by the research of Jack and Suri (2011) who explored the economics of M-Pesa in Kenya. According to their study, safety and ease of operation were the two main factors for adopting M-Pesa. Furthermore, they determined that the main reason for the non-use of M-Pesa was the simple fact of not owning a mobile phone (Jack & Suri 2011).

Regarding mobile phone diffusion in Africa, South Africa and Nigeria are in the pole position. More precisely, 89% of South African and Nigerian adults owned a mobile phone in 2014. This 89% is subdivided into 34% smartphones in South Africa, 27% smartphones in Nigeria and 55% mobile phones in South Africa and 62% mobile phones in Nigeria. Table 2 illustrates the top seven countries' diffusion of mobile phones and the use of mobile phones to perform payment transactions (Poushter & Oates 2015).

Although 89% of South African adults owned mobile phones in 2014, only 15% used them for mobile payments. Whereas users in Kenya exhibited a lower diffusion of mobile phones (82%), but the use of mobile phones for payment transaction was the highest in Africa at 61%. This inconsistency is discussed in the next section by comparing the South African M-Pesa with the Kenyan M-Pesa cases.

South African M-Pesa versus Kenyan M-Pesa

Two weeks after introducing M-Pesa in Kenya in 2007, Safaricom reported 20 000 active users (Bengelstorff 2015; Jack & Suri 2011). This success story continued, exhibiting 20 million customers and 83 000 agents by 2015 (Bengelstorff 2015; Jack & Suri 2011). Today, on this basis, M-Pesa enables customers to pay electricity and water bills, obtain cash from an ATM, buy airline tickets, pay taxi drivers and take out small loans (Bengelstorff 2015; Jack & Suri 2011). In contrast to Kenya, where Safaricom had the monopoly on mobile money during its launch, South Africa now exhibits a well-developed mobile banking system. More precisely, banks in South Africa provide reliable and easy access to banking services for all bank customers. This includes the lower-income customers, reducing the number of unbanked to a minimum (Abbott 2015). In order to compete, almost every South African bank provides online banking and mobile banking applications. Besides this well-developed banking system, South Africa's financial system provides similar money transfer systems to M-Pesa for the unbanked. For example, Shoprite, Africa's largest food retailer, provides money transfers countrywide for R15 per transaction (Shoprite 2016). Different preconditions, poor distribution and poor marketing resulted in only 1 million users of M-Pesa in South Africa by the end of March 2015, which was labelled as a failure by the two main investors, Vodacom and Nedbank (Bengelstorff 2015). Consequently, Vodacom South Africa made the decision to discontinue the M-Pesa product with effect from 30 June 2016. Potential new customers were not able to register, and the facility of person-to-person payments to unregistered customers was terminated on 9 May 2016 (Tshabalala 2015).

On the basis of these two cases, it can be concluded that technical preconditions alone, in this case, a high mobile phone density, are not a guarantor for a successful launch and that environmental conditions should not be disregarded. The environmental conditions in the South African context that might deserve further research are discussed later.

Zimbabwe's EcoCash

Regarding international, real-time, person-to-person payments in SSA EcoCash, a mobile money transfer system launched in Zimbabwe in 2011, enables users to receive money from more than 50 international countries and territories (Dann 2014). EcoCash is a person-to-person mobile transfer system developed by Econet Wireless, a privately held telecommunications group with operations and investments in Africa, Europe, South America, North America and the East Asia Pacific Rim. The product, EcoCash, is based on the development of a mobile payment system to help NGOs make cash transfers to refugees after the Burundian Civil War. By adopting M-Pesa's obscure lines between telecommunication and banking and with the aim of helping the lower class or the unbanked to save, transfer and purchase cashless, EcoCash symbolises a Zimbabwean copy of the Kenyan M-Pesa (EcoCash 2016; Econet 2016; Leach 2014). In contrast to where M-Pesa failed to succeed in South Africa, EcoCash was confronted by three preconditions in Zimbabwe, similar to M-Pesa in Kenya. Firstly, the Econet product provider of EcoCash and the Safaricom product provider of M-Pesa were both telecommunication providers during their launches. With regard to the launch date of their mobile money products, both providers were near-monopolistic players in their home market (Safaricom: 66.6% in 2007; Econet: 70% in 2011). Secondly, at the launch, both mobile phone penetration rates were high, with 40% for Safaricom in 2007 in Kenya and 74% for Econet in 2011 in Zimbabwe (Africa&middleeast 2011). Thirdly, with 70% unbanked in Zimbabwe in 2011 and a population that had lost trust in the banks, Zimbabwe's environmental preconditions for an independent banking service were high (Mangudya 2016). Because of these three preconditions and the advantage of technological progress over 4 years, EcoCash had 2.4 million subscribers in the first year, that is, 320 000 more subscribers than M-Pesa in its first year in Kenya (Kabweza 2012; Techzim 2011). Accompanied by a mobile penetration of 95.4% in the last quarter of 2015, the mobile money service, EcoCash, rapidly expanded in Zimbabwe. With 5.8 million subscribers in 2016 and 26 500 agents across Zimbabwe, EcoCash has become the largest financial service provider in the country (Gambanga 2016a). In addition to the national success, EcoCash allows users to send money to Zimbabwe from 57 countries worldwide (EcoCash 2016).

It is apparent that the environmental preconditions must be considered wisely when launching a mobile money service system. Furthermore, M-Pesa and EcoCash illustrated that mobile money services improve banking skills, particularly of the unbanked, simplify bank account maintenance and simplify money transfers in SSA. How mobile money services influence the adoption of information and communication technology (ICT) in South Africa is discussed in the next section.

Influence of information and communication technology on the adoption of mobile money

As illustrated by the three real-world examples above and underlined by Van de Ven (1986) and Rogers (2010), the implementation of ICT is always associated with organisational, environmental and individual changes. These changes and the accomplished implication challenges are theorised by researchers and practitioners in the research area that focuses on the acceptance and adoption of technology (Korpelainen 2011). According to Korpelainen, the most cited theories are the Technology Acceptance Model (TAM), the Theory of Reasoned Actions, Diffusion of Innovations and the Theory of Planned Behaviour. These theories mainly explore individual technology acceptance by analysing the organisation and the implementation of ICT.

TABLE 3: Sub-Saharan Africa literature concerning mobile money technology acceptance theories.

Main theory	Content	Research design	Author(s) and year
TAM	Explores the motivations of the unbanked to adopt mobile banking in Ghana	Qualitative research	Tobbin 2012
TAM	Examines the factors that influence the adoption of M-banking in Kenya	Quantitative research	Lule, Omwansa and Waema 2012
TAM; Diffusion of Innovation	Investigates the key factors that influence the Ghanaian consumers' acceptance of mobile money transfer technology	Quantitative research	Tobbin 2012
TAM	Investigates the success factors attributable to the use of mobile payments by micro-business operators in Kenya	Quantitative research	Mbogo 2010

TAM, Technology Acceptance Model

Source: Luarm, P. & Lin, H., 2005, 'Towards an understanding of the behavioral intention to use mobile banking', *Computers in Human Behaviour* 21(6), 873–891. https://doi.org/10.1016/j.chb.2004.03.003

Regarding the acceptance of the technology of mobile money in Africa, Table 3 outlines the literature using technology acceptance theories.

As can be seen in Table 3, TAM is a popular theory for the technology acceptance of mobile money in Africa. The TAM describes perceived usefulness and perceived ease of use as fundamental determinants to examine behavioural intentions concerning the use of technology and its acceptance. It is described by Luarm and Lin (2005) as the most widely accepted model in information system literature. Concerning the literature above and the use of the TAM, the two fundamental determinants mentioned above were extended with individual research perceptions. For example, Tobbin (2012) added the economic factor and perceived trust as two additional factors in order to explore the acceptance of mobile banking technology by the unbanked. On the basis of TAM, Lule et al. (2012) generated a generic mobile banking adoption framework. The literature above concludes without exception that TAM is a suitable technology acceptance theory for research in the mobile money field.

Taking these facts into account, the authors of this article illustrate how mobile money systems influence the adoption of ICT in South Africa with the help of: (1) organisational changes, (2) environmental changes, and (3) individual changes.

Organisational changes

Regarding organisational changes, the approach of Vodacom and Nedbank to implement M-Pesa in South Africa showed that not only environmental requirements but also organisational tasks were neglected (Bengelstorff 2015). According to Tshabalala (2015), the marketing and

TABLE 4: Meta-analysis of findings.

Empirical study	Findings	References
Kenya's M-Pesa	Kenya's mobile money project is regarded as one of the highly successful projects to have emerged in sub-Saharan Africa.	Bengelstorff (2015); Jack and Suri (2011).
South Africa's M-Pesa	Tshabalala (2015) asserts that the South African version of M-Pesa was a huge failure project, resulting in its closure.	Tshabalala (2015)
Zimbabwe's EcoCash	Compared to South Africa, Zimbabwe's EcoCash is regarded as a second success story after Kenya's M-Pesa. Reports indicate that EcoCash is the main mobile money transaction system in Zimbabwe.	Econet (2016); Leach (2014)
Present study	Mobile banking is the ideal alternative to traditional online banking. The failure of the South African project should be the basis for developing user-friendly and effective mobile banking platforms. The South African mobile money project is a clear indication that implementation of such systems is difficult because of a variety of factors. These factors include technology acceptance behaviour, risk associated with cyberspace transactions, technological infrastructure and lack of education relating to banking services. The Kenya and Zimbabwe success stories should act as sources of motivation for financial institutions and other players to propagate mobile banking. More efforts are required to educate users of mobile banking services so as to increase the uptake. Kenya has done and continues to excel in that aspect because of visible educational campaigns, while the current economic situation in Zimbabwe is compelling the financial and telecommunications industry to devise ways to curb shortages of money supply.	-

organisation of the agents, which are key points of the M-Pesa service system, were weakly implemented. As progressively claimed by the banks, the comparatively high bank account diffusion and accomplished low unbanked population share the organisational changes for mobile money adoption in South Africa. For example, Capitec Bank Holdings Limited provides unstructured supplementary service data, a mobile banking system applicable to almost every mobile phone. Because of the rapid technological progress, the smartphone applications provided by all large banks in South Africa have become particularly popular in the urban areas (Abbott 2015). Therefore, it can be said that organisational changes concerning mobile money systems in South Africa have a decentralised role, starting with the banks.

Environmental changes

Despite the influence of the international oil crisis in the 1970s, the international sanctions to end apartheid from 1985 onwards, democratisation in 1994 and the financial crisis from 2007 onwards, the economy of South Africa has been ranked in the top five in Africa continuously (Inglesi-Lotz et al. 2014). According to Inglesi-Lotz et al., growth-accounting calculations elucidate the progressive increase and importance of technological growth in contrast to the production factors of capital and labour during the 2000s. As reported by Debsu, Little, Tiki, Guagliardo, and Kitron (2016), the recent expansion of mobile phone use introduces the technological change in Africa. With the recent increased technical infrastructure, mobile technology that was predominantly used in urban areas has expanded to relatively remote areas. As illustrated in the previous sections, the use of ICTs has rapidly increased connectivity and aided in prosperity for Africa (Debsu et al. 2016). As one of the industrialised and westernised countries in Africa, environmental changes improved mobile banking skills in the rural areas.

Individual changes

With regard to 89% mobile phone diffusion 2014 in South Africa (Poushter & Oates 2015), the acceptance of mobile technology is high. However, the acceptance of the technology regarding mobile money is comparatively low at 15% (Poushter & Oates 2015). This low acceptancy might be reasoned by the relatively well-developed bank account diffusion. Nonetheless, future research is required to verify this speculation. Because of the decentralisation of mobile money providers and the large variety of them in comparison with other SSA countries, South Africa does not possess a high unbanked population. However, it is the corporation of the individual mobile money service provider that complicates transactions. More precisely, for individuals, it is more convenient to use a mobile money service when their transaction partner has the same mobile money service provider (Abbott 2015). Accordingly, the individual changes in South Africa are because of the advanced organisational and environmental progress in comparison with the remaining SSA countries and the smooth cooperation between the several mobile money service providers, not the actual mobile money service.

Findings

The findings from this study are illustrated in Table 4. A meta-analysis summary of findings from Kenya's mobile money project, South Africa's Vodacom M-Pesa and Zimbabwe's EcoCash project are presented in Table 4.

Limitations and suggestions for future research

This research is limited by the literature concerning mobile money in SSA and concentrating on the South African mobile money service market. Because this research is a literature survey, no quantitative or qualitative data were raised. Concerning future research, the sections above illustrate that because of a lack of academic literature concerning mobile banking in South Africa, both qualitative and quantitative research is required. More precisely, it would be promoting to investigate if an existing bank account has an influence on the adoption of mobile money in South Africa. This could be done through qualitative research (interviewing specialist) or quantitative research, taking TAM as a basic conceptual framework.

Conclusion

Whereas prior mobile banking research studies have explored consumers' intentions to adopt mobile banking services, the purpose of this research was to review existing research on mobile banking diffusion and investigate the adoption of mobile banking in SSA. In addition, the aim of this article was to provide suggestions for future research in the mobile money field in South Africa. The findings from this study revealed that both Kenya and Zimbabwe have recorded success stories in the areas of mobile banking, whereas the South African story is a sad note to discuss. This reveals that there is a great need to educate South African users on the importance of information communication technologies. The rate of ICT adoption in South Africa is relatively low despite a high number of mobile cellular phone users. In addition, private and public sector institutions have a big role to play to impart knowledge to users on the need to accept and embrace information communication technologies because the world has become a global village. Resistance to accepting and use of technologies may impede success in communities that were previously disadvantaged. The findings from this study also revealed that innovation is not a preserve of a rich economy, but when the economic and political conditions are stringent, entrepreneurial skills enhance innovation. The Zimbabwean political and economic situation is a clear example. Zimbabwe's Econet Wireless Holdings partnered and developed the highly successful EcoCash system because of the acute shortage of money supply. This system was ideal to alleviate traditional banking processes where clients spent time in banking halls queuing for cash or enquiries. EcoCash is establishing its operations in South Africa because there are many Zimbabwean nationals living in South Africa who send money back to Zimbabwe. Researchers established that South Africa is confronted with environmental, organisational and individual challenges compared to other SSA countries (23.5%). Consequently, future research exploring these different challenges could be conducted. With reference to research findings, it is difficult to deploy mobile money systems transnationally because of differences in the adoption and acceptance of information and communication technologies.

Acknowledgements

Competing interests

The authors declare that they have no financial or personal relationship(s) that may have inappropriately influenced them in writing this article.

Authors' contributions

Both the authors contributed significantly by drafting the article and revising it for important intellectual content. J.M.C. came up with the concept of developing the article on mobile banking and its success/failure in South Africa, by providing fundamental issues that formed the structure of the article. In addition, J.M.C. ensured that the article was edited through third party services. B.H. was responsible for collating the article through the collection of various pieces of literature on the research article. B.H. was also responsible for final editing and production of this presentation.

References

Abbott, D., 2015, *SA ripe for a mobile banking revolution*, viewed 17 May 2016, from http://www.fin24.com/Tech/Opinion/SA-ripe-for-a-mobile-banking-revolution-20150223

Africa&middleeast, 2011, *Kenya: Major African mobile market*, viewed 14 June 2016, from http://www.africantelecomsnews.com/resources/AfricaOpp_Kenya.html#Table2

Aker, J.C. & Mbiti, I.M., 2010, 'Mobile phones and economic development in Africa', *The Journal of Economic Perspectives* 24(3), 207–232. https://doi.org/10.1257/jep.24.3.207

Akhter, S.H., 2015, 'Impact of internet usage comfort and internet technical comfort on online shopping and online banking', *Journal of International Consumer Marketing* 27(3), 207–219. https://doi.org/10.1080/08961530.2014.994086

Akturan, U. & Tezcan, N., 2012, 'Mobile banking adoption of the youth market: Perceptions and intentions', *Marketing Intelligence & Planning* 30(4), 444–459. https://doi.org/10.1108/02634501211231928

AnswersAfrica, 2013, *How to open a bank account in South Africa*, viewed 13 May 2016, from http://answersafrica.com/how-to-open-a-bank-account-in-south-africa.html

Barbesino, P., Camerani, R. & Gaudino, A., 2005, 'Digital finance in Europe: Competitive dynamics and online behaviour', *Journal of Financial Services Marketing* 9(4), 329–343. https://doi.org/10.1057/palgrave.fsm.4770164

Bengelstorff, A., 2015, *A global success from Kenya*, viewed 8 June 2016, from https://www.credit-suisse.com/us/en/news-and-expertise/banking/articles/news-and-expertise/2015/08/en/a-global-success-from-kenya.html

Bluemagnet, 2014, *The state of social media in South Africa 2014*, viewed 20 February 2016, from http://www.bluemagnet.co.za/the-state-of-social-media-in-south-africa-2014/

Brown, M., 2014, *Ad reaction: Marketing in a multiscreen world*, viewed 20 February 2016, from https://www.millwardbrown.com/adreaction/2014/#/

BusinessTech, 2016, *How much money you need to be middle class in South Africa*, viewed 11 May 2016, from http://businesstech.co.za/news/wealth/111285/how-much-money-you-need-to-be-middle-class-in-south-africa/

Columinate, 2015, *Columinate 2015 internet banking SITEisfaction survey shows improvement from local banks*, viewed 16 May 2016, from http://www.bizcommunity.com/Article/196/19/128105.html.

Couse, L.J. & Chen, D.W., 2010, 'A tablet computer for young children? Exploring its viability for early childhood education', *Journal of Research on Technology in Education* 43(1), 75–96. https://doi.org/10.1080/15391523.2010.10782562

Dann, C., 2014, *Will EcoCash eat the banks' lunch? How mobile payments filled a financial services gap in Zimbabwe*, viewed 14 June 2016, from http://www.tfreview.com/news/regions/will-ecocash-eat-banks'-lunch-how-mobile-payments-filled-financial-services-gap-zimbabw

Debsu, D., Little, P., Tiki, W., Guagliardo, S. & Kitron, U., 2016, 'Mobile phones for mobile people: The role of information and communication technology (ICT) among livestock traders and Borana pastoralists of southern Ethiopia', *Nomadic Peoples* 20(1), 35–61. https://doi.org/10.3197/np.2016.200104

Department of Home Affairs (DHA), 2016, *Passport holders who are exempt from visas for South Africa*, viewed 13 May 2016, from http://www.dha.gov.za/index.php/immigration-services/exempt-countries

EcoCash, 2016, *EcoCash products & services*, viewed 14 June 2016, from https://www.econet.co.zw/ecocash/ecocash-products-and-services

Econet, 2016, *About us*, viewed 14 June 2016, from http://www.econetwireless.com/about_econet.php.

Euromonitor, 2015, *Mobile phones in South Africa*, viewed 20 February 2016, from http://www.euromonitor.com/mobile-phones-in-south-africa/report

Ferreira, J., 2016, *South Africa GDP growth rate 1993–2016*, viewed 10 May 2016, from http://www.tradingeconomics.com/south-africa/gdp-growth

FinScope, 2014, *FinScope South Africa 2014*, viewed 13 May 2016, from http://www.banking.org.za/docs/default-source/financial-inclusion/finscope/finscope-sa-2014.pdf

Gambanga, N., 2016a, EcoCash handles $6,6 billion in transactions, dominates Zimbabwean payments field, viewed 14 June 2016, from http://www.techzim.co.zw/2016/06/ecocash-handles-66-billion-transactions-dominates-zimbabwean-payments-field/#.V2QTYFexaqA

Gambanga, N., 2016b, *Latest POTRAZ report shows leaps in LTE & increase in Zimbabwe's internet penetration*, viewed 1 March 2017, from http://www.techzim.co.zw/2016/01/latest-potraz-report-shows-increase-in-zimbabwes-internet-penetration/

Gambanga, N., 2016c, *Mobile money subscribers in Zimbabwe increase by 7.1%*, viewed 1 March 2017, from http://www.techzim.co.zw/2016/01/mobile-money-subscribers-zimbabwe-increase-7-1/

Granado-Font, E., Flores-Mateo, G., Sorlí-Aguilar, M., Montaña-Carreras, X., Ferre-Grau, C., Barrera-Uriarte, M.L., 2015, 'Effectiveness of a smartphone application and wearable device for weight loss in overweight or obese primary care patients: Protocol for a randomised controlled trial', *BMC Public Health* 15(1), 531. https://doi.org/10.1186/s12889-015-1845-8

Inglesi-Lotz, R., Van Eyden, R. & Du Toit, C.B., 2014, 'The evolution and contribution of technological progress to the South African economy: Growth accounting and Kalman filter application', *Energy Policy* 39(6), 3690–3696. https://doi.org/10.1016/j.enpol.2011.03.078

Internetlivestats, 2016, *Internet users 2016*, viewed 10 January 2017, from http://www.internetlivestats.com/internet-users/

Internet Society, 2015, *Global internet report 2015*, viewed 25 April 2017, from http://www.internetsociety.org/globalinternetreport/#main-content

Jack, W. & Suri, T., 2011, *Mobile money: The economics of M-Pesa* (No. w16721), National Bureau of Economic Research.

Kabweza, L.S.M., 2012, *EcoCash adds 200,000 more subscribers in a month (Growth stats since launch)*, viewed 14 June 2016, from http://www.techzim.co.zw/2012/04/ecocash-adds-200000-subscribers-in-a-month-growth-trend-since-launch/#.V2QWpVexaqA

Karjaluoto, H., Mattila, M. & Pento, T., 2002, 'Factors underlying consumer attitude formation towards online banking in Finland', *International Journal of Bank Marketing* 20(6), 261–272. https://doi.org/10.1108/02652320210446724

KEDO, 2013, *South Africa's immigration problem*, viewed 13 May 2016, from http://fordhampoliticalreview.org/south-africa's-immigration-problem/

Khrais, L.T., 2015, 'Highlighting the vulnerabilities of online banking system', *Journal of Internet Banking & Commerce* 20(3), n.p. https://doi.org/10.4172/1204-5357.1000120

Koech, J., 2012, 'Bringing banking to the masses, one phone at a time,' *Economic Letter* 7.

Korpelainen, E., 2011, *Theories of ICT system implementation and adoption – A critical review*, Working Paper 2011, Department of Industrial Engineering and Management, Alto University Publication series (1), 14–17.

Laforet, S. & Li, X., 2005, '"Consumers" attitudes towards online and mobile banking in China', *International Journal of Bank Marketing* 23(5), 362–380.

Laukkanen, T. & Lauronen, J., 2005, 'Consumer value creation in mobile banking services', *International Journal of Mobile Communications* 3(4), 325–338. https://doi.org/10.1504/IJMC.2005.007021

Laukkanen, T. & Pasanen, M., 2008, 'Mobile banking innovators and early adopters: How they differ from other online users', *Journal of Financial Services Marketing* 13(2), 86–94. https://doi.org/10.1057/palgrave.fsm.4760077

Leach, A., 2014, 'Zimbabwe's Econet wireless and the making of Africa's first cashless society', viewed 14 June 2016, from http://www.theguardian.com/global-development-professionals-network/blog/2014/aug/18/econet-wireless-zimbabwe-cashless-society

Luarm, P. & Lin, H., 2005, 'Towards an understanding of the behavioral intention to use mobile banking', *Computers in Human Behaviour* 21(6), 873–891. https://doi.org/10.1016/j.chb.2004.03.003

Lule, I., Omwansa, T.K. & Waema, T.M., 2012, 'Application of technology acceptance model (TAM) in m-banking adoption in Kenya', *International Journal of Computing and ICT Research* 6(1), 31–43.

Maduku, D.K., 2014, 'Predicting retail banking customers' attitude towards internet banking services in South Africa', *Southern African Business Review* 17(3), 76–100.

Mangudya, J.P., 2016, *January 2016: Monetary policy statement*, viewed 14 June 2016, from http://www.rbz.co.zw/assets/monetary-policy-statement-january-2016.pdf.

Mankiw, N.G., 2015, *Macroeconomics*, 9th edn., International Edition, Macmillan Education, Cengage Learning, Boston, MA.

Mbogo, M., 2010, 'The impact of mobile payments on the success and growth of micro-business: The case of M-Pesa in Kenya', *Journal of Language, Technology & Entrepreneurship in Africa* 2(1), 182–203. https://doi.org/10.4314/jolte.v2i1.51998

Moloi, R., 2014, *Exploring the barriers to the sustainability of Spaza shops in Atteridgeville, Tshwane*, PhD dissertation, Unisa, Pretoria.

Online Dictionary, 2017, *Defining online banking*, viewed 24 January 2017, from http://www.dictionary.com.html

Poushter, J. & Oates, R., 2015, 'Cell phones in Africa: Communication lifeline texting most common activity, but mobile money popular in several countries', viewed 22 April 2016, from http://www.pewglobal.org/2015/04/15/cell-phones-in-africa-communication-lifeline/

Raitani, S. & Vyas, V., 2014, 'An exploratory study of factors influencing the e-loyalty of online banking consumers', *Journal of Bank Management* 13(3), 34.

Rogers, E.M., 2010, *Diffusion of innovations*, Simon and Schuster, New York.

Screen Africa, 2014, *Africa's digital penetration in 2014*, viewed 20 February 2016, from http://www.screenafrica.com/page/news/mobile-tv/1639686-Africas-digital-penetration-in-2014#.VshvBDaxYdV

Seidel, M. & Liebetrau, A., 2015, *Banking & innovation 2015: Ideen und erfolgskonzepte von experten für die praxis*, Springer-Verlag, Berlin.

Shoprite, 2016, *Money transfer service*, viewed 27 April 2016, from http://web.shoprite.co.za/money-market/money-transfers.html

Statista, 2015, *Online banking penetration in selected European markets in 2015*, viewed 15 May 2016, from http://www.statista.com/statistics/222286/online-banking-penetration-in-leading-european-countries/

Statistics South Africa, 2014, General household survey 2014, viewed 20 February 2016, from http://www.statssa.gov.za/publications/P0318/P03182014.pdf

Techzim, 2011, Econet announces the launch of EcoCash, *Press Release*, viewed 14 June 2016, from http://www.techzim.co.zw/2011/09/econet-announces-the-launch-of-ecocash/#.V2QVdVexaqA.

Tobbin, P., 2012, 'Towards a model of adoption in mobile banking by the unbanked: A qualitative study', *Info* 14(5), 74–88. https://doi.org/10.1108/14636691211256313

Tshabalala, S., 2015, *Why South Africa's largest mobile network, Vodacom, failed to grow M-Pesa*, viewed 14 June 2016, from http://qz.com/467887/why-south-africas-largest-mobile-network-vodacom-failed-to-grow-mpesa/

Ubuntu Connectors Club (UCC), 2016, *Working together for success*, viewed 14 June 2016, from http://www.ubuntuconnectors.co.za/contributions_5.html.

Van de Ven, A.H., 1986, 'Central problems in the management of innovations', *Management Science* 32(5), 590–607. https://doi.org/10.1287/mnsc.32.5.590

Van Wyk, M.W.T., 2012, *Mobile banking in south and beyond: SABRIC conference*, n.p., Midrand.

Vaupel, M. & Kaul, V., 2016, *Die geschichten des geldes: Von der kaurischnecke zum goldstandard – So entwickelte sich das finanzsystem*, Börsenbuch Verlag, Kulmbach.

Visagie, J., 2013, *Who are the middle class in South Africa? Does it matter for policy?*, viewed 11 May 2016, from http://www.econ3x3.org/article/who-are-middle-class-south-africa-does-it-matter-policy

14

An analysis of perceived usefulness of Google Scholar by the postgraduate students of the University of Ilorin, Nigeria

Authors:
Adeyinka Tella[1,2]
Michael Oyewole[1]
Adedeji Tella[3]

Affiliations:
[1]Department of Library and Information Science, University of Ilorin, Nigeria

[2]Department of Information Science, University of South Africa, South Africa

[3]Department of Teacher Education, University of Ibadan, Nigeria

Corresponding author:
Adeyinka Tella,
tellayinkaedu@yahoo.com

Background: Google Scholar provides user-friendly information resources and is very effective in finding information to satisfy various information needs, especially by the research students. However, despite its usefulness in satisfying information and research needs of the research students and researchers as a whole, the lingering effect associated with it is drawing students away from libraries. Similarly, there have been limited studies conducted to examine the level of perceived usefulness of Google Scholar by the graduate students, particularly in the context of the University of Ilorin, Nigeria.

Objectives: The study examined the perceived usefulness of Google Scholar by the postgraduate students of the University of Ilorin, Nigeria.

Methods: A total of 223 postgraduate students selected through simple random sampling from 15 faculties that made up the University formed the sample for the study. A survey approach was adopted using a questionnaire to gather data from respondents. Six research questions were developed to guide the study.

Results: The results demonstrate that the majority of respondents strongly agreed and agreed that they were aware of Google Scholar and usually used it. However, the respondents were not satisfied with Google Scholar as it does not either speed up their research or make their research easier. Google Scholar was considered useful because it covers broad topics in the area of interest and usually provides relevant articles related to the respondents' search done through this platform.

Conclusion: The study concluded by recommending, among others, that there is a need for orientation programmes to enhance the use of Google Scholar via the university library.

Introduction

Information is very essential in our day-to-day activities. It is needed for a variety of reasons which mostly involves solving problems. When faced with a problem, we search for information that will help us proffer solutions to remediate the problems. As Belkin and Croft (1992) pointed out, a search usually commences with a problem and the need to solve it. They explained that the gap between the two is the need for information, which now leads to information seeking.

The need for such information makes us use the library and other information repositories to find solutions to problems. Such problems may be academic, social, economic, health or financial. The need to use information in analysing, correcting, informing and solving problems is almost an unquenchable thirst as people demand information on a very large scale. In different walks of life, information is needed to get ahead of competition, market resources and to make informed decisions.

With the invention of technological devices such as cell phones, computers and others, information has become mobile in terms of accessibility. The Internet, for instance, is a huge repository of information that one can access anytime and anywhere for information. Internet is the interconnection of different networks and servers to form a giant network. The Internet has been defined as a network of networks. As the network includes different devices, it is easy to access vast amounts of information. There are thousands of websites which vary with the information they provide. While some provide academic information, others provide economic information, social information and so on.

Before the advent of the Internet, the library has been in existence as a veritable source for information. However, not everybody is capable of using the library and the materials in it. This has resulted in complications in the area of information retrieval, as users may either be far away from where a library is or been unable to access appropriate materials needed because of limitations in the searching strategy.

The revolution of the Internet has resulted in the availability of so many sources to access information. For instance, Google Scholar provides a new technique of locating a relevant article on a particular subject. This is done by identifying a subsequent publication that cites or references a previously published work. Features of Google Scholar identified by Noruzi (2005) include opportunity for researchers to trace interconnections among authors, citing articles on a relevant topic and determine the extent to which others cite a specific article, as it has a 'cited by' feature.

Information is essential to society. With the ever increasing need for information, especially in the academic world, there is a need for students to search for information to solve problems. The issue of information needs to be addressed as information is the bedrock for the survival and sustenance of the society. Lack of information in a society can lead to faulty decisions and decline in economic growth and academics. Once students are given tasks to perform, they need information to perform such tasks. This need will motivate research which will in turn produce a result which may be positive or negative depending on the information obtained. The need for information is a global issue as every society depends on it. The academic world hangs on information as it is used to carry out analysis and study data so as to make informed choices. The medium of accessing information is as important as information itself. When there is a need for information, the information seeker has to use a medium of information retrieval. This medium can be a library or other online applications such as Google Scholar.

Various studies by librarians and academics have demonstrated that Google Scholar provides friendly information resources to users; however, the lingering effect associated with this is drawing students away from libraries. There is no doubt that Google Scholar is very effective in finding information to satisfy various information needs, especially for research students. However, despite the usefulness of Google Scholar in satisfying information and research needs of research students and researchers as a whole, there have been limited studies conducted to examine the level of perceived usefulness of Google Scholar by the research students (postgraduate students), particularly in the context of the University of Ilorin, Nigeria.

The result of this research is significant in several ways. It will help in understanding the perspective of the postgraduate students of the University of Ilorin on the usefulness of the Google Scholar platform. The research will also create awareness on the part of other institutions' postgraduate students on how to effectively use Google Scholar for research. The outcomes from the research are expected to lead to a change of attitudes towards information searching as users will not be constrained to the use of a library. Also, it will help understand the advantages and reasons for using Google Scholar by postgraduate students.

Objective of the study

The broad objective of this study is to examine the perceived usefulness of Google Scholar by the postgraduate students of the University of Ilorin, Nigeria. The specific objectives of the study are to:

- identify the level of awareness of postgraduate students of the University of Ilorin towards the use of Google Scholar;
- examine the perception of postgraduate students of the University of Ilorin on the ease of use of Google Scholar;
- determine the perceived usefulness of Google Scholar to postgraduate students of the University of Ilorin;
- find out the degree of comprehensiveness and trust on information found on Google Scholar by the postgraduate students of the University of Ilorin;
- ascertain the satisfaction level of postgraduate students of the University of Ilorin with Google Scholar platform;
- identify the continued intention of postgraduate students of the University of Ilorin towards the use of Google Scholar platform.

Research questions

The following questions guided this study:

- What is the level of awareness of postgraduate students of the University of Ilorin towards the use of Google Scholar?
- What is the perception of postgraduate students of the University of Ilorin towards the ease of use of Google Scholar?
- What is the perceived usefulness of Google Scholar to postgraduate students of the University of Ilorin?
- What is the degree of comprehensiveness and trust on information found on Google Scholar by the postgraduate students of the University of Ilorin?
- What is the satisfaction level of postgraduate students of the University of Ilorin with Google Scholar platform?
- What is the intention of postgraduate students of the University of Ilorin towards the use of Google Scholar?

Literature review

Google Scholar describes a freely accessible search engine which enables users to search for print and electronic copies of published articles. The search engine searches various sources such as academic publishers, universities and preprint depositories by looking for articles, thesis and dissertations, citations and journals (Mikki 2009). It is a database that contains different databases majorly used in searching for text and scholarly articles that can either be digital or printed copies. According to Mikki, Google Scholar does this searching by linking with databases of some other academic institutions which it partners with. The coverage of Google Scholar is interdisciplinary because it covers almost all subjects in all disciplines. This allows it to generate a broad result when queries are entered into it. By linking with other databases, Google Scholar accesses their scholarly articles and publications, indexes and cites them on its own platform (Jasco 2005).

Since Google Scholar is a freely accessible search engine, it is being patronised by information users and libraries who cannot afford to increase their budget for information search facilities. Considering this factor, a lot of reviews have been done by librarians to check the credibility and reliability of the information obtained through Google Scholar (Adlington & Benda 2006; Callicott & Vaughn 2005). This also leads to questions regarding the efficiency and experience of users accessing Google Scholar, to understand their reactions to the search engine in assisting their research work.

Empirical framework

Shen (2012) conducted a study on the frequency of graduate students' usage of Google Scholar and the contributing factors to its adoption. The findings demonstrated that 45% of those who had used Google Scholar indicated its linkage to full text articles via the customised library link. On average, respondents found Google Scholar easy to use (M = 4.09 out of 5) and access (M = 3.86). Respondents also perceived Google Scholar as a useful resource for research because it enhanced their search effectiveness. On the other hand, respondents were not emphatic about whether or not they always found what they are searching for using Google Scholar or whether or not enough resources are available on it for their research. Nonetheless, most of the respondents were still convinced they made the right choice to use Google Scholar (M = 3.94). The results further revealed several factors that strongly influence graduate students' intention to use Google Scholar. These are perceived usefulness of Google Scholar, sense of loyalty, and perceived ease of use. The findings provide useful insights for librarians seeking to understand graduate students' perception of Google Scholar and practical implications on how best Google Scholar can be promoted to graduate students.

Cothran (2011) examined a quantitative analysis of Google Scholar acceptance and use among graduate students. By applying a web-based survey questionnaire, the results revealed that 73% of the respondents reported having used Google Scholar at least once before. However, 45% of those who had used Google Scholar reported its linkage to full text articles. The results revealed further that on average, respondents perceived Google Scholar as easy to use and easy to access. Hamid and Asadi (2010) investigated the role of Google Scholar in the information seeking behaviour of scientists including physicists and astronomers from the Department of Physics and Astronomy at the University College, London. A mixed method approach was adopted using semi-structured interview items, a questionnaire and information-event cards as instruments for the collection of data from 114 respondents. The results demonstrated that there is increasing reliance of scientists on general search engines, especially Google, for locating scholarly articles. Based on the findings, the study concluded that the increasing awareness of the large quantity of scholarly articles available and searchable via Google by the scientists make them rely on it for finding scholarly publications.

Neuhaus, Neuhaus and Asher (2008) conducted a study to determine the degree of Google Scholar adoption by academics. The authors analysed the frequency of Google Scholar appearances on 948 campus and library websites and established the link resolution between Google Scholar and library resources. The results showed that a positive correlation exists between the implementation of Google Scholar link resolution and the degree of Google Scholar adoption.

In a comparative analysis of Google Scholar interface and search engine Scirus conducted by Felter (2005), it was reported that although Scirus has a sophisticated interface, most researchers preferred the simplicity of Google and would more likely opt for it than other more capable and complicated databases. Henderson (2005) assessed the search capabilities of Google Scholar and reported a ranking bias towards older articles that has the passage of time been cited over a number times. The results also showed that Google Scholar lacked the standard search features such as 'similar pages' and 'did you mean' features for alternative spellings. Golderman and Connolly (2007) identified the compatibility of Google Scholar with bibliographic software such as Endnote and Reference works. However, they faulted Google Scholar for failing to include search histories, alert services, and utilities for sorting, marking and saving results.

Kousha and Thelwall (2006) in a study on Google Scholar citations indicated that there is a strong relationship between Google Scholar and ISI Web of Science for biology, computer science and physics journals. They also found moderate but statistically significant correlations between citations from Google Scholar and ISI for journals in sociology and psychology, education, chemistry and economics. The results showed further significant correlations between Google Scholar citation counts and ISI Journal Impact Factors. Noruzi (2006) in a related study tested the citation counts for 36 frequently cited papers in webometrics of both Google Scholar and Web of Science. The findings indicated that Google Scholar identified more citations than Web of Science for all but three of the articles. In another similar study, Bakkalbasi and Bauer (2005) compared citation counts in Google Scholar, Web of Science and Scopus for 1985 and 2000 using articles from the *Journal of the American Society of Information Science and Technology* (JASIST). The finding revealed that while Web of Science returned the most citation counts for 1985, Google Scholar tallied with the highest citation counts for all JASIST articles published in 2000.

Jasco (2005) in another study that compares Google Scholar, Scopus and Web of Science examined the relative coverage of the most cited papers from the journal *Current Science*. The report demonstrated that in a total citation count of 30 articles, both Web of Science and Scopus outperformed Google Scholar by a three to one margin.

Furthermore, Bakkalbasi et al. (2006) assessed the number of citing references on articles in the fields of oncology and condensed matter physics generated by Web of Science, Scopus and Google Scholar. They found that Web of Science and Scopus returned more citing references than Google Scholar, but Google Scholar returned the highest number of unique references. The study concluded that none of the three resources clearly outperformed the others and that a researcher relying on just one or even two of the resources might fail to find all references. In their comparative bibliometric study of Web of Science, Scopus, and Google Scholar, Meho and Yang (2007) reported that in the field of Library and Information Science, Google Scholar provides citations from a broader array of sources than either Scopus or Web of Science. However, many of the additional sources were from low-impact journals and conference proceedings.

Another comparative analysis of contents from 47 different databases with Google Scholar was conducted by Neuhaus et al. (2006). The results revealed that database contents inclusion in Google Scholar varies considerably from one database to another database and from one discipline to another discipline. A great variation was discovered between Google Scholar's coverage of freely accessible databases and restricted access databases. Based on the finding, the study concluded that Google Scholar coverage score was greater for databases within science, medicine and social science discipline categories. The drawbacks of Google Scholar identified included the lack of coverage of social science and humanities databases and a bias towards English language.

From the extant literature, it is evident that the use of search engines, particularly Google Scholar, is now common among undergraduate and graduate students. However, most of the available studies on the subject were conducted in the developed countries where there is a stable network and Internet connectivity (24×7). Graduates, undergraduates, scholars and researchers in developing countries also rely on Google Scholar in the conduct of their research; unfortunately, studies on the usefulness of this tool by these sets of users in developing countrie, particularly among the postgraduate students in Nigeria, are limited.

Methodology

Research design

A survey approach was adopted in the conduct of this research. This was to be able to reach out to a sizeable number of respondents. Similarly, survey has been the dominant approach used in previous related studies (e.g. Jasco 2005; Neuhaus et al. 2006).

Sample and sampling technique

The target population used in the study is the postgraduate students of the University of Ilorin, Nigeria. As at the 2015–2016 session, this population spread across 15 faculties that made up the postgraduate scheme of the university. The faculties are Faculty of Agriculture, Faculty of Arts, Faculty of Basic Medical Sciences, Faculty of Social Sciences, Faculty of Management Sciences, Faculty of Clinical Sciences, Faculty of Communication and Information Sciences, Faculty of Education, Faculty of Engineering and Technology, Faculty of Law, Faculty of Pharmaceutical Sciences, Faculty of Life Science, Faculty of Veterinary, Faculty of Physical Sciences and Faculty of Environment.

This study adopted the stratified sampling technique because the population has already been divided into natural strata (faculties). The population has homogenous groups known as strata. Each stratum is a representation of a faculty (postgraduate) in the university, bringing the total to 15 strata. Using simple random sampling method, the sample was drawn from the 15 strata. Fifteen respondents (postgraduate students) were selected from each of the faculties of the university, making a total of 225 postgraduate students who represent the sample for the study.

Data collection instrument

The main instrument used was a researcher-designed questionnaire tagged 'Perceived Usefulness of Google Scholar Questionnaire'. The questionnaire consists of a list of items relating to the research questions mentioned and the objectives. The questionnaire was divided into three sections. Section A requested the respondents' demography which includes age, gender and faculty. Section B contained the items that focus on each of the variables in the study and was further divided into parts. Each part focused on a variable in the objectives. For instance, Part 1 featured items on level of awareness of postgraduate students of the University of Ilorin towards the use of Google Scholar. Part B featured items on the perception of postgraduate students on the ease of use of Google Scholar. Part C featured the perceived usefulness of Google Scholar by postgraduate students. Part D featured items on the degree of trust in information found on Google Scholar by the postgraduate students. Part E featured items on the satisfaction level of the postgraduate students with Google Scholar platform, while Part F featured items on the intention of the postgraduate students towards the use of the Google Scholar platform. A Likert-type scale format with Strongly Agreed (SA), Agreed (A), Disagreed (D) and Strongly Disagreed (SD) was adopted for all items in Parts A–F of the instrument.

Validity of the instrument

In order to ensure the content and construct validity, the instrument was given to two specialists to scrutinise and check for appropriateness of language to examine its suitability for data collection before administering the instruments to the respondents. The suggestions made by the experts led to modifications of some items in the instrument before it was finally administered.

Reliability of the instrument

To study the reliability of the instrument, a split-half reliability method was adopted. This method involves administering the instrument to a set of 20 respondents outside the envisaged population. The responses collected were divided into two equal halves, while the data collected were subjected to Pearson's product moment correlation. The correlation coefficient returned an r of 0.88. This indicated that the instrument was highly reliable for data collection on the study.

Data collection procedures

The questionnaire on the perceived usefulness of Google Scholar by postgraduate students of the University of Ilorin was administered by the researcher to the respondents. The questionnaire was administered during the rainy semester of the 2015–2016 academic session. This is because that is the time when they could be easily reached. With the assistance of colleagues in different faculties of the university, the questionnaires administration exercise was an itch-free one and consequently resulted in no attrition rate. Fifteen copies of questionnaires were administered to respondents in each faculty, making a total of 225 copies. Out of the 225, a total of 223 copies of the questionnaire were returned properly filled and were thus good for data analysis given, representing a 99.1% return rate.

Methods of data analysis

Data analysis was carried out with the use of appropriate statistical methods. The researcher collated data by collecting responses on Sections A, B, C, D, E and F. The analysis was conducted using item by item analysis; the data collected were analysed with the use of simple percentage and frequency count. The data collected were coded using SPSS Version 21.0.

Data presentation and analysis and results

Table 1 shows that out of the 223 respondents, 142 (63.7%) were males while 81 (36.3%) were females. With this, it is clear that the population of male respondents is larger than the female population. On the age distribution of the respondents, the table also indicates that 60 (26.9%) respondents fall within the ages of 18–23 years; this is followed by the respondents within the ages of 24–29 years with 122 (54.7%). Next to it is the respondents who were between the ages of 30 years and above with 41 (18.4%). With the results presented, it is clear that students within the age range of 30 years and above represent the majority of the respondents. The results also revealed the statistics of the faculties in relation to the respondents. The lowest number of respondents was from the faculty of Basic Medical Sciences with 13 (5.8%), whereas the other 14 faculties had 15 (6.7%) respondents each.

Research Question 1

What is the level of awareness of postgraduate students of the University of Ilorin towards the use of Google Scholar?

Table 2 reveals that out of 223 (100%) students sampled, 21 (9.4%) respondents strongly agree to have awareness, 102 (45.7%) respondents agree to being aware, 71 (31.8%) disagree to being aware, while 29 (13.1%) strongly disagree to being aware. This shows that the majority of respondents are aware of Google Scholar. Of all the respondents, only 34 (15.3%) strongly agree that they can use Google Scholar. A total of 98

TABLE 1: Demography of the respondents.

Demographics	Frequency	%
Gender		
Male	142	63.7
Female	81	36.3
Total	223	100
Age		
18–23	60	26.9
24–29	122	54.7
30 above	41	18.4
Total	223	100
Faculties		
Agricultural science	15	6.7
Arts	15	6.7
Basic medical science	13	5.8
Clinical sciences	15	6.7
Communication and information sciences	15	6.7
Education	15	6.7
Engineering and technology	15	6.7
Environment	15	6.7
Law	15	6.7
Life sciences	15	6.7
Management sciences	15	6.7
Pharmaceutical sciences	15	6.7
Physical sciences	15	6.7
Social sciences	15	6.7
Veterinary	15	6.7
Total	**223**	**100**

TABLE 2: The level of awareness of Google Scholar.

Awareness of Google Scholar	SA		A		D		SD	
	n	%	*n*	%	*n*	%	*n*	%
1. I am aware of Google Scholar	21	9.4	102	45.7	71	31.8	29	13.1
2. I can make use of Google Scholar	34	15.3	98	43.9	84	37.7	7	3.1
3. I make use of Google Scholar via a library	1	0.4	6	2.7	195	87.5	21	9.4
4. I access Google Scholar via other medium	7	3.1	193	86.6	23	10.3	-	0
5. I use Google Scholar for research purposes	43	19.3	106	47.5	67	30.1	7	3.1

SA, strongly agree; A, agreed; D, disagreed; SD, strongly disagreed.

(43.9%) respondents agree to making use of Google Scholar, 84 (37.7%) respondents disagree to having made use of Google Scholar, while 7 (3.1%) strongly disagree to making use of Google Scholar. This shows that the majority of respondents strongly agree and agree with the fact that they can make use of Google Scholar.

As regards accessing Google Scholar via the library, one (0.4%) of the respondents attests that they strongly agree they often use Google Scholar through the library, while six (2.7%) of the respondents agree they often use Google Scholar via the library. However, 195 (87.5%) respondents disagree to have used Google Scholar via the library, while 21 (9.4%) strongly disagree. With this, it shows that respondents rarely use Google Scholar via the library. Furthermore, the results show the ratio of respondents that make use of Google Scholar via other mediums. A total of 7 (3.1%) respondents strongly agree using Google Scholar via other mediums, and 193 (86.6%) respondents agree to using Google Scholar via other mediums. From this, it is clear that the percentage of respondents using Google Scholar via other means trumps those using it via the library. With this result, it is clearly shown that the majority of respondents use Google Scholar via other mediums.

Of the 223 (100%) respondents, 43 (19.3%) strongly agree to using Google Scholar for research purposes, while 106 (47.5%) respondents agree to making use of Google Scholar for research purposes. However, 67 (30.1%) respondents disagree to using Google Scholar for research purposes, while 7 (3.1%) respondents strongly disagree. This shows that the majority of respondents use Google Scholar for research purposes.

Research Question 2

What is the perception of postgraduate students of the University of Ilorin towards the ease of use of the Google Scholar?

Table 3 shows the perceived ease of use of Google Scholar among the postgraduate students of the University of Ilorin. A total of 22 (9.9%) respondents strongly agree to finding Google Scholar easy to use; 121 (54.2%) respondents also agree to finding Google Scholar easy to use. However, 71 (31.8%) respondents disagree that Google Scholar is easy to use, while 9 (4.1%) strongly disagreed. With these results, it is clear that the majority of respondents agree that Google Scholar is easy to use. With regards to the mental effort required in interacting with Google Scholar, 37 (16.6%) respondents strongly agree that interacting with Google Scholar does not require a lot of mental effort, while 122 (54.7%) respondents agree with the statement. However, 56 (25.1%) respondents disagree with the statement that Google Scholar does not require a lot of mental effort in its interaction, while 8 (3.6%) strongly disagree. This shows that the majority of respondents agree that interacting with Google Scholar does not require a lot of mental effort.

Table 3 also confirms that 17 (7.6%) respondents strongly agree to finding it easy getting what they want on Google Scholar, while 114 (51.1%) agree to finding it easy getting what they want on Google Scholar. However, 81 (36.4%) respondents disagree to finding it easy to get what they want on Google Scholar, while 11 (4.9%) respondents strongly disagree. With this, it shows that the majority of respondents find it easy to get what they want on Google Scholar.

However, 46 (20.6%) respondents strongly agree to finding it easy to understand the terms used in Google Scholar; 86 (38.6%) respondents also agree with this statement. The remainder of the respondents, however, decided otherwise, with 79 (35.4%) of them disagreeing and 12 (5.4%) strongly disagreeing to finding it easy to understand the terms used in Google Scholar. This shows that the number of respondents who find it easy to understand the terms used in Google Scholar is slightly more than those who do not.

A total of 27 (12.1%) respondents strongly agree to finding it easy to learn to use Google Scholar and 103 (46.2%) also agree to finding it easy to learn to use Google Scholar. However, 77 (34.5%) of the remaining respondents disagree to finding it easy to learn to use Google Scholar, while 16 (7.2%) strongly disagree with the statement. This shows that the majority of respondents find it easy to learn to use Google Scholar.

Research Question 3

What is the perceived usefulness of Google Scholar to the postgraduate students of the University of Ilorin?

The results in Table 4 reveal that of the 223 (100%) respondents, only 36 (16.1%) strongly agree that using Google Scholar enables them to accomplish their tasks more quickly and 74 (33.2%) agree to the same statement. However, 92 (41.3%) respondents disagree and 21 (9.4%) strongly disagree. This shows that a slight majority of the respondents agree that Google Scholar enables them to accomplish their tasks faster. In terms of research, 29 (13.1%) respondents

TABLE 3: Perception of postgraduate students on the ease of use of Google Scholar.

Perceived ease of use	SA		A		D		SD	
	n	%	*n*	%	*n*	%	*n*	%
1. I find Google Scholar is easy to use	22	9.9	121	54.2	71	31.8	9	4.1
2. Interacting with Google Scholar does not require a lot of mental effort	37	16.6	122	54.7	56	25.1	8	3.6
3. I find it easy to get Google Scholar to do what I want it to do	17	7.6	114	51.1	81	36.4	11	4.9
4. I find it easy to understand the terms used throughout Google Scholar	46	20.6	86	38.6	79	35.4	12	5.4
5. Learning to use Google Scholar is easy for me	27	12.1	103	46.2	77	34.5	16	7.2

SA, strongly agree; A, agreed; D, disagreed; SD, strongly disagreed.

strongly agree to Google Scholar making it easier for them to do their research. A total of 52 (23.3%) respondents agree that Google Scholar makes their research work easier, but 93 (41.7%) respondents disagree and 49 (21.9%) of them strongly disagree. This statistics shows that the majority of respondents disagree that Google Scholar makes their research easier.

The results also confirm that of the 223 (100%) respondents, 25 (11.2%) strongly agree and 98 (43.9%) agree that using Google Scholar enhances their searching effectiveness. However, 84 (37.7%) respondents disagree and 16 (7.2%) strongly disagree. The numbers of respondents who agree that using Google Scholar enhances their searching effectiveness are almost the same as those who do not. However, those who agree are slightly more than those who do not. For any research to be useful, there is a need for finding relevant articles to assist the research. The table shows that 31 (13.9%) respondents strongly agree to finding many relevant articles with one search on Google Scholar. A total of 93 (41.7%) respondents also agree with this statement, but 77 (34.5%) disagree and 22 (9.9%) strongly disagree to finding many relevant articles on Google Scholar with one search. This statistic shows that a slight majority of the respondents agree to find many relevant articles on Google Scholar with one search. The results also show that 31 (13.9%) respondents strongly agree and 96 (43.1%) respondents agree that the resources found in Google Scholar relate well to their research. However, 54 (24.2%) and 52 (23.3%) respondents disagree and strongly disagree, respectively, that the resources found in Google Scholar relate well with their research. With this, it shows that a slight majority of the respondents agree that resources found in Google Scholar relate well with their research.

Research Question 4

What is the degree of comprehensiveness given to information found on Google Scholar by the postgraduate students of the University of Ilorin?

Table 5 shows how comprehensive Google Scholar is among the postgraduate students of the University of Ilorin. The table shows that 26 (11.6%) respondents strongly agree to easily understanding the resources found on Google Scholar while 103 (46.2%) respondents agree with the same statement. However, 78 (34.9) respondents disagree while 16 (7.2%) strongly disagree to understanding the resources found on Google Scholar. With this, it is obvious that majority of the respondents find it easy to understand resources on Google Scholar. The table also shows that 106 (47.5%) respondents strongly agree and 28 (12.6%) of them agree that Google Scholar has enough resources for their study. Of the respondents, 74 (33.2%) and 15 (6.7%) however disagree and strongly disagree, respectively, with the statement that Google Scholar has enough resources for their study. This shows that the majority of respondents agree that Google Scholar has enough resources for their study. In terms of the coverage of a wide range of topics in particular area of interest, 45 (20.2%) respondents strongly agree, 91 (40.8%) agree, 74 (33.2%) disagree and 13 (5.8%) strongly disagree that Google Scholar covers a wide range of topics in their particular area of interest; with this, it is clear that the majority of respondents agree that Google Scholar covers a wide range of topics in their particular area of interest. Also, 16 (7.2%) of the respondents strongly agree to often find exactly what they search for on Google Scholar. With 34 (15.2%) agreeing to this statement also, the remainder however do not share the same view. Of the respondents, 126 (56.5%) disagree and 47 (21.1%) strongly disagree to often finding exactly what they search for on Google Scholar. This shows that the majority of respondents do not find exactly what they search for on Google Scholar.

Table 5 also shows that 21 (9.4%) respondents strongly agree that Google Scholar usually provides details and in-depth information to them. Of the respondents, 92 (41.2%) also agree with the same statement. However, 88 (39.5%) disagree and 22 (9.9%) strongly disagree. This result shows that there is much difference between those agreeing and disagreeing with the above statement.

TABLE 4: Perceived usefulness of Google Scholar.

Perceived usefulness	SA		A		D		SD	
	n	%	*n*	%	*n*	%	*n*	%
1. Google Scholar enables quick completion of research	36	16.1	74	33.2	92	41.3	21	9.4
2. Google Scholar makes research work easier	29	13.1	52	23.3	93	41.7	49	21.9
3. Using Google Scholar enhances my searching effectiveness	25	11.2	98	43.9	84	37.7	16	7.2
4. I can find many relevant articles with one search in Google Scholar	31	13.9	93	41.7	77	34.5	22	9.9
5. The resources in Google Scholar relate well to my research	31	13.9	96	43.1	54	24.2	52	23.3

SA, strongly agree; A, agreed; D, disagree; SD, strongly disagreed.

TABLE 5: Comprehensiveness and subjective norm.

Comprehensiveness and subjective norm	SA		A		D		SD	
	n	%	*n*	%	*n*	%	*n*	%
1. The resources on Google Scholar are easy to understand	26	11.6	103	46.2	78	34.9	16	7.2
2. Google Scholar has enough resources for my study	106	47.5	28	12.6	74	33.2	15	6.7
3. Google Scholar covers a wide range of topics in my particular interest	45	20.2	91	40.8	74	33.2	13	5.8
4. I often find exactly what I search for while using Google Scholar	16	7.2	34	15.2	126	56.5	47	21.1
5. Google Scholar usually provides detail and in-depth information	21	9.4	92	41.2	88	39.5	22	9.9

SA, strongly agree; A, agreed; D, disagreed; SD, strongly disagreed.

Research Question 5

What is the satisfaction level of postgraduate students of the University of Ilorin with Google Scholar platform?

The results in Table 6 show satisfaction levels of the postgraduate students of the University of Ilorin with the use of Google Scholar. Of the 223 respondents, 58 (26.1%) strongly agree, 86 (38.6%) agree, 53 (23.7%) disagree and 26 (11.6%) strongly disagree that they made the correct decision to use Google Scholar. This shows that the majority of respondents agree that they made the correct decision to use Google Scholar. Also, 85 (38.1%) respondents strongly agree that they are satisfied with the results received from Google Scholar, and 120 (53.8%) also agree with this statement, but 15 (6.7%) disagree and 3 (1.4%) strongly disagree of being satisfied with the results received from Google Scholar. With this, it is clear that the majority of respondents are satisfied with the results received from Google Scholar. The table also shows 112 (16.6%) respondents strongly agree and indicate overall satisfaction with Google Scholar and 95 (42.6%) of them also agree with the same statement. However, 91 (50.2%) respondents disagree while 12 (5.4%) strongly disagree to being satisfied with Google Scholar. This shows that a considerable majority of the respondents are satisfied with Google Scholar.

Research Question 6

What is the loyalty and intention of postgraduate students of the University of Ilorin towards the use of Google Scholar platform?

Discussion of findings

The results demonstrate that the majority of respondents strongly agree and agree they are aware of Google Scholar and usually make use of it. This finding is in accordance with the findings of Hamid and Asadi (2010) that scientists are becoming more aware of the quantity of scholarly papers searchable by Google; they are increasingly relying on Google for finding scholarly literature. The fact that Google Scholar usually meets the information needs of the research might be the reason for its popularity and its awareness on the part of the respondents in this study. Any platform or site where users get what they want and provide the information the users want do not need any advertisement because that is enough to advertise itself. This is the case of Google Scholar as revealed in this study.

The results in this study show that majorities have trust in Google Scholar as a platform reliable for searching scholarly articles. This corroborates the earlier report by Shen (2012) whose results demonstrate that, on average, respondents found Google Scholar easy to use and access, and that Google Scholar is perceived as a useful resource for their research because it enhanced the respondents' searching effectiveness. Undoubtedly, Google Scholar is a veritable search tool; therefore, it is unexpected that the respondents in this study regarded it as being reliable for scholarly searching and it improves their search effectiveness.

The results in this study revealed continuous intention of using Google Scholar. This is also in support of the findings by Cothran (2011) who indicated that several factors influence graduate students' intention to use Google Scholar, including students' perceived usefulness of Google Scholar, their sense of loyalty towards the search engine and its perceived ease of use. As observed from the literature, any information system that is perceived as useful will attract continuous use by users. So, any information that is easier to use and access will attract increased patronage by the users. Therefore, the indication of continuous intention to use Google Scholar by the respondents in this study is not surprising. The argument by Felter (2005) that most researchers preferred the simplicity of Google and would likely opt for Google Scholar over many more capable, but complicated, databases may also be the rationale for the intention of the respondents in this study to use Google Scholar.

The findings in this study also reported the overall satisfaction with Google Scholar by the respondents. Undoubtedly, its usefulness in terms of providing relevance information, meeting users' needs, ease of use and access, and its perception of being useful by the respondents may be the reason for the overall satisfaction the respondents in this study indicated with Google Scholar.

The results also indicate respondents do not agree that Google Scholar makes research quicker and easier. There is no good thing without the side effect or shortcoming. Google Scholar is no exception. No wonder, Henderson (2005) tested the search capabilities of Google Scholar and found a ranking bias towards older articles that had, as a result of the passage of time, been cited the greatest number of times. Henderson (2006) also lamented that Google Scholar lacked the standard Google search features – 'Similar pages' and 'Did you mean' features for alternative spellings. On the other hand, Golderman and Connolly (2007) applauded the compatibility of Google Scholar with bibliographic software applications such as Endnote and RefWorks, but faulted Google Scholar for failing to include search histories, alert services and utilities for sorting, marking and saving results.

TABLE 6: Satisfaction of postgraduate students with Google Scholar.

Satisfaction	SA		A		D		SD	
	n	%	*n*	%	*n*	%	*n*	%
1. I think I made the correct decision to use Google Scholar	58	26.1	86	38.6	53	23.7	26	11.6
2. In general, I am satisfied with the results I received from Google Scholar	85	38.1	120	53.8	15	6.7	3	1.4
3. Overall, I am satisfied using Google Scholar	112	50.2	95	42.6	12	5.4	4	1.8

SA, strongly agree; A, agreed; D, disagreed; SD, strongly disagreed.

Recommendations

Based on the findings of this study, the following recommendations were made: There is a need for orientation programmes to be held to increase the level of awareness of people about Google Scholar and also make them understand the advantages of using Google Scholar via a library medium. One of the advantages of using Google Scholar via the library medium is that it makes available to users restricted access articles that have been subscribed for. Training should also be conducted to enhance searching on Google Scholar so as to assist researchers in making their research work easier and quicker.

There is also a need to include an 'Ask-a-Librarian' feature on Google Scholar so that it will assist users in retrieving exactly what they search for. This will in turn increase the satisfaction level of the postgraduate students using Google Scholar and increase the trust they have in using Google Scholar.

Conclusion

The study has examined the usefulness of Google Scholar for the postgraduate students of the University of Ilorin. So far, the results generally indicated that the postgraduate students are not only aware of Google Scholar but also that they can access it to get scholarly articles and literature. However, the respondents are not satisfied with using Google Scholar as it does not speed up their research nor does it make their research easier. Google Scholar was considered useful because it covers broad topics in the area of interest, and they also find relevant articles related to their search using Google Scholar. The flaws noted in this study are also relevant to those noted by Jasco (2005) when he stated that Google Scholar lacks sophisticated searches that can help users retrieve exactly what they search for.

Acknowledgements

We acknowledged all authors whose works were cited in this article. We also appreciate the Department of Information Science, UNISA for the funding of the publication of this article.

Competing interests

The authors declare that they have no financial or personal relationships that may have inappropriately influenced them in writing this article.

Authors' contributions

T.A. was involved in the writing and typing of the report for this article. O.M. collected the data that was used in this study while T.A. assisted in the analysis of the data collected in this study.

References

Adlington, J. & Benda, C., 2006, 'Checking under the hood: Evaluating Google Scholar for reference use', *Internet Reference Services Quarterly* 10(3–4), 135–148.

Bakkalbasi, N. & Bauer, K., 2005, 'An examination of citation counts in a new scholarly communication environment', *D-Lib Magazine* 11(September), 1–10, viewed 23 July 2016, from http://www.dlib.org/dlib/september05/bauer/09bauer.html

Bakkalbasi, N., Bauer, K., Glover, J. & Wang, L., 2006, 'Three options for citation tracking: Google Scholar, Scopus and Web of Science', *Biomedical Digital Libraries* 3, viewed 22 August 2015, from http://www.bio-diglib.com/content/3/1/7

Belkin, N.J. & Croft, A., 1992, 'Anomalous state of knowledge as the basis for information retrieval', *Canadian Journal of Library and Information Science* 5, 133–143.

Callicott, B. & Vaughn, D., 2005, 'Google Scholar vs. library scholar: Testing the performance of Schoogle', *Internet Reference Services Quarterly* 10(3–4), 71–88. https://doi.org/10.1300/J136v10n03_08

Cothran, T., 2011, 'Google Scholar acceptance and use among graduate students: A quantitative study', *Library & Information Science Research* 33, 293–301.

Felter, L.M., 2005, 'Google Scholar, Scirus, and the scholarly search revolution', *Searcher* 13, 43–48, viewed 23 July 2015, from http://www.scirus.com/press/pdf/searcher_reprint.pdf

Golderman, G. & Connolly, B., 2007, 'Who cited this?', *Library Journal* 132, 18–26.

Hamid, R. & Asadi, J.S., 2010, 'Google and the scholar: The role of Google in scientists' information seeking behavior', *Online Information Review* 34(2), 282–294. https://doi.org/10.1108/14684521011036990

Henderson, J., 2005, 'Google Scholar: A source for clinicians?', *CMAJ* 172, 1549–1550. https://doi.org/10.1503/cmaj.050404

Henderson, J., 2006, *Google Scholar goes to school the presence of Google Scholar on college and University web sites*, viewed 12 March 2016, from https://www.academia.edu/4056717/Google_Scholar_Goes_to_School_The_Presence_of_Google_Scholar_on_College_and_University_Web_Sites

Jasco, P., 2005, *The pros and cons of computing the h-index using Google Scholar*, University of Hawaii, Honolulu, HI.

Kousha, K. & Thelwall, M., 2006, 'Google Scholar citations and Google Web/URL citations: A multi-discipline exploratory analysis', Proceedings International Workshop on Webometrics, Informetrics and Scientometrics & Seventh COLLNET Meeting, Nancy, France, viewed 22 July 2015, from http://eprints.rclis.org/archive/00006416/

Mikki, S. 2009, 'Google Scholar Compared to Web of Science: A Literature Review', *Nordic Journal of Information Literacy in Higher Education* 1(1), 41–51.

Meho, L. & Yang, K., 2007, 'A new era in citation and bibliometric analyses: Web of Science, Scopus, and Google Scholar', *Journal of the American Society for Information Science and Technology* 58:1–21, viewed 30 April 2015, from http://arxiv.org/ftp/cs/papers/0612/0612132.pdf

Neuhaus, C., Neuhaus, E., & Asher, A., 2008, 'Google Scholar goes to school: The presence of Google Scholar on college and university web sites', *Journal of Academic of Librarianship* 34(1), 39–51.

Neuhaus, C., Neuhaus, E., Asher, A. & Wrede, C., 2006, 'The depth and breadth of Google Scholar: An empirical study', *Portal: Libraries and the Academy* 6(2), 127–141. https://doi.org/10.1353/pla.2006.0026

Noruzi, A., 2005, 'Web impact factor for Iranian universities', *Webology* 2(1), Article 11, viewed 12 March 2016, from: http://www.webology.ir/2005/v2n1/a11.html

Noruzi, A., 2006, 'Google Scholar: The new generation of citation indexes', *Libri* 55, 170–180, viewed 23 July 2015, from http://eprints.rclis.org/archive/00005542/01/Google_Scholar,_The_New_Generation_of_Citation_Indexes.pdf

Shen, L., 2012, 'Graduate students report strong acceptance and loyal usage of Google Scholar', *Evidence Based Library and Information Science* 7(4), 96–98. https://doi.org/10.18438/B8RW3P

Online Research Output Submission System as a mechanism to influence publication citations

Author:
Reetha Nundulall[1]

Affiliation:
[1]Research and Innovation Division, University of Johannesburg, South Africa

Corresponding author:
Reetha Nundulall,
reethan@uj.ac.za

Background: Higher Education Institutions (HEIs) need to ensure that the education provided meets the student's and employer's requirements, for today and the future. However, in addition to the challenges of teaching and learning, internationalisation, globalisation and world university rankings are rearing their heads thus increasing the demands made on many HEIs.

Objective: One of the ways in which HEIs can make their mark is through world university rankings. This may be achieved by exposing more information on new and innovative research knowledge to the broader community in the global market via research publications that attract citations on open access platforms, hence influencing the university's ranking. For this purpose and intent, a 'simple' and 'easy-to-use' online web tool was developed at a HEI. The aim was to have research publications submitted via the Online Research Output Submission System (OROSS) tool, screened and deposited in the institution's open access database.

Method: Training was provided to the relevant participants and a survey was conducted to ascertain the participants' perceptions about the utilisation of the OROSS tool and the training provided.

Conclusion: This article reflects on the pilot phase of a longitudinal study. Results of an evaluation conducted by the researcher of the OROSS application from a user perspective (process) are highlighted. In general, users rated OROSS favourably in terms of it being a useful, simple and easy-to-use web-based tool. The findings of this study may assist University of Johannesburg's executive management in deciding the fate of the OROSS tool for future use.

Introduction

'Higher education is rapidly growing and becoming a veritable global sector in its own right. That means challenges for educators, students and policy makers' (Yelland 2011:1).

Quality teaching in higher education matters for students learning outcomes. However, this presents higher education institutions (HEIs) with a range of challenges at a time when the higher education sector is coming under pressure from many different directions. HEIs need to ensure that the education provided meets the student's and employer's requirements, for today and the future. It is further elaborated that HEIs are complex organisations where the vision and strategy need to be well-aligned with bottom-up practices and innovations in teaching and learning (Henard & Roseveare 2012:3). Likewise, Eid (2014:1) is also of the view that higher education plays an essential role in society by creating new knowledge, transmitting it to students and fostering innovation.

However, in addition to the challenges of teaching and learning, internationalisation, globalisation and world university rankings are rearing their heads thus increasing the demands made on many HEIs.

According to Christopherson, Garretsen and Martin (2008:343), 'globalisation' has become increasingly prominent since the 1990s. It has become a feature of economic, social and political discourse, not just within the academic community but also in the popular press and in the world of policy-making. However, views tend to differ as to what this means and whether it is a trend for good or ill. In response to the issue of good and evil of globalisation, De Wit (2012:1) is of the view that there is a strong inclination to identify globalisation in higher education as 'evil' and internationalisation as 'good' although the reality is more complex. Similarly, the Centre for

Educational Research and Innovation (2009:23) is of the opinion that 'globalisation and internationalisation in higher education are potentially conflicting, while at the same time interactive and mutually generative'.

The differences and similarities between globalisation and internationalisation of higher education have been intensely debated over the past years with questions such as

> Is globalisation more an expression of the commercialisation of international higher education (education as a tradeable commodity) and internationalisation more the traditional concept of cooperation and exchange (higher education as a public good)? (De Wit 2012:1).

Blessinger (2015:1) is of the opinion that more internationalisation leads to more globalisation and that it can also be viewed as the integration of globalisation into the tripartite mission, that is, teaching, research and service of the university.

The view of Van Vught and Magnificus (2004:3) is that in higher education, the term 'internationalisation' is used to identify certain internal changes in HEIs, especially the integration of an international dimension into the functions of teaching, research and societal service. Internationalisation can also be interpreted as a process that can be shaped and influenced by HEIs themselves. 'Globalisation', on the other hand, is mostly seen as an external macro socio-economic process that cannot be influenced at the level of HEIs.

One of the ways in which HEIs can make their mark is through world university rankings. This may be achieved by exposing more information on new and innovative research knowledge to the broader community in the global market via research publications that attract citations on open access (OA) platforms, hence influencing the university's ranking. According to Jobbins (2014:1), the European University Association published a significant piece of research that highlighted one of the unintended consequences of university rankings. It validated the activities of national and international ranking agencies by recognising the role they played in the process of the continual improvement of higher education. However, Collyer (2013:257) argued that current debates about university ranking systems focussed on the need for improvement to ensure these measure 'output' and 'performance' rather than simply prestige and status. Although efforts to expand sources of data for these systems to eliminate bias towards science and Anglo-American university sector are welcomed, there is still a need to challenge and problematise the system of ranking itself. Consideration should also be given to the broad variety of work undertaken in diverse disciplines across the university sector, including efforts towards scholarship, when universities are being evaluated.

Public HEIs are also accountable in the marketisation of its institutions, and one of the elements is to profile themselves as leading institutions. One of the ways that this can be done is to set up quality mechanisms. A most significant and recent mechanism that most institutions are subjecting themselves to is the world ranking systems. Although there is a range of world ranking systems, not all of them use the same criteria for judging all the institutions. Nevertheless, the idea of subjecting themselves on the world ranking system requires institutions to introspect, plan, promote, strategise in meeting those objectives and go beyond the criteria for evaluation. Research production is increasingly becoming a focal point in higher education transformation to influence ranking (African Union 2007:8).

However, this research production must be made visible and accessible. One of the ways this may be achieved is through OA of research publications which in turn may influence citations, thus a rippling effect on university rankings. According to Gearing (2011:3), 'open access = accessibility = higher citations and research inquiries'. Similarly, Molecular Diversity Preservation International (MDPI) (1996–2016:1) concurred that the advantage of OA for authors is the high availability and visibility of articles. MDPI further elaborated that the higher citation impact of OA results from their high publicity and availability.

Citation can be defined as 'a written reference to a specific work or portion of a work by a particular author that identifies the document in which the work can be located' (Adriaanse & Rensleigh 2011:170).

In addition, De Groote (2015:2) stated that 'citation analysis is the process whereby the impact or "quality" of an article is assessed by counting the number of times other authors mention it in their work'. Citation analysis is used to establish the impact that a particular author or article had by showing which other authors cited the work within their own papers.

This article reflects on the pilot phase of a longitudinal study on the utilisation of the Online Research Output Submission System (OROSS) tool as a mechanism to influence citations of published research outputs on the OA database.

According to Graziano and Raulin (2013:148), longitudinal study follows the same people over time to observe development changes, thus controlling for cohort effects. However, the drawback is that this design has the disadvantage of taking a long time to complete. Arising out of the pilot study, the researcher will explore the implementation and utilisation of the OROSS tool by the larger community of University of Johannesburg (UJ). This will need to be monitored and evaluated over a period of time.

Literature review

Open access

It is more than a decade since the Budapest Open Access Initiative coined the term OA and united a movement to free scholarly literature from barriers. Incredible progress has been made in this time, and the momentum only seems to be increasing in recent year. OA is now considered to be inevitable, with one prediction estimating that it will be the dominant model for scholarly literature in the next decade (Dawson 2013:1).

According to Drahos and Braithwaite (2002:15), bulk of the intellectual property rights are owned by corporations instead of the initial creators. The corporations acquire intellectual property portfolios which end up in patent portfolios where citizens have to pay for the same knowledge again. Drahos and Braithwaite further added that the recycling of public knowledge for private reward is also occurring in the educational sector. Copyright owners uplift university-generated, publicly funded research into journals or databases and then charge universities and students for the use of them, incurring exorbitant costs. Hence, countries behind the development of the intellectual property and copyright systems are the major beneficiaries, with developing countries being the net importers of knowledge (Drahos & Braithwaite 2002:11).

However, the global shift towards making research findings available free of charge for readers, so-called OA, was confirmed in a study funded by the European Commission. The new research suggests that OA is reaching the tipping point, with around 50% of scientific papers published in 2011 is now available for free (European Commission 2013a:1).

The European Union Commission also announced new policies both for OA to publications and for access to data arising from research funded under Horizon 2020, the successor to Framework Programme 7, which will have come into effect in 2014 (Finch Report 2013:2). Similarly, in South Africa, in a statement released by the National Research Foundation (NRF) that as from 01 March 2015, authors of research papers generated from research either fully or partially funded by NRF are required to deposit their final peer-reviewed manuscripts that have been accepted by the journals to the administering institutional repository with an embargo of no more than 12 months. The NRF further requires its stakeholder community to actively seek collaboration with the international scientific community to facilitate the OA of publications generated from publicly funded research across the world (Sinha 2015:1). For Africa, OA allows those who have been largely silent and invisible contributors to global research production to express themselves freely (Botman 2012:3).

Open access in higher education

According to Botman (2012:2), 'knowledge production is important because it drives development, and open access accelerates that drive'.

Open access may be defined as the practice of providing online access to scientific information that is free of charge to the end user and that is reusable. In the context of research and innovation, 'scientific information' can refer to (I) peer-reviewed scientific research articles (published in scholarly journals) or (II) research data (data underlying publications, curated data or raw data). There are two main routes towards OA to publications, one of which is 'self-archiving'. This means that the published article or the final peer-reviewed manuscript is archived by the author or a representative in an online repository before, alongside or after its publication. Repository software usually allow authors to delay access to the article (embargo period) (European Commission 2013b:2).

The OA philosophy is transforming higher education. From the use of social media to engage students to tools designed to facilitate record keeping in higher education, it would seem the academic revolution will be digitised. Arguably no other aspects of digital hold the promise of the OA philosophy and open educational resources (OER). It seems that the benefits of OA in higher education could go beyond teaching and research. A report published by JISC (Joint Information Systems Committee, a United Kingdom not-for-profit company), showed that the private sector also benefitted from OA in higher education (The Guardian 2014:1).

A similar view is expressed by Hall (2014:1) who stated that universities are 'digital machines' and for the future research the need for openness is far more than a convenience. The rise in volume and rate of production of online publications and digital data sets has now outgrown the limits of conventional research methods, and it is changing the ways in which new knowledge is created. Without openness across global digital networks, it is doubtful that large and complex problems can be solved.

There are many arguments in favour of new OA publishing models providing cost-efficient methods for disseminating research findings, eradicating excess profits by publishers and massively widening the readership of scholarly works (Gatti 2014:1). There is even the boycotting of some academic publishers by Professor Randy Schekman who collected a Nobel Prize for physiology and medicine in December 2013. Professor Schekman boycotted three 'luxury' scientific journals stating that their decisions to publish work, or not, are made according to how fashionable it is, rather than its scientific merit, and pursuing their own agenda to publish work that will be cited (Livermore 2014:1). Likewise, Boswell (2014:2) stated that South African universities pay thrice for the privilege of publication – once for the cost of research, a second time for the page fees and a third time for institutional access to journal. Boswell further stated that it may be time for South African universities to pursue an international agreement that secures the publications' income of universities and academics. If they do not, then publishing houses will continue to tell stories about printing, distribution, marketing and administration costs.

However, Brown (2014:1–2) argued to the contrary. On pondering over many accusations made of publishers raking in profits while adding little value, he is of the opinion that publishers are doing a great deal to help move science forward. He stated that although the online space has afforded benefits to all, publishers have been presented with new challenges by this medium. Many assume that publishers' costs have declined because of non-printing and distribution of physical copies but there are important new functions requiring significant expenditures. Some of these are the need for strong, skilled editors to ensure that research can be universally understood, to recognise emerging fields and create new journals, and to build and maintain the brands and reputation of journals; recruitment and management of editorial review board; coordination of peer review to ensure integrity of scholarly record; and developing new ways for students, researchers and librarians to find and use content via metadata, XML generation, tagging and a host of other tools. This is concurred by Osborne (2014:2) who stated that there is no such thing as free access to academic research and for those who wish to have access, there is an admission cost. He is of the view that UK scholars who are obliged to publish in Gold OA journals will end up publishing in journals that are less international and, although all that access to them is cost-free, are in fact less accessed. UK research published via this medium will end up being ignored.

The argument by Brown regarding the important role that publishing houses play to ensure quality and integrity in research may be considered as valid in light of a new challenge that is now impacting on OA publishing, that is, the threat of predatory publishers and fake or hijacked journals.

The publishing of scholarly journals has undergone radical transformation because of the emergence of Internet.

According to Dadkhan and Maliszewski (2015:281), hijacked journals are launched by fraudulent cyber entities for financial gain by using names and ISSNs of reputable journals and cheat researchers. They publish papers by receiving publication charges similar to those of OA journals, but they are not authentic. Gunaydin and Dogan (2015:94) had similarly stated that recently scientists have been the targets for cybercrime in different ways. Hijacked or fake journals and predatory journals have emerged and many scientists have been victimised by these journals. Authors and readers are deceived by being charged for services that are not provided, like peer review or editorial review. The journals also do not follow traditional standards for the acceptance of articles published.

Likewise, Beall (2012:179) highlighted the signs of predatory publishers where they:

- set up websites that closely resemble those of legitimate online publishers
- publish questionable journals of low quality
- are dishonest and lack transparency
- solicit manuscripts from researchers but fail to mention the required author fee, which is revealed after the paper is accepted and published. The author is obliged to pay as they are often asked to sign over their copyright as part of the submission process.

Beall was of the opinion that the publishers are not totally responsible for this. The scientists who are taking the unethical shortcuts and paying for the publication of plagiarised or self-plagiarised work are also to be blamed. These unethical scientists gaming the system are earning tenure and promotion at the expense of the honest. This is concurred by Gunaydin and Dogan (2015:96) who stated that scientists are also to blame as by sending their work to predatory journals are in fact supporting the system and should resist the temptation of publishing their low quality work fast and with ease. However, Gunaydin and Dogan (2015:94) argued that because many scientists are under pressure to publish hence, they are 'forced' to publish to gain promotion, reputation, pay rise and so on.

The pressure on academics to publish in scientific journals is also highlighted by Singh and Remenyi (2016:54) who stated that the term *publish or perish* which originated in the United States of America in the 1930s has progressively spread throughout academe around the world in subsequent decades. Traditionally, to publish in a scientific journal is still a substantial challenge for most academics, whereby the research has to be relevant, rigorous and written in academic language. Added to this reviewers' feedback could result in considerable amount of additional work taking a long time to complete. There is also the issue of some leading journals having a backlog in their publications and that it may take a year or longer after the paper has been accepted before it appears in print.

The researcher is of the opinion that perhaps these may be some of the contributing factors tempting some academics to look for a 'quick solution' by publishing in these journals. The threats in publishing in these journals could result in poor quality work being published, and in large volumes, researchers' reputation may be comprised. This could also impact negatively on their affiliated institutions, especially if these HEIs are subjecting themselves to the world university ranking system.

Jalalian and Mahboobi (2014:394) are of the opinion that fake publishers and impact factors have created an urgent need to evaluate the methods that are currently used to assess academic research. As a long-term strategy, it is suggested to move from quantitative methods to qualitative approaches to assessing the quality of academic research to protect academia from all the obvious misconduct of fake publishers, hijacked journals, and the predatory, non-reviewed, low quality publications that are great threats to the validity and integrity to science.

Whatever the challenges and arguments for and against OA that may continue, ultimately the researchers must enjoy the academic freedom to choose their preferred channels of publications (Rice 2014:1).

Research problem

Challenges are experienced by researchers to make timeous submission of accredited research publications for the Department of Higher Education and Training (DHET) subsidy and accredited and non-accredited publications for depositing into the institutional repository for citation purpose.

In addition to their teaching and learning and community engagement roles, the academics are expected to do research and publish their work. Research publications are critical. Visibility of high quantity and quality of publications add to the stature of an institution, especially for those HEIs who are subjecting themselves to world university rankings. Saddled with these tasks, researchers have the administrative onus to submit these publications to the institution. Because it is the technology era, mechanisms should be in place to address these challenges.

The OROSS tool was developed to address the optimal way to manage and streamline the submission process. It is also to assist in ensuring that research publication information is managed effectively and efficiently, resulting in no financial and citation loss to the institution.

Development of the Online Research Output Submission System tool

University of Johannesburg, a comprehensive HEI in Gauteng, has a goal to be recognised globally and win a position in university rankings; planning, promoting and strategising is required to increase its visibility. The option of the 'self-archiving' route to deposit publications in OA in order to make research data visible and accessible, receive citations and improve the university's ranking was explored. This resulted in the development of a new and simple tool for this purpose, hence the birth of the OROSS tool. This tool was developed by Professor Alan Amory of UJ's Centre for Academic Technology (CAT), and the software is available under the General Public License (GPL). The purpose of this tool was to encourage researchers to submit all their research publications timeously without burdening them with too many administrative processes. The aim was to receive and screen as many publications as possible for depositing in the institutional repository without infringing any copyright. Hence, research information is being readily visible and accessible for referencing, influencing citations and thus a rippling effect on university rankings.

With the NRF's mandate (2015) that:

> from 1 March 2015, authors of research papers generated from research either partially or fully funded by NRF, when submitting and publishing in academic journals, should deposit their final peer-reviewed manuscripts that have been accepted, to the administering institution repository with an embargo period of no more than 12 months. (p. 1)

further supported the need for the OROSS tool.

According to Towert (2015),

> OROSS is not intended to be a database to store research output submission; it merely routes what has been captured within the faculties to the library for archiving in the institutional repository (UJDSpace) for web visibility/exposure. Research outputs are also routed to the Faculty Coordinators (FCs) responsible for managing research output in the faculties to screen and capture on the Research Information Management System (RIMS) for the Department of Higher Education and Training (DHET) subsidy purpose. (p. 1)

University of Johannesburg's institutional repository (UJDSpace) was started in the late 1990s. UJ was one of the first universities in Africa to implement the new software called DSpace. Many breakthroughs were achieved, one of which was the loading of theses and dissertations electronically. At the beginning of 2016, migration of the institutional repository to a new software started in order to improve the structure. This was successfully achieved by the end of April 2016. The institutional repository is no longer called UJDSpace but UJ Institutional Repository (UJIR) (University of Johannesburg 2016:11).

The need to drive online visibility is concurred by Louw (2014:1–2) who cited that researchers at cyber metrics use web content, web visibility and web impact to determine ranking. The number of links and pages on the site domain; files in online formats such as pdf and doc; articles, papers and citations in the academic domain; as well as articles published in high impact international journals all contribute to ranking. after University of Cape Town (UCT) recently launched the OpenUCT institutional repository, providing a platform for staff to share their research, teaching and learning content with the world.

In another briefing paper written by Swan (2017) for Open Access Scholarly Information Sourcebook (OASIS) is that at the beginning of 2009, there was over 1300 repositories around the world, and it has been growing at an average rate of one per day over the last 3 years. Swan further highlighted some of the advantages of an institutional repository as follows:

- opens up the university's outputs to the world hence maximising visibility and impact of these outputs
- showcases the university to prospective staff, students and other stakeholders
- enables and encourages interdisciplinary approaches to research
- supports student endeavours, providing access to theses and dissertations and a location for the development of e-portfolios.

One of the aims of developing OROSS is to allow the researcher to capture his or her outputs in a quick and simple way. It is also to avoid undue administrative burden on the researcher's teaching, learning and research work load. Once captured, the publication will be immediately available to the Library department for screening and uploading on OA. At the same time, the faculties will receive it for uploading it on RIMS for DHET subsidy purpose, as illustrated in the 'workflow' (Figure 1).

Implementation of Online Research Output Submission System: A pilot study

The pilot phase is part of a longitudinal study, as illustrated in Figure 2.

As a pilot study, OROSS was formally introduced in July 2014 in one of the nine faculties as requested by the Dean. Five out of fifteen departments volunteered to participate.

According to Vogt and Johnson (2016:326), a pilot study is 'a preliminary test or study to try out procedures and discover problems before the main study begins'. This enables researchers to make important corrections and adjustments. It is a research project's 'dress rehearsal'. In a pilot, the entire study with all its instruments and procedures is conducted in miniature (e.g. on a small sample). 'By contrast, a *pretest, definition (b), is used to assess some part of an instrument or procedure' (Vogt & Johnson 2016:326).

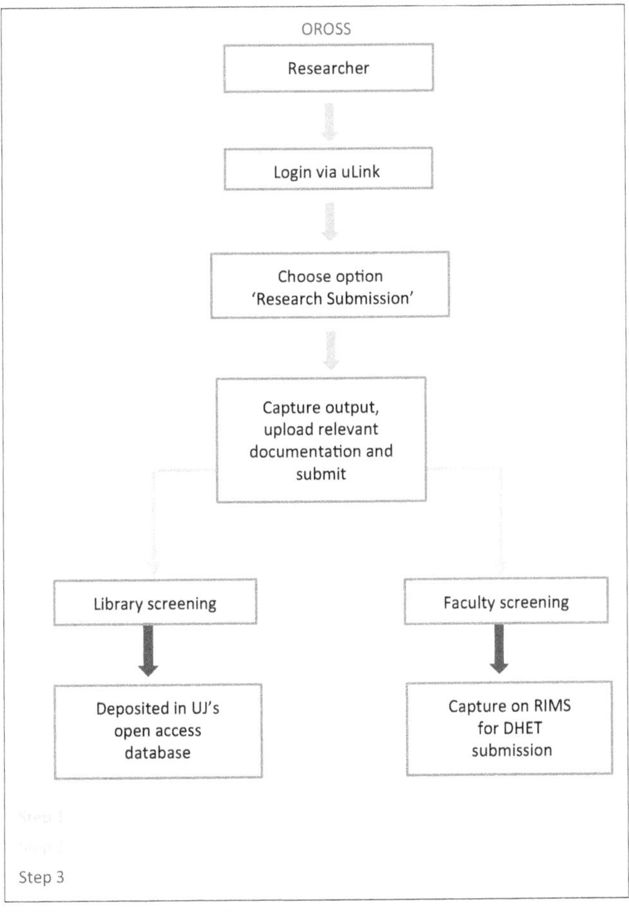

OROSS, Online Research Output Submission System

FIGURE 1: Online Research Output Submission System work flow.

Utilisation of OROSS involved the completion of a few online steps and providing the relevant documentation as required. Several hands-on training sessions were provided by the Library and Information Services Department in conjunction with the Research and Innovation Division to the volunteers (researchers and administrative support staff). Submissions were then viewed, screened for copyrights and deposited in the UJ's repository – that is, the OA database while at the same time these outputs were channelled to the faculty for DHET subsidy consideration.

The aim to pilot the utilisation of OROSS was to ascertain its influence on the timeframe submission on researchers to 'self-archive' their publications. An additional aim was to gauge the perception of the end users on OROSS and the value of the tool for future use.

Research methodology

According to Clough and Nutbrown (2012:21), the task of methodology 'is to explain the particularity of the methods made for a given study'. The purpose of a methodology is to show not how such and such appeared to be the best method available for the given purposes of the study, but how and why this way of doing it was unavoidable – was required by – in the context and purpose of this particular enquiry. Methodology requires researchers to justify their particular research decisions from the outset to the conclusion of their enquiry.

Study type

For the purpose of this study, the quantitative research method using the inductive strategy was chosen, as illustrated in Figure 3.

According to Neuman (2014):

> in quantitative studies, measurement is a distinct step in the research process that occurs prior to data collection. Quantitative measurement has a special terminology and set of techniques because the goal is to precisely capture details of the empirical social world and express what we find in numbers. (p. 203)

Similarly, Zappia (2015:1) described quantitative research as where the emphasis is on objectivity and the use of statistics or data gathered through polls, questionnaires or surveys. The data gathered are then generalised across groups of people to explain a trend or phenomena. Zappia further elaborated that this method can avoid personal bias in studying the research problem in the social sciences.

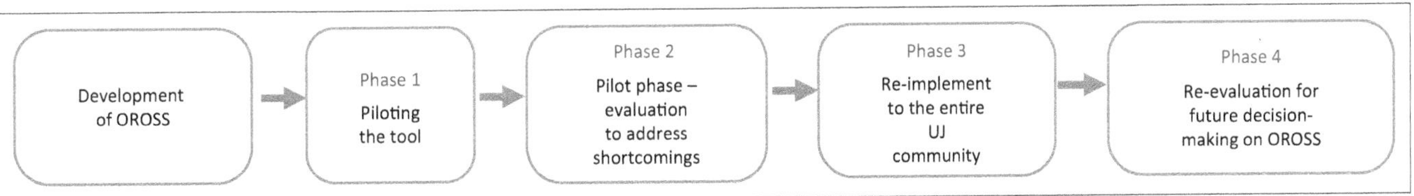

FIGURE 2: Online Research Output Submission System as a longitudinal study.

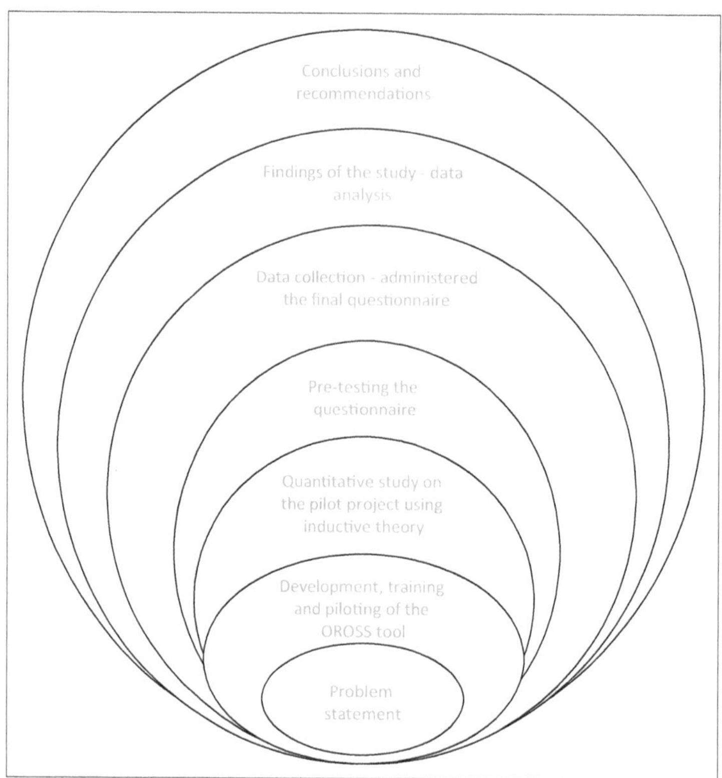

FIGURE 3: Research methodology.

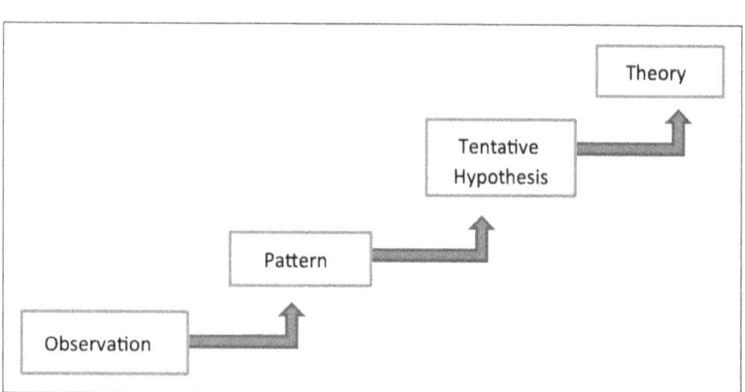

Source: Trochim, W.M.K. & Donnelly, J.P., 2008, *The research methods knowledge base*, 3rd edn., p. 17, Cengage Learning, Mason, OH.

FIGURE 4: A schematic representation of inductive reasoning.

Inductive reasoning or strategy is moving from specific observations to broader generalisations and theories. It starts with specific observations and measures, then detecting patterns and regularities, formulate some tentative hypotheses that can be explored, and finally end up developing some general conclusions or theories as indicated in Figure 4 (Trochim & Donnelly 2008:17).

A survey via a questionnaire was chosen to collect data. Key (1997:1) defined a questionnaire as a means of eliciting the feelings, beliefs, experiences, perceptions or attitudes of some sample of individuals. As a data collecting instrument, it could be structured or unstructured.

A semi-structured questionnaire was designed to obtain the perceptions, attitudes and preferences of the tool from the volunteers trained on OROSS, as well as the impact of the training provided. This method was a quick and easy means to reach the trained group in a short space of time.

Pre-testing of the instrument

Prior to administering the survey, a trial run was done to test the instrument. The purpose of this was to test the questionnaire for clarity, ascertain if there were any problems, and whether it was simple and easy to understand. Suggestions were received, reviewed and incorporated.

The final questionnaire was then administered as an online survey with the assistance from the UJ's Statkon Department. The URL link was emailed to the 41 staff members that made up the total sample size. With a slow response to the questionnaire by the deadline date, the researcher followed up with telephone calls to those staff members who were contactable. It was established that although the names of some of the staff members on the list did belong to the specific departments, they did not receive training. In two cases, the use of OROSS was not applicable to them, whereas in another two cases one person was no longer at the university while the other was overseas. The final target audience was 34 out of the 41 who did receive the training. Seventeen (50%) of the target audience responded to the questionnaire.

Ethical considerations

To conduct the online survey, an email was sent to the Dean of the pilot faculty who agreed via email dated 17 February 2015 and was also referred to the Vice-Dean: Research of the faculty for further liaison. Suggestion on data analysis and approval was provided by the Vice-Dean (Research) via email dated 22 July 2016.

Evaluation of the Online Research Output Submission System tool

Findings of the study

Data analysis

Quantitative data: For the purpose of this study, a survey via a questionnaire was chosen as one of the instruments to collect data. The questionnaire was designed to obtain feedback from the respondents on the training provided on the utilisation of OROSS and its user-friendliness.

The analysis of the data gathered via the questionnaires are revealed in Parts 1–5.

Part 1: Biographic data: A 50% return was received from respondents in the five departments. The only purpose of obtaining this data was to communicate with those respondents who may have indicated that they had experienced challenges when utilising OROSS. Data on race and gender were not relevant for this study.

Part 2: Evaluation of the training to use Online Research Output Submission System: This section was to ascertain feedback on the training provided. Figure 5 indicates that 50% or more respondents from four out of five departments, that is, Departments A, B, C and D agreed that their training requirements were met while Departments C and D (34%) strongly agreed. With respondents in departments choosing to remain neutral, in particular, Department E (100%) will provide the researcher an opportunity to do a follow-up to address the feedback provided.

Part 3: Evaluation of the Online Research Output Submission System tool: The purpose of this section was to obtain the respondents' perceptions about the OROSS tool. According to Singh (2013:5), 'website usability plays a vital role in the success of a website. Good usability helps to provide a seamless experience for users and improve the chance of successes'.

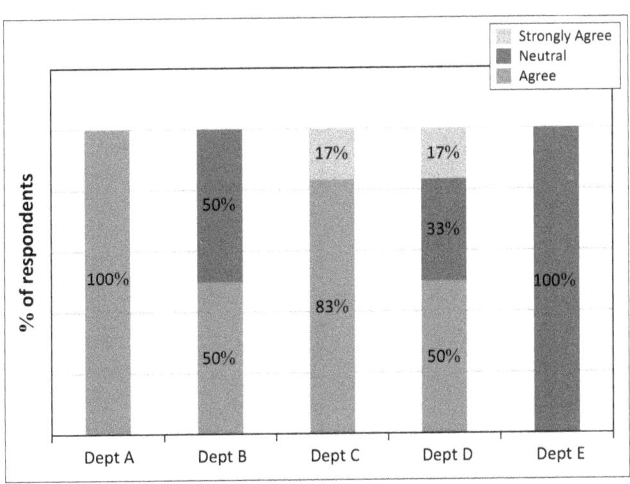

FIGURE 5: Online Research Output Submission System training met my requirements.

Figure 6 shows that more than 50% of the respondents agreed or strongly agreed that the OROSS app is user-friendly with Department E having a 100% agreement. The researcher is of the opinion that there is no cause for concern regarding those departments that remained neutral as the reasons provided did not make a significant impact on the overall data analysis, for example, 'haven't used it yet' and 'no outputs [to capture]'. Attempts will be made to address the issues raised by those respondents who have disagreed or strongly disagreed, that is, 34% in Department C and 20% in Department D.

Figure 7 indicates that more than 50% of the respondents agreed or strongly agreed that OROSS is a useful tool with Departments A and E having a 100% consensus. Reasons provided by those respondents who remained neutral did not make a significant impact on the overall data analysis, for example, 'haven't used it yet' and 'no output [to capture]'.

Figure 8 shows that more than 50% of the respondents agreed or strongly agreed that the OROSS has achieved the Vice Chancellor's directive for a simple, easy-to-use web-based tool for researchers to submit their research online for subsidy and archival with Department E having a 100% of

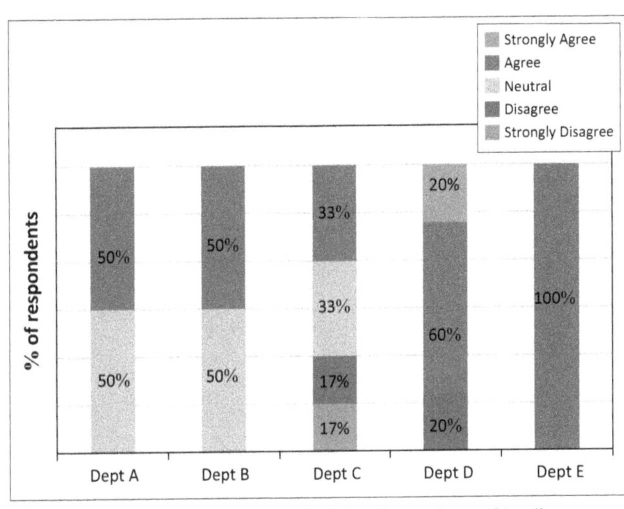

FIGURE 6: Online Research Output Submission System is user-friendly.

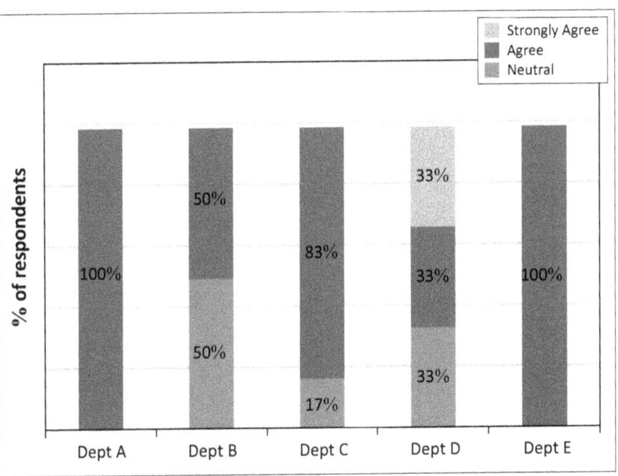

FIGURE 7: Online Research Output Submission System is a useful tool.

strongly agreeing. The researcher will attempt to address the issues raised by respondents who opted to be neutral.

Part 4: Conceptual outcome: This section was to ascertain the theoretic outcome of the OROSS training. Figure 9 indicates that respondents from all five departments agreed at varying percentage that the OROSS training provided them with a better insight regarding manuscripts and the publisher version PDF copy policies and institutional archiving in UJ's OA database. An overwhelming response of 100% was received from Departments A and E, whereas 83% from Department C. A fair response of 50% and 40% was received from Departments B and D, respectively. Feedback from respondents who remained neutral did not make a significant impact on the overall data analysis.

Part 5: Practical outcomes: This section was to gauge the impact of the training on the respondents and whether the tool is recommended for future use. According to Feghali, Zbib and Hallal (2011:84), the user attitude is important as it contributes to the user's intention to use the system.

Figure 10 indicates that there was an overwhelming response from all five departments where it was agreed or strongly agreed that they were confident to 'self-load' their outputs after the training. With the tool being user-friendly (Figure 6) and simple to use (Figure 8), a confident researcher can upload publications with minimal effort.

According to Feghali et al. (2011:84), the satisfied users of a website may recommend it to others.

Figure 11 shows that a fair percentage of respondents favoured OROSS be implemented on a permanent basis. However, there was a greater lean towards it being recommended for implementation on an optional basis.

Overall summary of the analysis

Overall analysis of the data leans towards a positive attitude on the utilisation of the OROSS tool, in particular, respondents found that OROSS was a 'useful tool' (Figure 7) and that it was also 'a simple and easy web-based tool' (Figure 8). A very significant finding is that an overwhelming percentage of respondents from all five departments agreed that the OROSS training provided them with a better insight regarding manuscripts and the publisher version PDF copy policies and institutional archiving in UJ's OA database (Figure 9). It is important for researchers to understand what is required, hence impacting on the 'buy-in' of the utilisation of the tool.

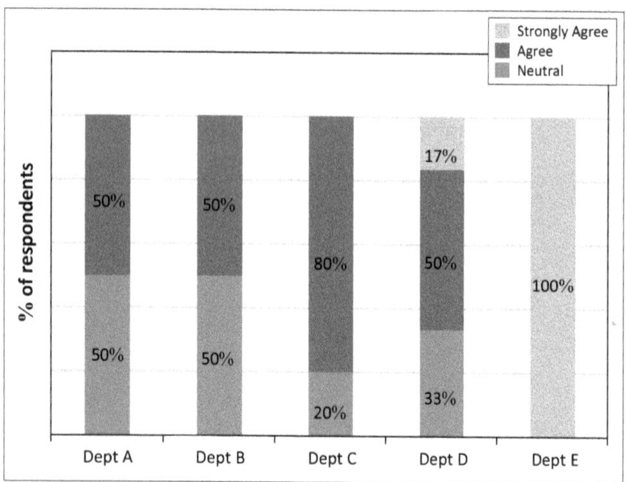

FIGURE 8: Online Research Output Submission System is a simple, easy-to-use web-based tool.

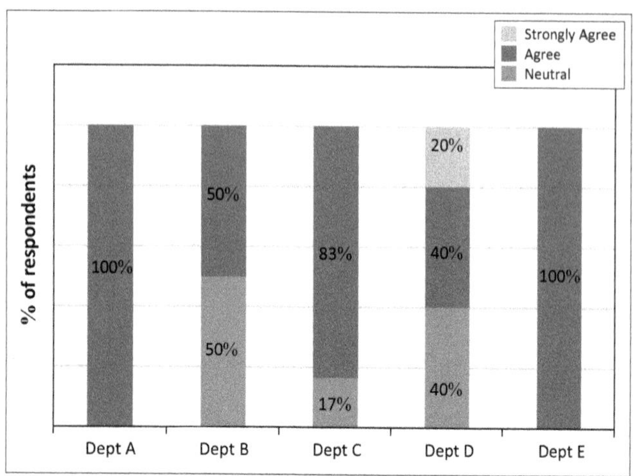

FIGURE 9: Better insight.

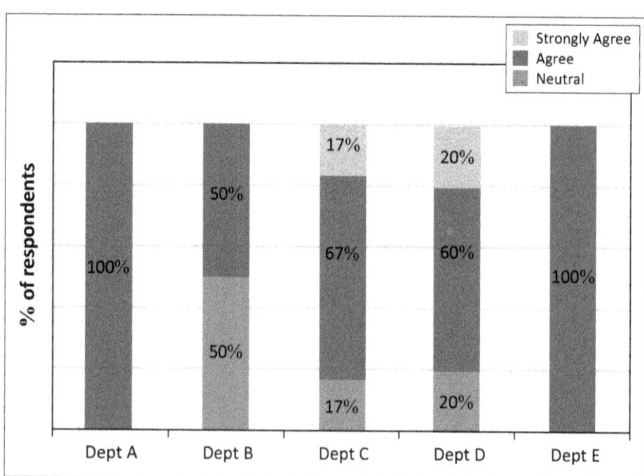

FIGURE 10: Confidence to 'self-upload' output.

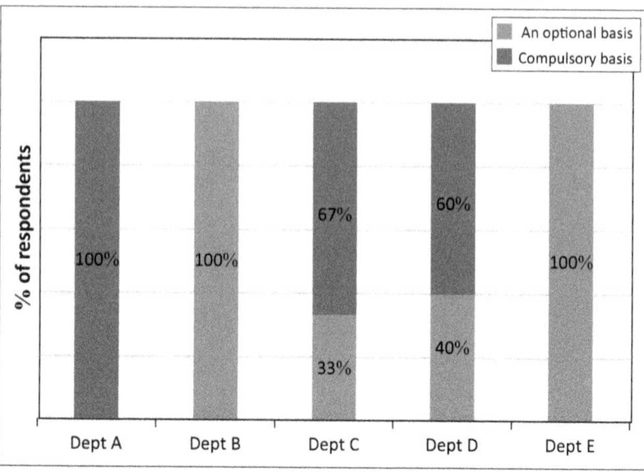

FIGURE 11: Utilisation of Online Research Output Submission System.

Feedback received from those respondents who have 'disagreed', 'totally disagreed' or opted to remain 'neutral' did not make a significant impact on the overall data analysis. However, this has provided the basis on which the tool may be reviewed for future enhancement and utilisation.

Review of the Online Research Output Submission System tool in its entirety

Feedback via the survey conducted indicated a positive uptake on the utilisation of OROSS. Data extracted in January 2016 (Macanda 2016) indicated that there had been a marked increase in publication volumes deposited in the UJ repository (Figure 12).

Figure 12 indicates that as on December 2015, there had been a marked increase in the volume of publications uploaded onto UJ's OA database in comparison with 2014, that is, from 499 to 698 publications (39.9% increase).

Development of the tool commenced in 2013. Once operational, it was left at the faculties' discretion to utilise this tool. Prior to the pilot study in July 2014, the submission of publications in UJ's OA database from January to June 2014 was 207, while for the same period in 2015 the volume of submission increased to 314, that is, by 51.7%.

The overall percentage increase of 39.9% of publications in UJ's OA database as on December 2015 is encouraging, especially for citation purposes. However, a shortfall in this process was noted. Because of there being no measuring mechanism in the OROSS tool, it cannot be confirmed that all the outputs deposited in the repository were received via the OROSS submission.

The researcher will explore possible solutions to address this shortcoming which will form another part of this longitudinal study.

Conclusion

The research arena has been steadily evolving and HEIs are continuously subjected to new challenges and demands nationally and globally.

One of the major challenges is that HEIs must increase their income apart from the dwindling funds received from government. It has now become crucial for HEIs to drive the process to increase research output publications in order to increase their subsidies from the DHET. To add to the funding challenges, focus on globalisation, internationalisation and world university ranking and recognition has gained momentum. Hence, universities

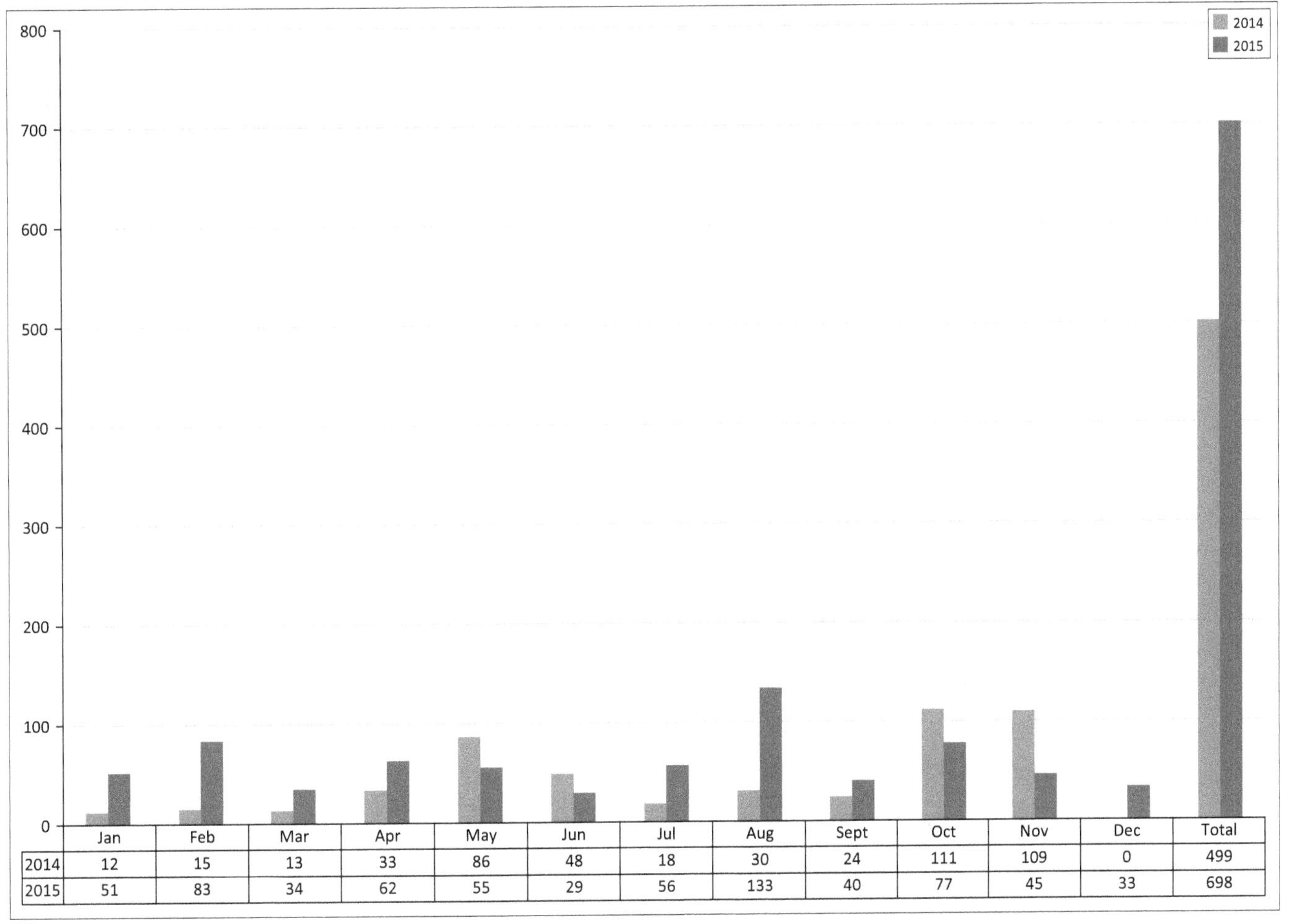

	Jan	Feb	Mar	Apr	May	Jun	Jul	Aug	Sept	Oct	Nov	Dec	Total
2014	12	15	13	33	86	48	18	30	24	111	109	0	499
2015	51	83	34	62	55	29	56	133	40	77	45	33	698

Source: Macanda, M., 2016, email, 04 January, macabam@uj.ac.za

FIGURE 12: Volume of publications uploaded in the open access database.

may focus on ranking and recognition to get the attention of their national and global stakeholders.

One of the ways to address some of these challenges is to get research publications in OA. This will assist universities and academics to get their research knowledge to a wider audience to make their work more relevant and have greater impact. It will also attract citations that will have a ripple effect on the university's ranking. The OA philosophy is transforming higher education as universities are now considered 'digital machines'. The rise in volume and rate of production of online publications has now outgrown the limits of conventional researcher methods. OA publishing models are considered as a cost-efficient method of disseminating research findings, eradicating excess profits by publishers and massively widening the readership of scholarly works.

University of Johannesburg is not immune to these challenges. Research is one of the critical key strategic goals of the institution and huge investments in various ways are made to promote this agenda. Hence, in addition to an institution achieving its goals to increase publications for subsidy purposes and promote research productivity, citations of publications play a key role in contributing to the institution's position in the world university rankings, globalisation and internationalisation.

One of the ways in which this may be achieved is the vigorous promotion of the utilisation of the OROSS tool. With a very positive feedback indicated in Figure 10 where an overwhelming response from all five departments agreed or strongly agreed that they were confident to 'self-load' their outputs after the training, the tool being user-friendly (Figure 6) and simple to use (Figure 8), a confident researcher can upload publications with minimal effort. This is advantageous as publications can be submitted speedily and timeously to the Library department for screening and depositing in the institutional repository, hence immediate accessibility to the wider market for citation.

The impact of citations influencing a university's ranking is highlighted in the latest 2015 QS World University of Rankings. Stellenbosch University (SUN) outranked the University of Witwatersrand (Wits) by becoming South Africa's second best university after UCT. SUN moved from 390th in 2014 to 302nd in 2015, and the reason attributed to this big climb has been credited to research output and impact measured – not only in terms of the number of papers but also citations (Staff Writer 2015:1–2).

Prior to the development of the OROSS tool, the depositing of research publications in the institutional repository was done via manual process. The documents loaded in a particular year were for the period n-1 (n=current year, 1=previous year), hence a delay in having documents readily available for public viewing, thus impacting on citations. With the implementation of the OROSS tool, current publications are made available to the Library department to deposit in the institutional repository for citation.

Figure 12 shows a marked increase in the volume of publications uploaded in the OA database. The assumption is that this has resulted from the utilisation of the OROSS tool. However, unfortunately because of a minor flaw in the development of the tool, there was no solid evidence to confirm that majority of the publications that were deposited in the repository were submitted via the OROSS tool.

An alternate way that researchers may capture research outputs is via the Research Information Management System (RIMS). This is a system purchased by the Department of Science and Technology with other consortium members being the DHET, NRF and some other South African HEIs, including UJ. This system is utilised by the UJ's Research and Innovation Division to make the final submission of accredited research publications to the DHET for subsidy purposes. There is also a provision in the system to upload the manuscript and the final officially published outputs. The Library department may then access the documentation via RIMS for screening and depositing in the UJ repository. However, the disadvantage of submitting via this system is that currently non-accredited outputs (i.e. publications not submitted for DHET subsidy) are not captured. Hence, the Library department will not be aware of these publications.

RIMS is a complex system requiring much training in capturing outputs as detailed information is required. This will be a time-consuming process that may lead to a possibility of researcher frustration and time delay in getting the research outputs in the UJ repository.

Hence, the development of OROSS with one of the aims being to allow the researcher to capture his or her outputs in a quick and simple way.

With the positive feedback received regarding the OROSS tool, the way forward is that the researcher will develop strategies for the promotion on the utilisation of the tool first to the entire academic community in the pilot faculty and then to the entire UJ community with the optimism of assisting UJ achieving a similar outcome as SUN's success rate in rankings.

After the post-pilot study, it can be assumed that the OROSS tool has partially solved the issues of some of the academics regarding the submission process. The interest in the utilisation of OROSS has spread to other faculties as the researcher has been providing training on an ad hoc basis.

This study has made a contribution to new research through the development of a new tool for the management research publication information, especially for the institutional repository for citation purposes, in a quick and simple way.

For further studies, the researcher will explore possible solutions to address all the shortcomings of the tool. Once the tool has been revised, tested and re-implemented, it will be re-assessed. The possibility of capturing dissertations via OROSS will also then be given attention.

The findings may assist UJ's executive management in deciding the fate of the OROSS tool for future use. The utilisation of this tool could either be made compulsory for all publishing researchers or defunct or left for use on an optional basis. It may also be of use to other HEIs on whether to adopt the strategy of utilising such a tool.

Acknowledgements

Thanks to Dr Richard Devey, UJ Statkon, for assisting in the questionnaire design and guidance on data analysis.

Competing interests

The author declares that he has no financial or personal relationships that may have inappropriately influenced him in writing this article.

References

Adriaanse, L.S. & Rensleigh, C., 2011, 'Comparing web of sciences, Scopus and Google scholar from an environmental sciences perspective', *South African Journal of Libraries and Information Science* 77(2), 169–178. https://doi.org/10.7553/77-2-58

African Union, 2017, 'Developing an African higher education quality rating system', Meeting of the Bureau of the Conference of Ministers of Education of the African Union (COMEDAF II+), Addis Ababa, Ethiopia, May 29–31, 2017.

Beall, J., 2012, 'Predatory publishers are corrupting open access', *Nature* 489, 179. https://doi.org/10.1038/489179a

Blessinger, P., 2015, 'The world needs more international higher education', *University World News*, 364, April, 2015, pp. 1–3.

Boswell, R., 2014, 'Milking the cash cow – how publishing houses suck academics dry', viewed 02 July 2014, from http://www.theguardian.com/higher-education-network/blog/2014/jul/02/research-pub

Botman, R., 2012, 'Open access to knowledge will boost Africa's development', *University World News*, 249, 25 November, pp. 1–4.

Brown, A., 2014, 'Open access: Why academic publishers still add value', viewed 02 July 2014, from http://www.theguardian.com/higher-education-network/blog/2012/nov/22/open-acces

Centre for Educational Research and Innovation, 2009, *Higher education to 2030, vol. 2, globalisation*, OECD.

Christopherson, S., Garretsen, H. & Martin, R., 2008, 'The world is not flat: Putting globalisation in its place', *Cambridge Journal of Regions, Economy and Society* 1, 343–349. https://doi.org/10.1093/cjres/rsn023

Clough, P. & Nutbrown, C., 2012, A *student's guide to methodology*, 3rd edn., Sage, London.

Collyer, F., 2013, 'The production of scholarly knowledge in the global market arena: University ranking systems, prestige and power', *Critical Studies in Education* 54(3), 245–259. https://doi.org/10.1080/17508487.2013.788049

Dadkhan, M. & Maliszewski, T., 2015, 'Hijacked journals – A threats and challenges to countries' scientific ranking', *International Journal of Technology Enhanced Learning* 7(3), 281–288. https://doi.org/10.1504/IJTEL.2015.072819

Dawson, D., 2013, 'Making your publications open access: Resources to assist researchers and librarians', *College and Research Libraries News* 74(9), 473–476.

De Groote, S., 2015, 'Measuring your impact: Impact factor, citation analysis, and other metrics: Citation analysis', viewed 16 September 2015, from http://researchguides.uic.edu/c.pho?g=252299andp=1683205

De Wit, H., 2012, 'From global to global citizen', *University World News,* 211, 04 March, pp. 1–2.

Drahos, P. & Braithwaite, J., 2002, 'Information feudalism: Who owns the knowledge economy?', 1st edn., Earthscan Publications Ltd, London.

Eid, F.H., 2014, 'Research, higher education and the quality of teaching: Inquiry in a Japanese academic context', *Research in Higher Education Journal* 24, 1–25.

European Commission, 2013a, *Open access to research publications reaching 'tipping point'*, viewed 17 November 2014, from http://europa.eu/rapid/press-release_IP-13-786_en.htm

European Commission, 2013b, 'The EU framework programme for research and innovation', *Horizon 2020: Guidelines on open access to scientific publications and research data in Horizon 2020*, Version 16, December, European Commission, Europe.

Feghali, T., Zbib, I. & Hallal, S., 2011, 'A web-based decision support tool for academic advising', *Educational Technology and Society* 14(1), 82–94.

Finch Report, 2013, *Report on the working group on expanding access to published research findings – the Finch Group*, viewed 17 November 2014, from http://www.researchinfornet.org/publish/finch

Gatti, R., 2014, *Open access: 'we no longer need expensive publishing networks'*, viewed 02 July 2014, from http://www.theguardian.com/higher-education-network/blog/2012/nov/08/open-acces

Gearing, E., 2011, *Increasing visibility, accessibility, and citations through open access publishing*. Johnson and Wales University, Providence, RI.

Graziano, A.M. & Raulin, M.L., 2013, *Research methods: A process of inquiry*, 8th edn., Pearson, Hoboken, NJ.

Gunaydin, G.P. & Dogan, N.O., 2015, 'A growing threat for academicians: Fake and predatory journals', *The Journal of Academic Emergency Medicine* 14, 94–96. https://doi.org/10.5152/jaem.2015.48569

Hall, M., 2014, *Why open access should be a key issue for university leaders*, viewed 02 July 2014, from http://www.theguardian.com/higher-education-network/blog/2014/feb/18/open-access

Henard, F. & Roseveare, D., 2012, *Fostering quality teaching in higher education: Policies and practices: An IMHE guide for higher education institutions*. OECD, Institutional Management in Higher Education.

Jalalian, M. & Mahboobi, H., 2014, 'Hijacked journals and predatory publishers: Is there a need to re-think how to assess the quality of academic research?', *Walailak Journal of Science and Technology* 11(5), 389–394.

Jobbins, D., 2014, *Europe: The role of rankings in improving higher education*, viewed 08 June 2016, from http://www.universityworldnews.com/article.php?story=20141113154912761&mode

Key, J.P., 1997, *Module R8. Questionnaire and interview as data-gathering tools*, viewed 27 July 2015, from http://okstate.edu/ag/agedcm4h/academic/aged5980a/5980/newpage16.htm

Livermore, T., 2014, *Boycotting academic publishers is a risk for young scientists*, viewed 02 July 2014, http://wwtheguardian.com/higher-education-network/blog/2014/jan/29/boycott-aca

Louw, P., 2014, *UCT at top of online table*, viewed 20 November 2014, from http://www.timeslive.co.za/thetimes/2014/08/07/uct-at-top-of-online-table?service=pr

Macanda, M., 2016, email, 04 January, macabam@uj.ac.za

Molecular Diversity Preservation International (MDPI), 1996–2016, *MDPI open access information and policy*, viewed 13 June 2016, from http://www.mdpi.com/about/openaccess

National Research Foundation, 2015, *Statement on open access to research publications from the National Research Foundation (NRF)-funded research*, viewed 27 July 2015, from http://www.nrf.ac.za/media-room/news/statement-open-access-research-publications-national-research-foundation-nrf-funded

Neuman, W.L., 2014, *Social research methods: Qualitative and quantitative approaches*, 7th edn., Pearson Education Limited, Essex.

Osborne, R., 2014, *Why open access make no sense*, viewed 02 July 2014, from http://www.theguardian.com/higher-education-network/blog/2013/jul/08/open-access-makes-no-sense

Rice, C., 2014, *Open access: Four ways it could enhance academic freedom*, viewed 02 July 2014, from http://www.theguardina.com/higher-educaiton-network/blog/2013/apr/22/open-access

Singh, K., 2013, *Web design: 11 characteristics of a user-friendly website*, viewed 08 February 2017, from http://www.socialmediatoday.com/content/web-design-11-characteristics-user-friendl

Singh, S. & Remenyi, D., 2016, 'Researchers beware of predatory and counterfeit journals: Are academics gullible?', *Electronic Journal of Business Research Methods* 14(1), 50–59.

Sinha, S., 2015, email, 22 January, reethan@uj.ac.za

Staff Writer, 2015, *New university rankings for South Africa*, viewed 16 September 2015, from http://businesstech.co.za/news/general/98423/university-rankings-insouth-africa/

Swan, A., 2017, 'Institutional repositories: A briefing paper', in *Open Access Scholarly Information Sourcebook*, viewed n.d., from http://www.openoasis.org/images/stories/briefing_papers/Institutional_repositories.pdf

The Guardian, 2014, *Exploring open access in higher education*, viewed 02 July 2014, from http://www.theguardian.com/higher-education-network/blog/2011/oct/25/open-access

Towert, D., 2015, email, 09 January, reethan@uj.ac.za

Trochim, W.M.K. & Donnelly, J.P., 2008, *The research methods knowledge base*, 3rd edn., Cengage Learning, Mason, OH.

University of Johannesburg, 2016, 'UJ Institutional repository', *Library News* 4(1), 1–12.

Van Vught, F. & Magnificus, R., 2004, *Internationalisation and globalisation in European higher education*, University of Twente, Enschede, The Netherlands.

Vogt, W.P. & Johnson, R.B., 2016, *Dictionary of statistics and methodology: A nontechnical guide for the social sciences*, 5th edn., Sage, Riverside County, CA.

Yelland, R., 2011, *The globalisation of higher education*, viewed 08 June 2016, from http://www.oecdobserver.org/news/printpage.php/aid/3731/The_gobalisation_of_hig

Zappia, S., 2015, *What is quantitative research?*, viewed 27 July 2015, from http://www.ehow.com/info_10018889_quantitative-research.html

16

Improvising information technology projects through the duality of structure

Author:
Tiko Iyamu[1]

Affiliation:
[1]Department of Information Technology, Cape Peninsula University of Technology, South Africa

Corresponding author:
Tiko Iyamu,
iyamut@cput.ac.za

Background: There is always emphasis on information technology (IT) projects because of their significance in organisations. Thus, efforts and resources are reciprocally committed to ensure the successes. Still, failure of IT projects in many organisations remains high and affects competitiveness. As recourse for remedy, different techniques and approaches have been employed. However, little or no progress has been made in increasing the success rate of IT projects in many organisations.

Objectives: The objective of this study was to examine the factors that influence and impact IT projects, improvisation and how improvisation manifests.

Method: The study was carried out using a single case study approach. Qualitative data were collected and duality of structure from the perspective of structuration theory was used as lens to guide the analysis.

Results: Findings from this study reveal how reproduction of actions manifests from non-technical factors, such as cultural value, organisational structure, power relationship, human capacity, know-how and change management. These factors help to gain a more constructive and better understanding of how IT projects improvisation is influenced or impacted by non-technical factors in organisations.

Conclusion: The study is intended to benefit both practitioners and academics. Some of the benefits will be gained from fresh perspectives on the complexities of IT projects improvisation, which are often caused by various seen and unforeseen non-technical factors. This includes how actions from relationship, know-how about facilities and communicative scheme are produced and reproduced.

Introduction

In the last two decades, the reliance on information technology (IT) by organisations has increased tremendously. Many organisations can hardly function or carry out their processes and activities without IT (Olugbode, Richards & Biss 2007). Organisations consider the capacity of the IT purposely for business objectives, which include services to their clients (Peak, Guynes & Kroon 2005). IT activities in organisations are normally carried out through projects. However, the nature of IT itself does and clearly creates challenges for the organisations that deploy and use it in their pursuit for competitive advantage (Drnevich & Croson 2013). The challenges are irrespective of the sector or organisation. According to Kellermann and Jones (2013), the disappointing performance of IT within the healthcare environment can be largely attributed to several factors, which affects its improvisation. Thus, Creswell and Sheikh (2013) relate to complex web of inter-related social and technical issues situated within an environment.

Improvisation of IT projects for organisations' competitiveness depends partly on actors' roles, responsibilities and competencies. According to Heeks (2006), actors play a key role in the improvisation of both design and reality, so as to help improve success rates. This could be attributed to the fact that improvisation is embedded into the intricate of activities of IT projects, which affects its success or failure (Ciborra 1996). Also, participating actors, such as IT managers and IT project managers must therefore be able to first competently make effective use of the technology that they are to manage its deployment and use (Schwalbe 2015). This requires knowledge that is based on convention, which is described in structuration theory by Giddens (1984), as a junction where two or more people possess, is a shared knowledge. The shared knowledge allows them to make sense or understand and interpret what is being communicated. The communication forms part of project to deliver IT solution. In Chae, Koh and Prybutok's (2014) argument, organisations with IT capability demonstrates better business performance than their counterparts.

Individuals' acceptance and use of IT has matured over the years (Venkatesh, Thong & Xu 2012). The usefulness and intention to use could also be influenced by their individual or group knowledge, common sense and sense-making of the technologies. Giddens (1984), through his structuration formation, argues that common sense is more than acts of habit, which is attributed to how employees fall in the habit of doing certain things in the organisation. The habits adopted, eventually become the norm, an accepted way of doing things, which is not necessarily the better way. Thus improvisation of IT projects involves both technical and non-technical factors (Rankin, Dahlbäck & Lundberg 2013), which manifest from human actions, based on their understanding and interpretations of its significance to them.

The study examines the factors which influences and impact IT projects, improvisation, and how improvisation manifests. Thus, the research question is, what are the non-technical factors that influence IT projects improvisation in organisations? The remainder of this article is structured into five main sections. The first section presents review of literature, which is split into two parts, to cover IT project and structuration theory. The approach that was employed in the study is discussed in the second section. The analysis, using structuration is presented in the third section. The findings and discussion are covered in the fourth section. Finally, a conclusion is drawn.

Literature review

Review of literature was conducted in the areas of IT project and structuration theory as they relate to improvisation:

Information technology project

One cannot deny the importance of IT projects in an organisation (Thomas & Fernández 2008), which are often undertaken by individuals or group on behalf of an organisation to deliver specific goal and objectives, overtime, using available resources (Bardhan, Krishnan & Lin 2013). As shown in Figure 1, IT project involves technology and non-technological capacity, which are further divided into units and sections of activities, depending on the nature and requirements for the project. The activities influence IT project improvisation through deliberate action of employees in their quest to deliver plan, on behalf of the organisation (Bansler & Havn 2004). As illustrated in Figure 1, the factors that are essentially required to engineer technology to desirability are of non-technology nature. For example, the process that is involved in the configuration of a technology in the context of an organisation is as important as the technology itself. This could be an opposing justification to actor–network theory of asymmetry formulation that human and non-human actors are equal within a network. According to Iyamu (2015:90), the fact is that non-human actors, such as technologies are created by humans, in essence, humans are competing with themselves for power through their own innovations, which inevitably cannot do without at times.

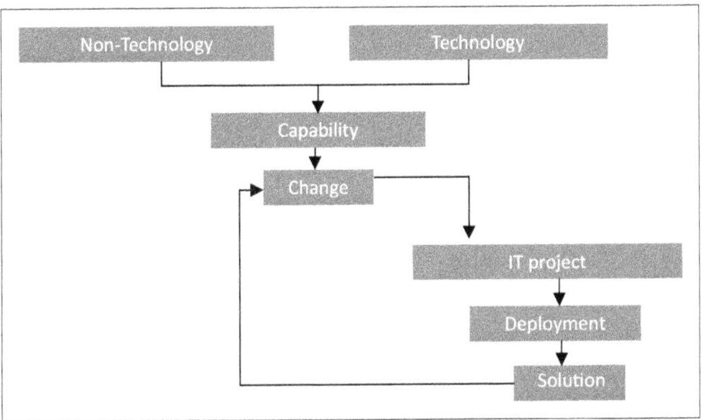

Source: Letseka, M. & Iyamu, T., 2011, 'The dualism of the information technology project,' in *The Proceedings of the 2011 Annual Conference of the South African Institute of Computer Scientists and Information Technologists*, Cape Town, October 3–5, pp. 294–297

FIGURE 1: Information technology project factors.

Technology is an object, external force which impact system within a social structure in IT projects improvisation (Rankin, Dahlbäck & Lundberg 2013). The relationship between technology and humans has been seen as a product of shared interpretations or interventions for many years (Orlikowski 1992). Improvisation of IT projects is primarily intended for organisational benefits and competitiveness. According to Carver and Turoff (2007), improvisation can be used to appraise how decision are made or formulated in carrying IT activities. Thus, Vaidya, Sajeev and Callendar (2006) propose a framework that could checkmate actors' activities towards assisting in projects, to minimise failure. In Sauer and Reich's (2009) assessment, there are five key 'directions' that could be employed in the implementation of projects, which include complexity, social process, value creation, broader conceptualisation of project and reflective practice.

Understanding of the word 'failure' in the context of IT projects could be associated with subjectivism. Thus, we clarify in perspective that under-utilisation or abandonment of an IT project represents failure (Yeo 2002). Failure has been synonymous with IT projects for many years, and across industries (Al-Ahmad et al. 2009). It could be caused by any or combination of factors, including people's efforts on the use of technology, which weakens or limits the strength of the relationship between behavioural intention and actual use of the technology use (Venkatesh, Thong & Xu 2012). However, Stoica and Brouse (2013) argue that many of the research that has been conducted on IT projects to date focus on 'success' factors, and less work focus on 'failures' and their respective potential root causes. Perhaps the subject of project failure is inevitably too soiled with managerialist, positivist or performative intent, which is based on thoughts and actions (Sage, Dainty & Brookes 2014). Improvisation occurs in an environment where there are various thinking and action of people happen simultaneously towards deliverable of (Ciborra 1996). Lind and Culler (2013) suggest that because IT projects involve many stakeholders, it take longer time to accomplish.

The stakeholders extend beyond the IT unit, to business personnel, users and executive managers, and they exercise different roles and responsibilities, which are influenced by their power to make a difference. Power is multidimensional, and it is directly or indirectly imbibed into human activity in accordance to individual interests and values (Castells 2011), which could have manifest in the process of improvisation. This could be attributed to the fact that power is a socially shaped construct, which focuses on building influence within network, and instrumental in decision making and planning (Beritelli & Laesser 2011). Also, actions from power could be attributed to manifestation of politics, which impact on how an organisation functions, the processes in the organisation and how decisions are made (Iyamu & Roode 2010), which is influenced by factors, such as processes, norms, culture and resources in their context and relevance. Improvisation appears to be a highly interactive process with social dimensions, which embeds human behaviour (Ciborra 1996). Thus, we employ structuration theory in order to gain better understanding of the factors that influence IT project improvisation in an organisation.

Structuration theory

Structuration is a sociotechnical theory which focuses on agent, structure and interaction. Interaction within a social system relies on how human actions are enabled or disabled through the organisational structures, which are interestingly a result of previous actions (Orlikowski & Robey 1991). Structuration, implicitly states that the agents' actions are conditioned by the organisational properties in social contexts (Iyamu & Roode 2010). The theory examines different assumptions include knowledge and techniques, which manifest from different practices and actions.

Structuration is a process of reproducing the duality of structure over time and space (Gao & Lyytinen 2003). As in Figure 2, the duality of structure contains three dimensions, which include structure, modality and interaction, in which both structure and interaction are linked through modalities: the interpretative schemes, resources and norms.

Structure comprises of three fundamental elements, signification, domination and legitimation. The structures are linked to agents through their interaction, which happens in dualism. Institutions are made up of the actions of agents in a social system, such as project team and an organisation. Agent actions are materialism of the structures. The modalities (interpretative schemes, facility and norms) link the process of interaction (communication, power and sanction) with the structural components (signification, domination and legitimation) of social, systems (Giddens 1984). The modalities are also the interaction between the agents and the structures in the features of a social system which are closely connected and yet the agents are capable of acting freely in the system (Giddens 1984). Bottom-line is that structuration is 'an effort to reconstruct the basic premises of social analysis' (Giddens 1991:205). The theory can therefore be used as a means to examine the interplay between the agent and structure (Buhr 2002).

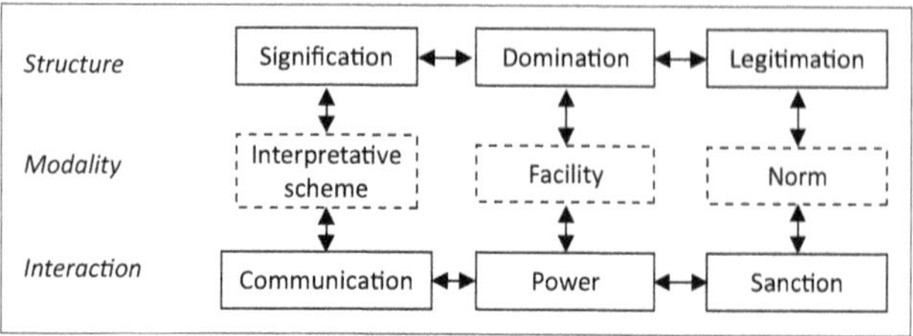

Source: Giddens, A., 1984, *The constitution of society: Outline of the theory of structure*, Berkley, CA, University of California Press

FIGURE 2: Duality of structure.

Research approach

The case study approach was applied in the study. Studying real-life situation, which the case study flexibly allows was the main justification for selecting the approach (Yin 2013). The other rationale was that the approach allows selection of vast pool of individuals and groups within a case (Ritchie et al. 2013). The IT department of a South Africa-based telecommunication organisation was used in the study. The company is listed in the Johannesburg Stock Exchange (JSE) since the year 2000. It had about 200 personnel in its IT department.

A total of 31 people at both senior and junior levels from IT (x21) and business (x10) units were interviewed at the point of saturation. The participants were labeled as follows: between TELIT01 and TELIT21 for IT; and between TELBU22 and TELBU31 for business.

Three main questions were used in the qualitative data collection: (1) How are IT projects improvised in the organisation? (2) What are the factors that influence improvisation of IT projects in the organisation? and (3) How are IT projects tasks assigned and carried out? The transcripts of the interviews were confirmed by the interviewees. The interpretive approach was employed to subjectively analyse the qualitative data that were gathered, with particular focus on the non-technical factors which manifest in the improvisation of IT projects in organisations. The interpretive approach is socially constructed in a natural setting of reality, and does not predefine variables, but aims to produce an understanding of the social context of the phenomenon (Rowlands 2005). In the use of interpretive approach, the duality of structure (see Figure 1) of the structuration theory was followed, as lens, to examine non-technical factors' reproductive actions, in order to gain better understanding of the factors that influences improvisation of IT projects in organisations.

As discussed in the 'Information technology project' section, the duality of structure from the perspective of structuration was employed in the analysis of the data for two main reasons: (1) the theory focuses on social process that involves the interaction amongst agents, using available structures, which can include technology designers, users and other decision makers in a project, and (2) it examines how events and interactions are reproduced over time within a social system, such as organisation and project team.

Information technology project viewed through the lens of duality of structure

Improvisation of IT project was viewed, using the duality of structure from structuration theory. Thus, structure, modality and interaction were followed in the analysis. This was to examine and understand non-technical factors manifest in the improvisation of IT projects, which influences success or failure in many organisations.

Duality of structure

As defined by Giddens (1984), duality of structure consists of three main components – structure: signification, domination and legitimation; modalities: interpretative schemes, facility and norms; and interaction: communication, power and sanction.

Signification and/or interpretative scheme and/or communication

The outcome, success or failure of improvisation of IT project is influenced by its significance to the organisation and the agents (stakeholders) that undertake the various sponsorship, technical and management tasks in a project. Signification illustrates the differentiation of values that is associated to object or subject within an entity, such as improvisation of IT project. Thus, the significance of an IT project is not always obvious as it is not necessarily its size or cost. The significance of IT projects is therefore influenced by how agents interpret the requirements including rules and regulations in the tasks that are assigned to them. According of one of the business analysts who participated in the study:

> 'some IT managers determine the importance of IT project improvisation based on the types of skill-set that are deployed in it. This is because our organisation sometimes deployment people into IT projects for the sake of keeping them busy.' [TELBU23]

The interpretation and subsequent understanding of requirements, rules and regulations is based on knowledge. Another critical factor that influences interpretations is individual's interest or organisation's or both interests. The interpretation that happens during improvisation of IT projects is primarily shaped by how the tasks and associated factors were communicated to the interpreters (stakeholders). What makes the interests more challenging towards the outcome of a project is that many managers take for granted how their subordinates understand their communication to them. Giddens (1984) attributes this type of behaviour to the unconscious categories of the mind that makes up the sentiments of the selfhood. Employees therefore act knowing fully that it impact the outcome of their IT project improvisation. This is attributed to the fact that some of them do not think that their expertise and opinion are taken seriously. This could be ascribed to some managers' over reliance on formal communication, which was well structured in the organisation as at the time of this study. One of the employees explains as follows:

> 'The Company has created website for communication and information purposes regarding projects. Our communications also happen through emails. There are collaboration tools, such as NetMeeting and Communicator, which we use as well in our IT projects. Yet, we have difficulty in understanding ourselves and gathering some relevance information about projects, such as interpretation of software development standards, and business and IT requirements' alignment.' [TELIT19]

This is primarily because many managers continue to pay attention to what they solely think it significance to the project, and not why things happen in the way that they did, such as how communication is carried out and received, how the interpretation of those communications. This affects team's cohesiveness and collectiveness, from the perspectives of allocation and execution of tasks. One of the business analysts who participated in the study shares her view as follows:

> 'The business architecture department is tasked with ensuring the requirements and scope provided to the project team is detailed enough to provide the business with their needs, of which we cannot be involved in the execution.' [TELBU25]

Managers and some employees seem, and continue to put emphasis on technology and other outcomes, and not the factors that manifest themselves into those outcomes. This could be attributed to some of the reasons why improvisation of IT projects continue to be challenged, after years of invented and application of sophisticated and improved processes. According to a software developer, he (the project manager):

> 'doesn't see the end-to-end picture. He doesn't care about the end-to-end picture. He only cares about the task that he must manage in the projects, which are basically to meet deadlines, save cost and fulfil requirements.' [TELIT09]

An agent can make sense of his or her own actions as well as other people's actions in the same social system, within the frame of their interest or knowledge, or both. The relationship between an agent and the system is therefore a methodological experience, which manifest from structure of signification overtime and space. Structures and communications are affected by individual or group of individuals' interpretative schemes within a social system, which manifest reproductively to give a certain favourable or unacceptable outcome. Agents interpret and internalise information that is communicated to them, and from this they act, which produces the end results. The agents may not justify the actions they take for various reasons, such as job security and know-how. Their actions are sometimes determined and influenced by the rules of a project or in the organisation. This could be ascribed to enact their source of power, to deterministically influence the facilities that are employed or not used in the improvisation of IT projects within the organisation.

Domination and/or facility and/or power

Improvisation of IT project happens within constitute of agents, which includes facilities, such as finance, rules, regulations and human capacity. The agents are used either as means or end towards achieving the objectives of the project. Therefore, a resource (facility) or combination of resources dominates or can be used to dominate in the process. This explains why in improvisation of IT project an activity can be held significantly high, and irrespective of the cost, to achieving the objectives of the project. This also reveals why individuals are able to use the facility within their means to influence activities in order to get favourable results, which are not necessarily for the interest of the organisation. According to one of the technical personnel in the organisation:

> 'Sometimes we were not privileged to how tasks were allocated. We often have little or no choice but to accept. Otherwise, we could be charged for insubordination. However, we make use of what means which is on our disposal to respond to the allocated task, such as requirements gathering and analysis, project design and technical documentation.' [TELIT13]

This was an interesting piece of revelation. However, the respondent was not comfortable in expanding further.

A facility become dominant factor, or is used to dominate based on agents' interpretation, which they envisaged it could make different in the activities or overall outcome of IT project improvisation. The dominant factor is therefore used as a source of individuals' power, to make a difference in a project within an environment. Sauer and Reich (2009) identify and emphasise the importance of being able to control the project team using the mandated power that is bestowed on the focal actor, as prescribed by the rules and regulations of the organisation. Power is a phenomenon, which involve control of resources for a specific task at different stages. The source of power varies, and it is not explicit or restricted to certain individuals or groups. They are identified as knowledgeable agents of domination, which is not permanent across projects. Employees' actions during a project have to demonstrate a certain kind of power to be able to make a difference, which determines the success or failure at the end. In the expression of a participant:

> 'We all have different types of skill, some are of technology know-how, and others are of social nature, such as how to get colleagues to do the right or wrong thing, which include adherence to standards, requirements and documentation in the process of project execution.' [TELIT15]

Thus, mangers of IT project do not take cognisance of, or do not know to do so. They begin and continue to look at results and not how they achieved the results or found themselves the position. An employee expressed his views as follows:

> 'Two things were primarily wrong with the allocation of tasks in the improvisation of many IT projects in our organisation: (1) imbalance of workload and (2) inappropriate alignment of individual skills with the tasks that are assigned to them, such as business analysts, software development and IT architects.' [TELIT08]

These are fundamental factors that develop into power that various actors tap upon, in attempt to assert themselves.

Power can be exercised by any individual or group in the improvisation of IT project in organisations. Every team member that is deployed to an IT has a certain level of power, by virtue of their knowledge of the project or the task that is assigned to them. Therefore, they have the ability to influence the outcome of the project, directly or indirectly. The source of power is extended to know-how of facility to a make a difference within the context of the task that was assigned to them in a project. Ignorantly, some IT project managers continue to undermine certain individuals by taking their power for granted, or lack the know-how to establish the extent of the influence of individuals' power to make a difference. This type of acts can be associated to Giddens (1984) description of practical unconsciousness, a certain type of action informed by knowledge that is implicitly carried out, but rarely expressed or articulated. Employees exhibit certain practical consciousness or stock of knowledge in an organisation, which with time are accepted and consequently considered norm, as they interpret their interactions during IT project improvisation. This stock of knowledge develops from a facility to source of dominant, and they are imprinted on others legitimately.

Legitimation and/or norm and/or sanction

An IT project takes effect after being approved by the relevant authority within an organisation. The approval legitimises the project, based on its adherence to the prescribed processes, which are considered to be norm in the organisation. This process or processes might not be perfect, but they are acceptable by majority of the agents who are involved or do have impact upon. As echoed by both software developers and IT project managers in the organisation:

> 'We do not follow process of best practices but our software that are developed in-house can be measured against the best'. [TELIT03]

Legitimisation of an IT project is done through structure, towards achieving its goal primarily for competitiveness. In duality, the structure of legitimation is created by agents, for the same agents, in the execution of their activities in IT projects. The structure of legitimation of IT project is carried out by agents through processes, using available facilities that are considered to be norm, which is not necessarily the correct approaches, but because they were sanctioned by those that are involved in the activity. This has serious impact on the project, which are often negative and challenging:

> 'It is better to embark on the right process, of innovative and creativity rather than this is how we have been doing it, according some of the employees who was relatively new, about three years in the organisation.' [TELIT02]

In the improvisation of IT projects, there are facilities that can or cannot be employed, do's and do not's, purposefully for the benefit of the project and the organisation at large. These are also to abide by the beliefs and culture of the organisation, including the requirements of the project. The dos and don'ts, which were created by an individual or group of them, become the norm overtime through which improvisation of IT projects were carried out in the organisation.

Employees endorse their actions by drawing on norms or standards of morality as they deemed acceptable within a project. The major implication of this is that in improvisation of many IT projects, the designers are not necessarily the implementers. Thus, there are sometimes conflicting views, which draws on the application of what is considered to be norm at the time, for resolution purposes. This could be attributed to why many IT projects are difficult to implement, as the users and implementers did not together sanction some of facilities and activities.

Employees' attitudes and behaviours can be linked to organisational structure and culture. Attitude inadvertently determines how individuals in an organisation respond to in-house and external changes, which does have a bearing on the outcome of IT project improvisation. The people in an organisation are most likely to behave in a similar manner when faced with a challenge. This is because they are together exposed to the same environment. This does not however suggest that people will always behave in the same manner; it merely suggests that they are inclined to reacting similarly unless one taps into their individual capabilities to make a difference.

Findings and discussion

The analysis as presented above through the duality of structure as a lens from the perspective of structuration theory reveals the non-technical factors, which influence and impact improvisation of IT projects in organisations. As shown in Figure 3, the factors include cultural value, organisational structure, power relationship, human capacity, know-how and change management. These factors are produced and reproduced over time through a duality in the improvisation of IT projects. The factors as depicted in Figure 3 should be read with the discussion that follows in order to gain a more constructive and better understanding of how improvisation of IT projects is influenced or impacted by non-technical factors.

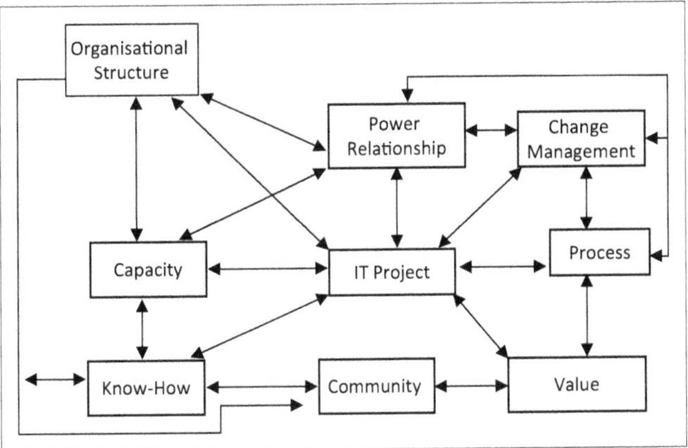

FIGURE 3: Dualism of information technology project improvisation.

Cultural value

Cultural value of an organisation is formulated overtime, primarily to uniformly guide their employees towards ensuring sustainability and competitiveness. It therefore drives the focus of the organisation, and influences the outcomes of its activities. Thus, IT project improvisation considers or aligns with the cultural value of the organisation. However, there are some fundamental that can be associated to the outcome of IT projects in an organisation. The challenges result from the following questions: (1) At what stage of the project is the cultural value considered? (2) How is the cultural value considered or aligned with the objectives of the project? and (3) Which of the entities takes priority, the IT project improvisation or cultural value?

The values of an organisation are enforced through a dualistic process in accordance to the structure (rules and resources), over dialogue as informed by interpretation within a communicative scheme. Organisational values are enforced because of their significance, mainly to dominate individuals' personal belief or interest, through a legitimate process.

Organisational structure

Organisational structure is different from structure in structuration theory, as defined by Giddens (1984) and clarified by Iyamu and Roode (2010), in that structure is rules and resource. Organisational structure is created or followed during IT project improvisation. This is to guide roles and responsibilities, which defines allocation of tasks. Also critically important in improvisation of IT projects are rules and resources, which are created by the employees, within which the creators themselves operate. The organisational structures help to define factors, such as rules, regulations, responsibilities, reporting lines, technology resource and the communication format amongst the stakeholders, which influence, not in a deterministic sense, the outcome of IT project improvisation, directly or through manifestation.

People and process constitute the entity known as the organisation, which consists of power, upon which relationships are built, and defines how communications are carried out amongst employees within an IT project. As communications of the same subject take place, but at different levels of the organisation, interpretation is enshrouded with various contexts, which has impact on IT project improvisation. The question is: how many IT projects managers consider this as a critical factor?

Many organisations follow hierarchical structures with defined reporting channels. This is referred to as a formal organisational structure. The hierarchical structure is argued to follow a rigid communication structure, where information is filtered from the top to bottom levels. One of the challenges is that the communication channel is not dualistically structured, to flow from bottom as it does from top to bottom.

An organisational structure dictates how the employees communicate and carry out their activities. Also, the organisational formal structure dictates the reporting lines as employees interact in the formal environment of the organisation. As a result of the lack of dualism in the communication channel that is caused by organisational structure, individuals begin to react through their personal interpretation of technology artefacts, as well as the processes that are involved in IT project improvisation. Through the interpretation, they begin to build their power as a form of self-defence or self-reliance.

Power relationship

As revealed in the analysis, employees do not only produce and reproduce rules and resources, they also have the ability to control and influence improvisation of IT projects in their organisations. This is often for their personal or organisation's or both interests, which of course influences the outcome of projects. In the course of producing and reproducing of activities, relationship is experienced. Thus, individuals and groups tap on available power to define a favourable relationship, which ultimately have impact on improvisation of IT projects. This has been difficult to identify by many IT project managers as they are not psychologists, who can possible read and understand the traces of the minds of the employees.

What makes the relationships that are founded on power to manage is that they are drawn and shaped legitimately through the rules and regulations, using the available resources of the organisation. Thus, power relationship enables and at the same time, constrain IT projects improvisation in organisations. IT project managers find it difficult to manage constrains that are caused by practical unconsciousness, in that the actions cannot be explained by the employees who carries out such acts. What makes it even more challenging for some IT project managers is the fact that human capacity is inseparable from their conscious and unconscious behaviours.

Human capacity

Human capacity is critically vital in some organisations, as it is considered to be the most valued resource in realisation of IT projects. People are the foundation of an organisation in that there is no organisation without people. People therefore make up the norms, values and culture of an organisation, through which they create capacity to make difference in the improvisation of IT projects, whether consciously or subconsciously.

The individual influences in an organisation have the potential to contribute to IT project improvisation through shared beliefs, practices and values. Values and practices within an IT project are found in the symbols, which reproduces the outcome. The challenges and gaps that exist in project managers' lack of ability to identify the values and practices from project team members' perspectives.

Employees in an organisation have their own perceptions, which allow them to accept or reject how activities of IT projects improvisation are problematised for them. This action of acceptance or rejection does not happen voluntarily. It is in fact driven by the leaders in the projects, in a reproductive manner. For example, the chief executive officer explores his or her ability and power to influence how improvisation of IT projects are shaped. The action could be as a result of know-how or lack of know-how.

Know-how

Agents have the ability to express reasons for why they do what they do in the improvisation of IT projects. They may however, not be able to explain the source of what drives their actions, but there are consequences and implications. Some of the things an employee does are intertwined in his or her mind as knowledge gained through practical consciousness. An agent does certain things without particularly being aware of their actions, which negatively or positively impact the project. The action of the agent takes place within rules and available resources, in that it legitimatises as part of the organisational norm. Based on their knowledge, actions are produced and reproduced with the duration of the IT project improvisation.

The unequivocal actions of employees, which affects IT projects improvisation, can be divided into two types of knowledge. In structuration, there are two types of knowledge: discursive knowledge and practical knowledge. Discursive knowledge is the knowledge which agents in an organisation are able to articulate, whilst practical knowledge refers to the tacit knowledge that agents draw from. When working in a project, there are activities or tasks an agent does, which he or she cannot explain. In some cases it might be things that they do because they knows just how to do them or the things an individual has been doing for so long, they have become a part of them. This is reproduction of results relatively to agents' reproductive actions. This therefore requires change management, which many IT project managers consider a different role and responsibility to theirs.

Change management

Change management seems inevitable in some organisations, in the improvisation of IT projects. Change management is a legitimate facility that is often used to support and enable processes and activities. Without change management, it is difficult to embark on during transition of events in IT projects improvisation. However, change management can also be a constraining factor to the events that it was supposed to support and enable. This could be attributed to interaction and interpretation of the communication about project tasks and activities. It therefore involves a process of negotiation between the focal actors and other stakeholders; hence the process has to be of dualism.

The change management process is not the function of the project manager alone, we do concede. Another important reveal in this study, and that must be taken cognisance of, is that change management happens at different, small- and large-scale levels. This is in lieu of the fact that the change manager is expected to ensure smooth transition of a technology into an environment, which this study empirically reveals is the responsibility of the IT project managers. Adopting a new system in an organisation is not an easy task; transition from current to desired state could be challenging. In an organisation, where changes are communicated and implemented as directives and instruction without exchange of information in the form of dualism, it becomes complicated in ensuring that enough is known for the decisions that were taken.

Process

Process is an ongoing activity in an organisation that entails engagement and interaction between employees in a specific purpose. Improvisation of IT project is unique irrespective of the technology and the organisation. It is carried out differently in organisations, by various people at a time. Also, it is simultaneously managed and constantly revisited with every new project in order to fulfill relevance, and to align with context. The process is a process in itself, in that through a process a process is formulated, resulting from dualism.

Improvisation of IT projects is process oriented. The rationale for implementing certain projects remains a challenge to those that are involved because of the nature of some processes. Each part that is involved in IT projects improvisation has a role to play, whether in the development or management process. In some instances, the role is determined by the individual's interest or the deterministic nature of the involving process. Hence communication amongst the stakeholders is critically important.

Conclusion

Improvisation of IT projects has been a cumbersome process or exercise in organisations for many years. The use of structuration theory as a lens in the empirical study helps in this regard, to examine, and reveals complexities of non-technical factors. The findings from the study provide a guide and facilitates improvisation of IT projects in an organisation. Thus, the study benefits both business and academia.

Managers will gain better understanding from how human actions are reproduced, to enable and at the same time constrain processes and activities in the improvisation of IT projects in their organisations. Academics will equally benefit from this study, particularly how structuration theory was employed to examine and understand the non-technical factors, which influence improvisation of IT in organisations. Also, the study contributes to existing literature in the areas of IT project and management. However, future studies can be undertaken to explore, examine and understand how human and non-human networks are formed, and how their roles can be used to assess the deployment of IT projects.

Acknowledgements

Competing interests

The author declares that he has no financial or personal relationship(s) that may have inappropriately influenced him in writing this article.

References

Al-Ahmad, W., Al-Fagih, K., Khanfar, K., Alsamara, K., Abuleil, S. & Abu-Salem, H., 2009, 'A taxonomy of an IT project failure: Root causes', *International Management Review* 5(1), 93.

Bansler, J.P. & Havn, E.C., 2004, 'Improvisation in information systems development', in B. Kaplan, D.P. Truex, D. Wastell, A.T. Wood-Harper & J.I. DeGross (eds.), *Information systems research*, pp. 631–646, Springer, Boston, MA.

Bardhan, I., Krishnan, V. & Lin, S., 2013, 'Team dispersion, information technology, and project performance', *Production and Operations Management* 22(6), 1478–1493. https://doi.org/10.1111/j.1937-5956.2012.01366.x

Beritelli, P. & Laesser, C., 2011, 'Power dimensions and influence reputation in tourist destinations: Empirical evidence from a network of actors and stakeholders', *Tourism Management* 32(6), 1299–1309. https://doi.org/10.1016/j.tourman.2010.12.010

Buhr, N., 2002, 'A structuration view on the initiation of environmental reports', *Critical Perspectives on Accounting* 13(1), 17–38. https://doi.org/10.1016/S1045-2354(00)90441-6

Carver, L. & Turoff, M., 2007, 'Human-computer interaction: The human and computer as a team in emergency management information systems', *Communications of the ACM* 50(3), 33–38. https://doi.org/10.1145/1226736.1226761

Castells, M., 2011, 'Network theory | A network theory of power', *International Journal of Communication* 5, 15.

Chae, C., Koh, E. & Prybutok, R., 2014, 'Information technology capability and firm performance: Contradictory findings and their possible causes', *MIS Quarterly* 38(1), 305–326.

Ciborra, C., 1996, 'Improvisation and information technology in organizations', in *The Proceedings of International Conference on Information Systems*, Association for Information Systems, Cleveland, OH, USA, December 16–18, 1996, pp. 369–380.

Creswell, K. & Sheikh, A., 2013, 'Organisational issues in the implementation and adoption of health information technology innovations: An interpretative review', *International Journal of Medical Informatics* 82(5), e73–e86. https://doi.org/10.1016/j.ijmedinf.2012.10.007

Drnevich, P.L. & Croson, D.C., 2013, 'Information technology and business-level strategy: Toward an integrated theoretical perspective', *MIS Quarterly* 37(2), 483–509.

Gao, P. & Lyytinen, J., 2003, 'China telecommunications transformation in globalization context: A structuration perspective', In *Proceedings of IFIP/TC8.2 and 9.4 Working Conference on IS Perspectives and Challenges in the Context of Globalization*, pp. 217–233, Athens, Greece, June 15–17.

Giddens, A., 1984, *The constitution of society: Outline of the theory of structure*, Berkley, CA, University of California Press.

Giddens, A., 1991, 'Structuration theory: Past, present and future,' in C. Bryant & D. Jary (eds.), *Giddens' theory of structuration: A critical appreciation*, pp. 201–221, Routledge, London, UK.

Heeks, R., 2006, 'Health information systems: Failure, success and improvisation', *International Journal of Medical Informatics* 75(2), 125–137. https://doi.org/10.1016/j.ijmedinf.2005.07.024

Iyamu, T. & Roode, D., 2010, 'The use of structuration theory and actor network theory for analysis: Case study of a financial institution in South Africa', *International Journal of Actor-Network Theory and Technological Innovation* 2(1), 1–9. https://doi.org/10.4018/jantti.2010071601

Iyamu, T., 2015, *Application of underpinning theories in information systems*, Heidelberg Press, Australia.

Kellermann, A.L. & Jones, S.S., 2013, 'What it will take to achieve the as-yet-unfulfilled promises of health information technology', *Health Affairs* 32(1), 63–68. https://doi.org/10.1377/hlthaff.2012.0693

Letseka, M. & Iyamu, T., 2011, 'The dualism of the information technology project,' in *The Proceedings of the 2011 Annual Conference of the South African Institute of Computer Scientists and Information Technologists*, Cape Town, October 3–5, pp. 294–297.

Lind, M.R. & Culler, E., 2013, 'Information technology project performance: The impact of critical success factors', *Perspectives and Techniques for Improving Information Technology Project Management* 39.

Olugbode, M., Richards, R. & Biss, T., 2007, 'The role of information technology in achieving the organisation's strategic development goals: A case study', *Information Systems* 32(5), 641–648. https://doi.org/10.1016/j.is.2006.04.001

Orlikowski, W.J., 1992, 'The duality of technology: rethinking the concept of technology in organisations', *Management of Technology* 3(3), 398–427. https://doi.org/10.1287/orsc.3.3.398

Orlikowski, W.J. & Robey, D., 1991, 'Information technology and the structuring of organisations', *Information Systems Research* 2(2), 143–169. https://doi.org/10.1287/isre.2.2.143

Peak, D., Guynes, C.S. & Kroon, V., 2005, 'Information technology alignment planning–A case study', *Information & Management* 42(5), 635–649. https://doi.org/10.1016/j.im.2004.02.009

Rankin, A., Dahlbäck, N. & Lundberg, J., 2013, 'A case study of factor influencing role improvisation in crisis response teams', *Cognition, Technology & Work* 15(1), 79–93. https://doi.org/10.1007/s10111-011-0186-3

Ritchie, J., Lewis, J., Nicholls, C.M. & Ormston, R. (eds.)., 2013, *Qualitative research practice: A guide for social science students and researchers*, Sage, Washington, DC.

Rowlands, B., 2005, 'Grounded in practice: Using interpretive research to build theory', *The Electronic Journal of Business Research Methodology* 3(1), 81–92.

Sage, D., Dainty, A. & Brookes, N., 2014, 'A critical argument in favor of theoretical pluralism: Project failure and the many and varied limitations of project management', *International Journal of Project Management* 32(4), 544–555. https://doi.org/10.1016/j.ijproman.2013.08.005

Sauer, C. & Reich, H., 2009, 'Rethinking IT project management: Evidence of a new mindset and its implications', *International Journal of Project Management* 27(2), 182–193. https://doi.org/10.1016/j.ijproman.2008.08.003

Schwalbe, K., 2015, *Information technology project management*, Cengage Learning, Boston, MA.

Stoica, R. & Brouse, P., 2013, 'IT project failure: A proposed four-phased adaptive multi-method approach', *Procedia Computer Science* 16, 728–736. https://doi.org/10.1016/j.procs.2013.01.076

Thomas, G. & Fernández, W., 2008, 'Success in IT projects: A matter of definition', *International Journal of Project Management* 26(7), 733–742. https://doi.org/10.1016/j.ijproman.2008.06.003

Vaidya, K., Sajeev, A.S.M. & Callender, G., 2006, 'Critical factors that influence e-procurement implementation success in the public sector', *Journal of Public Procurement* 6(1/2), 70.

Venkatesh, V., Thong, J.Y. & Xu, X., 2012, 'Consumer acceptance and use of information technology: Extending the unified theory of acceptance and use of technology', *MIS Quarterly* 36(1), 157–178.

Yeo, K.T., 2002, 'Critical failure factors in information system projects', *International Journal of Project Management* 20(3), 241–246. https://doi.org/10.1016/S0263-7863(01)00075-8

Yin, R.K., 2013, *Case study research: Design and methods*, Sage, California, CA.

17

Parallel search engine optimisation and pay-per-click campaigns: A comparison of cost per acquisition

Authors:
Wouter T. Kritzinger[1]
Melius Weideman[1]

Affiliations:
[1]Website Attributes Research Centre, Cape Peninsula University of Technology, South Africa

Corresponding author:
Melius Weideman,
melius@gmail.com

Background: It is imperative that commercial websites should rank highly in search engine result pages because these provide the main entry point to paying customers. There are two main methods to achieve high rankings: search engine optimisation (SEO) and pay-per-click (PPC) systems. Both require a financial investment – SEO mainly at the beginning, and PPC spread over time in regular amounts. If marketing budgets are applied in the wrong area, this could lead to losses and possibly financial ruin.

Objectives: The objective of this research was to investigate, using three real-world case studies, the actual expenditure on and income from both SEO and PPC systems. These figures were then compared, and specifically, the cost per acquisition (CPA) was used to decide which system yielded the best results.

Methodology: Three diverse websites were chosen, and analytics data for all three were compared over a 3-month period. Calculations were performed to reduce the figures to single ratios, to make comparisons between them possible.

Results: Some of the resultant ratios varied widely between websites. However, the CPA was shown to be on average 52.1 times lower for SEO than for PPC systems.

Conclusion: It was concluded that SEO should be the marketing system of preference for e-commerce-based websites. However, there are cases where PPC would yield better results – when instant traffic is required, and when a large initial expenditure is not possible.

Introduction

Websites are created for several reasons, one of which is the representation of the business on the Internet. Although a website is not always considered the only way to represent an online business's presence, a website is arguably the most important entity that a business can create online. The reason is that the website is the virtual representation of the organisation, brand and products or services. This online representation determines how current and potential customers perceive the business, and it will define how customers will interact with the business. This indicates that anything and everything implemented on the website is of paramount importance. Miller (2011:17–27) lists several web marketing methods that should be considered if a website is to be marketed effectively online:

- Search Engine Optimisation (SEO): The concept is based on applying a search engine best practice methodology to any given website (this may require website alterations architecturally and/or otherwise), which will result in improved organic search engine rankings for topic-related search queries (Weideman 2009).
- Pay-per-click (PPC) Advertising: PPC advertising is paid advertising on search engines and other display websites. It forms part of the search engine revenue model and functions on a keyword bidding system that depends on visitors who click on the advertisement.
- Online Advertising: This is commonly known as banner advertising; whereby graphical advertisements are placed on advertising publishing websites that have significant traffic volumes. The advertisements are paid for on a cost-per-impression basis and refer to the number of visitors who have viewed the advertisement.
- Email Marketing: Is referred to as 'push' marketing as the marketing message is pushed to the receiver's inbox. This also makes it a lot harder for the receiver to ignore the marketing message as opposed to an advertisement on a website. Email marketing is popular because of the following reasons: low cost, speed, simplicity, being proactive and targeting recipients.
- Blog Marketing: Blogs are used to make a more direct connection with customers. They are typically informative and personalise certain entities within the company. Blogs are often also used as a promotional channel for the business.

- Social Media Marketing: Although blogs form part of social media marketing, social media is more focused on creating communities of various types that share information and current activities. In addition, consumers prefer to connect with consumers as they no longer blindly trust what businesses say. Informal consumer discussions (horizontal trust) are beginning to take precedence over business promises (vertical trust) (Kotler, Kartajaya & Setiawan 2010:7).
- Online Public Relations: Also referred to as Press Releases, this is the publishing of press releases on other reliable, high-traffic volume and related industry websites that could drive traffic back to the business website.
- Multimedia Marketing: This includes both podcasting (audio) and digital video. The podcasts and videos could be hosted on other industry or topic-related websites as well as on the business website. Search engines often include different media formats in the search engine result pages (SERPs), which viewers often engage with owing to ease of use.
- Mobile Marketing: In recent years, more and more users have started to make use of mobile phones to access the Internet. This means that businesses need to re-evaluate not only websites and how they function on the mobile phone along with consumer expectations, but also other mobile advertising options such as SMS, banner and PPC advertising. More recently, the click-to-call function reduces the business response time delay, whereby the mobile user can simply click on the number on the advertisement to call the business without even visiting the website.

Each one of these marketing channels has a role to play in the overall marketing of a business website. However, for this study, a more in-depth analysis of PPC and SEO has been carried out. Why focus on PPC and SEO? According to Clarke and Clarke (2014), marketers typically use these two search engine marketing strategies. PPC is a scheme where marketers must submit a bid for one or more keywords or key phrases, then create the advertisements using minimal text to appear on user screens and pay the search engines only when a user clicks on one of the advertisements. The other strategy is SEO, which in turn involves many factors that the search engines use to determine relevance and ranking. These are normally categorised as being on-page, off-page and site-wide SEO.

Furthermore, the term 'cost per acquisition' (CPA) should be defined at this point because it has a prominent position in this research. In search engine marketing, the CPA is the average cost of acquiring customers or leads yielding customers. One accepted way of calculating the CPA is to divide the advertising cost by the number of customers (or leads) over a period. Some marketers use the terms CPA and cost per action interchangeably. CPA is one of a number of metrics used in measuring various attributes of e-commerce (Druckenmiller 2016; Pavel, Pauwels & Gupta 2016).

Most prospective online shoppers are often overwhelmed by an oversupply of information, provided by search engines and other channels to find a relevant answer to their information needs (Broilo, Espartel & Basso 2016). This further highlights the importance of providing answers to search queries high up on the SERPs, to ensure that user clicks are harvested. Both PPC and SEO strategies involve boosting rankings on a SERP, but there are key differences in where those results might appear (Olbrich & Schultz 2014; see Figure 1).

However, this layout has changed in February 2016 when Google started implementing a large overhaul, which moved some of the advertisements from the right side to the bottom of the screen. Google also stated that it may show an additional advertisement (one extra ad on top of the original three) above the organic search results for what they called 'highly commercial queries' (McGee 2016). Presumably, this was done to provide better exposure for paying clients, instead of giving away some precious real estate at the top of the ranking lists to non-paying search results (see Figure 2 for the new layout).

In summary, recent publications (both in the general news and academic publications) seem to have stressed the importance of using both SEO and PPC in tandem (Google Analytics 2015; Gudivada, Rao & Paris 2015; Jang, Lee & Oh 2016; PRN 2015, 2016). These claims confirm the validity of having embarked on this research path. At the same time, there are voices of concern about the accuracy of some of the existing metrics used for e-commerce performance (Clarke & Jansen 2017), but solutions proposed in this research have not been tested at the time of writing.

Aims and objectives

The aim of this study was to determine the best way to spend advertising resources. The objective was to measure and compare the CPA of SEO versus PPC, under comparable circumstances, which would give an indication of the most effective marketing spending pattern. These are critical issues, especially when companies are spending large amounts of money monthly to ensure the best possible exposure of their marketing efforts through websites and social media platforms (Baidya & Basu 2011).

Research problem

It is important to budget properly for marketing expenditure because large amounts could be involved in certain markets (Baidya & Basu 2011; Ford 1994). At the same time, money spent on marketing through PPC and SEO has been the topic of controversy (Kritzinger & Weideman 2015). It appears as if more marketing dollars are spent on SEO, while PPC seems to yield higher income.

It has also been claimed that expenditure on marketing in especially larger companies has increased from 20% to 50% in around 50 years (Baidya & Basu 2011).

The research problem is that financial losses can be incurred if marketing resources are misallocated, specifically when choosing between spending on SEO and PPC.

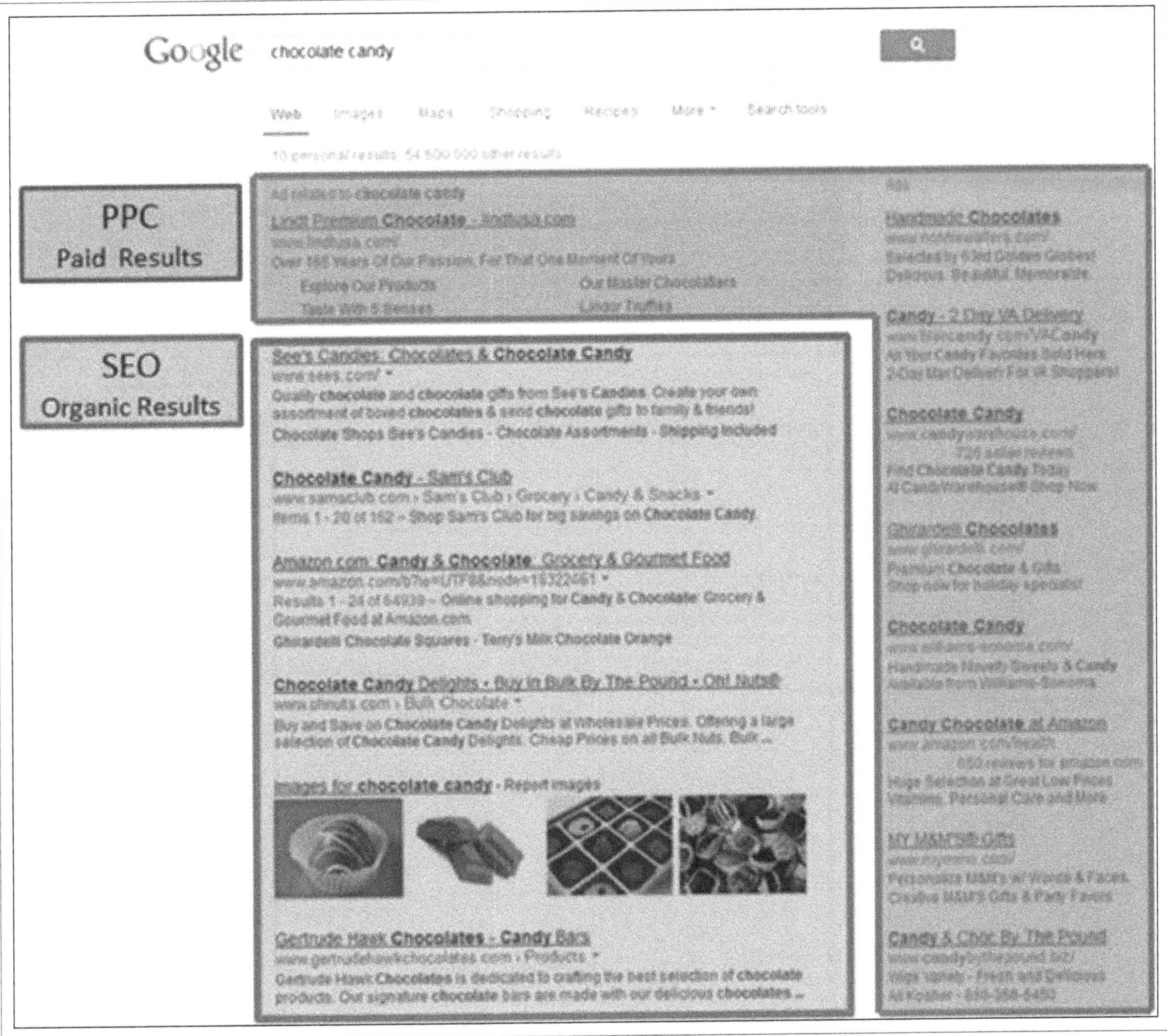

Source: Clarke, T.B. & Clarke, I., 2014, 'A competitive and experiential assignment in search engine optimisation strategy', *Marketing Education Review* 24(1), 25–30. https://doi.org/10.2753/MER1052-8008240104

FIGURE 1: Search engine result page locations for pay per click and search engine optimisation.

While attempting to address this problem through the research, a comparison will be made between cases where both SEO and PPC were used on different websites. The CPA will be calculated and compared because this figure is a good indication of the return on investment (ROI).

Literature review

A literature survey was conducted to determine what prior research has been done in this area. Key concepts such as SEO, PPC and CPA were studied.

Introduction

A brief explanation of how search engines index and rank web pages are given here for clarity. Search engines are companies that send programmes (called crawlers, robots, bots or spiders) to crawl the Internet, collecting the content of every web page they visit. This information is stored in an index (a complex database) for later use. When a user specifies a search query, the search engine algorithm examines the query, tries to determine what is that the user wants and then matches this information need as best it can with the website content it has stored in its index. The results are shown on the user's screen. Because there are almost always more than one possible answer, the search engine also has to decide in what order to display the answer, with the most relevant answer at the top (Weideman 2009).

Commercial motives coupled with inherent human laziness prescribes that the first few results on the results page are the ones that will receive the highest number of views. This has spawned the SEO industry, where websites are designed with search engine crawlers in mind, trying to ensure that every important web page will rank highly for a given search query. SEO techniques are divided into on-page and off-page types. On-page SEO refers to changes a

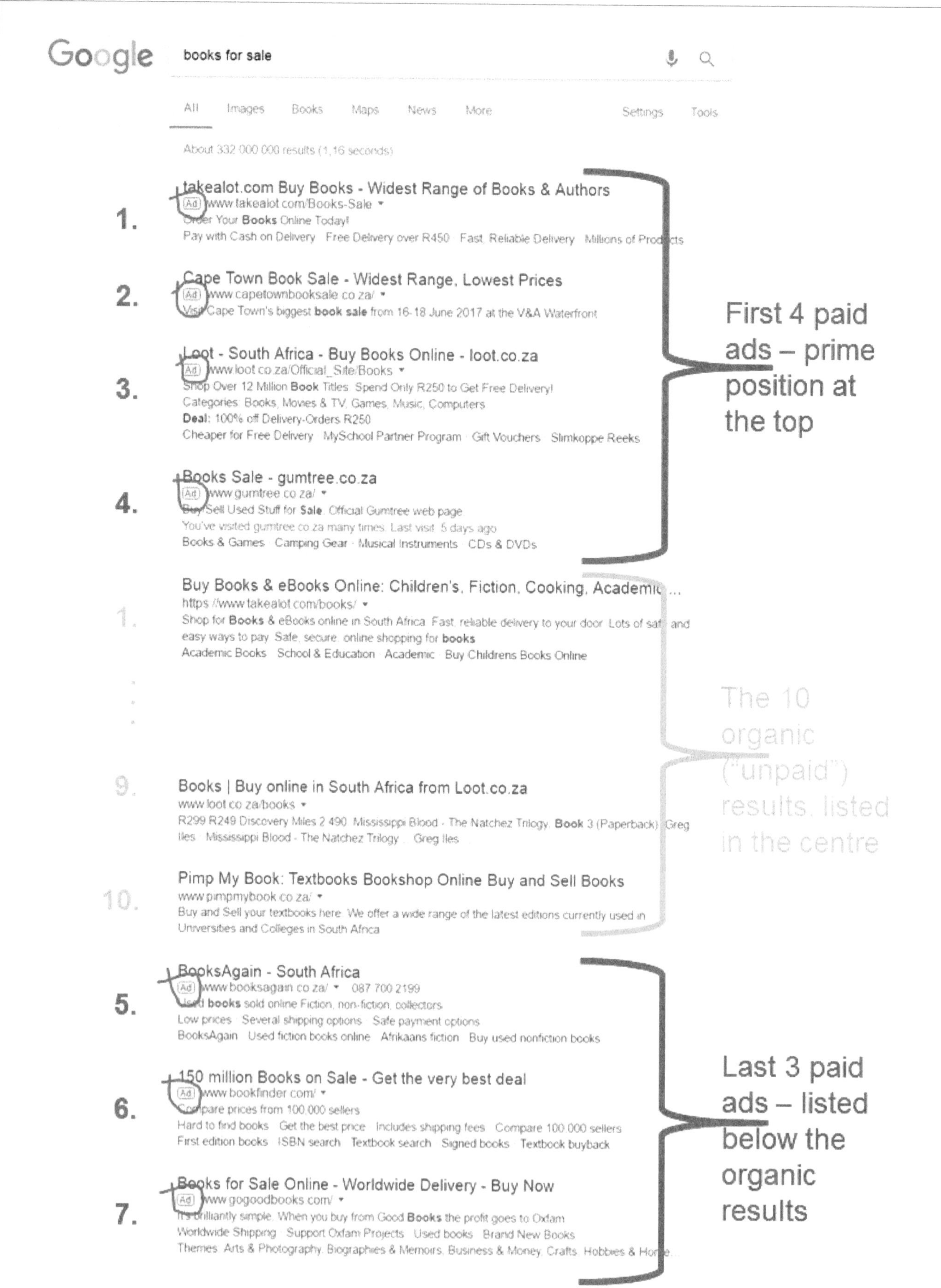

Source: Huck, L., Hamner, K. & Carpenter, C., 2016, *How Google's new desktop SERP layout has impacted marketers*, viewed 2 December 2016, from http://blog.360i.com/search-marketing/googles-new-desktop-serp-layout-impacted-marketers

FIGURE 2: New search engine result page locations for pay per click and search engine optimisation.

webmaster can make to the web pages under his or her control, where off-page techniques include things to be done outside the website at stake, to improve its ranking. Also, web page text must be written in an 'SEO-friendly' way, enabling crawlers and algorithms to easily detect what a given web page is really all about. On-page SEO includes the writing of 'good' meta-tags, Alt text for images, the correct use of H1 tags, well-written anchor text, file-name choices and others. Off-page SEO is mostly about creating an 'awareness' of the website at stake by building in-links (hyperlinks pointing from other website to the main website), and ensuring that many references about the main website are spread across the Internet. Unfortunately, the SEO industry also has its dark side – so-called black hat SEO is being practised, for example, by overstuffing a web page with keywords to appease the crawlers (Zuze & Weideman 2013).

Search engine optimisation

To ensure a higher volume of human visitors, websites need to be visible to search engine crawlers. One important element in high rankings is how closely the contents of any given web page match the specification of a search engine for a 'good' website. This match is determined by a search engine algorithm. A process termed SEO can be used to improve how closely a website's layout matches the guidelines of the search engine. This process includes writing good content, ensuring a high number of links pointing to the website, plus many other factors. These are sometimes classified as either:

- on-page SEO (elements that are present (or absent) on the actual web page); or
- off-page SEO (elements that are not part of the website, but exist outside).

SEO is theoretically a once-off process because these changes will remain on the website after being implemented. However, the SEO done on a website must be updated over time. Search engines change their algorithms regularly, and competitor websites with high rankings could push down a given website on the SERPs.

SEO mostly involves a relatively large investment when done for the first time, with a much lower expense over time after that. Much research has been conducted to determine the best strategy to leverage SEO into ranking better on Google. Luh, Yang and Huang (2016) claimed that important keywords on the website should be incorporated into the URL, the page title and the snippet. Both Sullivan (2016) and Weideman (2009) have developed models to rank the SEO elements used by Google algorithms in the commercially important ranking of results on SERPs. However, many large retrieval systems suffer from low efficiency because of badly designed systems (including the ignorance of SEO principles), which makes it difficult for search engine crawlers to find information and return relevant results (Weideman 2015).

Pay per click

According to Yang et al. (2012:1141), there has been tremendous growth of search auctions when, as these authors put it, 'economics meet search'.

The same authors continue and explain that search auctions (or PPC) have now become one of the most used online advertising channels. So much so that search auctions now produce the primary revenue source for major search engines. Google has reported a total revenue of $8.44 billion in the fourth quarter of 2010. Of this total, search auctions contributed 97% (Yang et al. 2012:1141). Prior research has been conducted to reduce the negative effect of inefficient keyword bidding when running a PPC campaign (Nabout 2015).

Some studies have shown that, when faced with the choice, more users will click on SEO results than those clicking on PPC results (Neethling 2008; Panda 2013). This seems to confirm the existence of an anomaly as noted by Kritzinger and Weideman (2015). However, the PPC industry has grown into a multibillion-dollar industry and generates a large income to its hosts, including Google and Bing (Gupta & Mateen 2014). This implies that the PPC system is successful and that it should be investigated.

Cost per acquisition

The CPA is an indication of the advertising cost of converting a human visitor into a paying client, producing revenue for the company. Ideally, the CPA should be low, which implies a higher profit rate. It has been claimed that acquiring a new customer could cost five times more than that to retain an existing one (Pfeifer 2005). This confirms the importance of determining which marketing method produces the lowest CPA.

Methodology

The best approach for this project was considered to be comparative and empirical. A convenience sample of three websites was used because all the historical data required for the research could be retrieved from these three, and all three had (a) product(s) to sell. Various user activities, as well as company expenditures were monitored and recorded over a period because they were all required to do the final CPA calculations.

For this research project, the authors examined the analytics and other statistical usage results of three real-life websites where both PPC and SEO of the marketing approaches were followed in tandem. The three websites are from three distinct industries and had no relation to each other.

The names of the three companies are not listed here – for brevity's sake, they will be referred to as Website 1, 2 and 3. All three companies invested in SEO and PPC on their websites. Website 1 is in the Bedding and Linen industry that is based in South Africa. They are an e-commerce concern.

In contrast, Website 2 is in the Toys Retail Industry and is based in the United Kingdom. Lastly, Website 3 is in the Road-Side Assistance Industry and is based in South Africa. Website 3 is not an e-commerce website, so an alternative way to measure transactions and actual income had to be found. For this research, the authors considered Goal Conversion specifically, that is, the number of new membership sign ups. This metric was roughly equivalent to an indication of sales because both generate direct income for the company.

The three websites were monitored for a period of 90 days (3 months). Usage behaviour and statistics were recorded and analysed to compare the expenditures with the gains, more specifically the CPA for each of these test websites.

Each of these websites was running an AdWords Campaign over the 90-day period they were monitored. All three were also running SEO campaigns alongside PPC Campaigns. The AdWords costs were recorded for each of the three websites as well as the monthly SEO cost over the 3-month period.

For the two e-commerce websites (Websites 1 and 2), the following statistics were recorded for both the PPC and SEO campaigns, for the 3-month period:

- the number of clicks received for both the paid and organic section of Google's search results page
- the number of user sessions recorded
- the average bounce rate
- the average number of pages per session
- the e-commerce conversion rate
- the number of transactions recorded
- the total revenue after 3 months for both PPC and SEO.

The e-commerce conversion rate is the percentage of sessions that resulted in an e-commerce transaction. For example, if a website had 17 352 sessions in a month and these sessions resulted in 188 transactions, then the e-commerce conversion rate would be (188/17 352) × 100 = 1.08%.

For Website 3 (the non-e-commerce website), the same statistics were also recorded for both PPC and SEO other the 3 months with these exceptions:

- The e-commerce conversion rate was replaced with 'goal conversion rate'.
- No revenue was recorded because the website is not e-commerce enabled.

Results and analysis

For the results and interpretation, the focus will firstly be on Websites 1 and 2 (the e-commerce websites).

Website 1

Clicks

For Website 1, the test period was from 07 September 2015 to 05 December 2015. The total number of organic clicks (SEO clicks) was retrieved from Google's Web Console.

Figure 3 indicates that Website 1 received 56 334 clicks from organic search results over the test period. This resulted in 57 475 organic sessions. The organic sessions were retrieved from Google Analytics (see Figure 4).

From the 57 475 organic sessions, the website analytics recorded 219 e-commerce transactions with a total revenue of R314 078.50, as shown in Figure 5.

Website 1 received 28 926 clicks from the Adwords Campaign (PPC Campaign) – this produced 29 795 PPC sessions. From these sessions, a total of 178 transactions were recorded over the 3-month period. This produced a PPC revenue of R238 925.60 (see Figure 6).

To summarise the results for Website 1, refer to Table 1.

Ratios

The values in the PPC and SEO columns were extracted from the Google Analytics records, while the Ratio column figures were calculated as a ratio of the previous two column values. Figures in the Ratio column were rounded to one decimal place. In all cases, a decision was taken in terms of how the ratio was to be calculated, to enable easier interpretation of the table data. For any given two sets of figures, a ratio of 1 (1:1) would mean that SEO and PPC performed identically. It was decided randomly (because

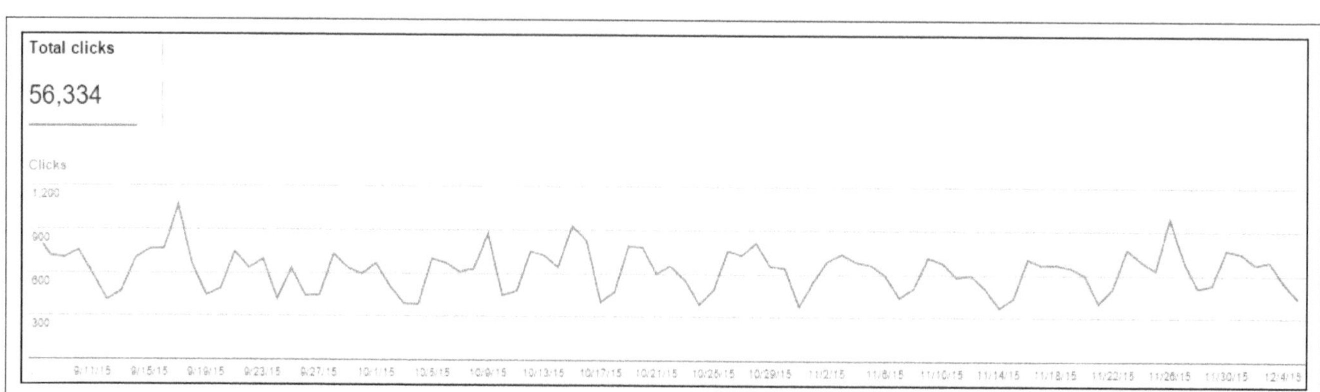

Source: Google Analytics, 2016, *Google Analytics Report*, viewed 16 May 2017, from https://www.google.com/analytics

FIGURE 3: Clicks harvested from Website 1.

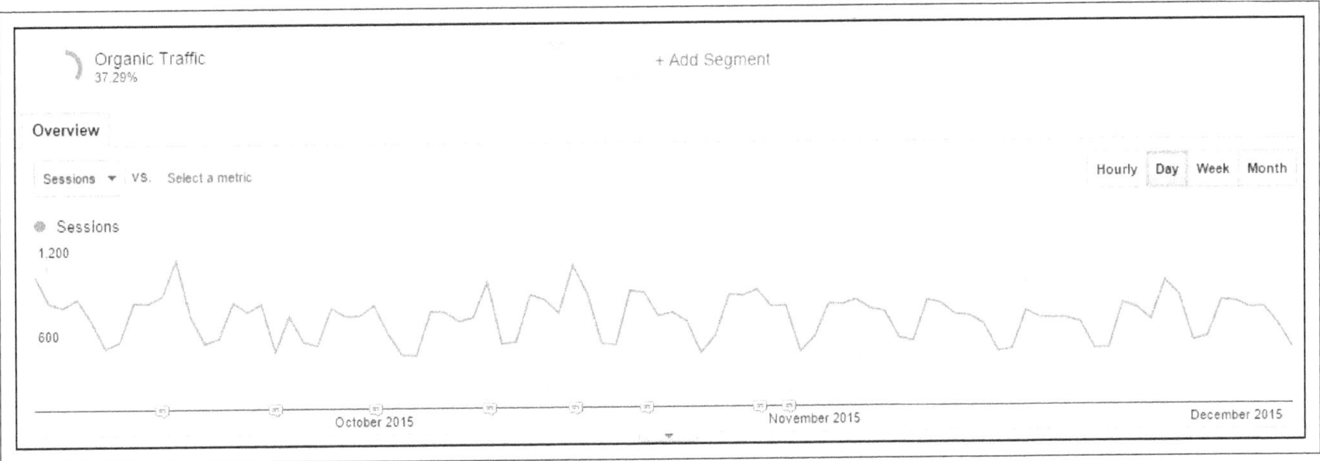

Source: Google Analytics, 2016, *Google Analytics Report*, viewed 16 May 2017, from https://www.google.com/analytics

FIGURE 4: User sessions recorded on Website 1.

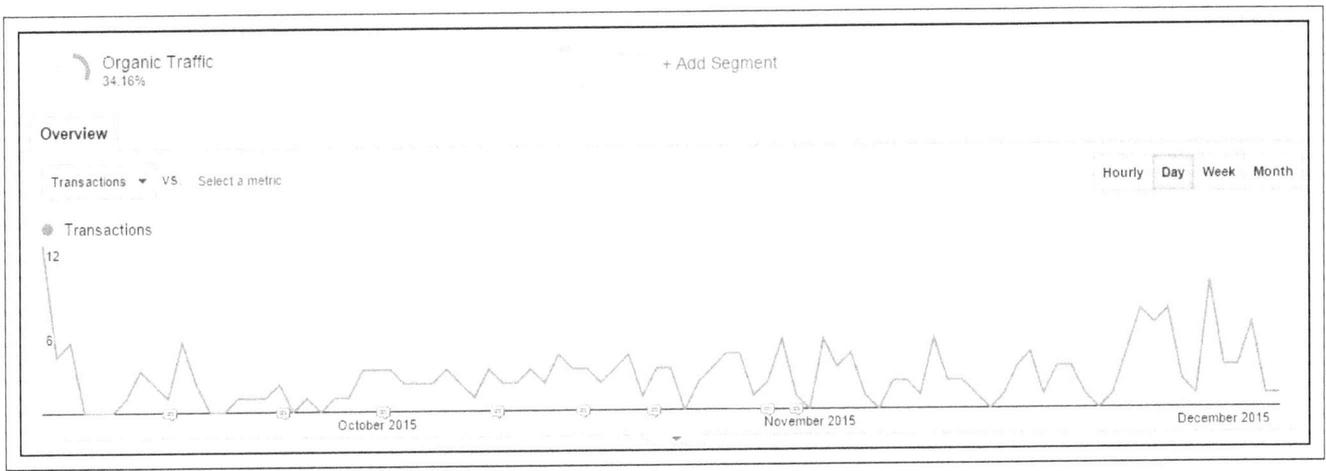

Source: Google Analytics, 2016, *Google Analytics Report*, viewed 16 May 2017, from https://www.google.com/analytics

FIGURE 5: The e-commerce transactions recorded on Website 1.

only the ratio and not the actual figures matter) that if the PPC and SEO figures for a given row indicated that SEO performed better than PPC (e.g. SEO produced more clicks, or SEO cost less than PPC), then the calculation would be performed in a way that the ratio would be above 1. This would allow for easier interpretation of results because a figure higher than 1 would always signify 'better' for SEO and 'worse' for PPC.

When considering the values of Table 1, note that higher values are more desirable than lower ones: Clicks, Sessions, Pages/session, e-commerce conversion rate, Transactions and Revenue. The remaining measures need to be lower to be better: Cost, Cost per click (CPC), Bounce rate and CPA. This difference is merely a result of the way these metrics were designed to indicate a given value for a given attribute. More clicks, more transactions and higher revenue are better, while lower values for expenditure (costs) and unimpressed users are better.

The figures in Table 1 can be classified into two types:

- those that do not have real value in terms of ROI, mostly isolated figures which do not depend on any other value (called incidental from here on – indicated in normal type)
- those that carry weight in terms of ROI, in the sense that they provide an indication of value (called indicative from here on – indicated in bold type).

From Table 1, over the test period of 3 months, a combined cost of R84 918.68 was incurred. PPC represents 68% of the total cost, while SEO represents the remaining 32%. The total number of clicks received was 85 260. SEO represents 66% of the total clicks, while PPC represents the remaining 34%. This is almost the exact reverse of the cost split between PPC and SEO.

Also from Table 1, the CPC for PPC was R1.99 and for SEO was R0.48 for SEO – the CPC for SEO is four times lower than the CPC for PPC. The bounce rates for PPC and SEO were relatively close to being the same at 29.61% and 23.59%, respectively. The e-commerce conversion rate for PPC is slightly higher than that of the SEO e-commerce conversion rate, at 0.6% and 0.38%, respectively. This indicates that PPC visitors are slightly more likely to convert than those arriving on a site through SEO results.

Finally, when comparing the total revenue, it was found that PPC resulted in R238 925.60 (or 43%) of the total revenue

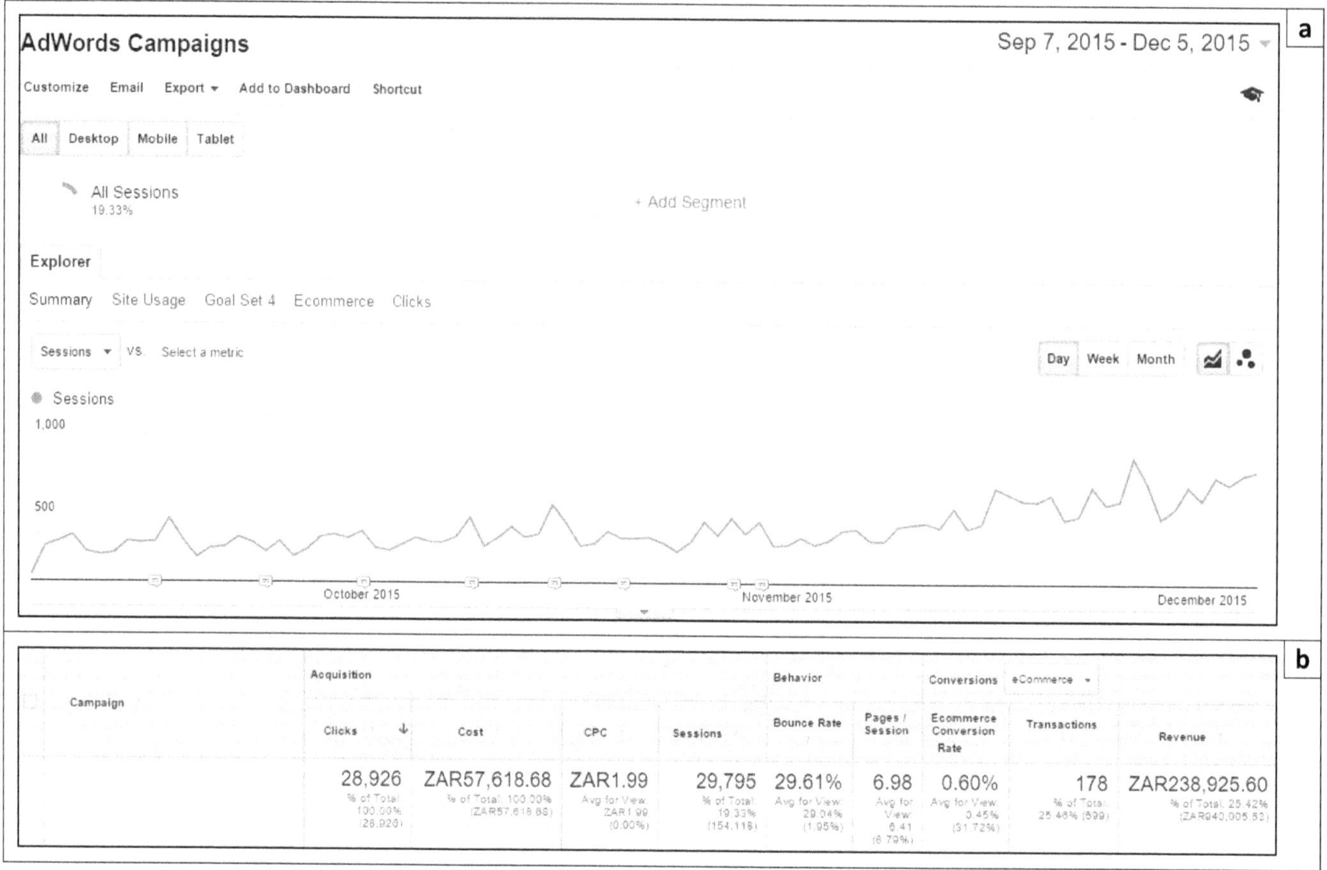

Source: Google Analytics, 2016, *Google Analytics Report*, viewed 16 May 2017, from https://www.google.com/analytics

FIGURE 6: Transactions recorded on Website 1: (a) number of user sessions recorded over the 3-month period and (b) session details: acquisition, behaviour and conversions.

TABLE 1: Results for Website 1.

Website 1	PPC	SEO	Ratio – PPC:SEO
Clicks	28 926	56 334	1.9
Cost	R57 618.68	R27 300.00	2.1
CPC	**R1.99**	**R0.48**	**4.1**
Sessions	29 795	57 475	1.9
Bounce rate	29.61%	23.59%	1.3
Pages/sessions	6.98	7.21	1.0
e-commerce conversion rate	**0.60%**	**0.38%**	**0.6**
Transactions	178	219	1.2
Revenue	R238 925.60	R314 078.50	1.3
CPA	**R333.43**	**R127.18**	**2.6**

Source: Google Analytics, 2016, *Google Analytics Report*, viewed 16 May 2017, from https://www.google.com/analytics

CPA, cost per acquisition; CPC, cost per click; PPC, pay per click; SEO, search engine optimisation.

received over the 3-month period. SEO resulted in R31 4078.50 (or 57%) of the total revenue.

In summary, three of the calculated ratios are indicative and two of the three favour SEO. This includes the most important measure, the CPA.

Website 2

Clicks

For Website 2 the test period was from 17 January 2016 to 15 April 2016. The total number of organic clicks (SEO clicks) was retrieved from Google's Web Console (see Figure 7).

As can be seen from Figure 7, Website 2 received 3 871 508 clicks from organic search results over the test period. This resulted in 4 872 537 organic sessions. The organic sessions were retrieved from Google Analytics (see Figure 8).

From the 4 872 537 organic sessions (see Figure 8), the website received 41 186 e-commerce transactions with a total revenue of £2 163 584.37 (see Figure 9).

From the Adwords Campaign (PPC Campaign), Website 2 received 322 483 clicks, which resulted in 442 399 PPC sessions. From the 442 399 PPC sessions, a total number of 7869 transactions were recorded over the 3-month period, which resulted in a PPC revenue of £354 876.22 (see Figure 10).

For a summary of the results for Website 2, see Table 2.

From Table 2, the authors found that over the test period of 3 months a combined cost of £88 966.82 was incurred. PPC represents 96% of the total cost, while SEO represents the remaining 4%. In contrast, the total number of clicks harvested over the 3-month period was 4 193 991. SEO represents 92% of the total clicks, while PPC represents the remaining 8%. This is almost the complete reverse of the cost split between PPC and SEO.

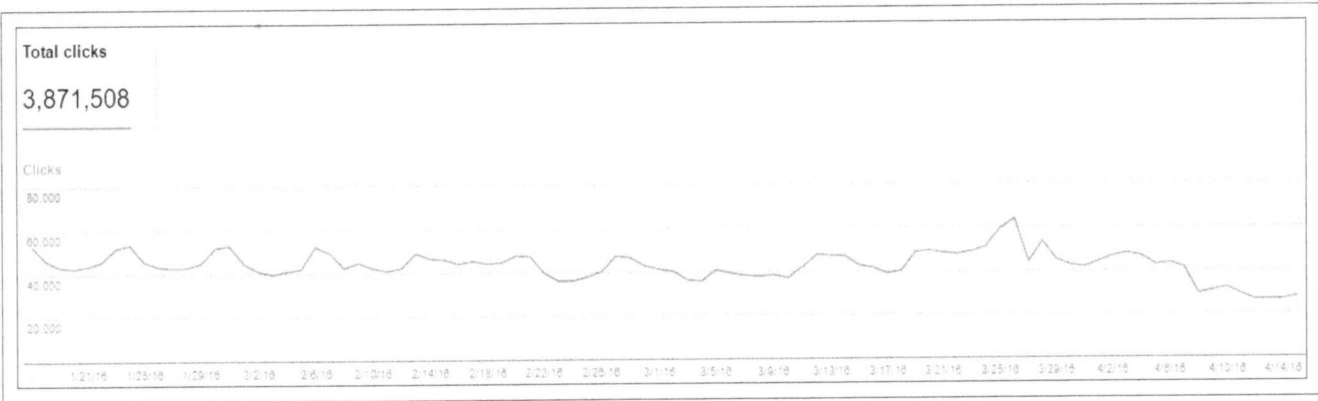

Source: Google Analytics, 2016, *Google Analytics Report*, viewed 16 May 2017, from https://www.google.com/analytics

FIGURE 7: Clicks harvested from Website 2.

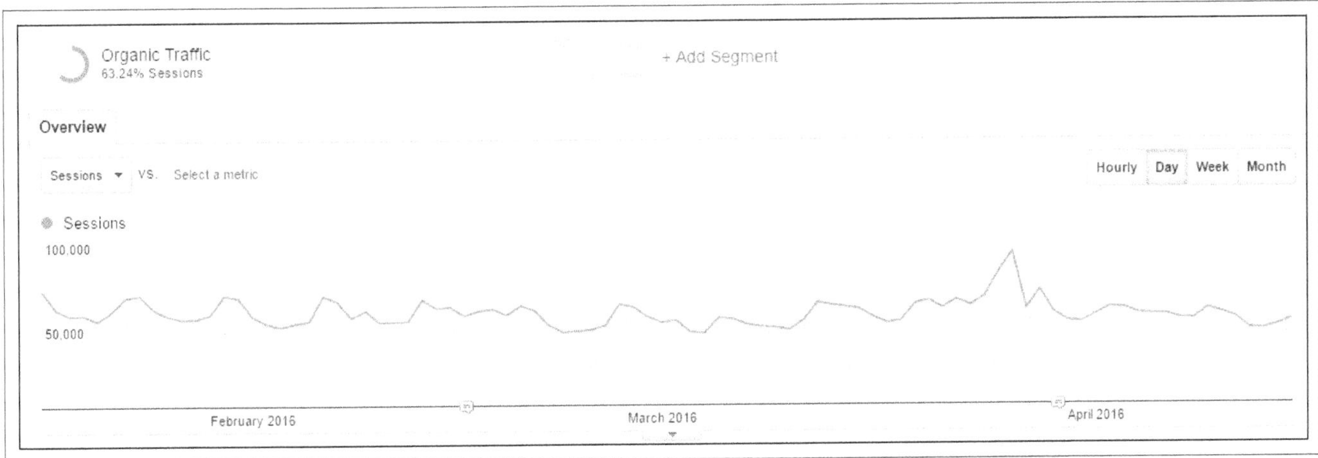

Source: Google Analytics, 2016, *Google Analytics Report*, viewed 16 May 2017, from https://www.google.com/analytics

FIGURE 8: User sessions recorded on Website 2.

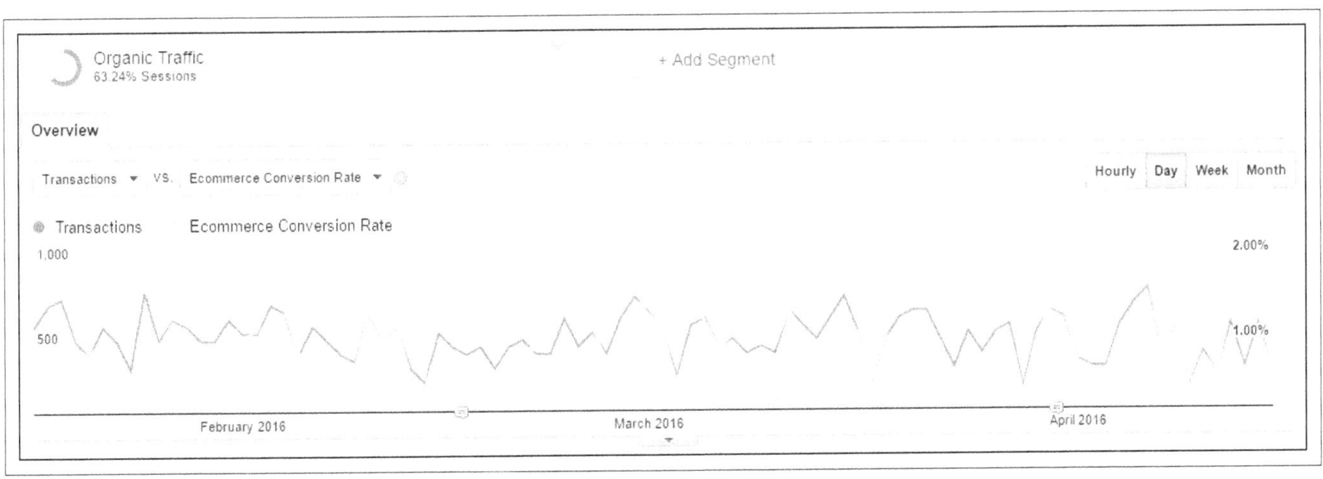

Source: Google Analytics, 2016, *Google Analytics Report*, viewed 16 May 2017, from https://www.google.com/analytics

FIGURE 9: The e-commerce transactions recorded on Website 2.

From the numbers in this table, it became clear that the CPC for PPC was £0.27 and £0.00087 for SEO. The CPC for SEO is significantly lower than the CPC for PPC. The bounce rates for PPC and SEO were very different at 59.55% and 26%, respectively. The e-commerce conversion rate for PPC is higher than that of the SEO e-commerce conversion rate – 1.78% and 0.85%, respectively. This means that PPC visitors are slightly more likely to convert.

Finally, when the authors compared the total revenue, it was found that PPC resulted in £354 876.22 (or 16%) of the total revenue received over the 3-month period. SEO resulted in £2 163 584.37 (or 84%) of the total revenue.

In summary, three of the calculated ratios are indicative, and two of the three favour SEO. This includes the most important measure, the CPA.

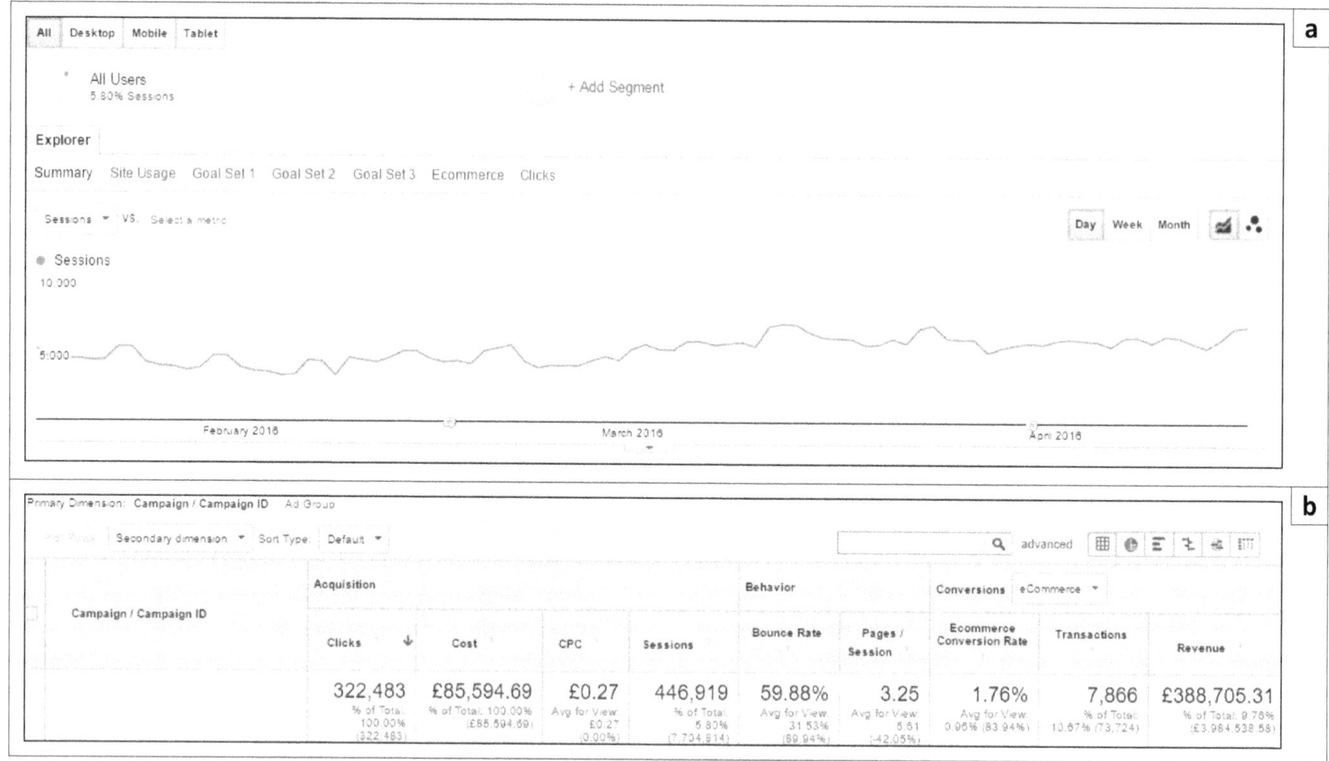

Source: Google Analytics, 2016, *Google Analytics Report*, viewed 16 May 2017, from https://www.google.com/analytics

FIGURE 10: Transactions recorded on Website 2: (a) number of user sessions recorded over the 3-month period and (b) session details: acquisition, behaviour and conversions.

TABLE 2: Results for Website 2.

Website 2	PPC	SEO	Ratio – PPC:SEO
Clicks	322 483	3 871 508	12
Cost	£85 594.69	£3372.13	25.4
CPC	**£0.27**	**£0.00087**	**310.3**
Sessions	442 399	4 872 537	11
Bounce rate	59.55%	26%	2.3
Pages/sessions	3.19	6.08	1.9
e-commerce conversion rate	**1.78%**	**0.85%**	**0.5**
Transactions	7869	41 186	5.2
Revenue	£354 876.22	£2 163 584.37	6.1
CPA	**£14.92**	**£0.10**	**149.2**

Source: Author's own based on data extracted from Google Analytics reports

CPA, cost per acquisition; CPC, cost per click; PPC, pay per click; SEO, search engine optimisation.

Website 3

Clicks

For Website 3, the test period was from 8 September 2015 to 6 December 2015. The total number of organic clicks (SEO clicks) was retrieved from Google's Web Console.

As can be seen from Figure 11, Website 3 received 296 101 clicks from organic search results over the test period. This resulted in 319 660 organic sessions. The organic sessions were retrieved from Google Analytics (see Figure 12).

From the 319 660 organic sessions, the website received 1573 goal completions (see Figure 13).

From the Adwords Campaign (PPC Campaign), Website 3 received 59 838 clicks, which resulted in 19 572 PPC sessions. From the 19 572 PPC sessions, a total number of 811 goals were recorded over the 3-month period (see Figure 14).

To summarise the results for Website 3, see Table 3.

From Table 3 the authors found that over the test period a combined cost of R315 592.29 was incurred. PPC represents 88% of the total cost, while SEO represents the remaining 12% of the total cost. In contrast, the total number of clicks received over the 3-month period was 355 939. SEO represents 83% of the total clicks, while PPC represents the remaining 17%. This is almost the complete reverse of the cost split between PPC and SEO.

From the figures in Table 3, the authors also found that the CPC for PPC was R4.68 and R0.13 for SEO. The CPC for SEO is 36 times lower than the CPC for PPC. The bounce rates for PPC and SEO were also very different at 66.73% and 41.29%, respectively. The goal conversion rate for PPC was higher than that of the SEO goal conversion rate – 4.14% and 0.49%, respectively. This means that PPC visitors are significantly more likely to convert.

In summary, three of the calculated ratios are indicative, and two of the three favour SEO. This includes the most important measure, the CPA.

Conclusion

Limitations and recommendations

It was considered necessary to investigate why Website 2 had such extreme figures favouring SEO. Website 2 is that

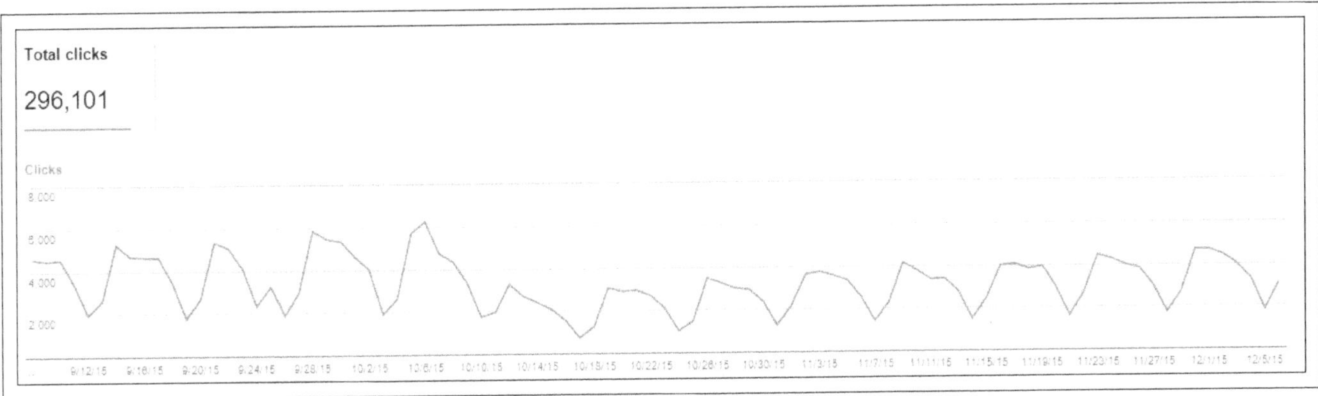

Source: Google Analytics, 2016, *Google Analytics Report*, viewed 16 May 2017, from https://www.google.com/analytics

FIGURE 11: Clicks harvested from Website 3.

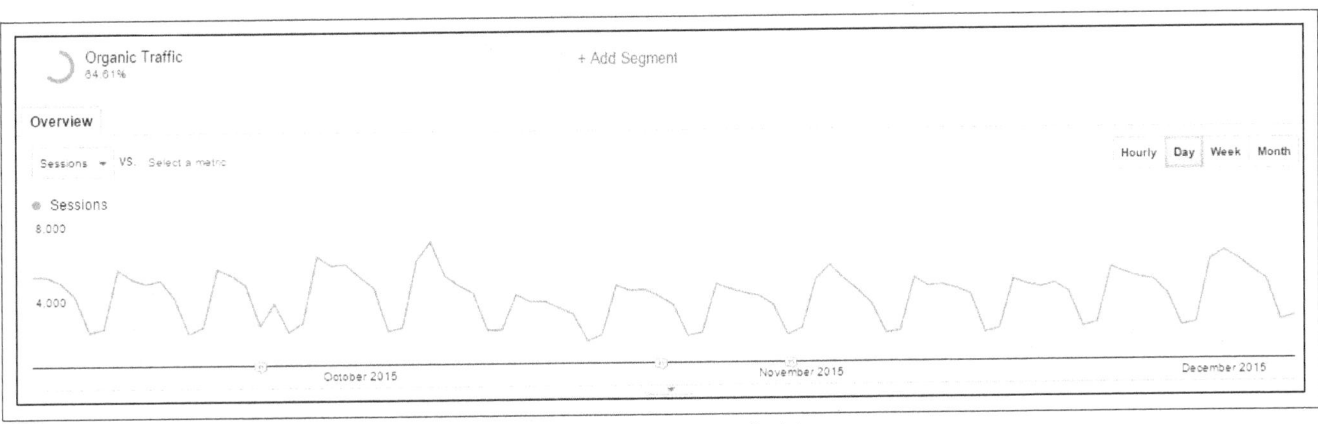

Source: Google Analytics, 2016, *Google Analytics Report*, viewed 16 May 2017, from https://www.google.com/analytics

FIGURE 12: User sessions recorded on Website 3.

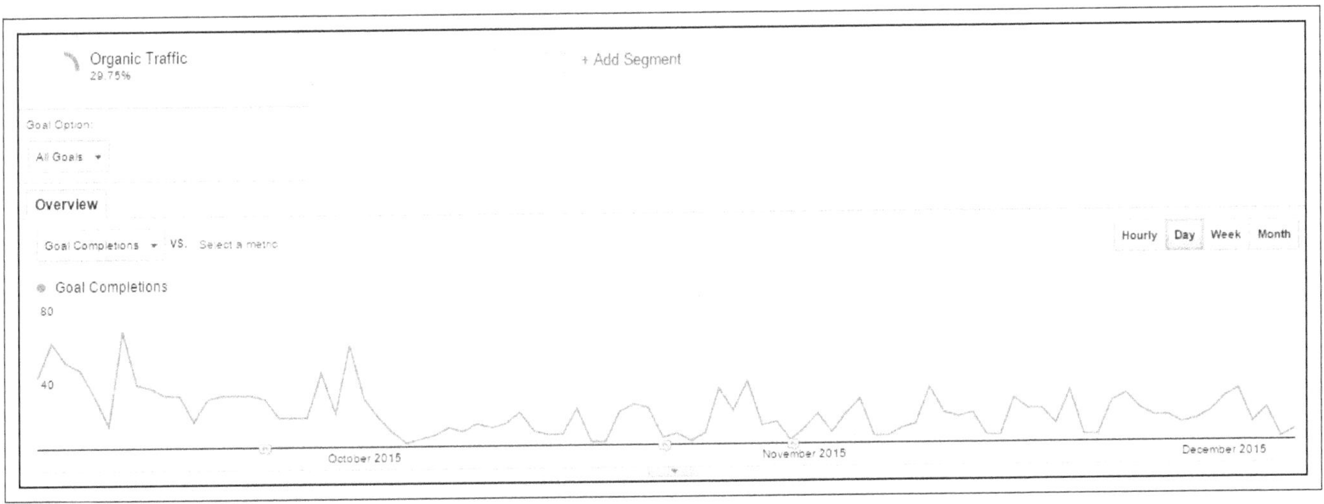

Source: Google Analytics, 2016, *Google Analytics Report*, viewed 16 May 2017, from https://www.google.com/analytics

FIGURE 13: The e-commerce transactions recorded on Website 3.

of 'n major toy retail store in the UK and Ireland. They have literally hundreds of different Product Categories and thousands of Products being sold. Each one of these category and product pages were built on SEO best practice. This has resulted in a very large number of web pages with a high search engine ranking, resulting in a high number of visits from searchers clicking on natural results. The large difference in user sessions between SEO and PPC (4 872 537 vs. 442 399) confirms this claim. Hence, this specific website has a much better ranking on natural results than the other two, smaller websites. This fact clarifies the higher SEO-supporting figures.

Finally, a further summary of the results from the three websites' figures and ratios was needed before drawing conclusions. In Table 4, the most indicative figures from the three website data tables are summarised.

It is clear that all three websites show the same trends, but to different degrees:

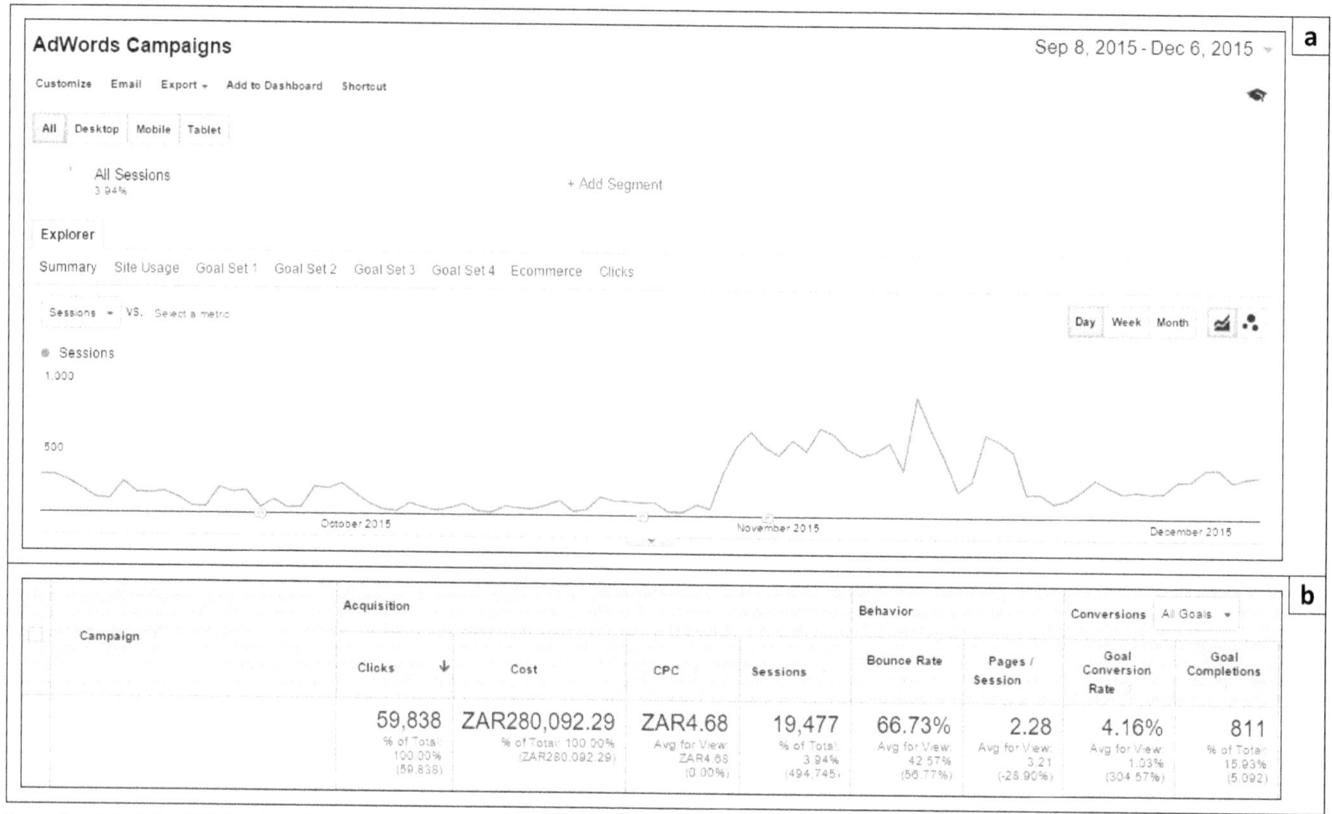

Source: Google Analytics, 2016, *Google Analytics Report*, viewed 16 May 2017, from https://www.google.com/analytics

FIGURE 14: Transactions recorded on Website 3: (a) number of user sessions recorded over the 3-month period and (b) session details: acquisition, behaviour and conversions.

TABLE 3: Results for Website 3.

Website 3	PPC	SEO	Ratio – PPC:SEO
Clicks	59 838	296 101	5.0
Cost	R280 092.29	R37 500.00	7.5
CPC	**R4.68**	**R0.13**	**36.0**
Sessions	19 572	319 660	16.3
Bounce rate	66.73%	41.29%	1.6
Pages/sessions	2.28	3.25	1.4
Goal conversion rate	**4.14%**	**0.49%**	**0.1**
Transactions	811	1573	1.9
CPA	**R112.96**	**R25.85**	**4.4**

Source: Author's own based on data extracted from Google Analytics reports

CPA, cost per acquisition; CPC, cost per click; PPC, pay per click; SEO, search engine optimisation.

- CPC: All three websites favour SEO, with Website 1 showing a relatively small difference and Website 2 showing a dramatic difference. A lower CPC can, therefore, be achieved through the use of SEO. Of all three measures, CPC has the highest degree of difference, with an average SEO preference of 116.8.
- Conversion rate: All three websites favour PPC, with Website 1 showing a relatively large difference and Website 3 showing a small difference. A higher Conversion Rate can be achieved using PPC. Of all three measures, Conversion Rate has the lowest degree of difference, with an average PPC preference of 0.4.
- CPA: All three websites favour SEO, with Website 1 showing a relatively small difference and Website 2 showing a dramatic difference. It can, therefore, be concluded that a lower CPA can be achieved using SEO. The average CPA for the three websites is 52.1.

TABLE 4: Website comparative results.

Measure	Website 1	Website 2	Website 3
CPC	4.1	310.3	36.0
Conversion rate	0.6	0.5	0.1
CPA	2.6	149.2	4.4

CPA, cost per acquisition; CPC, cost per click.

The focus of this research was on a comparison between the CPA of SEO versus PPC systems, so these figures require more attention. The CPA figure is 52.1 times higher on the average for PPC systems than for SEO. So, if an online retailer must spend, for example, R1000 per month to acquire sales through SEO, they will need to spend R52 100 during the same month through PPC for the same returns. A higher number of websites need to be compared for a reliable average figure, so this research can lead to some follow-up work using more websites.

In conclusion, the results clearly show that SEO produces a much lower CPA, which is, therefore, a better choice of marketing strategy for any online retailer.

Limitations of the study include that only three websites were used – more websites in the sample would yield more accurate results. Also, figures spanning a longer period would produce more stable results.

As recommendation, it is suggested that most of a company's marketing budget be spent on SEO. However, in certain isolated cases, PPC could be a better choice. Examples where this could be the case include:

- when immediate results are imperative
- when regular expenditure per month is preferable over an initial high investment.

In the first case, PPC would be better because one's PPC ads can start playing immediately after the system and accounting has been set up, possibly harvesting paying clients with virtually no delay (Kritzinger & Weideman 2013). With SEO, time must be allowed for SEO implementation, before search results could bring in clients.

Secondly, if SEO on a given website is non-existent or badly performed, it could require a major financial investment before results of an SEO campaign will become evident. In some situations, the client might not have the financial means to invest a large amount up front and might choose to rather spread the financial outlay over a period. In this case, after a given period the PPC expenditure might cross over that of what the SEO costs might have been and then an SEO investment might have been better in the long run. It has been proven in previous research that this time period can typically be around 6 months (Kritzinger & Weideman 2013).

Finally, the following recommendations were evident from this research:

- Use PPC if quick results are essential and if a more piecemeal way of spending a limited budget is needed.
- Use SEO for results at a lower overall cost, when considering the amount spent to achieve those results.
- Use both approaches in tandem in a systematic, carefully balanced long-term approach to ensure high rankings, high visitor counts, high income and eventually a higher ROI (Kritzinger & Weideman 2013).

Acknowledgements

Competing interests

The authors declare that they have no financial or personal relationships that may have inappropriately influenced them in writing this article.

Authors' contributions

W.T.K., the doctoral student, did the actual research, recorded the results and wrote 50% of the article. M.W., the supervisor, completed the other 50% of the article, did the proofreading, checked the content, formatted the article, added references and submitted the article for publication. After feedback from reviewers, he also did all corrections and improvements.

References

Baidya, M.K. & Basu, P., 2011, 'Allocation of budget on marketing efforts: An econometric approach in India', *Asia Pacific Journal of Marketing and Logistics* 23(4), 501–512. https://doi.org/10.1108/13555851111165057

Broilo, P.L., Espartel, L.B. & Basso, K., 2016, 'Pre-purchase information search: Too many sources to choose', *Journal of Research in Interactive Marketing* 10(3), 193–211. https://doi.org/10.1108/JRIM-07-2015-0048

Clarke, T.B. & Clarke, I., 2014, 'A competitive and experiential assignment in search engine optimisation strategy', *Marketing Education Review* 24(1), 25–30. https://doi.org/10.2753/MER1052-8008240104

Clarke, T.B. & Jansen, B.J., 2017, 'Conversion potential: A metric for evaluating search engine advertising Performance', *Journal of Research in Interactive Marketing* 11(2). https://doi.org/10.1108/JRIM-07-2016-0073

Druckenmiller, G., 2016, 'How to cut cost per acquisition in half and drive more leads without increasing budget', *Webinar Presented by Evariant*, 03 July 2016, Farmington, CT, Businesswire, bizwire.c67271458.

Ford, R.A.M.B.J., 1994, 'Relationship between marketing planning and annual budgeting', *Marketing Intelligence & Planning* 12(1), 22–28. https://doi.org/10.1108/02634509410052621

Google Analytics, 2015, 'Making sponsored search ads work better', *Strategic Direction* 31(1), 12–14. https://doi.org/10.1108/SD-10-2014-0155

Google Analytics, 2016, *Google Analytics Report*, viewed 16 May 2017, from https://www.google.com/analytics

Gudivada, V.N., Rao, D. & Paris, J., 2015, 'Understanding search-engine optimization', *Computer* 162(15), 43–52. https://doi.org/10.1109/MC.2015.297

Gupta, A. & Mateen, A., 2014, 'Exploring the factors affecting sponsored search ad performance', *Marketing Intelligence & Planning* 32(5), 586–599. https://doi.org/10.1108/MIP-05-2013-0083

Huck, L., Hamner, K. & Carpenter, C., 2016, *How Google's new desktop SERP layout has impacted marketers*, viewed 2 December 2016, from http://blog.360i.com/search-marketing/googles-new-desktop-serp-layout-impacted-marketers

Jang, W., Lee, E. & Oh, S.G., 2016, 'Search engine optimization', *Library Hi Tech* 34(2), 197–206. https://doi.org/10.1108/LHT-02-2016-0014

Kotler, P., Kartajaya, H. & Setiawan, I., 2010, *Marketing 3.0: From products to customers to the human spirit*, John Wiley, Hoboken, NJ.

Kritzinger, W.T. & Weideman, M., 2013, 'Search engine optimization and pay-per-click marketing strategies', *Journal of Organizational Computing and Electronic Commerce* 23(3), 273–286. https://doi.org/10.1080/10919392.2013.808124

Kritzinger, W.T. & Weideman, M., 2015, 'Comparative case study on website traffic generated by search engine optimisation and a pay-per-click campaign, versus marketing expenditure', *South African Journal of Information Management* 17(1), Art. #651, 1–12. https://doi.org/10.4102/sajim.v17i1.651

Luh, C.J., Yang, S.A. & Huang, T.L.D., 2016, 'Estimating Google's search engine ranking function from a search engine optimization perspective', *Online Information Review* 40(2), 239–255. https://doi.org/10.1108/OIR-04-2015-0112

McGee, M., 2016, *Confirmed: Google to stop showing ads on the right side of desktop search results worldwide*, viewed 05 December 2016, from http://searchengineland.com/google-no-ads-right-side-of-desktop-search-results-242997

Miller, M., 2011., *The ultimate web marketing guide*, Pearson Education, Indianapolis, IN.

Nabout, N.A., 2015, 'A novel approach for bidding on keywords in newly set-up search advertising campaigns', *European Journal of Marketing* 49(5/6), 668–691. https://doi.org/10.1108/EJM-08-2013-0424

Neethling, R., 2008, 'User profiles for preferences of search engine optimisation versus paid placement', Unpublished Master's Thesis, Cape Peninsula University of Technology, Cape Town.

Olbrich, R. & Schultz, C.D., 2014, 'Multichannel advertising: Does print advertising affect search engine advertising?', *European Journal of Marketing* 48(9/10), 1731–1756. https://doi.org/10.1108/EJM-10-2012-0569

Panda, T.K., 2013, 'Search engine marketing: Does the knowledge discovery process help Online retailers?', *The IUP Journal of Knowledge Management* XI(3), 56–66.

Pavel, K., Pauwels, K. & Gupta, S., 2016, 'Do display ads influence search? Attribution and dynamics in online advertising', *International Journal of Research in Marketing* 33(3), 475–490. https://doi.org/10.1016/j.ijresmar.2015.09.007

Pfeifer, P.E., 2005, 'The optimal ratio of acquisition and retention costs', *Journal of Targeting, Measurement and Analysis for Marketing* 13(2), 179–188. https://doi.org/10.1057/palgrave.jt.5740142

PRN, 2015, 'fishbat COO Scott Darrohn explains 4 reasons why companies should combine PPC with SEO', PR Newswire, TRIBECA, NY 2015 /PRNewswire-iReach/

PRN, 2016, 'Caroff communications reveals 5 ways PPC and SEO are used to enhance each other', PRNewswire, San Diego.

Sullivan, D., 2016, *The periodic table of SEO success factors*, SearchEngineLand, viewed 01 December 2016, from http://searchengineland.com/seotable/download-periodic-table-of-seo

Weideman, M., 2009, *Website visibility: The theory and practice of improving rankings*, Chandos Publishers, Oxford.

Weideman, M., 2015, 'ETD visibility: A study on the exposure of Indian ETDs to the Google Scholar crawler', Proceedings of the 18th International Symposium on Theses and Dissertations, New Delhi, India, November 2015.

Yang, Y., Zhang, J., Qin, R., Li, J. & Wang, F., 2012, 'A budget optimization framework for search advertisements across markets', *IEEE Transaction on Systems, Man, and Cybernetics* 42(5), 1141–1151. https://doi.org/10.1109/TSMCA.2011.2172418

Zuze, H. & Weideman, M, 2013, 'Keyword stuffing and the big three search engines', *Online Information Review* 37(2), 268–286, viewed 11 December 2016, from http://www.emeraldinsight.com/doi/abs/10.1108/OIR-11-2011-0193

18

Email communication in project management: A bane or a blessing?

Authors:
Marius C. Smit[1]
Taryn J. Bond-Barnard[1]
Herman Steyn[1]
Inger Fabris-Rotelli[2]

Affiliations:
[1]Department of Engineering and Technology Management, University of Pretoria, South Africa

[2]Department of Statistics, University of Pretoria, South Africa

Corresponding author:
Taryn Bond-Barnard,
taryn.barnard@up.ac.za

Background: Project success used to be measured solely in terms of efficiency metrics such as scope, cost and time; however, there are proposals that more attention should be paid to process-related performance factors such as communication. The advent of email has significantly impacted the way the world communicates.

Objectives: This study investigates the preference of email communication relative to other communication mediums in project environments and the effect of email communication on feelings of stress and overload in the workplace.

Method: A survey with 430 responses was conducted to determine the communication preferences of project practitioners in a typical project. The average rank and frequency response methods were used to analyse the data.

Results: The findings indicate that the communication preferences of project practitioners still support the media richness theory and that face-to-face communication is the preferred communication medium in most situations. Despite email being disruptive and a cause of stress, the respondents did not indicate being overloaded because of email.

Conclusion: Even though there has been a dramatic shift towards email and electronic communication in projects, face-to-face communication is still the most preferred communication type for most situations. Furthermore, email is perceived as an effective tool to delegate, can be used to build and develop relationships and trust, and is an efficient and effective tool that contributes to project communication success.

Introduction

Project management and project management principles are increasingly applied in the execution of projects and other endeavours not previously managed as projects (Crawford & Nahmias 2010). The narrow definition of project success as solely a function of efficiency metrics such as scope, cost and time is being challenged by authors who claim this to be a measure of project management success, rather than project success (Bryde & Robinson 2005; Frodell, Josephson & Lindahl 2008; Koops et al. 2016; Lim & Mohamed 1999; McLeod, Doolin & MacDonell 2012; Turner 2007). The importance of good communication to achieve success in projects is frequently outlined in the project management literature (Henderson, Stackman & Lindekilde 2016; Lehmann 2009; Müller & Turner 2001; Turner & Müller 2004). Padalkar and Gopinath (2016) noted that there was a significant increase in project communication research between 2011 and 2015. However, the topic is still minimally represented in research in comparison to the other project management body of knowledge (PMBOK) knowledge areas. Literature suggests that it will become a more important topic in future as communication research is vital for investigating knowledge acquisition and assimilation in projects, which is a trending topic (Padalkar & Gopinath 2016). This study investigates if practitioners' communication preferences are changing with the advent of the digital age, which contributes to a better understanding of how modern communication media impact practitioners and projects.

The advent of electronic mail (email) has significantly changed the way the world communicates and how communication media are defined. The immediacy of email and other electronic mail formats like text messaging is blurring the boundaries between synchronous and asynchronous media (Den Otter & Emmitt 2007). More focus is being placed on more frequent, informal project updates via email while formal reports are gradually being restricted to high-level feedback (Bond-Barnard, Fletcher & Steyn 2016).

The acceptance and use of email for conveying information that is both low and high in equivocality (this term is discussed later on in this paper) is greying the lines drawn by the theory of media richness and questions the measures used to define media richness. As project teams are often geographically dispersed, email is used to initiate and build relationships between project team members who will potentially never meet face-to-face (Cheshin et al. 2013). Email also has potential impediments because of its disruptive nature, opportunities for excessive delegation and its ability to overload users (Bawden & Robinson 2009; Gantz, Boyd & Dowling 2009; Sappelli et al. 2016). These impediments will be investigated in greater detail in this paper.

It is clear that communication is playing an increasingly important role in projects and project success (Ksenija & Skendrovic 2010). Communication and the way that communication impacts projects are receiving more attention in academic research (Bond-Barnard et al. 2016; Henderson et al. 2016). The transformation of communication because of the arrival of new electronic communication media is noted, but the impact thereof on organisations is not clearly understood. Attempts have been made to govern email in organisations (PwC South Africa 2017). However, the use of email as a preferred communication medium in the workplace and in the project management environment is growing, but its impact on individual and project performance is not clearly understood. Researchers are still trying to pin down the characteristics of email by making use of previously accepted communication media frameworks. In the process, previously held beliefs about communication in the workplace and in projects are being challenged.

Given the changes in the perceived importance of communication in projects, and the uncertainty surrounding the characteristics and impacts of email communication in the work environment, an opportunity exists to study the use and impact of electronic messages on individuals in the project environment. This study explores communication preferences, describes how individuals manage their email and gauges the impact of email communication on individuals, their relationships, efficiency and effectiveness in the project environment. Six hypotheses are proposed: (1) email is replacing other types of media in the project management environment; (2) email is disruptive; (3) users experience stress and overload because of email; (4) email is an effective tool to delegate tasks; (5) email supports building relationships and trust; and (6) email creates conflict.

The study provides insight into communication preferences and the use of email communication in projects. The perceived 'disruptive' impediments of email communication as well as email's impact on individual and project performance are investigated in more detail. The findings contribute to a better understanding of how modern communication media impact practitioners and projects. This information is useful for practitioners and academics as they grapple to understand the role and the do's and don'ts of electronic communication in project environments.

Literature review

The role of communication in projects

Teams are formed to work on projects, and team members need to work together to ensure successful project completion. Among the various aspects of how team members should work together are issues regarding communication and, more specifically, communication regarding tasks and coordination (Chiocchio 2007).

The emphasis on communication as it applies to project management may be understood as part of two interrelated trends. Firstly, teams are used more frequently because of the requirement for tasks to be performed using complex systems and processes where it is difficult to achieve success without teamwork (Kahai, Sosik & Avolio 2004 in Chiocchio 2007). This trend is related not only to globalisation and increased complexity but also to global and geographically dispersed project teams. Secondly, the way people communicate is modified by information technology such as email (Colquitt et al. 2002; Michinov, Michinov & Toczek-Capelle 2004 in Chiocchio 2007).

Communication and project success

Cserháti and Szabó (2014), Ngai, Law and Wat (2008), Pinto and Slevin (1987) identified critical success factors (CSFs) for projects which can be used as an instrument for measuring project success. Among the factors that they identified were adequate communication channels. Similarly, Fortune and White (2006) reviewed 63 publications on CSFs to formulate a summarised list of CSFs. They also identified that good communication or feedback was one of 27 CSFs of a project.

Experts interested in transforming organisations and also project management maintain that a large number of projects can fail because of shortcomings or errors in communication (Elovitz 1999 in Lehmann 2009). Lehmann (2009) stated that project management must take communication phenomena into account; if not, the project may fail.

Characteristics of communication mediums

Media richness: The media richness theory, which builds on the social presence theory, argues that communication media differ in their ability to facilitate understanding. It is the media's 'information richness', defined as the amount of information a medium can convey to change the receiver's 'understanding within a time interval', that differentiates richer media from leaner media. The use of richer media leads to better performance for tasks with greater equivocality or ambiguity (Robert & Dennis 2005).

Face-to-face communication is the richest medium and is preferred for highly equivocal tasks as it provides immediate feedback and allows that interpretation can be checked. Electronic media is generally believed to be leaner in richness and is preferred for non-equivocal tasks (Robert & Dennis 2005). Researchers classify email as falling between telephonic communication and non-electronic written communication in terms of richness (Markus 1994; Robert & Dennis 2005).

Mintzberg (1973) indicated that senior managers prefer verbal communication to written communication, mostly because of their need for a richer medium of communication. The need for richer media was attributed to the higher equivocality in the messages that they would generally convey.

If managers perceive email as higher in richness than the richness theory suggests, they might substitute email for some, possibly much of their telephonic communication. Media richness theory will therefore underestimate a manager's use of email to the extent that managers perceive email as higher in richness (Markus 1994).

Synchronous and asynchronous communication: Synchronous communication can be defined as direct communication where all parties involved in the communication are present at the same time. Synchronous communication includes face-to-face interactions such as meetings and informal discussions where the communication occurs at the same place and time. Moreover, electronic communication media such as video conferencing and instant messaging can also be viewed as synchronous communication; however, the communication in this instance occurs at different places at the same time (Den Otter & Emmitt 2007). Asynchronous communication does not require that all parties involved in the communication be present at the same time, such as email messages and text messaging.

Email is both written and asynchronous, although with the speed of modern computer technology and the email habits of users it is becoming a more synchronous communication medium. According to Renaud, Ramsay and Hair (2006), email does not fit neatly into established categories or behave according to well-established asynchronous communication rules. They termed email as e-synchronous, as it is unlike either synchronous or asynchronous media.

Equivocality: The term 'equivocality' is used to describe communication tasks high in ambiguity, such as settling a dispute. Tasks high in equivocality require a communication medium that is rich in information, while tasks low in equivocality do not require this (Robert & Dennis 2005). Different communication media vary in their ability to carry rich information. It is deemed to be important to match the richness of the medium with the equivocality of the communication task. Lean media lack adequate support for high equivocality tasks and may lead to miscommunication. The selection of the medium that matches the communication task leads to the most effective outcome.

The use of email for equivocal communication can largely be attributed to social behaviours that created richness by increasing the speed of email, rather than the capabilities of the medium itself (Markus 1994). The speed and convenience of email adds richness to the medium, which was previously associated with telephonic communication.

Multi-addressability: The ability to reach multiple persons simultaneously (multi-addressability) is a characteristic of both email and face-to-face communication, making it superior to telephonic communication. Multi-addressability results in individuals receiving more messages than they send, as email messages are often addressed to more than one recipient, or a number of recipients are included in the 'cc' field.

Multi-addressability can cause mistrust. Müller (2003) states that one-to-one communication is more informal and promotes trust and knowledge building. In contrast, one-to-many communication is more formal, creates mistrust and is controlled.

Another potential consequence of multi-addressability is the fact that email is not a collective means of communication, because senders choose to whom they send messages (Chiocchio 2007). As a result, team members can be kept out of the loop, intentionally or unintentionally.

Formal versus informal communication

Formal reports are perceived to be the most credible source of information (Johnson 1993 in Turner & Müller [2004]). Mullins 1999 in Turner and Müller (2004) found that informal communication is perceived to be high in speed and low in accuracy, while formal communication is perceived to be low in speed but high in accuracy. Research by Johnson et al. 1994 in Turner and Müller (2004) supported this finding by stating that formal communication is more credible than informal communication.

Bond-Barnard, Steyn and Fabris-Rotelli (2013) found that a reduction in mistrust and conflict of interest can be achieved through a balance of frequent informal and formal communication. Their findings support Turner and Müller's (2004) research, which states that trust exists where informal communication is used.

The application of email in organisations

The explosion in the use of email by all levels in organisations, including senior management, for a multitude of tasks including tasks with high equivocality, would suggest that the richness of email according to the richness theory is wrong. Workers conduct much of their business via email, because it is perceived to be less time-consuming, more reliable and efficient than phoning or meeting face-to-face (Berghel 1997 in Renaud et al. [2006]). Email also maintains a durable record of requests or instructions, which is useful to resolve future disputes (Renaud et al. 2006).

The aspects of email that made it popular in the first place, that is, brevity and accessibility to superiors, seem to cause some problems once email become ubiquitous in business

(Ramsay & Renaud 2012). People use email exclusively, instead of direct interaction with other people (even in the same building), often to the detriment of the communication process. The traditional measures of communication effectiveness are being ignored in the interest of convenience and brevity.

Email and relationships

Email lacks the personal connection allowed by face-to-face and telephonic communication. Renaud et al. (2006) found that email is impoverished as compared to other media, and yet users seem to prefer it. Email lacks the contextual details because people find it laborious to replicate in a written format all that is conveyed through voice intonation and body language when they convey a message verbally (Cramton & Orvis 2003 in Chiocchio [2007]). People, therefore, prefer to use telephonic communication to build and maintain relationships with people who are geographically dispersed. Markus (1994) interviewed several employees in his study that indicated that relationships with co-workers will become cold and impersonal if they communicated exclusively by email. It is appropriate and even necessary to use telephonic communication to prevent negative social outcomes and to maintain the personal connection. Frazee 1996 in Burgess, Jackson and Edwards (2005) highlighted the risk for misunderstanding and tension within the workplace because of ambiguous and poorly written email. Wilson (2002) stated that high-interaction participants found it frustrating to use email for developing relationships.

Email overload and stress

Whitaker and Sidner 1996 in Dredze, Blitzer and Pereira (2005) described the concept of 'email overload' and concluded that users performed a large variety of work-related tasks with email, and as a result, they are overwhelmed with the amount of information in their mailbox. Sumecki, Chipulu and Ojiako (2011) define email overload as the situation where possible business disruption because of email use may significantly harm the well-being of users and impair their productivity. The increase in workload attributable to email is one of the factors cited by Johnson et al. 2005 in Jerejian, Reid and Rees (2013) as contributing to office workers reporting the highest levels of stress in history.

Sproull and Kiesler 1991 in Renaud et al. (2006) attributed overload to the increased possibility and ease of making demands and requests of others. Mackay 1988 in Renaud et al. (2006) argued that the lower cost of delegating tasks to others increases the use of email. Worse than delegation by email, 'buck-passing' by means of email is bad work behaviour where work is dumped on a colleague by a sender without having faced him or her. Because the email is asynchronous, the person on which the work and associated responsibility is unexpectedly placed, often has no way of backing out (Ramsay & Renaud 2012). Correlation research by Jerejian et al. (2013) indicated that the more email messages people handle, the more they perceive email as a source of stress. This study aims to determine if email is perceived to be an effective task delegation tool and if project practitioners experience stress and overload because of email.

Email management

Dabbish and Kraut (2006) found that a higher email volume was associated with increased feelings of email overload, but the relationship was moderated by certain email strategies. Their analysis further suggested that checking whenever new messages arrive, rather than checking at restricted intervals, is one method for reducing email overload. Jerejian et al. (2013) also found that email volume significantly predicts email stress. In contrast to the moderating effect of email strategies found by Dabbish and Kraut (2006), the relationship between email management strategies and email stress was found to be non-significant. Jerejian et al. (2013) concluded that the moderating effect of email management strategies in the relationship between email volume and email stress was not supported by their research. One of the hypotheses of this study investigates this relationship in more detail; it proposes that users will experience stress and overload because of email.

An opposing view is raised by Kushlev and Dunn (2015), who found that limiting the number of times people check their email during the day lessened tension during a particular important activity and lowered overall day-to-day stress. This is supported by a multitude of popular publications and blogs (e.g. Ashton 2015; Bradberry 2016; Pearce 2014), which advise that restricting email access to set timeslots contributes to effective time management.

Email response pressure

The almost immediate delivery of messages has created a response expectation or pressure in the minds of the communicators. A response time much closer to synchronous media is expected (Renaud et al. 2006), even though the growth in volume of email has made it almost impossible to respond to all messages immediately. According to Renaud et al. (2006), the recipient will feel pressure to respond speedily to the request or execute the task without delay, if the sender has authority over the recipient. The response time is also affected by prior experience of the sender and the recipient's opinion of the sender.

Email interruptions

Renaud et al. (2006) noted the strange anomaly that people *want* to be interrupted even though they know that interruptions will probably make them feel overloaded. They found that their survey respondents did not perceive the disruptive potential of email to be anything as high as traditional synchronous communication mediums (like telephone calls). They propose that the benign view of the disruptive influence of email can be because of the perceptions of control over email that respondents expressed.

Adler and Benbunan-Fich (2013) investigated self-interruptions (such as checking messages) in discretionary multitasking. Multitasking was defined as interleaving independent tasks in the same time period and switching among them. Interspersing among different tasks contributes to the illusion of productivity, but studies show that performance degrades when attention is divided, particularly during complex tasks (Bailey & Konstan [2006]; Speier, Vessey & Valacich 2003 in Adler & Benbunan-Fich [2013]).

It is clear that communication is playing an increasingly important role in projects and project success. The transformation of communication because of the arrival of new electronic communication media formats is noted, but the impact it has on organisations is unclear. The growing use of email as a preferred communication medium in the workplace and in project environments is noted by practitioners and academics; however, its impact on individual and project performance is not clearly understood. Scholars are still trying to pin down the characteristics of email within previously accepted communication media frameworks. In the process, previously held beliefs about communication in the workplace are being challenged.

This study explores communication preferences, describes how individuals manage their email and gauges the impact of email communication on individuals, their relationships, efficiency and effectiveness in the project environment. Six hypotheses are proposed:

H1: Email is replacing other types of media in the project management environment.

H2: Email is disruptive.

H3: Users experience stress and overload because of email.

H4: Email is an effective tool to delegate tasks.

H5: Email supports building relationships and trust.

H6: Email creates conflict.

The study goes some way in providing insight into the communication preferences of project practitioners. Furthermore, the findings regarding the use of email communication in projects will assist project managers and team members to better understand the role of communication in the project and the impact of email communication on individuals and their relationships in the project environment.

Conceptual model

There are various opinions on how project success can be defined and what measures should be used to qualify as a successful project (Cooke-Davies 2002; Cserháti & Szabó 2014; Fortune & White 2006; Ngai et al. 2008; Pinto & Slevin 1988). From the literature review, it is clear that there is a relationship between project communication and project success, irrespective of which definition of project success is used. Successful project communication should therefore contribute to a successful project and several aspects can contribute to successful project communication. This study investigates a number of both contributing and detracting project success factors, within the context of email project communication. It is proposed that an increase in the use of appropriate communication media, communication efficiency, effectiveness, accuracy and trust will improve project communication and thereby project success. Similarly, an increase in overload and stress, disruption and conflict will result in a decrease in project communication success.

Research method and design

Research strategy

In this study, a post-positivist perspective was taken as described by Tashakkori and Teddlie (2009). These academics see post-positivism as 'currently the predominant philosophy for quantitative research in the human sciences'. Post-positivism 'assumes that the world is mainly driven by generalisable (natural) laws, but that their application and results are often situation dependent'. Post-positivist researchers therefore identify trends, that is, theories which hold in certain situations, but cannot be generalised (Biedenbach & Müller 2011 in Joslin & Müller [2015]). Tashakkori and Teddlie (2009) suggest that either quantitatively oriented experimental or survey research be used to assess relationships among variables and to explain those relationships statistically.

This study uses a deductive approach and cross-sectional questionnaire to test the following six hypotheses: (1) email is replacing other types of media in the project management environment; (2) email is disruptive; (3) users experience stress and overload because of email; (4) email is an effective tool to delegate tasks; (5) email supports building relationships and trust; and (6) email creates conflict. Purposive and self-selection sampling was used to conduct the web-based survey. It was important that the right sample group receives the email and self-selected sampling was used so that respondents that are familiar with the research topic respond.

Research instruments

A questionnaire was developed based on questions relating to the hypotheses and the underpinning literature. Two types of questions were used: ranking questions where respondents were asked to rank different types of communication media in order of communication medium preference for different situations and questions where respondents had to indicate their level of agreement with statements. A four-point Likert scale was used for the latter with the following levels: 1 – strongly disagree; 2 – disagree; 3 – agree; and 4 – strongly agree.

Data collection

The questionnaire was distributed in two separate campaigns. In the first campaign, email invitations to participate in the survey were sent to project practitioners and all current students and alumni of masters' projects and engineering management programmes in the Graduate School of

Technology Management at the University of Pretoria. One hundred and thirty responses were obtained during this first campaign.

The second campaign made use of an external consultancy that specialises in assisting researchers to obtain survey responses. The company distributed the survey to individuals of their project management database. The survey was closed after 300 responses were received.

In total, 430 responses were received. A small number of responses were not complete, possibly because of connectivity issues while respondents were completing the survey. Incomplete surveys were accepted. The response rate could not be calculated as the population that received the invitation is not known.

Data analysis

Questions were grouped according to the different hypotheses. An average rank was calculated for the ranking questions and the frequency of responses for the specific group of questions compiled. The valid dataset was analysed using IBM SPSS Statistics 22.

Results

Hypotheses testing

H1: Email is replacing other types of communication media in the project environment

Face-to-face communication was selected as the respondents' first preference across a range of questions, with an average rank of 1.80. This was followed by email (2.28), telephone calls (2.47), text messages (4.01) and written notes (4.44), where 1 was strongly agree and 4 strongly disagree.

Respondents indicated a preference for frequent informal feedback rather than formal progress reports (63.5% vs. 36.5%). They placed slightly more trust in the information contained in formal reports than email (53.3% vs. 46.7% agreeing with the statement), but substantially less trust in telephone calls compared with email (only 18.7% agreeing).

Four Likert scale questions were posed in the survey to address this hypothesis. The highest response frequency was at 2.5 (33.4% of responses). The average response was 2.6, with a maximum of 4. The highest response frequency and average response indicate a response between agreeing and disagreeing with the hypothesis. It can, therefore, not be strongly concluded that email is replacing other types of communication media in the project environment.

H2: Email is disruptive

Four Likert scale questions were posed in the survey to address this hypothesis. The highest response frequency was at 3 out of a maximum of 4, where 1 was strongly agree and 4 strongly disagree. It can be concluded that email is disruptive.

H3: Users experience stress and overload because of email

Six Likert scale questions addressed this hypothesis in the survey. The highest response frequency was at 3 out of a maximum of 4. It can be concluded that users experience stress and overload because of email.

H4: Email is an effective tool to delegate tasks

Face-to-face communication is the first preference of respondents, across the range of questions asked, with an average rank of 1.96. This preference is closely followed by email with 2.00, telephone calls with 2.52, text messages with 4.05 and written notes with 4.46. Four Likert scale questions were asked in the survey to address this hypothesis. The highest response frequency was at 3 out of a maximum of 4. The average response was 3.0, where 1 was strongly agree and 4 strongly disagree. It can be concluded that email is an effective tool to delegate tasks.

H5: Email communication supports building relationships and trust

Six Likert scale questions were asked to test for conflict emanating from email. The highest response frequency was at 3. The average response was 2.9. It can be concluded that email communication supports building relationships and trust.

H6: Email creates conflict

Four questions testing the ability to build and develop relationships and trust via email were asked. The highest response frequency was at 3 (out of a maximum of 4). The average response was 2.9. It can be concluded that email creates conflict.

Ethical consideration

The study was conducted in accordance with relevant national and international guidelines. Approval for all protocols followed in this study was obtained from the Research Ethics Committee of the University of Pretoria under permit number EBIT/GSTM/138/2016.

Trustworthiness

The study and all its findings are based on the respondents' perceptions regarding the subject matter and questions asked in the survey. Reliability was aided by a relatively large number (430) of responses received. Validity and reliability concerns were addressed in the study by utilising the services of a statistician for questionnaire design and data analysis. Key concepts and terms were defined upfront in the questionnaire so that all participants had a similar understanding of the topics being investigated. Furthermore, only close-ended questions were asked to reduce ambiguity and emotive responses.

Discussion

Communication medium preferences

Respondents indicated that face-to-face communication is their preferred communication medium for initial communication regarding project surprises (issues). This was followed by telephone calls with messages in the third place. Respondents preferred that further follow-ups be done either through face-to-face communication or by email (equal response frequency). Based on media richness theory, it can be assumed that face-to-face communication is preferred because of the nature of the message requiring high equivocality. This would also explain why telephone calls were indicated as the second highest preference. The use of email as a joint first choice for elaborating on the initial communication can be ascribed to the fact that email leaves a 'paper trail' for future reference, but also grants the author of the email the opportunity to construct his thoughts and explain the situation on his terms, without interruption.

This study found that, despite the convenience and prevalence of email, respondents appear to have an inherent understanding of the need for communication media richness when dealing with communication requiring high equivocality. Face-to-face communication was the preferred communication medium when dealing with minor and major disagreements and conflict. Email was the first preference only for the low equivocality task of requesting information from others. These findings support the work conducted by Robert and Dennis (2005). The majority of respondents selected email above telephone calls for general and day-to-day project communication. A fear expressed by the authors that people will use email for tasks for which it is not suited is therefore mostly unfounded. However, a significant number of respondents indicated a preference for email when dealing with major disagreements (23 respondents), conflict (34 respondents) and surprises (80 respondents). The potential risk of ineffective communication under these circumstances cannot be ignored.

The study reported higher email volumes for senior managers. It is not clear whether this is a function of the higher communication volumes associated with management responsibilities or whether it is in conflict with the media richness theory. Email appears to be replacing telephonic communication because of the fairly narrow gap in preference between the two media for situations requiring richer media, although email does not yet exceed it.

Email disruption

Email is perceived as being a very disruptive communication method especially when visual and audible notifications inform you of every email as it is received. Of the respondents, 74% indicated that they have either a visual or audible notification that informs them of new messages arriving. The majority of respondents are, therefore, constantly aware of new messages arriving.

More than half of the respondents (55.3%) indicated that they tend to interrupt activities to read or respond to email. An almost similar percentage (54.4%) indicated that excessive email prevents them from structuring their day and executing tasks according to their own daily schedule. The number of respondents agreeing with the statement that excessive email queries prevent them from structuring their day and executing tasks according to their own daily schedule increased with an increase in email volume.

Email overload and stress

A large source of stress at work originates from information overload, and more specifically email overload (Bawden & Robinson 2009; Gantz et al. 2009; Sappelli et al. 2016). However, the findings of this study showed that 82.3% of respondents indicated they are able to cope with current volume of email that they receive and therefore do not deem themselves to be overloaded because of email. In general, the findings support the statement that higher email volume was associated with increased feelings of email overload.

More than half of the respondents agreed that email is a contributor to stress at work. This increased with the number of messages received, with recipients of more email indicating higher levels of stress associated with email. This finding supports the research conducted by Jerejian et al. (2013).

Email response pressure

In total, 88.2% of respondents indicated that they respond to messages as quickly as possible to prevent messages from piling up in their inbox. It was interesting to note that the majority of the respondents (61.9%) agreed that the seniority of the sender is a significant determinant in the response time. The recipient's opinion of the sender was found to have limited influence on the speed of response.

Email and delegation of tasks

Email was found to be an easy and effective tool to request information, make demands and delegate tasks. It was the second most preferred communication medium for delegating tasks after face to-face communication (average rank 1.99 vs. 1.77 for face-to-face communication). The delegation of tasks did not result in abdication of ownership of the problem, despite requesting others for assistance or information regarding the problem.

Email and relationships

The majority of respondents indicated that they can build new work relationships with project members via email (60.3%). Even a greater proportion of the respondents (85.8%) agreed that they can maintain existing work relationships with project team members via email. Both these findings contribute to the work conducted by Cheshin et al. (2013). It was not tested whether email is exclusively used for communication in these instances, but it would appear as if respondents are comfortable to use email as a tool to develop and maintain relationships.

Email and conflict

Email can be manipulated to manage the flow of information by selecting the email recipients carefully. In total, 68.5% of respondents indicated that they exclude certain individuals from the distribution list to prevent negative consequences stemming from the contents of the email. The selective distributions lists can result in conflict, with 80.9% of respondents indicating that email creates conflict when they are excluded from email distribution lists on subjects that involve them. In addition, 64.7% of respondents agreed that email creates conflict when the sender and recipient's superior is copied in on messages.

The respondents were evenly divided regarding the need to follow up on messages to resolve misunderstandings arising from the original message and, as such, the risk of an ambiguous and poorly written message resulting in conflict did not materially realise. However, the tone of messages was found to have a much greater propensity to cause conflict; 80.4% of respondents indicated that conflict is created because of the tone of the email that some recipients deem to be offensive. Despite the confirmation that email causes conflict, this did not impact the ability to build and maintain relationships via email. The finding that the tone of an email can create conflict supports the research conducted by Turner and Müller (2004) and Bond-Barnard et al. (2013), which state that conflict can only be reduced by having a balance of informal and formal communication. A balance of communication types would assist the parties to address any issues face-to-face that may stem from formal, written communication such as an email.

Email and trust

Respondents indicated a slightly higher level of trust for information contained in formal reports when compared with information provided in an email, this aligns with Turner and Müller (2004). A significantly higher level of trust is placed in the accuracy of information contained in messages when compared with telephone calls. This can possibly be ascribed to the fact that messages produce a communication trail that can be accessed in the case of a dispute, whereas telephone calls are rarely recorded.

In total, 65.4% of respondents indicated that project communication by email increases the level of trust between the respondent and project team members. Respondents overwhelmingly agreed that email facilitates collaboration between them and the project team. Despite this, 92.3% of respondents indicated that they archive the majority of their mail as evidence in case of future disputes.

Email efficiency and effectiveness

Responses supported the notion that email is an efficient communication medium, with more than 85% of respondents indicating that email allows them to efficiently perform their duties, irrespective of the number of messages they receive each day. This percentage was independent of the number of messages received daily for the respondents receiving less than 25 messages per day, between 25 and 49 and between 50 and 74 messages per day (88.8%, 85.3% and 87.1%).

The contribution of email to project success

The vast majority of respondents indicated that email contributes more to successful project execution and success than hampering it (91.6%).

Limitations of the study

The study did not consider the age or computer literacy of respondents. Both these factors could potentially impact the participant's perception and preferences regarding email.

The survey made use of convenience sampling. The industries in which the respondents are working in were not surveyed, and a potential relationship between industry and responses was not investigated. The localities of respondents are not certain, although it can be assumed that the majority of the respondents are based in South Africa, and the results can therefore not necessarily be extrapolated to other countries or regions.

The study focused on communication preferences but did not measure actual experience of which communication media were used for the different situations.

Conclusion

The last two decades have witnessed an unprecedented shift in project communication from face-to-face conversations to email, short message service (SMS), instant messaging and video conferencing. The aim of this study was to assess current communication preferences of project practitioners to determine if and how these preferences have changed in comparison with literature from 20 years ago. The following hypotheses were tested in the study in order to address the aim of the study: (1) email is replacing other types of media in the project management environment; (2) email is disruptive; (3) users experience stress and overload because of email; (4) email is an effective tool to delegate tasks; (5) email supports building relationships and trust and (6) email creates conflict. The study found that communication media higher in richness than email are still preferred for most situations, especially for communication requiring higher equivocality. This supports the media richness theory. The findings indicate that email has replaced telephonic communication only for general communication, which is low in equivocality. Respondents also place more trust in information contained in messages than telephone calls.

The study found that email is indeed disruptive, but the majority of respondents allow themselves to be disrupted by using email notifications and also electing to disrupt other activities to read and respond to messages.

Email is a cause of stress in the workplace, and higher levels of stress are correlated with an increase in the number of email messages received. However, the majority of respondents indicated that they can cope with the number of messages that they receive and as such do not report to be overloaded by email.

Email is an effective tool to delegate work and was not found to be associated with abdication of accountability.

Email communication assists in building and maintaining project team relationships, despite agreement that email and specific uses of email can lead to conflict. Even though there was consensus that email communication creates trust, most respondents agreed that they archive the majority of their mail as evidence in case of future conflict. All the hypotheses except hypothesis 1, which states that email is replacing other types of media in the project management environment, are supported by the findings of the study.

Despite the disruptive nature of email and stress resulting from email, the respondents agreed that email contributes to task efficiency and effectiveness. The study found that email contributes more to project success than hampering it.

It is suggested that future studies should investigate whether project practitioner preferences correlate with their actual communication experiences. The demographical data did not include age, and it would be worthwhile to investigate whether a participant's perception of email, especially with regard to relationships and trust, is correlated with age.

Acknowledgements

Competing interests

The authors declare that they have no financial or personal relationship(s) that may have inappropriately influenced them in writing this article.

Authors' contributions

M.C.S. conceptualised the study topic, carried out the research and wrote the first draft of the manuscript. T.J.B-B. reviewed and critiqued the paper several times. She was responsible for putting the paper in the correct journal format and acting as the corresponding author. H.S. is M.C.S.'s supervisor for his master's mini dissertation. He also reviewed and critiqued the paper several times. I.F-R. assisted with questionnaire design and was responsible for performing all statistical calculations.

References

Adler, R.F. & Benbunan-Fich, R., 2013, 'Self-interruptions in discretionary multitasking', *Computers in Human Behavior* 29(4), 1441–1449. https://doi.org/10.1016/j.chb.2013.01.040

Ashton, R., 2015, *Email overload: How to escape the tyranny of the inbox*, viewed 12 October 2016, from https://www.theguardian.com/small-business-network/2015/aug/18/email-overload-escape-tyranny-inbox

Bailey, B.P. & Konstan, J.A., 2006 , 'On the need for attention-aware systems: Measuring effects of interruption on task performance, error rate, and affective state', *Computers in Human Behavior* 22(4), 685–708. https://doi.org/10.1016/j.chb.2005.12.009

Bawden, J.D. & Robinson, L., 2009, 'The dark side of information: Overload, anxiety and other paradoxes and pathologies', *Journal of Information Science* 35(2), 180–191. https://doi.org/10.1177/0165551508095781

Bond-Barnard, T.J., Steyn, H. & Fabris-Rotelli, I., 2013, 'The impact of a call centre on communication in a programme and its projects', *International Journal of Project Management* 31(7), 1006–1016. https://doi.org/10.1016/j.ijproman.2012.12.012

Bond-Barnard, T.J., Fletcher, L. & Steyn, H., 2016, 'Exploring the influence of instant messaging and video conferencing on the quality of project communication', *Acta Structilia* 23(1), 36–69.

Bradberry, T., 2016, *14 critical things ridiculously successful people do every day*, viewed12 October 2016, from http://www.huffingtonpost.com/dr-travis-bradberry/14-things-ridiculously-su_b_9760972.html

Bryde, J.D. & Robinson, L., 2005, 'Client versus contractor perspectives on project success criteria', *International Journal of Project Management* 23, 622–629. https://doi.org/10.1016/j.ijproman.2005.05.003

Burgess, A., Jackson, T. & Edwards, J., 2005, 'Email training significantly reduces email defects', *International Journal of Information Management* 25(1), 71–83. https://doi.org/10.1016/j.ijinfomgt.2004.10.004

Cheshin, A., Kim, Y., Nathan, D.B., Ning, N. & Olson, J.S., 2013, 'Emergence of differing electronic communication norms within partially distributed teams', *Journal of Personnel Psychology* 12, 7–21. https://doi.org/10.1027/1866-5888/a000076

Chiocchio, F., 2007, 'Project team performance: A study of electronic task and coordination communication', *Project Management Journal* 38(1), 97–110.

Colquitt, J.A., Hollenbeck, J.R., Ilgen, D.R., LePine, J.A. & Sheppard, L., 2002, 'Computer-assisted communication and team decision-making performance: The moderating effect of openness to experience', *Journal of Applied Psychology* 87(2), 402–410.

Cooke-Davies, T., 2002, 'The "real" success factors on projects', *International Journal of Project Management* 20, 185–190. https://doi.org/10.1016/S0263-7863(01)00067-9

Crawford, L. & Nahmias, A.H., 2010, 'Competencies for managing change', *International Journal of Project Management* 25(4), 405–412. https://doi.org/10.1016/j.ijproman.2010.01.015

Cserháti, G. & Szabó, L., 2014, 'The relationship between success criteria and success factors in organisational event projects', *International Journal of Project Management* 32(4), 613–624. https://doi.org/10.1016/j.ijproman.2013.08.008

Dabbish, L.A. & Kraut, R.E., 2006, 'Email overload at work: An analysis of factors associated with email strain', In *Computer Supported Cooperative Work '06*, Banff, Alberta, Canada, pp. 431–440. https://doi.org/10.1145/1180875.1180941

Den Otter, A. & Emmitt, S., 2007, 'Exploring effectiveness of team communication: Balancing synchronous and asynchronous communication in design teams', *Engineering, Construction and Architectural Management* 14(5), 408–419. https://doi.org/10.1108/09699980710780728

Dredze, M., Blitzer, J. & Pereira, F., 2005, 'Reply expectation prediction for email management', in *2nd Conference on Email and Anti-Spam*, pp. 2–3, Citeseer, Stanford, CA.

Elovitz, K.M., 1999, *Cultivating communication: A must*, Consulting-Specifying Engineer, Denver, CO.

Fortune, J. & White, D., 2006, 'Framing of project critical success factors by a systems model', *International Journal of Project Management* 24(1), 53–65. https://doi.org/10.1016/j.ijproman.2005.07.004

Frodell, M., Josephson, P.E. & Lindahl, G., 2008, 'Swedish construction clients' views on project success and measuring performance', *Journal of Engineering, Design and Technology* 6, 21–32. https://doi.org/10.1108/17260530810863316

Gantz, J., Boyd, A. & Dowling, S., 2009, *Cutting the clutter: Tackling information overload at the source*, International Data Corporation White Paper.

Henderson, L.S., Stackman, R.W. & Lindekilde, R., 2016, 'The centrality of communication norm alignment, role clarity, and trust in global project teams', *International Journal of Project Management* 34(8), 1717–1730. https://doi.org/10.1016/j.ijproman.2016.09.012

Jerejian, A.C.M., Reid, C. & Rees, C.S., 2013, 'The contribution of email volume, email management strategies and propensity to worry in predicting email stress among academics', *Computers in Human Behavior* 29(3), 991–996. https://doi.org/10.1016/j.chb.2012.12.037

Joslin, R. & Müller, R., 2015, 'Relationships between a project management methodology and project success in different project governance contexts', *International Journal of Project Management* 33(6), 1377–1392. https://doi.org/10.1016/j.ijproman.2015.03.005

Kahai, S.S., Sosik, J.J. & Avolio, B.J., 2004, 'Effects of participative and directive leadership in electronic groups', *Group & Organization Management* 29(1), 67–105.

Koops, L., Bosch-Rekveldt, M., Coman, L., Hertogh, M. & Bakker, H., 2016, 'Identifying perspectives of public project managers on project success : Comparing viewpoints of managers from five countries in North-West Europe', *JPMA* 34(5), 874–889. https://doi.org/10.1016/j.ijproman.2016.03.007

Ksenija, Č. & Skendrovic, V., 2010, 'Communication management is critical for project success', *Informatol* 43(3), 228–235.

Kushlev, K. & Dunn, E.W., 2015, 'Checking email less frequently reduces stress', *Computers in Human Behavior* 43, 220–228. https://doi.org/10.1016/j.chb.2014.11.005

Lehmann, V., 2009, *Communication and project management: Seeds for a new conceptual approach*, Administrative Sciences Association of Canada, Niagara Falls, Ontario.

Lim, C.S. & Mohamed, M.Z., 1999, 'Criteria of project success: An exploratory re-examination', *International Journal of Project Management* 17(4), 243–248. https://doi.org/10.1016/S0263-7863(98)00040-4

Markus, M.L., 1994, 'Electronic mail as the medium of managerial choice', *Organization Science* 5(4), 502–527. https://doi.org/10.1287/orsc.5.4.502

McLeod, L., Doolin, B. & MacDonell, S.G., 2012, 'A perspective-based understanding of project success', *Project Management Journal* 43, 68–86. https://doi.org/10.1002/pmj.21290

Michinov, N., Michinov, E. & Toczek-Capelle, M.-C., 2004, 'Social identity, group processes, and performance in synchronous computer-mediated communication', *Group Dynamics* 8(1), 27–39.

Mintzberg, H., 1973, *The nature of managerial work*, New Harper & Row, New York.

Müller, R., 2003, *Communication of information technology project sponsors and managers in buyer-seller relationships*, Brunel University, Henley-on-Thames, UK.

Müller, R. & Turner, J.R., 2001, 'The impact of performance in project management knowledge areas on earned value results in information technology projects', *International Journal of Project Management* 7(1), 44–50.

Ngai, E.W., Law, C.C. & Wat, F.K., 2008, 'Examining the critical success factors in the adoption of enterprise resource planning', *Computers in Industry* 59(6), 548–564. https://doi.org/10.1016/j.compind.2007.12.001

Padalkar, M. & Gopinath, S., 2016, 'Six decades of project management research: Thematic trends and future opportunities', *International Journal of Project Management* 34(7), 1305–1321. https://doi.org/10.1016/j.ijproman.2016.06.006

Pearce, R., 2014, *8 ways to reduce email overload,* viewed 25 October 2016, from http://www.pressreader.com/new-zealand/nz-business/20140501/281599533487907

Pinto, J. & Slevin, D., 1988, 'Critical success factors across the project life cycle', *Project Management Journal* 19(3), 67–75.

Pinto, J.K. & Slevin, D.P., 1987, 'Critical success factors in effective project implementation', *IEEE Transactions on Engineering Management* EM34, 22–28.

PwC South Africa, 2017, *Chapter 5: The governance of information technology*, viewed 05 February 2017, from http://www.pwc.co.za/en/king3/the-governance-of-information-technology.html

Ramsay, J. & Renaud, K., 2012, 'Using insights from email users to inform organisational email management policy', *Behaviour & Information Technology* 31(6), 587–603. https://doi.org/10.1080/0144929X.2010.517271

Renaud, K., Ramsay, J. & Hair, M., 2006, 'You've got email. Shall I deal with it now? Electronic mail from the recipient's perspective', *International Journal of Human-Computer Interaction* 21(3), 313–332. https://doi.org/10.1207/s15327590ijhc2103_3

Robert, L.P. & Dennis, A.R., 2005, 'Paradox of richness : A cognitive model of media choice', *IEEE Transactions on Professional Communication* 48(1), 10–21. https://doi.org/10.1109/TPC.2004.843292

Sappelli, M., Pasi, G., Verberne, S., De Boer, M. & Kraaij, W., 2016, 'Assessing e-mail intent and tasks in e-mail messages', *Information Sciences* 358–359, 1–17. https://doi.org/10.1016/j.ins.2016.03.002

Sumecki, D., Chipulu, M. & Ojiako, U., 2011, 'Email overload: Exploring the moderating role of the perception of email as a "business critical" tool', *International Journal of Information Management* 31(5), 407–414. https://doi.org/10.1016/j.ijinfomgt.2010.12.008

Tashakkori, A. & Teddlie, C., 2009, *Foundations of mixed methods research. Integrating quantitative and qualitative*, SAGE Publications Inc., Thousand Oaks, CA.

Turner, J.R., 2007, *Gower handbook of project management,* 4th edn., Gower, Aldershot.

Turner, J.R. & Müller, R., 2004, 'Communication and co-operation on projects between the project owner as principal and the project manager as agent', *European Management Journal* 22(3), 327–336. https://doi.org/10.1016/j.emj.2004.04.010

Wilson, E.V., 2002, 'Email winners and losers', *Communications of the ACM* 45(10), 121–126. https://doi.org/10.1145/570907.570908

The role of medical records in the provision of public healthcare services in the Limpopo province of South Africa

Authors:
Ngoako S. Marutha[1]
Mpho Ngoepe[1]

Affiliations:
[1]Department of Information Science, College of Human Sciences, University of South Africa, South Africa

Corresponding author:
Mpho Ngoepe,
ngoepms@unisa.ac.za

Background: The importance of medical records to the provision of healthcare services cannot be overemphasised. Medical practitioners need information about previous diagnoses, treatments and prescriptions in order to note the progress made with previous treatments and how to move forward. If medical records are not managed properly, it becomes difficult to retrieve such records, which results in hospitals not being able to render healthcare services or these services being rendered incorrectly, especially for chronic patients. Despite the importance of medical records, they are not being managed properly, resulting in a lack of effective systems for opening, tracking and indexing files.

Objective: This study seeks to investigate the role of medical records in the provision of public healthcare services in the Limpopo province of South Africa.

Method: Quantitative data were collected through questionnaires distributed to staff members in the records management unit and the information management unit in 40 hospitals in Limpopo. These units were relevant as they made use of patient files daily to discharge their duties.

Results: The study revealed that missing medical records negatively affected timely and effective healthcare service delivery. This resulted in patients having to wait longer to be treated and in some instances patients being treated without medical history.

Conclusion: The study concludes by arguing that missing files contribute to the length of time patients wait to be assisted. As a result, nurses and doctors are unable to assist patients or treat them immediately. The study recommends the introduction of an electronic records management system that can capture and provide access to a full patient record, as well as tracking paper records movement, irrespective of the location.

Introduction

Many professions such as accounting, auditing, health, finance, human resources and law rely on the strength of records management to perform their duties. Records are created and managed with the intention of supporting the accurate and efficient delivery of services in many areas. For example, Katuu (2016) highlights several studies within the public sector in South Africa that demonstrate the role of records management in various areas such as: the auditing process (Ngoepe 2012; Ngoepe & Ngulube 2016), provision of justice systems (Ngoepe & Makhubela 2015), service delivery and human rights (Ngoepe 2008) and healthcare services (Katuu 2015; Marutha 2011). Records are especially important in hospitals as they are needed for confirming background information (Marutha 2011:2).

Despite the importance of medical records, these are often not managed correctly, which results in medical practitioners being unable to access information about previous diagnoses, treatments and prescriptions. If medical records are not managed properly, they can be lost forever. Missing or incomplete files can have a negative impact on the lives of patients. Newspapers reported that Polokwane Hospital in Limpopo was unable 'to provide medical records for one of the chronic patients suffering from cervical cancer' (Maponya 2013:6). According to Marutha (2017:1):

> the file was to be used for further treatment by the patient's private doctor to conduct radiotherapy for the patient, but before that he needed medical records to get information about the patient's medical history.

However, medical records and X-rays of the patient could not be found. This resulted in the doctor being unable to proceed for fear of giving the patient wrong treatment. The life of the patient was at stake as a result of unavailability of records.

In another case, Marutha (2011:3) reports that at Nkhensani Hospital in Giyani town, Limpopo, doctors 'could not operate on a patient because of a missing file'. In this case, the patient was involved in a motor vehicle accident in 2005 which left her leg partially paralysed. The doctor needed the file that contained information about her accident and health problems to trace the history or the seriousness of the injuries before risking an operation. Unfortunately, the only available record was about the patient's diabetes. As a result, the Limpopo Department of Health and Social Development intervened and clarified that the hospital had a problem with the files. The reason given was that the hospital relocated in 2007 and the files were not lost, but were 'somewhere in the hospital'.

The ineffective management of records is not only a South African problem. In the United States, the Department of Health and Human Services (2006) reports that the ratio of missing files in healthcare institutions is one out of seven. This is attributed to poor records management. Therefore, it is important that medical records should be managed properly so that citizens can receive proper and accurate health care. The consequences of improper records management are that citizens can lose their lives or become permanently paralysed because of a wrong diagnosis based on a lack of medical history. This can result in the government being litigated and paying millions because of missing files. This study sought to investigate the role of medical records in the provision of healthcare in Limpopo.

Contextual setting

The Department of Health in the Limpopo province was established with the purpose to render healthcare services within the province. Limpopo is located in the far north of South Africa and it is divided into five districts, namely: Capricorn, Mopani, Sekhukhune, Vhembe and Waterberg. Each of these districts is further divided into five sub-districts or local municipalities. The Department, through its various hospital facilities, creates medical records when rendering healthcare service delivery (Marutha 2011:2). These records are used for various purposes, for example, 'for nursing and clinical audits in the peer review meetings which are conducted regularly in hospitals' (Marutha 2011:2). These records are used to:

> screen the business transactions conducted by doctors and nurses. They confirm the procedures followed when doctors and nurses conducted certain critical patients' treatment activities such as child delivery and operations, as well as investigating maternal death. The hospitals also regularly use medical records in response to legal actions/litigations or complaints from the patients or citizens about hospital services rendered. (Marutha 2011:3)

In addition, 'the patients' records are also used daily to further record information about the patients' personal details, prescriptions and diagnosis for future reference and for follow-up patients. The information recorded is eventually used to confirm the patients' health history during current and future consultations' (Marutha 2011:3). Marutha (2011:3) emphasises that 'the pace at which the records are retrieved and served for this purpose determine the patient waiting time for the services. This has an impact on the quality of the service rendered by the health institution'. By 2004, the average waiting period for a patient in Limpopo hospitals had been 5 hours and 5 minutes (Limpopo Department of Health and Social Development 2006:85). Even though the Limpopo Department of Health had planned to reduce the time to less than 3 hours, Marutha (2017:136) reports that it remained unchanged in 2017.

According to Marutha (2011:4):

> records in hospitals are used to collect and validate statistical information daily. The statistics collected are used to regularly review the hospital's monthly performance in all activities. It is through proper records management that the data collected can be complete and accurate.

Barry (2001) suggests that in order for records management to contribute meaningfully to health care provision, health care institutions need to implement a digital records system. According to Barry (2001), 'digital records system is a legitimate option which is cheaper in terms of money, time and energy to ensure speedy retrieval of records'.

The Department of Health in Limpopo uses a hybrid system for creating and managing records. However, even though the Department maintains medical records in digital and analogue format, the digital format is not complete as it excludes prescriptions, diagnoses and treatments. The digital format only covers personal details of the patient, dates of consultation and financial status regarding payments of consultation (Marutha 2011:4).

Research problem

In South Africa, it is often reported in the media that healthcare practitioners are unable to provide timeous and efficient healthcare services partly because of poor records management (Katuu 2015). This results in patients waiting long before they could be helped as the records cannot be retrieved or medical files are lost. In such instances, health workers are unable to assist patients. According to Marutha (2011:5):

> this is due to the fact that, if the health worker proceeds treating patients without enough information about patients' healthcare background, they may end up rendering poor health services that may be risky to the patients' health.

This can have serious repercussions for the health providers and hospital's service delivery reputation. It would seem that records are not managed properly because of a lack of skills from the staff, infrastructure, budget constraints and a lack of support from oversight mechanisms such as public archives repositories (Nengomasha 2013:66; Ngoepe 2016). Therefore, there is a need for proper records management practices to ensure efficient retrieval of records that supports the provision of medical healthcare service in hospitals (Robek, Brown & Stephens 1995). Otherwise, public hospitals will continue to be inefficient in providing services to patients and thus damaging their reputation.

Research purpose and objectives of the study

The purpose of this study was to investigate the role of records management in the provision of healthcare service delivery in Limpopo. The specific objectives were to:

- examine how records are managed to support healthcare services
- identify the root causes of missing medical records that hinder the provision of healthcare services in the Limpopo province
- make recommendations on the management of medical records.

Literature review

Besides their administrative value, records are managed in hospitals to support healthcare providers with patients' medical history. According to Marutha (2011:4), 'medical records assist the organisation with information about the treatment history and individual care experience that is regularly updated as the patient consults further. They are used for decision-making in the future course of treatment'. Therefore, these records need to be protected against destruction to ensure that they can be retrieved when needed. Several types of records created in hospitals include 'bed statistics, daily returns, day and night handover, nursing records and medical records' (Booyens 2001:153; Davidson 2000:199–200; Rampfumedzi 2006:18–19), 'patient information leaflets, handover books and records, maternity records and out of hours records' (Cowan & Haslam 2006:266–267). According to Marutha (2011:5):

> the bed statistics are created and preserved to provide information about bed occupancy in different wards, patients' conditions and discharges so that administrative staff knows which beds are available for new admissions while the daily returns are created and preserved to keep a written report about patients' admissions, discharges, deaths and transfers.

This assists with shift changes amongst 'day/evening shifting staff, administrative staff and management regarding the condition of patients in different wards' (Booyens 2001:153; Davidson 2000:199–200; Rampfumedzi 2006:18–19). In addition:

> day and night handover records are created during the formal shifting handover reporting to the nurse to check in for work. This is for them to know and understand the condition of each patient they will be nursing and the information about what happened before they took over. The nursing records are 'written nursing communication', and that makes all nurses aware of each patient's background.

According to Rampfumedzi (2006:19), 'this type of records also assists in planning for patients' needs'. It is important that records are created as Booyens (2001:153) argues that the 'creation of records also document the doctor's delegations, admissions, treatment of patients, investigations to be conducted by the doctor and the care necessary at home, if there is any need'. Therefore, it is important that records are created and managed properly in the healthcare institutions in order to support provision of health care.

Cowan and Haslam (2006:266) identify other types of records as 'the parent-held records which contain baby developmental information, immunisation details and milestones achieved, the refrigeration and freezer records/charts contain laboratory and equipment records'. To Davidson (2000:197–200):

> medical records are categorised into genre, such as nurses' notes, patient demographic data, physicians orders, progress reports, laboratory test results, pathology reports, radiology reports and images. The records are created based on observation, interpretation of data, treatment plans and patients outcomes. These records provide evidence of patient consultation, outcomes and health service rendered at the hospital.

It is important that these records are managed properly in future when diagnosing patients to prevent incorrect diagnoses resulting in death and litigations.

Research methodology

This study utilised quantitative data collected through questionnaires directed to staff members in the information management and records management unit at the hospitals in Limpopo. This study consisted of 40 hospitals in the province and the respondents were drawn from the records management and the information management units, which had a staff complement of 324 employees. These units were relevant for the study as they use medical records of patients daily to discharge their duties. The hospitals were first stratified and a proportion sampling of respondents was drawn from each hospital. As a result of using Rasoft sample calculator, out of 324 of the total population of the study, 65% (210) were sampled as guided by the scientific calculator for sampling. The study utilised the confidential level of 90% and 5% margin of error. From the sample of 210, the records management staff constituted 74% (155) while the information management proportion was 26% (55). Out of 210 questionnaires distributed, only 162 were returned, representing a response rate of 77%. The study utilised MS Excel® spreadsheet database to analyse the quantitative data. The tally-sheet was used to capture data from respondents as they responded and the spread sheet was used to capture the sum of data from the tally-sheet for each question and answer, calculate percentages, and sketch graphs based on the data captured.

Research findings

This section presents the results based on the objective of the paper.

Management and administration of medical records to support healthcare services

When asked to rate the state of records management, 15% (24) of respondents indicated that the state of records management in their institutions was very poor, 58% (94) stated that it was poor while 1% (2) were unsure about the state of records. Additionally, 22% (36) indicated that it was in a good state, while 4% (6) were of the view that the state of records in their institutions was very good. Figure 1 illustrates the results. Those who have indicated unsure, poor and very poor justified that at times records are requested in bulk, which makes the retrieval process lengthy. It was stated that there was too much paperwork, no proper filing/archiving system, poor planning, poor organisation and supervision, files are inexplicably lost as well as a lack of filing space. Furthermore, records management is a new concept in the hospitals; as a result, there is a lack of experienced officials and it is seen as an unimportant division, which leads to minimal budget allocation. The possible causes of the poor state of records management in hospitals which contributed to missing records were identified by respondents as:

- lack of good organisation and disciplinary measures for involved staff
- no proper filing system in place
- no designated staff
- lack of capacity, skills and training
- lack of administrative leadership and individual, official dedication
- usage of manual records management
- lack of filing space, which leads to a mixture of files in their different status like death and motor vehicle accidents
- staff are unfamiliar with records management, especially those who are also new to the field
- poor infrastructure
- little centralised budget
- poor planning

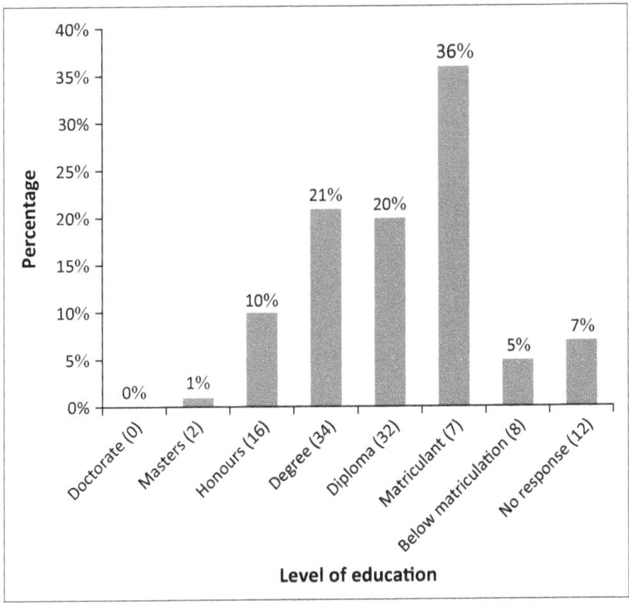

FIGURE 1: Respondents' educational levels (N = 162).

- lack of end users consultation when planning system and administration
- shortage of staff.

The root causes of missing files that hamper the provision of healthcare services

Proper implementation of records management policies, procedures and control measures

As indicated by 99% (161) of the respondents, some files were returned to the registry after more than a month. Files can be lost in the hands of users rather than those who are untrained in managing records. Proper records management ensures efficient retrieval of records to support healthcare service. Records that are managed properly can easily be tracked and thus minimise missing files. It was established that the hospitals did not have a standard, reasonable time frame for the returning of patient records when users borrow files. This was compounded by the fact that the records management policy and procedures were silent on the issue of returning files.

Medical records management resources

The study reported that 46% (75) of the respondents stated that the availability of resources for records administration was less than 25%, 35% (56) stated it was between 26% and 50%, 9% (14) stated it was between 51% and 75%, 7% (11) stated it was between 76% and 100% and 4% (6) of the respondents did not answer.

Records management education, training and knowledge

When asked about training received, 94% (153) of respondents indicated that they never received any training in policies, procedures, norms and standards for managing records, while only 6% (8) stated that they received such training. Respondents believed that the problems in records management emanated from lack of awareness and training; lack of system monitoring and auditing; unqualified records management staff; lack of space for filing and optimal filing system; no consultation with end users or records management staff by IT when planning system and administration.

In most instances, officials who are not trained in records management become demoralised and uninterested in the work and merely do it for the sake of receiving a salary. The educational level of respondents entails that none of the respondents had a doctorate, 1% (2) had a Master's degree, 10% (16) had an honours degree, 21% (34) had a degree, 20% (32) had a diploma, 36% (58) matriculated and 5% (8) had a qualification lower than matric while 7% (12) of the respondents did not respond. Figure 1 illustrates the results. The respondents stated percentages of officials trained in records management. Out of all respondents, 6% (10) stated that none of the officials were trained, 59% (96) stated that less than 25% were trained, 14% (23) stated that 50% were trained, 5% (8) stated that 75% of staff were trained, only 2% (3) stated that 100% records management staff were trained and 14% (22) did not answer. Respondents were also requested to state the kind of training that was offered in their institutions. Out of all respondents, 81% (132) stated that the training was offered in-house by internal staff, 36% (58) stated in-house by a private trainer, 51% (82) stated that the training was conducted by an external institution and 8% (13) did not respond. Furthermore, 58% (94) stated that in-house training was conducted by the manager, 53% (86) stated that it was by the supervisor, 44% (72) stated that it was by the provincial office and 19% (31) did not answer.

From the findings, it appears that only a few officials working for records management in the public hospitals completed qualifications in records management. That is one of the contributing factors to not being able to manage records properly. Considering the educational field of study, 6% (9) respondents studied records management, 39% (63) studied information management, 4% (7) knowledge management, 1% (2) studied history, 82% (134) studied public administration, 8% (13) studied nursing and 25% (41) studied other courses not listed, such as human resources, information and communication technologies (ICT) and financial management. Furthermore, 4% (6) respondents did not give an answer. Figure 2 indicates respondents' post-matriculation educational field of study. The study revealed that the majority 82% (134) of respondents had public administration qualifications, 39% (63) had information management qualifications and 25% (41) had other courses not listed, such as human resources.

When asked about experience, 82% (133) of the respondents had more than 5 years' experience in their current position while 86% (139) had more than 5 years of records management experience as illustrated by Figures 3 and 4, respectively.

The survey also discovered that 100% (162) of the respondents were confident about their knowledge of the meaning of records. Eighty-nine per cent (144) stated that records are recorded information and/or information created during communication or business transaction. The examples of records mentioned were 79% (128) memos and registers and 100% (162) said patient files.

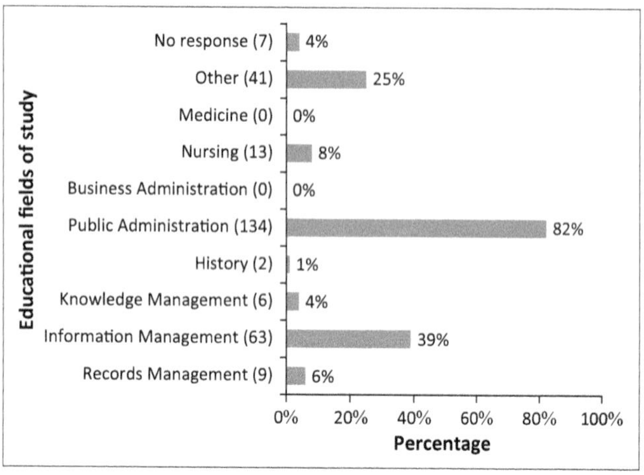

FIGURE 2: Respondents' post-matriculation educational fields of study (N = 162).

The survey indicated that 70% (114) of the respondents had never attended formal records management training and 88% (142) claimed that no formal records management training was offered to records management staff in their institutions. If the training was offered as stated by 63% (103), the competency level of the training was basic. When asked about training of officials on records management, only 6% (10) of the respondents stated that they were not trained in records management, while 94% (152) had received the training. Respondents indicated that training on records management was offered in-house by internal staff, by a private trainer such as consultants from Metrofile and the Document Warehouse (records management consultant companies) and institutions of higher learning, especially the University of South Africa. According to the respondents, the training offered covered records management areas such as classification systems, records creation, retention, appraisal and disposal as well as archival legislation. The respondents felt that the training was theoretical in nature with little practical training. As such, it was difficult to implement what they have learnt from the training. They felt that future training should cover digital records as it is a modern system of management.

Discussions of the findings

Ojo (2009:95) contends that 'development in Africa is still blocked by lack of ICT, illiteracy, politics, poor infrastructure

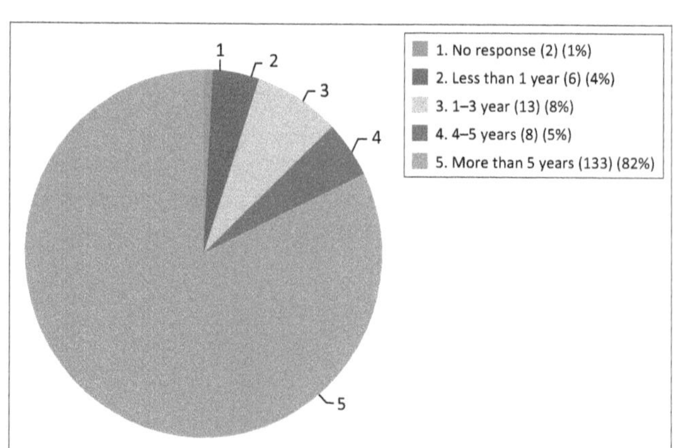

FIGURE 3: Respondents' length of service in the current position (N = 162).

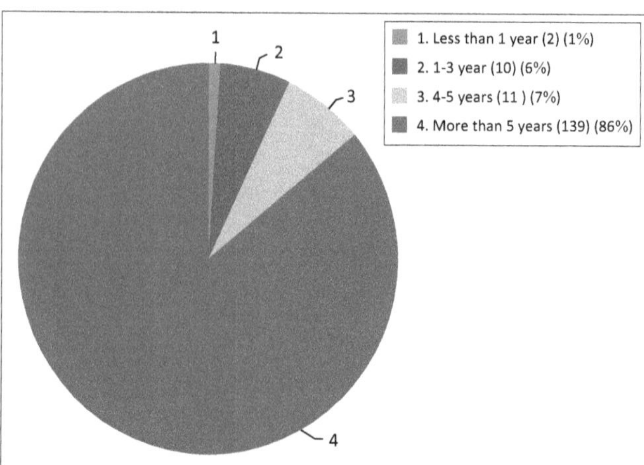

FIGURE 4: Respondents' length of experience in the current field of work specialisation (N=162).

and human resources'. This is the case in almost all countries in sub-Saharan Africa as they experience lack of support for resources, expertise and electronic media management facilities, which lead to poor management of digital records (Ngulube & Tafor 2006:69). This further had bad consequences for all citizens' information needs. For instance, missing files in the healthcare institutions may be emanated from several factors, including but not limited to: lack of or poor quality in the available policies; procedures and control measures that cover inappropriate scope and principles; lack of management support and inadequate resources and staff. Another major contributing factor to the missing files is the lack of appropriate education, training and knowledge for management of records, particularly medical records. The missing files have a negative impact on the provision of healthcare services. Marutha (2011:181) identifies issues contributing to missing files in the hospitals as 'vacancy rate, staff turnover, resources availability, management support, records management programmes functionality, staff competency and skills'. The missing files also contribute towards exceeding file retrieval turnaround time norm and/or target. Records that are not properly managed lead to time-consuming factors such as misfiling, untidy filing and challenges arising from a high records demand. If records are not managed properly in hospitals, this could result in a loss of human lives, as medical practitioners would not have any record to refer to. The problem of missing files was compounded by the fact that the hospitals were using manual systems as file tracking.

Many factors may contribute towards missing files in the healthcare institutions. Katuu and Ngoepe (2015:192) identify the education and training programme as a key challenge of addressing records management capacity deficit in South Africa. This is not only unique to South Africa as there are few archives and records management educational programmes throughout the African continent. As a result, very few practising archivists and records managers in Africa have the relevant qualification as evident by the Department of Health in Limpopo. Many public organisations in South Africa experienced challenges in managing records because of limited skills, infrastructure and lack of policies and controls (Nengomasha 2013:2). These challenges were also identified in this study. In most instances, 'poor record-keeping results in missing and lost files and documents, which leads to delayed service to citizens and poor image of the public service' (Marutha 2011:180). This poor state of records management also contributed to missing files in hospitals. Similarly, Limpopo healthcare service delivery hospitals experienced inadequate training, unrelated skills and competencies and inadequate record-keeping system. Looking at the education, training, skills and knowledge in the hospitals, most of the officials had more than 5 years of experience in their current position and more than 5 years of records management experience. The officials were confident about their knowledge of the meaning of records, which they indicated is recorded information and/or information created during communication or business transactions. The examples of records mentioned were memos, registers and patient files. The majority of officials in the hospitals did not attend formal records management training, as such training was not offered to the staff. The in-house training was conducted by the internal staff, although irregularly. The only training that was attended by less than 25% officials was at the basic competency level.

According to Chinyemba and Ngulube (2005), qualified records management staff in an organisation ensures that records management work is carried out efficiently. Employees need to be capacitated with the knowledge and skills to develop and maintain the records management programme. The knowledge required should cover all the processes of records management. According to Katuu (2015), this should be supplemented by contextual knowledge including 'administrative history, professional elements of law, social, cultural, legal and financial systems, information system and management of digital records'. Lack of training on records management may culminate into files missing as the officials might not have the skills to manage the records properly. In an organisation where the staff competency and skills are not developed, the survival of the organisation is not assured. Qualified and well-trained staff will lead the organisation to an advanced stage of operation, growth and quality of work (King 1997:658).

The hospitals were also disturbed by too much paperwork; no proper filing/archiving system; poor planning, organisation and supervision; many files lost with no known reason; lack of filing space; lack of experienced officials; records management division undermined; and little centralised budget. The poor state of records management in hospitals that resulted in records going missing and being misfiled also entails lack of good organisation and disciplinary measures for involved staff; no proper filing system in place; no properly designated staff; lack of capacity, skills and training; lack of administrative leadership and individual official dedication; use of manual records management; lack of filing space; a lot of staff not familiar with records management; poor infrastructure; poor planning; lack of end-user consultation when planning the system and administration; and shortage of staff (Marutha 2011:204).

The manual record-keeping, especially for a large volume of patient records, also led to most records going missing. The missing files were caused by, amongst others, misfiling, untidy filing, staff shortage and high records demand. Other reasons were incompetent/unskilled staff, damage to record and lack of general staff awareness about the importance of records and insufficient budget. It was also affected by lack of support for resources to support records management programmes. Poor records tracking system also led to records missing. The hospitals were using the manual file tracking system. They did not have a standard reasonable time frame for returning of patient records when clients borrowed files (Marutha 2011:204).

This was also discovered by Ngoepe and Van der Walt (2010:96) in their study about a framework for a records management programme in the Department of Cooperative Governance and Traditional Affairs in South Africa. 'This is the reason some files were returned after more than a month. The hospitals did not have policies, procedures, norms and standard documents that specifically govern patient records management' (Marutha 2011:205).

Conclusion and recommendations

It is clear from the discussion that missing files contributed to patients waiting long to be assisted. As a result, nurses and doctors are unable to assist patients or treat the patients immediately. In order to provide corrective measures to misfiling, it is necessary that experienced people are employed. These staff members should be trained regularly through short learning programmes offered at institutions of higher learning to keep their skills up to date. As Thurston (2005) would concur:

> Effective records management is important to avoid files piling up in different offices and corridors. Effective records management should be supported by avoiding sending difficult or poor performing personnel to the records management unit, by ensuring continuous training, creating policies, procedures and standards, and also ensuring that all officials consider records significant, as well as ensuring that proper disposal measures are put in place.

Furthermore, 'there should also be a political will and management support in hospitals to support the implementation of effective records management' (Marutha 2011:212).

The hospitals should adopt and implement an effective records system to avoid or minimise too much paper work. They should also fill their vacant posts as necessary and come up with a staff retention strategy to prevent high staff turnover. Hospitals should develop and implement a standard reasonable time frame for returning patients records when clients borrow files to measure their performance in terms of healthcare support and to prevent files from going missing (Marutha 2011:212).

They should also develop policies, procedures, norms and standard documents that specifically govern patient records management. Security measures in hospitals should also be maximally strengthened to avoid file theft, unauthorised destruction and alteration. As much as they had the basic security measures, they should consider moving to a higher level of security technology such as card or fingerprint access control, as well as surveillance cameras at strategic points of records custodies and registries. They should also bring about temperature and humidity control measures such as air conditioners in records custody places; air conditioners should be set at 18–20°C as guided by the National Archives and Records Service of South Africa (NARSSA) (Marutha 2011:212).

The Department should consider implementing an electronic records management system that is capable of capturing and providing access to a full patient record, as well as tracking paper records movement irrespective of the location. As records practitioners require skills in electronic records management, the Department should invest in capacity building, including training and provision of sustainable infrastructure required to manage digital records. As Ngoepe (2017:41) would attest, the skills acquired will enable records practitioners to fully participate in the planning of digital records systems and thus be able to support effective healthcare services.

Acknowledgements

Competing interests

The authors declare that they have no financial or personal relationship(s) which may have inappropriately influenced them in writing this article.

Authors' contributions

N.S.M. conceptualised the paper, collected data and wrote the article and contributed 60% to the article. M.N. assisted in conceptualisation, supervised the study and edited the article, contributing 40% to the article.

References

Barry, R.E., 2001, 'Electronic document and records management systems, towards a methodology for requirements definition', viewed 3 April 2016, from http://www.caldeson.com/RIMOS/barry1.html#six

Booyens, S.W., 2001, *Introduction to health services management*, 2nd edn., Kenwyn, Juta.

Chinyemba, A. & Ngulube, P., 2005, 'Managing records at higher education institution: A case study of the University of KwaZulu-Natal, Pietermaritzburg Campus', *South African Journal of Information Management* 7(1), viewed 24 July 2016, from http://www.sajim.co.za/index.php/SAJIM/article/download/250/241

Cowan, J. & Haslam, J., 2006, 'Clinical risk management managing NHS records: Complying with the new code of practice: Clinical governance', *An International Journal* 11(3), 262–269.

Davidson, E.J., 2000, 'Analyzing genre of organizational communication in clinical information system', *Information Technology and People* 13(3), 196–209. https://doi.org/10.1108/09593840010377635

Katuu, S., 2015, 'Managing records in South African public health care institutions: A critical analysis', PhD Thesis, University of South Africa.

Katuu, S., 2016, 'Transforming South Africa's health sector-the eHealth strategy and the implementation of electronic document and records management (EDRMS) and the utility of maturity models', *Journal of Science and Technology Policy Management* 7(3), 330–345. https://doi.org/10.1108/JSTPM-02-2016-0001

Katuu, S. & Ngoepe, M., 2015, 'Managing digital heritage: An analysis of the education and training curriculum for Africa's archives and records professionals', *Digital Heritage* 2, 191–194. https://doi.org/10.1109/DigitalHeritage.2015.7419488

King, L.A., 1997, 'Are you managing your vinyl effectively?', *Management Decision* 35(9), 656–659. https://doi.org/10.1108/00251749710186487

Limpopo Department of Health and Social Development, 2006, *Annual Report 2006/07 Health (Vote 7)*, viewed 20 November 2016, from http://www.dhsd.limpopo.gov.za/

Maponya, F., 2013, 'No medical records, no treatment', *Sowetan newspaper*, 10 April, p. 6.

Marutha, N.S., 2012, 'Electronic records management in the public health sector of the Limpopo province in South Africa', *Journal of the South African Society of Archivists* 45, 39–67.

Marutha, N.S., 2011, 'Records management in support of service delivery in the public health sector of the Limpopo province in South Africa', MINF Thesis, University of South Africa.

Marutha, N.S., 2017, 'A framework to embed medical records management into the healthcare service delivery in Limpopo Province of South Africa', PhD Thesis, University of South Africa.

Nengomasha, C.T., 2013, 'The past, present and future of records and archives management in sub-Saharan Africa', *Journal of the South African Society of Archivists* 46, 1–11.

Ngoepe, M., 2008, 'An exploration of records management trends in the South African public sector: A case study of the Department of Provincial and Local Government', MINF Thesis, University of South Africa.

Ngoepe, M., 2012, 'Fostering a framework to embed the records management function into the auditing process in the South African public sector', PhD Thesis, University of South Africa.

Ngoepe, M., 2016, 'Records management models in the public sector in South Africa: Is there a flicker of light at the end of the dark tunnel?', *Information Development* 32(3), 338–353. https://doi.org/10.1177/0266666914550492

Ngoepe, M., 2017. 'Archival orthodocy of post-custodial realities for digital records in South Africa', *Archives & Manuscript* 45(1), 31–44. https://doi.org/10.1080/01576895.2016.1277361

Ngoepe, M. & Van der Walt, T.B., 2010, 'A framework for records management programme: Lessons from the Department of Cooperative Governance and Traditional Affairs', *Mousaion* 28(2), 83–107.

Ngoepe, M. & Makhubela, S., 2015, 'Justice delayed is justice denied': Records management and the travesty of justice in South Africa', *Records Management Journal* 25(3), 288–305. https://doi.org/10.1108/RMJ-06-2015-0023

Ngoepe, M. & Ngulube, P., 2016, 'A framework to embed records management into the auditing process in the public sector in South Africa', *Information Development* 32(4), 890–903. https://doi.org/10.1177/0266666915573037

Ngulube, P. & Tafor, V.F., 2006, 'The management of public records and archives in the member countries of ESARBICA', *Journal of the Society of Archives* 27(1), 57–83. https://doi.org/10.1080/00039810600691288

Ojo, T., 2009, 'Communication networking: ICT and health information in Africa', *Information Development* 22(2), 94–101. https://doi.org/10.1177/0266666906065549

Rampfumedzi, D.P., 2006, 'Quality control of obstetric nursing records in a selected regional hospital', MA Health Studies Thesis, University of South Africa.

Robek, M.F., Brown, G.F. & Stephens, D.O., 1995, 'Why records management? Ten business reasons', viewed 30 July 2016, from http://www.epa.gov/records/what/quest1.htm

Thurston, A., 2005, 'Fostering trust and transparency through information system', PREM Notes Public Sector, no. 97, The World Bank, Washington, DC, viewed 30 July 2016, from http://documents.worldbank.org/curated/en/469671468329484494/Fostering-trust-and-transparency-through-information-systems

U.S. Department of Health and Human Services, 2006, 'Consumer awareness, addressing healthcare connectivity as a matter of life and death', viewed 31 July 2016, from http://www.hhs.gov/healthinformationtechnology/consumerAwareness.html

20

Successful IT governance in SMES: An application of the Technology–Organisation–Environment theory

Authors:
Olaitan Olutoyin[1]
Stephen Flowerday[2]

Affiliations:
[1]Department of Information Systems, University of Fort Hare, South Africa

Corresponding author:
Stephen Flowerday,
sflowerday@ufh.ac.za

Background: Small and medium-sized enterprises (SMEs) are the bedrock of most economies of the world. Due to global competition, SMEs are making significant investments in information technology (IT) to improve their business processes. However, a study of extant literature on the subject of IT governance in SMEs has highlighted the fact that the implementation of structural controls to enable effective IT governance is often difficult, resulting in project failures and loss of income.

Objectives: This paper seeks to examine ways by which SMEs can successfully adapt a suitable IT governance framework to manage its IT investments.

Method: A content analysis of extant literature was done in this paper. The Technology–Organisation–Environment theory forms the theoretical basis of the proposed key pillars for an SME to evaluate its capability to embark on an IT governance initiative in order to obtain the desired results.

Results: From the content analysis of relevant literature, the paper proposed three key pillars which should be in place before an SME adapts any IT governance framework to manage its IT investments. The key pillars are considered an important link between strategic IT governance plans and measurable successful outcomes.

Conclusion: It was concluded that an SME would be better positioned for successful IT governance if it were to conduct a careful analysis of the components of these key pillars before embarking on the implementation of any IT governance framework.

Introduction

As a sector, the small and medium-sized enterprises (SMEs) labour force is the largest sector of employees worldwide and contributes significantly to growth in developing economies (Apulu & Ige 2011). Because of global competition, SMEs are increasingly being forced to rethink their business processes and embrace agility in their work. The interconnectivity of the world has made it imperative for enterprises, both large and small, to rely on information technology (IT) in achieving their objectives (Devos, Van Landeghem & Deschoolmeester 2009a). As a result of this, SME owner-managers make significant investment in IT. They are therefore not immune from the governance debates on how to manage IT investments effectively and ensure its alignment to business strategies (Bloem, Van Doorn & Mittal 2007).

Following from this, it is apparent that a more structured system is required for the purpose of governing IT in SMEs. However, a study of extant literature on the subject of IT governance in SMEs has highlighted the problem, which is that implementation of structural controls to enable effective IT governance is often lacking, resulting in project failures and loss of income (Devos *et al.* 2009a).

This article proposes a set of constructs which are crucial for an SME to consider before implementing any IT governance framework. The Technology–Organisation–Environment (TOE) theory incorporates the three pillars on which an SME should evaluate its capability to embark on an IT governance initiative in order to obtain the desired results. The intrinsic value inherent in the ability of SME owner-managers to fully understand and articulate the business–IT fit in their particular environment before embarking on an IT governance initiative is also discussed in the article.

Research methodology

This section provides an overview of the research methods used.

Content analysis

Content analysis refers to a method for systematically exploring textual data to identify the patterns and structures in it, with the intention of identifying the important features of a given construct (Billore, Billore & Yamaji 2013). The purpose of such systematic data exploration in this research was to enable the author to decipher meanings and then draw inferences from the meanings with a certain degree of scientific precision (Vitouladiti 2014). In this article, the research methodology used is qualitative. The conclusions were drawn by using the six steps of content analysis as outlined by Krippendorff (2013). The following steps are involved:

1. **Unitising** – A systematic approach that involves delineating the text that is relevant to the content under investigation. This was done by mainly reviewing literature with a focus on IT governance in SMEs.
2. **Sampling** – The process of drawing a realistic sample of texts from the entire population, as it is impossible to perform a content analysis on the entire relevant population. A sample was selected from the range of available literature on IT governance based on the frequency of citation, relevance of empirical study of SMEs, and the focus on the challenges encountered when implementing IT governance in SMEs.
3. **Coding** – The process of stratifying similar contexts in sampled texts into the same units of analysis in order to deduce meaning. In this article, coding was done by categorising similar constructs under the relevant aspects of the TOE framework.
4. **Reducing** – The process of reducing the stratified data to manageable units in order for the results to be presented efficiently. The qualitative nature of this study implies that the reduced data is not coded when measured, but placed in a grouping of similar concepts.
5. **Inferring** – The process of enunciating the meaning, reference, and inference to be drawn from the data and the attendant thoughts or constructs these inferences provoke. The inferences drawn from a content analysis of secondary literature form the three pillars narrated in the conclusion to this study.
6. **Narrating** – The final step involves writing up the results of the preceding five steps in a way that answers the research question at hand. The narrative stage must ensure that the inferences drawn from the data are outlined in concise, clear language that directly addresses the research question. In this article, the narration is done as an application of the TOE framework and is presented in tabular form for easy assessment and understandability. (Krippendorff 2013).

Sampling procedure for the study

Because of the qualitative nature of this study, and the literature review being based on journals that include empirical studies on IT governance implementation in SMEs, quota sampling was the method used in selecting the journal articles surveyed in the course of writing this article. Quota sampling involves the selection of predetermined characteristics of units of the sample to be used for the research (Marshall & Rossman 2010). This article chose journals that discussed the common theme of IT governance challenges in SMEs, taking into consideration empirical studies on SME implementation of IT governance conducted across different sectors and countries. The TOE theory (Tornatzky & Fleischer 1990) was used to identify the tripartite pillars recommended for careful consideration before the implementation of IT governance frameworks in SMEs.

Validity and reliability

In a study of this nature, it is important to evaluate the quality of data interpretation. This is done by examining the reliability and validity of research findings, because these two attributes constitute a crucial test of trustworthiness for the credibility of the research (Miles, Huberman & Saldana 2013). For the purpose of this article, the validity and reliability of the findings are entrenched and inherent in the method of reviewing the scholarly articles on IT governance in SMEs. The most noteworthy articles were those which conducted case studies on IT governance implementation in SMEs. These were important to critically analyse the success of current IT governance processes in positioning SMEs competitively in the business community. The conclusions drawn from this study are therefore generalisable to the context of SMEs which plan to implement IT governance in their enterprises.

In addition, to ensure the validity and reliability of the constructs drawn from this study, the selection of the papers used for this exercise was based on how often they were cited by the academic community and their availability online as shown on the search engines Google Scholar and EBSCOhost.

Theoretical foundation

SME organisational structure

Worldwide, SMEs represent a means of distributing income among employees and their dependants (Bannock, 2005). Researchers estimate that SMEs are the source of 75% of employment in most economies (Apulu & Ige 2011). As a result of their peculiar ownership structure, mode of funding, and size, SMEs are less complex in both organisational structures and management processes than large organisations (Albayrak & Gadatsch 2012; Montazemi 2006). Additionally, because of financial constraints, SMEs are more inclined to hire personnel with adequate qualifications for the job specification rather than experts. SME owner-managers usually operate an informal reporting system, with the owner-managers as sole decision makers. This is contrary to what occurs in large corporations where decisions have to be ratified by the board or executive management.

Although there is usually good interaction between employees and the management of an SME, once decisions are made, the required implementation processes are cascaded down to employees without recourse to discussions and representations (Devos *et al.* 2009a). Accordingly, in the area of corporate and IT governance, SMEs are steered mainly by a microscopic unit of the enterprise, usually, the owner-manager, or, in a few cases, the top management team.

This article seeks to propose three pillars that a sound and successful IT governance program should be based on when introducing IT governance to SMEs. The proposed pillars will ensure that the governance of IT processes is aligned with organisational goals and achieves the desired results of improved operational efficiencies, profitability and strategic growth. The following section will discuss IT governance and its impact on the way IT is managed in SMEs.

IT Governance

Governance is described as the measurement and control systems of management, accountability, and supervision required to harness the complexity and competence of an enterprise in order to achieve the goals of that enterprise (Bloem *et al.* 2007). IT plays a central role in the crafting and introduction of new product offerings and serves as a tool in the implementation of strategic decision-making in enterprises (Montazemi 2006; Albayrak & Gadatsch 2012).

IT governance is defined as the processes that ensure the effective and efficient use of IT for enabling organisations to meet their business goals (Gerrard 2010). IT governance encompasses the decision framework, rights, responsibilities, and accountability required to ensure the desired behaviour in support of the organisation's business goals (Robinson 2007). The domain of IT governance relates to the systemic optimisation of the IT portfolio to ensure it delivers maximum value and manages the risks that may arise from IT investments (Gerrard 2010; Albayrak & Gadatsch 2012).

In an increasingly competitive environment, there are a number of IT best practices and processes that result from the need to achieve business goals and objectives. Some of these IT best practice frameworks are: Control Objectives for Information and related Technology (COBIT), published by the IT Governance Institute (ITGI 2007), the IT Service Management Forum, and ISO/IEC 38500 (International Organization for Standardization, 2008).

There are two important components of IT governance: the IT governance structure, and the operational governance processes. The IT governance structure refers to the enterprise's IT strategic plan which is based on its financial capabilities, business needs, and risk appetite. The second component of IT governance is an effective, well-laid-out, and unambiguous process for implementing the IT governance framework.

In an SME context, research findings on how the two aforementioned components are implemented are sparse (Huang, Zmud & Price 2010). According to Devos, Van Landeghem & Deschoolmeester (2012), the two components of IT governance cannot be implemented practicably in the SME context because structural controls in the SME environment are not mature enough to support strict compliance. Therefore we propose that IT governance for SMEs be reconsidered to find a way that consciously designs programs that can align the two components to the strategic goals of the SME in an implementable manner.

Ayat, Masrom & Sahibuddin (2011) contend that there is no framework for the implementation of IT governance in SMEs. In line with this, we outline the differences between large corporations and SMEs, concluding that these differences make the effective implementation of frameworks, such as COBIT Quickstart and ISO/IEC 38500, difficult in SME contexts. In this regard, Ayat *et al.* (2011) advocate further refinement of the ISO/IEC 38500 to better fit SMEs. In spite of this paucity of research findings on how to implement IT governance in SMEs, there is empirical evidence to show that SMEs that do so are better able to compete in the business world than their counterparts that do not (Huang *et al.* 2010). The next section of this article discusses factors that impede IT governance in SMEs and instances where IT governance frameworks designed for large corporations have been applied to SMEs.

IT Governance in SMEs

In light of globalisation, competition, and market convergence, SMEs are under increasing pressure to stay profitable, and are therefore in dire need of a system that ensures that IT investments, which are considerably high, deliver the expected value to keep the enterprise in business (Albayrak, Gadatsch & Olufs 2009).

The operational limitations and challenges faced by SMEs include a lack of specialists because of financial constraints that preclude them from attracting the most skilled personnel, and an inability to experiment with technological artefacts as they do not have resources to financially cushion them if the IT artefacts fail to achieve the desired goals. (Albayrak & Gadatsch 2012; Cocca & Alberti 2010).

Much of the research on IT governance has considered the organisational and structural composition of large corporations as being better able to benefit from, and institutionalise IT governance structures (Huang *et al.* 2010). Researchers have also conceded that large corporations have the financial, operational, and human capabilities required to implement the IT governance processes outlined in frameworks such as COBIT, TOGAF, and ITIL.

However, as discussed earlier in this article, SMEs invest a considerable amount of their limited resources in IT infrastructure; hence the need for these assets to have clear governance structures in place. This is important to ensure that their application aligns with the objectives of the enterprise (Albayrak *et al.* 2009). Also, extant literature has shown that the average SME manager does not base his IT decisions on any methodological metrics. This implies that IT artefacts in SMEs are being purchased and engaged on an *ad hoc* basis (Devos *et al.* 2009b; Apulu & Ige 2011; Huang *et al.* 2010).

In addition, because SMEs in the main do not have highly skilled personnel compared with large corporations, they depend heavily on external expertise for the adoption and implementation of IT (Devos *et al.* 2009b). The acquisition, implementation, and servicing of IT artefacts in SMEs are usually handled by external IT specialists acting as consultants or vendors. The effect of this is that IT governance is not considered an integral part of the enterprise, hence its value to the success of the business is not fully analysed or understood (Devos *et al.* 2009b; Jokonya, Kroeze & Van de Poll, 2012). A number of attempts have been made to tailor a scaled-down version of the IT governance frameworks designed for large corporations for SMEs. An example of this is COBIT Quickstart (ITGI 2007). However, reports from the IT Governance Institute (2007) suggest that the end result of the implementations has been disappointing, urging caution for enterprises with regard to the application of IT governance mechanisms in an SME environment (ITGI 2007).

The failure of these tailored IT governance frameworks in SMEs is attributable to the difference between SMEs and large corporations in terms of structure and operational processes (Albayrak & Gadatsch 2012; Teo, Manof & Choong 2013). IT governance in large corporations cannot be successfully extrapolated to SMEs because the managerial, cultural, and economic contexts are vastly different (Jokonya *et al.* 2012; Devos *et al.* 2012). The dearth of literature dedicated to SME adaptation of IT governance has also made it extremely difficult to draw general inferences about best practices in the implementation of IT governance in SMEs.

In view of the foregoing, this article proposes that a generic application of a structured IT governance framework is not the right fit for SMEs. It is opined that that there are important pillars to be considered before an SME embarks on adapting and implementing a particular IT governance framework in the enterprise. These key pillars form an important link between the strategic goals of the enterprise and the metrics that are conditional for successful IT governance in the SME context. This assertion has its theoretical grounding in the TOE framework. The framework is discussed in detail in the following section of this article.

Technology-Organisation-Environment framework

According to Tornatzky and Fleischer (1990), the TOE framework postulates that the implementation and use of a technology or information systems (IS) tool is influenced by the following contexts: technological, organisational, and environmental (Tornatzky & Fleischer 1990). For the purpose of this study, the technology environment is defined as the internal and external environment which has an impact on and is relevant to the SME. Major factors in this regard are the cost of procurement, maintenance, and adaptability of IT artefacts with existing skills and processes within the SME. All of these factors need to be governed in order for the SME to maximise the values derivable from IT (Ayat *et al.* 2011).

Major factors in the organisational context are the size, structure, internal processes, and disposition of the top management in an SME (Alston & Tippett 2009). The environmental context alludes to both the internal and external factors which may affect the IT in the SME. The external factors include government regulations, competition, and enabling infrastructure that mar or enhance the adaptation of new technology for the SME's business and market structure (Chen, Papazafeiropoulus & Wu 2011).

This article proposes that the TOE framework is applicable in formulating key pillars for the purpose of governing IT in SMEs. The relevance of the TOE framework for the successful implementation of IT governance in SMEs is discussed in the next section of this article.

An assessment of readiness for IT governance implementation in SMEs using the TOE framework

The technological context of an SME refers to the internal and external technologies that are applicable to the enterprise. These technologies may consist of hardware, software, and processes. The technology context mirrors and tracks the maturity level of technology in the enterprise (Tornatzky & Fleischer 1990). Oliviera and Martins (2010) assert that the technological context reflects both the physical and the human infrastructure that must be in place in order for an implemented IT governance framework to achieve its desired goal in the enterprise. Organisational context refers to factors such as management and managerial styles, degree of formalisation, available resources, and work culture within the enterprise. Environmental factors, on the other hand, are the elements that support or oppose the successful implementation of an IT governance framework in the enterprise. These factors could be government policy, competitors, and enabling infrastructure for carrying out the required processes to validate the IT governance framework and organisational structure (Tornatzky & Fleischer 1990).

Oliviera and Martins (2010) conducted an extensive survey of studies which used the TOE framework to analyse divergent IT adoptions such as e-commerce, enterprise resource planning, open systems, electronic data interchange, and knowledge management systems. It was their considered opinion that the TOE theory is the most complete framework for a rounded analogy of effective IT adoption in the enterprise. In the same vein, we contend, in agreement with Baker (2011) that the implementation of IT governance must follow a critical analysis of the competence- enhancing ability of the entire process to the SME.

Although many authors have used the TOE theory to understand factors which influence adoption, the applicable factors affecting the technological, organisational, and environmental contexts have differed slightly (Baker 2011).

This article has applied factors for each element of the theory relevant to the peculiar operating environments of SMEs in proposing its application in the adoption of IT governance in SMEs. We contend that the analogous investigation of the factors which should be in place for an effective IT governance program in SMEs are ingrained in the circumstances within which the SME operates, for example 'financial constraints' are more relevant to the organisational context of an SME than 'global scope'.

Based on the content analysis methodology chosen for this study, and the challenges identified in SME structures and management, it is postulated that the TOE framework serves as a useful tool in formulating the key pillars which enable an SME to delve into the critical issues that need to be addressed before the adaptation of an IT governance framework. These pillars relate to the conditions that should prevail in order for an IT governance framework in an SME to be implemented successfully. The key pillars are considered an important link between strategic plans and measurable successful outcomes (see Table 1).

Key Pillar 1 – Technology context of the enterprise

According to extant literature (Devos *et al.* 2012; Jokonya *et al.* 2012; Weill & Ross 2004), the research into IT governance in SMEs is an ongoing exercise. However, these authors agree that it is imperative that SMEs consider the stage and state of their technology artefact before adapting any IT governance framework or model. A situation where the technology context of the SME is purely based on outsourcing IT, including the management of the artefacts by specialists, raises questions about the need for a formal governance framework within the enterprise (Jokonya *et al.* 2012). According to Chen *et al.* (2011), many SMEs have a resource dependency outlook with regard to IT. The implication of this for IT governance is that the adaptation of a governance model may not be crucial to an SME with limited funding, it is thus advocated that an SME identify its dependency level before the adoption of an IT governance model or framework (Chen *et al.* 2011).

Owner-managers and CEOs of SMEs are typically the decision-makers regarding the extent and breadth of IT investments in the enterprise (Devos *et al.* 2012). Unfortunately, owner-managers often find it difficult to conceptualise the complicated thought processes behind the design of a framework for guiding IT in the enterprise, principally because they do not fully understand the immensely important role IT plays in the success and competitiveness of the enterprise (Huang *et al.* 2010). The components of the subpillars to be considered in the technology context are outlined as follows:

- Formal control of IT is the conceptual model of an IT governance framework; informal processes are the norm in the choice and deployment of IT in SMEs (Ayat *et al.* 2011). Thus, a decision to implement a governance model for IT in SMEs should first consider a needs analysis in relation to the current artefacts and business goals. Studies conducted by De Haes, Haest and Van Grembergen (2010) confirm this by showing that SMEs are challenged in the area of business–IT alignment and this has a negative impact on their IT governance efforts. It is thus surmised that, before deciding on a framework to govern IT, an SME must fully understand and be able to state the impact IT has on its business and the future plans it has for utilising IT to promote or position the enterprise for better competitiveness. In other words, the need for IT governance should be apparent before an SME considers adapting any framework.
- Following from this, a cost-benefit analysis of IT governance framework implementation should be carefully considered. In an SME where the IT in use is for process improvement or basic accounting, with the software sold and serviced by external vendors and specialists, the need for a rigorous process for IT governance does not seem apparent (Jokonya *et al.* 2012; Devos *et al.* 2012; Albayrak & Gadatsch 2012). The owner-manager may decide on a semiformal approach for managing IT risks, for example detailed and formalised Service Level Agreements which clearly outline the rules of engagement. However, in a technology context where the SME requires assembly line IT infrastructure, there may be a need for an internal IT specialist to be appointed to ensure the smooth running of artefacts; this would also necessitate the institutionalisation of strategic procedures to ensure no loopholes occur that may threaten the core of the business-production.
- The technological context of an SME is largely dependent on the financial strength of the enterprise. An SME that is struggling to find funding to improve its production processes, or has challenges keeping ahead of competitors, will not be in a position to execute an elaborate IT governance framework. Albayrak and Gadatsch (2012) confirmed this assertion through an empirical study of SMEs in Germany, which revealed that most managers and employees could not correctly estimate the cost outlay of their IT artefacts, nor could they estimate the cost of their IT and correlate it with value added to the enterprise.

Key Pillar 2 – Organisational context

As previously discussed in this article, the two sides of IT governance are the development of the framework and the actual implementation of processes and procedures to achieve the goals outlined in the framework. The TOE framework refers to the organisational context of an enterprise as its characteristics, which include its managerial structure, the extent of formalisation, and its human resources (Tornatzky & Fleischer 1990). The components of the subpillars to be considered regarding the organisational context and IT governance in an SME are outlined as follows:

- Although literature on SMEs and the availability of the organisational structure necessary for IT governance implementation is sparse, provision of quality IT services based on any IT governance framework in the enterprise depends on whether the human resources employed are equipped to carry out the required processes (Albayrak & Gadatsch 2012; Alston & Tippett 2009; Cocca & Alberti 2010; Montazemi 2006). It is critical for an SME to assess its readiness for IT governance in this respect before embarking on the implementation of any IT governance framework. This assessment should focus on two main factors:

- Are there skilled personnel available to ensure the correct, sustained, and measurable implementation of the IT processes outlined in the framework?
- Is the organisational context mature enough to ensure that the necessary controls and regulatory processes are in place for the governance of IT?

- The IT Governance Institute (2007) opines that extreme caution is required when applying IT governance measures in SMEs. In this article, we extend this notion further by stating that trust plays a major role in the organisational context of an SME, and should thus be regarded as a determining agent in the successful implementation of an IT governance framework in SMEs. According to Devos *et al.* (2012), trust limits the need for structural controls, which implies that the focus of IT governance in SMEs should not only be on the implementation of structures and processes, the organisational context should also be one that entrenches or engenders trust between the owner-manager and the personnel in order to encourage willing and committed participation in the IT governance processes required (Alston & Tippett 2009). Research has shown that organisational trust creates an enabling environment for process improvements in the workplace (Alston & Tippett 2009; Lippert & Davis 2006). To this end, it is opined that an organic culture, which is generally prevalent in SMEs, may not be suitable for rigid procedural compliance with an IT governance framework. The leadership in an SME should critically assess the organisational culture and determine the levels of employee trust before implementing any IT governance framework. Also, an employee's sense of belonging and community is enhanced by a high sense of organisational trust, which in turn contributes to the willingness to actively support required IT governance processes (Liu & Wang 2013).
- Furthermore, Devos *et al.* (2009) maintain that trust is more important than structural control in eliminating IS project failures in SMEs. These findings were based on an empirical study of eight SMEs, and the results indicated that trust played a greater role in ensuring IT project success than the controls that were in place for the same purpose. The implication of this finding for IT governance is therefore that the output-based contracts obtained in large corporations may not necessarily be a guarantee of successful IT governance in SMEs (Devos *et al.* 2009b).
- The organisational context also determines the level of communication within the enterprise. IT governance communication models for large corporations are structured and highly regulated. This structured, formalised model is unlikely to work in SMEs, where the organisational system is largely fluid and informal (Devos *et al.* 2012). Another crucial element which needs to be in place before the decision to choose any particular IT governance framework is a communication plan. The obvious challenge with formalising communication plans and implementing processes such as risk logs and issue logs in SMEs is that using these tools correctly involves training and a measurement metric to decipher compliance levels (Devos *et al.* 2012). Both of these elements, communication and documentation, must be enabled by the right human capital in the enterprise (Oliviera & Martins 2010).

Key Pillar 3 – Environmental context

The environmental context of an SME is of the utmost importance in the adoption of an IT governance framework. The regulatory environment in which an SME operates is fundamental to the successful adoption of IT governance (Jokonya *et al.* 2012) because an enabling environment in which SMEs can thrive and become innovative in delivering solutions to the industry is generally made possible by government support structures (Montazemi 2006). The components of the subpillars to be considered in the environmental context of an SME before the adaptation of an IT governance framework are outlined below:

- Enterprises that are situated in regions where government regulations and fiscal policies offer support to SMEs in the form of funding, infrastructural outlay, and other technicalities necessary for IT to thrive, will be better positioned to implement IT governance processes (Bloem *et al.* 2007). It is therefore important for an SME to ensure that the right support parameters are in place to actualise the IT governance framework it chooses for the enterprise (Ayat *et al.* 2011). Decision rights and accountabilities in the SME are centralised, with the owner-manager making the strategic decisions on the future of the enterprise. In the context of SMEs, this seemingly absolute power of the owner-manager may create an atmosphere of disenchantment. According to Devos *et al.* (2012), the concept of IT governance is rooted in IT strategic planning and management; however, in large corporations both of these elements are linked to a distinct and well-articulated corporate governance model. The operational environments of SMEs are typically devoid of such structures, hence the unsuitability of IT governance frameworks designed for large corporations (Devos *et al.* 2009b). It is therefore advocated that the adoption of an IT governance framework by SMEs should only be done after a thorough and detailed investigation of the peculiarities of that enterprise's environment. The next section of this article summarises these three pillars in a table format.

Conclusion

The TOE framework has been adopted for myriad innovations in both developed and developing countries. In this article, we contend that the TOE framework is a well-rounded theory for testing the core success factors

TABLE 1: Components of the key pillars of the TOE contexts for analysis before implementing IT governance in an SME.

Context	Justification	Support in literature
Technological (Pillar 1)		
A careful analysis of the state and stage of technology artefacts in SME is vital before any IT governance model is adapted.	This analysis will determine whether elaborate IT governance is essential or not.	Devos *et al.* (2012); Jokonya *et al.* (2012); Devos *et al.* (2009b); Weil & Ross (2004)
Cost-benefit analysis to determine the financial implications of implementing an IT governance model. This includes a business-IT alignment check to determine value delivery versus capital outlay for the enterprise.	SMEs do not have access to funds as readily as large firms, hence a need to watch the cost involved in implementing programs.	Jokonya *et al.* (2012); De Haes *et al.* (2010); Teo *et al.* (2013)
A consideration of the financial health of the SME is a necessary condition before the implementation of IT governance. The structures for managing IT governance processes successfully require both technical and human expertise. An SME must determine if it is ready for such capital outlay before committing to the adaptation of any IT governance model.	An adaptation of IT governance in an SME without the requisite financial muscle is futile and sure to fail, further eroding the SME's ability to compete in the marketplace.	Albayrak & Gadatsch (2012); Devos *et al.* (2012)
Organisational (Pillar 2)		
An assessment of the SME to determine whether there are skilled personnel to ensure the correct, sustained and measurable implementation of IT governance processes. SMEs that adapt a resource dependency outlook to the procurement of IT services have to be retrained to handle the tasks required by IT governance.	The processes require discipline, expertise and a level of tenacity in order to be successful, hence the need for skilled personnel.	Albayrak & Gadatch (2012); Cocca & Alberti (2010); Montezami (2006); Chen *et al.* (2011)
The maturity level of the organisation must be able to support the controls and regulatory processes required by IT governance framework.	The steps/ processes recommended by COBIT/ ISO/ IEC 38500/IEC 38500 for IT governance require certain structures to be in place, hence the need for pre-assessment of the organisation's context.	IT Governance Institute (2007)
Organisational culture - the level of trust between management and employees, the mode and effectiveness of communications play a role in the successful implementation of IT governance. Trust decreases the need for stringent controls and an effective communication plan encourages compliance with an IT governance framework.	An IT governance model requires the buy-in of personnel to succeed. It is even more important in an SME setting as processes are less automated and less rigid than in large corporations.	Devos *et al.* (2012); Alston & Tippett (2009); Liu & Wang (2013); Lippert & Davis (2006)
Environmental (Pillar 3)		
An analysis of the environmental context is fundamental. Support structures of government and industry/sector policy makers enhance IT performance in SMEs, hence a need to determine how this factor will impact on governance efforts before the choice of any framework.	Literature suggests that policy makers do not fully take into account the challenges and limitations of SMEs with regard to their IT use/governance.	Jokonya *et al.* (2012); Bloem *et al.* (2007); Montazemi (2006)
The peculiarities of the environment in which an SME is operating should be considered before an IT governance framework is adopted. This refers to the articulation of a corporate governance strategy which incorporates the need for IT governance and can clearly show the link between the two.	A clear understanding of the IT–business fit is important before adapting an IT governance framework.	Devos *et al.* (2009b); Ayat *et al.* (2011); Huang *et al.* (2010); Liu & Wang (2013)

of IT governance in SMEs. This article posits that the implementation of IT governance as it applies to the SME context is a complex, multifaceted endeavour. This is mainly because the very nature and structure of SMEs negate the clearly defined structural processes required for the actualisation of an IT governance program.

Based on the TOE framework, this article discussed three key pillars that should be in place in an SME before an IT governance framework can be adapted. The components of the three key pillars, the technological, environmental, and organisational contexts of the enterprise, were outlined. Some of the components discussed include the consideration of the financial health of the enterprise to ensure it has the resources it needs to successfully manage the technical and human resources required to actualise the processes of an adapted IT governance framework; a detailed assessment of the SME to determine whether there are skilled personnel to ensure the correct, sustained, and measurable implementation of the IT governance processes in the enterprise; and an evaluation of the support structures such as government policies and sector policymakers and how these may influence the success of the implementation of an IT governance framework in the enterprise.

These key pillars are considered to be a prerequisite to successful IT governance in SMEs as they highlight the peculiarities of the SME environment in order to ascertain whether the implementation of an IT governance framework in the enterprise is practicable. The article concluded by asserting that an SME would be better positioned for successful IT governance if it were to conduct a careful analysis of the components of these key pillars before embarking on the implementation of any IT governance framework.

A limitation of this article is that the application of the TOE framework, which is discussed and forms the foundation of this article, is theoretical. Thus, the direction for future research is an empirical, quantitative investigation of SMEs in order to test the validity of the components of the key pillars outlined in this study.

Acknowledgements

Competing interests

The authors declare that they have no financial or personal relationships which may have inappropriately influenced them in writing this article.

Authors' contributions

O.O. (University of Fort Hare): lead author and writing up of article. S.F. (University of Fort Hare): Postgraduate supervisor of the lead author.

References

Albayrak, A.C. & Gadatsch, A., 2012, 'IT Governance model for small and medium sized enterprises', *Munich, European, Mediterranean & Middle East Conference on Information Systems (EMOIS)*, pp. 380–390.

Albayrak, A.C., Gadatsch, A. & Olufs, D., 2009, 'Life cycle model for IT performance measurement: A reference model for small and medium enterprises (SME)', in G. Dhillon, C.B Stahl, & R. Bakersdale (eds.), *Information systems-creativity and innovation in small and medium sized enterprises: Proceedings of IFIP W.G 8.2 conference*, pp. 180–191. http://dx.doi.org/10.1007/978-3-642-02388-0_13

Alston, F. & Tippett, D., 2009, 'Does a technology-driven organization's culture influence the trust employees have in their managers?', *Engineering Management Journal* 21(2), 3–10. http://dx.doi.org/10.1080/10429247.2009.11431801

Apulu, I. & Ige, E., 2011, 'Are Nigerian SMEs Effectively Utilising ICT?', *International Journal of Business and Management* 6(6), 207–214. http://dx.doi.org/10.5539/ijbm.v6n6p207

Ayat, M., Masrom, M., Sahibuddin, S. & Sharifi, M., 2011, 'Issues in implementing IT Governance in small and medium enterprises', *California, USA, second international conference on Intelligent Systems, Modelling and Simulation (ISMS)*, pp. 197–201. http://dx.doi.org/10.1109/isms.2011.40

Baker, J., 2011, 'The technology-organisation-environment framework', in Y. K. Dwivedi, M.R. Wade & S.L. Schneberger (eds.), *Information systems theory: Explaining and predicting our digital society*, pp. 231–245, Springer.

Bannock, G., 2005, *The Economics and Management of Small Business: An international perspective*, 1st edn., Taylor & Francis, London.

Billore, S., Billore, G. & Yamaji, K., 2013, 'The online corporate branding of banks-a comparative content analysis of Indian and Japanese Banks', *The Journal of American Business Review* 1(2), 90–96.

Bloem, J., Van Doorn, M. & Mittal, P., 2007, *Making IT Governance work in a Sarbanes Oxley world,* 2nd edn., Wiley & Sons, New York.

Chen, H., Papazafeiropoulus, A. & Wu, C., 2011, 'An E-government initiative to support supply chain integration for small to medium sized enterprises', *The Database for Advances in IS -Communications of the ACM* 42(4), 63–99. http://dx.doi.org/10.1145/2096140.2096145

Cocca, P. & Alberti, M., 2010, 'A framework to assess performance measurement systems in SMEs', *International Journal of Productivity and Performance Management* 59(2), 186–200. http://dx.doi.org/10.1108/17410401011014258

De Haes, S., Haest, R. & Van Grembergen, W., 2010, 'IT governance and business IT alignment in SMEs', *ISACA: Serving IT Governance Professionals* 6, 1–7.

Devos, J., Van Landeghem, V.H. & Deschoolmeester, D., 2009a, *IT Governance in SMEs: A theoretical framework based on the outsourced information systems failure*, Academic Publishing, Sweden, pp. 213–246.

Devos, J., Van Landeghem, H. & Deschoolmeester, D., 2009b, 'IT Governance in SMEs: Trust or control?', in G. Dhillon, C.B. Stahl & R. Bakersville, (eds.), *Information systems-creativity and innovation in small and medium-sized enterprises*, pp. 135–149, Springer, Germany. http://dx.doi.org/10.1007/978-3-642-02388-0_10

Devos, J., Van Landeghem, H. & Deschoolmester, D., 2012, 'Rethinking IT Governance for SMEs', *Industrial Management and Data Systems* 112(2), 206–223. http://dx.doi.org/10.1108/02635571211204263

Gerrard, M., 2010, viewed 15 August 2014, from http://www.gartner.com/IT/initiatives

Huang, R., Zmud, R.W. & Price, L.R., 2010, 'Influencing the effectiveness of IT Governance practices through steering committees and communication policies', *European Journal of Information Systems* 19, 288–302. http://dx.doi.org/10.1057/ejis.2010.16

International Organization for Standardization, 2009, *ISO/IEC 38500,* viewed 5 September 2014, from http://www.itgovernance.co.uk/iso38500

ITGI, 2007, 'CobiT 4.1: Executive summary', viewed 13th July 2013, from http://www.isaca.org/

Jokonya, O., Kroeze, J. & Van der Poll, J.A., 2012, *Towards a framework for decision making regarding IT adoption.* Pretoria, Association for Computer Machinery (ACM), pp. 316–325. http://dx.doi.org/10.1145/2389836.2389874

Krippendorff, K., 2013, *Content analysis: An introduction to its methodology,* 3rd edn., Sage Publications, Thousand Oaks.

Lippert, S.K. & Davis, M., 2006, 'A conceptual model integrating trust into planned change activities to enhance technology adoption behaviour', *Journal of Information Science* 32(5), 434–448. http://dx.doi.org/10.1177/0165551506066042

Liu, X.P. & Wang, Z.M., 2013, 'Perceived risk and organizational commitment: The moderating role of organisational trust', *The Journal of Social Behaviour and Personality* 41(2), 229–240. http://dx.doi.org/10.2224/sbp.2013.41.2.229

Marshall, C. & Rossman, G.B., 2010, *Designing qualitative research*, 5th edn., Sage Publications, Thousand Oaks.

Miles, M.B., Huberman, M.A. & Saldana, J., 2013, *Qualitative data analysis: A methods sourcebook,* 3rd edn., Sage Publications Inc, Thousand Oaks.

Montazemi, A., 2006, 'How they manage IT: SMEs in Canada and the US', *Communications of the ACM* 49(12),109–112. http://dx.doi.org/10.1145/1183236.1183240

Oliviera, T. & Martins, F.M., 2010, 'Firm patterns of E-business adoption: Evidence for the European Union-27', *The Electronic Journal of Information Systems Evaluation* 13(1), 47–56.

Robinson, N., 2007, viewed 17 August 2014, from http//www.isaca.org

Teo, W.L., Manof, A. & Choong, L.F.P., 2013, 'Perceived effectiveness of information technology governance initiatives among IT practitioners, *International Journal of Engineering Business Management* 5, 1–9.

Tornatzky, L.G. & Fleischer, M., 1990, *The process of technological innovation,* Lexington Books, United Kingdom.

Vitouladiti, O., 2014, 'Content analysis as a research tool for marketing, management and development strategies in Tourism', *Procedia Economics and Finance* 9, 278–287. http://dx.doi.org/10.1016/S2212-5671(14)00029-X

Weill, P. & Ross, J.W., 2004, *IT Governance on one page*, MIT Sloan Working Paper, vol. 349, pp. 1–18.

Assessing the legislative and regulatory framework supporting the management of records in South Africa's public health sector

Authors:
Shadrack Katuu[1,2]
Thomas van der Walt[1]

Affiliations:
[1]Department of Information Sciences, University of South Africa, South Africa

[2]Head of Records Unit, International Atomic Energy Agency, Austria

Corresponding author:
Shadrack Katuu,
skatuu@gmail.com

Background: The process of improving the quality of health care delivery requires that health systems function efficiently and effectively. A key component of health care systems' efficiency is the administration of records that are often poorly managed. Any improvement in the management of records has to be done in full cognisance that records are generated in an organisational setting and based on a national legislative and regulatory framework.

Objectives: The purpose of this article is to assess the contextual legislative and regulatory framework of South Africa's health care system and its impact on the effectiveness of records management in public health care institutions.

Method: Data for the study were obtained from two sources. On the one hand, the study conducted a review of literature that not only provided background information but also informed the research process. On the other hand, a varied number of respondents were identified through purposive sampling, and their expert knowledge solicited through semi-structured interviews.

Results: The literature review, as well as the interviews, revealed that findings on the legislative and regulatory environment are multi-layered. For instance, respondents echoed observations made from the literature review that, whilst South Africa had a complex array of legal instruments, compliance levels at public health institutions were very rudimentary and contrary to the levels of sophistication expected by the legal instruments. A number of respondents noted the lack of specific guidelines for health records and that in most government departments there was 'a very low key focus on the regulatory issues'. Several respondents stated that even when there were general guidelines for managing records, very few public institutions were compliant. A majority of the respondents noted a lack of an integrated approach in the different legislative and regulatory instruments, for instance, on the issue of records retention.

Conclusion: The study revealed three related observations: firstly, that there is substantial legislative and regulatory dissonance in the management of health records in the country's public health sector; secondly, understanding the complex interplay of different legal and regulatory instruments in the country's public health sector is a critical first step, but it remains the beginning of the process; thirdly, there are lessons to be drawn from the extensive experiences of other countries such as the United Kingdom in addressing the legislative and regulatory challenges.

Introduction

Jonas, Goldsteen and Goldsteen (2007:9) argue that health is the product of multiple factors including 'genetic inheritance, the physical environment, and the social environment, as well as an individual's behavioural and biologic response to these factors'. The central focus of health care systems is to restore health or prevent exacerbation of health problems. Any nation's health care system is influenced by both external and internal factors. The combined interaction of these internal and external forces determines the quality of health care delivered.

The process of improving the quality of health care delivery requires that health systems function efficiently and effectively. A key component of health care systems functioning effectively is the management of records. Several studies in South Africa have demonstrated that if health facilities are to provide quality services then they need efficient record management programmes (Brink 2004; Katuu 2015a; Mahoro 2013; Marutha 2011).

Problem Statement

The provision of health care in any country is often one of the most fundamental rights of its citizens. In South Africa, the right to health is enshrined in Chapter 2 of the Constitution. However, throughout South Africa's history, both during its colonial period and apartheid era, the racial segregation that permeated every aspect of the country was also reflected in the health system. At the dawn of South Africa's new political dispensation in 1994 there was great expectation that there would be greater equity in all aspects of life, including the provision of health services. By 1996 the national Health Department had acknowledged the continuing inequality in health expenditure in the country (Harrison, Barron & Edwards 1996:xv). The private sector, for example, accounted for approximately 60% of resources spent on health for about 20% of the population. Within the public sector there was also gross inequity in per capita spending amongst the provinces (Ngwena & Cook 2005:127–130). In addition, a disproportionate amount of resources was spent on tertiary health care as opposed to primary health care (Harrison *et al.* 1996:xv). The distribution, physical state and functional design of facilities in the public sector needed to serve the majority of the citizens in the new nation was gravely inadequate.

Research objective

The key to transforming any society often begins with reviewing its legislative and regulatory framework and this is particularly critical in the health sector. Legislative reforms have been the subject of debates all over the world, from the US with the *Affordable Care Act* to the UK's reform of the National Health Service (Dusheiko 2014; Sommers, Kenney & Epstein 2014). Considering South Africa's quest for transformation of the public health sector, the assessment of the legislative and regulatory framework is foundational to eventual success of the transformation process (Whiteside 2014). A number of media reports have highlighted the negative effects of poor records management in South Africa's public health sector. This was demonstrated in the case where the health records of a former Minister of Health in South Africa were published in a weekend newspaper. The Minister sued 'the editor, two journalists, and the publisher of the *Sunday Times* for allegedly violating her right to privacy' by obtaining and disclosing her health records without her consent (Berger, Hassim, Heywood, Honermann, Krynauw & Rugege 2013:33; De Lange & Caelers 2007). There have been a number of cases of negligence within the health sector that have resulted in the maiming or death of patients (Slabbert 2011:108–109; Walker, Darer, Elmore & Delbanco 2014). Whilst in most cases probes have been launched in order to curb the acts of negligence, in one sad case not even an investigation could be launched into the case of the death of a baby because the deceased's records could not be found (Khoza 2008). In this regard, this study assessed the legislative and regulatory framework in South Africa and its impact on the management of records in public health institutions.

Literature review

The history of South Africa's health sector is intricately connected to the history of the country. For many decades, events within the health sector have, either directly or indirectly, contributed to the national narrative. For example, during the Soweto uprising of 1976, it was the hospital in Soweto that became the epicentre of interest from national and international media who, not having eye witness evidence from the school children protests and subsequent shooting by police forces, went to the hospital to verify the evidence of the police brutality (Ndlovu 2006:343–349).

Over the period of its long history, the governance of the country's health system had been both inequitable and fragmented. The inequity was most obvious in the racially divided health system during the apartheid period, whose vestiges are still very evident almost two decades since apartheid was officially dismantled (South Africa Department of Health 2010:5). During the apartheid period, the health system consisted of 14 different operating health authorities, ten in the Homelands and the other four in what was known as White South Africa. The legacy of this fragmentation is a system divided into two parallel sectors – 'a public sector financed through general taxation for the majority and a private sector' (Schneider, Barron & Fonn 2007:290). Whilst the majority of the population accessed a weak and dysfunctional public system, a few privileged people accessed a very strong private health sector. The private sector included health professionals in private practice, private hospitals, pharmaceutical manufacturers and distributors and Medical Aid Schemes (Cullinan 2006:3).

According to Schneider *et al.* (2007:294), the new administration in 1994 inherited a reasonably well-resourced health system, able to offer quality services to segments of the population. However, it was also deeply inequitable, disorganised and inefficient, with powerful private sector interests and limited institutional intelligence in the form of knowledge and information to plan restructuring of the health sector (Thiede & Mutyambizi 2010:192). To this end, the new democratic government sought to consolidate the fragmented health authorities. In addition, the health services were 'doctor-dependent medical services biased towards curing existing diseases (i.e. providing medical care) rather than preventing disease (through provision of services such as clean water and sanitation and education)' (Cullinan 2006:3). The new government sought to reorient the doctor dependence towards preventive health and to widen their services to all the population through the public health system.

The democratic changes that took place in the 1990s necessitated drastic legislative, regulatory and organisational changes to address the inequity. The legislative and regulatory aspects are the core of this discussion. South Africa has a 'hybrid' or 'mixed' legal system, formed by the interweaving of three distinct legal traditions (Du Bois 2004:9–16). The first legal tradition is a civil law system inherited from the Dutch and commonly referred to as Roman Dutch law, which draws from two sources: 'judicial decisions and the writing of the old Dutch jurists' (Madhuku 2010:50). The second legal tradition is a common law system inherited from the British, and the third a customary law system inherited from indigenous Africans and is often termed as African Customary Law (Alberts & Mollema 2014; Du Bois 2010). These traditions have had complex interrelationships with each other, causing areas of strain in the past, not only in South Africa but also other parts of the African continent (Toufayan 2014). The complexity of the interrelationships has contributed to making it difficult to efficiently address transformation of the legacy of the deeply inequitable, disorganised and inefficient system.

In South Africa, the Constitution's Sections 27 and 28 embodies the inalienable rights to health for all South Africans. In addition, children have the right to basic nutrition, shelter and social services (South Africa 1996a). According to the Constitution, health is a 'concurrent' function of both national and provincial spheres of government with the national government largely responsible for setting policies and provinces largely responsible for implementing these policies (Cullinan 2006:3). The current *National Health Act* was promulgated in 2003 and further elaborates how the Constitutional rights can be accessed. It provides 'a framework for a structure uniform health system within the Republic, taking into account the obligations imposed by the Constitution and other laws on the national, provincial and local governments with regard to health services' (South Africa 2003:2).

Within the context of continuously striving for transformation in the public health sector, it is worth exploring the extent to which records in public health institutions have been managed. There have been a number of media reports illustrating instances of poor records management. These reports paint a gloomy picture of the extent to which records in public health institutions are managed. This leads to the fundamental question of the extent to which legislative and regulatory instruments are providing guidance in the management of records in supporting the fulfilment of the constitutional rights of South Africa's citizens. Therefore, this study sought to explore the current state of the legislative and regulatory framework in order to support the management of records in the country's public health care institutions.

Research methodology

This research study was conducted at two levels: first, review of literature and second, the interviewing of 22 respondents from different professional backgrounds in three main sectors: the public health sector, the private health sector as well as those in academic and research institutions.

The review of literature not only provided a background to the study, it also informed as well as actively fashioned the discussions throughout the research process. The literature review process informed the framing of the interview questions for the respondents as well as contextualising the kinds of responses received from the interviewees.

The interview questions were semi-structured and sought for information from respondents about their practical experience with legislative and regulatory instruments. This information included the impact of the legal and regulatory framework on the management of records in public health care instruments touching on issues such as retention and disposition, privacy as well as soliciting information on future trends based on global developments.

The professional backgrounds of the respondents were deliberately diverse in order to solicit varied perspectives that would demonstrate the nuanced understandings required to understanding the complex dynamics in the health sector, as well as within the records management profession in South Africa.

Data analysis and research findings

Findings on the legislative and regulatory environment were multi-layered. The literature review revealed that South Africa's legislative terrain is complex. There are two categories of legislative instruments. The first category oversees the management of records within the health sector. The fundamental act at the heart of the country's health framework is the *National Health Act* which stipulates that a health record should be 'created and maintained at that health establishment for every user of health services' and protected (South Africa 2003:ss. 13, 17). In addition, the Act adds that the Minister may make regulations on how particular records should be managed even though at the time of the study none had been published (South Africa 2003:ss. 68, 90). Additional legislative instruments within the health sector include:

- *Academic Health Centres Act 86 of 1993*
- *Allied Health Professions Act 63 of 1982*
- *Choice on Termination of Pregnancy Act 92 of 1996*
- *Council of Medical Schemes Levy Act 58 of 2000*
- *Dental Technicians Act 19 of 1979*
- *Foodstuffs, Cosmetic and Disinfectants Act 54 of 1972*
- *Hazardous Substances Act 15 of 1973*
- *Medical Schemes Act 131 of 1998*
- *Medicines and Related Substances Act 101 of 1965*
- *Mental Health Care Act 17 of 2002*
- *Nursing Act 33 of 2005*
- *Occupational Diseases in Mines and Works Act 78 of 1973*
- *Pharmacy Act 53 of 1974 as amended (South Africa, 1974)*
- *Sterilisation Act 44 of 1998*
- *Tobacco Products Control Amendment Act 63 of 2008*

Each of these instruments is expected to address the management of records within its own context.

The second category of legislative instruments oversees different aspects of the management of records in the public sector and therefore encompasses the health sector. These include: the *National Archives Act 43 of 1996* (South Africa 1996b), the *Electronic Communications and Transactions Act 25 of 2002* (South Africa 2002), the *Promotion of Access to Information Act 2 of 2000* (South Africa 2000), the *Protection of Personal Information Act 4 of 2013* (South Africa 2013), and the *Protection of Information Act 84 of 1982* (South Africa 1982).

Both the *Promotion of Access to Information Act* (PAIA) and the *Protection of Personal Information Act* (POPIA) have made special mention of health records. PAIA, which facilitates access to records, notes that access to health records should be done to ensure that the disclosure does not 'cause serious harm' to the physical or mental health, or well-being of the requester (South Africa 2000:s. 30). POPIA, which regulates the processing of personal information by both public and private institutions, notes that health information is considered a special kind of personal information and has to be managed effectively (South Africa 2013, s. 32).

One of the respondents argued that, whilst South Africa had put together a number of 'very sophisticated legislative instruments which were comparable to those in any country in the world', the compliance levels at health institutions were very rudimentary and contrary to the levels of sophistication expected by the legal instruments. A number of respondents attributed this poor compliance to the lack of awareness of the legislative provisions dealing with the management of records. This was most apparent when health institutions received PAIA requests and could not provide access to records, in part, because of their poor records management systems.

In addition, the respondents also noted a lack of an integrated approach in the different legislative instruments, for instance, on the issue of records retention. Many acts did not specify retention periods for records and the few that did would often appear contradictory. According to the respondents, most health institutions did not have a common understanding of how long records could be kept. For instance, one of the respondents had spoken with key managers at health institutions who believed records should be kept for five years but did not have a legal or procedural basis for this view, except that this was information passed on from their predecessors. Other respondents argued that either the *Archives Act* or the *Health Act* stated that certain records, for instance X-rays, had to be kept for five years or 15 years. However, the relevant acts did not specify any of these periods thus demonstrating the extent of the discrepancy amongst some of the respondents.

Whilst the legislative environment could be considered extensive and well structured, the regulatory framework was less structured but complex nonetheless. The literature revealed that, whilst there were numerous regulations within the health sector, very few provided detailed guidance on the management of records. For instance, there are five documents outlining Standard Operating Procedures for District Health Information System (DHIS) that record data about facility services as well as infrastructure and human resources at the primary care level. Three of those are: facility level (South Africa Department of Health 2012), sub-district level (South Africa Department of Health 2013d), and district level (South Africa Department of Health 2013a), which state that patient records need to be filed, warn against inaccuracy and duplication of the records and prescribe for their safe storage. The two additional standard operating procedures are: the provincial level (South Africa Department of Health 2013c) and national level (South Africa Department of Health 2013b). These procedures require that all staff, supervisors, line and programme managers involved in information management have relevant levels of knowledge and skills in the management of paper and electronic records. However, none of these regulations provide definitions, processes and methodologies required to manage these health records. They also do not provide a breakdown of the aspects that would constitute 'relevant levels of knowledge and skills' for the staff.

Beyond the national Department of Health, the most comprehensive guidelines for records in the health sector were developed by the Health Professions Council of South Africa (HPCSA) and published in three editions between 2002 and 2008 (Health Professions Council of South Africa 2002; Health Professions Council of South Africa 2007; Health Professions Council of South Africa 2008). The guidelines provided a definition of the health records, what they constitute and how they should be managed, addressing aspects such as storage, ownership as well as access. Several respondents stated that even when there were general guidelines for managing records, very few public institutions were compliant.

The literature revealed that the National Archives did not have specific guidelines for health records, but the institution had published regulatory guidance on the management of records in the form of Advisory Pamphlets (AP) that provide general, rather than specific, guidance to the health sector. AP no. 1 addressed the management of public records (National Archives and Records Service of South Africa 2007c), AP no. 2 addressed the management of electronic records (National Archives and Records Service of South Africa 2007a) and AP no. 3 outlined the responsibilities of records professionals within a public institution and the prerequisite qualifications and experience for them to be appointed (National Archives and Records Service of South Africa 2007b). All the regulatory guidance from the National Archives remained very general rather than specific to the health sector. One respondent noted that the National Archives had little direct contact with health institutions, whilst another respondent argued that the National Archives was a weak institution and could not impose compliance.

Similar to the case of legislative instruments, there was a lack of uniformity on the issue of retention and disposal of records in regulatory instruments. This was most evident in

TABLE 1: Retention periods for different categories of health records.

Type of record	Retention period
Most health records	Stored for a period of 6 years 'from the date they become dormant'
Records belonging to individuals under the age of 18 and obstetric records	Stored until the individual reaches the age of 21
Records of mentally incompetent patients	Stored for the duration of their life
Records related to the Occupational *Health and Safety Act*	Stored for 20 years subsequent to patient receiving treatment
Records related to the exposure to asbestos	Stored for 25 years or more

guidelines issued by the HPCSA as summarised in the table above (Health Professions Council of South Africa 2008:4).

As shown in Table 1, most health records should be stored for a period of six years or more 'from the date they became dormant' (Health Professions Council of South Africa 2008:4). This requirement suggests that records have to be continuously monitored in order to determine when they initially become dormant and, from that point on, kept for at least six years. The additional challenge, which is already arduous to address, is monitoring the specific categories of records that differ from the general rule.

Several respondents echoed this lack of consistency on retention periods for similar health records, drawing from their varied experiences and knowledge. Not only did their views on retention periods of specific records vary vastly from one other, often they also failed to link their views with precise legal or regulatory provisions. This suggested that their views may have been developed through tradition, the result of lacking clear guidelines for the health sector. For two of the respondents, the responsibility for the development of retention and disposal guidelines lay directly on the national and provincial archival institutions. Some respondents noted that, historically, there had been records retention guidelines for hospitals in the Transvaal Provincial Administration, but these had not been updated. One respondent argued that, because of the confusing nature of retention and disposal requirements, some health institutions had resorted to keeping everything indefinitely. However, this came with huge cost implications related to space, equipment and human resources and resulted in poor access to health records when required for clinical activities. In addition, records with historical value need to be managed in archival institutions that undergo archival processing, including appraisal, arrangement and description in order to facilitate provision of records access to a wider audience beyond just the health institution (Katuu 2015b; Williams 2006).

Finally, discussions with respondents revealed that the issue of retention and disposal also needed to address discrepancies when the same type of record in a health institution existed in different formats (i.e. hard copy and digital). For one respondent, this was exemplified by the challenge of keeping digital x-rays, yet film copies also existed. The respondent added that the challenge of long-term preservation of digital records would be whether or not to retain digital copies. In this regard, a review of literature revealed that long-term preservation of digital records was a complex subject, one that required concerted efforts in order to be fully addressed (Brown, Katuu, Sebina & Seles 2009:33–46; Katuu 2012; Katuu & Ngoepe 2015).

Conclusions and recommendations

There are three concluding remarks that were drawn from the research process. First, there is substantial legislative and regulatory dissonance in the management of health records in the country. South Africa has more than 200 years of legislative history in the health sector with the current legislative and regulatory instruments straddling both the apartheid and post-apartheid eras. Whilst there are extensive legislative and regulatory instruments that could facilitate the management of records in the health sector, a considerable number lack strategic coherence as a result of their legacy. For instance, the retention period for health records is not substantially addressed in current legislative or regulatory instruments within the ambit of the National Archives or any national or provincial Department of Health.

Second, understanding the complex interplay of different legal and regulatory instruments in the country's public health sector is a critical first step, but it remains the beginning of the process. One respondent acknowledged that, over time, the public sector had evolved from being ignorant of legislative instruments. The respondent added:

> 'Nine years ago nobody knew about these laws and nobody cared. Then they did know and they didn't care. And then they did know and did care but they didn't know what to do about it. Now they do know and they do care and they are saying help. That's a big change' (Respondent no. 8)

However, beyond having a sophisticated understanding of the legislative and regulatory instruments, there is need for an equally sophisticated implementation process. This means that knowledge of the instruments has to be translated to practice through compliance in order to ultimately improve the quality of health services. For a number of respondents, effective records management in the health sector was intricately linked to compliance. According to one of the respondents:

> Records compliance is the backbone of all the other compliance. For ...a health care institution or anyone in the public sector, if you want to comply with the Public Finance Act or the Municipal Finance Act, whichever level you are, then it's very difficult to comply with it without having proper records systems (Respondent no. 6)

Third, there are lessons to be drawn from the extensive experiences of other countries. For instance, between 2006 and 2009, the UK National Health Service published two parts of the Code of Practice for Records Management which included: guidelines, responsibilities and processes of managing records as well as details on records retention and disposal schedules for the different kinds of health, as well as business and corporate records (GB. Department of Health 2006; GB. Department of Health 2009). The strength of the Code of Practice is that it is based on both legal requirements as well as professional best practice (GB. Department of Health 2006:1). It draws on 'advice and published guidance available from the Ministry of Justice and The National Archives as well as from best practices followed by a wide range of organisations in both the public and private sectors' (GB. Department of Health 2006:3). In addition, the Code of Practice is part of a larger framework of an information governance policy and implementation toolkit (GB. Department of Health 2006:3–4) that is necessary to meet the requirements set out under the *Data Protection Act 1998* (GB. Parliament 1998) and the *Freedom of Information Act 2000* (GB. Office of Public Sector Information 2000). As an example for South Africa, this code of practice ensures there is increased legal and regulatory certainty for health institutions by providing components that include:

- A model records management policy.
- A model records management strategy.
- A records inventory survey template.
- An approach to records management audit.
- Electronic records inventory form definitions.
- Electronic records inventory survey form.
- Manual records inventory form definitions.
- Manual records inventory survey form.
- Raising the profile of records management – 'getting started'.
- The Roadmap Framework (Great Britain, Department of Health [United Kingdom] 2014).

The lesson to be drawn is that legislative and regulatory certainty on the management of records requires adequately defined roles, responsibilities and obligations of both public entities and the managers that run them.

In conclusion, this research study has revealed that whilst a number of sophisticated legislative instruments and a few regulatory instruments exist in the health sector, they do not comprehensively address the needs within health institutions. In addition, the health sector instruments are largely divorced from those addressing records management in the wider public sector. For this trend to be reversed a lot of work needs to be done to address the legislative and regulatory dissonance and there are lessons to be learnt from the experiences of other countries. The changes are not only required within the health sector but across the public sector in general (Ngoepe 2013:167).

Acknowledgements

Competing interests

The authors declare that they have no financial or personal relationships which may have inappropriately influenced them in writing this article.

Authors' contributions

S.K. conducted the research as part of his doctoral studies under the supervision of T.W.

References

Alberts, M. & Mollema, N., 2014, 'Developing legal terminology in African languages as aid to the court interpreter: A South African perspective', *Lexikos* 23(1), 29–58.

Berger, J., Hassim, A., Heywood, M., Honermann, B., Krynauw, M. & Rugege, U. (eds.), 2013, *The National Health Act 61 of 2003 - A guide*, Siber Ink, Cape Town.

Brink, I., 2004, *Records management in health Institutions: A Department of Health project - North West Province, South Africa, Johannesburg*, viewed 27 August 2015, from http://esarbica.com/ESARBICAnews2.pdf

Brown, A., Katuu, S., Sebina, P. & Seles, A., 2009, *Module 4: Preserving electronic records*, International Records Management Trust, London, viewed 02 November 2014, from http://www.irmt.org/documents/educ_training/term%20modules/IRMT%20TERM%20Module%204.pdf

Cullinan, K., 2006, 'Health Services in South Africa: A Basic Introduction', Health-e News Service, Cape Town, viewed 27 August 2015, from http://www.health-e.org.za/wp-content/uploads/2013/04/Health_services_briefing_doc.pdf

De Lange, D. & Caelers, D., 2007, 'Missing Manto Records baffle Clinic', IOL News, Cape Town, viewed 27 August 2015, from http://mobi.iol.co.za/#!/article/missing-manto-records-baffle-clinic-1.366413

Du Bois, F., 2004, 'Introduction: History, system and sources', in C.G. Van der Merwe & J.E. Du Plessis (eds.), *Introduction to the Law of South Africa*, pp. 1–54, Kluwer law international, The Hague.

Du Bois, F., 2010, 'State liability in South Africa: A constitutional remix', *Tulane European & Civil Law Forum* 25, 139–172.

Dusheiko, M., 2014, 'Patient choice and mobility in the UK health system: Internal and external markets', in R. Levaggi & M. Montefiori (eds.), *Health Care Provision and Patient Mobility*, pp. 81–132, Springer, Milan.

Great Britain. Department of Health, 2006, *Records Management: NHS Code of Practice Part 1, Department of Health, London,* viewed 27 August 2015, from https://www.gov.uk/government/uploads/system/uploads/attachment_data/file/200138/Records_Management_-_NHS_Code_of_Practice_Part_1.pdf

Great Britain. Department of Health, 2009, *Records Management: NHS Code of Practice Part 2*, Department of Health, London, viewed 27 August 2015, from https://www.gov.uk/government/uploads/system/uploads/attachment_data/file/200139/Records_Management_-_NHS_Code_of_Practice_Part_2_second_edition.pdf

Great Britain. Department of Health, 2014, *NHS Records Management*, Department of Health, London, viewed 27 August 2015, from http://www.connectingforhealth.nhs.uk/systemsandservices/infogov/records

Great Britain. Office of Public Sector Information, 2000, *Freedom of Information Act 2000*, The Stationery Office, London.

Great Britain. Parliament, 1998, *Data Protection Act of 1998*, 1st March 2010 edn., The Stationery Office, London.

Harrison, D., Barron, P. & Edwards, J., 1996, 'Preface', in *South African Health Review*, pp. ix-x, Health Systems Trust, Durban. http://dx.doi.org/10.1017/cbo9780511523625.001

Health Professions Council of South Africa, 2002, *Guidelines on the keeping of patient records - Booklet 11*, Health Professions Council of South Africa, Pretoria, viewed 27 August 2015, from http://www0.sun.ac.za/ruralhealth/ukwandahome/rudasaresources2009/More/Guidelines%20on%20Keeping%20of%20Patient%27s%20Records.pdf

Health Professions Council of South Africa, 2007, *Guidelines on the keeping of patient records - Booklet 15*, Health Professions Council of South Africa, Pretoria, viewed 27 August 2015, from http://www.hpcsa.co.za/downloads/conduct_ethics/rules/guidelines_patient.pdf

Health Professions Council of South Africa, 2008, *Guidelines on the keeping of patient records - Booklet 14*, Health Professions Council of South Africa, Pretoria, viewed 27 August 2015, from http://www.hpcsa.co.za/downloads/conduct_ethics/rules/generic_ethical_rules/booklet_14_keeping_of_patience_records.pdf

Jonas, S., Goldsteen, R. & Goldsteen, K., 2007, *Introduction to the US Health Care system*, Springer Publishing Company, New York.

Katuu, S., 2012, 'Enterprise content management and digital curation applications – Maturity Model Connections', paper presented at the The Memory of the World in the Digital Age: Digitization and Preservation Conference, Vancouver, September 26-28, 2012, viewed 27 August 2015, from http://www.unesco.org/new/fileadmin/MULTIMEDIA/HQ/CI/CI/pdf/mow/VC_Katuu_28_D_1130.pdf

Katuu, S., 2015a, 'Managing records in South African public health care institutions: A critical analysis', PhD thesis, University of South Africa.

Katuu, S., 2015b, 'User studies and user education programmes in archival institutions', *Aslib Journal of Information Management* 67(4), 442–457. http://dx.doi.org/10.1108/AJIM-01-2015-0005

Katuu, S. & Ngoepe, M., 2015, 'Managing digital records within South Africa's legislative and regulatory framework', paper presented at the 3rd International Conference on Cloud Security and Management ICCSM-2015, Tacoma, WA, viewed n.d., from http://academic-conferences.org/iccsm/iccsm2015/iccsm15-home.htm

Khoza, T., 2008, 'Dead Baby's Records Missing', *News24*, viewed 27 August 2015, from http://www.news24.com/SouthAfrica/News/Dead-babys-records-missing-20080707

Madhuku, L., 2010, *An introduction to Zimbabwean law*, Weaver Press, Harare.

Mahoro, A., 2013, 'Examining the inventory management of antiretroviral drugs at community health centres in the Cape Metropole, Western Cape', Masters thesis, University of the Western Cape.

Marutha, N.S., 2011, 'Records management in support of service delivery in the public health care sector of the Limpopo Province in South Africa', Masters thesis, University of South Africa.

National Archives and Records Service of South Africa, 2007a, *Advisory pamphlet no 2: Electronic records and the law: What governmental bodies need to know*, National Archives and Records Service of South Africa, Pretoria, viewed 27 August 2015, from http://www.national.archives.gov.za/Advisory%20Pamplet%20No%202%20April%202012.pdf

National Archives and Records Service of South Africa, 2007b, *Advisory pamphlet no 3: Records managers and the law: What governmental bodies need to know*, National Archives and Records Service of South Africa, Pretoria, viewed 27 August 2015, from http://www.national.archives.gov.za/rms/ad_pamphlet3.PDF

National Archives and Records Service of South Africa, 2007c, *Advisory pamphlet no. 1: Managing Public Records and the Law: What governmental bodies need to know*, National Archives and Records Service of South Africa, Pretoria, viewed 27 August 2015, from http://www.national.archives.gov.za/rms/ad_pamphlet1.PDF

Ndlovu, S.M., 2006, 'The Soweto Uprising', in B. Magubane (ed.), *The road to democracy in South Africa, vol. 2, 1970-1980*, pp. 317–368, South African Democratic Education Trust, Pretoria.

Ngoepe, M., 2013, 'Fostering a framework to embed the records management function into the auditing process in the South African public sector', PhD thesis, University of South Africa.

Ngwena, C. & Cook, R., 2005, 'Rights concerning Health', in D. Brand & C. Heyns (eds.), *Socio-economic rights in South Africa*, Pretoria University of Law Press, Pretoria.

Schneider, H., Barron, P. & Fonn, S., 2007, 'The Promise and the Practice of Transformation in South Africa's Health System', in S. Buhlungu, J. Daniel, R. Southall & J. Lutchman (eds.), *State of the nation: South Africa 2007*, pp. 289–311, HSRC Press, Cape Town.

Slabbert, M.N., 2011, *Medical Law in South Africa*, Kluwer Law International, Bedfordshire.

Sommers, B.D., Kenney, G.M. & Epstein, A.M., 2014, 'New evidence on the Affordable Care Act: Coverage impacts of early Medicaid expansions', *Health Affairs* 33(1), 78–87. http://dx.doi.org/10.1377/hlthaff.2013.1087

South Africa, 1974, *Pharmacy Act (Act 53 of 1974)*, Government Printer, Pretoria.

South Africa, 1982, *Protection of Information Act (Act 84 of 1982)*, Government Printer, Pretoria.

South Africa, 1996a, *Constitution of the Republic of South Africa (Act 108 of 1996)*, Government Printer, Pretoria.

South Africa, 1996b, *National Archives Act (Act 43 of 1996)*, Government Printer, Pretoria.

South Africa, 2000, *Promotion of Access to Information Act (Act 2 of 2000)*, Government Printer, Pretoria.

South Africa, 2002, *Electronic Communications and Transactions Act (Act 25 of 2002)*, Government Printer, Pretoria.

South Africa, 2003, *National Health (Act 61 of 2003)*, Government Printer, Pretoria.

South Africa, 2013, *Protection of Personal Information Act (Act 4 of 2013)*, Government Printer, Pretoria.

South Africa. Department of Health, 2010, *National Service Delivery Agreement: A long and healthy life for all South Africans*, Department of Health, Pretoria, viewed 07 March 2014, from http://www.hst.org.za/sites/default/files/NSDA_booklet.pdf

South Africa. Department of Health, 2012, *District Health Information System - Standard Operating Procedure: Facility level*, Department of Health, Pretoria, viewed 05 October 2014, from http://www.health.gov.za/docs/Policies/2014/5SOPFacilitylevel.pdf

South Africa. Department of Health, 2013a, *District Health Information System – Standard Operating Procedure: District level*, Department of Health, Pretoria, viewed 05 October 2014, from http://www.health.gov.za/docs/Policies/2014/3SOPDistrictlevel29Jan2014.pdf

South Africa. Department of Health, 2013b, *District Health Information System – Standard Operating Procedure: National level*, Department of Health, Pretoria, viewed 05 October 2014, from http://www.health.gov.za/docs/Policies/2014/1SOPNationallevel27Jan2014.pdf

South Africa. Department of Health, 2013c, *District Health Information System - Standard Operating Procedure: Provincial level*, Department of Health, Pretoria, viewed 5 October 2014, from http://www.health.gov.za/docs/Policies/2014/2SOPProvinciallevel29Jan2014.pdf

South Africa. Department of Health, 2013d, *District Health Information System - Standard Operating Procedure: Sub-District Level*, Department of Health, Pretoria, viewed 05 October 2014, from http://www.health.gov.za/docs/Policies/2014/4SOPSubdistrict29Jan2014.pdf

Thiede, M. & Mutyambizi, V., 2010, 'South Africa', in A.S. Preker, P. Zweifel, P. & O.P. Schellekens (eds.), *Global marketplace for private health insurance: strength in numbers*, World Bank, Washington.

Toufayan, M., 2014, 'When British Justice (in African Colonies) Points Two Ways: On Dualism, Hybridity, and the Genealogy of Juridical Negritude in Taslim Olawale Elias', in O. Onazi (ed.), *African legal theory and contemporary problems*, pp. 31–70, Springer, Dordrecht. http://dx.doi.org/10.1007/978-94-007-7537-4_3

Walker, J., Darer, J.D., Elmore, J.G. & Delbanco, T., 2014, 'The road toward fully transparent medical records', *New England Journal of Medicine* 370(1), 6–8. http://dx.doi.org/10.1056/NEJMp1310132

Whiteside, A., 2014, 'South Africa's key health challenges', *The ANNALS of the American Academy of Political and Social Science* 652(1), 166–185. http://dx.doi.org/10.1177/0002716213508067

Williams, C., 2006, *Managing archives: Foundations, principles and practice*, Chandos Publishing, Oxford. http://dx.doi.org/10.1533/9781780630892

Comparative case study on website traffic generated by search engine optimisation and a pay-per-click campaign, versus marketing expenditure

Authors:
Wouter T. Kritzinger[1]
Melius Weideman[1]

Affiliations:
[1]Website Attributes Research Centre (WARC), Cape Peninsula University of Technology, South Africa

Correspondence to:
Melius Weideman

Email:
weidemanm@cput.ac.za

Postal address:
PO Box 652, Cape Town 8000, South Africa

Background: No empirical work was found on how marketing expenses compare when used solely for either the one or the other of the two main types of search engine marketing.

Objectives: This research set out to determine how the results of the implementation of a pay-per-click campaign compared to those of a search engine optimisation campaign, given the same website and environment. At the same time, the expenses incurred on both these marketing methods were recorded and compared.

Method: The active website of an existing, successful e-commerce concern was used as platform. The company had been using pay-per-click only for a period, whilst traffic was monitored. This system was decommissioned on a particular date and time, and an alternative search engine optimisation system was started at the same time. Again, both traffic and expenses were monitored.

Results: The results indicate that the pay-per-click system did produce favourable results, but on the condition that a monthly fee has to be set aside to guarantee consistent traffic. The implementation of search engine optimisation required a relatively large investment at the outset, but it was once-off. After a drop in traffic owing to crawler visitation delays, the website traffic bypassed the average figure achieved during the pay-per-click period after a little over three months, whilst the expenditure crossed over after just six months.

Conclusion: Whilst considering the specific parameters of this study, an investment in search engine optimisation rather than a pay-per-click campaign appears to produce better results at a lower cost, after a given period of time.

Introduction

The growth of the Internet has produced an important information resource during the last two decades that has advanced at a much faster rate than was previously envisaged. It took seven years to reach a 25% international market share – 70% faster than the development of the radio and 80% faster than the development of the telephone. This growth makes the Internet the fastest growing technology the world has ever encountered (Singh 2002). Boyes and Irani (2004:191) support this trend by claiming that the Internet had acquired 50 million global users in five years as opposed to the 38 years it took for radio and 13 years for television.

The implementation of the World Wide Web (WWW) has seen the world confronted with the concept of a website. Websites act as connection and communication points between the user and digital information. Therefore, most corporations (according to Akakandelwa 2011), organisations or institutions have been making efforts to launch themselves into the virtual world using this modern platform. The WWW is more than two decades old and, due to its complexity, its size is impossible to measure with regard to the number of websites or servers. It is claimed that, for January 2014, the nine most popular websites in the United States of America (USA) drew between 100 million and 370 million visitors each (Nielsen 2014). The WWW is a decentralised environment constructed and controlled by various people and access to it is less restricted than access to the common information media (Brunn & Dodge 2001).

The base of Internet users is massive; hence, there is much interest in leveraging this user base for commercial gain. This commercial gain could be realised by ensuring that many thousands of users view a given website daily, with some of them being converted from browsers to buyers. It is generally accepted that the two types of interventions which could be implemented to increase the traffic to a website are search engine optimisation (SEO) and a paid campaign. However, no research could be found which compares the expenditure in a controlled environment with the value received from that expenditure for these two approaches. It is against this background that this study has originated.

The research problem on which this project was based is the fact that the respective value of the two marketing methods has not been directly compared, leading to resources being wasted on marketing. The purpose of this study was to compare these two categories to see how they produce traffic over a period of time, and to offset them against the expenditure.

Literature review

Search engines

According to Green (2000), a search engine is a search service that uses retrieval software called crawlers that examine websites and then index them in a database of website listings according to their relevancy. Search engines use their own indexing software and strategies to continuously traverse the Web, searching for the most up-to-date content possible. The indexing software (also referred to as spiders or bots) is responsible for visiting webpages following links between pages. The pages found are then analysed, parts are copied back to the site running the indexing software and added to the database for the purpose of including them in the search engine results (Weideman 2009).

Even though search engines use different algorithms to rank a webpage, they operate on similar principles. All search engines, primarily, strive to retrieve and display relevant results (webpages) that contain words or terms that match the user's search query (Green 2000; Guenther 2004:47).

Oppenheim *et al.* (2000:191) are of the opinion that, although search engines search a vast amount of information at impressive speeds, they are criticised on issues such as the retrieval of duplicate and irrelevant records owing to spamming techniques. The sheer mass of these irrelevant results is one of the main user complaints against search engines.

Much research has been done recently on search engines, the way they operate, the way users generate queries, and the way they affect our lives. Moreno and Martinez (2013) indicated that webpages can be designed to be both SEO and human friendly. This was confirmed by another study on the effect of usability elements on the way search engine crawlers view websites (Visser & Weideman 2011).

In summary, the availability and use of search engines affect our lives on a regular basis through user interaction with results produced by them. It is now certain that the use of search engines, together with the power of advertising, plays a role in peoples' daily decisions on various aspects and is not limited to purchasing only.

Search engine marketing

Search engine marketing (SEM) is a strategy that makes use of the power of search engines to potentially attract millions of views per day to websites. Even academic universities need to consider how they should market themselves to prospective students as they are the paying clients (Weideman 2013). Crowley (2014) discusses some of these strategies, including SEO and tracking analytics, to determine user behaviour. Many systems are fighting for 'eyeballs'; these are users reading and responding to advertisements on websites. Social media has added to the frenzy through their advertisement offerings, although research has proven that it has not been all that successful. Barreto (2013) indicated that Facebook banner advertisements have less business value than recommendations from friends, possibly because of banner blindness. These ads (advertisements) were located outside the main viewing area first scanned by most users.

A recent study was done to determine the effectiveness of a search marketing campaign and the effect of print advertising on SEM (Olbrich & Schultz 2014). It was found that the budget and the degree of keyword matching had the largest effect on the yield in business gained, followed by the click-through rate and the bid amount. This result seems to indicate that SEM needs to be planned with care as a larger budget might reduce expenditure on other marketing efforts. This fact supports the current study. SEO and pay-per-click schemes (PPC) are generally considered to be the two main categories of SEM which are to be investigated.

Pay-per-click

PPC schemes, producing non-natural rankings, are systems which display advertisements on a search result screen, co-located with organic results but ranked separately. The location of these advertisements is normally to the right and above the organic search engine listings (Chen *et al.* 2011). This sharing of the prime real estate space on the user's screen has caused some problems for users. No longer can they simply evaluate the quality of answers based on which answer is listed the highest on the result screen as they have to also consider the ranking difference between organic and paid results. Even libraries have found this to be an obstacle for their users (Moxley, Blake & Maze 2004). However, many industries, particularly the tourism sector, have been making extensive use of this marketing opportunity. In some cases even small businesses went to extremes to do research to identify the better search engine PPC scheme to use (Kennedy & Kennedy 2008). At the same time, the 'newness' of this form of marketing initially scared off other smaller businesses for example some smaller hotels did not make use of PPC (Murphy & Kielgast 2008).

PPC, as the name suggests, charges the advertiser the bid amount every time an Internet user clicks on an advertisement. The keywords all have different competition ratings and the more popular a keyword, the higher the cost per click would be (Chen *et al.* 2011). A recent study on the value of the bid price per keyword for a new PPC campaign determined the best of a number of methods to determine this price (Nabout 2015). This study confirms the importance of financial expenditure, which could easily grow beyond what a company decided they could spend on a marketing campaign.

The PPC ranking system operates in stark contrast to the value associated with the quantity and quality of inlinks, in other words SEO (Thelwall 2001). In the past Google specifically used a simple formula to determine the ranking of PPC results: Rank = Bid price X Quality Score (Sagin 2013). The bid price is the amount the advertisement owner is prepared to pay per user click on the ad, and the quality score is Google's interpretation of the quality of the landing page. However, in October 2013 Google announced a third factor, namely ad extensions (Mancuso 2013). Where two competing advertisements achieve an equal score, the use of ad extensions is used to determine the highest ranker.

A recent study was done on the relationship between print and search engine advertising (Olbrich & Schultz 2014). The results proved that print advertising did not directly affect the number of advertisements impressions produced by the search engine. However, there was an indirect relationship between print advertising and the number of conversions indicating that e-commerce marketers cannot ignore the traditional advertising methods and focus only on SEM. Since exposure through PPC requires constant and accumulative expenditure, past research has also focused on maximising this expense. The performance of PPC advertisements is crucial in recapping the expense, hopefully bypassing it to provide a profit. Another recent study determined the role of ranking of these advertisements, branding, and the role of the device used to search (Gupta & Mateen 2014).

In summary, PPC has been a successful business model. In the case of Google, it has produced the bulk of its profits over the years, playing a major role in its financial success (Kumar & Kohli 2007). At the same time, an e-commerce business running PPC schemes on multiple keywords across many campaigns is advised to budget for specialised staff to manage these campaigns. Still, some authors actually prescribe that PPC is a better way to spend marketing dollars than SEO (Sen 2005).

Search engine optimisation

SEO is a method that uses data observation and marketing research to identify the most suitable keyword for a website (Malaga 2010). However, it requires a base of knowledge to implement, such as how to choose keywords and how to use keywords in order to enhance a website's ranking, etc.

There is a need for any e-commerce business to be ranked highly with search engines (Kent 2012). Another author states that to increase the volume of traffic to individual websites from search engines, SEO must be considered and invested in (Kisiel 2010). For successful SEO there are many concepts that need to be understood and applied; some of these are discussed later. The ultimate goal of SEO is to increase a website's ranking with search engines, thus increasing the traffic to the website, which should result in increased sales (Lee 2010; Lee, Chen & Wu 2010; Lee & Lin 2011).

Lately, much research has been done on the visibility of content to search engine crawlers. Onaifo and Rasmussen (2013) found that the principles of SEO can, and should, be applied to increase the visibility of library content to search engines. A number of elements affect SEO; it is not just a case of implementing a simple set of rules, thereby ensuring high visibility. Some of these elements are listed below.

Another recent study considered the value of using search query data to obtain business information. Search query data is much more recent than, for example, business reports published at the end of a financial year. A significant correlation was found between business performance and position and search query data (Vaughan 2014). This kind of timely information could be used to predict business performance, leading to financial gains.

It is clear that both SEO and PPC could play a role in marketing a website to the search engine crawlers. The purpose of this study was to determine how much traffic each of SEO and PPC produces and to measure and compare the expenditure in each case.

Some of the aspects of SEO are considered below. They are all discussed with regard to the components of a webpage over which the website owner has direct control.

Header tags

Metatags are elements of a webpage that are mostly optional, invisible to the casual browser, but which could affect the way a crawler views a webpage. One of these is the H (Heading) meta tag.

A Web designer can choose whether or not to highlight headings inside a block of text on a webpage. To this effect, there are six levels of heading tags. H1 is the most important (biggest text); H2 is slightly less important, down to H6 which is the least important. Some search engines recognise the use of header tags as a safe method to weight keywords, owing to its connection with a heading of a paragraph. Henzinger, Motwani and Silverstein (2002:9) state that the higher the importance of the headings, the more weight a search engine could assign to a given webpage. For example, text in an <H1> would appear prominently on a webpage and therefore some search engines could see it as safe to assign a high weight to the text in that heading.

Research by Craven (2003) to determine the relevant weight of meta tags indicates that the H1 (heading 1) and H2 (heading 2) tags are the second and third most highly weighted (after the TITLE tag) of all the meta tags. As with Microsoft Word, the hypertext mark-up language (HTML) has built-in styles for headings to differentiate between importance levels of text that are usually used to break up text into paragraphs. The different options allow the designer to develop large and bold text in an HTML document, marking the beginning of a new paragraph or section (Henzinger *et al*. 2002:9).

Image filenames

Search engine crawlers cannot interpret the content of an image, a video or an audio file. The designer has to provide text-based information to allow the crawler to make some association between this type of file and its contents (Weideman 2009). For still images, the name of the file is the most obvious way of establishing this association. A simple experiment can prove that the name of an image file does play a role in its visibility. When doing an image search on Google or Bing for the term 'rolls royce' for example, page after page of images of this car are produced. Upon closer inspection of the first result page, virtually every image has those two words as part of the file-name.

Image alternative tags

ALT (alternative) tags are used to display text in the place of an image on a webpage if graphics are turned off. The ALT text will also display if a user places his or her mouse pointer over an image for a few seconds. Currently, automated crawlers can read only text elements within a webpage and are unable to read multimedia elements, as discussed earlier. For this reason, it is of importance to apply ALT tags, where possible, that accurately describe the graphics on the webpage (Hubbard 2004).

By implementing ALT text within a webpage, the developer ultimately caters for users who turn graphics off to increase loading speed. Without the use of ALT tags a site could become impossible to navigate when graphics are turned off. The use of ALT tags also provides the ability to cater for users with a visual impairment. Voice-output screen readers (benefiting those users) will not 'read' a non-text element (Oppenheim *et al*. 2000:204), but will do so if an ALT element is provided. Ironically, the implementation of techniques to allow the visually impaired to better interpret website contents could also play a major role in improving the user experience of other users, as well as the way crawlers interpret webpages.

Metadata

Another meta tag which plays a role in visibility is the TITLE tag. It is also invisible as part of the body text of a webpage being displayed, but it is often displayed on a user screen as part of search engine results. Search engines often claim that the presence of a well-written TITLE tag can positively influence a webpage's visibility (Guenther 2014).

In summary, only a few of the many elements affecting the crawler visibility of a webpage have been discussed. There are many others (keyword usage, HTML file-names, links, etc.), as well as a long list of negative elements that should specifically not be implemented (Weideman 2009).

Methodology

Data were gathered from a real-life website where first the one (PPC) and then the other (SEO) of the marketing approaches were followed exclusively. Usage behaviour and statistics were recorded and analysed in an attempt to compare the expenditure with the gain from each approach.

A company in Cape Town, South Africa, manufactures PVC, polypropylene and leather promotional and stationery products. The company's name is not listed; for the purposes of recording they will be named XYZ. The company invested in PPC from May 2010 to May 2011 in an attempt to drive traffic to the website. During that time no SEO implementation was done on the website. Each month XYZ spent, on average, R3000 on PPC. However, after the PPC campaign was terminated, they paid a once-off fee of R19 000 for the SEO project.

The XYZ concern is a relatively small company. Considering that they have a typical monthly website traffic figure of hundreds as compared to millions for large companies, their business model must be sound to run a successful e-commerce concern. The most important requirement of the client was that their website remained optimised in such a way that it could lead to sales. The authors did a detailed investigation of the XYZ website, identifying elements that could be improved through SEO with the estimated short-term cost it may entail.

The following elements which needed improvement were identified:

- Header tags (were not being used).
- Image filenames (were inappropriate and non-descriptive).
- Metadata (was outdated).
- Alternative tags (were inappropriate and non-descriptive).
- Product descriptions (were too short or non-existent).
- The bounce rate (was too high).

Header tags

All the headings on the XYZ website were placed in strong tags. Best practice prescribed that all strong tags be replaced with H1 and H2 Tags. This would imply that the authors would have to inspect every one of the 55 webpages and either write new H1 tags, or rewrite the existing ones.

Image filenames

Some of the image filenames did not contain relevant keywords. An example of this was '_MG_2174.jpg'. Again, best practice was that these filenames be renamed with appropriate keywords that reflect the objects on each image. A total of 246 images were found and renamed in the 55 HTML pages.

Metadata

Throughout the year the website was updated with new products, whilst older products were removed. However, the metadata was not updated accordingly. It was recommended that the metadata of all 55 HTML pages be updated to reflect the new content. This was done, and it included updating the TITLE-, DESCRIPTION- and KEYWORD tags of all 55 HTML pages.

Image alternative tags

Some of the ALT tags of the images were too long. These ALT tags, in accordance with best practice, needed to be shortened and rewritten to contain relevant keywords that reflect the images that they are associated with. There were a total of 256 images whose ALT tags were reviewed and rewritten.

Product descriptions

Some of the products listed on the XYZ website were identified by only one short sentence. It was decided, based on best practice, that all product descriptions be rewritten to have at least two to three descriptive sentences each. Sixty four of the 128 products did not have sufficient descriptive text and were subsequently rewritten. The remaining 64 descriptions were also reviewed to ensure that they contained relevant keywords.

Bounce rate

The XYZ website had a bounce rate of 48%, where a lower figure is considered to be better (Plaza 2009). In industry, a bounce rate of 30% is considered to be a breakpoint; higher than 30% is 'bad' and lower is 'good'. It was necessary that the homepage text be reviewed with the aim to reduce the high bounce rate. However, the bounce rate is not an element that a Web developer can improve by doing coding updates or any other direct actions. It is a figure which will decrease (i.e. improve) as users spend more time on webpages as a result of other elements described here being put into place.

Project plan

The project was thus split into three stages:

- Throughout June 2011 the header tags were modified.
- Throughout July 2011 the image filenames and image ALT tags were modified.
- Throughout August 2011 the product descriptions, copy, and metadata were modified.

These timescales appear in the figures following, to indicate the effect of each alteration.

Results and interpretation

Header tags

The effect (if any) of the header tag improvement, as discussed earlier, was measured by viewing statistics on website usage as from when the header tags were redone. Refer to Figure 1.

The company stopped their PPC campaign on 31 May 2011. The immediate effect of this action was a drop in total traffic by 15.42% (1130 vs 1336) when comparing June 2011 with May 2011. The authors then proceeded to review and modify all headings on the website. This process involved modifying the CSS file and defining the Header Tags. There were 244 instances where strong tags were used, and all of them were replaced with H1 and H2 tags.

Also, the headings were modified to include appropriate keywords. The authors ensured that each page only had one instance of the H1 tag, which is considered the most important of the heading tags. The work was conducted throughout June 2011 and was completed in the final week of June 2011. It must be noted that all the work was completed on the live website. As the authors progressed a slight increase in traffic in the second week of June 2011 was noted.

It must also be noted that 01 May 2011 and 02 May 2011 were Worker's Day and a public holiday respectively in South Africa. These two calendar events would have had a negative impact on the statistics as the biggest part of the workforce would not be at work on those days. However, this pattern repeated the next month: 16 June 2011 and 17 June 2011 were Youth Day and a school holiday respectively. These two calendar events would have had a similar effect on the figures of June 2011. Also, during 25 June to 18 July 2011 the schools in South Africa were closed for recess which would also have had a negative impact on the June 2011 statistics.

By this time half of the 244 instances of strong tags were replaced by either H1 tags or H2 tags. The fact that the authors saw an increase in organic traffic was somewhat unexpected, since it can take search engines up to a month (Zuze & Weideman 2013) to re-index and rank webpages after significant changes have been implemented. From the author's point of view this highlights the importance search engines place on Header tags. For any website it is a simple matter to assign header tags to headings. The website, from a search engines perspective, was seen in a more favourable position because of the above action taken.

ALT tags

The effect of the updating of the ALT tags was also measured by viewing the relevant statistics – see Figure 2.

The modifications of the image ALT tags were completed in the final week of July 2011. Whilst performing this task

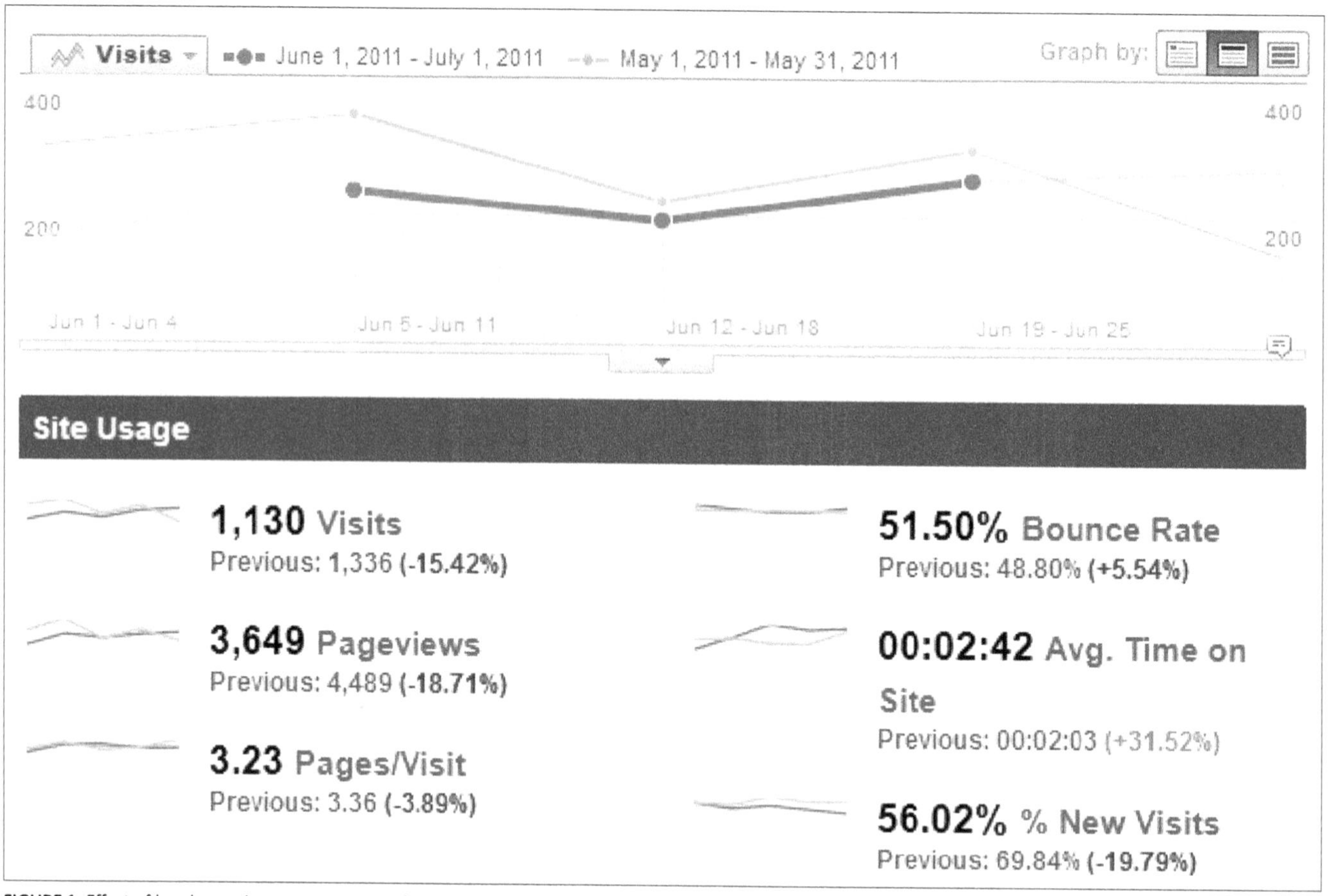

Visits ▾ June 1, 2011 - July 1, 2011 May 1, 2011 - May 31, 2011 Graph by:

400 400

200 200

Jun 1 - Jun 4 Jun 5 - Jun 11 Jun 12 - Jun 18 Jun 19 - Jun 25

Site Usage

1,130 Visits
Previous: 1,336 (-15.42%)

3,649 Pageviews
Previous: 4,489 (-18.71%)

3.23 Pages/Visit
Previous: 3.36 (-3.89%)

51.50% Bounce Rate
Previous: 48.80% (+5.54%)

00:02:42 Avg. Time on Site
Previous: 00:02:03 (+31.52%)

56.02% % New Visits
Previous: 69.84% (-19.79%)

FIGURE 1: Effect of header tag improvement on website visitations.

Visits ▾ July 1, 2011 - July 31, 2011 June 1, 2011 - July 1, 2011 Graph by:

300 300

150 150

Jul 1 - Jul 2 Jul 3 - Jul 9 Jul 10 - Jul 16 Jul 17 - Jul 23 Jul 24 - Jul 30

Site Usage

825 Visits
Previous: 1,130 (-26.99%)

2,785 Pageviews
Previous: 3,649 (-23.68%)

3.38 Pages/Visit
Previous: 3.23 (+4.54%)

46.67% Bounce Rate
Previous: 51.50% (-9.39%)

00:02:06 Avg. Time on Site
Previous: 00:02:42 (-22.21%)

62.06% % New Visits
Previous: 56.02% (+10.79%)

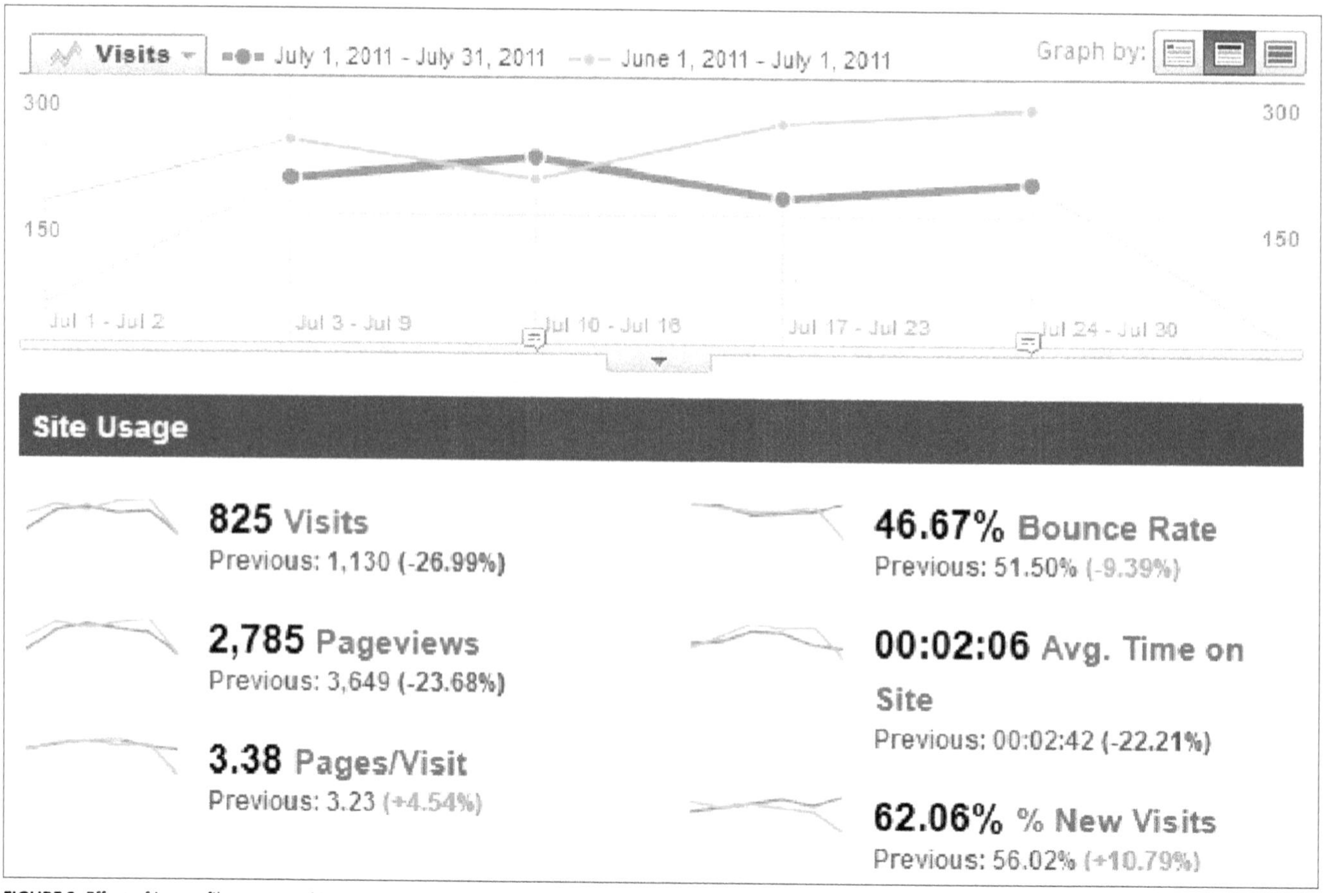

FIGURE 2: Effect of image file-name and image ALT improvement on website visitations.

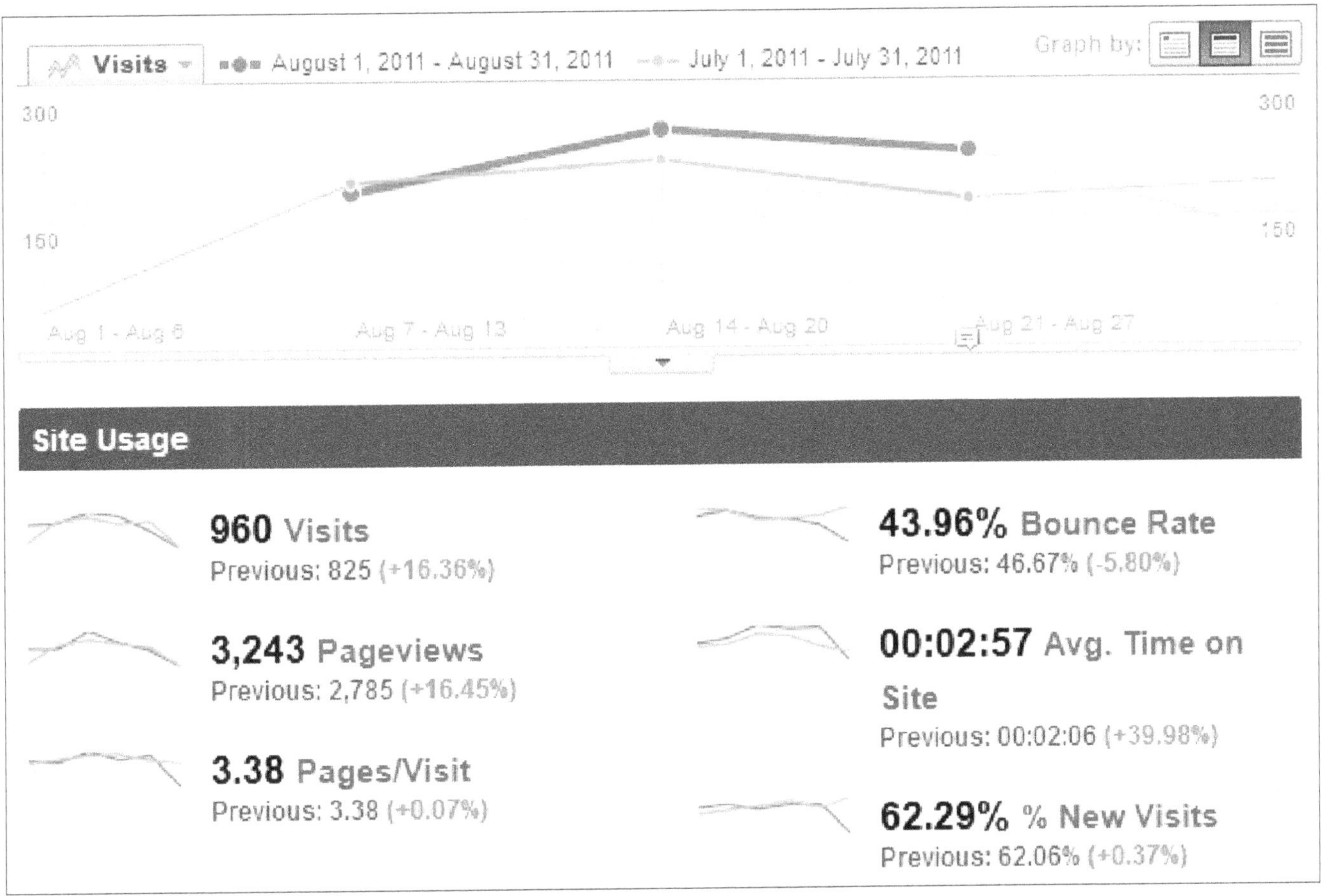

FIGURE 3: Effect of product descriptions, content and metadata improvement on website visitations.

the authors observed a slight decrease in traffic from the second week to the third week of July 2011. However, a slight increase in total traffic followed the initial decline as the month of July 2011 drew to a close. By this time, the total number of visitors dropped from 1336 (May 2011) to 825 (July 2011). As mentioned previously, during the month of June the holiday events would have impacted on these figures. Some users at that time would have gone on family holidays, reducing Internet activity to an extent.

It is expected to note decreases in traffic when extensive work is being performed on a website. Search engines take note of content changes after which they have to re-index and rank the individual webpages. This process can take anything from a few days to months. The increase by the end of July 2011 was also, in a sense, unexpected as the authors argued that the process of re-indexing and ranking would take longer than it did. This increase also indicates the value basic SEO elements can have on a website's ranking.

Body content

The role of body text and the use of keywords have been noted many times in previous research. As mentioned above, sections of this body text had to be rewritten and the graphs of Figure 3 indicate the effect of these changes.

A lack of regular updating of HTML metadata content was noted in the webpages of the company. Whilst descriptive text in the body was updated, the relevant metadata was simply left with the original content, leading to a severance of the connections between these two elements.

Care was taken to ensure that all three meta-elements were rewritten according to Google's guidelines. The new version contained relevant keywords and reflected the product that it related to. This work was completed in the last week of August 2011.

The August 2011 total traffic increased compared to July 2011 (16.36%). This indicated to the authors that Google was starting to re-index the text website with the modifications. It must also be noted that the schools in South Africa were closed for recess between the periods of 24 June 2011 and 18 July 2011, which would have negatively impacted the statistics for the month of July 2011. However, August 2011 did have two public holidays on 08 August 2011 (school holiday) and 09 August 2011 (Women's Day). These two calendar events would have had a similar negative effect on the August 2011 figures.

A relative simple update to the content, and ensuring that the metadata was reflective of the new content, produced a significant increase in website traffic. This was mostly because of the presence of relevant, unique, keyword rich and regularly updated content. This increase in traffic confirms

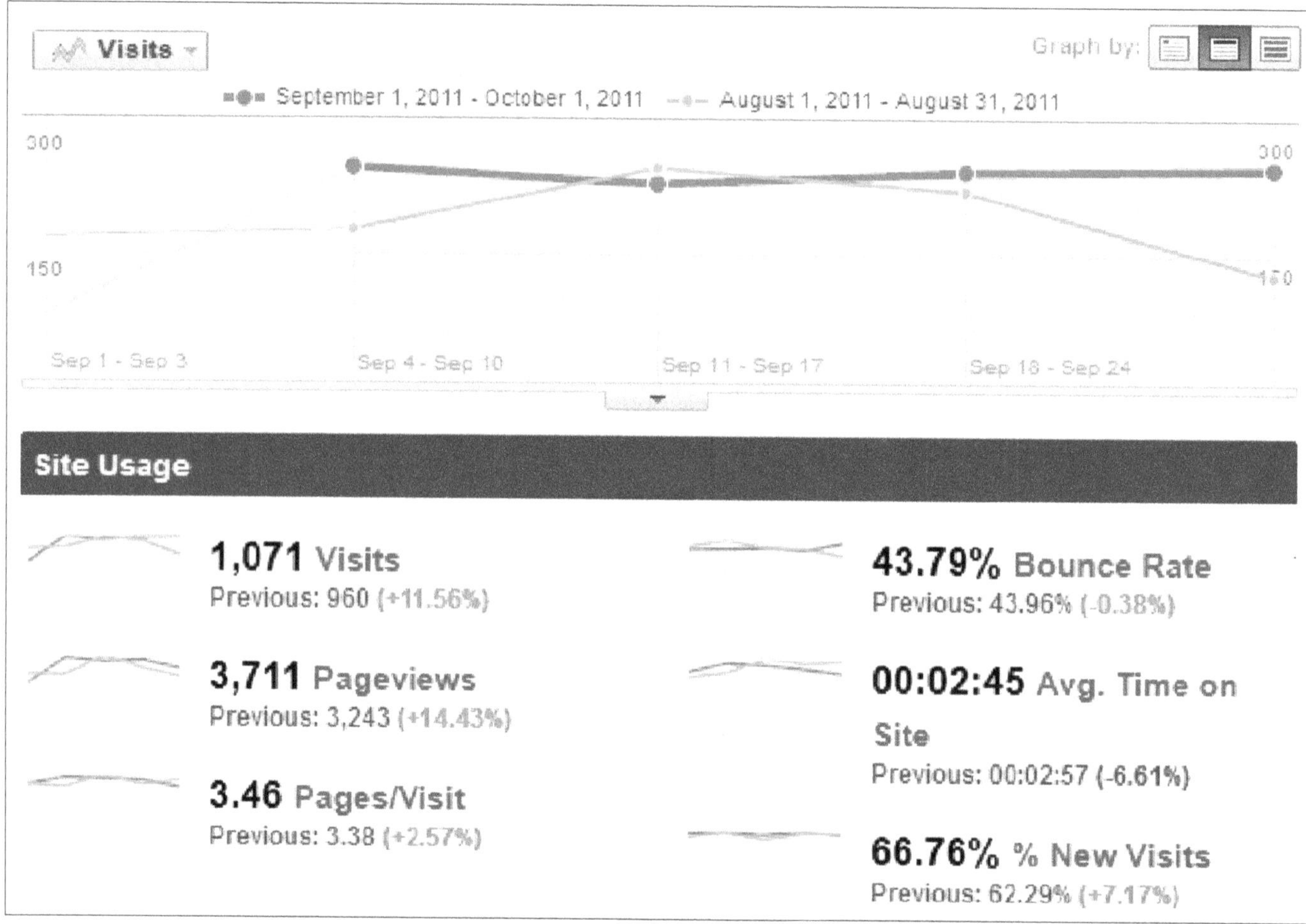

FIGURE 4: Total website traffic: September 2011 compared to August 2011.

this conclusion and website authors should seriously consider this crucial aspect of a website.

Overall traffic trends

Month 1

Next, two one-month periods are compared to determine whether a trend is evident. See Figure 4.

During the month of September 2011 no work was conducted on the test website. In this time, the total traffic increased further compared to August 2011; 11.56% in total. Although August 2011 had not quite reached the traffic levels of May 2011, which included the PPC traffic, the data looked promising. Also note that August 2011 had two calendar events that would have negatively impacted the results for August 2011, as noted earlier. Furthermore, September 2011 also had one event on 24 September 2011 when South Africans celebrated Heritage Day.

By this time it was safe to assume that Google had indexed all the on-site changes. It was evident that all the website's pages were being re-indexed and ranked. However, the continuing climb in traffic indicated that rankings were indeed improving and more and more users were finding the website via Google's search result pages. This has to be seen against the fact that no further investment in PPC was done after campaign shutdown in May 2011.

Month 2

In October 2011 the authors continued to monitor the results and noted another slight increase in total traffic (1.21%). This was an indication that Google had completed the re-indexing of the modified test website. By this time the website traffic had increased from 825 visits to 1084 (31.4% increase) in a period of four months. It should be noted that, in October 2011, the schools in South Africa closed for recess from 01 October 2011 to 10 October 2011. This would have had a negative impact on the October 2011 data. Also, as mentioned before, Heritage Day was celebrated on 24 September 2011.

Annual comparison

Finally, a year on year comparison is performed – see Figure 6.

In Figure 6 the authors compare the period 01 June 2011 to 31 October 2011 (no PPC included) to 01 June 2010 to 31 October 2010 (PPC traffic included). In June, the data regarding website traffic for the two years appear similar, however a sharp decrease in traffic can be observed when the PPC campaign was shut down and the modifications to the website started. By August 2011 the traffic already started increasing to just below the levels of the previous year after the header tags, image file names and image ALT tags were modified. Then, in August 2011 when the product descriptions, new homepage content, and

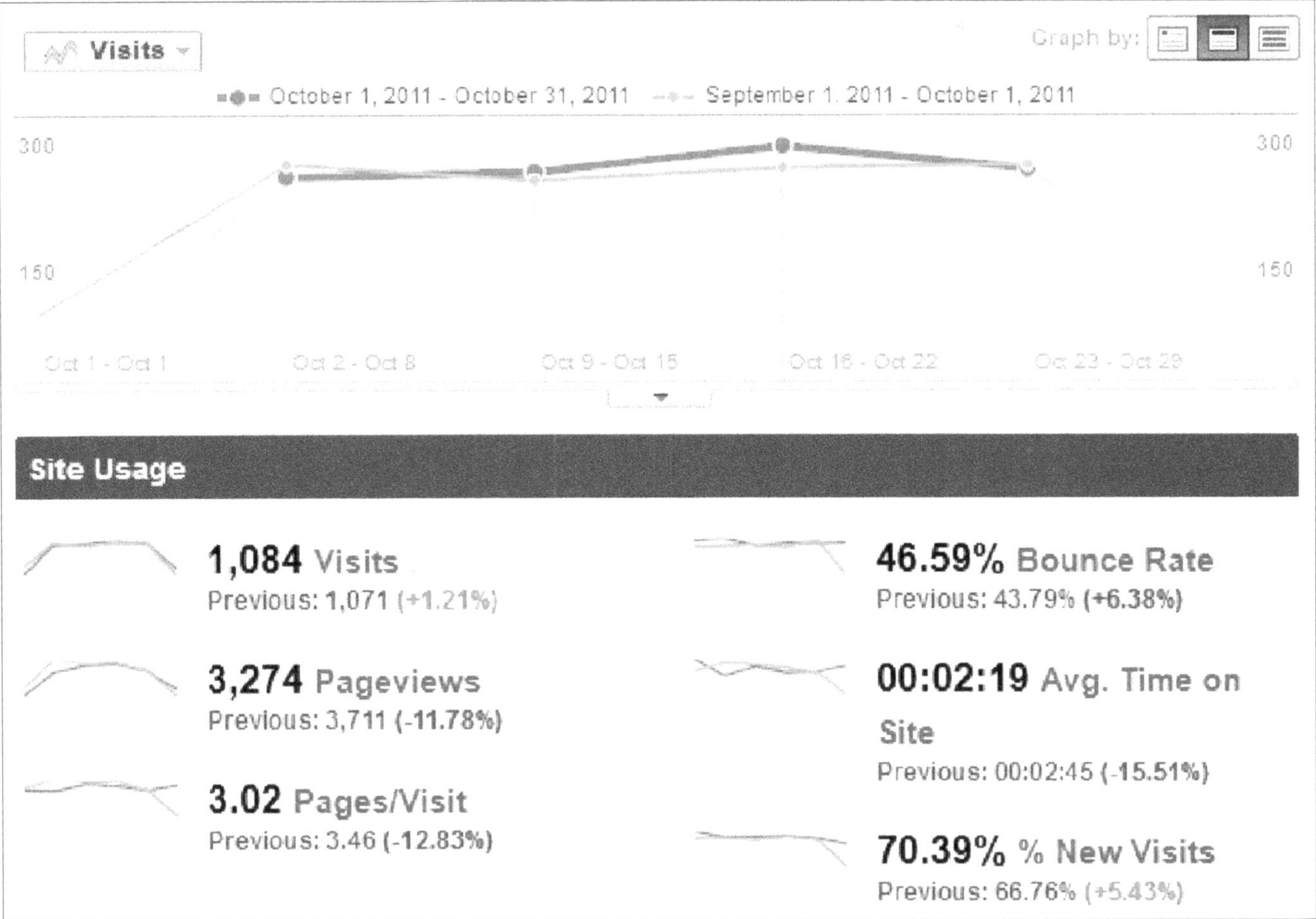

FIGURE 5: Total Traffic October 2011 compared to September 2011.

metadata were concluded the traffic increased further. By end of September 2011 the total traffic had increased to levels higher than the previous year, which included the PPC traffic.

Final traffic or expenditure summary

The results of this study are best described by summarising traffic to the XYZ website during the two test periods, whilst comparing it to the expenditure. Table 1 summarises the relevant figures.

The date column lists the date of measurement of both traffic values and the expenditure of company XYZ on SEM. 'Traffic PPC' lists the number of visitors for the period originating from all search traffic; direct, referral and PPC sources. However, the actual figures for November 2010 until May 2011 were not available, and these figures were taken to be the average of the preceding months (718).

The 'Traffic SEO' column contains the number of visitors for the relevant period, all of which is search traffic. However, by this time the PPC campaign had been terminated, so part of the source is SEO-generated traffic. The 'Expenses Original' column is a summary of the SEM expenditure of the XYZ Company, being R3000 per month spent on PPC for 11 consecutive months. In May 2011 there was no expenditure, since the PPC campaign was terminated. Then, in June 2011, an amount of R19 000 was paid (once-off) to do the SEO as agreed.

Finally, the 'Expenses Adjusted' column is simply the 'Expenses Original' figure divided by 21. The figure of 21 was chosen as a scale-down factor to bring the Rand values in line with the other figures in the table. This would ensure that graphs of these values plotted on the same scale (see Figure 7) would be comparable in amplitude.

A graphical presentation of the relevant figures as noted above is done in Figure 7.

An analysis of the graphs in Figure 7 is required. The PPC graph indicates that the amount of search traffic had stabilised over the 12 month period from June 2010 to May 2011. Since this component consists of three parts and the split is unknown, it cannot be determined what the exact contribution of PPC was to the monthly figure. However, it is assumed that it must have been substantial considering the steep drop in traffic in the months (June and July 2011) directly following the termination of the PPC campaign.

The SEO graph of Figure 7 again lists all search traffic to the website, but this time with the PPC component having been

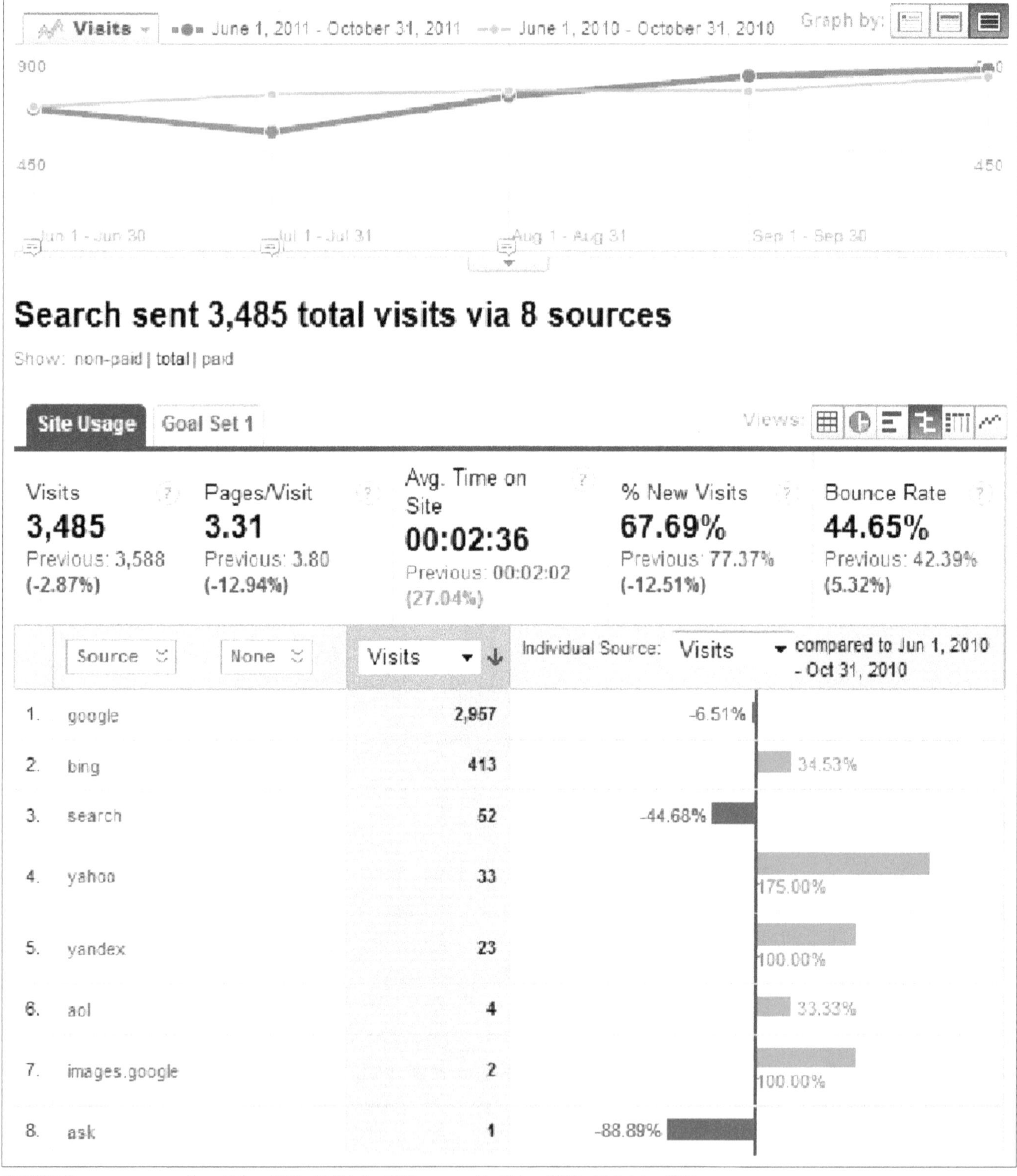

FIGURE 6: Year on year comparison: 01 June 2011 – 31 October 2011 compared to 01 June 2010 – 31 October 2010.

replaced by the newly introduced SEO component. The initial drop over the first two months is owing to the SEO campaign taking time to influence rankings and therefore traffic. However, as from the third month into the SEO section, the graph shows a continued rise indicating a growing trend in traffic volumes. This resulted from the fact that search engine crawlers had started visiting the site, indexing the new content, and their algorithms had started giving the site an ever increasing rank in the result listings. The rising trend appears to flatten towards the last recorded month, but without more figures this trend cannot be confirmed past the last recorded month.

Finally, the expenses of XYZ to achieve this increase in traffic need to be put into perspective – refer to the 'R' line on Figure 7. At a fixed rate of R3000 per month, XYZ had spent

TABLE 1: Comparative traffic during two periods.

Date	Traffic PPC	Traffic SEO	Exp. Adj.	Exp. Orig.
Jun-10	650	-	142.8571	3000
Jul-10	706	-	142.8571	3000
Aug-10	723	-	142.8571	3000
Sep-10	721	-	142.8571	3000
Oct-10	788	-	142.8571	3000
Nov-10	718	-	142.8571	3000
Dec-10	718	-	142.8571	3000
Jan-11	718	-	142.8571	3000
Feb-11	718	-	142.8571	3000
Mar-11	718	-	142.8571	3000
Apr-11	718	-	142.8571	3000
May-11	718	-	0	0
Jun-11	-	639	904.7619	19000
Jul-11	-	536	0	0
Aug-11	-	696	0	0
Sep-11	-	792	0	0
Oct-11	-	822	0	0

PPC, pay-per-click; SEO, search engine optimisation; Exp. Adj.; Expenses Adjusted; Exp. Orig.; Expenses Original'.

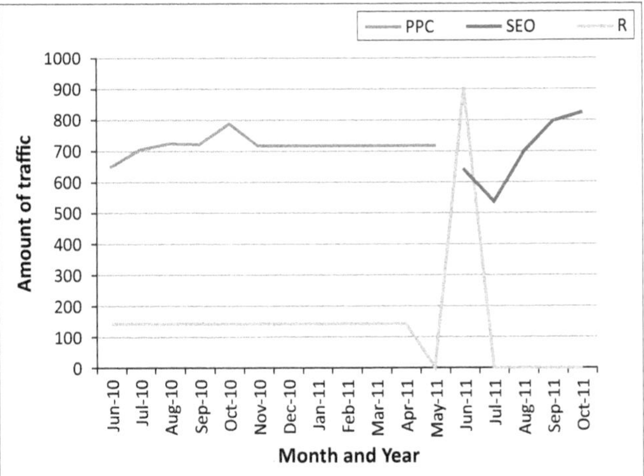

FIGURE 7: Summary of traffic versus expenditure.

R33 000 over the 11 month period in an attempt to maximise the number of visitors to their site. This expenditure played a large part in achieving the traffic volumes listed as the PPC line as noted above. During June 2011 there was a sharp increase to R19 000, but this was a once-off expenditure. After that time it dropped to zero for the rest of the recording period.

It should be noted that the traffic volume during the SEO period had bypassed the highest level achieved during the PPC period after only three months of running on SEO. This occurred whilst the average monthly PPC expense of R3000 compared well to the R3800 (R19 000/5) average per month spent on SEO for this short period. However, this R3800 average figure is for only five months as compared to the PPC figure of 11 months. The average cost for SEO, if calculated further, would decrease dramatically as follows:

- November 2011: R3167 per month
- December 2011: R2714 per month
- May 2012: R1727 per month

In both cases, after 11 months the PPC expense would still be R3000 per month with the SEO averaging out at R1727 per month. This trend of downward spiralling costs for SEO would continue. At the same time, if the SEO graph is extrapolated, it can be expected that the traffic volumes could increase past those achieved during the PPC period.

It should be noted that in a real-life SEO campaign there will be further expenses past the initial layout, but not necessarily of the monthly recurring type. In the time period of this case study there were none, bar the initial amount. However, a study over a much longer period of time is needed to do a long-term comparison. It is likely that the longer an SEO campaign is running, the lower the average monthly costs will become.

Limitations of this study include that the data were obtained from a relatively low-traffic site. Also, data across a longer period of time would provide a clearer trend. Finally, a comparison was done on the traffic generated from certain marketing expenses only, not the profit eventually generated by that traffic.

Conclusion

An existing commercial website (that of company XYZ) was considered as the central object of this research project. An experiment was done on the XYZ website to start implementing SEO immediately after the PPC was terminated. At the same time, monitoring was done of traffic to the website and of other relevant analytic measures. The SEO was done based on industry best practice supported by academic research.

The owners had been spending 'marketing dollars' on this website, using firstly, only one of the two main types of SEM for a period: PPC. The main disadvantage of PPC is that expenditure has to be consistent for results to appear; the moment a PPC budget is cut, the resultant traffic drops to zero immediately. Therefore, the overall PPC expenditure should be calculated from the monthly expenditure; in the case of XYZ, R3000.

After the PPC campaign was terminated, XYZ spent R19 000 once-off on SEO. This amount was for the implementation of the elements as listed under 'Methodology' above. As noted from the literature, where PPC produces immediate ranking improvements once payment has been arranged, SEO takes longer to affect rankings. This is mostly due to the waiting period for search engine crawlers to visit or refresh their copy of the website content.

When these expenditure figures are compared, it can thus be claimed that, after 6.33 months, the expenditure on the two systems for XYZ would have been the same. From this point in time onwards, SEO would continue to provide a growing return on investment over PPC, assuming that no further expenses would be required for SEO.

In conclusion, it can be claimed that, in this specific case, SEO provides a better investment than PPC. It is also predictable that this advantage will increase as time goes by. It should also be noted that traffic to a website on its own is not the only indicator of success. A high conversion rate, leading to more revenue generated, and eventually leading to increased profit would be the final indicator of the success of an e-commerce website. However, owing to the sensitivity of company financial information, this kind of evidence will be harder to come by and use as proof.

Acknowledgements

Competing interests

The authors declare that they have no financial or personal relationships which may have inappropriately influenced them in writing this article.

Authors' contributions

Both W.T.K. (Cape Peninsula University of Technology) and M.W. (Cape Peninsula University of Technology) worked together in conceptualising the research work, completing the literature survey and reference hunting, doing the write-up and checking results. W.T.K. gathered and summarised the data, checked accuracy and did the write-up of the skeleton of the whole article, specifically the results section. M.W. did the conclusion, abstract, proofreading, editing and overall checking.

References

Akakandelwa, A., 2011, 'An exploratory survey on the SADC e-government web sites', *Library Review* 60(5), 421–431. http://dx.doi.org/10.1108/00242531111135317

Barreto, A.M., 2013, 'Do users look at banner ads on Facebook?', *Journal of Research in Interactive Marketing* 7(2), 119–139. http://dx.doi.org/10.1108/JRIM-Mar-2012-0013

Boyes, J.A. & Irani, Z., 2004, 'An analysis of the barriers and problems to web infrastructure development experienced by small businesses', *International Journal of Information Technology and Management* 3(2/4), 189–207. http://dx.doi.org/10.1504/IJITM.2004.005032

Brunn, D.S. & Dodge, M., 2001, 'Mapping the "worlds" of the World Wide Web: (Re) structuring global commerce through hyperlinks', *American Behavior Scientists* 44(10), 1717–1739. http://dx.doi.org/10.1177/0002764201044010011

Chen, C.-Y., Shih, B.-Y., Chen, Z.-S. & Chen, T.-H., 2011, 'The exploration of internet marketing strategy by search engine optimization: A critical review and comparison', *African Journal of Business Management* 5(12), 4644–4649.

Craven, T.C., 2003, 'HTML tags as extraction cues for webpage description construction', *Information Science Journal* 6, 1–12.

Crowley, M., 2014, 'Take the guesswork out of your marketing strategy', *Journal of Financial Planning* 27(1), 16.

Green, D., 2000, 'The evolution of Web searching', *Online Information Review* 24(2), 124–137. http://dx.doi.org/10.1108/14684520010330283

Guenther, K., 2014, 'Getting your website recognized', *Online Magazine*, Issue May/June, 47–49. *Guidelines for optimising and making your site searchable*, 2014, viewed 01 March 2015, from http://www.ananzi.co.za/submit/guidelines

Gupta, A. & Mateen, A., 2014, 'Exploring the factors affecting sponsored search ad performance', *Marketing Intelligence & Planning* 32(5), 586–599. http://dx.doi.org/10.1108/MIP-05-2013-0083

Henzinger, M.R., Motwani, R. & Silverstein, C., 2002, 'Challenges in web search engines', viewed 30 April 2015, from http://www.acm.org/sigs/sigir/forum/F2002/henzinger.pdf

Hubbard, J., 2004, 'Indexing the Internet', in *Essay for Drexel University College of Information Science and Technology*, viewed 25 April 2015, from http://www.tk421.net/essays/babel.html

Kennedy, K. & Kennedy, B.B., 2008, 'A small company's dilemma: Using search engines effectively for corporate sales', *Management Research News* 31(10), 737–745. http://dx.doi.org/10.1108/01409170810908499

Kent, P., 2012, *Search engine optimization for dummies*, 5th edn., Wiley and Sons, Hoboken.

Kisiel, R., 2010, 'Dealers get on top of search engine results', *Automotive News* 84(6408), 24–25.

Kumar, E. & Kohli, S., 2007, 'A strategic analysis of search engine advertising in web based-commerce', *Journal of Internet Banking & Commerce* 12(2), 1–13.

Lee, W.I., 2010, 'The development of a qualitative dynamic attribute value model for healthcare institutes', *Iranian Journal of Public Health* 39(4), 15–25. PMID: 23113034.

Lee, W.I., Chen, C.W. & Wu, C.H., 2010, 'Relationship between quality of medical treatment and customer satisfaction - A case study in dental clinic association', *International Journal of Innovative Computing, Information and Control* 6, 1805–1822.

Lee, W.I. & Lin, C.H., 2011, 'Consumer hierarchical value map modeling in the healthcare service industry', *African Journal of Business Management* 5(3), 722–736.

Malaga, R.A., 2010, 'Search engine optimization - Black and white hat approaches', *Advances in Computers* 78, 1–39. http://dx.doi.org/10.1016/S0065-2458(10)78001-3

Mancuso, A., 2013, 'How Google AdWords' Ad Rank Algorithm Update Increased Brand CPC's by 600 Percent', viewed 12 May 2015, from http://www.seerinteractive.com/blog/how-google-adwords-ad-rank-algorithm-update-increased-brand-cpcs-by-600

Moreno, L. & Martinez, P., 2013, 'Overlapping factors in search engine optimization and web accessibility', *Online Information Review* 37(4), 564–580. http://dx.doi.org/10.1108/OIR-04-2012-0063

Moxley, D., Blake, J. & Maze, S., 2004, 'Web search engine advertising practices and their effect on library service', *The Bottom Line: Managing Library Finances* 17(2), 61–65. http://dx.doi.org/10.1108/08880450410536080

Murphy, H.C. & Kielgast, C.D., 2008, 'Do small and medium-sized hotels exploit search engine marketing?', *International Journal of Contemporary Hospitality Management* 20(1), 90–97. http://dx.doi.org/10.1108/09596110810848604

Nabout, N.A., 2015, 'A novel approach for bidding on keywords in newly set-up search advertising campaigns', *European Journal of Marketing* 49(5/6), 668–691. http://dx.doi.org/10.1108/EJM-08-2013-0424

Nielsen, J., 2014, 'Top ten global web parent companies', viewed 08 March 2015, from http://www.nielsen.com/us/en/top10s.html

Olbrich, R. & Schultz, C.D., 2014, 'Multichannel advertising: Does print advertising affect search engine advertising?', *European Journal of Marketing* 48(9/10), 1731–1756. http://dx.doi.org/10.1108/EJM-10-2012-0569

Onaifo, D. & Rasmussen, D., 2013, 'Increasing libraries' content findability on the web with search engine optimization', *Library Hi-Tech* 31(1), 87–108. http://dx.doi.org/10.1108/07378831311303958

Oppenheim, C., Morris, A. & McKnight, C., Lowley, S., 2000, 'The evaluation of WWW search engines', *Journal of Documentation* 56(2), 190–211. http://dx.doi.org/10.1108/00220410010803810

Plaza, B., 2009, 'Monitoring web traffic source effectiveness with Google Analytics: An experiment with time series', *Aslib Proceedings* 61(5), 474–482. http://dx.doi.org/10.1108/00012530910989625

Sagin, E., 2013, 'What the new AdWords ad rank algorithm really means', viewed 29 January 2015, from http://www.wordstream.com/blog/ws/2013/10/24/adwords-ad-rank-algorithm

Sen, R., 2005, 'Optimal search engine marketing strategy', *International Journal of Electronic Commerce* 10(1), 9–25.

Singh, A.M., 2002, 'The Internet – Strategies for optimal utilization in South Africa', *South African Journal of Information Management* 4(1). http://dx.doi.org/10.4102/sajim.v4i1.152

Thelwall, M., 2001, 'Commercial web site links', *Internet Research* 11(2), 114–124. http://dx.doi.org/10.1108/10662240110388224

Vaughan, L., 2014, 'Discovering business information from search engine query data', *Online Information Review* 38(4), 562–574. http://dx.doi.org/10.1108/OIR-08-2013-0190

Visser, E.B. & Weideman, M., 2011, 'An empirical study on website usability elements and how they affect search engine optimisation', *South African Journal of Information Management* 13(1). 9 pages. http://dx.doi.org/10.4102/sajim.v13i1.428

Weideman, M., 2013, 'Comparative analysis of homepage website visibility and academic rankings for UK universities', *Information Research* 18(4), viewed 30 April 2015, from http://InformationR.net/ir/18-4/paper599.html

Weideman, M., 2009, *Website visibility: The theory and practice of improving ranking*, Chandos Publishers, Oxford.

Zuze, H. & Weideman, M., 2013, 'Keyword stuffing and the big three search engines', *Online Information Review* 37(2), 268–286. http://dx.doi.org/10.1108/OIR-11-2011-0193

The mobile application preferences of undergraduate university students: A longitudinal study

Author:
Andrea Potgieter[1]

Affiliation:
[1]Department of Information and Knowledge Management, University of Johannesburg, South Africa

Correspondence to:
Andrea Potgieter

Email:
apotgieter@uj.ac.za

Postal address:
PO Box 524, Aucklandpark 2006, South Africa

Background: Smartphones and similar mobile devices have changed the way individuals interact with technology and with each other. The app preferences of smartphone users are vitally important to those seeking to understand the motivation behind app downloads and usage.

Objective: The research problem of this article is centred on the preferences for smartphone apps by the growing market of smartphone users in South Africa. The study includes a demographic profile of the users to establish what attracts this market into downloading smartphone apps.

Methodology: The study employed a mono-method, quantitative methodological framework with an online survey as the data collection instrument. The survey was conducted amongst undergraduate university students in 2013 and repeated again in 2014.

Results: It was found that the 'young adult' demographic, of which the sample of undergraduate university students formed a part, was discerning about which apps they downloaded and that the frequency of downloads occurred less than once a month in most cases. Information and entertainment needs were amongst the top reasons users indicated as motivations for downloading apps.

Conclusion: The study's findings confirmed that the sample had definite preferences regarding which apps the users were downloading, and these preferences depended on the needs that they wished to fulfil. The study also revealed that, even though users were aware of security threats associated with downloading apps, this knowledge did not deter them from continuing to download apps. Future research recommendations also arose from the study, giving direction to prospective studies.

Introduction

Smartphones and similar mobile devices have changed the way individuals interact with technology and with one other. According to Böhmer *et al.* (2011:47), these devices have 'evolved from single-purpose communication devices into dynamic tools that support their users in a wide variety of tasks'. This support is mainly offered through mobile application interfaces (apps) that are designed for specific tasks and downloaded, via an app store, onto the user's smartphone. Based on trends from the literature, it is clear that changes in mobility are continuous and may branch out into many different areas, but for now apps are the main contenders (Lynch 2012; McCarthy 2014).

The effect of mobile connectivity through apps amongst students is also a global phenomenon, as 79% of young adults (ages 18–24) own smartphones, and 70% of these students are using their devices in class to stay connected (Skiba 2014). This article aims at discussing the preferences regarding mobile apps of undergraduate university students, who typically fall within the 'young adult' age group. In addition, it attempts to reveal why the respondents in the study download certain apps by highlighting the respondents' preferences for these mobile apps.

Background to research problem

According to a comprehensive Groupe Speciale Mobile Association (GSMA) study of the socio-economic impact of the mobile industry in sub-Saharan Africa (SSA), over 6% of the region's gross domestic product (GDP) is contributed by mobile operations, which is 'higher than any other comparable region globally' (GSMA 2013). Furthermore, according to the GSMA (2014a) country dashboard, South Africa specifically is 'a Fast Grower market in Southern Africa with four operators and 70.4 million mobile connections'.

The latest GSMA (2014b) Mobile Economy report predicts that SSA is estimated to experience the highest growth of any region with regard to the number of smartphone connections over the next six years. According to the report, there will be 525 million smartphone connections in the region by 2020, and 'for the majority of users, smartphones will be the first device over which to access the Internet and to use new applications and services, as well as to explore digital content'.

It stands to reason that the app preferences of these smartphone users are vitally important to those seeking to understand the motivation behind app downloads and usage, especially when taking into account that 80.2% of South African Internet users use their app-enabled smartphones to access the Internet (Effective Measure 2014). Monica Bannan, vice president of product leadership at Nielsen, agrees that app developers should remain in the know regarding what app users expect:

> As mobile consumption habits evolve, it's imperative that app developers continue to add functionality and robustness to their offerings. Although there does appear to be a limit to the number of apps people are willing to access on a monthly basis, [*app users*] are spending 31 percent more time than they were last year, proving that it's the content that counts. (Nielsen 2014)

Srivastava (2014), discussing the Nielsen (2014) study, argues that, due to the fact that smartphones have become an integral part of users' lives, 'the selection of specific apps has become more precautionary'. Although the number of app downloads is increasing, users have shown that they prefer to uninstall or delete any apps 'which fail to lure them within a few hours', which leads to new app developers struggling to find new and devoted users (Srivastava 2014). The research problem of this study is centred on the preferences for smartphone apps by the growing market of smartphone users in South Africa. The study includes a demographic profile of the users to establish what attracts this market into downloading smartphone apps.

To highlight these preferences, this study will present findings regarding the app proclivities of 'young adults' (a group of students in this case, the majority of whom were between the age of 18 and 25), as this group of consumers spends the most average hours on their smartphone interacting on apps when compared to other age groups. This age group attributes an average of 5.2 hours daily to smartphone use (Salesforce Marketing Cloud 2014).

The students in this sample typically fell within the 18–25 year age group, with 70% of the 2014 respondents indicating that they fall within the 18–21 year age group and 25% within the 22–25 year age group. This concentration of 'young adult' ages was also prevalent with the 2013 survey, with 73% of those respondents belonging to the 18–21 year age group and 18% within the 22–25 year age group; see Figure 1. It has been established that this age group boasts the most active smartphone and app users, which supported the goal of this research, the search for preferences regarding mobile apps.

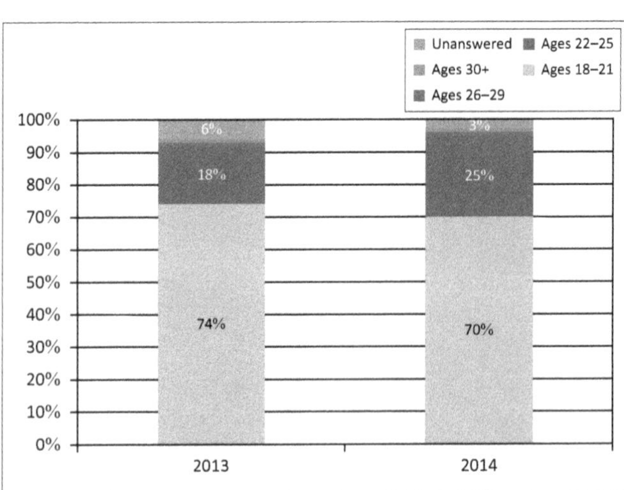

FIGURE 1: Age distribution of samples: 2013 and 2014.

Research methodology

This section constitutes the theoretical perspective of the research, discussing the overall nature of the research activity (Pickard 2013:xviii).

Research design

The research paradigm for this study was quantitative in nature, with a limited number of open-ended questions in the survey, allowing for qualitative interpretation. The philosophical paradigm in which the study was performed was one of positivism, allowing for the creation of broader generalisations based on casual relationships revealed in the data.

The research approach of this study was abductive, where the researcher aimed at generalising from the interactions between the specific and the general. The phenomenon of app choices amongst the sample group was explored in an attempt to identify themes and patterns in order to modify existing theories, or build new theories, about the subject at hand (Saunders, Lewis & Thornhill 2012:144). The researcher employed the use of an online questionnaire to this end.

Research method

The methodological framework prevalent in this study was mono-method quantitative. Although two open-ended questions were present in the survey, the terms that arose from those questions were analysed based on the frequency of each term appearing. The data from these open-ended questions were inducted in a quantitative format, as was the case with the typical Likert-scale questions collected throughout the rest of the questionnaire.

Data collection instrument

The online survey used in the 2014 study was a marginally modified version of the survey implemented by Mashiane and Potgieter in 2013 (Mashiane & Potgieter 2014) for the purpose of comparing results longitudinally. In both 2013 and 2014, the survey was deployed to the sample group through the use of the online university student portal, ULink. This portal offers a survey facility which deploys a survey directly to the relevant users – in this case, undergraduate university students.

The questionnaire consisted of 28 questions, four of which were open-ended questions where respondents could type in the relevant answer. The remaining 24 questions were delivered in a multiple-choice style, giving the respondents the option of choosing the appropriate answer, or a neutral answer ('I don't know' or 'Other') where applicable.

The findings of the 2013 Mashiane and Potgieter (2014) survey were presented at the Pan-Pacific Conference XXXI in Japan in June 2014. The findings of the 2014 survey were presented at the Annual Information and Knowledge Management Conference in South Africa in November 2014. This article will compare and discuss the findings of these two data collection instances.

Survey samples

The sampling technique applied in both data collection instances was one of non-probability convenience sampling, which is appropriate in the quantitative nature of the study's research method (Kumar 2014:242). Saunders *et al.* (2012:176) notes that samples that are selected based on convenience are characteristically easier to access, because these samples are typically familiar to the researcher. Saunders *et al.* (2012:291) also state that, in many instances, samples chosen for convenience seemingly 'meet purposive sample selection criteria that is relevant to the research aim'. Since this study focused on the tendencies of young adults and their preferences regarding app downloads, the sample was both convenient whilst also meeting the purposive criteria of falling within the 'young adult' range.

Using the University of Johannesburg's (UJ) online student portal ULink, the survey was made available to all undergraduate Information Management students at the UJ in June 2013 and again in September 2014. The survey was developed by taking into consideration global trends in mobile app usage surveys. Contemporary surveys were used as guidelines in this endeavour.

In 2013, the survey was made available to 1161 students, the total number of students registered for the subject Information Management on an undergraduate level at the time of the study. A response rate of 62% was achieved with a total of 717 responses successfully captured.

During the 2014 data collection period, September to November, the survey was posted to all undergraduate Information Management students at the UJ. In September 2014, the survey was made available to 1256 undergraduate students, and by 05 November 2014, 522 responses had been captured, amounting to a response rate of 42%.

In both instances, an online survey was selected, since these students access their student portal on a regular basis. The suitability of being able to participate in the survey by using a portal they are familiar with was considered to be an advantage.

Findings

Survey respondents were asked whether they owned an Internet-enabled smartphone. There was a slight increase in the number of respondents as 79% of respondents in 2013 indicated that they owned a smartphone, compared to 84% in 2014. In both instances, this percentage was higher than the smartphone penetration reported for urban dwellers in South Africa, which is 62% (On Device Research 2014).

Subsequently, respondents were asked whether they downloaded apps to their smartphones. This number increased to 77% in 2014, and the increase was to be expected, since apps have been described as 'the single most significant tool driving the mobile economy in South Africa' (World Wide Worx 2013).

In 2013, 44% of respondents indicated that they owned a smartphone with a BlackBerry operating system (OS), and only 13% of respondents owned an Android enabled smartphone. In 2014, BlackBerry was no longer the leader amongst the sample, with only 25% of respondents indicating that they owned a Blackberry device and 37% representing Android; see Figure 2. The loss of market share by BlackBerry had been predicted by Effective Measure (2014); it had also been predicted that the market share would be lost to Samsung (an Android device) and – at least from an OS point of view – is seemingly confirmed in this instance.

When respondents were asked when they searched for an app, the motivation for 2013 and 2014 searches were relatively similar; see Figure 3. A notable difference between the two instances was the most popular reason respondents had pointed out as motivation for searching for an app. In 2013, 48% of respondents indicated that they searched for an app when they 'need information on a brand, its product or its services', whereas the most popular reason in 2014 for

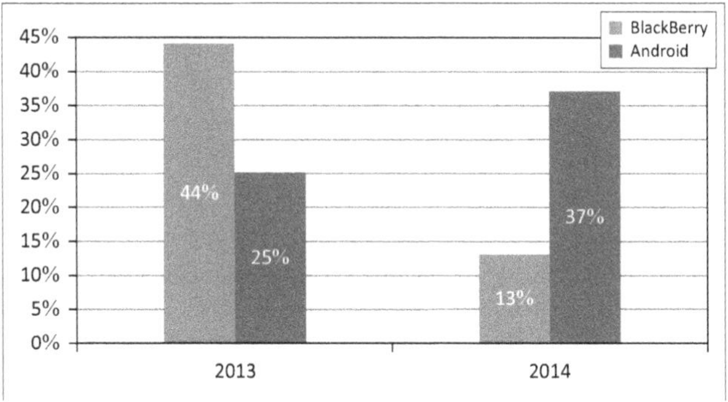

FIGURE 2: Growth of Android adoption from 2013–2014.

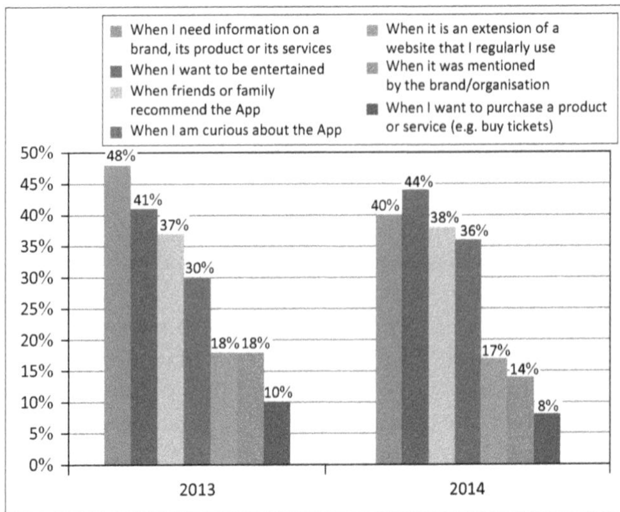

FIGURE 3: Motivation for searching for an app, 2013 vs. 2014.

searching for an app was that respondents 'wanted to be entertained'.

In both 2013 and 2014, the remaining reasons noted for searching for an app were indicated as follows, in descending order of preference:

- When friends or family recommend the app.
- When I am curious about the app.
- When it is an extension of a website that I regularly use.
- When it was mentioned by the brand and/or organisation.
- When I want to purchase a product or service (e.g. buy tickets).

What these findings imply, is that an information need and a need to be entertained are evidently equally important to this sample. The reasons for searching for an app as listed above, are typically less important, but also indicate a hierarchy in the samples' motivations for searching for apps to download. Based on this finding, one could infer that a respondent will most probably search for an app when he or she is bored, or needs information about a product. They will be less likely to do so if an app is an extension of a website that they typically use, or if they want to purchase a product or service.

Respondents were also asked what they considered before downloading an app that they had searched for. Respondents indicated, in both 2013 and 2014, that the price of the app was the most important feature. It must, however, be noted that Pengnate and Delen (2014:7), when controlling for confusing factors such as price, found a strong relationship between 'emotions and the number of an app downloaded', and state that this relationship can hypothetically be described 'by the affect-as-information model and theory of reasoned action'. Therefore, even though the respondents in this sample indicated that price plays a very important role in their selection of an app, they may not be aware of the underlying emotional triggers affecting their choices.

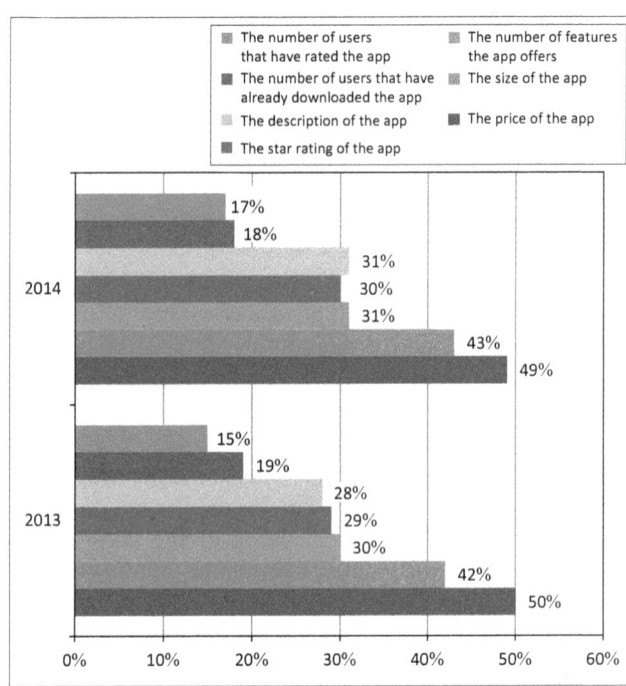

FIGURE 4: Considerations before downloading an app, 2013 vs. 2014.

An important secondary consideration was the size of the actual app, possibly implying that device memory is a consideration for this demographic as it influences device performance (Huang *et al.* 2010). Khalid *et al.* (2015:74) confirm this notion by remarking that app users notably complained about 'resource heavy' apps; these apps consumed too much battery life or memory on mobile devices, which caused frustration with regard to performance.

Equally important to one another, but less important overall, was the number of features the app had to offer, the star rating of the app on the app store platform, and the app's description. Pagano and Maalej (2013:132) note a bias in user rating of apps, as users may consider feedback which gives an app a low rating as less helpful than feedback giving an app a higher rating. It becomes evident that feedback which gives an app a better rating is considered more helpful by users, who then rate these positive reviews as more helpful. Taking the partiality of the app rating system into account, it is satisfactory to note that the least consequential of considerations that the respondents in this study took into account before downloading an app were the number of users that have rated the app, and the number of users that have already downloaded the app. This was the case with both the 2013 and the 2014 respondents; see Figure 4.

The issue of security risks was raised with respondents. In 2013, 53% of the respondents indicated a concern regarding security risks when downloading apps, and in 2014, 51% of the respondents indicated a similar concern. The risks associated with downloading mobile apps are real as a MetaIntell study found that 92% of the top 500 downloadable Android apps carry security or privacy risks (Business Wire 2014). Although it is evident that these respondents are aware and concerned about the security risks associated with downloading apps to their phones, it did not deter the majority of respondents from downloading apps regardless of these risks.

Respondents were asked to indicate how many apps they download per month. In 2013, 33% of respondents noted that they do not download apps every month. This percentage remained similar in 2014, when 34% of respondents indicated that they do not download apps on a monthly basis. In 2013 and 2014 respectively, 25% and 22% of respondents indicated that they downloaded at least one app per month; 17% and 16% agreed that they downloaded two to five apps per month. Very few of the respondents downloaded more than five apps per month, with only 5% of respondents in 2013 and 6% in 2014 indicating that they downloaded apps at this rate.

This finding supported the exploration of the research problem of this study, as it was evident that this demographic, although actively using their smartphones according to global standards, were very discerning when downloading apps. The majority of respondents, in both instances, indicated that they do not download apps more than once a month. This suggested that specific criteria were taken into account by these users when they decided to download an app.

The app that most respondents had downloaded at the time of the survey changed from 2013–2014. In 2013, Facebook was a clear favourite with 75% of respondents indicating that they had this app on their smartphone, whereas in 2014, WhatsApp had been installed by 73% of respondents – the highest instance compared to other apps. Unfortunately, many smartphones have Facebook pre-installed at purchase; therefore, it is not a clear indication of whether the respondents had downloaded the app out of their own volition. It does however confirm that this app had not been uninstalled once the device had been personalised by the respondents. Further study of the issue could possibly explore which pre-installed apps remain installed and used on users' phones after purchase.

The fact that WhatsApp was to be found on the majority of the 2014 sample's smartphones was a testament to this app's popularity, as WhatsApp is not typically pre-installed at purchase. The attractiveness of WhatsApp was further confirmed when respondents selected this app as 'the most useful app they had ever downloaded'; 18% of respondents in 2013 and 22% in 2014 sided with WhatsApp in their answers to this open-ended question. The remaining responses were divided, in less frequent instances, between apps such as Facebook, News24 and Opera Mini.

When the question of whether respondents would consider downloading paid-for apps was asked, the response was mostly negative from the 2013 (42%) and the 2014 (46%) sample groups. Considering that 32% of respondents in 2013 and 25% of respondents in 2014 'did not have a monthly income', and 43% of respondents in 2013 and 28% in 2014 had a monthly income of less that R1000, it was to be expected that paying for apps would not be a priority.

Even though the general attitude seemed to be not to pay for apps, 22% of respondents in 2013 and 17% in 2014 indicated that they had at least one paid-for app installed on their smartphone. The main reasons indicated by respondents that led them to consider paying for an app were 'if the paid-for app appeared to be of a higher quality than a free app that offers the same function' (33% in 2013 and 30% in 2014), or 'if a paid-for app fulfilled a specific need that the respondent considered vital' (28% in both 2013 and 2014).

In 2013, 28% of respondents also indicated that the most they had ever paid for an app had been 'less than R10', whereas 23% indicated the same in 2014. A smaller percentage of respondents in 2013 (18%) and 2014 (19%) confirmed that the most they had ever paid for an app had been 'between R11 and R50'. Even fewer respondents indicated that they had ever paid 'between R51 and R100' for an app, with merely 5% of respondents in 2013 and 4% in 2014. Only 1% of respondents in both 2013 and 2014 indicated that they had ever paid 'more than R100' for an app. This finding can also be linked to the low income bracket of the sample in both 2013 and 2014.

Conclusion and recommendations

This longitudinal study set out to establish the preferences regarding downloading apps of undergraduate university students. Following the analysis of data from two samples, one surveyed in 2013 and the other in 2014, it was found that these groups of 'young adults' were discerning about which apps they download, as the frequency of downloads was relatively low. It was found that less than one app per month was being downloaded by the respondents.

The main motivation for downloading apps was found to be either a need for specific information (in 2013), or a need to be entertained (in 2014). It was also found that the price and size of an app were important considerations when respondents considered downloading an app. The recurring theme of app price was evident, as respondents either had a very small monthly income or no income at all, making the downloading of paid-for apps a non-probability.

On the rare occasions where respondents did download paid-for apps, the motivation had been a perceived higher quality of the paid-for app compared to its free counterparts. In addition to a perceived higher quality of paid-for apps, respondents also indicated that they would choose to purchase one if they considered the paid-for app to be vital to fulfil a specific need. When respondents committed to paying for an app, it was found that most chose an app that cost less than R10 to download.

WhatsApp was found to be a very popular app downloaded by the sample groups. It is suggested that a follow-up study be conducted to establish whether 'popular' apps are apps that had been pre-installed before purchase, as was the case with Facebook. Since respondents indicated that the need to access information and to be entertained were important considerations when downloading apps, it stands to reason that these two popular apps, WhatsApp and Facebook, most likely fulfilled these needs.

The study also showed that app users were aware of the security risks associated with downloading apps to their smartphones, but that these risks were not deterring the download of apps. This is an interesting finding, as it could indicate that these respondents did not regard a threat to their information privacy as a cause for concern; further investigation is needed to explore the issue of security risks in the downloading of apps.

Although some insight was given into the preferences of this demographic with regard to app use, this area of study still poses many unanswered questions, the disregard of risk regarding security when downloading apps being one example. As the use of apps increases, as it has in recent times, these questions need to be explored in order for app developers to create useful products, and also for researchers to gain insight into the interaction of users with their smartphones.

It is further suggested, for future research, to not exclude older generations from research in smartphone and app usage research simply because they have been slower in adopting the technology. For the purpose of this study, the sample explored 'young adults' as this demographic was found to spend the most time interacting using their smartphones. According to Deloitte (2014), however, smartphone penetration by individuals over 55 is on the rise and by 2020 the current gap between this age group and younger demographics will be negligible. A study comparing the differences in app usage amongst all age groups, in South Africa specifically, will offer crucial insight.

Acknowledgements

Competing interests

The authors declare that they have no financial or personal relationships which may have inappropriately influenced them in writing this article.

References

Böhmer, M., Hecht, B., Schöning, J., Krüger, A. & Bauer, B., 2011, 'Falling asleep with Angry Birds, Facebook and Kindle – A large scale study on mobile application usage', *Proceedings of the 13th International Conference on Human Computer Interaction with Mobile Devices and Services*, Stockholm, Sweden, August 30 - September 2, 2011, pp. 47–56.

Business Wire, 2014, *MetaIntell identifies enterprise security risks, privacy risks and data leakage in 92% of top 500 android mobile applications*, viewed 22 January 2014, from http://www.businesswire.com/news/home/20140122006295/en/MetaIntell-Identifies-Enterprise-Security-Risks-Privacy-Risks#.VlcDp9KUcrV

Deloitte, 2014, *The smartphone generation gap: Over-55? There's no app for that*, viewed 26 October 2014, from http://www2.deloitte.com/content/dam/Deloitte/global/Documents/Technology-Media-Telecommunications/gx-tmt-2014prediction-smartphone.pdf

Effective Measure, 2014, *South African mobile report: A survey of desktop user's attitudes and uses of mobile phones*, viewed 26 October 2014, from http://www.effectivemeasure.com/south-african-mobile-report-march-2014

GSMA, 2013, *New GSMA report shows sub-Saharan Africa lea ds the world in mobile growth and impact*, media release, viewed 11 November 2013, from http://www.gsma.com/newsroom/sub-saharan-africa-leads-world/

GSMA, 2014a, *Data » Markets » Africa » South Africa*, viewed 28 October 2014, from https://gsmaintelligence.com/markets/3788/dashboard/

GSMA, 2014b, *The mobile economy: Sub-Saharan Africa 2014*, viewed 28 October 2014, from http://ssa.gsmamobileeconomy.com/

Huang, J., Xu, Q., Tiwana, B., Mao, Z.M., Zhang, M. & Bahl, P., 2010, 'Anatomizing application performance differences on smartphones', *Proceedings of the 8th international conference on mobile systems, applications, and services*, San Francisco, USA, June 15–18, 2010, pp. 165–178.

Khalid, H., Shihab, E., Nagappan, M. & Hassan, A.E., 2015, 'What do mobile app users complain about?', *Software, IEEE* 32(3), 70–77. http://dx.doi.org/10.1109/MS.2014.50

Kumar, R., 2014, *Research methodology: A step by step guide for beginners*, 4th edn., Sage Publishing Ltd., London.

Lynch, W., 2012, *How apps are taking over computing and content*, Web Log Post, viewed 20 November 2012, from http://www.realmdigital.co.za/post/how-apps-are-taking-over-computing-and-content/

Mashiane, S. & Potgieter, A., 2014, 'Enterprise apps: What do consumers really think?', *Proceedings of the Pan-Pacific Conference XXXI*, Osaka, Japan, June 2–5, 2014, pp. 70–72.

McCarthy, N., 2014, 'Mobile app usage by the numbers [infographic]', viewed 29 October 2014, from http://www.forbes.com/sites/niallmccarthy/2014/10/29/mobile-app-usage-by-the-numbers-infographic/

Nielsen, 2014, *Smartphones: So many apps, so much time*, viewed 01 July 2014, from http://www.nielsen.com/us/en/insights/news/2014/smartphones-so-many-apps--so-much-time.html

On Device Research, 2014, *Impact of the mobile Internet in Africa vs UK*, viewed 22 October 2014, from http://www.slideshare.net/OnDevice/impact-of-the-mobile-internet-in-african-lives?redirected_from=save_on_embed

Pagano, D. & Maalej, W., 2013, 'User feedback in the AppStore: An empirical study', *Proceedings of the IEEE 21st International Requirements Engineering Conference (RE)*, Rio de Janeiro, Brazil, July 15–19, 2013, pp. 125–134.

Pengnate, S.F. & Delen, D., 2014, 'Evaluating emotions in mobile application descriptions: Sentiment analysis approach', *Proceedings of the 20th Americas Conference on Information Systems*, Savannah, USA, August 7–9, 2014.

Pickard, A.J., 2013, *Research methods in information*, Facet Publishing, London.

Salesforce Marketing Cloud, 2014, *2014 mobile behavior report*, viewed 26 October 2014, http://www.exacttarget.com/2014-mobile-behavior-report

Saunders, M., Lewis, P. & Thornhill, A., 2012, *Research methods for business students*, Pearson, Essex.

Skiba, D.J., 2014, 'The connected age: Mobile apps and consumer engagement', *Nursing Education Perspectives* 35(3), 199–201. http://dx.doi.org/10.5480/1536-5026-35.3.199

Srivastava, B., 2014, *Mobile app usage to rise, but new apps struggle to find market!*, viewed 17 July 2014, from http://www.dazeinfo.com/2014/07/17/mobile-app-usage-us-2013-catagory-interest-age-group-study/

World Wide Worx, 2013, *The time of the app*, viewed 28 November 2013, from http://www.worldwideworx.com/mobileinternet2014/

Permissions

All chapters in this book were first published in SAJIM, by African Online Scientific Information Systems (Pty) Ltd; hereby published with permission under the Creative Commons Attribution License or equivalent. Every chapter published in this book has been scrutinized by our experts. Their significance has been extensively debated. The topics covered herein carry significant findings which will fuel the growth of the discipline. They may even be implemented as practical applications or may be referred to as a beginning point for another development.

The contributors of this book come from diverse backgrounds, making this book a truly international effort. This book will bring forth new frontiers with its revolutionizing research information and detailed analysis of the nascent developments around the world.

We would like to thank all the contributing authors for lending their expertise to make the book truly unique. They have played a crucial role in the development of this book. Without their invaluable contributions this book wouldn't have been possible. They have made vital efforts to compile up to date information on the varied aspects of this subject to make this book a valuable addition to the collection of many professionals and students.

This book was conceptualized with the vision of imparting up-to-date information and advanced data in this field. To ensure the same, a matchless editorial board was set up. Every individual on the board went through rigorous rounds of assessment to prove their worth. After which they invested a large part of their time researching and compiling the most relevant data for our readers.

The editorial board has been involved in producing this book since its inception. They have spent rigorous hours researching and exploring the diverse topics which have resulted in the successful publishing of this book. They have passed on their knowledge of decades through this book. To expedite this challenging task, the publisher supported the team at every step. A small team of assistant editors was also appointed to further simplify the editing procedure and attain best results for the readers.

Apart from the editorial board, the designing team has also invested a significant amount of their time in understanding the subject and creating the most relevant covers. They scrutinized every image to scout for the most suitable representation of the subject and create an appropriate cover for the book.

The publishing team has been an ardent support to the editorial, designing and production team. Their endless efforts to recruit the best for this project, has resulted in the accomplishment of this book. They are a veteran in the field of academics and their pool of knowledge is as vast as their experience in printing. Their expertise and guidance has proved useful at every step. Their uncompromising quality standards have made this book an exceptional effort. Their encouragement from time to time has been an inspiration for everyone.

The publisher and the editorial board hope that this book will prove to be a valuable piece of knowledge for researchers, students, practitioners and scholars across the globe.

List of Contributors

Thinamano C. Ramavhona and Sello Mokwena
Department of Informatics, Tshwane University of Technology, South Africa

Herring Shava and Willie Chinyamurindi
Department of Business Management, University of Fort Hare, South Africa

Anathi Somdyala
Business Management Unit, East London Management Institute, South Africa

Peterson Dewah and Stephen Mutula
School of Social Sciences, Information Studies Programme, University of KwaZulu-Natal, South Africa

Tanya du Plessis and Mzoxolo Gulwa
Department of Information and Knowledge Management, University of Johannesburg, South Africa

Willie Chinyamurindi
Department of Business Management, University of Fort Hare, South Africa

Grace Msoffe
University of Dodoma Library, University of Dodoma, United Republic of Tanzania

Patrick Ngulube
Department of Interdisciplinary Research and Postgraduate Studies, University of South Africa, South Africa

Oliva Muwanga-Zake and Marlien Herselman
Department of Information Systems, University of Fort Hare, South Africa

Craig Fleisher
Aurora WDC, United States

Rostyk Hursky
Saskatchewan Research Council, Canada

Elizabeth Bosha, Liezel Cilliers and Stephen Flowerday
Department of Information Systems, University of Fort Hare, South Africa

Liezel Cilliers
Department of Information Systems, University of Fort Hare, South Africa

Rodreck David
Department of Records and Archives Management, National University of Science and Technology, Zimbabwe

Cornelius J.P. Niemand and Hlelo Chauke
Department of Information and Knowledge Management, University of Johannesburg, South Africa

Joel M. Chigada and Benedikt Hirschfelder
School of Management Studies, University of Cape Town, South Africa

Adeyinka Tella
Department of Library and Information Science, University of Ilorin, Nigeria
Department of Information Science, University of South Africa, South Africa

Michael Oyewole
Department of Library and Information Science, University of Ilorin, Nigeria

Adedeji Tella
Department of Teacher Education, University of Ibadan, Nigeria

Reetha Nundulall
Research and Innovation Division, University of Johannesburg, South Africa

Tiko Iyamu
Department of Information Technology, Cape Peninsula University of Technology, South Africa

Wouter T. Kritzinger and Melius Weideman
Website Attributes Research Centre, Cape Peninsula University of Technology, South Africa

Marius C. Smit, Taryn J. Bond-Barnard and Herman Steyn
Department of Engineering and Technology Management, University of Pretoria, South Africa

Inger Fabris-Rotelli
Department of Statistics, University of Pretoria, South Africa

Ngoako S. Marutha and Mpho Ngoepe
Department of Information Science, College of Human Sciences, University of South Africa, South Africa

Olaitan Olutoyin and Stephen Flowerday
Department of Information Systems, University of Fort Hare, South Africa

Shadrack Katuu
Department of Information Sciences, University of South Africa, South Africa
Head of Records Unit, International Atomic Energy Agency, Austria

Thomas van der Walt
Department of Information Sciences, University of South Africa, South Africa

Andrea Potgieter
Department of Information and Knowledge Management, University of Johannesburg, South Africa

Index

P

Q

R

S

T

U

V

W

Printed in the USA
CPSIA information can be obtained
at www.ICGtesting.com
JSHW051438221024
72173JS00006B/1503